INTERPRETING CRIMES
IN THE ROME STATUTE OF THE
INTERNATIONAL CRIMINAL COURT

The Rome Statute of the International Criminal Court defines more than ninety crimes that fall within the Court's jurisdiction, including genocide, other crimes against humanity, war crimes and aggression. How these crimes are interpreted contributes to findings of individual criminal liability and moreover affects the perceived legitimacy of the Court. And yet, to date, there is no agreed-upon approach to interpreting these definitions. This book offers practitioners and scholars a guiding principle, arguments and aids necessary for the interpretation of international crimes. Leena Grover surveys the jurisprudence of the International Criminal Tribunal for the former Yugoslavia (ICTY) and International Criminal Tribunal for Rwanda (ICTR) before presenting a model of interpretive reasoning that integrates the guidance within the Rome Statute into articles 31–33 of the Vienna Convention on the Law of Treaties (1969).

LEENA GROVER is a Habilitation Candidate in the Faculty of Law at the University of Zurich. She is a member of the Law Society of Upper Canada and has worked for a number of adjudicatory bodies including the ICTY and International Criminal Court.

INTERPRETING CRIMES IN THE ROME STATUTE OF THE INTERNATIONAL CRIMINAL COURT

LEENA GROVER

CAMBRIDGE
UNIVERSITY PRESS

CAMBRIDGE
UNIVERSITY PRESS

University Printing House, Cambridge CB2 8BS, United Kingdom

Cambridge University Press is part of the University of Cambridge.

It furthers the University's mission by disseminating knowledge in the pursuit of
education, learning and research at the highest international levels of excellence.

www.cambridge.org
Information on this title: www.cambridge.org/9781107688773

© Leena Grover 2014

First published 2014
First paperback edition 2015

A catalogue record for this publication is available from the British Library

Library of Congress Cataloguing in Publication data
Grover, Leena, author.
Interpreting crimes in the Rome Statute of the International Criminal Court / Leena Grover.
pages   cm
Includes bibliographical references and index.
ISBN 978-1-107-06772-1 (hardback)
1. International criminal law.   2. Rome Statute of the International Criminal Court
(1998 July 17)   I. Title.
KZ7070.G76   2014
345′.02 – dc23   2014007599

ISBN 978-1-107-06772-1 Hardback
ISBN 978-1-107-68877-3 Paperback

For all who toil to nurture the international criminal
justice enterprise

Practitioners and courts often seem not to regard it as a subject at all... Academics have not yet given sufficient attention to the doctrinal aspects.... [W]e neglect issues of interpretation at our peril.[1]

[1] A Ashworth, 'Interpreting Criminal Statutes: A Crisis of Legality?' (1991) 107 Law Quart Rev 419, 449.

CONTENTS

vii

FOREWORD

The Rome Statute of the International Criminal Court marks a turning point in the development of international criminal justice. That the Statute defines crimes in some detail instead of referring judges to customary international law is just one important innovation. And it gives rise to the challenge of interpreting these new treaty definitions. But is this really a challenge? In light of the well-established rules of interpretation in the *Vienna Convention on the Law of Treaties* (1969), one may wonder whether there is anything special or new about construing the relevant provisions of the Rome Statute. In Dr Leena Grover's well-considered view, the matter is not quite that simple, though. She believes that a treaty defining 'the most serious crimes of concern to the international community as a whole' does indeed pose specific questions of interpretation. She points out that the Rome Statute itself recognizes this fact by setting out several rules to assist judges with answering these questions. Her ambitious goal is to formulate a method for construing the definitions of crimes enshrined in the Rome Statute in accordance with the rules of interpretation contained therein, and to integrate this method into the general 'Vienna framework on treaty interpretation', thereby forming a coherent whole. International legal practitioners might question the usefulness of such an 'abstract' scholarly exercise, and judges perhaps even fear that an elaborate doctrine of interpretation could only unduly tighten their hands in the necessary development of the law. Dr Grover anticipates both possible concerns. To the first, she responds with the conviction that nothing is more useful for practitioners than an organized toolbox of interpretive principles, arguments and aids. Accordingly, her reflections, while certainly most inspiring from a scholarly perspective, are directly addressed to judges at the International Criminal Court, their teams and lawyers appearing before them. Dr Grover takes great pains to address the second possible objection. She does not dispute the fact that her doctrine of interpretation would restrain judicial development of the law to some degree. On the contrary, this is precisely the intended effect of her book. In Dr Grover's view, the first permanent international criminal court is exposed to a more stringent legitimacy test than its predecessors. It no longer suffices to refer to international criminal law's benign mission in order to justify the Court's decisions; in accordance with the overarching principle of legality, the latter must also duly respect the protected liberties of the international *citoyen* and maintain a proper balance of powers on the international plane. These latter considerations, according to the author, require a methodology that enhances the foreseeability and transparency of judicial reasoning. In her search for a comprehensive doctrine of interpretation for the Court, Dr Grover covers vast ground, including some thorny territory, and many of the insights gained along the way are precious in themselves; I just mention her efforts to elucidate more precisely the Rome Statute's principle of strict construction and the significance of customary international law within the interpretive process. All of this eventually results in a thoughtfully composed and elegantly formulated interpretive doctrine. I very much hope that practitioners and scholars alike will soon subject this doctrine to close scrutiny. It would be pretentious to predict at this moment in time whether the edifice Dr Grover has erected will withstand all future objections. But it can be stated with confidence that the edifice is an impressive one, based on the courageous, rigorous and dedicated work of a very promising scholar.

Claus Kreß
Director of the Institute of International Peace and Security Law,
University of Cologne

ACKNOWLEDGEMENTS

The kindness of many people made this book possible. Starting at the beginning, it was Morten Bergsmo at the Office of the Prosecutor (OTP) of the International Criminal Court who sowed the seed to pursue doctoral studies and relentlessly nurtured it in the early days. The result is this book. Thank you Morten, Gilbert Bitti, Christine Chung and other members of the OTP, as well as Susanne Malmström and everyone in Trial Chamber I at the International Criminal Tribunal for the former Yugoslavia for invaluable exposure to the practice of international criminal law, including its interpretation.

My most profound gratitude goes to Professor Claus Kreß, who has immeasurably enriched my life. Beyond supervising my doctoral work for four years, he has supported me professionally in every way possible. He is a teacher who dreams big dreams for his students and inspires them daily through his keen intellect, integrity, kindness and passion for the study and practice of international law. To my good friends at the University of Cologne, thank you for going above and beyond to make Germany feel like my second home. A third home was found at the University of Zurich thanks to Professor Helen Keller, now judge at the European Court of Human Rights, who introduced me to the fascinating work of the United Nations Human Rights Committee, as well as my friends at her chair, who made me feel so welcome.

An enormous thank you is warmly extended to Professor Angelika Nußberger for serving as the second corrector of my doctoral thesis despite her very demanding schedule as judge at the European Court of Human Rights. Several other people also gave of their precious time to read portions of this manuscript, comment on a related article published in the *European Journal of International Law* or help with footnotes. I therefore wish to convey my heartfelt thanks to Professors Dapo Akande, Roger Clark, Anne Peters, Darryl Robinson, Richard Vernon, Thomas Weigend and Joseph Weiler, as well as Nicole Bürli, Nikolaos Gazeas, Till Gut, Mareike Herrmann, Raji Mangat and Leigh Salsberg.

During the course of writing this book, I had the incredibly good fortune of working as a legal adviser to Ambassador Christian Wenaweser, His Royal Highness Prince Zeid Ra'ad Zeid Al-Hussein and Deputy Ambassador Stefan Barriga on the crime of aggression negotiations within the Court's Assembly of States Parties and at the first Review Conference of the Rome Statute. I am forever grateful for this exhilarating once-in-a-lifetime opportunity to experience how, through multilateral negotiations, international crimes are defined. I am also deeply indebted to Benjamin and Don Ferencz for so generously supporting this work.

It is with immense gratitude that I acknowledge the Canadian Council on International Law for funding my research, as well as Professor Peter Hogg and Dean Mayo Moran in Canada for their academic support and encouragement. To Elizabeth Spicer, Cassie Tuttle and the entire Cambridge University Press team, I wish to express my sincere appreciation for your belief in and work on this project. For their most constructive comments and time, I kindly thank the manuscript's blind reviewers. This book was initially completed in March 2011. I am therefore indebted to Professor Christian Walter and members of his chair at Ludwig Maximilian University in Munich for providing me with an ideal environment in which to update it.

Finally, a book is not written in a bubble – life intervenes. I therefore wish to acknowledge the wonderful support of friends and family near and far, especially Susan, Kelly, Gerli, Wolfgang, Sasha and mom. Christian, my greatest blessing, words fail me; you make all dreams possible and I can never thank you adequately. Julian, our lives know no greater love or joy than you.

1

Introduction

1.1 Introduction

Interpretation is central to the practice of law. Sometimes a legal victory or defeat turns on the meaning a judge attributes to a single word in a legal text. The stakes may be low or incredibly high. For example, the International Court of Justice (ICJ) in its *Genocide Decision* (2007) held that the killing of approximately 7,000 Muslim men in Srebrenica between 13 and 15 July 1995 was an act of genocide and that Serbia was responsible for failing to prevent and punish the individuals involved.[1] For conduct to qualify as genocide in a legal sense, the victim group must be protected by the *Convention on the Prevention and Punishment of the Crime of Genocide* (1948) (*Genocide Convention*).[2] Accordingly, the judges had to satisfy themselves that the victims formed whole or 'part' of a national, ethnical, racial or religious 'group'.

The parties disputed inter alia whether the death of 7,000 Muslim men satisfied this element of the crime. Given the gravity of genocide, does the killing of 7,000 men result in the destruction of 'part' of a group? If the argument is that the number of people forming 'part' of the group is substantial in a quantitative sense, should this be assessed in absolute terms or relative to the size of the whole group? On this point, can 'group' be defined in geographically limited terms even if large diasporas of persons exist who share the same nationality, ethnicity, race or religion as the victim group? Ultimately, one important justification for the ICJ's finding that genocide occurred in Srebrenica was its interpretation of the words 'part' and 'group'.

Judges deciding cases at the International Criminal Court (Court) will be forced to engage in similar interpretive exercises. The difference is that their decisions will be used to justify findings of individual culpability for the most serious crimes of concern to the international community as a whole. Indeed, one judge of the International Criminal Tribunal for the former Yugoslavia

---

[1] *Case Concerning the Application of the Convention on the Prevention and Punishment of the Crime of Genocide (Bosnia-Herzegovina v. Serbia and Montenegro)* Judgment (26 February 2007).

[2] 78 UNTS 277 (adopted 9 December 1948, entered into force 12 January 1951).

(ICTY) described the task of interpreting the law as 'both the most challenging and the most anxiety-ridden part of the job'.[3] These decisions could lead to the imprisonment of individuals and the compensation of victims, contribute to or disturb transitional justice efforts in situation countries, influence the development of customary international law, encourage or dissuade Non-States Parties to join the Court and help to strengthen or undermine the Court's legitimacy as an independent and impartial international judicial organ.

The Rome Statute has to date been ratified by 122 States Parties, thirteen of which have ratified the aggression amendments and sixteen the recently added crimes committed in the course of a non-international armed conflict. The Court is seized of situations in Uganda, the Democratic Republic of the Congo, Darfur (the Republic of the Sudan), the Central African Republic, Kenya, Libya and Cote d'Ivoire. It is investigating eight situations, conducting preliminary examinations of an additional eight, is considering the appeals of two cases, has acquitted one individual, has one ongoing trial, is scheduled to commence two more trials, has several cases that are at the pretrial stage and has twelve arrest warrants that remain outstanding, the oldest ones dating back to 2005 (e.g., Joseph Kony).[4]

Given that the Court is the world's first permanent international criminal court, the legitimacy factor is a serious concern. As a young judicial body that only came into existence in 2004, it does not have the luxury of being able to rest on its laurels as an established and well-respected institution. Unlike domestic criminal courts, any missteps the Court might make will occur under the watchful gaze of those who thumb their noses at the international criminal justice enterprise and would welcome the Court's failure. Unfortunately, judges do not currently have an agreed method for interpreting the more than ninety international crimes that fall within the Court's jurisdiction. One of its strongest critics suggested that 'the Court's discretion ranges far beyond normal or acceptable judicial responsibilities, giving it broad and unacceptable powers of interpretation that are essentially political and legislative in nature'.[5]

The purpose of this book is to offer judges of the Court and counsel appearing before them a tool known as a 'legal methodology' for interpreting

---

[3] PM Wald, Interview for The Third Branch (2002), www.uscourts.gov/News/ TheThirdBranch/02-03-01/An_Interview_with_Judge_Patricia_Wald.aspx, accessed 23 April 2014.

[4] Report of the International Criminal Court to the UN General Assembly (13 August 2013), UN Doc. A/68/314, 2, 4; The Global Campaign for Ratification and Implementation of the Kampala Amendments on the Crime of Aggression, 'Status of Ratification and Implementation', http://crimeofaggression.info/the-role-of-states/ status-of-ratification-and-implementation/, accessed 23 April 2014.

[5] JR Bolton, former Under Secretary for Arms Control and International Security, 'The United States and the International Criminal Court', Remarks to the Federalist Society in Washington, DC, 2002, www.iccnow.org/documents/USBoltonFedSociety14Nov02. pdf, accessed 2 November 2013.

the definitions of crimes that fall within the Court's jurisdiction. The Rome Statute of the International Criminal Court (Rome Statute or Statute) grants the Court jurisdiction to hear cases of genocide, other crimes against humanity, war crimes and, once States Parties activate the Court's jurisdiction for this crime not earlier than 2017, aggression.[6] These crimes are currently defined in articles 6, 7, 8 and 8 *bis* of the Rome Statute.[7] These provisions resemble a criminal code of sorts. Part III of the Statute sets out general principles of criminal law, and articles 55, 66 and 67 contain various due process guarantees for individuals. Other parts of the Rome Statute deal with diverse subject matter. For example, part IV is concerned with the composition and administration of the Court, part IX with international cooperation and judicial assistance, part X with enforcement and part XII with financing. A method of interpretation for these other parts of the Rome Statute might well differ from anything developed for crimes in the Rome Statute and be informed inter alia by international institutional law.

To understand the exact scope of this study and its import, this introductory Chapter will set out the following: (1) a working definition of interpretation; (2) sources of interpretive problems; (3) a working definition of legal methodology; (4) an explanation of the method for developing this methodology; (5) the practical benefits of this study; and (6) how to use this book.

1.2 Interpretation

In this section and the one that follows, a working definition of 'interpretation' will be introduced in three stages. First, the concept of operative interpretation will be defined. Second, this concept will be distinguished from gap filling and other judicial responsibilities. Finally, the line between operative interpretation and gap filling will be brought into sharper relief by introducing the reader to all of the interpretive problems that are covered by this study.

1.2.1 Operative interpretation

Every time a court publicly expresses its view on how a legal text should be construed, it engages in the act of interpretation.[8] Recognizing that no universally accepted legal definition of interpretation exists, the following definition of 'operative interpretation' will be adopted in this study:

---

[6] Article 5, Rome Statute for the Establishment of the International Criminal Court, 2187 UNTS 90 (adopted 17 July 1998, entered into force 1 July 2002).

[7] See also First Review Conference of the Rome Statute, Official Records, Resolution on the Crime of Aggression (adopted 11 June 2010) RC/Res.6, www.icc-cpi.int/iccdocs/asp_docs/Resolutions/RC-Res.6-ENG.pdf, accessed 2 November 2013.

[8] Z Bankowski, DN MacCormick, RS Summers and J Wróblewski, 'On Method and Methodology' in DN MacCormick and RS Summers (eds.), *Interpreting Statutes: A Comparative Study* (Ashgate 1991) 9, 12.

Interpretation in its narrow sense (*sensu stricto*) is a subclass of interpretation *sensu largo* and occurs where there are doubts in the understanding of
a language when it is used, in a particular context, in an act of communication. . . . For example, if I say I will meet you at ten o'clock on Wednesday,
you may experience doubt as to which Wednesday I mean (this Wednesday? next Wednesday?) and as to whether I mean ten in the morning or
ten at night. However you resolve this doubt (and perhaps even if you
do so by asking me for a clarification), you make an interpretive choice
among possibilities which you view as conceivable but conflicting . . . Such
a choice among alternatives in a setting of real doubt or dispute is a case
of interpretation *sensu stricto*.

   Interpreting in this strict sense often occurs in law. A jurist preparing a
commentary on some statute may find significant ambiguity in some of its
provisions. The commentary should draw attention to these and should
state a reasoned preference for one or other of the possible interpretations.
Again, a legal adviser seeking to advise a client on, for example, the tax
implications of some transaction or another may encounter doubt as to the
meaning of the tax statute for this purpose. The giving of advice requires
some resolution of this doubt. The citizen who receives a contractual offer
through the post may notice an ambiguity and respond to the offer on the
basis of the seemingly most reasonable interpretation in view. None of these
instances of interpretation *sensu stricto*, however, is what we call 'operative
interpretation'. That occurs only when there is an act of interpretation *sensu
stricto* performed by a judicial or other tribunal for the purpose of making
a binding legal decision in an actual trial or litigated controversy. That is,
it takes place when a court or other legal tribunal has to determine the
meaning of legal language in a way sufficiently precise to make a decision in
the case and to provide a justification for the decision on the ground of the
interpreted meaning of the provision in issue. Operative interpretation,
then, occurs in the official application of law and is determined by the
requirements of justified decision making in concrete cases.[9]

By adopting a narrow definition of interpretation, one that is limited to 'operative interpretation', it is important to be clear about what the present study
does not address. This study does not concern itself with non-public interpretive processes experienced by judges prior to writing a decision. These
processes are acknowledged by the author but set aside in favour of making public interpretive processes the subject of this study.[10] Judgments from
courts and tribunals are authoritative and binding on the parties to the dispute. They are read, reported and critiqued. But judges, like all people, cannot
escape the fact that their understanding of words is informed by everything

---

[9] Ibid. 12–13.

[10] For a short discussion on the merits of concentrating on published written opinions as
opposed to looking behind them in search of judges' real motives, see Bankowski and
Others (n. 8) 16–18.

that is in their minds at the time of reading a text. This information comprises 'linguistic and social conventions which the reader has internalized and the broad range of cultural assumptions absorbed through family, school, religion, work and leisure activities like reading and watching television. It includes everything the reader knows or thinks she knows...'[11] If one accepts that judges cannot avoid experiencing internal, subjective, interpretive processes, this entails the impossibility of any legal methodology on interpretation being able to fully guide them. This observation is not intended, however, to suggest that the non-public interpretive dialogue is very different from the public one that appears in judgments. What matters is how legal analysis on the construction of a treaty is disciplined by the formal requirement to provide public and legally compelling written reasons. Interpretive reasoning is not an internal psychological thought process but an exercise in 'competent legal argument'.[12] This is one of the highest aspirations that those concerned with the rule of law can have. Indeed, these are reasons that must be able to withstand the scrutiny of appellate judges, lawyers, commentators and other interested parties.

Briefly, the Rome Statute expressly admits both the real possibility of interpretive problems arising as well as their judicial resolution. Article 9(1) provides that the Elements of Crimes shall assist judges in the 'interpretation and application of articles 6, 7, 8 and 8 *bis*'. Article 22(2) requires judges to strictly construe the definitions of crimes in the Rome Statute. It also prohibits judges from expanding the definitions of these crimes by analogy and states that in case of ambiguity, the definition of a crime 'shall be interpreted in favour of the person being investigated, prosecuted or convicted.' Article 21(3) requires judges to, above all else, interpret the Rome Statute consistent with internationally recognized human rights. In light of these express references to interpretation, it seems untenable to suggest that judges have not been tasked with interpreting the Rome Statute. While drafters of the Statute are to be commended for attempting to provide as much detail and clarity to the text as possible, they nevertheless anticipated interpretive issues arising and made provision for their judicial resolution.

Even if the Rome Statute contains these imperatives, does this logically entail that judges are required to provide public reasons every time they interpret the definitions of genocide, other crimes against humanity, war crimes and aggression? The better legal view suggests that it does. Interpretation is a major judicial function that the system admits, and judges are obliged to issue written

---

[11] R Sullivan, 'The Plain Meaning Rule and Other Ways to Cheat at Statutory Interpretation', http://aix1.uottawa.ca/~resulliv/legdr/pmr.html, accessed 5 November 2013.

[12] M Koskenniemi, 'Fragmentation of International Law: Difficulties Arising from the Diversification and Expansion of International Law: Report of the Study Group of the International Law Commission' (4 April 2006), UN Doc. A/CN.4/L.682, 197.

decisions containing 'full and reasoned' statements of their conclusions.[13] As well, both the prosecutor and the convicted individual have an automatic right to appeal alleged errors of law.[14] A number of legal objections to an interpretive outcome could be raised, such as its inconsistency with a particular human right or its failure to favour the accused. All of this renders it likely that judges are obliged to provide reasons for their interpretation of crimes in the Statute. Even if one doubts the existence of a legal obligation in this regard, it is nevertheless good policy for the Court to provide reasons; it is young and in need of establishing its legitimacy among States Parties upon which it heavily relies for its successful operation.

To be clear, this study does not advance a utopic vision of how a methodology can assist with the task of interpretation. An attempt is made to constrain the interpretive choices available, but there is no denying that interpretation includes an essential discretionary creative or developmental component; laws rarely, if ever, have a single, clear meaning that a method of interpretation can simply discover. This study also does not assume that interpretation is the most decisive factor in all judicial decisions – other legal tasks or ascertaining the facts may be as or even more important in individual cases.[15]

1.2.2 Interpretation versus gap filling

In addition to excluding non-public interpretive processes, the narrow working definition of interpretation for this study must be distinguished from gap filling and other judicial tasks. In deciding a case, judges are expected to move through different stages of legal analysis that are often reflected in their decisions, including: statement of the issue(s); identification of potentially relevant provision(s) in the Rome Statute, Elements of Crimes and Rules of Procedure and Evidence; interpretation of these provisions; identification of outstanding legal issues not addressed by these instruments (gaps); resolution of these issues through the analysis of applicable law set out in article 21 of the Rome Statute (gap filling); identification of legally relevant facts; application of all relevant law to the facts; and statement of finding(s). The reasons in a judgment might not appear in the order presented or contain all of these stages. For example, if the Rome Statute adequately resolves an issue, there is no need to apply other law to the facts of a case. As well, a judgment will likely contain several non-reasoning components, such as statements describing the facts, the procedural background of a case or the arguments of the parties.

---

[13] Article 74(5), Rome Statute.   [14] Articles 81(1)(a)(iii), 81(1)(b)(iii), Rome Statute.
[15] J Pauwelyn and M Elsig, 'The Politics of Treaty Interpretation: Variations and Explanations Across International Tribunals' (3 October 2011), 1, 5, http://ssrn.com/abstract=1938618, accessed 16 October 2013.

This study is concerned with only one of the aforementioned stages of reasoning: interpretation of crimes in the Rome Statute. While other stages of legal analysis may be characterised as interpretive *sensu largo* insofar as judges are explaining the meaning of the law, the word interpretation in this study is intended to capture the judicial function of giving meaning to words in the Rome Statute. Perhaps the hardest distinction to be drawn between the aforementioned stages of legal analysis is the task of interpreting the Rome Statute, maybe with the aid of applicable law set out in article 21 and the analysis and application of law set out in article 21 *directly* to the facts of a case – gap filling. The task of gap filling in the Rome regime has been usefully defined as follows:

> [A] gap in the Statute may be defined as an "objective" which could be inferred from the context or the object and purpose of the Statute, an objective which would not be given effect by the express provisions of the Statute or the Rules of Procedure and Evidence, thus obliging the judge to resort to the second or third source of law – in that order – to give effect to that objective. In short, the subsidiary sources of law described in Article 21(1)(b) or (c) cannot be used just to add . . . to the Statute and the Rules of Procedure and Evidence.[16]

As can be seen from this definition, the line between interpreting the Rome Statute using an aid to interpretation, such as treaty or customary law, and directly applying treaty or custom to the facts of a case may be fine in some cases.[17] One gap that ICTY judges have had to fill in their statute is determining whether duress is a defence to killing innocent human beings.[18] The practical significance of the distinction between interpretation and gap filling can also be understood by considering which materials might aid each process. Article 21 provides:

1. The Court shall apply:
   (a) In the first place, this Statute, Elements of Crimes and its Rules of Procedure and Evidence;

---

[16] G Bitti, 'Article 21 of the Statute of the International Criminal Court and the Treatment of Sources of Law in the Jurisprudence of the ICC' in C Stahn and G Sluiter (eds.), *The Emerging Practice of the International Criminal Court* (Brill 2009) 281, 295.

[17] Consider, for example, the difficulty of interpreting article XX(1)(d) of the *Treaty of Amity, Economic Relations and Consular Rights between US and Iran* (1955), 284 UNTS 93 (adopted 15 August 1955, entered into force 16 June 1957), against the backdrop of customary law on the use of force in *Case Concerning Oil Platforms (Islamic Republic of Iran v. United States of America)* [2003] ICJ Rep. 161, especially the separate opinions of Judges Higgins, Buergenthal and Kooijmans.

[18] *Prosecutor v. Erdemović*, Judgment, ICTY-96–22-A, 7 October 1997.

(b) In the second place, where appropriate, applicable treaties and the principles and rules of international law, including the established principles of the international law of armed conflict;

(c) Failing that, general principles of law derived by the Court from national laws of legal systems of the world including, as appropriate, the national laws of States that would normally exercise jurisdiction over the crime, provided that those principles are not inconsistent with this Statute and with international law and internationally recognized norms and standards.

2. The Court may apply principles and rules of law as interpreted in its previous decisions.

3. The application and interpretation of law pursuant to this article must be consistent with internationally recognized human rights, and be without any adverse distinction founded on grounds such as gender as defined in article 7, paragraph 3, age, race, colour, language, religion or belief, political or other opinion, national, ethnic or social origin, wealth, birth or other status.

Whereas the task of gap filling is limited to applicable law set out in article 21 of the Rome Statute, interpretation might be aided by sources of law set out in article 21 but also by dictionary definitions, UN General Assembly resolutions, *obiter* statements contained in post-WWII jurisprudence, expert commentaries to relevant conventions and so on. Because some aids to interpretation are also applicable law for purposes of gap filling, any resulting confusion about the performance of these distinct legal tasks is understandable. At the very outset, the distinction requires one to not presume that the hierarchy of sources of law set out in article 21 is the same relationship that these sources of law will have to one another as aids to interpreting the Rome Statute. For example, whereas customary and treaty law must be analysed to fill a legal gap not adequately addressed by the Rome Statute, Elements of Crimes and Rules of Procedure and Evidence, their roles as interpretive aids might be more or less prominent.

1.3 Sources of interpretive problems

Thus far, interpretation has been defined as the public or external expression by judges of how the Rome Statute is to be construed. As well, interpretation has been distinguished from the judicial task of filling gaps in the Rome Statute. However, these elaborations only take us so far. It remains unclear which types of issues necessitate interpreting the Rome Statute. For example, is a judicial statement about the relationship between the Rome Statute and the four *Geneva Conventions on the Laws of War* (1949)[19] (*Geneva Conventions*) an act of interpretation or gap filling? What about a judicial statement on so-called 'unstated assumptions' underlying the Rome Statute?

Before it is possible to develop a legal methodology on how to interpret the crimes in the Rome Statute, it is necessary to understand which legal issues are considered interpretive for the purposes of this study. After all, it is precisely these problems that this study seeks to address. The definition of operative interpretation was coined by Jerzy Wróblewski. He was a member of the 'Bielefelder Kreis', an academic group that carried out a landmark comparative study of the interpretive practices of appellate courts in nine countries.[20] In the course of their study, Robert Summers, another member of the group, identified several common sources of interpretive problems. As will be seen, these sources also exist at the international level.

Judges of the International Criminal Tribunals for the former Yugoslavia and Rwanda (ICTY and ICTR respectively) have had the unenviable task of resolving a huge number of interpretive problems over the years in the absence of any guidance from their constitutive statutes.[21] At first blush, this jurisprudence appears to comprise a random universe of single and unique interpretive instances. However, a careful examination of these decisions renders discernable the same sources of interpretive problems that Summers identified. It is anticipated that judges of the Court will be similarly challenged.

The following sources of interpretive problems, which are not necessarily mutually exclusive, are introduced below: (1) linguistic issues; (2) background principles; (3) internal structure; (4) inadequate design; (5) value conflicts; (6) methodology; (7) special features of the case; (8) drafting errors; (9) inherent indefiniteness; (10) Elements of Crimes; (11) inter-treaty relationships; (12) the relationship between a constitutive statute or treaty and customary international law; and (13) subsequent agreements, practice and law.[22] The final four

---

[19] *Convention (I) for the Amelioration of the Condition of the Wounded and Sick in Armed Forces in the Field*, 75 UNTS 31; *Convention (II) for the Amelioration of the Condition of Wounded, Sick and Shipwrecked Members of Armed Forces at Sea*, 75 UNTS 85; *Convention (III) relative to the Treatment of Prisoners of War*, 75 UNTS 135; *Convention (IV) relative to the Protection of Civilian Persons in Time of War*, 75 UNTS 287 (all adopted 12 August 1949, all entered into force 2 October 1950).

[20] Bankowski and Others (n. 8). Nine countries were studied: Argentina, Germany, Finland, France, Italy, Poland, Sweden, United Kingdom and the United States.

[21] ICTY statute, annexed to UNSC Res. 827 (25 May 1993, as amended); ICTR statute, annexed to UNSC Res. 955 (8 November 1994, as amended).

[22] Several but not all of these interpretive issues take their inspiration from those identified in RS Summers, 'Statutory Interpretation in the United States' in DN MacCormick and RS Summers (eds.), *Interpreting Statutes: A Comparative Study* (Ashgate 1991) 407, 408–11.

interpretive problems may be understood more generally as problems arising from interpretive aids.

1.3.1 Linguistic

Linguistic interpretive issues encompass syntactical[23] ambiguities in respect of ordinary words or sentences.[24] In these situations, judges must choose which ordinary (and there may be more than one), standard technical (legal or non-legal) or special (non-standard) meaning should be ascribed to a statutory (or treaty) term.[25] This category of interpretive issues also encompasses problems of vagueness,[26] generality and deciding what meaning to attribute to evaluative words.[27] The crimes of genocide and other crimes against humanity illustrate this point.

Article 4 of the ICTY statute and article 2 of the ICTR statute respectively define these tribunals' jurisdiction over the crime of genocide. These definitions are identical to one another and were taken from the *Genocide Convention* (1948). Numerous linguistic interpretive problems have arisen from this definition. In particular, judges have struggled to interpret what it means to '*destroy,* in whole or in part, the group *as such*'.[28] Equally difficult was deciding whether to define the targeted 'group' positively or negatively[29] and how to define 'part' of the group.[30] There was also some confusion about whether a crime as grave as genocide committed by 'killing' required proof of intent to kill. The prosecutor argued that whereas '*meutre*' means deliberate homicide in French, the

---

[23] Syntax means: (1) 'orderly or systematic arrangement of parts or elements; constitution (of body); a connected order or system of things'; and (2) 'The order and arrangement of the words or symbols forming a logical sentence; the rules operating in formal systems.' Syntactical means 'belonging or relating to grammatical syntax.' Oxford English Dictionary, 2nd edn (Oxford University Press 1989).

[24] Summers (n. 22) 408.   [25] Ibid.

[26] A famous hypothetical of vagueness in a statute is repeated ibid. 409: '"No vehicles may be taken into the park." Borderline cases can easily be imagined here: a military jeep no longer in running condition which is placed on a pedestal in the park as a war memorial; a toy airplane with a motor for flight subject to remote control from the ground; a motorized wheelchair; a horse; roller skates; a pram.'

[27] Evaluation means: (1) 'The action of appraising or valuing (goods, etc.); a calculation or statement of value;' or (2) 'The action of evaluating or determining the value of (a mathematical expression, a physical quantity, etc.), or of estimating the force of (probabilities, evidence, etc.).' Evaluative means: 'Of, pertaining to, or tending to evaluation; appraisive, estimative.' Oxford English Dictionary (n. 23).

[28] *Prosecutor v. Jelisić*, Judgment, ICTY-95–10-T, 14 December 1999, paras. 78ff. (emphasis added); *Prosecutor v. Blagojević and Others*, Judgment, ICTY-02–60-T, 17 January 2005, para. 665.

[29] *Prosecutor v. Stakić*, Judgment, ICTY-97–24-A, 22 March 2006, paras. 12ff.

[30] See, e.g., *Prosecutor v. Krstić*, Judgment, ICTY-98–33-A, 19 April 2004, paras. 6ff.; *Blagojević* (n. 28) para. 668.

word 'killing' in English only means the act of causing another person's death. Ultimately, proof of intent to kill was held to be necessary.[31]

Article 5 of the ICTY statute and article 3 of the ICTR statute respectively define crimes against humanity. In contrast to genocide, the statutes define crimes against humanity differently. The ICTY statute expressly states that such crimes must be committed in armed conflict, whereas the ICTR statute does not. As well, article 5 of the ICTY statute fails to mention in its chapeau that the acts enumerated constitute crimes against humanity *when committed as part of a widespread or systematic attack* against any civilian population. Relative to other crimes, both the chapeaus to these provisions and the list of enumerated crimes contained thereunder have given rise to the greatest number of linguistic interpretive issues. Within the chapeaus, content has had to be provided to the phrases 'when committed in armed conflict',[32] 'attack',[33] 'widespread or systematic'[34] and 'directed against any civilian population'.[35] The elements of the following crimes against humanity also have had to be interpreted: 'murder';[36] 'extermination';[37] 'enslavement';[38] 'unlawful transfer';[39] 'torture';[40] 'rape';[41] 'persecutions';[42] and 'other inhumane acts'.[43]

Modes of liability have also given rise to linguistic interpretive problems. Both statutes assign criminal responsibility to individuals who 'planned, instigated, ordered, committed or otherwise aided and abetted in the planning, preparation or execution of a crime' within the tribunals' jurisdiction.[44] Each

---

[31] *Prosecutor* v. *Kayishema and Others*, Judgment, ICTR-95–1-T, 21 May 1999, paras. 101–14 (emphasis added).

[32] *Prosecutor* v. *Tadić*, Judgment, ICTY-94–1-T, 7 May 1997, para. 629, emphasis added (*Tadić Trial Judgment*).

[33] Ibid. para. 251 (attack distinguished from armed conflict); *Prosecutor* v. *Musema*, Judgment, ICTR-96–13-A, 27 January 2000, para. 205 (attack can be non-violent).

[34] *Prosecutor* v. *Akayesu*, Judgment, ICTR-96–4-T, 2 September 1998, paras. 578–580.

[35] *Prosecutor* v. *Blaškić*, Judgment, ICTY-95–14-T, 3 March 2000, para. 208; *Prosecutor* v. *Kupreškić and Others*, Judgment, ICTY-95–16-T, 14 January 2000, paras. 521ff.; *Prosecutor* v. *Martić*, Judgment, ICTY-95–11-T, 12 June 2007, paras. 50ff.

[36] *Blaškić* (n. 35) paras. 216–217.

[37] *Blagojević* (n. 28) paras. 571ff.; *Prosecutor* v. *Krstić*, Judgment, ICTY-98–33-T, 2 August 2001, para. 490; *Prosecutor* v. *Vasiljević*, Judgment, ICTY-98–32-T, 29 November 2002, paras. 216ff.

[38] *Prosecutor* v. *Kunarac and Others*, Judgment, ICTY-96–23-A & ICTY-96–23/1-A, 12 June 2002, paras. 116ff.

[39] *Prosecutor* v. *Naletilić and Martinović*, Judgment, ICTY-98–34-T, 31 March 2003, paras. 512ff.

[40] *Prosecutor* v. *Furundžija*, Judgment, ICTY-95–17/1-T, 10 December 1998, paras. 250ff.

[41] Ibid. paras. 174ff.; *Prosecutor* v. *Kvočka and Others*, Judgment, ICTY-98–30/1-T, 2 November 2001, paras. 174ff.; *Akayesu* (n. 34) paras. 597–598.

[42] *Blaškić* (n. 35) para. 234.   [43] Ibid. paras. 239–242.

[44] Article 7(1), ICTY statute; article 6, ICTR statute.

generally stated mode of liability has required judicial clarification.[45] In particular, judges have struggled to interpret the word 'committing' when defining the concept of joint criminal enterprise.[46] Command responsibility is also recognized in each of the statutes,[47] and judges have had to determine whether liability attaches to a commander for the crimes of his subordinates or for dereliction of duty.[48] Definitive content has also had to be provided for the vague phrases 'acts',[49] 'superior'[50] and 'had reason to know'.[51]

Apart from the definitions of crimes, judges have had to clarify the rights of the accused. For example, they have had to interpret the phrases '[a]ll persons shall be equal before the International Tribunal'[52] and the right of the accused to 'defend himself in person or through legal assistance of his own choosing'.[53] Interpretive issues have also arisen with respect to understanding judges' legal obligations, such as the requirement to 'have recourse to' the sentencing practices of the courts of the former Yugoslavia when determining terms of imprisonment.[54] It has also been necessary to clarify the obligation of States and others to cooperate with the tribunals.[55] Indeed, judges have had to give content to words as weighty as 'jurisdiction'[56] and 'established by law'[57] as well as to words as innocuous and seemingly clear as 'shall'[58] and 'includes'.[59]

The linguistic interpretive problems that judges confront are not restricted to words within the four corners of their governing statute and rules of procedure and evidence. Judges at the ICTY and ICTR have also been forced to define

---

[45] See, e.g., *Furundžija* (n. 40) para. 235.

[46] See, e.g., *Prosecutor v. Limaj and Others*, Judgment, Partially Dissenting and Separate Opinion and Declaration of Judge Schomburg, ICTY-03-66-A, 27 September 2001, paras. 10ff.

[47] Article 7(3), ICTY statute; article 6(3), ICTR statute.

[48] *Prosecutor v. Halilović*, Judgment, ICTY-01-48-T, 16 November 2005, para. 50.

[49] *Prosecutor v. Orić*, Judgment, ICTY-03-68-T, 30 June 2006, para. 302.

[50] *Prosecutor v. Delalić and Others*, Judgment, ICTY-96-21-T, 16 November 1998, paras. 355–363.

[51] Ibid. paras. 387–393; *Blaškić* (n. 35) paras. 314ff.

[52] *Prosecutor v. Tadić*, Judgment, ICTY-94-1-A, 15 July 1999, paras. 44, 56 (*Tadić Judgment*); *Prosecutor v. Delalić and Others*, Decision on the Prosecution's Motion for an Order requiring Advance Disclosure of Witnesses by the Defense, ICTY-96-21, 4 February 1998, para. 49.

[53] *Prosecutor v. Milosević*, Decision on Interlocutory Appeal of the Trial Chamber's Decision on the Assignment of Defense Counsel, ICTY-02-54-AR73.7, 1 November 2004, paras. 11ff.

[54] *Kunarac* (n. 38) paras. 348–349.

[55] *Prosecutor v. Simić and Others*, Motion for Judicial Assistance to be provided by SFOR and Others, ICTY-95-9- PT, 18 October 2000, paras. 38ff.

[56] *Prosecutor v. Tadić*, Decision on the Defence Motion for Interlocutory Appeal on Jurisdiction, ICTY-94-1-AR72, 2 October 1995, paras. 4ff. (*Tadić Jurisdiction Decision*).

[57] Ibid. paras. 43ff.

[58] *Barayagwiza v. Prosecutor*, Decision, ICTR-97-19.AR72, 3 November 1998, para. 110.

[59] *Delalić* (n. 50) paras. 1156ff.

key terms in the *Geneva Conventions* (1949) such as 'protected person'[60] and 'armed conflict'.[61] On occasion, they have also had to interpret phrases in the first two *Additional Protocols* (1977) to the *Geneva Conventions* (1949),[62] the Charter of the United Nations,[63] and the Report of the Secretary-General on the ICTY.[64]

This brief survey of interpretive issues arising from linguistic problems illustrates that they are the most common source of such issues. Judges repeatedly confronted with linguistic ambiguity, vagueness and generality are forced to resolve these problems lest they abdicate their responsibility to adjudicate the cases before them. In this regard, the jurisprudence suggests that the experience of ICTY and ICTR judges has been trying and perhaps even overwhelming at times. Because of what was regarded by the Security Council as an urgent need to establish these tribunals,[65] judges have been forced to work with statutes that contain vague jurisdictional headings and articulate neither fundamental principles of interpretation nor sources of applicable law.

This methodological deficit necessarily led these judges to look beyond the content of their governing statutes for guidance. What they found took them in many directions and is discussed in Chapter 2. In light of this odyssey and its results, one cannot resist regarding the code-like nature of the Rome Statute and supplementary Elements of Crimes was a backlash to the judicial creativity that some perceived in the judgments of the ICTY and ICTR.[66] This backlash has been characterized by one commentator as an 'overwhelming exercise in legal positivism'.[67] One might add that the effort is misguided if it was intended to forever stifle the act of judging by judges or fortify the Rome Statute against the mounting of linguistically inspired attacks by counsel

---

[60] Ibid. para. 265.

[61] *Tadić Jurisdiction Decision* (n. 56) paras. 67ff.

[62] *Protocol Additional to the Geneva Conventions of 12 August 1949, and relating to the Protection of Victims of International Armed Conflicts* (first *Protocol*), 1125 UNTS 3; *Protocol Additional to the Geneva Conventions of 12 August 1949, and relating to the Protection of Victims of Non-International Armed Conflicts* (second *Protocol*), 1125 UNTS 609 (both adopted 8 June 1977, both entered into force 7 December 1978); *Delalić* (n. 50) paras. 390–393.

[63] *Tadić Jurisdiction Decision* (n. 56) para. 30: whether 'threat to the peace' in article 39 of the UN Charter includes internal armed conflicts.

[64] UNSC, 'Report of the Secretary-General Pursuant to Paragraph 2 of Security Council Resolution 808' (1993), UN Doc. S/25704; *Tadić Jurisdiction Decision* (n. 56) paras. 291, 297.

[65] UNSC, ibid. para. 22; Preamble, UNSC Res. 955 (8 November 1994).

[66] D Hunt, 'The International Criminal Court – High Hopes, "Creative Ambiguity" and an Unfortunate Mistrust in International Judges' (2004) 2:1 J Int'l Crim Justice 56; W Schabas, 'Customary Law or "Judge-Made" Law: Judicial Creativity at the UN Criminal Tribunals' in J Doria, H-P Gasser and MC Bassiouni (eds.), *The Legal Regime of the International Criminal Court: Essays in Honour of Professor Igor Blishchenko* (Martinus Nijhoff 2009) 77.

[67] Hunt, ibid. 59.

appearing before the Court.[68] As Thomas Hobbes astutely observed: 'The written Laws, if they be short, are easily misinterpreted, from the diverse significations of a word, or two: if long they be more obscure by the diverse significations of many words . . . .'[69] Words are a medium for ideas and therefore are intrinsically imprecise. The most optimistic drafter should therefore accept that written laws will always give rise to linguistic interpretive problems.

1.3.2 Background principles

The issue here is whether any principle that exists outside of the legal text being interpreted – in the background – informs, modifies or renders a legal provision inapplicable in spite of the fact that, on its face, it is applicable.[70] A domestic example is the case of a man who kills his wife and then seeks to inherit half of her estate in accordance with a statute that expressly provides for this entitlement in cases where the deceased does not have a will.[71] In the absence of a statutory exception or qualifier to this entitlement, a judge would consider invoking the background principle that one is not entitled at law to profit from his own wrongdoing. In every jurisdiction, judges must decide what to do when the facts of the case lend themselves to the application of a background principle and the drafters of the applicable legal instrument have not made express provision for this scenario.[72]

In the jurisprudence of the ICTY and ICTR, this type of interpretive problem does not consciously arise very often. One can, however, discern instances of it. For example, article 24(2) of the ICTY statute offers judges almost no guidance on the scale of penalties that can be imposed for each crime within the jurisdiction of the tribunal. Judges have therefore interpreted this provision against the background principle of proportionality.[73] Another example can be found where the Appeals Chamber of the ICTR had to interpret rule 40 *bis* of its rules of procedure and evidence.[74] This rule states that an arrested person can be released if a confirmed indictment is not presented to him or her within a maximum of ninety days. In this case, the prosecutor had constructively detained the suspect twice, once for over seven months, before his indictment was confirmed. Among other things, the Appeals Chamber interpreted rule

---

[68] As Lord Simon of Glaisdale in the House of Lords once remarked: 'Words and phrases of the English language have an extraordinary range of meanings. This has been a rich resource in English poetry . . . but it has a concomitant disadvantage in English law (which seeks unambiguous precision, with the aim that every citizen shall know, as exactly as possible, where he stands under the law)'. *Stock* v. *Frank Jones (Tipton) Ltd.* [1978] 1 WLR 231 (HL) 236.

[69] *Leviathan* (JM Dent & Sons Ltd 1970) 146.

[70] Summers (n. 22) 409.   [71] Ibid.   [72] Ibid.   [73] *Blaškić* (n. 35) para. 796.

[74] Adopted on 5 July 1995 (as amended); *Barayagwiza* (n. 58).

40 *bis* against the background principles that prohibit abuses of process and require the prosecutor to perform her functions with due diligence.[75] The suspect was subsequently released, and all charges against him were dropped.

A background principle qualifies the meaning of a statutory provision and thereby limits its application to a particular set of facts. A judge does not invalidate the provision but instead avoids an absurd or patently unjust outcome by 'reading down'. This technique enables a court to give general words a more specific meaning in light of the background principle.[76] For example, a reverse onus provision requiring an individual to 'prove' something could be read down to mean 'give sufficient evidence', thereby reducing a legal burden to an evidential burden.[77]

Use of the term 'background principle' can serve as judicial shorthand for signalling to the reader that the judge must step outside the four corners of a legal instrument to make sense of the meaning contained therein. The impact of a background principle on the interpretation of a statute or treaty is to expand the relevant context in which it is to be interpreted. To make the best use of a background principle as an interpretive aid, judges should express in their decisions awareness that they are expanding their interpretive context. In the aforementioned examples, judges interpreted a provision or rule in a manner that was consistent with or comprehensible against a background principle but without calling it that.

A lawyer trained in the common law might regard a background principle as similar to a principle derived from equity, the common law or the constitution, which is invoked by judges to interpret statutes. While they are similar, insofar as a background principle may be derived from an applicable source of law, it is used as an interpretive aid, not necessarily as a binding source of law to remedy a legislative gap or silence. At the international level, a background principle might have its source in customary law or general principles common to all civilized nations. Principles originating from these legal sources only become background principles if they become contextually relevant to the interpretive task at hand. Finally, a background principle is a legally relevant principle, not a policy consideration.

1.3.3 *Internal structure*

An internal structural interpretive issue arises when a legal text contains an asymmetry or inconsistency or is incoherent in some respect. Otherwise

---

[75] Ibid., *Barayagwiza* v. *Prosecutor*, Decision, Separate Opinion of Judge Shahabuddeen, ICTR-97–19-AR72, 3 November 1999, ss. 4 and 5.

[76] RS Geddes, 'Purpose and Context in Statutory Interpretation' (2005) 2 Univ of New England LJ 5, 24–25.

[77] *R* v. *Lambert* [2001] 3 WLR 206 (HL).

parallel or functionally similar provisions may contain slight linguistic differences. This begs the question whether this difference is indicative of a difference in meaning.[78] One major structural issue that the ICTY Appeals Chamber confronted in *Prosecutor* v. *Tadić* (1995) was reconciling the relationship between articles 2 and 3 of the ICTY statute.[79] Article 2 refers to 'grave breaches' of the *Geneva Conventions* (1949), which are widely understood to be committed only in international armed conflicts. Article 3, however, gives the tribunal the power to 'prosecute persons violating the laws or customs of war', also without expressly referring to the requisite nature of the underlying conflict. A literal reading of article 3 might lead to the conclusion that it applies to all violations of the laws or customs of war, irrespective of whether they occur in the context of an internal or international armed conflict. However, article 5 explicitly states that crimes against humanity may be prosecuted by the tribunal irrespective of whether they are committed in armed conflict of an internal or international character. Arguably, the drafters could have added the same express reference to article 3 if its application was intended to have the same breadth. An argument *a contrario* based on the absence of similar wording in article 3 might suggest that it applies only to one class of conflict rather than to both of them.

Ultimately, the Appeals Chamber held that article 2 applies only to international conflicts and article 3 applies to both internal and international armed conflicts.[80] It held that article 3 functions as a residual clause, which is intended to ensure that no serious violation of international humanitarian law is removed from the jurisdiction of the ICTY. According to the Appeals Chamber, 'Article 3 aims to make such jurisdiction watertight and inescapable.'[81]

Two other major structural issues arising from within the ICTY and ICTR statutes pertain to modes of participation and crimes against humanity. First, it was unclear whether the doctrine of superior responsibility in both statutes applies to all modes of participation in a crime – 'planned, instigated, ordered, committed or otherwise aided and abetted in the planning, preparation or execution of a crime'.[82] Second, judges had to resolve whether their jurisdiction over crimes against humanity was limited to conduct connected to another crime within their jurisdiction, as was the case under the Charter of the International Military Tribunal for Nuremberg.[83]

1.3.4 Inadequate design

Design inadequacies encompass legislative misunderstandings, miscategorizations in legal texts, faulty and indeterminate ends of those texts, mistaken or

---

[78] Summers (n. 22) 410. [79] *Tadić Jurisdiction Decision* (n. 56) paras. 87, 91.
[80] Ibid. paras. 84, 91. [81] Ibid. para. 91.
[82] *Orić* (n. 49) para. 296; *Prosecutor* v. *Blagojević*, Judgment, ICTY-02–60-A, 9 May 2007, para. 280.
[83] *Kupreškić* (n. 35) para. 573.

unstated assumptions about means, inapposite means and bad drafting.[84] Several examples of inadequate design are evident with respect to the ICTY and ICTR tribunals' jurisdiction over crimes against humanity. Judges have had to determine whether these crimes are limited to conduct that is committed in the course of an armed conflict, internal or international.[85] Another design issue is whether a single act can constitute a crime against humanity[86] and whether proof of the existence of a government policy is required to make out the offence.[87] Judges have also had to determine whether persecution as a crime against humanity can cover acts not enumerated elsewhere in the ICTY statute.[88]

The absence of express mental elements for crimes that fall within the jurisdiction of the ICTY and ICTR has also been a huge source of interpretive problems. Some illustrative examples include determining the *mens rea* requirements for persecution,[89] extermination[90] and deportation[91] as crimes against humanity, as well as the *mens rea* for superior responsibility[92] and for wilful killing and murder.[93] With respect to genocide, defining the specific intent to destroy a group in whole or in part has been particularly challenging.[94] The ICTY has also had to articulate the customary elements of the following grave breaches that are listed in its statute but are not defined therein or in the *Geneva Conventions* (1949): 'torture', 'wilfully causing great suffering', 'inhuman treatment' and 'serious injury to body or health'.[95]

Article 3 of the ICTY statute is also susceptible to interpretive problems arising from its design. Arguably, all residual clauses are deliberately 'under-detailed' or 'under-designed'. Still, some are better than others. In spite of its express wording, parties still asked judges to clarify whether the list of acts enumerated in article 3 is illustrative or exhaustive.[96] The tribunal has also had to repeatedly clarify whether particular crimes are covered under article 3 by determining whether the test it set out in *Tadić* (1995) has been met.[97] Other interpretive issues caused by design inadequacies include the following: (1) the features of the doctrine of joint criminal enterprise as a means of assigning individual responsibility;[98] (2) whether causality is an element of

---

[84] Summers (n. 22) 410.   [85] *Tadić Jurisdiction Decision* (n. 56) paras. 140–141.
[86] *Kupreškić* (n. 35) para. 550.   [87] Ibid. para. 551.   [88] Ibid. para. 608.
[89] *Blaškić* (n. 35) paras. 235ff.   [90] *Stakić* (n. 29) paras. 252ff.   [91] Ibid. paras. 304ff.
[92] *Prosecutor* v. *Blaškić*, Judgment, ICTY-95–14-A, 29 July 2003, paras. 54ff.
[93] *Delalić* (n. 50) paras. 437–439.
[94] *Krstić* (n. 30) paras. 24ff.; *Blagojević* (n. 28) paras. 655ff.
[95] *Delalić* (n. 50) paras. 441, 498ff.   [96] *Blaškić* (n. 35) paras. 162ff.
[97] *Tadić Jurisdiction Decision* (n. 56) paras. 87, 91; *Delalić* (n. 50) paras. 278ff. See, e.g., *Prosecutor* v. *Furundžija*, Decision on the Defendant's Motion to Dismiss Counts 13 and 14 of the Indictment (Lack of Subject Matter Jurisdiction), ICTY-95–17/1-T, 29 May 1998, paras. 13–14, 18.
[98] *Prosecutor* v. *Brđanin*, ICTY-99–36-A, 3 April 2007, paras. 389ff.

superior responsibility;[99] and (3) in respect of the United Nations Charter, determining which measures the Security Council may take in accordance with articles 41 and 42 to maintain or restore international peace and security.[100] Inadequate design issues perhaps come closest to blurring the line between operative interpretation and gap filling. Indeed, reasonable people may disagree about which of these legal tasks confronts judges in a given case.

1.3.5 Value conflicts

A value conflict arises when language in a legal text restates or renders unresolved a value controversy in the international community. Examples of value conflicts in the ICTY and ICTR statutes are difficult to find, largely because they lack preambular paragraphs that outline the goals of these tribunals. Nevertheless, the report of the UN Secretary-General on the establishment of the ICTY inelegantly states that the tribunal was intended to 'bring about the achievement of the aim of putting an end to such crimes and of taking effective measures to bring to justice the persons responsible for them, and would contribute to the restoration and maintenance of peace'.[101]

Two value conflicts identified by judges are between deterrence and individual responsibility, and between applying customary law, which may be inadequate in places, and achieving the ICTY's goal to 'bring to justice' persons responsible for serious crimes committed in the former Yugoslavia. In *Prosecutor v. Erdemović* (1997), Judges McDonald and Vohrah of the Appeals Chamber rejected the defence of duress in cases of killings in part because they believed that this would undermine the tribunal's goal of deterrence.[102] These judges reasoned that negating individual responsibility in the case before them would send the wrong message to others forced to commit crimes under duress.[103]

In *Tadić* (1995), the Appeals Chamber acknowledged that its jurisdiction was mainly limited to crimes under customary international law, but it also held that article 3 of the ICTY statute covers violations of the laws or customs of war committed in both international and internal conflicts. The latter finding was supported in part by the argument that the tribunal must be free to realize its mandate.[104] Such tensions have the potential to influence the interpretive principle by which a judge chooses to be guided. For example, a purposive interpretation might be favoured where the rights of the accused are pitted

---

[99] *Delalić* (n. 50) paras. 396ff.   [100] *Tadić Jurisdiction Decision* (n. 56) paras. 31ff.

[101] UNSC (n. 64) para. 26. See also the purposes of the ICTR and ICTY tribunals, as expressed in UNSC Res. 955 (8 November 1994) and UNSC Res. 808 (22 February 1993).

[102] *Prosecutor v. Erdemović*, Judgment, Joint Separate Opinion of Judges McDonald and Vohrah, ICTY-96–22-A, 7 October 1997, para. 75.

[103] Ibid. para. 80.   [104] *Tadić Jurisdiction Decision* (n. 56) para. 93.

against the need for the prosecutor to be in a position to exercise all powers necessary for her to fulfil the tribunal's mandate.[105]

Judges of the Court will also be forced to resolve value conflicts. To give just one example, article 8(2)(b)(iv) of the Rome Statute prohibits deliberate attacks that cause 'clearly excessive' collateral damage to civilians, civilian objects or the natural environment. Judges will have to weigh the permissibility of collateral damage during armed conflict against the legally protected status of civilians and non-military objects.

1.3.6 Methodology

Even in a system where a general method of interpretation prevails, interpretive issues may arise about the application of this method. For example, a general method of treaty interpretation that emphasizes literal or plain meaning can raise questions about the meaning of 'literal' or 'plain'. The same is true of a method that emphasizes a treaty's 'purpose', which can be a vague or ambiguous concept if left undefined.

Articles 31–33 of the *Vienna Convention on the Law of Treaties* (1969) (*Vienna Convention*)[106] have been described as articulating the general principles of interpretation in the international legal system[107] and forming a part of customary law.[108] The initial hurdle for the ICTY and ICTR judges was to determine whether to be guided by these provisions in the *Vienna Convention* (1969).[109] Both tribunals' constitutive statutes are annexes to Security Council resolutions and therefore not technically treaties. Even after deciding to be guided by these provisions, judges continued to face methodological hurdles. Article 31(1) of the *Vienna Convention* (1969) states that a treaty shall be interpreted 'in good faith in accordance with the ordinary meaning to be given to the terms of the treaty in their context and in the light of its object and purpose'. However, this methodological imperative itself gives rise to interpretive issues about its precise meaning. Context is defined in article 31(2) as follows:

> The context for the purpose of the interpretation of a treaty shall comprise, in addition to the text, including its preamble and annexes:
>
> (a) any agreement relating to the treaty which was made between all the parties in connexion with the conclusion of the treaty;

---

[105] *Furundžija* (n. 40) paras. 738–739.
[106] 1155 UNTS 331 (adopted 23 May 1969, entered into force 27 January 1980).
[107] *Delalić* (n. 50) para. 1161.
[108] Koskenniemi (n. 12) 181; MT Kamminga, 'Final Report on the Impact of International Human Rights Law on General International Law' in MT Kamminga and M Scheinin (eds.), *The Impact of Human Rights Law on General International Law* (Oxford University Press 2009) 1, 10.
[109] See Chapter 2, Section 2.2.

(b) any instrument which was made by one or more parties in connexion
with the conclusion of the treaty and accepted by the other parties as
an instrument related to the treaty.

A contextual interpretation has been understood as requiring consideration
of the text in the statutes, situating the statutes in their historical context,
considering the nature of international law and the international system, as
well as considering the nature of the conflict that gave rise to the creation of the
tribunals.[110] As well, a purposive interpretation has been understood to mean
a contextual interpretation, an interpretation that accords with the purpose of
the treaty to which a term in the statutes can be traced, the purpose of the
tribunals as well as the purpose of the statutes.[111]

In addition to leaving key terms undefined, article 31(1) of the *Vienna Convention* (1969) contains the following imperatives, which could each lead one
in different directions in the absence of knowing which principle is paramount:
'in *good faith* in accordance with the *ordinary meaning* to be given to the terms
of the treaty *in their context* and in the light of *its object and purpose*'.[112]

1.3.7 Special features of the case

Facts that are difficult to ascertain or characterize can sometimes be the main
cause of an interpretive issue.[113] For example, use of the term 'ethnic cleansing'
raised questions about whether it describes acts of genocide.[114] As well, the
circumstances surrounding the conflicts in the former Yugoslavia and Rwanda
raised the issue of whether civilians in positions of authority may incur criminal responsibility under the doctrine of command or superior responsibility.[115]
Another issue for the ICTY was whether deportation as a crime against humanity can occur when the border of a State is not yet fixed and instead is a
'constantly changing frontline'.[116]

1.3.8 Drafting errors

Odd or erroneous punctuation and other drafting errors may give rise to an
interpretive ambiguity or even a literal absurdity.[117] For example, the French
version of the ICTR statute erroneously referred to a 'widespread *and* systematic
attack' in article 3, which deals with crimes against humanity.[118] Another
famous drafting error was the appearance of a semicolon in the English and
French versions of article 6(c) of the Charter for the International Military
Tribunal for Nuremberg. This provision defined the tribunal's jurisdiction
over crimes against humanity as follows:

---

[110] See Chapter 2, Section 2.3.1.3.   [111] See Chapter 2, Section 2.3.1.4.
[112] Emphasis added.   [113] Summers (n. 22) 411.   [114] *Krstić* (n. 30) paras. 567, 578.
[115] *Delalić* (n. 50) paras. 355–363.   [116] *Stakić* (n. 29) paras. 301ff.
[117] Summers (n. 22) 411.   [118] *Musema* (n. 33) para. 202.

CRIMES AGAINST HUMANITY: namely, murder, extermination, enslavement, deportation, and other inhumane acts committed against any
civilian population, before or during the war; or persecutions on political,
racial or religious grounds in execution of or in connection with any crime
within the jurisdiction of the Tribunal, whether or not in violation of the
domestic law of the country where perpetrated.[119]

The semicolon between the words 'war' and 'or' gave rise to two doubts. The
first was whether the acts listed before the semicolon could fall within the
tribunal's jurisdiction without being connected to another crime within its
jurisdiction. The second was whether those acts could be justified by arguing
that they were perpetrated in conformity with the domestic law of the country
where they were committed. Drafters intended neither of these possibilities,
and the semicolon was eventually replaced with a comma.[120]

1.3.9 Inherent indefiniteness

A legal concept may be inherently indefinite, thus rendering the task of interpretation extremely difficult. A good example of this is the crime of 'other inhumane acts' as a crime against humanity under article 5 of the ICTY statute.[121]
The tribunal consequently defined the crime in relative terms (relative to torture and degrading treatment)[122] and in the negative (inhumane treatment
is treatment that is not humane).[123] Other words and terms that have given
rise to this kind of interpretive problem include the following: 'instigated';[124]
'*serious* bodily or mental *harm*';[125] 'persecution';[126] 'torture';[127] 'outrages upon
personal dignity';[128] 'wilfully causing great suffering or serious injury to body
and health';[129] 'cruel and inhumane treatment';[130] and 'serious injury'.[131]

1.3.10 The Elements of Crimes

Following the Rome conference, a Preparatory Commission was established
to draft an Elements of Crimes (Elements) document, which the Assembly of
States Parties to the Rome Statute adopted at its first session on 9 September
2002.[132] The Elements set out the mental and material elements that are to be

---

[119] Agreement for the Prosecution and Punishment of the Major War Criminals of the
European Axis, and Charter of the International Military Tribunal, 82 UNTS 279 (No.
251) (adopted and entered into force 8 August 1945).

[120] Protocol Rectifying Discrepancy in the Charter (6 October, 1945).

[121] *Delalić* (n. 50) paras. 516ff.   [122] Ibid. para. 542.

[123] Ibid. para. 532; *Kupreškić* (n. 35) paras. 562ff.   [124] *Akayesu* (n. 34) para. 481.

[125] (emphasis added); *Blagojević* (n. 28) para. 645; *Krstić* (n. 30) para. 506.

[126] *Kupreškić* (n. 35) para. 567; *Naletilić and Martinović* (n. 39) paras. 632ff.

[127] *Kunarac* (n. 38) para. 149.   [128] Ibid. para. 161.   [129] *Delalić* (n. 50) paras. 506ff.

[130] *Krstić* (n. 37) paras. 515ff.   [131] *Delalić* (n. 50) paras. 509ff.

[132] ICC-ASP/1/3 (part II-B), adopted by consensus.

proven in order to reach a finding of guilt. Article 9(1) of the Rome Statute provides that the Elements 'shall assist' judges in the 'interpretation and application of articles 6, 7, 8 and 8 *bis*'. Article 21(1)(a), however, reads: 'The Court shall apply: (a) In the first place, this Statute, Elements of Crimes and its Rules of Procedure and Evidence.' The primacy of the Elements of Crimes as an interpretive aid is therefore also a subject of inquiry in this study, as is its relationship to other aids.

1.3.11 The Rome Statute and other treaties

Judges of the ICTY and ICTR have had to reconcile the relationship between their constitutive statutes and treaties that deal with the same conduct. Where terminology from other treaties is transplanted into the constitutive statutes of the tribunals, judges have had to determine the following: (1) whether to ascribe the same meaning to these words as was ascribed to them in the donor treaty; and (2) whether these words require the importation of legal concepts that attach to them in the donor treaty. Where the language in the constitutive statute differs from the terminology contained in prior law, or omits it, the question arises whether the drafters of the constitutive statute intended to signify a legal conceptual departure from established law. One such task has been to interpret the scope of article 3 of the ICTY statute, including how it relates to other legal instruments.[133] The Appeals Chamber in *Tadić* (1995) held that article 3:

> is a general clause covering all violations of humanitarian law not falling under Article 2 or covered by Articles 4 or 5, more specifically: (i) violations of the Hague law on international conflicts; (ii) infringements of provisions of the Geneva Conventions other than those classified as 'grave breaches' by those Conventions; (iii) violations of common Article 3 and other customary rules on internal conflicts; [and] (iv) violations of agreements binding upon the parties to the conflict, considered qua treaty law, i.e. agreements which have not turned into customary international law.[134]

A related and equally significant challenge was determining the relationship between the ICTY and ICTR statutes, the four *Geneva Conventions* (1949) and the jurisdiction of these tribunals. The Secretary-General in his report on the establishment of the ICTY stated that these conventions are reflective of custom and that the tribunal should apply rules that are undoubtedly reflective of custom.[135] In a landmark decision, the Appeals Chamber in *Tadić* (1995) held that the tribunal's jurisdiction extends to violations of the laws and customs of war committed in a non-international armed conflict and that common article 3

---

[133] *Tadić Jurisdiction Decision* (n. 56) paras. 87, 91; *Delalić* (n. 50) para. 300.
[134] *Tadić Jurisdiction Decision* (n. 56) para. 89.   [135] UNSC (n. 64) paras. 34–35.

to the *Geneva Conventions* (1949) forms part of customary international law.[136] These findings cemented the relationship between the ICTY statute and these conventions insofar as judges draw heavily from the latter when interpreting the former. This is, however, not always the case. For example, one judge remarked: 'I do not believe that it is necessary to decide whether deportation has the same meaning under the Geneva Conventions and under Article 5 of the Statute.'[137] Judges of the ICTY also held that large parts of the two *Additional Protocols* (1977) to the *Geneva Conventions* (1949) form part of customary international law and that the formulation of superior responsibility in the ICTY statute is based on article 86(2) of the first *Additional Protocol* (1977).[138]

1.3.12 The Rome Statute and customary law

Adjudicating upon genocide, other crimes against humanity and war crimes, judges of the ICTY and ICTR have had to determine to what extent their interpretation of the definitions of these crimes in their constitutive statutes can deviate from what they ascertain to be customary law. According to one ICTY Trial Chamber:

> [What] the Security Council has enacted under Chapter VII is the creation of a tribunal whose jurisdiction is expressly confined to the prosecution of breaches of international humanitarian law that are beyond any doubt part of customary law, not the establishment of some eccentric and novel code of conduct . . . [139]

The Report of the Secretary-General on the establishment of the ICTY states that the tribunal should apply rules that are 'beyond doubt' customary.[140] Some judges have gone so far as to suggest that customary law is 'imported' into the ICTY and ICTR statutes.[141] However, the Appeals Chamber of the ICTY held that it was open to the Security Council of the United Nations to expressly depart from custom in the ICTY statute.[142]

Significantly, no similar authoritative document exists for the Rome Statute. There is only article 10 of the Statute, which provides that nothing in the jurisdiction, admissibility and applicable law section of the Statute 'shall be interpreted as limiting or prejudicing in any way existing or developing rules of international law for purposes other than this Statute'. Judges will therefore be left with the extremely difficult task of determining the relationship between the Rome Statute and customary law. For example, does language in the Rome Statute mirroring that contained in treaties reflecting customary law

---

[136] *Tadić Jurisdiction Decision* (n. 56) paras. 102ff.

[137] *Prosecutor v. Krnojelac*, Judgment, ICTY-97–25-A, 17 September 2003, para. 14.

[138] *Blagojević* (n. 82) para. 281.   [139] *Tadić Jurisdiction Decision* (n. 56) para. 19.

[140] UNSC (n. 64) para. 34.   [141] *Tadić Trial Judgment* (n. 32) para. 559.

[142] *Tadić Judgment* (n. 52) para. 296.

incorporate by reference legal concepts in those treaties that are not expressly mentioned in the Rome Statute? Clarifying this relationship is a fundamental question that any proposed interpretive methodology for the Rome Statute must resolve in order to determine custom's role, if any, as an aid to interpreting these crimes.[143]

1.3.13 Subsequent agreements, practice and law

Interpretive issues arise when, subsequent to the adoption of a treaty, a seemingly relevant and applicable agreement among States Parties, practice or law emerges. According to article 31(3) of the *Vienna Convention* (1969), judges are required to take into account subsequent agreements, practice and law when interpreting a treaty. For example, in *Tadić* (1995), subsequent practice was considered by Judge Abi-Saab to determine whether articles 2 and 3 of the ICTY statute applied to both international and internal armed conflicts.[144] In the Rome regime, judges will have to decide whether the crimes defined in the Statute are intended to be frozen in time and, if applicable, how much weight to place on these subsequent developments. For example, at the 2010 Review Conference for the Rome Statute, seven interpretive Understandings on the crime of aggression were adopted. Do these have a role to play as aids to interpretation, and, if so, what role is this relative to other aids?

In sum, while the working definition of interpretation in this study might seem narrow at first blush, it in fact extends beyond the resolution of linguistic ambiguities in articles 6, 7, 8 and 8 *bis* of the Rome Statute to cover a range of interpretive issues that are expected to confront judges. And although the origins of interpretive problems may be the same across many legal systems, each system may need to develop its own methodology or tools for resolving them. Finally, in spite of the above effort to clarify which issues are interpretive, this study does not exclude the possibility that there will remain a grey area where reasonable disagreement is possible on whether an issue gives rise to an interpretive or gap-filling problem.

1.4 Legal methodology

While the practise of law is multifaceted and the practitioner is constantly confronted with new facts and issues, there are some skills that are kept sharpened for the simple reason that their usefulness is proven time and again. These include issue spotting, research, legal drafting and interpreting legal instruments to name a few. These skills are taught in law schools, honed over time through practise and sometimes guided and governed by principles and

---

[143] See Chapters 6–8.
[144] *Tadić Jurisdiction Decision* (n. 56) Separate Opinion of Judge Abi-Saab.

standards. What then is a legal methodology? A legal methodology may be defined 'as a systemic general approach to the duly purposive and consistent execution of a recurrent type of major task arising in the making or application of law'.[145] Simply put, it is a template or guide for the consistent performance of a recurring legal task.

A legal methodology for the 'operative' interpretation of crimes in the Rome Statute is understood to mean a systemic general approach to reasoning through the resolution of interpretive issues arising from the definitions of these crimes. A fully developed method has three tiers. It offers its user, in this case judges and lawyers in the field of international criminal law, the following levels of assistance: (1) a primary interpretive principle to guide their reasoning process when confronted with interpretive issues; (2) arguments or reasons that support (and perhaps also do not support) this interpretive principle; and (3) a catalogue of materials or aids that must, may and, if applicable, may not be taken into account in support of these arguments.[146] An example from Canada might help to illustrate the work that such a methodology is intended to do – or at least what can happen in the absence of a methodology.

In 1928, the Supreme Court of Canada held that women are not eligible to be members of the Senate.[147] Section 24 of the British North America Act (1867) (BNA Act or Act) stated that 'qualified persons' could be summoned to the Senate. While the word 'persons' was held to be gender neutral, the Court interpreted the word 'qualified' as excluding women. The Court justified its interpretation by pointing to its consistency with the common-law disability of women to hold public office and case law arising under other legislation dealing with the right of women to vote for a Member of Parliament. The Court held that if the Imperial Parliament intended to make such a marked departure from the common law, this intention must be clearly expressed. In a historic judgment, the Privy Council overruled the Supreme Court's decision in *Edwards* v. *Canada (Attorney General)* (1928) (*Edwards*) and held that women are eligible to become senators.[148] Their Lordships held that when interpreting an act of Parliament, it is permissible to consider 'external evidence derived from extraneous circumstances such as previous legislation and decided cases' and 'internal evidence derived from the Act itself'.

The external evidence considered included the circumstances that led to the passing of the BNA Act. Their Lordships concluded that the Act granted a written constitution to Canada that is 'subject to development through usage and convention'. They described it as a 'living tree capable of growth and expansion

---

[145] RS Summers, *Form and Function in a Legal System: A General Study* (Cambridge University Press 2006) 241.

[146] This definition takes its inspiration from the study in MacCormick and Summers (n. 8).

[147] *Edwards* v. *Canada (Attorney General)* [1928] SCR 276.

[148] *Edwards* v. *Canada (Attorney General)* [1930] AC 124.

within its natural limits'. Consequently, their Lordships considered it their duty to give the provisions in the Act a large and liberal interpretation in contrast to narrow and technical constructions. Additionally, outdated case law arising under other legislation was not considered particularly useful. Because customs 'are apt to develop into traditions [that] . . . remain unchallenged long after the reason for them has disappeared', the 'appeal to history . . . in this particular matter is not conclusive'. The Privy Council observed that women are currently entitled to vote and to be candidates in all Dominion and provincial elections except for where they have been expressly excluded from the right to vote.

The internal evidence also proved to be useful. Their Lordships reasoned that the word 'persons' was used in other sections of the Act where one could be certain that the term included females. They also observed that other sections of the Act contained express references to 'male persons'. The Interpretation Act (1889) even stated that words importing the masculine gender shall include females. In an effort to harmonize section 24 with the rest of the Act, their Lordships interpreted the word 'persons' to include men and women. On the meaning of the word 'qualified', their Lordships held that it was a reference to the list of qualifications for senators contained in section 23 of the Act. In contrast to the Supreme Court, the Privy Council held that if Parliament intended to limit the word 'persons' in section 24 to male persons, 'it would surely have manifested such intention by an express limitation as it has done' in other sections.

The foregoing example highlights a number of issues that a methodology on interpretation can address and attempt to resolve. One of the most fundamental issues that the Privy Council confronted was identifying a governing interpretive principle. By reading the Act and considering the circumstances that led to its drafting, their Lordships were able to discern that it was a written constitution and thus were able to identify a corresponding interpretive principle to govern their analysis. The Privy Council decided to be guided by the principle of progressive interpretation. They invoked the image of a living tree that grows as a society changes. Similarly, the present study seeks to identify a governing interpretive principle that achieves the greatest degree of faithfulness to the definitions of crimes in the Rome Statute.

Once the Privy Council articulated the interpretive principle that would guide its reasoning, their Lordships began to offer arguments in support of their analysis. For example, the Privy Council accepted the argument of giving a large and liberal interpretation to the words in section 24 of the Act. This argument was qualified by an argument against stretching the ordinary meaning of words beyond their 'natural limits'. As well, a complementary argument was accepted that favoured adopting an interpretation that is harmonious with the structure of the Act and the meaning of 'persons' in other sections. All of these arguments were accepted under the umbrella of a progressive approach to interpretation. The Supreme Court failed to identify a guiding interpretive principle as well as interpretive arguments in support of this principle. In this study, arguments that support and undermine the guiding interpretive principle are discerned.

Another critical issue was whether the common law created a rebuttable interpretive presumption. The Supreme Court's analytical point of departure was that the Act could only displace the common law in express terms. The Privy Council's approach was just the opposite. The Act was considered to be paramount, and constitutional rights arising from the ordinary meaning of words therein could be narrowed only by express language. To guide judges and counsel in interpreting the Rome Statute, the present study will attempt to reconcile the relationship between the Rome Statute and customary international law. Article 21 of the Rome Statute articulates a hierarchy of legal sources for gap-filling purposes. It does not, however, instruct judges on whether to presume that the definitions of crimes in the Rome Statute accord with customary international law. As *Edwards* (1928) demonstrates, the creation of such a presumption could have enormous implications for the work of the Court. In fact, the Appeals Chamber of the ICTY held that such a presumption exists in respect of its statute.[149] Whether such a presumption should inform a methodology for interpreting crimes in the Rome Statute is therefore a question of central importance that is addressed.

The parties involved in litigating the *Edwards* (1928) case submitted to the Supreme Court and Privy Council various materials in support of their positions including similar legislative texts and case law. The Supreme Court navigated its way through these materials without an overarching interpretive approach in mind, apart from the common-law disability presumption. By contrast, the Privy Council was guided by a progressive interpretative approach and a keen awareness that it was interpreting a written constitution, meaning the supreme law in Canada. With these considerations in mind, their Lordships were able to justify their decision not to give weight to subsidiary legislation and case law that no longer reflected prevailing values. Like the Privy Council, judges at the Court will have to sift through and make sense of the materials submitted by counsel in support of interpretive arguments. A methodology for interpreting crimes in the Rome Statute can help judges assess the relevance and weight to be given to these materials in a principled manner.

In conclusion, the present study will attempt the following: (1) identify the guiding interpretive principle or primary criterion for achieving the greatest

---

[149] *Tadić Trial Judgment* (n. 32) paras. 292, 296. However, the Appeals Chamber in *Tadić* qualified this rule in the following terms: '[A]s a general principle, provisions of the Statute defining the crimes within the jurisdiction of the Tribunal should always be interpreted as reflecting customary international law, unless an intention to depart from customary international law is expressed in the terms of the Statute, or from other authoritative sources'.

degree of faithfulness to crimes in the Rome Statute (e.g., literal, drafters' intent, purposive, contextual interpretation); (2) identify which types of arguments respect and undermine this principle (e.g., strict construction, deterrence, textual coherence, making the Court effective and so on); (3) discern the relationship between customary international law and the Rome Statute for the purposes of interpretation; and (4) analyze the role of and relationship over time between material aids in support of these arguments (e.g., Elements of Crimes, custom, treaties, *travaux préparatoires*, interpretive Understandings on aggression, case law, expert opinions, etc.).

1.5 Method for developing a legal methodology

1.5.1 International dimension

The method for carrying out this study merits some explanation, not least because it does not sail a traditional course of comparative research.

In Chapter 2, a narrow international comparative approach is taken in assessing the state of the art rather than studying the interpretation of (international) criminal statutes in a select number of domestic jurisdictions. Why? While a domestic comparative approach could very well yield valuable insights, this study assumes for three reasons that international law boasts nearly[150] all of the tools necessary for crafting a method of interpretation for crimes defined in an international treaty. Further, it is submitted that judges of the Court should approach the task of interpretation as an international legal exercise.

First, there are articles 31–33 of the *Vienna Convention* (1969), which have guided the reasoning of diverse international and regional courts, tribunals, treaty bodies and States for decades. Sure, these provisions have been criticized inter alia for being both under- and overinclusive as well as too general. But perhaps that is the fate of any set of guidelines that seek to assist with the interpretation of every treaty for all time. Still, their enduring usefulness to many suggests that it would be hard to do better or, for those more sceptical, that they are entirely unhelpful. Rather than reinvent the wheel, therefore, and barring strong evidence of States Parties contracting out of these provisions in the Rome Statute, this study seeks to build upon the wisdom of those who drafted the *Vienna Convention* (1969) provisions.[151] It does not question their

---

[150] When examining arguments that support and undermine the principle of legality as well as operationalizing it, consideration is given to relevant domestic material.

[151] For a different approach, see D Jacobs, 'Positivism and International Criminal Law: The Principle of Legality as a Rule of Conflict of Theories' in J d'Aspremont and J Kammerhofer (eds.), *International Legal Positivism in a Post-Modern World* (Cambridge University Press, forthcoming October 2014), 1, 27, http://papers.ssrn.com/sol3/papers.cfm?abstract_id=2046311, accessed 16 October 2013.

widely acknowledged customary status or the Court's rulings that they apply to the interpretation of the Rome Statute.[152] Recourse to the *Vienna Convention* (1969) provisions is also rooted in the idea that international criminal law treaties do not *ipso facto* create entirely self-contained regimes such that methods of interpretation for them are completely incompatible with the general rules of treaty interpretation. This idea might appeal to those who think that articles 31–33 of the *Vienna Convention* (1969) have the potential to work against the fragmentation of international law.

Second, this study tries to draw from the rich experiences of two ad hoc international criminal tribunals that have been in operation for nearly twenty years. In comparison to their domestic counterparts, these tribunals perhaps more closely resemble the Rome regime in terms of legal heritage, culture and constraints. The legitimacy factor is also worth considering. It might be risky to construct a method of interpretation for international crimes defined in a multilateral treaty that is inspired by the interpretive practices of a handful of national courts.

Third, and most important, the Rome Statute itself contains two interpretive imperatives and a provision on applicable law; it is also accompanied by an Elements of Crimes document to assist with the interpretation of crimes in the Statute. These imperatives and aids arguably lie at the heart of any interpretive method developed, which is why the comparative approach taken is narrow, looking only at the jurisprudence of two other international criminal tribunals.

The ultimate goal is in fact to graft the method of interpretation developed in this study *onto* articles 31–33 of the *Vienna Convention* (1969), which offers a common and familiar interpretive framework for international criminal lawyers and judges hailing from all over the world. Indeed, the Court should treat the interpretation of crimes as an international legal exercise.

The Court is an international judicial body that is based on the law of nations and established by a multilateral treaty. Its object and purpose are unique,

---

[152] Koskenniemi (n. 12); Kamminga (n. 108); R Gardiner, *Treaty Interpretation* (Oxford University Press 2008) 12–13 and relevant international and national case law. On the Court accepting the applicability of the *Vienna Convention* (1969), see *Prosecutor v. Lubanga Dyilo*, Judgment on the Prosecutor's Application for Extraordinary Review of the Pre-Trial Chamber I's 31 Mar. 2006 Decision Denying Leave to Appeal, ICC-01/04–168, 13 July 2006, paras. 33–42, cited in G Bitti, 'Article 21 of the Statute of the International Criminal Court and the Treatment of Sources of Law in the Jurisprudence of the ICC' in C Stahn and G Sluiter (eds.), *The Emerging Practice of the International Criminal Court* (Martinus Nijhoff 2009) 281, 295. See also *Prosecutor v. Lubanga Dyilo*, Decision on the Final System of Disclosure and the Establishment of a Timetable, ICC-01/04–01/06, 15 May 2006, Annex I, para. 1; *Prosecutor v. Lubanga Dyilo*, Decision on the Practices of Witness Familiarisation and Witness Proofing, ICC-01/04–01/06, 8 November 2006, para. 8.

as is the context in which it operates. International courts have consistently held that reliance on domestic legal notions is justified only if 'international rules make explicit reference to national law or if such reference is necessarily implied by the very content and nature of the concept'.[153] Even then, a judge must consider whether the transplant of a national law, concept or method of reasoning needs to be adapted or adjusted to make sense in an international context.[154] 'Only if this enquiry leads to negative conclusions is one warranted to draw upon' the law, concept or method as it is conceived at the national level.[155]

Another way to understand the obligation to develop a method of interpretation that is grounded in international law is by drawing an analogy to John Rawls' concept of public reason.[156] Public reason respects that citizens have conflicting reasonable comprehensive doctrines – whether religious, moral, philosophical or cultural.[157] It respects this reasonable pluralism.[158] However, Rawls maintained that in a well-ordered constitutional democratic society, fundamental political questions need to be resolved and justified by citizens to one another using public reason.[159] In particular, the discourse of judges in their decisions must apply public reason.[160] This reason is public insofar as it applies to free and equal citizens, it is concerned with questions of fundamental political justice and its nature and content are public.[161]

Similarly, judges of the Court should invoke international public reason in their judgments rather than plucking interpretive principles from their domestic legal systems. The domestic legal system of a State is somewhat analogous to the comprehensive doctrine of a citizen living in a constitutional democracy. It is therefore anathema to international public reason for judges to fall back on the method of interpretation that exists in their domestic legal system. The State Party whose legal system is represented cannot reasonably

---

[153] *Erdemović* (n. 102), Separate and Dissenting Opinion of Judge Cassese, para. 3. Judge Cassese made these comments when deciding whether to import the national concept of guilty pleas to the international level. Although the present context is different, it nevertheless seems appropriate to heed his comments.

[154] Ibid. para. 6.   [155] Ibid.

[156] J Rawls, 'Public Reason Revisited' (1997) 64 U Chi L Rev 765. See also J Rawls, *Justice as Fairness* (Belknap 2001) 27–29.

[157] Rawls, 'Public Reason Revisited', ibid. 766.

[158] Ibid. 765.   [159] Ibid. 765–76.   [160] Ibid. 767.

[161] Ibid. Public reason is also necessary to ensure reciprocity and cooperation among States Parties: 'the idea of political legitimacy based on the criterion of reciprocity says: Our exercise of political power is proper only when we sincerely believe that the reasons we would offer for our political actions – were we to state them as government officials – are sufficient, and we also reasonably think that other citizens might also reasonably accept those reasons' (771).

expect other States Parties to endorse reasons in a judgment that reflect a legal system to which they do not belong. The legal reasons in the Court's judgments are of interest to all States Parties (and perhaps also Non-States Parties) and should therefore, to the extent possible, respect their freedom and equality.

1.5.2 Logical progression

A legal methodology for interpreting crimes in the Rome Statute has been defined above as comprising three tiers. However, the manner for developing this methodology does not always proceed cleanly from tier to tier. Four apparent detours warrant explanation. First, after identifying legality as the primary principle of interpretation in Chapter 3 and reconciling it with a human rights interpretive imperative in the Rome Statute, the Chapter closes by introducing readers to an issue that surfaces from this reconciliation yet remains unresolved: that of systemically integrating the background regimes of international human rights and humanitarian law as aids to interpreting crimes in the Rome Statute. This is an example of a step forward in the development of an interpretive methodology that at the same time exposes an important outstanding interpretive issue, a limitation.

A second apparent detour is then taken in Chapter 4, which is in the form of identifying the interests that underlie the principle of legality and arguments that might undermine these interests. The motivation for identifying supporting and non-supporting arguments for this principle before assigning it content – building the second tier of the method before the first – is the belief that legality can most effectively be operationalized by first sketching the essential context of interests it is intended to protect and those which threaten its primacy. It is only when these underlying and competing interests are identified and evaluated that legality can be given meaningful and principled content as well as surgically reconciled with the *Vienna Convention* (1969) provisions. The goal is to ensure the primacy of legality while avoiding any unnecessary slicing and dicing of the *Vienna Convention* (1969) provisions.

Having settled the first two tiers of the method, the study turns finally in Chapter 6 to the third tier, ascertaining the role of various interpretive aids and their relationship to one another. The inquiry commences in a possibly surprising way, by assessing customary law's relationship to the Rome Statute's definitions of crimes – a third apparent detour that requires explanation. Because of the historic importance of custom as an aid to interpreting international crimes as well as the careful drafting and adoption of the Elements of Crimes document, a central interpretive aid, special emphasis is placed on ascertaining the role of these aids relative to one another, as they may at times conflict. The difficulty with trying to answer this question by employing the usual analytical tools is set out in greater detail at the beginning of Chapter 6 before considering how a codification study might be undertaken to help resolve the issue. An extensive codification study follows in Chapters 7 and 8, which necessarily delays consideration of the role of other interpretive aids. However, given the centrality of this inquiry, the most rigorous and scientific method for resolving it was conjured.

In Chapter 9, the role of all interpretive aids as well as their relationship to one another is considered within the framework of the *Vienna Convention* (1969) provisions. However, a fourth apparent detour is taken in the middle of this Chapter to consider how time affects the use of these interpretive aids. The issue of intertemporality implicit in article 31(3)(c) of the *Vienna Convention* (1969) casts the aids to interpretation along a temporal dimension and asks whether the definitions of crimes in the Rome Statute are frozen or whether they can be interpreted in light of the content of these aids as they appear at the time the crime was allegedly committed or at the time of trial. This foray into the issue of intertemporality is a necessary juncture if one seeks to advance an interpretive method that can be used over time. It is to be expected that custom will evolve, that new and relevant treaties will be enacted, that general principles of law will grow and change and that subsequent practice and agreements will emerge that could influence the interpretation of the Rome Statute as well as treaties upon which it is based.

The method developed for developing a method of interpretation in this study – word play intended – may well be controversial. Some might find all or some of its elements inelegant, unnecessary, illogical in their ordering or too extensive (at the expense of overlooking other interpretive issues). Whatever the critiques may be, the motivation behind each step was borne out of a sincere interest in proceeding in a logical, principled and scientifically rigorous manner for the purpose of developing a method of interpretation for crimes in the Rome Statute. For those who find the method useful, it is worth noting that elements of it might be employed to develop interpretive methodologies for other international legal regimes.

Finally, to be clear, this study does not purport to be non-normative,[162] nor does it claim that a method of interpretation can yield 'correct' outcomes.[163] Rather, the goal is to develop 'mandatory guidelines'[164] that assist with how interpretive issues are thought of and resolved.

---

[162] M Ajevski, 'Interpretation and the Constraints on International Courts', 13 June 2012, MultiRights Research Paper No. 12–05, 1, 35, 37, 39, http://papers.ssrn.com/sol3/papers. cfm?abstract'id=2083616, accessed 20 October 2013.

[163] A von Bogdandy and I Venzke, 'Beyond Dispute: International Judicial Institutions as Lawmakers' (2011) 12 German LJ 979, 984.

[164] See Chapter 2, Section 2.2.

1.6 Practical merits of this study

The legal methodology developed in the Chapters that follow cannot serve as a lone guarantor of the Court's legitimacy or as a panacea for constraining every stage of legal analysis in the Court's judgments. Hopefully it does, however, promote the rule of law and thereby enhances the Court's image as respectful of this value. Legal theorist Jeremy Waldron describes the rule of law as follows:

> The Rule of Law celebrates features of a well-functioning system of government such as publicity and transparency in public administration, the generality and prospectivity of the norms that are enforced in society, the predictability of the social environment that these norms help to shape, the procedural fairness involved in their administration, the independence and incorruptibility of the judiciary, and so on. It looks to a world where people in positions of power exercise their power within a constraining framework of public rules rather than on the basis of their own preferences, their own ideology, or their own individual sense of right and wrong.[165]

The rule of law is therefore intended to constrain the judicial exercise of power by urging judges to be candid and to base their decisions on guidelines that are public, are prospective in their application and respect the equality of States Parties and individuals appearing before the Court. The rule of law also concerns itself with procedural fairness, judicial independence and impartiality. While no methodology for interpreting crimes in the Rome Statute can guarantee 'just' or unanimous outcomes, this study can help to discipline judicial reasoning on interpretation in the aforementioned ways and generate a principled dialogue among judges and counsel on the rules of interpretation for crimes within the Court's jurisdiction.

A possible criticism of this study is that the use of a methodology concedes the existence of ambiguities in how international crimes are defined in the Rome Statute. Without commenting on the soundness of this concern, it ignores the fact that the Rome Statute itself recognizes the possibility of these definitions being ambiguous. The legitimacy of the judiciary is therefore not pitted against candour. The two are reconciled within the Rome Statute by instructing judges to acknowledge the existence of interpretive problems and then resolve them in a principled manner. The method developed in this study is intended to assist judges in this effort.

Another criticism might be that judges could use the method in this study to expand, restrict or modify words and phrases in the Rome Statute to develop or create law. However, this risk always exists, even (or perhaps especially) in

---

[165] J Waldron, 'The Concept and the Rule of Law', Paper read at the NYU Colloquium in Legal, Political and Social Theory (14 September 2006) (on file with author).

the absence of a methodology. The judicial interpretation of treaty provisions through the medium of words necessarily adds a layer of meaning to them. This cannot be avoided. But supplying additional words so as to increase understanding is precisely the point of having judges interpret legal texts. The goal of a method of interpretation based on international legal imperatives is to guide and constrain, in a principled manner, the judicial exercise of discretion in the interpretive process. Beyond this, this study cannot guarantee that all concerned will embrace every interpretive outcome. In spite of their best efforts, allegations of judges legislating will remain a risk. Behind critiques of judicial activism, however, lies the myth of legal certainty, 'the myth that if the judge looks long enough and hard enough the law will always provide a clear, indisputable answer upon which all will agree'.[166] Indeed, a degree of judicial development of the law is inevitable.

Additionally, concerns about developing a methodology must be weighed against the risk of not doing so. Legal findings would be open to scrutiny without the shield that reasons can sometimes offer. While judges hearing the same case might not support the same interpretive outcome, their reasons will demonstrate to others that a reasonable basis for disagreement exists within the adopted method of interpretation. Interested parties can then compare these decisions and assess their merit based not just on the outcome but also on the soundness of the legal analysis contained therein. If no reasons are provided or judges' interpretive methods are completely different, concerns about bias or outcome-driven reasoning might be fuelled, and meaningful comparison will not be possible.

Indeed, a methodology for interpretation can generate vertical and horizontal consistency. Vertical consistency refers to the internal coherence of a decision that a judge writes. Adhering to a particular methodology rather than engaging in freestyle reasoning throughout a judgment reduces the chances of a contradiction in the interpretive analysis. Horizontal consistency refers to the consistent use of a method across several judgments. This consistency can discourage judges from deciding to 'go it alone' by invoking their own brand of interpretation in the face of a widespread practice of using a different methodology.

Another important benefit of a commonly used methodology is the legal certainty and shared dialogue it generates. By confining a discussion on interpretation to the guidelines set out in a methodology, it is possible for judges and counsel to address their arguments to one another secure in the knowledge that they will be understood and that their arguments fall within the scope of what

---

[166] B McLachlin, 'Judging in a Democratic State', Speech (3 June 2004), www.cjc-ccm.gc .ca/cmslib/general/Matlow_Docs/Authorities/Book%20of%20Authorities%20-%20Tab% 20E%20Rt.%20Hon.%20Beverley%20McLachlin%20article%20-%20Judging%20in% 20a%20Democratic%20State.pdf, accessed 23 April 2014.

is defined by the methodology as reasonable. A methodology can also weed out arguments that cannot be expressed using this shared language and can even help to garner support for arguments that are not popular at first blush. The debate on interpretive issues will be rich and informed by many different principled views. By gathering counsel and judges under the same methodological umbrella for the purposes of interpretation, a measure of accountability in this regard might also emerge.

Ultimately, all of this candour, structure and predictability can enhance the efficiency of Court proceedings. Judges and counsel come from many different cultural and legal backgrounds. This can create difficulties in communication, as a legal concept that may exist in one language might have no parallel in another language.[167] Instead of negotiating a hybrid of interpretive rules on a case-by-case basis, an interpretive methodology that is known to judges and counsel in advance of a hearing will exist. Before trial, counsel will know which interpretive principle will govern judges' deliberations and which supporting arguments and materials will most appeal to them. Counsel will therefore be able to efficiently draft their submissions to the Court and present their cases in the strongest possible terms. Lawyers for the defence are often especially pressed for time and have relatively fewer resources to prepare their legal briefs. Similarly, judicial deliberations will also be more focussed.

By enhancing the rule of law and efficiency of Court proceedings, a method of interpretation may also indirectly attract greater support for the Court from States Parties. It is well known that the Court relies on States Parties inter alia for its budget, the gathering of evidence, relocating witnesses, conducting investigations, carrying out arrests and enforcing sentences. The Rome Statute represents a delicate compromise struck by States, and it is important that the work of judges in interpreting its provisions remains faithful to the text and does not wholly undermine these underlying agreements. By the same token, decisions of the Court that uphold the rule of law may help attract Non-States Parties that are otherwise sceptical of the Court's agenda to join the Rome regime. States Parties dissatisfied with the work of the Court retain the option to exit the regime.[168]

Finally, there is the educative function of judicial decisions for observers of the Court, including national and international courts deciding cases involving the same crimes. A method of interpretation fosters transparent reasoning, allowing these judges to discern the interpretive principle, supporting arguments and aids to interpretation that lead the Court to prefer a particular interpretive outcome over several other options.

There are some who will, against all evidence to the contrary, argue that the Court is merely a pawn in international relations, the embodiment of victors'

---

[167] Wald (n. 3).   [168] Article 127, Rome Statute.

justice. Perhaps these voices will never be silenced. This study, however, seeks to strengthen the Court's respect for the rule of law and thereby reduce the audience that these voices command. Whatever its shortcomings, this study seeks, at the very least, to begin an important dialogue on interpretation in the field of international criminal law.

1.7 How to use this book

For scholars, this book might be read cover to cover or else portions of it might be of particular interest. For practitioners, it might be useful to begin by reading Chapter 10, which contains the entire method of interpretation in its final form, meaning grafted onto the *Vienna Convention* (1969) provisions. Having done this, the reader might have questions about elements of the proposed method in which case the relevant section(s) of the book could be read.

One important qualification is in order about the extent to which articles 31–33 of the *Vienna Convention* (1969) are discussed herein. The goal in this book is not to rehearse all of the literature on the meaning of interpretive mandates contained in these provisions – a great many treatises already do this expertly – but rather to comment on those aspects of these provisions that would substantively be affected by a method of interpretation for crimes in the Rome Statute. In this way, the method of interpretation in this study serves as a supplement to this general literature, which should also be consulted. Such an approach was already contemplated by Special Rapporteur Sir Humphrey Waldock: 'It is true that the character of a treaty may affect the question whether the application of a particular principle, maxim or method of interpretation is suitable in a particular case.'[169]

In Chapter 2, an attempt is made to survey the state of the art and to understand what guidance can be gleaned from the *Vienna Convention* (1969) and jurisprudence of the ICTY and ICTR for developing a method of interpretation for crimes in the Rome Statute. Some salient features of the Rome regime are also identified, which have the potential to influence the task of interpretation. In Chapter 3, two potential guiding interpretive principles for crimes in the Rome Statute are examined and arguments for their relative roles advanced. In Chapter 4, values underlying the preferred guiding interpretive principle, legality, are identified, and the merits of common interpretive arguments advanced to weaken or undermine this principle are critically analyzed. In Chapter 5, meaningful content is given to the principle of legality for guiding the task of interpretation by trying to understand the interpretive imperatives in article 22 of the Rome Statute, such as strict construction and interpretation in favour of the accused. In Chapter 6, the concept of codification is introduced and the

---

[169] H Waldock, 'Third Report on the Law of Treaties' (1964) II Ybk of the ILC 5, 55.

need to study the relationship between custom and crimes in the Rome Statute explained. In Chapters 7 and 8, a careful codification study is carried out to ascertain this relationship. In Chapter 9, the role of and relationship between aids to interpretation over time are analyzed, and this effort is informed by the outcome of the codification study. Chapter 10 closes the study by setting out a methodology for interpreting crimes in the Rome Statute, based on the findings reached in previous Chapters, which is grafted onto articles 31–33 of the *Vienna Convention* (1969).

2

The state of the art

2.1 Introduction

The task of developing a legal methodology begins with a moment of hesitation. One cannot resist glancing across the vast horizon of international law in search of anything that might inform this effort. It must be recalled that judges of the International Criminal Court (Court) are not the first to interpret the definitions of international crimes. At the international level, the rules of interpretation in the *Vienna Convention on the Law of Treaties* (1969) (*Vienna Convention*) have been guiding judges' interpretations for decades. And judges of the International Criminal Tribunals for the former Yugoslavia (ICTY) and Rwanda (ICTR) have been interpreting their governing statutes since 1994 and 1995 respectively.[1] While the jurisdiction of both tribunals is limited territorially and temporally, their subject matter jurisdiction is similar to that of the Court. The ICTY's jurisdiction extends to grave breaches of the *Geneva Conventions on the Laws of War* (1949) (*Geneva Conventions*), genocide, other crimes against humanity and violations of the laws or customs of war. The ICTR's jurisdiction is limited to genocide, other crimes against humanity and violations of article 3 common to the *Geneva Conventions* (1949) and the second *Additional Protocol* (1977).

The *Vienna Convention* (1969) as well as ICTY and ICTR jurisprudence beg the question: has a methodology for interpreting international crimes already emerged organically in the case law of these tribunals? Have judges widely recognized certain principles or rules of interpretation governing international criminal law and arguments in support of them? If so, how can these developments assist one in building a methodology that is suitable for judges interpreting crimes in the Rome Statute of the International Criminal Court (Rome Statute or Statute)? And what roles, if any, have ICTY and ICTR judges assigned to various interpretive aids? As for the Rome regime proper, what idiosyncratic aspects of its Statute and Court will potentially influence

---

[1] Before the ICTY and ICTR judges, judges at Nuremberg and Tokyo shouldered the same responsibility, albeit without the benefit of the *Vienna Convention* (1969).

interpretation by judges even while largely falling outside the purview of a methodology for performing this task?

This Chapter is divided into three parts. In the first part, whether articles 31–33 of the *Vienna Convention* (1969) offer a methodology for interpreting crimes in the Rome Statute will be considered. In the second part, a representative sample of the jurisprudential landscape that the ICTY and ICTR have populated will be canvassed and an attempt made to unearth any methodological insights that might be rooted in this terrain. Even if judges have not explicitly identified the components of a methodology in their reasoning, rudimentary features or seeds of an interpretive methodology for international criminal law may nevertheless exist. In the third and final part, some salient features of the Rome regime will be highlighted for their potential to influence judges in the task of interpretation.

2.2 Articles 31–33 of the *Vienna Convention* (1969)

A method of interpretation is understood to mean a systemic general approach to reasoning through the resolution of interpretive issues. The development of international rules of interpretation beginning with the work of Grotius and now reflected in the *Vienna Convention* (1969) is rehearsed elsewhere.[2] The scope and content of these rules, their status under customary law and their application by international and national tribunals is also the subject of many books and articles.[3] Generally, '[w]ith varying degrees of success, international

---

[2] For an excellent and succinct summary of this history, see R Gardiner, *Treaty Interpretation* (Oxford University Press 2008) ch. 2.

[3] Some more recent books include: O Dörr and K Schmalenbach (eds.), *Vienna Convention on the Law of Treaties* (Springer 2012); O Corten and E Klein (eds.), *The Vienna Conventions on the Law of Treaties: A Commentary* (Oxford University Press 2011); E Cannizzaro (ed.), *The Law of Treaties Beyond the Vienna Convention* (Oxford University Press 2011) pt. II; M Fitzmaurice, O Elias and P Merkouris, *Treaty Interpretation and the Vienna Convention on the Law of Treaties: 30 Years On* (Martinus Nijhoff 2010); I Van Damme, *Treaty Interpretation by the WTO Appellate Body* (Oxford University Press 2009); Gardiner (n. 2); A Orakhelashvili, *The Interpretation of Acts and Public Rules in Public International Law* (Oxford University Press 2008); U Linderfalk, *On the Interpretation of Treaties: the Modern International Law as Expressed in the 1969 Vienna Convention on the Law of Treaties* (Springer 2007); R Kolb, *Interprétation et Création du Droit International: Equisse d'une herméneutique juridique modern pour le droit international public* (Bruylant 2006); A Aust, *Modern Treaty Law and Practice* (Cambridge University Press 2000). Classic texts include: HWA Thirlway, 'The Law and Procedure of the International Court of Justice: 1960–1989 (Part Three)' (1991) 62:1 British Ybk Int'l L 1; HWA Thirlway, 'The Law and Procedure of the International Court of Justice: 1960–1989 (Part Two)' (1990) 61(1) British Ybk Int'l L 1; HWA Thirlway, 'The Law and Procedure of the International Court of Justice 1960–1989 (Part One)' (1989) 60(1) British Ybk Int'l L 1; I Sinclair, *The Vienna Convention on the Law of Treaties*, 2nd edn (Manchester University Press 1984); M Bos, 'Theory and Practice of Treaty Interpretation' (1980) 27 Netherlands Int'l L Rev 3, 135; TO Elias, *The Modern Law of Treaties* (Oceana 1974); MS McDougal, 'The International Law Commission's Draft Articles Upon Interpretation: Textuality Redivivus', (1967) 61 AJIL 992; AD McNair, *The Law of Treaties* (Oxford University Press 1961); GG Fitzmaurice, 'The Law and Procedure

courts and tribunals have responded well to these principles, using them as guidance and justification, as tools to build credibility and to exercise and assert their judicial function, as instruments to achieve accountability, as techniques to order and structure their reasoning process, and, as aids to making their decisions acceptable and comprehensible.'[4]

What follows, therefore, are some salient observations about the viability – or lack thereof – of deriving a method for interpreting crimes in the Rome Statute wholly from articles 31–33 of the *Vienna Convention* (1969). A fully developed method has three tiers. It offers its user, in this case judges and lawyers in the field of international criminal law, the following levels of assistance: (1) a primary interpretive principle to guide their reasoning process when confronted with interpretive issues; (2) arguments or reasons that support this interpretive principle; and (3) a catalogue of materials or aids that must, may and, if applicable, may not be taken into account in support of these arguments.[5]

The ICTY, ICTR and the Court have recognized the applicability of articles 31–33 of the *Vienna Convention* (1969) to the interpretation of their respective statutes.[6] In terms of offering a 'primary interpretive principle', article 31(1)

---

of the International Court of Justice 1951–1954: Treaty Interpretation and Other Treaty Points' (1957) 33 British Ybk Int'l L 203; GG Fitzmaurice, 'The Law and Procedure of the International Court of Justice: Treaty Interpretation and Other Treaty Points' (1951) 31 British Ybk Int'l L 1.

[4] I Van Damme, 'Treaty Interpretation by the WTO Appellate Body' (2010) 21:3 EJIL 605, 639.

[5] This definition takes its inspiration from DN MacCormick and RS Summers (eds.), *Interpreting Statutes: A Comparative Study* (Ashgate 1991). A legal methodology may be defined 'as a systemic general approach to the duly purposive and consistent execution of a recurrent type of major task arising in the making or application of law': RS Summers, *Form and Function in a Legal System: A General Study* (Cambridge University Press 2006) 241.

[6] Even though the ICTY and ICTR statutes are not technically treaties, both tribunals have held that the interpretive rules in the *Vienna Convention* (1969) are relevant and applicable to their work: *Prosecutor v. Tadić*, Decision on the Defence Motion for Interlocutory Appeal on Jurisdiction, ICTY-94–1-AR72, 2 October 1995, para. 18 (*Tadić Jurisdiction Decision*); *Prosecutor v. Erdemović*, Judgment, Joint Separate Opinion of Judges McDonald and Vohrah, ICTY-96–22-A, 7 October 1997, para. 3; *Prosecutor v. Bagosora and Others*, Decision on the Admissibility of the Prosecutor's Appeal from the Decision of a Confirming Judge Dismissing an Indictment against Theoneste Bagosora and 28 Others, ICTR 98–37-A, 8 June 1998, paras. 28–29; *Prosecutor v. Delalić and Others*, Judgment, ICTY-96–21-T, 16 November 1998, para. 1161. On the merits of the reasons given by the ICTY and ICTR for applying the *Vienna Convention* (1969) to their statutes, see W Schabas, 'Interpreting the Statutes of the Ad Hoc Tribunals' in LC Vohrah (ed.), *Man's Inhumanity to Man: Essays on International Law in Honour of Antonio Cassese* (Kluwer Law International 2003) 847, 849–52; J Powderly, 'Judicial Interpretation at the Ad Hoc Tribunals: Method from Chaos' in S Darcy and J Powderly (eds.), *Judicial Creativity at the International Criminal Tribunals* (Oxford University Press 2010) 17. On the Court accepting the applicability of the *Vienna Convention* (1969), see *Prosecutor v. Lubanga Dyilo*, Judgment on the Prosecutor's Application for Extraordinary Review of the Pre-Trial Chamber I's 31 Mar. 2006 Decision Denying Leave to Appeal, ICC-01/04–168,

provides: 'A treaty shall be interpreted in good faith in accordance with the ordinary meaning to be given to the terms of the treaty in their context and in the light of its object and purpose.' From this imperative, one can derive various arguments or reasons in support of a preferred interpretation. Additionally, articles 31(4) and 33 outline two more interpretive arguments that can be made. Article 31(4) states: 'A special meaning shall be given to a term if it is established that the parties so intended.' Article 33 reads:

1. When a treaty has been authenticated in two or more languages, the text is equally authoritative in each language, unless the treaty provides or the parties agree that, in case of divergence, a particular text shall prevail.
2. A version of the treaty in a language other than one of those in which the text was authenticated shall be considered an authentic text only if the treaty so provides or the parties so agree.
3. The terms of the treaty are presumed to have the same meaning in each authentic text.
4. Except where a particular text prevails in accordance with paragraph 1, when a comparison of the authentic texts discloses a difference of meaning which the application of articles 31 and 32 does not remove, the meaning which best reconciles the texts, having regard to the object and purpose of the treaty, shall be adopted.

As for materials that must, may and may not aid in the interpretation of a treaty, articles 31(2) and (3) provide:

2. The context for the purpose of the interpretation of a treaty shall comprise, in addition to the text, including its preamble and annexes:
   (a) any agreement relating to the treaty which was made between all the parties in connection with the conclusion of the treaty;
   (b) any instrument which was made by one or more parties in connection with the conclusion of the treaty and accepted by the other parties as an instrument related to the treaty.
3. There shall be taken into account, together with the context:
   (a) any subsequent agreement between the parties regarding the interpretation of the treaty or the application of its provisions;
   (b) any subsequent practice in the application of the treaty which establishes the agreement of the parties regarding its interpretation;

13 July 2006, paras. 33–42, cited in G Bitti, 'Article 21 of the Statute of the International Criminal Court and the Treatment of Sources of Law in the Jurisprudence of the ICC' in C Stahn and G Sluiter (eds.), *The Emerging Practice of the International Criminal Court* (Martinus Nijhoff 2009) 281, 295. See also *Prosecutor* v. *Lubanga Dyilo*, Decision on the Final System of Disclosure and the Establishment of a Timetable, ICC-01/04–01/06, 15 May 2006, Annex I, para. 1; *Prosecutor* v. *Lubanga Dyilo*, Decision on the Practices of Witness Familiarisation and Witness Proofing, ICC-01/04–01/06, 8 November 2006, para. 8.

(c) any relevant rules of international law applicable in the relations between the parties.

And article 32 states:

> Recourse may be had to supplementary means of interpretation, including the preparatory work of the treaty and the circumstances of its conclusion, in order to confirm the meaning resulting from the application of article 31, or to determine the meaning when the interpretation according to article 31:
>
> (a) leaves the meaning ambiguous or obscure; or
> (b) leads to a result which is manifestly absurd or unreasonable.

The International Law Commission (ILC) in its commentary to article 31 stated:

> The Commission, by heading the article 'General Rule of Interpretation' in the singular and by underlining the connection between paragraphs 1 and 2 and again between paragraph 3 and the two previous paragraphs, intended to indicate that the application of the means of interpretation in the article would be a single combined operation. All the various elements, as they were present in any given case, would be thrown into the crucible and their interaction would give the legally relevant interpretation.[7]

In fixing the ordinary meaning of a treaty term, judges often must choose from more than one possible meaning. To make this choice, they are to consider the context in which the term is used, good faith (meaning the element of reasonableness[8]) and the treaty's object and purpose. Accordingly, the meaning of a term is not merely the result of consulting a dictionary or parsing the language of a treaty.[9] The interpretive imperatives in articles 31–33 are reflective of customary international law but not an exhaustive catalogue of interpretive techniques used by international judges.[10] They do not exclude other principles compatible with these general rules, leaving open to the interpreter's discretion recourse to the wealth of material on treaty interpretation which preceded

---

[7] ILC, 'Reports of the International Law Commission on the Second Part of its Seventeenth Session and Eighteenth Session' (1966) II Ybk of the ILC 169, 219–20.

[8] R Jennings and A Watts, *Oppenheim's International Law*, 9th edn (Longman Harlow 1992) 1272 fn. 7.

[9] Gardiner (n. 2) 145.

[10] M Koskenniemi, 'Fragmentation of International Law: Difficulties Arising from the Diversification and Expansion of International Law: Report of the Study Group of the International Law Commission', UN Doc. A/CN.4/L.682 (2006) 181; MT Kamminga, 'Final Report on the Impact of International Human Rights Law on General International Law' in MT Kamminga and M Scheinin (eds.), *The Impact of Human Rights Law on General International Law* (Oxford University Press 2009) 1, 10; Gardiner (n. 2) 12–13 and relevant international and national case law cited therein.

the Convention'.[11] Some supplementary principles that courts have invoked include *in dubio mitius*, interpretation *contra proferentem*, the maxim *expressio unius est exclusio alterius*, the rule *ejusdem generis* and *generalia specialibus non derogant*.[12] There are also the interpretive arguments of special meaning in article 31(4) and article 33.

Because the crucible approach does not expressly single out one interpretive principle as being superior to all others, it has spawned three schools of interpretation, which are not necessarily mutually exclusive, each of which promotes a different guiding interpretive principle or approach: (1) textual; (2) drafter's intent; and (3) object and purpose.[13] Stated differently, the *Vienna Convention* (1969) 'avoids taking a stand on any of the great doctrinal debates on interpretation. The articles adopt both an "ordinary meaning" and a "purposive" approach; they look for Party consent as well as what is in accordance with good faith. It is in fact hard to think of any approach to interpretation that would be excluded from articles 31–32'.[14] In addition, no clear distinction is drawn between the idea of a guiding interpretive principle and arguments in support of this principle. The interpretive imperatives in article 31(1) could be invoked as guiding interpretive principles but also as arguments in support of one of them acting as a guiding principle. For example, one could invoke good faith as a guiding interpretive principle and then proceed to argue that an interpretation consistent with a treaty's object and purpose most faithfully upholds that principle. Or, one might invoke the object and purpose of a treaty as a guiding interpretive principle and then argue that the ordinary meaning of a term is consistent with this principle.

In an established area of law that includes detailed treaty texts and a well-accepted normativity, the crucible approach might yield the prevalence of one of these three schools of interpretation as well as a coherent and stable body of jurisprudence on this issue. However, as will be seen in the next section, international criminal law has not benefited from the *Vienna Convention* (1969) rules in this manner. While some judges have invoked article 31(1) to emphasize giving words their ordinary meaning,[15] others have used it to adopt a more purposive approach to interpretation.[16] Others still have been inspired by this rule to focus on drafters' intent.[17] On their face, none of these approaches are

---

[11] Ibid. 51.   [12] Jennings and Watts (n. 8) 1276–81.   [13] Sinclair (n. 3) 115.

[14] Koskenniemi (n. 10) 181. Brownlie observed that '[m]any of the rules and principles offered are general, question-begging and contradictory': I Brownlie, *Principles of Public International Law*, 6th edn (Oxford University Press 2003) 602.

[15] *Delalić* (n. 6) paras. 163, 438.

[16] *Kanyabashi v. Prosecutor*, Judgment, Joint Separate and Concurring Opinion of Judge Wang Tieya and Judge Rafael Nieto-Navia, ICTR-96–15-A, 3 June 1999, para. 13; *Kanyabashi v. Prosecutor*, Judgment, Dissenting Opinion of Judge Shahabuddeen, ICTR-96–15-A, 3 June 1999, para. 21.

[17] *Kanyabashi*, Wang Tieya and Nieto-Navia Opinion, ibid. para. 13.

'wrong' in light of the wording of article 31(1), but they do raise the issue of paramountcy – deciding which interpretive principle might prevail in the field of international criminal law.

Thus, articles 31–33 of the *Vienna Convention* (1969) can be said to provide 'a generic, "off the rack" approach to treaty interpretation that does not contain special consideration for penal treaties'.[18] They are inspired by the saying that interpretation is an art and not a science.[19] The *Vienna Convention* (1969) cannot be faulted for this feature, as it was intended to offer guidance on the interpretation of all kinds of treaties. However, absent further guidance from the regime in which a treaty is being interpreted, the 'very choice of any single rule or of a combination or cumulation of them is the result of a judgement arrived at, independently of any rules of construction, by reference to considerations of good faith, of justice, and of public policy within the orbit of the express or implied intention of the parties or of the legislature'.[20] Accordingly, it has been said that 'it is a fallacy to assume that the existence of these rules is a secure safeguard against arbitrariness or partiality'.[21] In fact, some have criticized the general rule of interpretation as disguising arbitrary decision making and called for it to be replaced with a more 'honest' interpretive reasoning process that acknowledges the weighing of important values.[22]

For an international criminal law treaty, however, it is submitted that the ingredients of articles 31–33 can be refined to suit its object and purpose. An attempt can be made to fix some relationships between the interpretive principles, arguments and aids mentioned therein; to graft a constraining method of interpretation onto it. However, such efforts should not be taken too far as there is likely an important lesson to be learned from the International Law Commission (ILC) in its efforts to draft articles 31–33. It could have drafted a code of rules and fixed their relationship to one another or, at the other extreme, rendered all rules of interpretation entirely discretionary. Instead, it chose to draft *mandatory guidelines*.[23]

> The Commission was fully . . . conscious . . . of the undesirability – if not impossibility – of confining the process of interpretation within rigid rules, and the provision of [the draft Articles] . . . do not appear to constitute a code of rules incompatible with the required degree of flexibility . . . In a sense all 'rules' of interpretation have the character of 'guidelines' since

---

[18] B Van Schaack, 'Crimen Sine Lege: Judicial Lawmaking at the Intersection of Law and Morals' (2008) 97 Georgetown LJ 119, 149.

[19] RY Jennings, 'Amendment and Modification of Treaties' (1967) 121 Recueil des Cours de l'Académie de Droit International 544; M Koskenniemi, *From Apology to Utopia: The Structure of International Legal Argument* (Cambridge University Press 2006) 340 fn. 106 (citing the works of CE Rousseau, VD Degan and D Anzilotti).

[20] H Lauterpacht, 'Restrictive Interpretation and the Principle of Effectiveness in the Interpretation of Treaties' (1949) 26 British Ybk Int'l L 48, 53.

[21] Ibid.   [22] Koskenniemi (n. 10) 341.   [23] Gardiner (n. 2) 38.

their application in a particular case depends so much on the appreciation of the context and the circumstances of the point to be interpreted.[24]

Accordingly, the present study will take a cue from the ILC insofar as it will seek to address major issues expected to arise when interpreting crimes in the Rome Statute but not offer guidance that is too formal. An excessively rigid methodology may prove to be useless in a number of situations, politically unrealistic and, or, rejected by the wider interpretive community.[25] The *Vienna Convention* (1969) also reminds those developing a methodology to try to maintain the distinction between interpretation and application of a treaty: 'Interpretation is the process of determining the meaning of a text; application is the process of determining the consequences which, according to the text, should follow in a given situation.'[26]

As has been alluded to already, the crucible approach contains rules that, if construed absolutely, can abrogate one another because they are said to be 'mutually exclusive and contradictory'.[27] Examples of this are the imperatives of effective and strict construction, both of which may be derived from the reference to good faith in article 31(1) of the *Vienna Convention* (1969). Effective interpretation bars rendering a treaty term meaningless, and some understand it to require assigning a treaty term a meaning that is most consistent with a treaty's object and purpose but without offending the text of the treaty.[28] On the other hand, strict construction in cases of ambiguity is understood by some to prefer imposing the least burdensome interpretation of a term on the Party to a treaty that is obligated.[29] Underlying these rules, therefore, are the opposing presumptions of giving a treaty term the fullest possible meaning and assigning it minimal content. This problem surely must

---

[24] H Waldock, 'Sixth Report on the Law of Treaties' (1966) II Ybk of the ILC 51, 94; Jennings and Watts (n. 8) 1270.

[25] J Tobin, 'Seeking to Persuade: A Constructive Approach to Human Rights Treaty Interpretation' (2010) 23 Harvard HR J 1, 14–15.

[26] Research in International Law of the Harvard Law School, 'Harvard Draft Convention on the Law of Treaties' (1935) 29 AJIL, Supp. 657, 938. The distinction has also been explained as follows: 'Interpretation is the process of establishing the legal character and effects of consensus achieved by the parties. In contrast, application is the process of determining the consequences of such an interpretation in a concrete case. Thus, interpretation of a treaty is independent of, and need not be followed by, the application of the treaty. Any application of a treaty, including its execution, presupposes, however, a preceding conscious or subconscious interpretation of the treaty.' G Schwarzenberger, 'Myths and Realities of Treaty Interpretation: Articles 31–33 of the Vienna Convention on the Law of Treaties' in G Schwarzenberger, *International Law and Order* (Stevens & Sons 1971) 110, 116.

[27] JHW Verzijl in 1928 before the Royal Netherlands Academy of Science, cited in Lauterpacht (n. 20) 52.

[28] Jennings and Watts (n. 8) 1278–81.   [29] Ibid. 1278–79.

be examined and ideally resolved for purposes of interpreting crimes in the Rome Statute.[30] Indeed, articles 21(3) and 22(2) of the Rome Statute seem in part to embody precisely this problem. Article 21(3) obliges judges to interpret the Rome Statute 'consistent with internationally recognized human rights', whereas article 22(2) provides: 'The definition of a crime shall be strictly construed and shall not be extended by analogy. In case of ambiguity, the definition shall be interpreted in favour of the person being investigated, prosecuted or convicted.'

Beyond the problems that the crucible approach presents in terms of not offering up a guiding interpretive principle for crimes in the Rome Statute, article 31(3) gives rise to serious questions about aids to interpreting these crimes, their relationship to one another and their role over time. Article 31(3) obliges judges to consider all three aids to interpretation, and, because they have no hierarchical relationship to one another, no guidance is offered on how to resolve conflicts that might arise between them. For example, the Elements of Crimes (Elements), which supplement the definitions of crimes in the Rome Statute, are a subsequent agreement in the sense of article 31(3)(a). What happens, then, if the Elements conflict with customary international law, which might be relevant and applicable international law under article 31(3)(c) of the *Vienna Convention* (1969)?[31] Additionally, article 31(3) does not indicate whether subsequent agreements, practice and legal developments may always influence the interpretation of a treaty or whether certain treaties are 'frozen' in time and may only be interpreted in light of the law that existed when they were adopted.[32]

Finally, the literature on the rules of interpretation in the *Vienna Convention* (1969) exposes two (possibly necessary) myths that are germane to the present study and should therefore be kept in mind. The first is the myth of a common intention underlying a treaty text. Application of the rules of interpretation in the *Vienna Convention* (1969) are supposed to lead one to the intention of the Parties to the treaty, not in the abstract but to their common intention regarding the question of interpretation at issue.[33] As early as 1950, it was argued that 'it is unrealistic to attempt to find a common intention of the Parties when, in fact, they never had a common intention on the point that has arisen, but simply agreed on a text'.[34] International treaties are often negotiated with a view to achieving consensus rather than clarity, meaning creative ambiguities might abound to mask the lack of common intent.[35] Where such intent is lacking, judges do not have the option to refrain from resolving the interpretive issue

---

[30] See Chapter 3.   [31] See Chapter 9, Sections 9.2.2 and 9.2.6.
[32] See Chapter 9, Section 9.3.   [33] Jennings and Watts (n. 8) 1267.
[34] E Beckett, 'Comments on the Report of Sir Hersch Lauterpacht' (1950) 43 Annuaire de l'Institut de Droit International 435, 438.
[35] Lauterpacht (n. 20) 52.

that arises in a particular case.[36] Accordingly, the interpretive rules in articles 31–33 of the *Vienna Convention* (1969) are invoked to *attribute* a common intention to the Parties even if none existed and in light of a set of facts that might never have been contemplated by them.[37] This leads to the second myth of interpretation.

The exercise of interpretation claims its legitimacy from purporting to yield an outcome that reflects the common intention of the Parties to a treaty and is therefore based on consent. One might therefore expect that heavy reliance on the *travaux préparatoires* for a treaty would be permissible. However, it is widely acknowledged that article 31 of the *Vienna Convention* (1969) regards the text of the treaty as the 'only authentic and the most recent expression of what the parties intended, and consequently interpretation may be thought of as essentially a textual matter'.[38] Accordingly, the intent derived from (or attributed to) the text of a treaty may well prevail over the actual intent of the Parties as evidenced in *travaux* or other material, thereby undercutting its own claim to legitimacy.

> Intent can be known only in its manifestations – which manifestations (text, behaviour, teleology etc.) count depends on whether they express intent. . . . The indeterminacy of treaty interpretation follows from [the] doctrine's inability to prefer consistently subjective and objective points. The structure of treaty interpretation is governed by the *constant shift from a subjective into an objective position and vice-versa*. . . . Preferring non-consensualism will either result in holding the State bound irrespectively of its will, in which case the problem-solver will lack criteria for justifying the adopted standard, or it will result in consensualism, holding the standard binding only to the extent that it expresses the real consent of the parties. . . . In order for closure to emerge priority should be established between the subjective and objective approaches, or the ascending and descending modes of argument. This, however, is impossible within the conceptual structures of the liberal doctrine of politics which requires, on the one hand, that law be justified by recourse to the legal subjects' subjective behaviour, will or interest and that its application must be divorced from them. The distinction between a level of justification and a level of ascertainment does not hold within the argument.[39]

Both of these legal fictions, the existence of a common intention and the idea that subjective intent can be ascertained from an objective treaty text, perhaps need to endure so that judges can offer reasons in their decisions that are perceived as legitimate and objective, and so the work of developing a methodology to constrain this reasoning can move forward.

---

[36] Ibid.   [37] Jennings and Watts (n. 8) 1287–88.
[38] Ibid. 1271–72; ILC (n. 7) 220.   [39] Koskenniemi (n. 10) 337, 342, 345.

2.3 Jurisprudence of the ICTY and ICTR

The ICTY and ICTR statutes ushered in the modern era of international criminal law under relatively impoverished circumstances. They have been described as comprising 'an incomplete shopping list of ancient treaties'.[40] Neither of the statutes contains interpretive guidance, and each provides little more than vague jurisdictional headings for entire categories of crimes, some of which are not exhaustively listed, with little indication of requisite mental and material elements that must be proven or possible defences to crimes. And while the rights of the accused are briefly mentioned, the rules of procedure and evidence for the ICTY and ICTR were left to judges to adopt. Further, as will be seen, the normativity of international criminal law when these tribunals began their work was (and is) far from settled.[41]

It is against this backdrop of vague and scant statutes as well as serious normative tensions that judges at the ICTY and ICTR have had to put flesh on the bones of modern international criminal law. What they have achieved under these circumstances is extraordinary. However, from the perspective of interpretation, such a state of affairs opened the door for judges to develop their own methods, which were perhaps inspired inter alia by their legal training,[42] their understanding of articles 31–33 of the *Vienna Convention* (1969) and, or, understanding of international criminal law's normativity.

What follows is an attempt to produce a coherent survey of different interpretive principles, arguments and supporting materials that appear in a representative sample of ICTY and ICTR jurisprudence covering a period of fourteen years.[43] This survey should be read heuristically and not as a definitive or exhaustive portrayal of how interpretive principles, arguments and material aids are related to one another in the jurisprudence.[44] The goal is not to dissect the case law of these tribunals in search for subtle tendencies, which could be a study in itself, but to canvass it in search of well-established and common interpretive practices. As well, although the jurisprudence of the ICTY and ICTR were equally researched, it will become apparent that the ICTR's jurisprudence contains relatively little legal analysis on issues of interpretation. This is perhaps because of the comparatively strong civil law influence on this tribunal or because it chose, on occasion, to adopt interpretive outcomes reached by the ICTY.

---

[40] Schabas (n. 6) 848.   [41] See Chapter 3, Section 3.2.

[42] J Wessel, 'Judicial Policy-Making at the International Criminal Court: An Institutional Guide to Analyzing International Adjudication' (2006) 44 Columbia J Transnat'l L 377.

[43] 1994 to April 2008.

[44] As well, the distinction between principles and arguments is made by the author and does not necessarily reflect how judges invoking these concepts would regard them.

2.3.1 *Interpretive principles and arguments*

2.3.1.1 Literal interpretation

The reference in article 31(1) of the *Vienna Convention* (1969) to 'ordinary meaning' has been described as a natural starting point for interpreting a treaty term and not a complete or independent interpretive process.[45] This is because the meaning of 'ordinary' is itself a relative notion that is dependent on the context in which the term is being used.[46] Applying the rules of interpretation in articles 31–33 of the *Vienna Convention* (1969) provides that context. The concept of literal interpretation has been endorsed by several judges[47] and held to mean that words in a statute must be given their clear,[48] plain or ordinary meaning.[49] This does not take judges very far.[50] Without a common under-standing of what an ambiguity is,[51] the discretion that judges have to pronounce that a term is clear or ambiguous (and therefore in need of interpretation) is virtually unfettered. Indeed, a methodology cannot eliminate discretion at this first stage of interpretation. Furthermore, a literal interpretation does not spec-ify whether judges should favour a broad or strict interpretation of words and phrases.

On occasion, judges have endorsed definitions of words contained in law dictionaries, such as 'jurisdiction'.[52] Other times, the literal interpretation has admitted giving words their technical meaning.[53] If a literal or grammatical reading of the word or phrase results in an absurdity, injustice, anomaly or con-tradiction, this meaning will be disregarded on the assumption that the drafters or 'legislature' could not have intended such an outcome.[54] Without elaborating

---

[45] Gardiner (n. 2) 162.   [46] Ibid.

[47] *Prosecutor* v. *Tadić*, Judgment, ICTY-94-1-A, 15 July 1999, para. 296 (*Tadić Judgment*); *Tadić Jurisdiction Decision* (n. 6) paras. 35, 71; *Prosecutor* v. *Krnojelac*, Judgment, Separate Opinion of Judge Schomburg, ICTY-97-25-A, 17 September 2003, para. 13.

[48] *Delalić* (n. 6) paras. 161, 170, 438; *Barayagwiza* v. *Prosecutor*, Decision, Separate Opinion of Judge Shahabuddeen, ICTR-97-19-AR72, 3 November 1999, s. 4.

[49] *Prosecutor* v. *Blagojević and Others*, Judgment, ICTY-02-60-A, 9 May 2007, para. 281; *Prosecutor* v. *Kupreškić and Others*, Judgment, ICTY-95-16-T, 14 January 2000, para. 569; *Prosecutor* v. *Krstić*, Judgment, ICTY-98-33-T, 2 August 2001, para. 496; *Kanyabashi* v. *Prosecutor*, Decision on the Defence Motion for Interlocutory Appeal on the Jurisdiction of Trial Chamber I, Joint and Separate Opinion of Judges McDonald and Vohrah, ICTR-96-15-A, 3 June 1999, para. 13.

[50] 'The difficulty about this approach to the issue is that almost any word has more than one meaning. The word "meaning" itself, has at least sixteen different meanings.' G Schwarzenberger, 'Myths and Realities of Treaty Interpretation: Articles 27–29 of the Vienna Draft Convention on the Law of Treaties' (1968) 9 Virginia J Int'l L 1, 13, cited in Gardiner (n. 2) 161.

[51] See, e.g., Section 2.2 above.   [52] *Tadić Jurisdiction Decision* (n. 6) para. 10.

[53] *Delalić* (n. 6) para. 166.

[54] Ibid. para. 162; *Kanyabashi*, McDonald and Vohrah Opinion (n. 49) para. 19.

on the point, judges have stated that if a word is ambiguous, a method must exist for determining how to give effect to the legislative intention.[55] At the same time, judges have endorsed the idea of resorting to analogy to extract the meaning of a word when the literal meaning of the provision does not resolve the issue.[56]

2.3.1.2 Logical interpretation

Judges at the ICTY and ICTR appeal to the concept of interpreting statutory provisions in a logical[57] or reasonable manner.[58] The concept of logical interpretation is not defined, although various interpretive rules or arguments that appeal to logic can be found throughout the case law. *Expressio unius est exclusio alterius* means that mention of one or more things of a particular class may be regarded as silently excluding all other members of the class.[59] *Ejusdem generis* means that general words are to be taken as referring only to those things of the same class as specifically mentioned.[60] On at least one occasion, this maxim was held to lack precision and be 'too general to provide a safe yardstick for the work of the Tribunal'.[61] Instead, the maxim was thought to be a useful 'supplementary tool, to establish whether certain acts . . . reach the level of gravity required'[62] by a particular provision. Both the *expressio unius* and *ejusdem* rules are grammatical rules of construction that have been applied by international tribunals over the years.[63] *Noscitur a sociis* means that words can be understood by looking to the words around them and the context in which they are used.[64] *Reductio ad absurdum* means that judges should avoid interpreting words in such a way as to produce an absurd outcome.[65] Indeed, the interpretive presumption of a rational legislator that exists in many countries seems to find expression at the international level in article 32 of the *Vienna Convention* (1969).[66] Judges have also referred to logical inferences.[67] For example, the ICTR reasoned:

> [T]he logical inference from the foregoing is that an individual cannot thus be both the principal perpetrator of a particular act and the accomplice thereto. An act with which an accused is being charged cannot, therefore, be characterized both as an act of genocide and an act of complicity in genocide as pertains to this accused. Consequently, since the two are

---

[55] *Delalić*, ibid. para. 161.   [56] Ibid. para. 162.

[57] Ibid. paras. 166, 400; *Tadić Jurisdiction Decision* (n. 6) paras. 79–95; *Kupreškić* (n. 49) para. 571; *Kanyabashi*, Shahabuddeen Dissent (n. 16) 16, 21; *Tadić Judgment* (n. 47) para. 284.

[58] *Kanyabashi*, Shahabuddeen Dissent, ibid. 21.   [59] *Delalić* (n. 6) para. 166.

[60] Ibid.; *Kupreškić* (n. 49) paras. 564, 620.   [61] *Kupreškić*, ibid. para. 564.

[62] Ibid. para. 620.   [63] See Jennings and Watts (n. 8) 1279–80 for case law.

[64] *Delalić* (n. 6) para. 166.   [65] *Tadić Jurisdiction Decision* (n. 6) para. 76.

[66] 1155 UNTS 331 (adopted 23 May 1969, entered into force 27 January 1980).

[67] *Prosecutor v. Akayesu*, Judgment, ICTR-96–4-T, 2 September 1998, para. 532.

mutually exclusive, the same individual cannot be convicted of both crimes for the same act.[68]

The aforementioned rules or maxims need to be distinguished from guiding principles of interpretation.

> [The former] convey rational ideas in clarifying the meaning of written provisions [while] . . . the latter derive their legitimacy from the Vienna Convention which is also part of customary law. . . . Although resorted to in several cases, the maxims of interpretation are valuable only in so far as they constitute the application of the principles of interpretation. Where a recognised principle of interpretation disposed of the issue, the maxims of interpretation are irrelevant. Another factor preventing the maxims of interpretation from having direct normative impact is that they are so specific in scope that, given the context of individual situations of interpretation, they can lead to mutually incompatible outcomes in different cases.[69]

On other occasions, less obviously logical arguments have been presented as just that and subsequently endorsed. Judges have held that loose language favours a broad interpretation,[70] that nothing prevents the interpretation contemplated,[71] that no express limitation is made restricting the interpretation contemplated[72] and that a generic term provides enough scope for the interpretation contemplated.[73] On one occasion, the ICTY held that 'there is no reason why Article 29 should not apply to collective enterprises undertaken by States, in the framework of international organisations . . .'[74] On its face, article 29 of the ICTY Statute, which deals with cooperation obligations, was limited to States. What these arguments have in common is that they appeal to logic to favour the broad interpretation of a statutory provision. The absence of a prohibition against a broad interpretation is regarded as permitting it. This 'logic' needs to be critically evaluated in the context of interpreting crimes that, by definition, must be of concern to the international community as a whole.

2.3.1.3 Contextual interpretation

The principle of contextual interpretation has also garnered some favour. Pursuant to article 31(2) of the *Vienna Convention* (1969), context encompasses not just a treaty text, including its preamble and annexes, but also 'any agreement relating to the treaty and made between all the parties in connection with the conclusion of the treaty, and any instrument made by one or more parties in

---

[68] Ibid.   [69] Orakhelashvili (n. 3) 317.   [70] *Tadić Jurisdiction Decision* (n. 6) para. 69.

[71] *Prosecutor* v. *Stakić*, Judgment, Partly Dissenting Opinion of Judge Shahabuddeen, ICTY-97–24-A, 22 March 2006, para. 12.

[72] *Delalić* (n. 6) para. 356.   [73] Ibid.

[74] *Prosecutor* v. *Simić and Others*, Decision on Motion for Judicial Assistance to be provided by SFOR and Others, ICTY-95–9-PT, 18 October 2000, para. 46.

connection with the conclusion of the treaty and accepted by the other parties as an instrument related to the treaty'.[75] The instrument need not have been made exactly when the relevant treaty was concluded. A short lapse of time between them is permitted, but this length is not defined.[76] The function of context in article 31 is twofold. First, context qualifies what is meant by ordinary meaning in article 31(1), thereby discouraging an overly literal method of interpretation.[77] Second, context is a reference to interpretive aids that are to assist in interpreting a treaty term.[78]

What is encompassed by context for judges at the ICTY and ICTR is not always clear. Often it has been understood as requiring a provision to be read in the context of the ICTY or ICTR statute as a whole, with special emphasis being placed on neighbouring provisions.[79] This is sometimes referred to as textual interpretation.[80] It might mean looking at the subparagraphs of a provision to better understand the chapeau[81] or taking into account a statute as a whole and systematically constructing it.[82] Sometimes the goal is to interpret a concept in a manner that is consistent with a similar concept (e.g., that the mental element for harm is consistent with the mental element for cruel treatment, wilfully causing great suffering and inhumane treatment).[83] Other times, it is to interpret a word in a manner consistent with how the same word has been interpreted in other sections of the statute (e.g., the broad meaning of 'commit',[84] or that 'acts' encompass acts and omissions).[85] The interpretive technique of cross-referencing could also be described as logical, as it treats the drafters of the text as rational actors who create an internally coherent instrument.

Context, however, has not always been limited to the statutory text. Some judges have adopted a more expansive understanding of context to include treaty provisions that form the basis of the provision being interpreted.[86] Others have understood context to mean situating the statutes in their historical context,[87] considering the nature of international law and the international system,[88] as well as considering the nature of the conflicts that gave rise to the creation of the tribunals.[89]

---

[75] Jennings and Watts (n. 8) 1273–74.   [76] Ibid.

[77] Gardiner (n. 2) 177–78.   [78] Ibid.

[79] 'The method of analyzing ordinary usage invites us to consider what these terms mean as they are used, not what they "mean" when wrenched out of context and defined for the purposes of legal analysis.' G Fletcher, *Rethinking Criminal Law* (Little, Brown 1978) 451; *Barayagwiza*, Shahabuddeen Separate Opinion (n. 48).

[80] *Tadić Jurisdiction Decision* (n. 6) para. 68.

[81] *Prosecutor v. Blaškić*, Judgment, ICTY-95–14-T, 3 March 2000, para. 202.

[82] *Tadić Jurisdiction Decision* (n. 6) para. 90.   [83] *Blagojević* (n. 49) para. 645.

[84] *Blagojević and Others v. Prosecutor*, Judgment, ICTY-02–60-A, 7 May 2007, para. 280.

[85] *Prosecutor v. Orić*, Judgment, ICTY-03–68-T, 30 June 2006, para. 302.

[86] *Blaškić* (n. 81) para. 168.   [87] *Tadić Jurisdiction Decision* (n. 6) para. 93.

[88] Ibid. paras. 11, 43ff.   [89] Ibid. para. 73.

2.3.1.4 Purposive interpretation

The reference to object and purpose in article 31(1) read alongside the definition of context in article 31(2) of the *Vienna Convention* (1969) means that the object and purpose of a treaty is to be gleaned not only from its preamble but from all of its provisions as well as any related concluding agreements.[90] In fact, international tribunals such as the Appellate Body of the World Trade Organisation will often examine in detail the impugned treaty provision to gain a fuller understanding of its purpose rather than merely recite the purpose gleaned from a treaty's preambular paragraphs.[91] The 'purpose of a particular provision [as opposed to the purpose of the treaty], in the sense of its role in the structure of the treaty and its delineating function in the scheme of the treaty is as much (or more) part of the context as an aid to identifying the ordinary meaning.'[92] While the object and purpose of a treaty or any of its provisions cannot modify the treaty, they can assist with deciding which of several definitions should be deemed the 'ordinary meaning' of a term.[93] Considerations of object and purpose might also come into play when the scope of a treaty provision is raised, whether it applies to a certain category of persons for example.[94] In practice, courts and tribunals tend not to distinguish between or define the concepts of object and purpose.[95] As well, some have argued that the reference in article 31(1) of the *Vienna Convention* (1969) to this does not signify a distinct approach to interpretation – that it is not meant to be a guiding interpretive principle.[96]

That said, references to purposive interpretation can be found in the jurisprudence of the ICTY and ICTR,[97] although the principle is not consistently defined. Purposive interpretation has been understood to encompass a contextual interpretation,[98] the purpose of the tribunal,[99] as well as the purpose of the statute.[100] For example, when defining the liability of a superior under article 7(3) of the ICTY statute for a crime 'committed' by a subordinate, a broad meaning was assigned to the word 'commit' to include all modes of participation, inter alia because of the object and purpose of this provision but also that of the tribunal. The ICTY's mandate is to 'put an end to [widespread violations of international humanitarian law] and to take effective measures to bring to justice the persons who are responsible for them.'[101] Judges have also invoked the principle of purposive interpretation to consider the purpose of a

---

[90] Gardiner (n. 2) 197.   [91] Ibid.   [92] Ibid. 193–94.   [93] Ibid. 190.
[94] Ibid. 199.   [95] Ibid. 193–94.   [96] Ibid. 190.
[97] *Prosecutor* v. *Orić* (n. 85) para. 300; *Kanyabashi*, McDonald and Vohrah Opinion (n. 49) paras. 16, 17, 19; *Simić* (n. 74) paras. 46, 48; *Kanyabashi* (n. 16) Wang Tieya and Nieto-Navia Opinion, para. 13; *Delalić* (n. 6) paras. 163–165, 170.
[98] *Kanyabashi*, McDonald and Vohrah Opinion (n. 49) para 16.
[99] *Blagojević* (n. 49) para. 281.   [100] *Tadić Jurisdiction Decision* (n. 6) para 78.
[101] *Blagojević* (n. 49) para. 281.

treaty to which a statutory provision can be traced, such as the purpose of the *Convention on the Prevention and Punishment of the Crime of Genocide* (1948) (*Genocide Convention*).[102]

2.3.1.5 Effective interpretation

Another interpretive approach is adhering to the principle of 'effectiveness'. This principle 'is directed to the adoption of an interpretation that would give effect to the substantial purpose of the text; it is not directed to changing the substance or the purpose of the text'.[103] This rule may also be expressed as *ut res magis valeat quam pereat*, which is tantamount to the imperative of interpreting a treaty in accordance with the intention of the Parties and its object and purpose.[104] This broad definition of the rule of effective interpretation should be contrasted with the narrower version of this rule: 'all provisions of the treaty or other instrument must be supposed to have been intended to have significance and to be necessary to convey the intended meaning; that an interpretation which reduces some part of the text to the status of a pleonasm, or mere surplusage, is prima facie suspect'.[105]

The broader principle of effective interpretation gives serious consideration to the result that a particular interpretive argument produces. It has been described as 'elementary'[106] and 'a well-established principle under international law',[107] and as creating a presumption 'that law-makers enact or agree upon rules that are well thought out and meaningful in all their elements'.[108] One argument that adheres to the broader principle of effective interpretation is the completeness argument. For example, when choosing not to define persecution as a crime against humanity in too precise a manner, the ICTY held that it 'does not see fit to identify which rights constitute fundamental rights for the purposes of persecution. The interests of justice would not be served by so doing, as the explicit inclusion of particular fundamental rights could be interpreted as the implicit exclusion of other rights (*expressio unius est exclusio alterius*).'[109] The ICTY added:

> [I]f persecution was given a narrow interpretation, so as not to include the crimes found in the remaining sub-headings of Article 5, a lacuna would exist in the Statute of the Tribunal. There would be no means of conceptualising those crimes against humanity which are committed on

---

[102] Ibid.; *Prosecutor* v. *Krstić*, Judgment, ICTY-98–33-A, 19 April 2004, para. 8.

[103] *Barayagwiza* v. *Prosecutor*, Decision, Separate Opinion of Judge Shahabuddeen, ICTR-97–19-AR72, 3 November 1999, s. 4: 'Within reasonable limits the principle of the maxim in question is a good servant . . . outside of reasonable limits it is a bad master. . . . '

[104] H Thirlway, 'The Law and Procedure of the International Court of Justice: 1960–1989, Part Three' (1991) 62 British Ybk of Int'l L 1, 44.

[105] Ibid.   [106] *Tadić Judgment* (n. 47) para. 284.

[107] *Kanyabashi*, Shahabuddeen Dissent (n. 16) para. 46.

[108] *Tadić Judgment* (n. 47) para. 284.   [109] *Kupreškić* (n. 49) para. 623.

discriminatory grounds, but which, for example, fall short of genocide, which requires a specific intent 'to destroy, in whole or in part, a national, ethnical, racial, or religious group.[110]

Effective interpretation is also supported by arguments about preventing redundancy, giving each concept in a statute meaningful content. For example, judges held that '[e]xtermination differs from murder in that it requires an element of mass destruction which is not required for murder'.[111] This reasoning seems to also underlie the interpretation that 'wilfully causing great suffering or serious injury to body or health' covers those acts that do not satisfy the purpose requirement for the offence of torture.[112] Just as murder is the 'residual clause' for extermination, so too is wilfully causing great suffering or serious injury to body or health the 'residual clause' for torture. Despite the popularity of effective interpretation, it is not expressly mentioned in article 31(1) of the *Vienna Convention* (1969). What then, are its origins?

It has been said that all rules of interpretation are manifestations of the meta-imperative to interpret treaties in good faith.[113] Good faith has been understood to mean that Parties should perform and interpret their obligations or exercise their rights in a manner that does not result in an abuse of rights.[114] For purposes of interpretation, good faith is sometimes used (1) as a synonym for a 'reasonable' interpretation; (2) to justify finding the intention of the Parties; or (3) as encompassing the principle of effectiveness.[115] The narrow meaning of effectiveness, that 'an interpretation should be preferred which gives [a word] . . . some meaning and role rather than one which does not' can be accommodated here.[116] However, effective interpretation may not override a treaty's text, which is why express reference to it was removed from article 31 of the *Vienna Convention* (1969).[117] Where a treaty embodies communal values, good faith has been invoked to limit the powers of States Parties to it in order to render it effective.[118] Good faith and effectiveness might also result in judges seeking to reasonably balance competing elements of a treaty.[119] The principle of effectiveness has also been derived on occasion from the imperative in article 31(1) of the *Vienna Convention* (1969) to interpret a treaty provision in light of its object and purpose.[120] A broad definition of effective interpretation, giving terms in a treaty meanings that most advance the goals of the treaty as a whole,[121] can also be situated here.

2.3.1.6 Drafters' intent

Article 32 of the *Vienna Convention* (1969) permits recourse to supplementary means of interpretation, including preparatory work, to determine the meaning

---

[110] Ibid. para. 606.   [111] *Akayesu* (n. 67) para. 591.   [112] *Delalić* (n. 6) para. 511.
[113] Lauterpacht (n. 20) 56.   [114] Gardiner (n. 2) 148.   [115] Ibid.   [116] Ibid.
[117] Ibid. 190.   [118] Ibid. 157–58 (case law omitted).   [119] Ibid. 158–59.
[120] Ibid.; Van Damme (n. 3).   [121] Gardiner, ibid. 148.

of a treaty term where application of the general rule of interpretation in article 31 yields a meaning that is ambiguous or obscure, or an outcome that is manifestly absurd or unreasonable. The *Vienna Convention* (1969) is therefore clear about the secondary role of preparatory work as an aid to interpretation. Accordingly, it stands to reason that adherence to drafters' intent as manifested in this work is not a good candidate for a guiding interpretive principle and that the text of a treaty is the authoritative expression of the Parties' intent.

In the jurisprudence of the ICTY and ICTR, however, the principle of adhering to drafters' intent is used in a unique manner. It is most often the underlying justification for interpreting a statutory word or phrase in accordance with the meaning given to it under customary international law.[122] The rationale is that drafters of the ICTY statute expressly stated that judges are supposed to apply only customary international law to the facts before them.[123] It is arguably rare to find an express and common intention such as this in an aid to interpretation external to a treaty. This has led the ICTY, for example, to adopt definitions in the four *Geneva Conventions* (1949) and their commentaries, as they are considered to reflect customary law.[124] At least once, however, judges held that a statutory phrase deliberately departed from customary law and used this to justify broadly interpreting the word 'civilians' in the definition of crimes against humanity.[125]

Interestingly, judges at the ICTY and ICTR have not always limited themselves to the intent underlying their own constitutive statute. For example, ICTR judges relied on the intention of the drafters of the *Genocide Convention* (1948) to protect any stable or permanent group when determining that Rwanda's Tutsis were a protected group.[126] The principle of adhering to drafters' intent has led to the problem of identifying which materials provide evidence of this intent or form part of the *travaux préparatoires*. In addition to the Report of the Secretary-General on the ICTY,[127] records of Security Council debates on the establishment of the ICTY and opinions expressed by members of the Security Council when voting on the relevant resolutions have aided

---

[122] *Delalić* (n. 6) paras. 357, 390, 439; *Blaškić* (n. 81) paras. 219, 314ff; *Prosecutor* v. *Simić*, Judgment, Dissenting Opinion of Judge Schomburg, ICTY-95–9-A, 28 November 2006, para. 3; *Tadić Judgment* (n. 47) para. 713; *Prosecutor* v. *Musema*, Judgment, ICTR-96–13-T, 27 January 2000, paras. 202ff.;

[123] UNSC, 'Report of the Secretary-General Pursuant to Paragraph 2 of Security Council Resolution 808' (1993) UN Doc. S/25704, para. 34 (ICTY Report). In contrast to the ICTY statute, the Secretary-General admitted that article 4 of the ICTR statute goes somewhat beyond custom by including violations of the second *Additional Protocol* (1977): UNSC, 'Report of the Secretary-General Pursuant to Paragraph 5 of Security Council Resolution 955' (1994) UN Doc. S/1995/134, para. 12. On this point, it is interesting to note that Rwanda acceded to the second *Additional Protocol* on 19 November 1984.

[124] *Delalić* (n. 6) para. 439.   [125] *Kupreškić* (n. 49) para. 547.

[126] *Akayesu* (n. 67) para. 516; *Musema* (n. 122) para. 162.

[127] UNSC, ICTY Report (n. 123).

interpretation.[128] Judges of the ICTY have also considered what members of the Security Council knew about the nature of the Balkan conflict when they adopted the ICTY statute.[129]

2.3.1.7 Progressive interpretation

In contrast to drafters' intent, some judges have availed themselves of the principle of progressive interpretation. This concept is used here to capture the practice of judges taking into account changes in the law, as reflected in subsequent practice, as well as evolving norms or values that inform the interpretation of a term. Examples of subsequent practice being taken into account include the ICTY considering how the ICTR interpreted the same terms in its statute or how States defined crimes in the Rome Statute that are also listed in the ICTY statute.[130] In *Kunarać* (2002), the ICTY Appeals Chamber held that what constitutes a war crime depends on the development of the laws and customs of war.[131] In *Simić* (2006), Judge Schomburg sought to recognize indirect perpetratorship as a distinct mode of liability on the basis of developments in modern national and international criminal law.[132] Curiously, both of these decisions cite in support of their reasoning the Nuremberg tribunal for the proposition that the laws of war 'are not static, but by continual adaptation follow the needs of a changing world'.[133] However, this statement could speak equally to changes in social mores or technology rather than legal developments. An example of this second understanding of progressive interpretation, that of evolutive interpretation, is the ICTR holding in respect of the crime of rape that 'a conceptual definition is preferable to a mechanical definition [as it] ... will better accommodate evolving norms of criminal justice.'[134] Similarly, in *Tadić* (1995), the Appeals Chamber of the ICTY rejected a narrow interpretation of jurisdiction advanced by the prosecutor, reasoning inter alia that it 'falls foul of a modern vision of the administration of justice'.[135]

---

[128] *Tadić Jurisdiction Decision* (n. 6) para. 74; *Delalić* (n. 6) para. 169; *Prosecutor* v. *Kordić and Others*, Decision on the Joint Defence Motion to Dismiss the Amended Indictment for Lack of Jurisdiction Based on the Limited Jurisdictional Reach of Articles 2 and 3, ICTY-95–14/2-A, 2 March 1999, para. 29; *Prosecutor* v. *Kordić and Others*, Decision on the Joint Defence Motion to Strike Paragraphs 20 and 22 and All References to Article 7(3) as Providing a Separate or an Alternative Basis for Imputing Criminal Responsibility, ICTY-95–14/2-A, 2 March 1999, para. 5.

[129] *Tadić Jurisdiction Decision* (n. 6) paras. 72ff.

[130] *Prosecutor* v. *Jelisić*, Judgment, ICTY-95–10-T, 14 December 1999, para. 61; *Tadić Jurisdiction Decision*, Separate Opinion of Judge Abi-Saab (n. 6).

[131] *Prosecutor* v. *Kunarac*, Judgment, ICTY-96–23 & ICTY-96–23/1-A, 12 June 2002, para. 67.

[132] *Simić*, Schomburg Dissent (n. 122) paras. 17–21.

[133] *Kunarac* (n. 131) para. 67; *Simić*, Schomburg Dissent (n. 122) para. 17.

[134] *Musema* (n. 122) para. 228.   [135] *Tadić Jurisdiction Decision* (n. 6) paras. 4–6.

2.3.1.8 Human rights standards and fairness to the accused

Other judges have focused on interpreting words and phrases in a manner that is consistent with human rights or is fair to the accused. For example, the ICTY has held that Bosnian Serbs detained by the Bosnian government forces are 'protected persons' under the fourth *Geneva Convention* (1949) because the Bosnian authorities clearly regarded them as belonging to the opposing Party in an armed conflict and as posing a threat to the Bosnian State. The Trial Chamber held:

> This interpretation of the Convention is fully in accordance with the development of the human rights doctrine which has been increasing in force since the middle of this century. It would be incongruous with the whole concept of human rights, which protect individuals from the excesses of their own governments, to rigidly apply the nationality requirement of article 4 that was apparently inserted to prevent interference in a State's relations with its own nationals.[136]

In another decision, respect for human dignity guided judges in defining rape on the basis that this principle underpins international law.[137]

Sometimes concerns about fairness have inspired judges to invoke the rule of *in dubio pro reo* ('when in doubt, in favour of the accused') to resolve an evidentiary issue,[138] and also to resolve differences between French and English versions of their governing statute.[139] For example, it was used to justify imposing an intent requirement for killings as genocide.[140] Whereas the word *meurtre* in French is understood to mean deliberate homicide, killing means the act of causing another person's death and therefore is silent on the question of whether intent is required. It was also used to impose the mental element of intent for the crime of murder as a crime against humanity.[141] Some judges have rejected *in dubio pro reo* as an interpretive rule.[142]

---

[136] *Delalić* (n. 6) paras. 265–266.

[137] *Prosecutor* v. *Furundžija*, Judgment, ICTY-95–17/1-T, 10 December 1998, para. 183.

[138] *Prosecutor* v. *Tadić*, Decision on Appellant's Motion for the Extension of the Time-Limit and Admission of Additional Evidence, ICTY-94–1-A, 15 October 1998, para. 73.

[139] *Prosecutor* v. *Rutaganda*, Judgment, ICTR-96–3-T, 6 December 1999, para. 50; *Akayesu* (n. 67) para. 501; *Musema* (n. 122) para. 155.

[140] *Blagojević* (n. 49) para. 642 fn. 2057; *Akayesu* (n. 67) para. 501.

[141] *Prosecutor* v. *Kayishema*, Judgment, ICTR-95–1-T, 21 May 1999, para. 103.

[142] Judge Schomburg has taken the position that the rule *in dubio pro reo* applies only to findings of fact and 'legal facts' and not to interpreting the ICTY's statute or rules of procedure and evidence. *Prosecutor* v. *Limaj and Others*, Judgment, Partially Dissenting and Separate Opinion and Declaration of Judge Schomburg, ICTY-03–66-A, 27 September 2007, paras. 15ff.

Other judges have invoked the rule of *contra proferentem* ('against the one bringing forth'),[143] a rule of interpretation that was originally used in contract law and provides that 'in case of doubt the contract must be interpreted in favour of or against the party bound by the obligation'.[144]

> The essence of the contractual relation consists in the mutually conform-
> ing declaration of will as to the contents of the obligation. Accordingly,
> the party which undertakes the drafting of the contract undertakes the
> responsibility for such conformity. It follows that in case of an ambiguity
> the drafting party is responsible for any mistake of the other party. For
> the party responsible for the drafting either deliberately introduces the
> ambiguity in order to lead the other party or he was negligent. In either
> case the interpretation must be against him.[145]

Unlike a bilateral contract, however, a multilateral treaty is negotiated, drafted and ratified by many States. When interpreting a treaty, therefore, it means the following: 'If two meanings are admissible, the provision should be interpreted *contra proferentem*, ie. that meaning which is least to the advantage of the party which prepared and proposed the provision, *or for whose benefit it was inserted in the treaty, should be preferred*.'[146] This rule of interpretation has had to compete with the principle of effective interpretation, the two often being mutually incompatible if understood in absolute terms.[147] In practice, international tribunals have favoured the rule of effective interpretation, even when paying lip service to the idea of restrictive interpretation.[148]

Where a multilateral treaty creates international criminal jurisdiction, it might be said that the *contra proferentem* rule requires interpretation in favour of the accused, as the treaty is intended to benefit the international community as a whole and was drafted by its member States. Article 22(2) of the Rome Statute embodies this notion. However, the ICTY and ICTR seem to have largely ignored this and the rule of strict construction while at the same time acknowledging its importance.[149] In *Delalić* (1998), the ICTY held:

---

[143] *Delalić* (n. 6) paras. 408–413; *Kanyabashi*, Shahabuddeen Dissent (n. 16) 21. For more on the national and international origins of this rule and its content for purposes of interpreting crimes in the Rome Statute, see Chapter 5, Section 5.5.

[144] Lauterpacht (n. 20) 56 (citing provisions of the French Civil Code, Italian Civil Code, Roman law and the American Law Institute's Restatement of Contract Law).

[145] Ibid. 57.   [146] Jennings and Watts (n. 8) 1279 (emphasis added).

[147] Lauterpacht (n. 20) 67.

[148] See ibid. generally for ICJ *contra proferentem* case law and ibid. 63 fn. 4 for more on this conflict of rules.

[149] *Tadić* Judgment (n. 47) 73; see also *Prosecutor v. Erdemović*, Judgment, Separate and Dissenting Opinion of Judge Cassese, ICTY-96–22-A, 7 October 1997, para. 49; *Kayishema* (n. 141) para. 103; *Akayesu* (n. 67) para. 319; *Rutaganda* (n. 139) para. 51; *Musema* (n. 122) para. 155, cited in W Schabas, *The International Criminal Court: A Commentary on the Rome Statute* (Oxford University Press 2010) 409–10.

To put the meaning of the principle of legality beyond doubt, two important corollaries must be accepted. The first of these is that penal statutes
must be strictly construed, this being a general rule which has stood the
test of time.... The rule of strict construction requires that the language
of a particular provision shall be construed such that no cases shall be held
to fall within it which do not fall both within the reasonable meaning of
its terms and within the spirit and scope of the enactment. In the construction of a criminal statute no violence must be done to its language
to include people within it who do not ordinarily fall within its express
language.... The paramount object in the construction of a criminal provision, or any other statute, is to ascertain the legislative intent. The rule of
strict construction is not violated by giving the expression its full meaning
or the alternative meaning which is more consonant with the legislative
intent and best effectuates such intent.... The effect of strict construction
of the provisions of a criminal statute is that *where an equivocal word
or ambiguous sentence leaves a reasonable doubt of its meaning which the
canons of construction fail to solve, the benefit of the doubt should be given
to the subject and against the legislature* which has failed to explain itself.
This is why ambiguous criminal statutes are to be construed *contra proferentem*.[150]

Accordingly, the ICTY would permit consideration of all canons of interpretation (including effective interpretation) and interpretive aids (including
preparatory work) before resorting to strict construction should an ambiguity
still linger.[151] However, it is hard to imagine that the canons of interpretation
in the *Vienna Convention* (1969) and beyond could produce no result – that
an ambiguity would remain.[152] Still, the ICTY and ICTR have, on occasion,
given priority to the rule of strict construction over those rules in the *Vienna
Convention* (1969). For example, the ICTR Appeals Chamber in *Nahimana and
Others* (2007) overruled the Trial Chamber's finding that the accused could
be convicted for criminal conduct that occurred prior to 1994. The Appeals
Chamber held that strict construction requires an accused to be charged with
a crime that he or she allegedly committed in 1994 and that all of the elements
of that crime must have been present in that year.[153]

---

[150] *Delalić* (n. 6) paras. 408, 410, 412, 413 (emphasis added). On *contra proferentum*, see also
Prosecutor v. *Tadić*, Opinion and Judgement, ICTY-94–1-T, 7 May 1997, para. 713 (*Tadić
Trial Judgment*).
[151] B Broomhall, 'Article 22' in O Triffterer (ed.), *Commentary on the Rome Statute of the
International Criminal Court*, 2nd edn (CH Beck/Hart/Nomos 2008) 713, 726; A Cassese,
International Criminal Law, 2nd edn (Oxford University Press 2008) 51.
[152] Lauterpacht (n. 20) 61–62.
[153] *Prosecutor* v. *Nahimana and Others*, Judgment, ICTR-99–52-A, 28 November 2007, paras.
313–314.

2.3.1.9 Customary international law

In the *Vienna Convention* (1969), custom is conceived of as an *aid* to interpretation and not a guiding interpretive principle.[154] However, the UN Secretary-General's report on the establishment of the ICTY expressly states that its jurisdiction is limited to conduct that is, 'beyond doubt', criminal under customary international law.[155] The ICTR is empowered to apply both custom and applicable treaty law but was implicitly encouraged to apply custom to its material jurisdiction.[156] Accordingly, the ICTR's jurisprudence has made a more modest contribution to clarifying the content of custom.[157] Still, the ICTR Appeals Chamber has held that it is 'unfair' to hold an individual accountable for conduct that was not clearly defined under international criminal law at the time it occurred.[158] The ICTY and ICTR are not the first tribunals to give prominence to custom when interpreting the definitions of crimes:

> From the earliest days of the international criminal tribunals, customary international law has played an extraordinary and unprecedented role. It is relied upon to delimit the scope of the crimes themselves, building upon the often laconic provisions drawn from aging treaties. Judges also use customary international law to address challenges to retroactivity, answering claims that a prosecution violates the principle of *nullum crimen sine lege* by arguing that the law could be found in custom even if it had not been written down.[159]

Judges have sometimes resolved an ambiguity in the ICTY or ICTR statute by adopting a definition or concept that most adheres to customary international law, even if this interpretation is not the most favourable to the accused.[160] Accordingly, a presumption of interpretation consistent with custom has operated as an interpretive principle or argument. For example, crimes against

---

[154] Article 31(3)(c), *Vienna Convention* (1969).   [155] UNSC, ICTY Report (n. 123).

[156] UNSC, 'Comprehensive Report of the Secretary-General on Practical Arrangements for the Effective Functioning of the International Criminal Tribunal for Rwanda, Recommending Arusha as the Seat of the Tribunal' (1995) UN Doc. S/1995/134, para. 12; see, e.g., *Akayesu* (n. 67) paras. 604–607; *Kayishema* (n. 141) paras. 156–158, 597–598; *Musema* (n. 122) para. 242; *Prosecutor* v. *Semanza*, Judgment, ICTR-97–20-T, 15 May 2003, para. 353, cited in G Mettraux, *International Crimes and the Ad Hoc Tribunals* (Oxford University Press 2006) 10.

[157] T Meron, 'Revival of Customary International Humanitarian Law' (2005) 99 AJIL 817, 831.

[158] *Prosecutor* v. *Bagilishema*, Judgment, ICTR-95–1A, 3 July 2002, para. 34.

[159] WA Schabas, 'Customary Law or "Judge-Made" Law: Judicial Creativity at the UN Criminal Tribunals' in J Doria, H-P Gasser & MC Bassiouni (eds.), *The Legal Regime of the International Criminal Court: Essays in Honour of Professor Igor Blishchenko* (Brill 2009) 77.

[160] See Section 2.3.1.8 above.

humanity were held to be defined by a widespread *or* systematic attack even though the French version of the ICTR statute referred to a widespread *and* systematic attack.[161] While few would contest the ICTR's correction of this drafting error, the point is that the decision fails to explain why customary law was applied rather than an interpretation that favours the accused. In the ICTY statute, no reference appears at all to a widespread or systematic attack, and the requirement was read in as an element of a crime against humanity on the basis that this element is present in other statutes, namely the ICTR statute and Rome Statute.[162] In that case, reading in the requirement significantly limited the situations that would rise to the level of a crime against humanity, thereby favouring the accused.

In the Nuremberg judgment, the tribunal wrote that 'in many cases treaties do no more than express and define for more accurate reference the principles of law already existing'.[163] In *Tadić* (1995) the ICTY held that the only reason that the report of the UN Secretary-General referred to the tribunal's jurisdiction being limited to crimes that undoubtedly exist under customary international law was the goal of respecting the principle of legality, as Parties to the conflict in the former Yugoslavia might not have ratified relevant treaties on the laws of war.[164] Perhaps this is why the UN Secretary-General in his report on the draft statute for the Special Court for Sierra Leone expressly linked the presumption of consistency with customary international law to the principle of legality and specifically the prohibition against retroactive application of criminal law.[165] However, the ICTY Appeals Chamber went on in *Tadić* (1999) to hold that the Security Council is entitled to define crimes in the ICTY statute in a manner that departs from custom so long as *jus cogens* norms are not violated, thereby rendering the presumption of consistency with custom rebuttable.[166] Other judges, however, have linked the presumption of consistency with custom not only to the principle of legality but also to the idea that the Security Council is not empowered to legislate crimes for the international community, therefore transforming this presumption into a legal requirement.[167]

In practice, the presumption of consistency with custom has given rise to several methodological problems at the ICTY. First, it has been pointed out that, in practice, judges have adopted diverging positions on the customary status of certain treaty provisions.[168] More problematic is the reproach that judges have not taken a sufficiently rigorous approach to the ascertainment

---

[161] *Musema* (n. 122) paras. 202ff.   [162] *Blaškić* (n. 81) para. 202.
[163] *France and Others* v. *Göring and Others* (1946) 13 ILR 203, (1947) 41 AJIL 172, 219.
[164] *Tadić Jurisdiction Decision* (n. 6) para. 143; UNSC, ICTY Report (n. 123).
[165] UNSC, 'Report of the Secretary-General on the Establishment of a Special Court for Sierra Leone' (2000) UN Doc. S/2000/915, para. 12.
[166] *Tadić Judgment* (n. 47) paras. 287, 296.   [167] *Delalić* (n. 6) para. 417.
[168] Schabas (n. 159) 82.

of custom, focusing disproportionately on *opinio juris* and not inquiring fully into State practice – even using the concept of custom to mask judicial law making.[169] Indeed, '[o]n several occasions it is not State practice but rather its absence that has been invoked as evidence of customary international law'.[170] Not everyone is in agreement with this assessment.[171] And even those who are do not necessarily regard this practice as objectionable on legal policy grounds. It has been observed that '[i]n reality, the judges are exercising leadership not so much in the judicial codification of State practice as in the progressive development of a legal system that would never have emerged in the way that it has if this had been left the initiative of States alone'.[172]

2.3.1.10 Conclusions

No prevailing hermeneutic has emerged, and the jurisprudence contains inconsistent reasoning with references inter alia to the following principles of interpretation: literal, logical, contextual, purposive, effective, drafters' intent and progressive. Human rights standards, including fairness to the suspect or accused, as well as interpretation most consistent with customary law have also been invoked as guiding considerations. Adding to this confusion is that none of the aforementioned interpretive principles have been authoritatively defined, and so their meanings vary throughout the jurisprudence and sometimes even overlap. Not surprisingly, therefore, arguments supporting interpretive principles are not clearly connected to the interpretive principle to which they adhere. For example, judges have used the principle of literal interpretation to endorse arguments favouring both strict and broad interpretations of impugned words.[173] On other occasions, bald statements about the prudence of adopting a broad interpretation of a phrase, for example, are not buttressed by an explanation about how this argument achieves the greatest faithfulness to a particular interpretive principle (e.g., progressive interpretation, effective interpretation). Accordingly, the development of a method of interpretation, as defined above, has not been possible.

The practice of identifying but not describing the interpretive rule being applied is not unique to the ICTY and ICTR. It has also been described as a

---

[169] M Swart, 'Judicial Lawmaking at the Ad Hoc Tribunals: The Creative Use of the Sources of International Law and "Adventurous Interpretation"' (2010) 70 ZaöRV 459, 461, 464; Schabas (n. 159) 99–100 (citing *Prosecutor* v. *Hadzihasanovic and Others*, Judgment, Separate and Partially Dissenting Opinion of Judge David Hunt, ICTY-01–47-AR72, 16 July 2003, para. 3 as hinting at this).

[170] Schabas (n. 159) 89.   [171] See, e.g., Meron (n. 157) 831.   [172] Schabas (n. 159) 101.

[173] *Blaškić* (n. 81) para. 328; *Tadić Trial Judgment* (n. 148) para. 639; *Blagojević* (n. 47) para. 281; *Prosecutor* v. *Martić*, Judgment, ICTY-95–11-T, 12 June 2007, para. 50.

'constant feature' of the International Court of Justice.[174] However, as perplexing as it may be to see different (and sometimes contradictory) interpretive principles and arguments being invoked in the jurisprudence of the ICTY and ICTR, it is even more curious to find the use of none at all.[175]

More than half a century ago, the ability of rules of interpretation to absolutely check judicial discretion was rejected for three reasons:

> In the first instance, the selection of any particular rule, out of a number of competing and occasionally mutually inconsistent rules, is necessarily a matter of discretion. The discretion is proportionate to the number and the elasticity of the rules available. Secondly, there is no assurance that a judge, bent upon achieving a desired result, will not purport to base his or her decision on a rule that nominally covers the issue but in fact has little to do with it. Thirdly, it is not necessary for the judge formally to use any rules of interpretation at all – even as a mere device for achieving a desired result which he considers to be consistent with the common intention of the parties or, in its absence, with justice and good faith.[176]

A methodology for interpretation can address the first reason only by fixing the relationship between rules of interpretation that are most inconsistent with one another. However, it cannot force judges to adhere to this method. Judges of the ICTY and ICTR have accomplished the laudable task of defining in detail the crimes that fall within their respective jurisdictions. They have also identified numerous interpretive principles and arguments that could possibly guide judges at the International Criminal Court in the future. Most important, however, their experience can serve as a cautionary tale for these judges. The jurisprudence of the ICTY and ICTR reveals the legal uncertainty that can plague interpretative reasoning when judges are not equipped with a shared legal methodology. Going forward, therefore, the focus should not be on 'criticism of rules of interpretation in general, or of their number, as to the accuracy of particular rules, the manner of their application, and their hierarchical importance when viewed in their totality'.[177]

2.3.2 Aids to interpretation

References to supporting materials abound in the jurisprudence of the ICTY and ICTR. A large representative sample of this case law over a period of fourteen years (1994–2008) was carefully examined to identify the frequency with which various materials have been used by judges in support of their interpretive arguments. These findings are summarized in this section. Owing

---

[174] Lauterpacht (n. 20) 55.
[175] The tribunal was attempting to define torture under customary international law. *Delalić* (n. 6) para. 442; *Blaškić* (n. 81) para. 208 fn. 401.
[176] Lauterpacht (n. 20) 53–54.   [177] Ibid. 55.

to the sheer volume of jurisprudence that was reviewed, the case law supporting these findings is listed in an annex at the end of this Chapter. Interpretive aids may be authoritative, that is, binding or non-binding materials that must be taken into account if they are relevant, or non-authoritative, meaning materials that may be taken into account.[178] In the jurisprudence of the ICTY and ICTR, it is difficult to ascertain the admissibility or persuasiveness of the materials that have aided judges in the interpretive process – the extent to which judges must, may or may not consider these materials. Further, the scant detail in the ICTY and ICTR statutes understandably leads to greater than normal convergence of interpretation and application of the law, with judges not always specifying whether they are invoking a legal source as an aid to interpreting a statutory provision or applying it directly to a set of facts. In spite of this, it is still possible to roughly approximate the prevalence of these materials being invoked as interpretive aids in the jurisprudence of these tribunals.

Expert materials are the interpretive aids most often relied upon by judges, perhaps to clarify the content of the statutes and crimes under customary international law. These materials include expert and academic commentary, the International Law Commission's (ILC) *Draft Code of Offences against the Peace and Security of Mankind* (1996) and commentary to it,[179] ILC reports, views expressed by the International Committee of the Red Cross, commentaries to the four *Geneva Conventions* (1949) and commentaries to the *Additional Protocols* (1977).

In second place are domestic legal instruments and decisions, including case law arising under Control Council Law No. 10 (Punishment of Persons Guilty of War Crimes, Crimes against Peace and against Humanity).[180] The invocation of domestic law has been the most varied and unexplained. The ICTR and ICTY have resorted to substantive laws applicable to the territory of the former Yugoslavia and Rwanda, with the ICTR showing more deference to Rwandan law than the ICTY to its counterpart. Judges have also undertaken detailed comparative analyses on legal definitions in different national jurisdictions as well as less detailed comparisons of civil and common law understandings of a legal concept. Domestic war crimes jurisprudence of all kinds has been considered, as well as codes, legislation and principles of criminal law common

---

[178] RS Summers and M Taruffo, 'Interpretation and Comparative Analysis' in DN MacCormick and RS Summers (eds.), *Interpreting Statutes: A Comparative Study* (Ashgate 1991) 461, 475–76. This distinction has been acknowledged on occasion by judges at the ICTY: *Delalić* (n. 6) paras. 168–169. However, unlike the judges in *Delalić*, Summers and Taruffo define authoritative aids as including non-binding materials, such as official regulations and similar statutes in other jurisdictions.

[179] ILC (1996) II (Part Two) Ybk of the ILC 17.

[180] Adopted at Berlin on 20 December 1945, Official Gazette of the Control Council for Germany No. 3, Berlin, 31 January 1946, reprinted in B Ferencz, *An International Criminal Court: A Step Toward World Peace*, vol. I (Oceana 1980) 488.

to the major legal systems of the world. This is perhaps in an effort to identify a general principle of law or custom. When a provision in the ICTY or
ICTR statute is unclear, it is understandable that judges would turn to a well-
developed national law that reflects a reasonable, fair and workable solution.
This reliance, however, must not undermine express terms in these statutes
or fail to make due allowance for the unique nature of international criminal
law.[181] Perhaps in response to this practice, the drafters of the Rome Statute
deliberately steered clear of terms that implicate a particular legal system.

Coming in third is the jurisprudence of the ICTY and ICTR tribunals themselves. While the concept of binding precedents does not exist under international law, trial judges at the tribunals tend to follow the interpretive findings
of the Appeals Chamber, and judicial comity fosters respect for the interpretive findings of their peers in other trial chambers. The Appeals Chamber
of the ICTY has observed that the principle of stare decisis (binding precedent) tends to underpin general trends detected in both common and civil
law jurisdictions.[182] However, the ranking of these tribunals' jurisprudence as
the third most frequented aid to interpretation is somewhat misleading; the
decisions relied upon likely invoked an aid to interpretation other than the
tribunals' own jurisprudence. In fourth place is customary law, which has been
held to include the four *Geneva Conventions* (1949), parts of the *Additional
Protocols* (1977), the *Genocide Convention* (1948) as well as Hague law.[183] To
the extent that domestic law is used to discern custom, the latter may be one of
the highest-ranking interpretive aids invoked by the tribunals.

In fifth place are the preparatory works for the tribunals' statutes as well
as those for other treaties, including the Rome Statute. This low ranking for
preparatory works exists despite some judges regarding them as mandatory
interpretive aids: '[they] cannot be ignored in the interpretation of provisions
that might be deemed ambiguous. The vast majority of the members of the
international community rely upon such sources in construing international
instruments.'[184] One explanation for this low ranking is that preparatory works

---

[181] In *Erdemović* (n. 149), paras. 2–6, the Appeals Chamber had to consider the meaning of a
        guilty plea. While Judges McDonald and Vohrah turned to the common law for guidance
        as to the proper meaning of the term and for an understanding of safeguards surrounding
        the concept, Judge Cassese expressed caution about reliance upon a particular legal
        family, finding that that such an approach is only admissible where the term used in the
        international legal instrument indisputably is derived from that legal family or 'where no
        autonomous notion can be inferred from the whole context and spirit of international
        norms'.

[182] *Prosecutor* v. *Aleksovski*, Judgment, ICTY- 95–14/1-A, 24 March 2000, paras. 92ff.

[183] *Convention (IV) respecting the Laws and Customs of War on Land and its annex: Regulations
        concerning the Laws and Customs of War on Land* with Annex of Regulations (adopted
        18 October 1907, 26 January 1910) 35 Stat. 2277, TS 539, 1 Bevans 631.

[184] *Delalić* (n. 6) paras. 168–169.

do not form part of the ICTY and ICTR statutes' 'context' as defined in article 31(1) of the *Vienna Convention* (1969) unless they are agreements between the Parties.[185] As well, preparatory works, which are mentioned in article 32, 'constitute a supplementary means of interpretation and may only be resorted to when the text of the treaty or any other international norm-creating instrument is *ambiguous or obscure*'.[186] Given the comparative relevance and irrelevance of contextual and preparatory materials respectively, these labels become very important. Some materials have been difficult to classify. For example, Security Council resolutions and the Report of the UN Secretary-General on the establishment of the ICTY have been held to form part of the 'context' of the ICTY statute pursuant to article 31.[187] Elsewhere, the ICTY has held that the Report is more akin to a preparatory work.[188] The ICTY has also, on occasion, treated the statements of members of the Security Council on the establishment of the tribunal as preparatory work.[189]

In sixth place are the Charters for the International Military Tribunals (IMTs) at Nuremberg and Tokyo,[190] IMT case law and the principles derived therefrom. Again, if these materials are considered to be reflective of customary law, then the ranking of custom as an interpretive aid becomes even higher. In seventh place are treaties, including the Rome Statute, dealing with various issues such as torture, apartheid, crimes against humanity and civil and political rights. Sometimes a legal standard in the Rome Statute is rejected as being a step beyond customary law.[191] Other times, the Rome Statute is resorted to because of the limited number of precedents on the matter.[192] In eighth place are comparisons between the French and English versions of the ICTY or ICTR statutes in accordance with article 33 of the *Vienna Convention* (1969).

In ninth place is the jurisprudence of the International Court of Justice and European Court of Human Rights. In tenth and final place is a potpourri of materials, including dictionary definitions and United Nations General Assembly materials (e.g., statements and resolutions), historic events and even a speech by Robert Jackson.

In spite of the seemingly random use of such a wide variety of materials, some important general trends are discernable. Judges seem to be keenly aware

---

[185] *Tadić Judgment* (n. 47) paras. 300–304.

[186] Ibid. paras. 303–304 (emphasis in original).

[187] *Prosecutor* v. *Tadić*, Decision of the Prosecutor's Motion Requesting Protective Measures for Victims and Witnesses, ICTY-94-1-A, 10 August 1995, para. 18.

[188] *Tadić Judgment* (n. 47) paras. 293–295.

[189] Ibid. paras. 300, 303–304.

[190] London Agreement 1945 establishing the Nuremberg Tribunal, 82 UNTS 279 (No. 251); Tokyo Tribunal Charter (1946) 15 AD 356 254. The Tokyo Tribunal was established by special proclamation of General MacArthur.

[191] *Delalić* (n. 6) para. 393; article 28(1)(a), Rome Statute.   [192] *Krstić* (n. 49) para. 498.

of the fact that so many of the words and phrases in the ICTY and ICTR statutes were taken directly from treaties and have special technical (legal or non-legal) meanings. The strongest evidence of this is their deference to interpretive arguments that are supported by expert opinions as opposed to dictionary definitions of words – the former ranking first among interpretive aids and the latter ranking last. The hardest cases seem to be those where expert materials at the international level do not offer much guidance to judges. Here, they often turn to what can be described as content-rich materials from domestic legal systems. This practice needs to be carefully scrutinized given the cautionary remarks of Judge Cassese about legal transplants to the international level.[193] It is also noteworthy that once judges interpret a word or phrase in a particular way, later judges tend to respect this construction.

Most important, judges seem to rely on authoritative and non-authoritative aids to interpretation, which suggests that judges implicitly regard the tasks of interpretation and gap-filling as distinct. In spite of these positive developments, the generality of the preceding comments is symptomatic of the absence of a methodological framework. The starting point for resolving interpretive issues is not fixed. Sometimes judges turn first to jurisprudence that dates back to Nuremberg; other times they look to the decisions of the ICTY or ICTR; and other times, the starting point is a domestic law or the Rome Statute. This lack of predictability arguably undermines the rule of law. Defining the content and scope of core international crimes is the object of these ad hoc interpretive approaches, and it is one that warrants more coherence and consistency. For example, it would be most helpful if, when invoking an aid such as IMT or domestic law, some clarification were provided as to whether this is for the purpose of ascertaining custom, which is also an aid, or whether these laws are being invoked as interpretive aids in their own right.

2.4 Features of the Rome regime

With the advent of the Court, some methodological progress has been made. First, the Rome Statute contains articles 21(3) and 22(2), both of which contain interpretive guidance and will be studied in subsequent Chapters. Second, whereas the distinction between interpretation and application of the law has not always been identified in the jurisprudence of the ICTY and ICTR, this distinction has not only been entrenched in article 21 of the Rome Statute, which makes alternating references to 'interpretation' and 'application', but also recognized by judges of the Court.[194] By referring expressly to interpretation, the Rome Statute legitimates the role of judges as interpreters and not only

---

[193] *Erdemović* (n. 149) paras. 4–6.

[194] See, e.g., article 21, Rome Statute; *Prosecutor* v. *Lubanga Dyilo*, Judgment on the Appeal of Mr Thomas Lubanga Dyilo against the Decision on the Defence Challenge to the

appliers of international criminal law, a notion that was perhaps on shaky or contested ground in the past. Third, judges have acknowledged that the Rome regime is distinct from the ICTY and ICTR regimes.[195] The jurisprudence of the ad hoc tribunals is so rich that it is perhaps tempting for those working at the Court, many of whom spent time working at the tribunals, to mistakenly transpose familiar legal approaches on a wholesale basis. In the final part of this Chapter, consideration will be given to some unique features of the Rome regime – relative to the ICTY and ICTR regimes – that may be expected to influence how judges approach the task of interpretation. These include: (1) the drafting of the Rome Statute; (2) the division of powers in the Rome regime; (3) dialogue and political constraints in this regime; (4) the nature of the Statute and Court; and (5) the selection and removal of judges. What these features have in common is that they do not per se form part of a legal methodology for interpretation but may indirectly, from the perspective of legal policy, hint at or influence some of its contours and even impact its effectiveness. Some have also suggested that the legitimacy of an interpretive approach hinges on its ability to respond to the 'particular needs and characteristics of the treaty being interpreted'.[196]

2.4.1 Drafting of the Rome Statute

How was the Rome Statute drafted? In this section, consideration will be given to what the process of political bargaining leading up to the adoption of the Rome Statute suggests about the potential role of the drafters' intent as evidenced by preparatory work serving as a guiding principle of interpretation for crimes in the Rome Statute.

The drafting process for the Rome Statute differs markedly from that for the ICTY and ICTR statutes. When the UN Security Council requested a report from the Secretary-General on its decision to establish the ICTY, the latter swiftly responded with a report and a single draft statute for the future ICTY.[197] Remarkably, members of the Security Council unanimously approved

---

Jurisdiction of the Court pursuant to Article 19(2)(a) of the Statute of 3 October 2006, ICC-01/04–01/06–772, 14 December 2006, para. 34, cited in Bitti (n. 6).

[195] See, e.g., *Prosecutor* v. *Kony and Others*, Decision on the Prosecutor's Position on the Decision of Pre-Trial Chamber II to Redact Factual Descriptions of Crimes in the Warrants of Arrest, Motion for Reconsideration, and Motion for Clarification, ICC-02/04–01/05–60, 28 October 2005, para. 19, cited in Bitti (n. 6) 297.

[196] DM McRae, 'Approaches to the Interpretation of Treaties: the European Court of Human Rights and the WTO Appellate Body' in S Breitenmoser and Others (eds.), *Human Rights, Democracy and the Rule of Law: Liber amicorum Luzius Wildhaber* (Nomos 2007) 1407, 1420.

[197] R Zacklin, 'Some Major Problems in the Drafting of the ICTY Statute' (2004) 2 J Int'l Crim Justice 361.

it, without changes.[198] The ICTR statute is an adaptation of the ICTY statute; it was drafted by some members of the Security Council, including Rwanda, and it was endorsed by all members of the Security Council except Rwanda and China.[199] The principal drafters for both statutes were lawyers in the Legal Affairs section at the United Nations.[200]

In contrast to the ICTY and ICTR statutes, which were drafted in a short period of time by a small circle of lawyers, the road to Rome was paved with years of painstaking preparatory negotiations involving many actors. The history of these negotiations is documented elsewhere.[201] It is well known that serious efforts to establish the Court date back to the Draft Statute prepared by the International Law Commission (ILC) in 1994, that an Ad Hoc Committee on the establishment of the Court met for a total of nineteen days in April and August of 1995 and that a Preparatory Committee was subsequently convened for a total of thirty-seven days in March, April and August in 1996 and nine additional weeks in 1997 and 1998. It is important to note that to give the Preparatory Committee sufficient time to revise the work of the ILC, it was excused from preparing a report on these nine additional weeks of debates.[202] Consequently, drafting revisions were recorded as UN documents without being supplemented with any sort of explanatory text.[203] As one commentator and participant in these debates rightly remarks, this procedure 'makes it more difficult to trace the history of the text of the articles of the Statute'.[204] As well, an intersessional meeting in Zutphen in January 1998 and annual intersessional meetings in Siracusa from 1995–1998 were integral to the final outcome and involved experts from government, universities and the ICTY and ICTR.

The Rome Diplomatic Conference convened from 15 June until 17 July 1998. The negotiations leading up to the conference revealed deep and diverging national positions. In fact, it began with a consolidated draft text that contained 116 articles and more than 1,300 brackets, as well as more than 2,000 State delegates and 238 non-governmental organizations (NGOs) ready to get involved in the drafting process.[205] State delegates included career UN diplomats, politicians, senior civil servants and legal experts.[206] Observers,

---

[198] Ibid.; UNSC Res. 827 (25 May 1993).

[199] Rwanda voted against it and China abstained.   [200] Zacklin (n. 197).

[201] See, e.g., A Bos, 'From the International Law Commission to the Rome Conference (1994–1999)' in A Cassese and Others (eds.), *The Rome Statute of the International Criminal Court: A Commentary*, vol. I (Oxford University Press 2002) 35; J Crawford, 'The Work of the International Law Commission' in A Cassese and Others (eds.), *The Rome Statute of the International Criminal Court: A Commentary*, vol. I (Oxford University Press 2002) 23.

[202] Bos, ibid. 51.   [203] Ibid.   [204] Ibid.

[205] MC Bassiouni, *The Legislative History of the International Criminal Court: Introduction, Analysis, and Integrated Text* (Transnational Publishers 2005) 72, 79, 86.

[206] Ibid. 79.

United Nations staff members and media representatives were also in attendance.[207] To increase their impact, NGOs formed the Coalition for the Establishment of an International Criminal Court and provided substantive input during the negotiations.[208] They and the International Committee of the Red Cross (ICRC) also lobbied delegations, monitored negotiations and provided delegations with technical expertise and helpful research papers.[209] Whereas some delegates had knowledge of the draft text on which the negotiations were based, others had little or no knowledge of it.[210] Over five weeks, this draft statute was the subject of intensive multilateral negotiations and political bargaining.

The outstanding issues were both complex and contentious. Responding to specific issues and clusters of issues gave rise to the formation of groups of States at the conference.[211] The Like-Minded Group (LMG) consisted of more than sixty States that were committed to an independent and effective Court.[212] The permanent members of the Security Council (P-5) shared a number of concerns, with the exception of the United Kingdom, which joined the LMG.[213] There was also a non-aligned movement (NAM), which included States that were inside and outside the LMG. Delegations in the NAM had diverging views on most issues.

Unlike the small group of lawyers working on the ICTY and ICTR statutes who were able to draft these documents together, time pressure in Rome coupled with the size of the draft text and the number of players meant that articles were drafted in smaller working groups. The negotiations at Rome proceeded as follows: the Committee of the Whole would debate an issue, refer further discussions and the drafting of a compromise text to a Working Group on the matter, discuss the results of the Working Group and transmit an approved text to the Drafting Committee for a technical review, which then referred the text back to the Committee of the Whole. The Committee of the Whole was responsible for developing a Draft Statute that could be referred to the Plenary for final adoption.[214] According to the Chairman of the Committee of the Whole,

---

[207] P Kirsch and D Robinson, 'Reaching Agreement at the Rome Conference' in A Cassese and Others (eds.), *The Rome Statute of the International Criminal Court: A Commentary*, vol. I (Oxford University Press 2002) 67.

[208] Bos (n. 201) 62. For an account of the contribution made by NGOs to these and the Rome negotiations, see WR Pace and J Schense, 'The Role of Non-Governmental Organizations' in A Cassese and Others (eds.), *The Rome Statute of the International Criminal Court: A Commentary*, vol. I (Oxford University Press 2002) 105; WR Pace and M Thieroff, 'Participation of Non-governmental Organizations' in RS Lee (ed.), *The International Criminal Court: The Making of the Rome Statute: Issues, Negotiations, Results* (Kluwer Law International 1999) 391.

[209] Kirsch and Robinson (n. 207) 71–72.   [210] Bassiouni (n. 205) 79.

[211] Kirsch and Robinson (n. 207) 70.   [212] Ibid. 70.   [213] Ibid. 71.   [214] Ibid. 73.

'the philosophy of the final package was to reflect the strong majority trends, but with efforts to accommodate minority views to the extent possible'.[215] Thus, no common intent existed, but rather desirable elements and compromises that delegations could tolerate. It was mandatory under the rules of procedure for the conference that actors try to attract the broadest possible support for each text at issue.[216] No mention was made of adopting the clearest possible language evidencing a singular intent. Creative ambiguities therefore undoubtedly exist in the resulting text. It has been suggested that the rules of interpretation in the *Vienna Convention* (1969) are accordingly 'meaningless', as the latter are intended to distil the intent of States when this is ambiguous as a result of poor drafting and not because of a lack of agreement.[217] Then again, all treaties are said to be 'disagreement reduced to writing'.[218]

As pieces of this jigsaw puzzle trickled in on a daily basis, the Drafting Committee worked hard at fitting these pieces together and trying to maintain a uniform style, form and usage of terms in the provisions as well as appropriate cross-references to related articles.[219] They might not have always succeeded. As well, the final product benefited more from informal and informal-informal negotiations at Rome than formal ones.[220] Unfortunately, hardly any preparatory works exist on the conference negotiations.[221] 'The need for informal, off-the-record discussions clearly arose out of the necessity to overcome major rifts in a smooth manner and in such a way as to avoid States losing face by changing their position.'[222] The records that do exist are thousands of pages long, incomplete in places, not publicly accessible in one place and not easily searchable.[223] Interestingly, some have characterized the absence of an official legislative history as a 'blessing':

> [I]t frees those in the future who will interpret the Statute from the shackles of a historic record. This will no doubt allow the Statute to evolve with the needs of the international community and with the shifting demands of international criminal justice. In short, the Statute's interpretation will evolve similar to that of a national constitution and will likely change in relation to international developments. The less dogmatic [the] approach that is taken, the more likely it is that the ICC will be able to go through its

---

[215] Ibid. 76.
[216] Rules 34 and 52, Rules of Procedure for the Rome Conference (23 June 1998) UN Doc. A/CONF.183/6.
[217] Wessel (n. 42) 415.
[218] P Allott, 'The Concept of International Law' (1999) 10 EJIL 31.
[219] Bassiouni (n. 205) 82.   [220] Ibid. 80.   [221] Ibid. xix.
[222] A Cassese, 'The Statute of the International Criminal Court: Some Preliminary Reflections' (1999) 10 EJIL 144, 145.
[223] See, however, the Legal Tools project on the website of the International Criminal Court, which is a commendable and enormous effort to improve this situation: www.legal-tools. org/en/what-are-the-icc-legal-tools/, accessed 1 May 2014.

own historic stages, as has been the case with the most successful judicial institutions throughout the world.[224]

All of the above should arguably give pause to anyone who might seek to develop a method for interpreting crimes in the Rome Statute with drafters' intent as a guiding interpretive principle and based on arguments supported by preparatory materials. While thousands of pages of preparatory work exist, one questions the sense in binding judges to a perfectly coherent 'truth' that might be pieced together therein when the final outcome is the merging of various definitions from various drafting phases that involved numerous and diverse actors. How can one speak of a common and uncontested intent? The existence of expert works explaining the drafting history of these provisions is highly informative but cannot overcome all problems arising from these fragmented and unrecorded negotiations.

It became apparent at Rome that five weeks was insufficient time to facilitate the drafting of instruments subsidiary to the Statute, including the Elements of Crimes (Elements).[225] Thus, the Final Act of the Rome Conference mandated the participation of States that signed this Act in a Preparatory Commission following the conference, which was instructed inter alia to draft the Elements.[226] The ICRC assisted the Preparatory Commission with drafting the Elements by submitting to it a comprehensive study of existing case law and international humanitarian and human rights law instruments relevant to the crimes.

This study was a key working tool for government delegations. It provided delegates with the necessary legal background, guided their discussions and assisted them in their drafting efforts. The Assembly of States Parties to the Rome Statute (ASP) adopted the Elements of Crimes during its first session from 3–10 September 2002. The ICRC went on to prepare a commentary to the Elements of Crimes, which sets out the *travaux préparatoires* or understandings of the Preparatory Commission during the drafting process and relevant legal sources pertaining to each crime.[227] This commentary renders the *travaux préparatoires* easily accessible to judges. However, as at Rome, it is possible that many difficult issues were resolved in informal sessions. As well, the status of the Elements as a material aid for interpreting crimes in the Rome Statute

---

[224] Bassiouni (n. 205) xix–xx.

[225] P Kirsch and V Oosterveld, 'The Post-Rome Conference Preparatory Commission' in A Cassese and Others (eds.), *The Rome Statute of the International Criminal Court: A Commentary*, vol. I (Oxford University Press 2002) 94.

[226] Final Act of the United Nations Diplomatic Conference of Plenipotentiaries on the Establishment of an International Criminal Court (17 July 1998) UN Doc. A/CONF.183/19, Resolution F, preambular para. 2.

[227] K Dörmann, *International Committee of the Red Cross, Elements of War Crimes under the Rome Statute of the International Criminal Court: Sources and Commentary* (Cambridge University Press 2003).

appears ambiguous when one juxtaposes articles 9(1) and 21(1)(a). Article 9(1) provides that 'Elements of Crimes *shall assist* the Court in the interpretation and application of articles 6, 7, 8 and 8 *bis*.'[228] Article 21(1)(a) states that the Court 'shall apply' the Elements of Crimes. It remains to be seen how this ambiguity is to be resolved and the corresponding implications this will have for the preparatory work and commentary as aids to interpreting crimes in the Rome Statute.[229]

2.4.2 Division of powers

It has been said that the detailed definitions of crimes in the Rome Statute and the Elements of Crimes instrument evidence 'mistrust' for judges at the Court.[230] In the Nuremberg Charter, war crimes were defined within 73 words, the ICTY statute uses 239 words and article 8 of the Rome Statute contains 1,594 words.[231] Further, unlike its predecessors, the work of judges at the Court will be carried out alongside the work of the Assembly of States Parties to the Rome Statute (ASP). The ASP is the permanent 'management oversight and legislative body' of the Court.[232] Its members are States that have ratified the Rome Statute, and it has the exclusive capacity to make binding decisions concerning the Court.[233] Accordingly, a methodology for interpreting crimes in the Rome Statute should respect the division of powers envisioned in the Statute so as not to undermine the legitimacy of judicial reasoning and decisions. It should avoid suggesting that judges are empowered to perform tasks that have been entrusted to the ASP. In this section, who has the power to correct drafting errors, amend provisions, 'correct' judicial misinterpretations and invalidate provisions of the Rome Statute will be identified with a view to bringing into sharp relief the outer limits of a method of interpretation for crimes defined therein.

2.4.2.1 Corrections

In the Rome regime, the process for correcting drafting errors differs from that for the ad hoc tribunals. Whereas ICTR judges 'corrected' the French version of their statute when it erroneously referred to a 'widespread and systematic attack'

---

[228] Emphasis added.

[229] See Chapter 7, Section 7.9, and Chapter 9, Sections 9.2.6 and 9.4.

[230] D Hunt, 'The International Criminal Court – High Hopes, "Creative Ambiguity" and an Unfortunate Mistrust in International Judges' (2004) 2 J Int'l Crim Justice 56.

[231] W Schabas, 'Follow Up to Rome: Preparing for Entry into Force of the International Criminal Court Statute' (1999) 20 Human Rights LJ 157, 163.

[232] Article 112, Rome Statute; Assembly of States Parties, www.icc-cpi.int/en_menus/asp/assembly/Pages/assembly.aspx, accessed 1 May 2014.

[233] Kirsch and Oosterveld (n. 225).

in article 3 as an element of crimes against humanity,[234] drafting errors in the Rome Statute have been corrected by the ASP using *procès-verbaux*. Corrections have thus far not been subject to any objection. To date, this process has been used on six occasions to correct drafting errors: 10 November 1998, 12 July 1999, 30 November 1999, 8 May 2000, 17 January 2001 and 16 January 2002. While most of these corrections have been of linguistic discrepancies between the official language versions of the Rome Statute, one correction is noteworthy.

On 10 November 1998, no State Party objected to an arguably substantive 'correction' to article 121(5), and it was not discussed within the Preparatory Commission or at a meeting of the ASP.[235] This provision previously provided that amendments to article 5 of the Rome Statute shall enter into force only for those States that accept the amendment by depositing their instruments of ratification or acceptance. This provision was corrected to refer to articles 6, 7 and 8 as well. Rather than this amendment procedure applying only to the addition of new crimes to the Court's jurisdiction, reference to articles 6, 7 and 8 results in amendments to the definitions of existing crimes in the Court's jurisdiction also becoming subject to a purely consent-based model. One drafter of article 121 was surprised that no State objected to the correction of this drafting error, given its significance and substantive nature.[236] Unlike the other corrections, it was not limited to discrepancies in language. All of the aforementioned errors were corrected before the Rome Statute entered into force on 1 July 2002. However, it is reasonable to assume that States Parties will retain the competence to correct drafting errors now that the Rome Statute has entered into force. Nothing suggests that States Parties have delegated this power to judges of the Court. What is less clear, however, is what the procedure would be if a State Party were to object to a correction, a matter that is not addressed by article 79 of the *Vienna Convention* (1969).[237] It is not clear

---

[234] *Prosecutor* v. *Musema*, Judgment, ICTR-96-13-A, 16 November 2001, para. 202.
[235] R Clark, 'Article 121' in Triffterer (n. 151) 1751, 1755–56.   [236] Ibid.
[237] Article 79 provides:
  1. Where, after the authentication of the text of a treaty, the signatory States and the contracting States are agreed that it contains an error, the error shall, unless they decide upon some other means of correction, be corrected . . .
  2. Where the treaty is one for which there is a depositary, the latter shall notify the signatory States and the contracting States of the error and of the proposal to correct it and shall specify an appropriate time-limit within which objection to the proposed correction may be raised. If, on the expiry of the time-limit:
    (a) no objection has been raised, the depositary shall make and initial the correction in the text and shall execute a procès-verbal of the rectification of the text and communicate a copy of it to the parties and to the States entitled to become parties to the treaty;
    (b) an objection has been raised, the depositary shall communicate the objection to the signatory States and to the contracting States.

whether consent to correct a mistake in the Rome Statute must be unanimous or follow the relevant amendment formula in articles 121 or 122, or whether a lower threshold might suffice, such as the approval of two-thirds of all members of the ASP. This lack of clarity is likely largely academic, at least for crimes in the Rome Statute, as it is hard to imagine that a drafting error in these provisions escaped the notice of all States Parties for over a decade. What is important is that judges are not competent to adopt an interpretation of a provision in the Rome Statute that 'corrects' a drafting error.

2.4.2.2 Amendments

While the correction of a drafting error is an attempt to bring the Statute in line with an intention already expressed by its drafters, an amendment is presumably a new legislative act that embodies a new drafters' intent. This distinction, however, might not be particularly helpful in practice.

As of 20 February 2008, the Security Council adopted resolutions to amend the ICTY statute nine times and the ICTR statute twice.[238] All of these amendments concerned judicial appointments. A review of these Security Council resolutions suggests that the process for amending the ICTY and ICTR statutes is as follows: the president of the tribunal is informed about an issue and writes a letter to the Secretary-General of the United Nations requesting the appropriate statutory amendment; the Secretary-General writes a letter to the Security Council informing it of the issue and recommending a course of action; and the Security Council passes a resolution on the issue, annexing to it the necessary statutory amendment(s). This amendment procedure can be carried out in three weeks or can take a year to be completed. Most amendments take several months to implement.

The Rome Statute contemplates substantive legal amendments in addition to those of an institutional nature. Article 122 provides that amendments to the Statute that are of an exclusively institutional nature may be proposed at any time and by any State Party. The proposed amendment shall be adopted by the ASP by a two-thirds majority of States Parties and enter into force for all States Parties six months thereafter, or as may be determined by the ASP. Article 121 permits substantive or non-institutional amendments to the Statute beginning seven years after the Statute's entry into force. The ASP or a Review Conference (which is a special sitting of the ASP) must adopt the proposed amendment by at least a two-thirds majority of States Parties.[239]

---

[238] UNSC Res. 1166 (13 May 1998); UNSC Res. 1329 (30 November 2000); UNSC Res. 1411 (17 May 2002); UNSC Res. 1431 (14 August 2002); UNSC Res. 1481 (19 May 2003); UNSC Res. 1597 (20 April 2005); UNSC Res. 1660 (28 February 2006); UNSC Res. 1668 (10 April 2006); UNSC Res. 1800 (20 February 2008).
[239] Article 121(3), Rome Statute.

However, the amendment only enters into force for all States Parties one year after seven-eighths of them deposit their instrument of ratification or acceptance with the Secretary-General of the United Nations.[240] In 2013, the ASP established a Working Group on Amendments to review, report on and recommend the adoption of amendment proposals submitted to it by States Parties.

An exception to the substantive amendment procedure is any amendment to articles 5, 6, 7 or 8 of the Rome Statute.[241] Article 5 lists crimes that fall within the jurisdiction of the Court, and articles 6, 7 and 8 define the crimes of genocide, other crimes against humanity and war crimes. After such an amendment is adopted by two-thirds of all States Parties in attendance at a meeting of the ASP or Review Conference, it will enter into force only for those States Parties that accept the amendment and only one year after they deposit their instruments of ratification or acceptance.[242] States Parties that do not accept an amendment to one of these provisions are not subject to the Court's jurisdiction in respect of that crime when committed by nationals of that State Party or on its territory.

Concern has been expressed about how difficult it is to amend definitions of crimes in the Rome Statute, warning that it leaves judges with considerable discretion to make law.[243] However, perhaps this is an oversimplification of the relationship between judges and the ASP. The option of States to decline the jurisdiction of the Court over amendments to existing crimes and the seven-eighths threshold for recognizing new categories of crimes may signal to judges that they are to interpret the Rome Statute in a manner that respects the text of the provisions as much as possible. As well, the procedure for amending the Elements of Crimes, which is more relaxed, can facilitate a dialogue between the Court and the ASP, one that can encourage judges to exercise their discretion in a way that results in incremental legal developments that enjoy widespread support. Amendments to the Elements of Crimes can be adopted by a two-thirds majority of the members of the ASP and proposed by any State Party, the judges acting by an absolute majority or the prosecutor.

2.4.2.3 Invalidation

The ICTY and ICTR judges have not, to date, invalidated any provision in their constitutive statutes. This is perhaps because they perceived their jurisdiction to be mainly limited to crimes under customary international law, which concern peremptory norms. Both statutes also ensure minimum fair trial guarantees and

---

[240] Article 121(4), Rome Statute.   [241] Article 121(5), Rome Statute.
[242] There was a difficult and ongoing debate about whether the crime of aggression is subject to this amendment procedure.
[243] Wessel (n. 42) 428.

provide that '[a]ll persons shall be equal before the International Tribunal'.[244]
What about the International Criminal Court?

The Rome Statute does not expressly state that judges are empowered to
invalidate provisions of the Statute. However, article 53 of the *Vienna Convention* (1969) would suggest that judges have the inherent power to invalidate a
provision – or at least render it inapplicable – should it violate a peremptory
norm (*jus cogens*):

> A treaty is void if, at the time of its conclusion, it conflicts with a peremptory norm of general international law. For the purposes of the present
> Convention, a peremptory norm of general international law is a norm
> accepted and recognized by the international community of States as a
> whole as a norm from which no derogation is permitted and which can be
> modified only by a subsequent norm of general international law having
> the same character.

In addition to expressly protecting certain rights of a person investigated for
or accused of committing crimes in the Court's jurisdiction,[245] article 21(3) of
the Rome Statute provides:

> The application and interpretation of law pursuant to this article must be
> consistent with internationally recognized human rights, and be without
> any adverse distinction founded on grounds such as gender as defined
> in article 7, paragraph 3, age, race, colour, language, religion or belief,
> political or other opinion, national, ethnic or social origin, wealth, birth
> or other status.

It remains to be seen what role, if any, international human rights might have as
a guiding or background principle for the interpretation of crimes and whether
this provision thereby empowers judges to invalidate, choose not to apply or
read down provisions that offend it. Reading down the language of a provision
to bring it into conformity with a background principle is arguably a mild
form of legislating but is the only alternative available in the absence of powers
to invalidate or not apply it. However, given the strong presence of NGOs
at Rome and the expertise of some of the delegates involved in drafting the
Statute's provisions, it may be expected that conflicts between the definitions
of crimes and background principles, such as *jus cogens* norms, are unlikely to
arise.

---

[244] *Tadić Judgment* (n. 47) paras. 44, 56; *Prosecutor* v. *Delalić and Others*, Decision on the
Prosecution's Motion for an Order requiring Advance Disclosure of Witnesses by the
Defense, ICTY-96–21-T, 4 February 1998, para. 49.
[245] Articles 55, 66 and 67, Rome Statute.

2.4.3 Dialogue and political constraint

The Security Council has refrained from engaging in a formal dialogue with judges of the ICTY and ICTR on their judicial findings. This restraint suggests that the Security Council respects the findings of these bodies and their inherent competence to determine their own jurisdiction, which is necessitated by the absence of an integrated international judicial system.[246] The ICTY Appeals Chamber conceded that this inherent jurisdiction, which is a general principle of international law, may be limited by an express provision, but that this limitation becomes controversial when it undermines the judicial character or independence of the judicial organ in question.[247] The ICTY's recognition of its inherent competence is consistent with the jurisprudence of the International Court of Justice.[248]

States have the opportunity to engage in a dialogue with the Court prior to its determination of jurisdiction. The judicial task of interpretation plays a critical role when the Court considers preliminary objections, which will often include objections to the Court's jurisdiction over the alleged conduct. The Court may determine matters of justiciability on its own motion or upon the filing of a motion by the accused, a person subject to an arrest warrant or a summons to appear, a State that has jurisdiction over a case or a State that must consent to the jurisdiction of the Court. Either Party may appeal this decision.

The International Criminal Court's competence to determine its jurisdiction is not merely inherent but express. Article 19(1) of the Rome Statute obliges the Court to 'satisfy itself that it has jurisdiction in any case brought before it'. As well, article 119(1) provides: 'Any dispute concerning the judicial functions of the Court shall be settled by the decision of the Court.' Dispute has been defined by the International Court of Justice as 'disagreement on a point of law or fact, a conflict of legal views or interests between parties'.[249] Disputes concerning the judicial functions of the Court are likely to include 'questions of jurisdiction and interpretation of the definitions of crimes within the jurisdiction of the Court'.[250]

It has been argued that multilateral treaty regimes tend towards judges de facto possessing greater discretion owing to the difficulty of amending the treaty in order to 'overrule' the findings of judges and that a large number of

---

[246] *Tadić Jurisdiction Decision* (n. 6) paras. 10ff.   [247] Ibid.

[248] Article 36(6) of the Statute of the International Court of Justice provides: 'In the event of a dispute as to whether the Court has jurisdiction, the matter shall be settled by the decision of the Court.' See also *Case Concerning Oil Platforms (Islamic Republic of Iran v. United States of America)* [2003] ICJ Rep. 161.

[249] *Case Concerning East Timor (Portugal v. Australia)* [1995] ICJ Rep. 90, 99.

[250] R Clark, 'Article 119' in O Triffterer (ed.), *Commentary on the Rome Statute of the International Criminal Court*, 1st edn (NVG Baden-Baden 1999) 1241.

States Parties increases the political cost for any State exiting that regime.[251] In practice, therefore, a perceived misinterpretation of the crimes as defined in the Rome Statute is unlikely to inspire States Parties to amend these definitions so as to expressly exclude the offensive judicial interpretation. As well, it is unlikely that one offensive judgment would cause a State Party to exit the Rome regime pursuant to article 127(1) of the Statute. However, this does not mean that States Parties are without recourse.

A State Party might choose to ignore the offending decision.[252] A more moderate option would be for the State Party to voice its disapproval of the Court's ruling in a formal setting, such as at an annual meeting of the ASP.[253] Such voiced admonition could 'discipline' or influence judicial behaviour in the future. States can also 'quasi-exit' from the Rome regime by refusing to cooperate with the Court in its investigations or by not signing agreements on the enforcement of sentences and witness relocation. The Court is dependent on States for evidence, defendants and witnesses. Article 86 of the Rome Statute obliges States Parties to cooperate with the Court, a judicial body that is largely dependent on political will, in the prosecution of crimes. While the Court can also obtain the cooperation of Non-States Parties and the United Nations to carry out its work, the non-cooperation of a State Party that is essential to the work of the Court in a particular case may send a strong message of disapproval to the Court.

If enough States Parties are dissatisfied with the work of the Court, they may express their disapproval by voting in favour of reducing the Court's budget as well as making smaller donations (or none at all) to the Victims Trust Fund. Similarly, it has been suggested that standing bodies, like the ASP, can even reward a court for decisions they approve of through the provision of material incentives. States Parties can also promote an attitude of judicial passivity through the appointments process, discussed below.[254] Given these means to exert political constraints on the Court, it has rightly been argued that the differences between domestic and international courts in this regard is 'only of degree rather than kind'.[255]

2.4.4 Nature of the Rome Statute and Court

In this section, the nature of the Rome Statute and the Court is examined for possible implications on a method of interpretation.

As early as 1930, it was observed that treaties are a 'sadly overworked instrument' that international society uses to perform a wide variety of

---

[251] T Ginsburg, 'Bounded Discretion in International Judicial Lawmaking' (2005) 45 Virginia J Int'l L 631, 670.
[252] Ibid. 659.   [253] Ibid. 666.   [254] Ibid. 660.   [255] Ibid. 669.

transactions.[256] It is questioned whether treaties with different functions can be governed by the same rules of interpretation. One fundamental distinction is between treaties that have the essential juridical character of a contract and those that have that of law making or legislation.[257] A contractual treaty may be bilateral or multilateral and creates reciprocal obligations (which may or may not be identical), the breach of which by one Party gives rise to rights of termination or suspension of performance by other Parties.[258] It has been suggested that the interpretation of contractual treaties can be relatively better aided by preparatory work because the number of Parties is likely to be smaller than for a law-making treaty, and there might therefore exist a common understanding about the meaning of ambiguous treaty terms.[259] It has also been argued that judges can adapt a contractual treaty to respond to changes in circumstances but that the same for law-making treaties is best left to States; then again, the opposite has also been suggested.[260]

A law-making treaty can be subdivided into two classes: those that create constitutional international law (or public international law) and those that create or declare 'ordinary' international law.[261] Public or constitutional international law treaties are understood here to 'create a kind of public law transcending in kind and not merely in degree the ordinary agreements between states' and be concerned with maintaining great public principles.[262] Because of this character, constitutional treaties may well impose rights and obligations on third States, perhaps because the laws they embody are reflective of customary law or peremptory norms.[263] By contrast, 'ordinary' law-making treaties are 'not concerned with constitutional relations of the members of the society of states' and

---

[256] AD McNair, 'The Functions and Differing Legal Character of Treaties' (1930) 11 British Ybk of Int'l L 100, 101. See also J Pauwelyn and M Elsig, 'The Politics of Treaty Interpretation: Variations and Explanations Across International Tribunals' (3 October 2011), http://ssrn.com/abstract=1938618, accessed 16 October 2013.

[257] Ibid. 105.

[258] Ibid.; article 60, *Vienna Convention* (1969); J Crawford, *The International Law Commission's Articles on State Responsibility: Introduction, Text and Commentaries* (Cambridge University Press 2002).

[259] McNair (n. 256) 107.

[260] Ibid. 110; J Arato, 'Subsequent Practice and Evolutive Interpretation: Techniques of Treaty Interpretation over Time and their Diverse Consequences' (2010) 9:3 *The Law & Practice of International Courts and Tribunals* 443, 486–87.

[261] McNair, ibid. 112.

[262] Ibid. 112–13; see also B Simma, 'From Bilateralism to Community Interest in International Law' (1994) 250 Recueil des Cours de l'Académie de Droit International 217; S Villalpando, 'The Legal Dimension of the International Community: How Community Interests are Protected in International Law' (2010) 21:2 EJIL 387.

[263] McNair, ibid. 113; Villalpando, ibid. 402:

> In its codification of the law of treaties, the Commission thus identified the emergence of a certain category of international rules characterized by 'the particular nature of

may regulate topics such as labour standards.[264] What all law-making treaties have in common is that they are 'multilateral; they make rules of pure law [as opposed to reciprocal obligations], and they are intended to be permanent'.[265] There is one more type of treaty that might also be described as a sort of law-making treaty, one that creates a permanent international organization and is thereby akin to a charter of incorporation.[266]

In the introduction to Chapter 1, it was recalled that the Rome Statute is a treaty that itself performs different functions, which is why this study is concerned with developing a method of interpretation only for crimes defined therein. The question raised here is: what is the nature of the definitions of crimes in the Rome Statute? They hardly seem contractual, but what law-making characteristics do they possess? Are they constitutional or 'ordinary' laws? Similar to international human rights and humanitarian law treaties, it might be said that the definitions of these crimes are expressions of community values and that the protection of the individual lies at their core. However, is it perhaps an oversimplification to characterize these definitions as being concerned only with victims of serious crimes under international law? Unlike a treaty that protects individuals against human rights violations committed by a government or that regulates means of warfare, the Rome Statute seems to be concerned with not only victims of human rights and humanitarian law violations but also those investigated, arrested and criminally charged with

> the subject-matter' with which they deal, including the prohibition of the use of force, slavery, piracy, or genocide. (footnotes omitted)

However, read the following for the general rule on the contractual nature of treaties: C Laly-Chevalier, 'Observance, Application and Interpretation of Treaties, s. 4 Treaties and Third States, art. 35, 1969 Vienna Convention' in O Corten and E Klein (eds.), *The Vienna Conventions on the Law of Treaties: A Commentary*, vol. I (Oxford University Press 2011) 903; M Fitzmaurice, 'Third Parties and the Law of Treaties' (2002) 6 Max Planck Yb of UN Law 37.

Articles 35, 36(1) and 38 of the *Vienna Convention* (1969) provide:

> [Article 35] An obligation arises for a third State from a provision of a treaty if the parties to the treaty intend the provision to be the means of establishing the obligation and the third State *expressly accepts* that obligation in writing. (emphasis added)

> [Article 36] 1. A right arises for a third State from a provision of a treaty if the parties to the treaty intend the provision to accord that right either to the third State, or to a group of States to which it belongs, or to all States, and the third State assents thereto. Its assent *shall be presumed* so long as the contrary is not indicated, unless the treaty otherwise provides. (emphasis added)

> [Article 38] Nothing in articles 34 to 37 precludes a rule set forth in a treaty from becoming binding upon a third State as a *customary rule of international law*, recognized as such. (emphasis added)

[264] McNair, ibid. 115.   [265] Ibid. 116.   [266] Ibid. 116–17.

committing these acts. In fact, the latter group of individuals is arguably the focal point of the Rome Statute. Accordingly and without further consideration, it seems inappropriate to assume the wholesale transferability of any methods of interpretation that have been developed in the fields of international human rights or humanitarian law to the context of international criminal law. The normativities underlying the Rome Statute are the subject of the next Chapter.

The relative detail of the Rome Statute is also noteworthy. It contains 128 articles and more than ninety substantive crimes (excluding various forms of vicarious liability).[267] This unprecedented degree of specificity in an international criminal law statute is perhaps also an important clue about the method of interpretation that is appropriate for crimes in the Statute. A method of interpretation that places little importance on the text of the Rome Statute is obviously inapt. It also reveals the extent to which the content of international criminal law has been identified and agreed upon by States Parties, and so the field of law's maturity. Perhaps this detail is indicative of the ripeness of international criminal law and its readiness to begin a new phase in its development, such as rules of interpretation.[268]

Given the odd amalgam of functions that the Rome Statute performs[269] and its focus on persons suspected or accused of committing crimes, it might reasonably be asked whether the *Vienna Convention* (1969) can offer any guidance on its interpretation. However, as discussed at the beginning of this Chapter, the rules of interpretation in the *Vienna Convention* (1969) adopt a crucible approach to interpretation by putting forward a general rule of interpretation that seems to definitively exclude nothing. It is therefore difficult at this stage to conceive of a methodology being developed for crimes in the Rome Statute that could not somehow benefit from the rules of interpretation in the *Vienna Convention* (1969) and, although unique to the Rome Statute, even be grafted onto it. The Appeals Chamber of the Court seems to agree, holding that articles 31 and 32 of the *Vienna Convention* (1969) apply to interpreting the Rome Statute and that the latter 'is no exception'.[270]

Finally, there is the matter of the nature of the Court. In addition to being a permanent judicial organ, paragraph 10 of the Rome Statute's preamble emphasizes that it 'shall be complementary to national criminal jurisdictions'. Articles 17(1)(a) and (b) elaborate on this relationship as follows:

---

[267] WK Lietzau, 'Checks and Balances and Elements of Proof: Structural Pillars for the International Criminal Court' (1999) 32 Cornell Int'l LJ 477, 487.

[268] HLA Hart, *The Concept of Law* (Oxford University Press 1961).

[269] See Chapter 1, Section 1.1.

[270] *Situation in the Democratic Republic of the Congo*, Judgment on Extraordinary Review, ICC-01/04–168 OA3, 13 July 2006, para. 33.

[T]he Court shall determine that a case is inadmissible where:

(a) The case is being investigated or prosecuted by a State which has jurisdiction over it, unless the State is unwilling or unable genuinely to carry out the investigation or prosecution;

(b) The case has been investigated by a State which has jurisdiction over it and the State has decided not to prosecute the person concerned, unless the decision resulted from the unwillingness or inability of the State genuinely to prosecute;

The Court is therefore one of 'last resort'. The relationship of complementarity suggests that, ideally, the crimes defined in the Rome Statute will be prosecuted before national courts. The decisions of these courts and the decisions of the Court may employ different methods of interpretation, the former perhaps being influenced by domestic rules for interpreting criminal statutes. What does this mean for purposes of developing a method of interpretation? Whether the jurisprudence of the Court is useful to these national courts will depend in part on the interpretive methodology employed by judges and the extent to which it is compatible with that which national judges feel compelled to apply. For example, the interpretation of criminal statutes in a domestic jurisdiction may be subject to the rule of strict construction. If the method of interpretation invoked by the Court were to ignore this rule in favour of a progressive approach to interpretation, national judges may distinguish this jurisprudence on the grounds that their criminal statutes are subject to different interpretive rules. Given that the Court is a permanent international criminal court intended to try persons for crimes that a country was unwilling or unable to prosecute nationally, the interpretive approach it adopts would ideally resonate with national judges and not give them pause or concern when consulting the Court's jurisprudence. And since judges of the Court will likely decide fewer cases than their national counterparts, such an interpretive approach would perhaps enable them to benefit from the insights gleaned by their national colleagues, who may well acquire relatively greater exposure to interpretive issues.

2.4.5 Selection and removal of judges

No matter how well developed a method of interpretation for crimes in the Rome Statute is, it is unlikely to be able to secure or preserve on its own the legitimacy of the Court if judges lack professionalism, independence and, or, impartiality. In this section, the judicial appointments and removal procedures for the Court will be examined to ascertain how they might influence these essential characteristics for preserving the rule of law.

ICTY, ICTR and International Criminal Court judges must all be 'persons of high moral character, impartiality and integrity who possess the qualifications required in their respective countries for appointment to the highest judicial offices'.[271] In the 'overall composition' of each ICTY and ICTR chamber, due account 'shall be taken of the experience of the judges in criminal law, international law, including international humanitarian law and human rights law'.[272] The Rome Statute imposes relatively stricter standards:

> *Every candidate* for election to the Court shall:
>
> (i) Have established competence in criminal law and procedure, and the necessary relevant experience, whether as judge, prosecutor, advocate or in other similar capacity, in criminal proceedings; or
> (ii) Have established competence in relevant areas of international law such as international humanitarian law and the law of human rights, and extensive experience in a professional legal capacity which is of relevance to the judicial work of the Court.[273]

Growth in the study and practice of international criminal law has given rise to corresponding expertise, and the Rome Statute attempts to ensure that judges elected to office possess demonstrated competence in either international law or criminal law and procedure. In the future, once a larger bar of international criminal lawyers emerges, this provision may be amended to require that every candidate for election possess established competence in international criminal law. Judges at the Court must be fluent in at least French or English, the two official languages of the Court.[274] Factors to be taken into account when nominating and electing judges include the need for judges with legal expertise on specific issues, such as violence against women or children.[275]

The process for electing ICTY and ICTR judges begins with the UN Secretary-General inviting States to nominate up to two candidates.[276] The Secretary-General forwards the list of nominees to the UN Security Council, which then establishes a short list of candidates taking 'due account of the adequate representation of the principal legal systems of the world'.[277] This short list is submitted to the UN General Assembly. Judges are appointed to the ICTY and ICTR upon receiving an absolute majority of votes in the General Assembly.[278]

---

[271] Article 13, ICTY statute; article 12(1), ICTR statute; article 36(3)(a), Rome Statute.

[272] Article 13, ICTY statute; article 12(1), ICTR statute.

[273] Article 36(3)(b), Rome Statute (emphasis added).

[274] Article 36(3)(c), Rome Statute.   [275] Article 36(8)(b), Rome Statute.

[276] Article 13 *bis*(1)(a), ICTY statute; article 12(3)(a), ICTR statute.

[277] Article 13 *bis*, ICTY statute: 'not less than twenty-eight' and 'not more than forty-two' candidates. In respect of the ICTR, the list ranges from eighteen to twenty-seven candidates: article 12(3)(c), ICTR statute.

[278] Article 13 *bis*, ICTY statute; article 12(3)(d), ICTR statute. In the UN General Assembly, members of the UN and Non-Member States maintaining permanent observer missions at the UN headquarters are permitted to vote on the election of judges to the ICTY and ICTR.

By contrast, the ASP, on the basis of nominations submitted by States Parties, carries out the election of judges to the Court.[279] States nominating a candidate for judicial office must provide the ASP with a detailed statement explaining how the candidate meets the aforementioned requirements. Judges are elected by secret ballot from two lists of candidates: criminal law practitioners and international humanitarian and human rights lawyers.[280] Factors to be taken into account when nominating and electing judges include representing the principal legal systems of the world, equitable geographical representation and fair representation of female and male judges.[281] The NGO community, under the umbrella organization of the Coalition for the International Criminal Court, has established an independent expert panel that evaluates judicial candidates. NGOs also attend meetings of the ASP with a view to informally lobbying for and against the appointment of certain candidates in the days leading up to the vote. In 2012, the ASP established its own expert advisory committee for judicial nominations and tasked it with reviewing and recommending judicial candidates for election after ensuring that they met the requirements set out in the Rome Statute.

Whereas ICTY and ICTR judges are elected for four-year terms and are eligible for re-election, judges of the Court with some limited exceptions are elected to serve for a term of nine years without the possibility of re-election.[282] During their term, neither the UN General Assembly nor an individual State may dismiss ICTY and ICTR judges. They can, however, be disqualified for lack of impartiality and independence. The respective bureaus of these tribunals, which is the presidency, determine objections against an ICTY or ICTR judge.[283] At the International Criminal Court, judges may be disqualified for lack of impartiality or independence by an absolute majority of judges, excluding the judge in question.[284] It is important to note that judges at the Court may also be removed from office for serious misconduct or a serious breach of their duties under the Rome Statute.[285] Removal for misconduct or serious breach requires the support of two-thirds of the judges and two-thirds of States Parties.[286] Salaries for ICTY and ICTR judges were initially paid on an ad hoc basis, but

[279] Article 36(4)(a), Rome Statute.
[280] Articles 36(3)(b)(i), 36(3)(b)(ii) and 36(5), Rome Statute. More generally, see D Terris, CPR Romano and L Swigart, *The International Judge – An Introduction to the Men and Women Who Decide the World's Cases* (Brandeis University Press 2007).
[281] Article 36(8)(a), Rome Statute.
[282] Article 13(4), ICTY statute; article 12(5), ICTR statute. For example, a judge appointed to fill a vacancy for a period of less than three years is eligible for re-election: article 37(2), Rome Statute.
[283] JRWD Jones, 'Composition of the Court' in A Cassese and Others (eds.), *The Rome Statute of the International Criminal Court: A Commentary*, vol. I (Oxford University Press 2002) 235, 253.
[284] Articles 40(4) and 41(2)(c), Rome Statute.   [285] Article 46(1)(a), Rome Statute.
[286] Article 46(2)(a), Rome Statute.

regular salaries were eventually implemented.[287] Salaries for judges at the Court are determined by the ASP prior to judges taking office and cannot be reduced during their service.[288] Judges also enjoy full diplomatic immunity, unless this is waived by an absolute majority of judges.[289]

On balance, the Rome Statute tries to ensure judicial professionalism and independence through its election procedure, the length of terms, security of tenure and appropriate remuneration. Concerns have been expressed, however, about ensuring the impartiality of judges.[290] Whereas judges are required to refrain from 'any activity which is likely to interfere with their judicial functions or to affect confidence in their independence', the same is not stated in the Statute in respect of impartiality. This requirement can, however, be inferred from the aforementioned reference to judicial functions. Part of the judicial function is surely to be and appear to be impartial.

Additionally, concerns have been expressed about judges' prior links with human rights or humanitarian law associations. It is predicted that judges with such affiliations possess 'preformed, professional norms' that will push them towards 'robust judicial policy-making' at the cost of rigorous legal analysis.[291] This assertion evidences some distrust of judges with expertise in human rights and humanitarian law. While international criminal law has a moral or natural law core, this does not mean that judges will turn away from their judicial responsibilities in order to advance a progressive legal agenda. There are plenty of practitioners who, because of their desire to preserve the legitimacy of international criminal law, would discourage such interpretive practices. At the same time, given the number of international judicial bodies, it seem untenable to suggest that judges play no role in developing international law.[292] Concerns about judges' legal background are not, however, without merit. But rather than go to the issue of actual impartiality, they speak perhaps more to the appearance of impartiality. For example, of the first eighteen judges appointed to the Court, eleven had either an academic or advocacy background, and none of their biographies mention military service. As well, it is not clear how many possess experience working as defence counsel. This imbalance in relative expertise may create the appearance of partiality or bias, could deprive the Court of rich and relevant expertise[293] and creates a bench that does not

---

[287] Jones (n. 283) 251–52.   [288] Articles 35(4) and 49, Rome Statute.

[289] Articles 48(2) and 48(5), Rome Statute.

[290] J Wessel, 'Judicial Policy-Making at the International Criminal Court: An Institutional Guide to Analyzing International Adjudication' (2006) 44 Columbia J Transnat'l L 377, 444.

[291] Ibid. 377.

[292] Terris, Romano and Swigart (n. 280) 104.

[293] RV Meyer, 'Following Historical Precedent: An Argument for the Continued Use of Military Professionals as Triers of Fact in Some Humanitarian Law Tribunals' (2009) 7 J Int'l Crim Justice 43.

reflect the diversity of the interpretive community[294] within which it operates. The consequence may be judgments that do not speak to those whom they are intended to persuade.

Finally, despite the wording of the Rome Statute, it must be recalled that vote trading is a notoriously engrained practice within the UN system. Unfortunately, the judicial appointments process within the ASP does not seem to have escaped this phenomenon. States that have nominated a judicial candidate will often host social events at which States are encouraged to vote for their candidate in exchange for promised support in elections of interest to the other States. As well, nominees do not always possess as much expertise as they should. For example, Japan nominated Ms Kuniko Ozaki to serve as a judge at the Court. While Ms Ozaki undoubtedly possesses relevant legal experience, she does not have a law degree, and her knowledge of international criminal law is limited relative to her Japanese peers. Nevertheless, she was elected to the Court for a term of nine years. If a trend emerges towards appointments being predominantly political and ignoring or downplaying professional requirements set out in the Rome Statute, a method of interpretation may not be able to save the Court from the charge that its work is political, not judicial, or fails to observe the rule of law.

2.5 Conclusions

On balance, there are a few lessons that can be taken away from the state of the art and features of the Rome regime. First, the rules of interpretation in articles 31–33 of the *Vienna Convention* (1969) remind one of the need for interpretive guidance that is somewhat open-ended or flexible (mandatory guidelines) and not overly rigid so as to prove unworkable in the face of problems that were not anticipated. There is an essential discretion that judges must retain, as the task of interpretation is hardly mechanical. Second, without more, these rules appear to be inadequate for fixing a method of interpretation for crimes in the Rome Statute, although one could be grafted onto them. This is perhaps best evidenced by the experience of the ICTY and ICTR, which acknowledged the applicability of these rules but did not go on to discern a prevailing guiding interpretive principle for their work and corresponding supporting arguments and material aids. Third, the jurisprudence of these tribunals offers insight into principles, arguments and aids that a method of interpretation for crimes in the Rome Statute might incorporate but also warns of the perils of invoking these tools outside the constraining framework of a method of interpretation.

Fourth, certain features of the Rome regime remind one of the environment in which an interpretive methodology is to function and the limits that flow from this. For example, judges will be constrained by their inability to 'correct'

---

[294] S Fish, *Is There a Text in This Class? The Authority of Interpretive Communities* (Harvard University Press 1980).

drafting errors and to amend the Rome Statute and possibly their inability to invalidate or choose not to apply its provisions, unless they violate *jus cogens* norms. In addition, the drafting history of the Rome Statute calls into question the existence of common intentions discernible from an incomplete body of preparatory work. This and the relative detail of the Rome Statute necessarily increase the importance of the text for purposes of interpretation and possibly other aids to interpreting it. With the advent of the ASP, judges interpreting the Rome Statute are subject to certain political constraints and a dialogue with States Parties about their work. As well, a methodology that resonates with national courts can spark a dialogue between the Court and national judges who interpret the same crimes. Finally, the selection and removal procedures for judges serve as a reminder that no matter how thoughtful and coherent a methodology for interpretation is, it cannot shield the Court from critiques of failing to uphold the rule of law if judges are not highly qualified, independent and impartial.

Annex

Aids to interpretation[295]

Rank	Category	Aid	Case Law
1	Expert material	General expert and academic materials	*Tadić*, Decision on the Defence Motion for Interlocutory Appeal on Jurisdiction, ICTY-94–1-AR722, 2 Oct. 1995, paras. 45ff.; *Delalić and Others*, Judgment, ICTY-96–21-T, 16 Nov. 1998, paras. 539–541; *Kunarac and Others*, Judgment, ICTY-96–23-A & ICTY-96–23/1-A, 12 June 2002, para. 100 fn. 119; *Musema*, Judgment and Sentence, ICTR-96–13-A, 27 Jan. 2000, para. 188; *Vasiljević*, Judgment, ICTY-98–32-T, 29 Nov. 2002, para. 220; *Krstić*, Judgment, ICTY-98–33-T, 2 Aug. 2001,
			(cont.)

---

[295] This chart does not list every instance of a particular interpretive aid being used in the case law of the ICTY and ICTR between 1994 and 2008. Rather, it contains a representative sample of how these materials have been used by these tribunals. This chart also does not differentiate between consideration of the material, reliance on it and its use to buttress other arguments. Rankings are based on the number of decisions that refer to aids belonging in each category.

(*Cont.*)

Rank	Category	Aid	Case Law
			paras. 541 fn. 1197, 571, 575, 587; *Blaskić*, Judgment, ICTY-95–14-T, 3 Mar. 2000, paras. 213, 330; *Jelisić*, Judgment, ICTY-95–10-T, 14 Dec. 1999, para. 822; *Halilović*, Judgment, ICTY-01–48-T, 16 Nov. 2005, para. 51; *Tadić*, Judgment, ICTY-94–1-T, 7 May 1997, paras. 644, 650 fn. 154; *Stakić*, Judgment, ICTY-97–24-A, 22 Mar. 2006, para. 13; *Simić*, Dissenting Opinion of Judge Schomburg, ICTY-95–9-A, 28 Nov. 2006, paras. 13ff.; *Blagojević and Others*, Judgment, ICTY-02–60-T, 17 Jan. 2005, paras. 660 fn. 2094, 663; *Krnojelac*, Judgment, ICTY-97–25-T, 15 Mar. 2002, para. 476 fn. 1437; *Naletilić and Martinović*, Judgment, ICTY-98–34-T, 31 Mar. 2003, para. 258 fn. 694; *Krstić*, Judgment, ICTY-98–33-A, 19 Apr. 2004, paras. 10ff.; *Simić*, Judgment, ICTY-95–9-T, 17 Oct. 2003, para. 133 fn. 238; *Kanyabashi*, Joint Separate and Concurring Opinion of Judge Wang Tieya and Judge Rafael Nieto-Navia, ICTR-96–15-A, 3 June 1999, para. 11 fn. 4.
1	Expert material	ILC Draft Code of Crimes (1996), commentary to it and reports	*Delalić and Others*, Judgment, ICTY-96–21-T, 16 Nov. 1998, paras. 395, 532; *Blaskić*, Judgment, 3 Mar. 2000, ICTY-95–14-T, paras. 205–206, 216–217, 221, 225, 231, 239, 242; *Jelisić*, Judgment, ICTY-95–10-T, 14 Dec. 1999, paras. 79–80, 82; *Tadić*, Judgment, ICTY-94–1-A, 15 July 1999, para. 291; *Tadić*, Opinion and Judgment, 7 May 1997, ICTY-94–1-T, paras. 647–648, 652; *Halilović*, Judgment, ICTY-01–48-T, 16 Nov.

(*Cont.*)

Rank	Category	Aid	Case Law
			2005, para. 52; *Kupreskić and Others*, Judgment, ICTY-95–16-T, 14 Jan. 2000, para. 590; *Krstić*, Judgment, ICTY-98–33-T, 2 Aug. 2001, paras. 497, 500, 552, 571, 575–576, 586; *Blagojević and Others*, Judgment, ICTY-02–60-T, 17 Jan. 2005, paras. 571, 645 fn. 2065, 657; *Kunarac and Others*, Judgment, ICTY-96–23-A & ICTY-96–23/1-A, 12 June 2002, para. 98 fn. 114; *Krstić*, Judgment, ICTY-98–33-A, 19 Apr. 2004, para. 11; *Akayesu*, Judgment, ICTR-96–4-T, 2 Sept. 1998, paras. 556, 587.
1	Expert material	Views of the ICRC	*Tadić*, Decision on the Defence Motion for Interlocutory Appeal on Jurisdiction, ICTY-94–1-AR722, 2 Oct. 1995, para. 73.
1	Expert material	*Geneva Conventions* (1949) commentaries	*Delalić and Others*, Judgment, ICTY-96–21-T, 16 Nov. 1998, paras. 439, 519–532; *Tadić*, Judgment, ICTY-94–1-T, 7 May 1997, para. 639; *Krnojelac*, Judgment, ICTY-97–25-T, 15 Mar. 2002, para. 475 fn. 1434; *Kupreskić and Others*, Judgment, ICTY-95–16-T, 14 Jan. 2000, para. 562; *Naletilić and Martinović*, Judgment, ICTY-98–34-T, 31 March 2003, paras. 256ff.; *Simić and Others*, Judgment, ICTY-95–9-T, 17 Oct. 2003, para. 132; *Vasiljević*, Judgment, ICTY-98–32-T, 29 Nov. 2002, para. 223.
1	Expert material	*Additional Protocols* (1977) commentaries	*Blaskić*, Judgment, 3 Mar. 2000, ICTY-95–14-T, paras. 328–329; *Strugar*, Judgment, ICTY-01–42-T, 31 Jan. 2005, para. 375; *Martić*, Judgment, ICTY-95–11-T, 12 June 2007, para. 56.; *Musema*, Judgment and Sentence, ICTR-96–13-A, 27 Jan. 2000, paras. 130, 146.

(*cont.*)

(*Cont.*)

Rank	Category	Aid	Case Law
2	Domestic law	Law of former Yugoslavia	*Simić*, Dissenting Opinion of Judge Schomburg, ICTY-95–9-A, 28 Nov. 2006, para. 13.
2	Domestic law	Rwandan law	*Akayesu*, Judgment, ICTR-96–4-T, 2 Sept. 1998, para. 537; *Musema*, Judgment and Sentence, ICTR-96–13-A, 27 Jan. 2000, para. 179.
2	Domestic law	Comparative analyses	*Simić*, Dissenting Opinion of Judge Schomburg, ICTY-95–9-A, 28 Nov. 2006, para. 14; *Akayesu*, Judgment, ICTR-96–4-T, 2 Sept. 1998, paras. 481, 527, 533, 535, 539, 552, 555ff.; *Musema*, Judgment and Sentence, ICTR-96–13-A, 27 Jan. 2000, paras. 169, 186ff.; *Furundžija*, Judgment, ICTY-95–17/1-T, 10 Dec. 1998, paras. 177ff.; *Blaskić*, Judgment, ICTY-95–14-T, 3 Mar. 2000, paras. 324ff.; *Delalić and Others*, Judgment, ICTY-96–21-T, 16 Nov. 1998, para. 1161.
2	Domestic law	Codes and other legislation	*Furundžija*, Judgment, ICTY-95–17/1-T, 10 Dec. 1998, para. 254 fn. 286; *Blaskić*, Judgment, ICTY-95–14-T, 3 Mar. 2000, para. 212; *Kupreskić and Others*, Judgment, ICTY-95–16-T, 14 Jan. 2000, para. 577; *Vasiljević*, Judgment, ICTY-98–32-T, 29 Nov. 2002, para. 224 fn. 579; *Krstić*, Judgment, ICTY-98–33-T, 2 Aug. 2001, para. 541; *Blagojević and Others*, Judgment, ICTY-02–60-T, 17 Jan. 2005, para. 664.
2	Domestic law	National war crimes trials	*Blagojević and Others*, Judgment, ICTY-02–60-T, 17 Jan. 2005, para. 646; *Krnojelac*, Judgment, ICTY-97–25-A, 17 Sept. 2003, para. 15; *Kupreskić and Others*, Judgment, ICTY-95–16-T, 14 Jan. 2000, paras. 548, 568; *Kunarac and Others*, Judgment, ICTY-96–23-A &

(*Cont.*)

Rank	Category	Aid	Case Law
			ICTY-96–23/1-A, 12 June 2002, para. 98 fn. 114; *Vasiljević*, Judgment, ICTY-98–32-T, 29 Nov. 2002, paras. 216ff.; *Akayesu*, Judgment, ICTR-96–4-T, 2 Sept. 1998, paras. 503, 542–543, 567ff.; *Furundžija*, Judgment, ICTY-95–17/1-T, 10 Dec. 1998, para. 254 fn. 286; *Blaskić*, Judgment, ICTY-95–14-T, 3 Mar. 2000, paras. 212, 221, 224; *Tadić*, Judgment, ICTY-94–1-T, 7 May 1997, paras. 638 fn. 120, 650–651, fn. 154–155; *Simić*, Dissenting Opinion of Judge Schomburg, ICTY-95–9-A, 28 Nov. 2006, para. 18.
2	Domestic law	Control Council Law No. 10 jurisprudence	*Blaskić*, Judgment, ICTY-95–14-T, 3 Mar. 2000, paras. 221, 223, 229, 230; *Delalić and Others*, Judgment, ICTY-96–21-T, 16 Nov. 1998, paras. 388–390; *Tadić*, Judgment, ICTY-94–1-T, 7 May 1997, para. 649 fn. 153; *Orić*, Judgment, ICTY-03–68-T, 30 June 2006, para. 304; *Kupreskić and Others*, Judgment, ICTY-95–16-T, 14 Jan. 2000, paras. 550, 577, 611ff.; *Kunarac and Others*, Judgment, ICTY-96–23-A & ICTY-96–23/1-A, 12 June 2002, paras. 98 fn. 114, 123; *Krstić*, Judgment, ICTY-98–33-T, 2 Aug. 2001, para. 575; *Strugar*, Judgment, ICTY-01–42-T, 31 Jan. 2005, para. 376; *Vasiljević*, Judgment, ICTY-98–32-T, 29 Nov. 2002, paras. 221–222.
2	Domestic law	Commission of Inquiry	*Blaskić*, Judgment, ICTY-95–14-T, 3 Mar. 2000, para. 331.
3	Tribunals' jurisprudence	ICTR	*Blagojević and Others*, Judgment, ICTY-02–60-T, 17 Jan. 2005, paras.

(*cont.*)

(*Cont.*)

Rank	Category	Aid	Case Law
			645ff.; *Kvočka and Others*, Judgment, ICTY-98–30/1-T, 2 Nov. 2001, paras. 175ff.; *Krnojelac*, Judgment, ICTY-97–25-A, 17 Sept. 2003, para. 4; *Krstić*, Judgment, ICTY-98–33-T, 2 Aug. 2001, paras. 485, 492, 495, 509–510, 513, 541, 552, 571, 587, 589; *Musema*, Judgment and Sentence, ICTR-96–13-A, 27 Jan. 2000, paras. 112–113, 135ff., 153, 161ff., 199ff., 220ff.; *Furundžija*, Judgment, ICTY-95–17/1-T, 10 Dec. 1998, paras. 176, 254 fn. 286; *Blaskić*, Judgment, ICTY-95–14-T, 3 March 2000, paras. 166, 202–204, 207, 209–211, 216–217, 226, 232, 235, 239–240, *Strugar*, Judgment, ICTY-01–42-T, 31 Jan. 2005, paras. 307, 310–311; *Kupreskić and Others*, ICTY-95–16-T, Judgment, 14 Jan. 2000, paras. 548, 568, 577; *Kunarac and Others*, Judgment, ICTY-96–23-A & ICTY-96–23/1-A, 12 June 2002, para. 98 fn. 114; *Naletilić and Martinović*, Judgment, ICTY-98–34-T, 31 Mar. 2003, paras. 519, 634; *Krstić*, Judgment, ICTY-98–33-A, 19 Apr. 2004, paras. 8–9; *Martić*, Judgment, ICTY-95–11-T, 12 June 2007, paras. 50ff.; *Simić and Others*, Judgment, ICTY-95–9-T, 17 Oct. 2003, paras. 125ff.; *Akayesu*, Judgment, ICTR-96–4-T, 2 Sept. 1998, para. 524; *Halilović*, Judgment, ICTY-01–48-T, 16 Nov. 2005, paras. 51, 53; *Tadić*, Judgment, ICTY-94–1-T, 7 May 1997, para. 647; *Simić*, Dissenting Opinion of Judge Schomburg, ICTY-95–9-A, 28 Nov. 2006, para. 18.

(*Cont.*)

Rank	Category	Aid	Case Law
3	Tribunals' jurisprudence	ICTY	*Blagojević and Others*, Judgment, ICTY-02–60-T, 17 Jan. 2005, paras. 645ff.; *Kvočka and Others*, Judgment, ICTY-98–30/1-T, 2 Nov. 2001, paras. 175ff.; *Strugar*, Judgment, ICTY-01–42-T, 31 Jan. 2005, paras. 307, 310–311; *Krnojelac*, Judgment, ICTY-97–25-A, 17 Sept. 2003, para. 4; *Kupreskić and Others*, Judgment, ICTY-95–16-T, 14 Jan. 2000, paras. 548, 568, 577; *Kunarac and Others*, Judgment, ICTY-96–23-A & ICTY-96–23/1-A, 12 June 2002, para. 98 fn. 114; *Krstić*, Judgment, ICTY-98–33-T, 2 Aug. 2001, paras. 485, 495, 509, 511ff., 589; *Naletilić and Martinović*, Judgment, ICTY-98–34-T, 31 Mar. 2003, paras. 519, 634; *Krstić*, Judgment, ICTY-98–33-A, 19 Apr. 2004, paras. 8–9; *Martić*, Judgment, ICTY-95–11-T, 12 June 2007, paras. 50ff.; *Simić and Others*, Judgment, ICTY-95–9-T, 17 Oct. 2003, paras. 125ff.; *Akayesu*, Judgment, ICTR-96–4-T, 2 Sept. 1998, para. 524; *Musema*, Judgment and Sentence, ICTR-96–13-A, 27 Jan. 2000, paras. 112, 136ff., 223ff.; *Blaskić*, Judgment, ICTY-95–14-T, 3 Mar. 2000, paras. 166, 202–204, 207, 209–211, 226, 232, 235; *Halilović*, Judgment, ICTY-01–48-T, 16 Nov. 2005, paras. 51, 53; *Tadić*, Judgment, 7 May 1997, ICTY-94–1-T, para. 647; *Simić*, Dissenting Opinion of Judge Schomburg, ICTY-95–9-A, 28 Nov. 2006, para. 18.
4	Customary law	*Geneva Conventions* (1949)	*Furundžija*, Judgment, ICTY-95–17/1-T, 10 Dec. 1998, para. 175; *Stakić*, Judgment, ICTY-97–24-A, 22 March

(*cont.*)

(*Cont.*)

Rank	Category	Aid	Case Law
			2006, para. 307; *Krnojelac*, Judgment, ICTY-97–25-T, 15 Mar. 2002, para. 475 fn. 1432; *Kupreskić and Others*, Judgment, ICTY-95–16-T, 14 Jan. 2000, para. 523; *Naletilić and Martinović*, Judgment, ICTY-98–34-T, 31 Mar. 2003, paras. 250ff.; *Simić and Others*, Judgment, ICTY-95–9-T, 17 Oct. 2003, paras. 125, 127; *Vasiljević*, Judgment, ICTY-98–32-T, 29 Nov. 2002, para. 223; *Musema*, Judgment and Sentence, ICTR-96–13-A, 27 Jan. 2000, para. 150.
4	Customary law	*Additional Protocols* (1977)	*Furundžija*, Judgment, ICTY-95–17/1-T, 10 Dec. 1998, para. 175; *Tadić*, Judgment, ICTY-94–1-T, 7 May 1997, paras. 638 fn. 120, 639; *Strugar*, Judgment, ICTY-01–42-T, 31 Jan. 2005, paras. 306ff.; *Kupreskić and Others*, Judgment, ICTY-95–16-T, 14 Jan. 2000, paras. 524, 566; *Martić*, Judgment, ICTY-95–11-T, 12 June 2007, paras. 50–51; *Simić and Others*, Judgment, ICTY-95–9-T, 17 Oct. 2003, paras. 125, 127; *Musema*, Judgment and Sentence, ICTR-96–13-A, 27 Jan. 2000, paras. 128, 143ff.
4	Customary law	*Genocide Convention* (1948)	*Kupreskić and Others*, Judgment, ICTY-95–16-T, 14 Jan. 2000, para. 577; *Krstić*, Judgment, ICTY-98–33-T, 2 Aug. 2001, para. 541; *Krstić*, Judgment, ICTY-98–33-A, 19 Apr. 2004, paras. 6ff., 25, 29; *Akayesu*, Judgment, ICTR-96–4-T, 2 Sept. 1998, paras. 494ff.; *Musema*, Judgment and Sentence, ICTR-96–13-A, 27 Jan. 2000, para. 161.
4	Customary law	Hague law	*Strugar*, Judgment, ICTY-01–42-T, 31 Jan. 2005, paras. 304–305, 307, 309;

(*Cont.*)

Rank	Category	Aid	Case Law
			Kupreskić and Others, Judgment, ICTY-95–16-T, 14 Jan. 2000, paras. 523, 525.
5	Preparatory work	Report of the Secretary-General on the ICTY	*Blaskić*, Judgment, ICTY-95–14-T, 3 Mar. 2000, paras. 164ff.; *Halilović*, Judgment, ICTY-01–48-T, 16 Nov. 2005, para. 51; *Tadić*, Decision on the Defence Motion for Interlocutory Appeal on Jurisdiction, ICTY-94–1-AR72, 2 Oct. 1995, paras. 75, 79, 86, 87; *Tadić*, Judgment, ICTY-94–1-T, 7 May 1997, paras. 646–647, 652; *Simić*, Dissenting Opinion of Judge Schomburg, ICTY-95–9-A, 28 Nov. 2006, para. 3; *Akayesu*, Judgment, ICTR-96–4-T, 2 Sept. 1998, para. 495.
5	Preparatory work	UNSC Res. 808 establishing the ICTY	*Krnojelac*, Judgment, ICTY-97–25-A, 17 Sept. 2003, para. 14; *Kunarac and Others*, Judgment, ICTY-96–23-A & ICTY-96–23/1-A, 12 June 2002, para. 98 fn. 114.
5	Preparatory work	Security Council debates on the ICTY	*Tadić*, Decision on the Defence Motion for Interlocutory Appeal on Jurisdiction, ICTY-94–1-AR72, 2 Oct. 1995, para. 88.
5	Preparatory work	*Genocide Convention* (1948)	*Jelisić*, Judgment, ICTY-95–10-T, 14 Dec. 1999, paras. 69, 100; *Blagojević and Others*, Judgment, ICTY-02–60-T, 17 Jan. 2005, para. 657; *Krstić*, Judgment, ICTY-98–33-T, 2 Aug. 2001, paras. 510 fn. 1158, 571, 585; *Rutaganda*, Judgment and Sentence, ICTR-96–3-T, 6 Dec. 1999, para. 50; *Akayesu*, Judgment, ICTR-96–4-T, 2 Sept. 1998, paras. 501, 519, 551, 557, 561; *Musema*, Judgment and Sentence, ICTR-96–13-A, 27 Jan. 2000, paras. 161, 172, 187, 198.

(*cont.*)

(*Cont.*)

Rank	Category	Aid	Case Law
5	Preparatory work	Rome Statute	*Krstić*, Judgment, ICTY-98–33-T, 2 Aug. 2001, paras. 498, 509–510, 541; *Tadić*, Judgment, ICTY-94–1-T, 7 May 1997, para. 647; *Bagosora and 28 Others*, Decision on the Admissibility of the Prosecutor's Appeal From the Decision of a Confirming Judge Dismissing an Indictment against Theoneste Bagosora and 28 Others, ICTR-98–37-A, 8 June 1998, para. 40.
5	Preparatory work	Other treaties	*Delalić and Others*, Judgment, ICTY-96–21-T, 16 Nov. 1998, para. 391; *Vasiljević*, Judgment, ICTY-98–32-T, 29 Nov. 2002, para. 217.
6	IMT law	Nuremberg judgment	*Krnojelac*, Judgment, ICTY-97–25-A, 17 Sept. 2003, para. 15; *Kupreskić and Others*, Judgment, ICTY-95–16-T, 14 Jan. 2000, paras. 576, 610; *Kunarac and Others*, Judgment, ICTY-96–23-A & ICTY-96–23/1-A, 12 June 2002, para. 98 fn. 114; *Vasiljević*, Judgment, ICTY-98–32-T, 29 Nov. 2002, para. 219; *Musema*, Judgment and Sentence, ICTR-96–13-A, 27 Jan. 2000, para. 128; *Blaskić*, Judgment, ICTY-95–14-T, 3 Mar. 2000, paras. 221–222, 228, 316–322; *Delalić and Others*, Judgment, ICTY-96–21-T, 16 Nov. 1998, paras. 388–390; *Simić*, Dissenting Opinion of Judge Schomburg, ICTY-95–9-A, 28 Nov. 2006, paras. 17, 67.
6	IMT law	Nuremberg Charter	*Krstić*, Judgment, ICTY-98–33-T, 2 Aug. 2001, para. 575.
6	IMT law	Nuremberg principles	*Vasiljević*, Judgment, ICTY-98–32-T, 29 Nov. 2002, para. 221; *Akayesu*, Judgment, ICTR-96–4-T, 2 Sept. 1998, para. 526; *Tadić*, Judgment,

(*Cont.*)

Rank	Category	Aid	Case Law
			ICTY-94–1-T, 7 May 1997, paras. 644, 651.
6	IMT law	Tokyo judgment	*Strugar*, Judgment, ICTY-01–42-T, 31 Jan. 2005, para. 374; *Musema*, Judgment and Sentence, ICTR-96–13-A, 27 Jan. 2000, paras. 128ff.; *Blaskić*, Judgment, ICTY-95–14-T, 3 Mar. 2000, paras. 221–222, 228, 316–322; *Delalić and Others*, Judgment, ICTY-96–21-T, 16 Nov. 1998, paras. 388–390.
6	IMT law	Tokyo Charter	*Vasiljević*, Judgment, ICTY-98–32-T, 29 Nov. 2002, para. 221.
7	Treaties	*Torture Convention* (1984)	*Kupreskić and Others*, Judgment, ICTY-95–16-T, 14 Jan. 2000, para. 566; *Kunarac and Others*, Judgment, ICTY-96–23-A & ICTY-96–23/1-A, 12 June 2002, para. 142; *Akayesu*, Judgment, ICTR-96–4-T, 2 Sept. 1998, para. 597.
7	Treaties	*Apartheid Convention* (1973)	*Kupreskić and Others*, Judgment, ICTY-95–16-T, 14 Jan. 2000, para. 577; *Akayesu*, Judgment, ICTR-96–4-T, 2 Sept. 1998, para. 581; *Musema*, Judgment and Sentence, ICTR-96–13-A, 27 Jan. 2000, para. 205.
7	Treaties	International and regional human rights instruments	*Blaskić*, Judgment, ICTY-95–14-T, 3 Mar. 2000, para. 220; *Kupreskić and Others*, Judgment, ICTY-95–16-T, 14 Jan. 2000, paras. 566, 621; *Delalić and Others*, Judgment, ICTY-96–21-T, 16 Nov. 1998, para. 541.
7	Treaties	Rome Statute	*Delalić and Others*, Judgment, ICTY-96–21-T, 16 Nov. 1998, para. 393; *Blaskić*, Judgment, ICTY-95–14-T, 3 Mar. 2000, paras. 205, 216, 239, 241; *Tadić*, Judgment, ICTY-94–1-A, 15 July 1999, para. 291; *Simić*, Dissenting Opinion of

(*cont.*)

(*Cont.*)

Rank	Category	Aid	Case Law
			Judge Schomburg, ICTY-95–9-A, 28 Nov. 2006, para. 16; *Kupreskić and Others*, Judgment, ICTY-95–16-T, 14 Jan. 2000, paras. 565, 578–580, 617; *Krstić*, Judgment, ICTY-98–33-T, 2 Aug. 2001, paras. 498, 502; *Musema*, Judgment and Sentence, ICTR-96–13-A, 27 Jan. 2000, paras. 230–231; *Akayesu*, Judgment, ICTR-96–4-T, 2 Sept. 1998, para. 577.
8	Treaties	Other	*Kupreskić and Others*, Judgment, ICTY-95–16-T, 14 Jan. 2000, para. 577.
8	French and English versions of the tribunals' statutes	ICTR	*Rutaganda*, Judgment and Sentence, ICTR-96–3-T, 6 Dec. 1999, para. 50; *Kayishema and Others*, Judgment, ICTR-95–1-T, 21 May 1999, para. 101; *Akayesu*, Judgment, ICTR-96–4-T, 2 Sept. 1998, paras. 481, 500, 588; *Musema*, Judgment and Sentence, ICTR-96–13-A, 27 Jan. 2000, para. 155.
8	French and English versions of the tribunals' statutes	ICTY	*Delalić and Others*, Judgment, ICTY-96–21-T, 16 Nov. 1998, para. 392; *Blaskić*, Judgment, ICTY-95–14-T, 3 Mar. 2000, paras. 216, 326; *Blagojević and Others*, Judgment, ICTY-02–60-T, 17 Jan. 2005, para. 642 fn. 2057.
9	Other case law	International Court of Justice	*Blagojević and Others*, Judgment, ICTY-02–60-T, 17 Jan. 2005, para. 663; *Kupreskić and Others*, Judgment, ICTY-95–16-T, 14 Jan. 2000, para. 524; *Krstić*, Judgment, ICTY-98–33-T, 2 Aug. 2001, paras. 552, 571, 587; *Kanyabashi*, Joint Separate and Concurring Opinion of Judge Wang Tieya and Judge Rafael Nieto-Navia, ICTR-96–15-A, 3 June 1999, para. 11 fn. 4; *Akayesu*, Judgment, ICTR-96–4-T, 2 Sept. 1998, paras. 495, 512.

(*Cont.*)

Rank	Category	Aid	Case Law
9	Other case law	European Court of Human Rights	*Delalić and Others*, Judgment, ICTY-96–21-T, 16 Nov. 1998, paras. 534–538.
10	Miscellaneous	Ordinary and legal dictionaries	*Delalić and Others*, Judgment, ICTY-96–21-T, 16 Nov. 1998, paras. 518, 1194; *Krnojelac*, Judgment, ICTY-97–25-A, 17 Sept. 2003, para. 13; *Tadić*, Decision on the Defence Motion for Interlocutory Appeal on Jurisdiction, ICTY-94–1-AR722, 2 Oct. 1995, para. 10.
10	Miscellaneous	UN General Assembly statements and resolutions	*Krstić*, Judgment, ICTY-98–33-T, 2 Aug. 2001, para. 589; *Blagojević and Others*, Judgment, ICTY-02–60-T, 17 Jan. 2005, para. 663; *Krstić*, Judgment, ICTY-98–33-T, 2 Aug. 2001, para. 552.
10	Miscellaneous	Historic events and speeches	*Krstić*, Judgment, ICTY-98–33-A, 19 Apr. 2004, para. 13; *Vasiljević*, Judgment, ICTY-98–32-T, 29 Nov. 2002, para. 218.

3

Guiding interpretive principle

3.1 Introduction

In Chapter 2, a representative sample of the ICTY's and ICTR's jurisprudence was canvassed in order to glean insights on developing a method of interpretation. One of the findings of that study is that no widely accepted and recognized primary principle has emerged to guide judges in their interpretive reasoning. Accordingly, the next three Chapters are dedicated to identifying a guiding interpretive principle for crimes in the Rome Statute, articulating that principle's content in a manner that could be useful to judges and lawyers and cataloguing arguments that are (in)consistent with it.

To appreciate the interpretive imperatives set out in the Rome Statute, this Chapter begins by recalling the normative tensions underlying international criminal law. Next, the interpretive imperatives in articles 21(3) and 22 of the Rome Statute – interpretation consistent with international human rights and interpretation consistent with the principle of legality – will be examined. It will be argued that the guiding interpretive principle for crimes in the Rome Statute is legality. An attempt will therefore be made to reconcile article 21(3) with this reading and to give it content that is consistent with legality.

3.2 Normative tensions that influence the interpretation of crimes

The normative tensions underlying international criminal law can be understood in at least two ways: (1) as an 'identity crisis' owing inter alia to its mixed legal parentage;[1] and (2) as a tension between its substantive justice origins and strict legality aspirations.[2] Each will briefly be explained.

International criminal law is a 'hybrid branch of law' as it is the child of a tripartite marriage between international human rights law, its *jus in bello*

---

[1] D Robinson, 'The Identity Crisis of International Criminal Law' (2008) 21 LJIL 925; AM Danner and JS Martinez, 'Guilty Associations: Joint Criminal Enterprise, Command Responsibility, and the Development of International Criminal Law' (2005) 93 California L Rev 75. See also SR Ratner, 'The Schizophrenias of International Criminal Law' (1998) 33 Texas Int'l LJ 237.
[2] A Cassese, *International Criminal Law*, 2nd edn (Oxford University Press 2008) 36ff.

cousin, international humanitarian law and domestic criminal law.[3] Whereas the fundamental principles underpinning a liberal criminal justice system are those of personal culpability, legality and fair labelling,[4] international human rights law is focused on State responsibility and harm to the victim.[5] Thus, while the object and purpose of criminal justice favour the strict construction of statutes, the object and purpose of international human rights instruments are invoked to justify generally broad interpretations of crimes to ensure that 'harms are recognized and remedied, and that, over time, there is progressively greater realisation of respect for human dignity and freedom'.[6] Further, international human rights increasingly takes aim at the 'culture of impunity' so that the failure to provide a remedy for a human rights violation may in and of itself amount to a violation by a State of an international human rights treaty it has ratified.[7]

Of course, there is some overlap in the objectives of these normative frameworks, such as fair trial protections for the accused and victim participation rights in legal proceedings. Additionally, whereas both international human rights and humanitarian law aim to protect the individual, the latter generally (but not always) admits more rights limitations, as it seeks to strike an acceptable 'compromise between humanitarian ideals and the desire to ensure military effectiveness in warfare'.[8] At the same time, it has been demonstrated that international human rights has had a 'humanizing effect' on international humanitarian law.[9] Thus, while many international crimes initially 'emerged directly from'[10] international humanitarian law or were at least characterized

---

[3] Ibid. 6–7: 'ICL also presents the unique characteristic that, more than any other segment of international law, it simultaneously *derives its origin from* and continuously *draws upon* both *international humanitarian law and human rights law*, as well as *national criminal law.*'

[4] Robinson (n. 1) 930–31.   [5] Danner and Martinez (n. 1) 87–89.

[6] Ibid. 89. On the imprecise meaning of human dignity, see C McCrudden, 'Human Dignity and Judicial Interpretation of Human Rights' (2008) 19 EJIL 655. On the evolutive interpretation of human rights treaties, see R Bernhardt, 'Evolutive Treaty Interpretation, Especially of the European Convention on Human Rights' (1999) 42 German Ybk Int'l L 11; M Fitzmaurice, 'Dynamic (Evolutive) Interpretation of Treaties' (2008) 21 Hague Ybk Int'l L 101; J Christoffersen, 'Impact on General Principles of Treaty Interpretation' in MT Kamminga and M Scheinin (eds.), *The Impact of Human Rights Law on General International Law* (Oxford University Press 2009) 37.

[7] UNHRC, 'General Comment No. 32' (2007) UN Doc. CCPR/C/GC/32, para. 18. To trace the evolution of this line of reasoning, see also 'General Comment No. 7' (1982) UN Doc. HRI/GEN/1/Rev.6, 129 (2003) and 'General Comment No. 20' (1992) UN Doc. HRI/GEN/1/Rev.6, 151 (2003).

[8] R Provost, *International Human Rights and Humanitarian Law* (Cambridge University Press 2002) 136; J Pictet, *Development and Principles of International Humanitarian Law* (Martinus Nijhoff 1985).

[9] See generally T Meron, 'International Law in the Age of Human Rights' (2003) 301 Recueil des Cours de l'Académie de Droit International 9.

[10] Danner and Martinez (n. 1) 81.

as such, this relationship is weakening, and international criminal law's direct ties to international human rights is strengthening.[11] In light of this 'cross-fertilization'[12] and the influence of three sets of parent norms, it is not surprising that international criminal law suffers from an identity crisis. Indeed, the ICTR has apparently gone so far as to conclude that 'what may constitute a prohibition in international human rights law is also an international crime'.[13]

A second way to understand the uncertain normativity of international criminal law is to consider its substantive justice origins and strict legality aspirations. A legal order modelled on the substantive justice doctrine has as its aim the punishment of socially harmful or dangerous conduct, even if this requires retroactive application of the law.[14] One premised on the doctrine of strict legality purports to punish an individual only for acts that were criminal when performed so as to protect individuals against the harsh and arbitrary exercise of State power to curtail or deprive them of their liberty.[15] The influence of strict legality on the task of interpretation is to ensure fair warning, limit the power of unelected judges illegitimately to restrain individual autonomy[16] and ensure respect for the law-making role of the 'legislature' as distinct from the law interpretation and application role of the judiciary.[17]

The genesis of modern international criminal law can be traced to the trial of war criminals at Nuremberg and Tokyo after the Second World War.[18] These trials have been criticized inter alia for offending the principle of legality because certain crimes contained in their governing statutes, namely crimes against peace and crimes against humanity, were said to have become crimes after the conduct in question occurred. Confronted with an objection to the retroactive application of these laws, the Nuremberg tribunal responded:

> In the first place, it is to be observed that the maxim *nullum crimen sine lege* is not a limitation of sovereignty, but is a general principle of justice. To assert that it is unjust to punish those who in defiance of treaties and assurances have attacked neighbouring states without warning is obviously

---

[11] The implications of this shift for purposes of interpretation are discussed in Section 3.6 of this Chapter.

[12] This term is borrowed from P Sands, 'Treaty, Custom and the Cross-fertilization of International Law' (1998) 1 Yale Human Rights & Development LJ 85.

[13] WA Schabas, 'Customary Law or "Judge-Made" Law: Judicial Creativity at the UN Criminal Tribunals' in J Doria, H-P Gasser and MC Bassiouni (eds.), *The Legal Regime of the International Criminal Court: Essays in Honour of Professor Igor Blishchenko* (Martinus Nijhoff 2009) 77, 99 (no cases cited).

[14] B Broomhall, 'Article 22' in O Triffterer (ed.), *Commentary on the Rome Statute of the International Criminal Court*, 2nd edn (CH Beck/Hart/Nomos 2008) 713, 719; Cassese, *International Criminal Law* (n. 2) 36–37; A Ashworth and J Horder, *Principles of Criminal Law*, 7th edn (Oxford University Press 2013) 69–71.

[15] Cassese (n. 2) 37.   [16] Ashworth and Horder (n. 14) 70.

[17] Ibid. 67–69.   [18] Cassese (n. 2) 319ff.

untrue, for in such circumstances the attacker must know that he is doing wrong, and so far from it being unjust to punish him, *it would be unjust if his wrong were allowed to go unpunished.*[19]

The Nuremberg and Tokyo trials evidently attempted to derive some of their legitimacy from the substantive justice doctrine.[20] In recent times, where dynamic interpretation likely motivated by substantive justice considerations has been perceived as offending the principle of legality, a distinction has been drawn between the jurisdiction of international criminal tribunals and the criminality of the conduct being adjudicated:

> Some criminal defence lawyers from national systems may be scandalised at the ease with which the [international criminal law] judges have enlarged the definitions of crimes and the general principles of criminal responsibility. But this writer is not overly troubled by the point, because whether or not criminal behaviour falls within the scope of international prosecution by the ad hoc Tribunals is fundamentally a jurisdictional issue. Even if we suppose, for the sake of argument, and as many believed before the *Tadić Jurisdiction Decision,* there was no individual criminal liability at international law in internal armed conflict, the underlying acts of killing, torture and rape remained crimes under general principles of law. An offender can plead that the Tribunal is without jurisdiction, based on a certain interpretation of the subject-matter provisions, but it cannot be argued that he or she did not know it was wrong.[21]

The above passage may be seen as the modern manifestation of the substantive justice and strict legality tension within international criminal law. It is thought that notions of fair warning and individual autonomy that the principle of legality is intended to protect are not undermined in certain situations. However, legality is also intended to safeguard the rule of law and the separation of powers doctrine.[22]

The absence of a prevailing method of interpretation in the jurisprudence of the ICTY and ICTR is perhaps symptomatic in part of the aforementioned normative tensions.[23]

---

[19] International Military Tribunal (Nuremberg), 'Judgment and Sentences' (1947) 41 AJIL (1947) 172, 217 (emphasis added).

[20] Cassese (n. 2) 39.

[21] WA Schabas, 'Interpreting the Statutes of the Ad Hoc Tribunals' in LC Vohrah (ed.), *Man's Inhumanity to Man: Essays on International Law in Honour of Antonio Cassese* (Kluwer 2003) 887.

[22] Ashworth and Horder (n. 14) 81–82; A Ashworth, 'Interpreting Criminal Statutes: a Crisis of Legality?' (1991) 107 LQR 419, 420ff.; A Cassese, 'The Statute of the International Criminal Court: Some Preliminary Reflections' (1999) 10 EJIL 144, 152.

[23] Robinson (n. 1).

3.3 Legality and article 22

At the Rome Diplomatic Conference in 1998, delegates were familiar with the experiences of the ICTY and ICTR judges adjudicating cases of individual criminal liability.[24] They were also familiar with the critique that international criminal law lacks specificity in the following respects as compared to domestic criminal sanctions: (1) prohibited conduct is not described in detail; (2) some prohibited conduct is especially vague (e.g., 'other inhumane acts' as a crime against humanity); and (3) mental elements for crimes are not accurately defined.[25] Keenly aware that the treaty they were negotiating was for establishing an international criminal court with permanent jurisdiction to try inter alia their own State agents, delegates were guided by the principle of specificity, meaning they attempted 'to set out in detail all the classes of crimes falling under the jurisdiction of the Court, so as to have a *lex scripta* laying down the substantive criminal rules to be applied by the ICC'.[26] Their goal was exhaustively to list crimes within the Court's jurisdiction and in as detailed and clear a manner as possible so that States and their agents could know with reasonable certainty what the outer reaches of prohibited conduct are and what obligations they have under the Rome Statute.[27] Put simply, the principle of specificity is 'an injunction to take care in the framing of criminal statutes, that no more power be given to call conduct into question as criminal, with all the destruction of human autonomy that this power necessarily imports, than is reasonably needed to deal with the conduct the lawmakers seek to prevent'.[28]

The principle of legality was said to require specificity at the drafting stage.[29] And while not perfect,[30] four aspects of the Rome Statute evidence extraordinary advances relative to the ICTY and ICTR statutes in terms of

---

[24] WA Schabas, *An Introduction to the International Criminal Court*, 2nd edn (Cambridge University Press 2004) 94: 'Article 22(2) [of the Rome Statute] is in many respects a reaction to the large and liberal approach to construction taken by the judges of the International Criminal Tribunal for the Former Yugoslavia. The approach to the definitions of crimes taken in such cases as the *Tadić* jurisdiction decision, which quite dramatically opened up the category of war crimes to include offences committed in non-international armed conflict, was rather clearly not within the spirit of strict construction.'

[25] Cassese (n. 22) 148–49.　　[26] Ibid. 152.　　[27] Broomhall (n. 14) 713–17.

[28] HL Packer, *The Limits of the Criminal Sanction* (Stanford University Press 1968) 94–95.

[29] Ad Hoc Committee, 'Report of the Ad Hoc Committee on the Establishment of an International Criminal Court' (1995) UN Doc. A/50/22, paras. 52, 57; Preparatory Committee, 'Report of the Preparatory Committee on the Establishment of an International Criminal Court (Proceedings of the Preparatory Committee during Mar.–Apr. and Aug. 1996)', vol. I, UN Doc. A/51/22, paras. 52, 180, 185, cited in S Lamb, '*Nullum Crimen, Nulla Poena Sine Lege* in International Criminal Law' in A Cassese and Others (eds.), *The Rome Statute of the International Criminal Court: A Commentary*, vol. I (Oxford University Press 2002) 733, 747.

[30] See, e.g., K Ambos, '*Nulla Poena Sine Lege* in International Criminal Law' in R Haveman and O Olusanya (eds.), *Sentencing and Sanctioning in Supranational Criminal Law* (Intersentia 2006) 17.

legal certainty. First, it not only contains categories of offences but also nearly exhaustively lists more than ninety crimes,[31] which are supplemented by the Elements of Crimes. Second, article 21 contains a hierarchy of law that judges are to apply if interpretation of the Rome Statute, Elements of Crimes and Rules of Procedure and Evidence fail to resolve an issue. Third, the Rome Statute contains numerous procedural protections for suspects and the accused, which are further supplemented by Rules of Procedure and Evidence.[32] Fourth, part III of the Rome Statute sets out, for the first time, general principles of international criminal law applicable to crimes within the Court's jurisdiction. These address inter alia basic concepts and modes of individual criminal responsibility, requisite mental elements, grounds for excluding criminal responsibility and mistakes of fact and law.

For purposes of interpretation, one of the most important developments at Rome was the express mention of the principle of legality in article 22(2):

> The definition of a crime shall be strictly construed and shall not be extended by analogy. In case of ambiguity, the definition shall be interpreted in favour of the person being investigated, prosecuted or convicted.

Article 22(2) obliges judges to construe crimes strictly, not extend them by analogy and to interpret them in favour of the suspect or accused in case of ambiguity.[33] The perceived liberal interpretive reasoning of the ad hoc tribunals was a motivating factor for States to adopt this provision.[34] The principle of

---

[31] Non-exhaustive provisions such as articles 7(1)(g) ('any other form of sexual violence of a comparable gravity') and (k) ('other inhumane acts of a similar character') leave the list of crimes against humanity in the Rome Statute somewhat (perhaps unavoidably) open-ended. See also articles 8(b)(xxii) and (e)(vi) on sexual violence as a war crime.

[32] ICC-ASP/1/3, adopted by the ASP on 9 September 2002.

[33] The content to be given to these concepts is discussed in detail in Chapter 6. There is an abundance of literature on the rationale for and content of the legality principle. See, e.g., Ashworth and Horder (n. 14) 56ff.; Broomhall (n. 14) 714–17; Cassese (n. 14) 36ff; KS Gallant, *The Principle of Legality in International and Comparative Criminal Law* (Cambridge University Press 2009); Lamb (n. 29); C Kreß, 'Nullum Crimen, Nulla Poena Sine Lege' in R Wolfrum (ed.), *Max Planck Encyclopedia of Public International Law* (2008–), online edition, www.mpepil.com, accessed 15 March 2011; PJA Ritter von Feuerbach, 'The General Principles of International Criminal Law: The Foundations of Criminal Law and the Nullum Crimen Principle' in *Lehrbuch des gemeinen in Deutschland gültigen peinlichen Rechts*, 11th edn (Heyer 1832) 12–19, translation by IL Fraser in (2007) 5 J Int'l Crim Justice 1005; F von Liszt, 'The Rationale for the Nullum Crimen Principle' (2007) 5 J Int'l Crim Justice 1009; MC Bassiouni, 'Principles of Legality in International and Comparative Criminal Law' in MC Bassiouni (ed.), *International Criminal Law*, vol. II, 3rd edn (Martinus Nijhoff 2008) 73; R Haveman, 'The Principle of Legality' in R Haveman, O Kavran and J Nicholls (eds.), *Supranational Criminal Law: A System Sui Generis* (Intersentia 2003) 39; J Hall, 'Nulla Poena Sine Lege' (1937) 47 Yale LJ 165; JC Jeffries Jr, 'Legality, Vagueness, and the Construction of Penal Statutes' (1985) 71 Virginia L Rev 189; A Mokhtar, 'Nullum Crimen, Nulla Poena Sine Lege: Aspects and Prospects' (2005) 26 Statute L Rev 41.

[34] Broomhall (n. 14) 725; Schabas (n. 24).

legality is further manifested in the following three prohibitions: (1) retroactive exercise of jurisdiction by the Court (article 11(1)); (2) conviction for a crime which is not within the Court's jurisdiction at the time it is perpetrated (articles 22(1) and 24(1)); and (3) retroactive application of all applicable law set out in article 21 prior to a final judgment unless the new law is more favourable to the person being investigated, prosecuted or convicted (article 24(2)). In light of the principle of specificity guiding drafters of the Rome Statute and their decision to firmly embed a robust articulation of the principle of legality in article 22(2), the normative dilemma confronting international criminal law has arguably been resolved for the Court with respect to interpreting articles 6, 7, 8 and eventually 8 *bis* of the Rome Statute. Whether the principle of legality may appropriately influence the interpretation of other parts of the Rome Statute is not considered here. And while the content of the legality principle is the focus of the next two Chapters, a few preliminary marks are appropriate.

At its core, the principle of legality takes very seriously the power of the 'legislator' to curtail individual liberty through the enactment of criminal laws and the power of police, prosecutors and judges to deprive individuals of their liberty as a consequence of enforcing these laws. The domestic and international origins of the legality principle dating back to Roman and Greek law are well rehearsed elsewhere.[35] Suffice it to mention that a recent study on legality concluded that the most important constituent elements of legality in criminal law, the non-retroactive application of criminal laws and punishment of crimes, are so widely recognized (albeit to varying degrees) that they bind national and international judges as a matter of customary international law[36] or at least as a general principle of law recognized by the community of nations.[37] Indeed, all major human rights instruments protect the principle of legality.[38] However, the diversity of legality definitions at the national level and

---

[35] See, e.g., Hall (n. 33); Bassiouni (n. 33) 73; S Glaser, 'Nullum Crimen Sine Lege' (1942) 24 J Comp Legis & Int'l L 29; Mokhtar (n. 33) 41–47; M Boot, *Genocide, Crimes Against Humanity, War Crimes: Nullum Crimen Sine Lege and the Subject Matter Jurisdiction of the International Criminal Court* (Intersentia 2002). For its evolution in international law, see Lamb (n. 29) 735; in a nutshell, 'the English tradition of the rule of law, translated by eighteenth century French philosophers into terms expressive of the Revolutionary ideology, joined with the continental movement for codification to provide *nulla poena* with its particular, current meanings.' The French Declaration of the Rights of Man (1789), which was inspired by the Virginia Declaration of Rights (1776) 'fixed the prevailing meanings of *nulla poena* not only as a basic constitutional safeguard of the individual against oppressive government but also as a cardinal tenet of penal law. . . . [T]he rule was incorporated in the Bavarian Code drafted by Feuerbach in 1813. . . . Feuerbach is generally credited with the Statement *nulla poena* in its current form.' Hall (n. 33) 168–71.

[36] Gallant (n. 33) 8–9.

[37] R Higgins, 'Time and the Law: International Perspectives on an Old Problem' (1997) 46 Int'l Comp LQ 501, 507–08; Gallant (n. 33) 8–9.

[38] Article 11 (2), *Universal Declaration of Human Rights*, UNGA Res. 217 A (III) (10 December 1948); article 99, third *Geneva Convention* (1949); articles 65 and 67, fourth *Geneva*

their fitful and qualified application has led to problems with authoritatively determining its content at the international level.[39] In various jurisdictions, the legality principle's scope reveals a persistent albeit attenuated tension between compelling considerations of substantive justice and strict legality. While most criminal law jurisdictions have adopted a doctrine of strict legality in theory and invoke it to justify the principle of legality,[40] considerations of substantive justice have, in practice, qualified the principle's application in absolute terms. In fact, the European Court of Human Rights has accepted this. For example, it held in *SW v. United Kingdom* (1995)[41] that the principle of strict construction is satisfied when a judicial interpretation, while not strictly in conformity with the wording of a criminal prohibition or relevant case law, is nonetheless reasonably foreseeable – even if this requires obtaining legal advice – and is consistent with the 'essence' of an offence.[42] The Rome Statute does not expressly admit the qualification of foreseeability, and so it remains to be seen whether the Court will recognize it.[43]

As in some domestic jurisdictions,[44] the legality principle for crimes under international law may also be 'subject to a number of significant qualifications'.[45] Some crimes are inherently vague;[46] some vagueness is inevitable to avoid 'excessive rigidity and to keep pace with changing circumstances';[47] and in the absence of a world legislature, universally binding written criminal prohibitions (and defences to them) do not exist.[48] Further, while

Convention (1949); article 7, *European Convention for the Protection of Human Rights and Fundamental Freedoms* (adopted 4 November 1950, entered into force 3 September 1953) 213 UNTS 221; article 15, *International Covenant on Civil and Political Rights*, 999 UNTS 171 (adopted 19 December 1966, entered into force 23 March 1976); article 9, *American Convention on Human Rights*, 1144 UNTS 123 (adopted 22 November 1969, entered into force 18 July 1978); article 7(2), *African Charter on Human and Peoples' Rights*, 1520 UNTS 217 (adopted 27 June 1981, entered into force 21 October 1986); article 40(2)(a), *Convention on the Rights of the Child*, 1577 UNTS 3 (adopted 20 November 1989, entered into force 2 September 1990); article 15, *Arab Charter on Human Rights* (revised), (2005) 12 IHRR 893 (adopted 22 May 2004, entered into force 15 March 2008); article 49, *Charter of Fundamental Rights of the European Union* (2001) 40 ILM 266 (adopted 7 December 2000, entered into force 1 December 2009), cited in Kreß (n. 33) para. 15. At the very least, the legality principle is thought to bind international criminal tribunals as a matter of treaty law 'because such institutions are created via multilateral action whereby formative and member states bring their treaty obligations with them when they launch and associate with such bodies.' B Van Schaack, '*Crimen Sine Lege*: Judicial Lawmaking at the Intersection of Law and Morals' (2008) 97 Georgetown LJ 119, 176.

[39] Van Schaack, ibid. 134.
[40] J Raz, *The Authority of Law* (Oxford University Press 1979) 214–15.
[41] App. No. 20166/92, ECHR (1995) Series A, No. 335-B, para. 36.   [42] Ibid.
[43] See Chapter 4, Section 4.3.8 on the merits of this reasoning and Chapter 5 on the recommended content of this rule.
[44] Gallant (n. 33); Bassiouni (n. 33).   [45] Cassese (n. 2) 41.
[46] Article 7(1)(k), Rome Statute ('other inhumane acts of a similar character').
[47] App. No. 14307/88, *Kokkinakis v. Greece*, ECHR (1993) Series A, No. 260, para. 52.
[48] Cassese (n. 2) 42.

courts and tribunals have worked hard to give clear content to vague international criminal law concepts, the absence of a supreme international criminal
court means that this work has occurred in a decentralized manner through ad
hoc international tribunals, hybrid tribunals and domestic courts.[49] In addition to the qualifications of foreseeability and constructive knowledge of the
illegality of criminal conduct, it is often asserted that strict construction cannot surreptitiously gut the concept of interpretation of all meaning. Judges are
mandated to interpret and apply the law, which requires giving content in good
faith to the text in light of its ordinary or special meaning, context, object and
purpose, as well as subsequent practice, subsequent agreements and applicable
law.[50] The ICTY accordingly reasoned:

> The effect of strict construction of the provisions of a criminal statute is that
> where an equivocal word or ambiguous sentence leaves a reasonable doubt
> of its meaning *which the canons of construction fail to solve*, the benefit of
> the doubt should be given to the subject and against the legislature which
> has failed to explain itself.[51]

Both strict construction and the ban on analogy are said 'not [to] stand in
the way of progressive juridical clarification of the content of an offence'.[52]
This interpretive exercise is not considered to undermine the notions of fair
warning, rule of law or separation of powers so long as the Court's reasoning
does not yield a new crime not contemplated by States Parties.[53] Indeed, in hard
cases, these liberal standards will render a fine line between the interpretation
of existing crimes and the retroactive application of judge-made law. Like the
principle of strict construction, the ban on analogy has enjoyed qualified use
at the national level[54] and remains to be defined in the Rome Statute regime.

---

[49] Ibid. 42–43.

[50] *United States* v. *Davis*, 576 F.2d 1065, 1069 (3d Cir. 1978) (Aldisert, J. concurring), cited
in JJ Paust, 'Nullum *Crimen* and Related Claims' (1997) 25 Denver J Int'l L & Policy 321,
325.

[51] *Prosecutor* v. *Delalić and Others*, Judgment, ICTY-96–21-T, 16 November 1998, para. 413
(emphasis added). D Akande suggests that where an ambiguity exists, the legality principle bars resort to *travaux préparatoires* pursuant to article 32 of the *Vienna Convention*
(1969) to resolve it in a manner unfavourable to the suspect or accused. 'The Sources of
International Criminal Law' in A Cassese (ed.), *The Oxford Companion to International
Criminal Justice* (Oxford University Press 2009) 41, 45.

[52] *S.W.* v. *United Kingdom* (n. 41); Broomhall (n. 14) 724; Cassese (n. 2) 44–47; Shahabuddeen, 'Does the Principle of Legality Stand in the Way of Progressive Development of
Law?' (2004) 2 J Int'l Crim Justice 1007.

[53] On fair warning and the surreptitious broadening of crimes see Cassese, *International
Criminal Law* (n. 2) 48. For a critique of strict construction and the concept of fair
warning see Jeffries Jr (n. 33).

[54] Broomhall (n. 14) 724.

While the exact content of legality in article 22 remains to be determined, it is arguable that, at a minimum, it requires the textual approach in article 31 of the *Vienna Convention* (1969) to prevail for interpreting crimes – as opposed to the drafters' intent or object and purpose approaches.[55] This means, quite simply, textual primacy:

> This aspect of the primacy of the text has been recognized by international tribunals in a number of recurring situations. First, it seems to be generally recognized that an interpretation that does not emerge from the text cannot be accepted, however plausible it may be in view of the circumstance, unless failure to do so would lead to an obviously unreasonable result. Accordingly, tribunals have usually rejected otherwise reasonable interpretations because to accept them would have been tantamount to rephrasing or otherwise altering the actual text. Second, interpretations suggested by means of interpretation not derived from the text cannot be justified by referring to general custom, usage, or even recognized rules of international law unless sufficiently supported by the text. Last, when two or more reasonable interpretations exist, all of which are consistent with the text, the one that appears to be the most compatible with the text should prevail in the absence of persuasive evidence in support of another interpretation.[56]

International tribunals that are associated with the textual school of interpretation are the International Court of Justice and the World Trade Organization's Appellate Body (WTO).[57] And while some have characterized the ICTY and ICTR as favouring a teleological approach to interpretation and the Court a textual approach,[58] others have asserted that the approach of all three bodies falls somewhere in between the textual approach of the WTO and the teleological approach of the European Court of Human Rights.[59]

---

[55] *Kokkinakis* v. *Greece* (n. 47): A clear definition of the law in accordance with the legality principle requires that 'the individual can know *from the wording* of the relevant provision, and if need be, with the assistance of the courts' interpretation of it, what acts and omissions will make him liable' (emphasis added). On the three schools, see I Sinclair, *The Vienna Convention on the Law of Treaties*, 2nd edn (Manchester University Press 1984) 115.

[56] R Gardiner, *Treaty Interpretation* (Oxford University Press 2008) 145 (citing RH Berglin, 'Treaty Interpretation and the Impact of Contractual Choice of Forum Clauses on the Jurisdiction of International Tribunals: the Iranian Forum Clause Decisions of the Iran-United States Claims Tribunal' (1986) 21 Tex Int'l LJ 39, 44 (footnotes omitted)).

[57] J Pauwelyn and M Elsig, 'The Politics of Treaty Interpretation: Variations and Explanations Across International Tribunals' (3 October 2011) 1, 9, 18, http://ssrn.com/abstract=1938618, accessed 16 October 2013.

[58] Ibid.

[59] G Nolte, 'Second Report for the ILC Study Group on Treaties over Time: Jurisprudence under Special Regimes relating to Subsequent Agreements and Subsequent Practice' in G Nolte (ed.), *Treaties and Subsequent Practice* (Oxford University Press 2013) 210, pt. IV, s. 2.

To be clear, textual primacy is not incompatible with the 'crucible' approach to interpretation. In practice, dictionary meanings without consideration of the treaty's context, purpose and relevant interpretive aids may well prove unhelpful and should therefore be seen as a starting point rather than conclusive. Stated differently, it is acknowledged that the idea of textual determinacy is a myth and that context is highly relevant; it is, however, equally acknowledged that texts are not open to an infinite number of meanings and that context has a constraining function.[60]

Considerations of context, object and purpose as well as interpretive aids such as the Elements of Crimes and *travaux préparatoires* cannot be invoked to modify or override the plain meaning of provisions in the Rome Statute or inappropriately restrict or broaden them. But the devil lies in the details. While it is relatively easy to identify the modification or overriding of language in articles 6, 7, 8 and 8 *bis* of the Rome Statute, it is more difficult to identify which interpretive arguments otherwise offend the principle of legality and would thereby 'inappropriately' alter the scope of these provisions if accepted by judges.[61] This matter is taken up in the next two Chapters. But first, it must be determined whether legality is to be the guiding interpretive principle for crimes in the Rome Statute.

3.4 Internationally recognized human rights and article 21(3)

While article 22(2) of the Rome Statute might be invoked in support of an open and shut case for legality emerging as the primary or guiding interpretive principle for crimes in the Court's jurisdiction, drafters of the Rome Statute, ironically in their zeal to safeguard this principle, may have created serious competition for it by inadvertently reviving the normative tensions described in Section 2 of this Chapter.

In order of hierarchy, article 21 of the Rome Statute sets out the law to be applied by the Court, including the Rome Statute, Elements of Crimes, 'applicable treaties and the principles and rules of international law', 'the established principles of the international law of armed conflict', general principles of law and national laws as appropriate. Article 21(2) also permits the Court to apply 'principles and rules of law as interpreted in its previous decisions'. Article 21(3) closes the provision and provides:

> The application and interpretation of law pursuant to this article must be consistent with internationally recognized human rights, and be without

---

[60] A Bianchi, 'Textual Interpretation and (International) Law Reading: The Myth of (In)determinacy and the Genealogy of Meaning' in *Making Transnational Law Work in the Global Economy: Essays in Honour of Detlev Vagts* (Cambridge University Press 2010) 34, 36.

[61] See Chapter 4.

any adverse distinction founded on grounds such as gender as defined in article 7, paragraph 3, age, race, colour, language, religion or belief, political or other opinion, national, ethnic or social origin, wealth, birth or other status.

The latter part of this provision contains a fairly straightforward prohibition on adverse distinction when interpreting and applying the Rome Statute. The focus of this section is therefore on the meaning of the first part of this provision, the general consistency requirement. On its face, article 21(3) appears to create what has been termed a 'super-legality',[62] a normative superiority for international human rights, which can be invoked to override all applicable sources of law, including the Rome Statute and established principles of the international law of armed conflict. For example, it has been argued that the absolute ban on torture under international human rights law is a *jus cogens* norm and that, accordingly, article 21(3) should operate to exclude application of the defences available under articles 31(c) (self-defence of oneself or others) and 31(d) (necessity) of the Rome Statute for cases of 'preventive torture'.[63] While the aforementioned argument is based on *jus cogens* and not just on the torture ban originating from international human rights law, it nevertheless illustrates how article 21(3) might be invoked to exclude the application of certain Rome Statute provisions on the basis of an internationally recognized human right.

As a super-legal norm, it could also be understood as requiring the interpretation of crimes consistent with internationally recognized human rights in all cases, thereby resolving the normative tensions underlying international criminal law in favour of human rights as opposed to liberal criminal justice. As well, the conclusion of the ICTR that 'what may constitute a prohibition in international human rights law is also an international crime'[64] could take hold. One might argue that in light of the international human rights movement

---

[62] A Pellet, 'Applicable Law' in A Cassese and Others (eds.), *The Rome Statute of the International Criminal Court: A Commentary*, vol. II (Oxford University Press 2002) 1051, 1080–81; MH Arsanjani, 'The Rome Statute of the International Criminal Court' (1999) 93 AJIL 22, 28–29; B Perrin, 'Searching for Law While Seeking Justice: The Difficulties of Enforcing International Humanitarian Law in International Criminal Trials' (2008) 39 Ottawa L Rev 367, 398; Akande (n. 51) 46–47.

[63] F Jessberger, 'Bad Torture – Good Torture? What International Criminal Lawyers may Learn from the Recent Trial of Police Officers in Germany' (2005) 3 J Int'l Crim Justice 1059 (citing therein for reaching the same conclusion P Gaeta, 'May Necessity be Available as a Defence for Torture in the Interrogation of Suspected Terrorists?' (2004) 2 J Int'l Crim Justice 785). On the inapplicability of exclusionary grounds in a case before the Court, see also article 31(2) of the Rome Statute and A Eser, 'Article 31' in O Triffterer (ed.), *Commentary on the Rome Statute of the International Criminal Court*, 2nd edn (CH Beck/Hart/Nomos 2008) 863, 888ff.

[64] Schabas (n. 13) 99.

providing the necessary political momentum for the creation of the Court, such a super-legal status would be fitting.[65]

While this status for article 21(3) finds support in the ordinary meaning of its words, article 31 of the *Vienna Convention* (1969) requires these words to be read in context and in light of the object and purpose of the Rome Statute. A contextual reading of article 21(3) would draw the reader's eye to article 22(2) and specifically its opening words, 'The definition of a crime shall be', followed by the interpretive imperatives of legality. Notable is that article 22(2) deals expressly with the interpretation of crimes, whereas article 21(3) applies to all provisions of the Rome Statute, not just crimes. As well, there is a difference in the active and passive construction of the imperatives in these provisions. Article 21(3) informs judges that the definition of a crime 'shall be' interpreted in accordance with the legality principle. Article 22(2) provides that the 'application and interpretation of law . . . must be consistent with internationally recognized human rights'. What significance might this have, if any?

As for the object and purpose of the Rome Statute, its preamble signals several, including ending impunity for the perpetrators of the most serious crimes of concern to the international community as a whole, thereby contributing to the prevention of these crimes, reaffirming the purposes and principles of the Charter of the United Nations, establishing an independent permanent Court that is complementary to national criminal jurisdictions and resolving to guarantee lasting respect for and the enforcement of international justice. However, the object and purpose of the definitions of crimes also deserve consideration. Certainly one of their purposes is to uphold respect for the principles of specificity and legality. Accordingly, assigning article 21(3) a super-legal status that obliges judges to be guided by interpretation in favour of international human rights and norms, including maximum protection for the victim, would seriously undermine the express wording of article 22(2). This seems unreasonable.

In fact, the intent of the drafters at Rome confirms that the scope of article 21(3) is rather modest with respect to the interpretation of crimes. Article 32 of the *Vienna Convention* (1969) provides:

> Recourse may be had to supplementary means of interpretation, including the preparatory work of the treaty and the circumstances of its conclusion, in order to confirm the meaning resulting from the application of article 31, *or to determine the meaning when the interpretation according to article 31:*

---

[65] WA Schabas, *The International Criminal Court: A Commentary on the Rome Statute* (Oxford University Press 2010) 397: 'The drive to establish the Court is associated with the emergence of concerns about accountability and impunity in human rights bodies like the Inter-American Court of Human Rights and the United Nations Sub-Commission on the Protection and Promotion of Human Rights during the 1980s.'

(a) leaves the meaning ambiguous or obscure; or

(b) leads to a result which is *manifestly* absurd or *unreasonable*.[66]

In spite of the sparse legislative history for this provision, experts and commentators agree that consistency with internationally recognized human rights was intended to require consistency with the principle of legality,[67] to limit judicial discretion[68] and to maximize other fair trial protections for the *alleged perpetrator*, which originate from international human rights law.[69] Indeed, a great deal of work has been done in the area of human rights in criminal proceedings, looking at inter alia the following rights of the accused: the scope of the right to a fair trial in criminal matters, the right to a public hearing before an independent and impartial tribunal, the right to be tried within a reasonable time, the right to be presumed innocent, the right to be informed of the accusation(s), the right to defend oneself and to have the assistance of counsel, the right to adequate time and facilities to prepare one's defence, the right to test witness evidence, the right to free assistance of an interpreter, the privilege against self-incrimination, the right to appeal, the right to compensation for wrongful conviction, the protection against double jeopardy and so on. There are also rights concerning the liberty and security of the person, which are relevant to criminal proceedings and imprisonment: the right to be informed of the reasons for one's arrest, the right to habeas corpus proceedings and the special rights of persons detained on remand (the right to be brought before a judge, the limitation in time of detention on remand, release on bail, possibility of redress etc.). Finally, other rights may be affected by criminal proceedings as a result of interferences with one's private life and property.[70]

In addition to legality, some specific fair trial issues that were raised at Rome include the age of persons over which the Court would have jurisdiction, respect for the fair trial standards set out in article 14 of the *International Covenant on Civil and Political Rights* (1966) (*ICCPR*)[71] and ensuring that any recourse to national law is consistent with international human rights law.[72] Indeed, this latter role for article 21(3) may, in the longer term, prove to be its main field of application. Interestingly, the limited debate on article 21(3) focussed

---

[66] Emphasis added.

[67] Preparatory Committee, 'Report of the Preparatory Committee on the Establishment of an International Criminal Court' (1998) UN Doc. A/CONF.183/2/Add.1, 47 (fn. 63), 48.

[68] Arsanjani (n. 62) 22.

[69] M McAuliffe de Guzman, 'Article 21' in O Triffterer (ed.), *Commentary on the Rome Statute of the International Criminal Court*, 2nd edn (CH Beck/Hart/Nomos 2008) 701, 711; G Hafner and C Binder, 'The Interpretation of Article 21(3) ICC Statute Opinion Reviewed' (2004) 9 Austrian Rev Int'l and Eur L 163, 166–67; N Roht-Arriaza, Letter to the Office of the Prosecutor on the Meaning of Article 21(3) (14 December 2004) 2 (on file with author); Perrin (n. 62) 403.

[70] See generally S Trechsel, *Human Rights in Criminal Proceedings* (Oxford University Press 2005).

[71] *ICCPR* (1966) (n. 38).   [72] Roht-Arriaza (n. 69) 2.

on the non-discrimination clause and the meaning to be given to 'gender'.[73] Thus, in terms of a hierarchy of applicable sources of law for purposes other than protecting the rights of the accused, little or no thought was given to the relationship between internationally recognized human rights and the Rome Statute. Ironically, the drafting of article 21 was motivated by the principle of legality and the desire to limit judicial discretion in the interpretation and application of the Rome Statute.[74] And in terms of normative hierarchies, little or no thought was given to the relationship between internationally recognized human rights and the 'international law of armed conflict'. Indeed, it is the reference in article 21 to both sources of law as well as fields of law that is curious and confusing.

In addition to the drafting history of this provision, several reasons have been provided for rejecting the systemic supremacy of article 21(3) relative to the Rome Statute.[75] First, article 21(3) is at the end of this provision rather than at the beginning, thereby suggesting a lack of supremacy.[76] Second, article 21(3) does not refer to internationally recognized human rights as *jus cogens* norms.[77] Third, the crimes in the Rome Statute are likely to be of a 'general', '*ordre public*', or *jus cogens* character themselves, and so there is no a priori reason to privilege article 21(3) in this context.[78] Fourth, if article 21(3) could be invoked to override the Rome Statute, no alternative rule would exist, and the Court would have to apply judge-made law.[79] Fifth, if article 21(3) were to operate in the manner contemplated, this mandate could be more clearly expressed.[80] Sixth, because of the reference in article 69(7) of the Rome Statute to the exclusion of evidence that violates the Rome Statute *or* internationally recognized human rights, these two bodies of law do not have a hierarchical relationship to one another.[81]

On balance, none of these arguments seem sufficiently compelling to override the clear and ordinary meaning of this provision and would render article 21(3) largely redundant. For this reason, perhaps the better legal approach is to assign meaning to article 21(3) that respects its wording and the fair trial protections it is intended to safeguard, but is also consistent with the legality provision, which is specifically addressed to the interpretation of crimes. The drafters of the Rome Statute 'are assumed to intend the provision . . . to have a certain effect, and not to be meaningless: the maxim is *ut res magis valeat quam pereat*. Therefore, an

---

[73] McAuliffe de Guzman (n. 69) 712.

[74] Ibid. 702ff.; Arsanjani (n. 62) 28–29; J Verhoeven, 'Article 21 of the Rome Statute and the Ambiguities of Applicable Law' (2002) 33 Netherlands Ybk Int'l L 3, 17; Hafner and Binder (n. 69) 175; KS Gallant, 'Individual Human Rights in a New International Organization: The Rome Statute of the International Criminal Court' in MC Bassiouni (ed.), *International Criminal Law*, 2nd edn (Transnational Publishers 1999) 693, 702–03.

[75] Hafner and Binder (n. 69) 173–74.   [76] Ibid. 174.

[77] Gallant (n. 74) 702; Hafner and Binder (n. 69) 173–74.   [78] Verhoeven (n. 74) 15.

[79] Ibid. 14.   [80] Hafner and Binder (n. 69) 174.   [81] Ibid. 174.

interpretation is not admissible which would make a provision meaningless, or ineffective.'[82] The principle of legality seems poised to emerge as a central pillar in the Rome Statute regime and would be seriously undermined if, as in the past,[83] a neighbouring and vast body of law that is undefined in the Rome Statute were used to widen the scope of individual criminal liability under international law.

Unfortunately, the phrase 'internationally recognized human rights' has no obvious or fixed meaning. It was borrowed from article 69(7) of the Rome Statute, which provides:

> Evidence obtained by means of a violation of this Statute or internationally recognized human rights shall not be admissible if: (a) The violation causes substantial doubt on the reliability of the evidence; or (b) The admission of the evidence would be antithetical to and would seriously damage the integrity of the proceedings.[84]

Prior to March 1998, delegates could not agree on how to define or refer to human rights in this provision.[85] During the March–April 1998 session of the Preparatory Committee, the phrase 'internationally recognized human rights' was coined and replaced 'internationally protected human rights' in article 69(7).[86] The latter phrase was intended to include soft law instruments, such as criminal justice norms and standards developed and recognized by the United Nations.[87] Problems arose, however, with the reference to 'protected' rights, which tended to suggest that some international human rights are not protected without offering more guidance.[88] By replacing 'protected' with 'recognized', drafters hoped to remedy this ambiguity and allow for all internationally recognized human rights norms to benefit the accused.[89] Another debate leading up to the Rome Diplomatic Conference was whether only 'universally' recognized human rights may be applied by the Court.[90] Delegates agreed that this reference could unduly limit the Court and decided to replace it with 'internationally' so as to be specific but flexible and allow for 'growth and application'.[91]

---

[82] R Jennings and A Watts, *Oppenheim's International Law*, 9th edn (Longman, Harlow 1992) 1280.

[83] Robinson (n. 1) 75.

[84] DK Piragoff, 'Article 69' in O Triffterer (ed.), *Commentary on the Rome Statute of the International Criminal Court*, 2nd edn (CH Beck/Hart/Nomos 2008) 1301, 1333.

[85] Ibid. 1309.   [86] Ibid. 1310.

[87] 1996 Preparatory Committee Report (n. 29) para. 289, cited in Piragoff, ibid. 1333.

[88] Piragoff, ibid. 1310.   [89] Ibid.

[90] In this regard, notice the difference between articles 21(3) and 69(7), which refer to '*internationally* recognized' and article 7(1)(h) (regarding persecution as a crime against humanity), which refers to grounds of persecution 'that are *universally* recognized as impermissible under international law' (emphasis added).

[91] Piragoff (n. 84) 1333.

Against this backdrop, it is interesting to observe that almost no commentators have suggested that the term 'internationally recognized human rights' is sufficiently broad to include non-treaty and non-customary norms. It is variously understood to include international human rights standards that have a *jus cogens* character, have a general customary legal character, are contained in one of the seven 'global' or 'core' international human rights instruments or are in the *Universal Declaration of Human Rights* (1948).[92] A brief survey reveals that the term is used 'extensively in international relations and appears to be a generally accepted standard of reference but that its content is neither precisely defined nor consistently detailed'.[93] As for regional human rights standards, such as those contained in the *European Convention on Human Rights* (1950) (*ECHR*),[94] it has been suggested that the term 'internationally recognized' excludes their application.[95] Others have suggested that, to the extent regional bodies 'have interpreted identical or substantially similar provisions, their rulings could be used as persuasive interpretive tools to flesh out the meaning of the provisions of the global treaties, and in addition be considered a binding part of "internationally recognized human rights" when the issue concerns the territory or nationals of a state that is party to one of the regional treaties'.[96] Despite the views of many commentators, however, the Court – which has to date refrained from explaining its approach to and the content of article 21(3) – has frequently invoked soft law instruments as well as regional treaties and jurisprudence under this provision when determining issues of international criminal procedure.[97] In conclusion, there is no consensus on the content of internationally recognized human rights as a source of law, which is consistent with the larger debate about the content of international human rights. And while the International Court of Justice has expressly recognized an obligation under general international law to respect fundamental human rights, it has deftly avoided identifying the source of 'fundamental' rights, avoiding

---

[92] Ibid.; Verhoeven (n. 74) 14–15; Hafner and Binder (n. 69) 186–89; Roht-Arriaza (n. 69) 2. However, R Young has suggested that the term is sufficiently broad to encompass soft law instruments: '"Internationally Recognized Human Rights" before the International Criminal Court' (January 2011) 60 Int'l Crim LQ 189, 193, 205–06.

[93] Hafner and Binder (n. 69) 183.   [94] *ECHR* (n. 38).

[95] Hafner and Binder (n. 69) 187–88.

[96] Roht-Arriaza (n. 69) 2. For a slight variation of this argument, see also D Sheppard, 'The International Criminal Court and "Internationally Recognized Human Rights": Understanding Article 21(3) of the Rome Statute' (2010) 10 Int'l Crim L Rev 43, 65.

[97] See Sheppard, ibid. 50–53 and Young (n. 92) 205 for a discussion of the relevant case law; G Sluiter, 'Human Rights Protection in the ICC Pre-Trial Phase' in C Stahn and G Sluiter (eds.), *The Emerging Practice of the International Criminal Court* (Brill 2009) 459, 466; R Clark, 'Article 106' in O Triffterer (ed.), *Commentary on the Rome Statute of the International Criminal Court*, 2nd edn (CH Beck/Hart/Nomos 2008) 1663, 1665; *Prosecutor* v. *Lubanga Dyilo*, Decision on the Final System of Disclosure and the Establishment of a Timetable, ICC-01/04–01/06, 15 May 2006, Annex I, paras. 2–3.

references to custom for example.[98] Whatever meaning is to be given to article 21(3), the Rome Statute at a minimum recognizes customary international human rights, treaties and general principles as applicable sources of law in article 21(1)(b) of the Rome Statute, as confirmed by the Court.[99]

3.5 Reconciling articles 21(3) and 22

Apart from where a provision in the Rome Statute conflicts with a *jus cogens* norm and thereby becomes void or inapplicable,[100] what content can be given to article 21(3)? Should it have any other role to play in the interpretation and application of crimes in the Rome Statute? It appears that the motivation for article 21(3) was to protect the rights of the accused and that these rights were envisaged as mainly procedural. However, a suspect or accused may have other rights protected under customary international law, a treaty ratified by the State of which he or she is a national or a general principle of law. In this regard, what role, if any, could these rights have where the Court interprets the definition of a crime to be in conflict with such a right or where States Parties include a crime in the Rome Statute that does this? Does article 21(3) give the suspect or accused the right to challenge the interpretation and application of crimes in the Rome Statute which conflict with such rights? It is submitted that it does.

For example, were the Court to interpret the crime of directly and publicly inciting others to commit genocide to include hate speech, could the suspect or accused not rely on article 21(3) to argue that the Court's interpretation conflicts with his or her right to freedom of expression, assuming that this right was protected under customary international law, a treaty ratified by the relevant State or a general principle of the law and the hate speech had not been criminalized under international law?[101] Here, international human

---

[98] B Simma and P Alston, 'The Sources of Human Rights Law: Custom, Jus Cogens, and General Principles' (1988–1989) 12 Australian Ybk Int'l L 82, 105–06 (citing *Corfu Channel Case (United Kingdom* v. *Albania)* [1949] ICJ Rep. 4, 22: 'obligations . . . based . . . on certain general and well-recognized principles', among them 'elementary considerations of humanity').

[99] Article 21(1)(b) states: 'The Court shall apply: . . . In the second place, where appropriate, applicable treaties and the principles and rules of international law, including the established principles of the international law of armed conflict'; Schabas (n. 24) 93; Schabas (n. 65) 339.

[100] Article 53, *Vienna Convention* (1969); Jennings and Watts (n. 82) 1282.

[101] Article 19(3), *ICCPR* (n. 38) provides: 'The exercise of the rights provided for in paragraph 2 of this article [which includes freedom of expression] carries with it special duties and responsibilities. It may therefore be subject to certain restrictions, but these shall only be such as are *provided by law* and are necessary: (a) For respect of the rights or reputations of others; (b) For the protection of national security or of public order (ordre public), or of public health or morals' (emphasis added). On this point, it is interesting to note that the *travaux préparatoires* for the *Genocide Convention* (1948) reveal a clear intent

rights norms would be invoked in a manner consistent with the principle of legality, as there would be no concerns about retroactive application of the law. As well, if States Parties were to add to the Court's jurisdiction a panoply of terrorism-related offences which violated the suspect's or accused's right to liberty or freedom of association – again assuming these were protected by an applicable source of law – could article 21(3) not be invoked by the accused to argue that the Court cannot apply these provisions to the extent that they are inconsistent with internationally recognized human rights? It is submitted that this role is ideal for article 21(3) of the Rome Statute. As for interpreting internationally recognized human rights to include custom, treaty law and general principles, this is particularly important given how difficult it is for the elements of custom – *opinio juris* and State practice – to be established in respect of human rights, which 'run between' a State and individuals within its jurisdiction as opposed to between States:

> The performance of most substantive human rights obligations . . . lacks this element of interaction proper; it does not "run between" States in any meaningful sense. Thus, one reason why the claims to the existence of such a number of substantive human rights obligations under customary law remain unconvincing, and even do violence to some degree, to the established formal criteria of custom, can be seen in the fact that an element of interaction – in a broad sense – is intrinsic to, and essential to, the kind of State practice leading to the formation of customary international law.[102]

Custom, treaties and general principles are recognized sources of law in article 38 of the Statute of the International Court of Justice but also in article 21 of the Rome Statute. While an international custom and a general principle of law would, by definition, meet the requirement of 'internationally recognized', care would have to be taken to ensure that the treaty applicable to the individual meets this requirement. A right contained in just one regional treaty but not in any widely ratified international treaty might fall short of this requirement. The role contemplated for article 21(3) would roughly resemble that which

---

to exclude hate speech from the definition of this crime and that the ICTR Appeals Chamber stopped short of holding that there is no norm under customary international law criminalizing hate speech: *Nahimana and Others* v. *Prosecutor*, Judgment, ICTR-99–52-A, 28 November 2007, paras. 692ff., 985; D Orentlicher, 'Criminalizing Hate Speech in the Crucible of Trial: Prosecutor v. Nahimana' (2005) 12 New England J Int'l & Comp L 17. See also A Cassese, 'The Influence of the European Court of Human Rights on International Criminal Tribunals – Some Methodological Remarks' in M Bergsmo (ed.), *Human Rights and Criminal Justice for the Downtrodden: Essays in Honour of Asbjørn Eide* (Martinus Nijhoff 2003) 157.

[102] Simma and Alston (n. 98) 99. The 'ICTR Appeals Chamber has referred to the International Covenant on Civil and Political Rights as well as the relevant regional human rights treaties as 'persuasive authority and evidence of international custom'. Schabas (n. 13) 81.

constitutional rights and freedoms or human rights play in many domestic criminal justice systems by virtue of their character as background individual rights, their status as relevant and applicable norms, and the presumption that the 'legislature' would not enact laws that are inconsistent with these norms.[103] It has therefore been said to be rich with potential because it could 'disallow' interpretations and applications of articles 6, 7, 8 and 8 *bis* of the Rome Statute 'to the extent they are incompatible with fundamental human rights standards or that they are discriminatory'.[104] Its role is therefore fundamental.

This understanding of article 21(3) would presume that definitions of crimes are consistent with the rights of the person being investigated, prosecuted or convicted, unless a rights violation is proven. Indeed, a leading comparative study on interpretation concluded that the 'higher courts of all countries [studied] also invoke certain "presumptions" as to legislative intention . . . [including] that the legislature intends its enactments to be constitutionally valid'.[105] Similarly, in the *Rights of Passage (Preliminary Objections)* case (1957), the International Court of Justice stated that 'it is a rule of interpretation that a text emanating from a Government must, in principle, be interpreted as producing and as intended to produce effects in accordance with existing law and not in violation of it'.[106] Article 21(3) may also be regarded as a subordination clause of sorts. Article 30(2) of the *Vienna Convention* (1969) prescribes: 'When a treaty specifies that it is subject to, or that it is not to be considered as incompatible with, an earlier or later treaty, the provisions of the other treaty prevail.'

> [W]hen a treaty in effect subordinates itself to extrinsic (treaty and customary) restrictions of this kind, the subordination must not be misunderstood. There is no attempt to construct a conceptual hierarchy between norms that are lower and higher in rank, as is the case with *jus cogens* . . . All

---

[103] A Ashworth, B Emmerson and A Macdonald, *Human Rights and Criminal Justice*, 2nd edn (Sweet & Maxwell 2007); R Clayton and H Tomlinson, *The Law of Human Rights*, vol. I, 2nd edn (Oxford University Press 2009) ss. 4.05–4.20. For example, it is not dissimilar to the role of fundamental human rights guarantees in the interpretation and application of criminal law in England. The *Human Rights Act* (1998) (HRA) incorporates the *EHCR* into domestic law. Article 3 of the HRA requires judges to 'interpret statutory provisions, so far as is possible, in such a way as is compatible with Convention rights', something that domestic judges in other jurisdictions have also had to do against the backdrop of their constitutions or bills of rights. Such mandates pose unique challenges in the realm of criminal law, where judges take seriously respect for the principle of legality.

[104] Schabas (n. 65) 398.

[105] RS Summers and M Taruffo, 'Interpretation and Comparative Analysis' in DN MacCormick and RS Summers (eds.), *Interpreting Statutes: A Comparative Study* (Dartmouth Publishing Company 1991) 461, 471.

[106] *Case Concerning Right of Passage over Indian Territory (Portugal v. India)*, Preliminary Objections [1957] ICJ Rep. 125, 142; Jennings and Watts (n. 82) 1275.

that transpires is that the authors of a given treaty deem fit to apply their text (in whole or in part) in a manner consistent with a normative matrix *dehors* the instrument.[107]

The presumption that articles 6, 7, 8 and 8 *bis* are interpreted and applied in a manner that does not offend international human rights of the individual investigated, prosecuted or convicted and does not adversely distinguish on prohibited grounds would place the evidentiary burden on the person claiming otherwise. As in domestic criminal justice systems, it is expected that this issue is likely to arise in respect of the 'outer edges' of crimes defined in the Rome Statute, whether they implicate recognized freedoms or not.[108] These will be the hard cases.

This role as a background presumption also happens to be consistent with the 'passive' construction and wording of article 21(3) as well as the 'active' wording of article 22. Such a role is markedly different from imputing to article 21(3) a mandate to interpret crimes in the Rome Statute in order to attain the maximum protection of victims' international human rights. The proposed relationship between these provisions is also consistent with the notion that the Rome Statute defines crimes within the Court's jurisdiction, not (customary) international human rights law (see article 22(3)).[109] Thus, with legality as a guiding interpretive principle for crimes in the Rome Statute, the interpretive principles prevalent in international human rights jurisprudence (e.g., effective) would lose much of their currency or could not convincingly be advanced solely by relying on the wording of article 21(3), an argument that implicitly asks one to ignore the wording of article 22(2) (which expressly refers to the devices of strict construction, prohibition against analogy and interpretation in favour of the individual being investigated, prosecuted or convicted in case of ambiguity).

Four caveats are in order. First, the principle of legality in article 22 applies to the interpretation of crimes and would not therefore have to guide interpretation of the scope and content of internationally recognized human rights.[110] Second, the 'background role' for article 21(3) – requiring that the interpretation of crimes in the Court's jurisdiction does not violate internationally recognized human rights of the person investigated, prosecuted or convicted – would not prevent the Court from deeming it a guiding interpretive principle for another part of the Rome Statute (e.g., fair trial provisions). For example, article 67 on rights of the accused is based on article 14(3) of the *ICCPR*

---

[107] Y Dinstein, 'Interaction Between Customary International Law and Treaties' (2006) 322 Recueil des Cours de l'Académie de Droit International 243, 392.

[108] Jeffries Jr (n. 33) 196.   [109] I am grateful to Thomas Weigend for this observation.

[110] International human rights scholars have observed that the interpretation of human rights is generally subject to what is variously termed teleological, dynamic, progressive, effective or liberal interpretation as well as interpretation consistent with the 'living tree' doctrine. See, e.g., Christoffersen (n. 6) 37.

(1966), and article 21(3) is a powerful aid to interpreting the general right to a fair hearing in the chapeau of this provision 'to keep pace with the progressive development of human rights law'.[111] Indeed, human rights have been invoked several times to interpret provisions of the Rome Statute consistent with this law. Human rights law has aided the interpretation of 'reasonable grounds to believe' in article 58, the right of the accused to disclosure of the ground for detention, the recognition of the possibility of ordering a stay of proceedings in the event of breaches of the rights of the suspect or accused and the right to habeas corpus.[112] International human rights treaties and soft law instruments have also usefully aided judges in resolving matters relating to victim participation and protection.[113]

Third, understanding 'internationally recognized human rights' as limited to custom, applicable treaties and general principles for purposes of interpreting articles 6, 7, 8 and 8 *bis* in the aforementioned manner would not prevent the Court from interpreting this term more broadly in another context to include soft law human rights instruments, for example.[114] Fourth, the role proposed for article 21(3) should not be understood as empowering judges to frustrate the intent of the Rome Statute's drafters or amenders to impose legally permissible limits on international human rights within it. For example, article 19(2) of the ICCPR (1966) guarantees inter alia the freedom to receive information, but article 19(3)(b) permits this right to be limited for the protection of national security.[115] Accordingly, article 21(3) could not convincingly be invoked to argue that article 72 of the Rome Statute, which permits the non-disclosure to a defendant of information that is protected for reasons of national security, is inconsistent with internationally recognized human rights.

In conclusion, the viability of legality as a primary or guiding interpretive principle for crimes in the Rome Statute is due in no small part to the detail contained in articles 6, 7, 8 and 8 *bis* and the maturation of international criminal law in recent years. Indeed, 'we are now heading for the formation of a fully-fledged body of law in this area'.[116] The existence of several treaties which have attained the status of custom as well as case law that has contributed to

---

[111] Schabas (n. 24) 98: 'Fair trial rights are set out in very comprehensive provisions elsewhere in the *Rome Statute*. The effect of article 21(3) is both to expand such texts, to the extent it may permit other procedural and substantive rights not listed in the provisions to be invoked before the Court, and also by ensuring that they apply to all proceedings before the Court, at every stage.'

[112] Schabas (n. 65) 399 and accompanying footnotes for case law citations. For some methodological remarks on interpreting rules of international criminal procedure arising from the Rome Statute, including the role of human rights, see C Safferling, *International Criminal Procedure* (Oxford University Press 2012) 109ff. (especially 120).

[113] Ibid. 399–400 and accompanying footnotes for citations.

[114] See, e.g., Hafner and Binder (n. 69); Roht-Arriaza (n. 69) 2; Piragoff and Robinson (n. 84) 1301, 1309, 1310, 1333.

[115] See article 72, Rome Statute.   [116] Cassese (n. 2) 7; Van Schaack (n. 38) 189.

crystallizing and clarifying the content of crimes under international law and defences to them has been key to making this transition possible.[117] Because of these developments, international criminal law is able gradually to move away from the substantive justice doctrine and towards strict legality.[118] Further, unlike international criminal law generally, the Rome Statute regime could be said to have a 'supreme court', the International Criminal Court, and a legislature, the Assembly of States Parties (ASP).[119] While the normative tensions underlying international criminal law may continue to play out in other respects, these tensions have, to some degree, been resolved for purposes of interpreting crimes within the jurisdiction of the Rome Statute.

As for the shape that the principle of legality will take, this is the focus of the next two Chapters, although it will ultimately be for judges to develop this through the Court's jurisprudence. Article 21(2) provides: 'The Court may apply principles and rules of law as interpreted in its previous decisions'. While not creating a binding system of precedents, article 21(2) is arguably intended to promote consistency and certainty in the jurisprudence of the Court.[120] By defining the contours of the principle of legality in its early case law and declaring it the centrepiece for interpreting crimes in the Rome Statute, the Court could go a long way towards realizing this goal.

3.6 Systemic integration dilemma

It has been argued that the principle of legality is the primary principle for guiding the interpretation of crimes in the Rome Statute. To a large degree, this position attenuates the normative tensions arising from international criminal law's identity crisis and its substantive justice origins. However, caution is needed so as not to overstate matters. This is because nothing has so far been said about the relationship between 'internationally recognized human rights' in article 21(3) and 'established principles of the international law of armed conflict' in article 21(1)(b) for purposes of interpretation. Although an examination of this relationship is beyond the scope of this study, it is necessary to highlight how this relationship will pose problems for the Court when taking applicable law into account for the purpose of interpreting crimes in the Rome Statute. Recall that article 31(3)(c) of the *Vienna Convention* (1969) provides: 'There shall be taken into account, together with the context: ... any relevant rules of international law applicable in the relations between the parties.'[121]

---

[117] Cassese, ibid. 40–41.
[118] Ibid. 10, 40. This evolution bears some resemblance to that experienced in countries where common law offences were gradually codified in or displaced by criminal law statutes.
[119] See Chapter 4 on the separation of powers doctrine.
[120] McAuliffe de Guzman (n. 69) 701, 711.
[121] Hafner and Binder note that article 21(3) should be interpreted in light of article 31(3)(c) of the *Vienna Convention* (1969) but do not identify the possibility of human rights

In article 21, international human rights and humanitarian law appear to have been inadvertently cited hierarchically, with the former having supremacy. In practice, however, their relationship to one another and to international criminal law is complex and seems to defy such absolute and abstract ordering. It is well known that many international crimes have 'emerged directly' from international humanitarian law.[122] However, it is also true that the crime of genocide and other crimes against humanity 'belong more properly to the law of human rights', as the former developed to address atrocities committed in peacetime, and the latter was conceived to deal with Nazi persecution of Germans, which, at the time, was understood as not being covered by international humanitarian law.[123] As well, international human rights is said to have had a 'humanizing' effect on international humanitarian law, and the latter a 'humanitarianizing' effect on the former.[124]

Examples of the 'humanizing' trend include: (1) expanding the notion of 'protected persons';[125] (2) otherwise using human rights norms to interpret the content of international humanitarian law and thereby offer greater protection to victims;[126] and (3) trying to recognize minimum standards of humanity.[127] In respect of international criminal law, international human rights considerations have also had a 'humanizing' influence[128] with the advent of greater protections for the accused but also in respect of the definitions of crimes, including (1) the criminalization under international law of some violations of international humanitarian law committed during an armed conflict not of an international character;[129] (2) the removal of a nexus that previously required crimes against humanity to have been committed in connection with an armed conflict;[130] and (3) the emergence of an extensive list of acts amounting to crimes against humanity in article 7 of the Rome Statute that is 'replete

---

and humanitarian law conflicting with one another, the systemic integration dilemma, stating simply that applicable law should be interpreted consistent with international human rights. Hafner and Binder (n. 69) 171.

[122] See generally Meron (n. 9) 112ff.

[123] W Schabas, 'Lex Specialis? Belt and Suspenders? The Parallel Operation of Human Rights Law and the Law of Armed Conflict, and the Conundrum of Jus ad Bellum' (2007) 40:2 Israel L Rev 592, 602.

[124] J d'Aspremont, 'Articulating International Human Rights and International Humanitarian Law: Conciliatory Interpretation under the Guise of Conflict of Norms-Resolution' in M Fitzmaurice and P Merkouris (eds.), *The Interpretation and Application of the European Convention on Human Rights: Legal and Practical Implications* (Martinus Nijhoff 2013) 4, 26.

[125] Meron (n. 9) 54ff.   [126] Ibid. 68.

[127] Ibid. 82ff.; A Eide, A Rosas and T Meron, 'Combating Lawlessness in Gray Zone Conflicts Through Minimum Humanitarian Standards' (1995) 89 AJIL 215.

[128] Cassese (n. 101); E Møse, 'Impact of Human Rights Conventions on the Two Ad Hoc Tribunals' in M Bergsmo (ed.), *Human Rights and Criminal Justice for the Downtrodden: Essays in Honour of Asbjørn Eide* (Martinus Nijhoff 2003) 179.

[129] Meron (n. 9) 155ff.   [130] Ibid. 116–21.

with language derived from sources of human rights law'.[131] In respect of crimes against humanity, while '[a]ll delegations agreed that the Court's jurisdiction relates to serious violations of international criminal law, not international human rights law',[132] it is admitted by some that it is hard to distinguish the list of acts in article 7 of the Rome Statute from serious violations of human rights apart from their 'egregiousness and systemic nature'.[133]

Where international human rights norms are invoked to interpret crimes that result in the violation of non-derogable rights, such as torture, rape and enslavement as crimes against humanity,[134] their use is not terribly controversial. However, where international human rights and humanitarian law norms diverge in their content and this content is relevant to the interpretation of a crime in the Rome Statute, a problem of 'systemic integration' arises. To appreciate the importance and sensitivity of this dilemma, it might be helpful to recall that crimes against humanity as defined in article 7 can occur during times of armed conflict, peace and occupation and can include 'other inhumane acts of a similar character intentionally causing great suffering, or serious injury to body or to mental or physical health'.[135] Further, the Court has hinted at the possibility that private persons may perpetrate crimes against humanity.[136] With this in mind, the following should also be recalled: (1) international human rights treaties do apply extraterritorially, although there are differing views on the conditions that need to be met for this to occur;[137] (2) proportionality assessments under international human rights law differ

---

[131]   Ibid. 68; Schabas (n. 65) 397.

[132]   D Robinson, 'Defining "Crimes against Humanity" at the Rome Conference' (1999) 93 AJIL 43, 53.

[133]   T Meron, 'The Humanization of Humanitarian Law' (2000) 94 AJIL 239, 265.

[134]   Møse (n. 128) 184–85.

[135]   Article 7(1)(k), Rome Statute; M Boot, R Dixon and C Hall (revised by C Hall), 'Article 7' in O Triffterer (ed.), *Commentary on the Rome Statute of the International Criminal Court*, 2nd edn (CH Beck/Hart/Nomos 2008) 159, 230ff.

[136]   *Prosecutor* v. *Bemba Gombo*, Decision Pursuant to Article 61(7)(a) and (b) of the Rome Statute on the Charges of the Prosecutor Against Jean-Pierre Bemba Gombo, ICC-01/05–01/08, 15 June 2009, para. 81: 'The requirement of "a State or organizational policy" implies that the attack follows a regular pattern. Such a policy may be made by groups of persons who govern a specific territory *or by any organization with the capability to commit a widespread or systematic attack against any civilian population.*' (emphasis added). For a challenge to this interpretation, see *Situation in the Republic of Kenya*, Decision Pursuant to Article 15 of the Rome Statute on the Authorization of an Investigation into the Situation in the Republic of Kenya, Dissenting Opinion of Judge Hans-Peter Kaul, ICC-01/09, 31 March 2010.

[137]   See, e.g., MJ Dennis, 'Application of Human Rights Treaties Extraterritorially in Times of Armed Conflict and Military Occupation' (2005) 99 AJIL 119; H Duffy, 'Human Rights Litigation and the 'War on Terror'' (2008) 90: 871 Int'l Rev of the Committee of the Red Cross 573, 581ff.; FJ Hampson, 'The Relationship between International Humanitarian Law and Human Rights Law from the Perspective of a Human Rights Treaty Body' (2009)

from those under international humanitarian law;[138] (3) permissive rights limitations and derogability vary depending on whether international human rights or humanitarian law is applied to a given situation;[139] (4) international human rights do not automatically cease to apply during times of war or occupation;[140] and (5) while it remains controversial whether international human rights obligations can be borne by non-State actors,[141] international humanitarian law binds all 'parties to the conflict'.[142] Where rights or norms in these two bodies of law diverge or conflict[143] and could aid in the interpretation of crimes in the Rome Statute, what is the Court to do?

Decisions of international criminal tribunals illustrate that questions about the application and interpretation of international human rights and international humanitarian law are not likely to go away any time soon. In *Prosecutor* v. *Brima, Kamara and Kanu* (2008), the Appeals Chamber of the Special Court for Sierra Leone overturned a Trial Chamber decision by recognizing forced marriage as an 'inhumane act' amounting to a crime against humanity.[144] In its reasoning, the Appeals Chamber referred to international human rights instruments. While this decision has been praised,[145] the impact of international human rights on crimes against humanity in other cases has been criticized for inappropriately diluting international humanitarian law. For example, in *Prosecutor* v. *Gotovina* (2007),[146] an ICTY Trial Chamber had to determine whether,

---

90:871 Int'l Rev of the Committee of the Red Cross 549, 566ff.; W Kälin and J Künzli, *The Law of International Human Rights Protection* (Oxford University Press 2009) 132ff.

[138] D Kretzmer, 'Rethinking Application of IHL in Non-International Armed Conflicts' (2009) 42 Israel L Rev 32, 50ff.

[139] See, e.g., UNHRC, 'General Comment No. 29' (2001) UN Doc. CCPR/C/21/Rev.1/Add.11.

[140] *Legality of the Threat or Use of Nuclear Weapons*, Advisory Opinion [1996] ICJ Rep. 226, 240; *Legal Consequences of the Construction of a Wall in the Occupied Territory*, Advisory Opinion [2004] ICJ Rep. 136, 178; *Case Concerning Armed Activities on the Territory of the Congo (DRC* v. *Uganda)* [2005] ICJ Rep. 116, 242–23; Meron (n. 9) 73ff.

[141] Kälin and Künzli (n. 137) 81ff.

[142] Common article 3 to the *Geneva Conventions* (1949); Kälin and Künzli (n. 137) 159ff.

[143] The ILC has formulated a definition of conflict in respect of treaties, but it seems generally useful: '[T]he test of whether two treaties deal with the "same subject matter" is resolved through the assessment of whether the fulfilment of the obligation under one treaty affects the fulfilment of the obligation of another. This "affecting" might then take place either as strictly preventing the fulfilment of the other obligation or undermining its object and purpose in one or another way.' M Koskenniemi, 'Fragmentation of International Law: Difficulties Arising from the Diversification and Expansion of International Law: Report of the Study Group of the International Law Commission' (4 April 2006) UN Doc. A/CN.4/L.682, 109.

[144] Also known as the 'AFRC Trial', Judgment, SCSL-04–16-A, 22 February 2008, para. 175ff.

[145] TA Doherty, 'The Application of Human Rights Treaties in the Development of Domestic and International Law: A Personal Perspective' (2009) 22:4 LJIL 753.

[146] Decision on Several Motions Challenging Jurisdiction, ICTY-06–90-PT, 19 March 2007, paras. 24–28.

during hostilities, the crime against humanity of deportation or forcible transfer should be interpreted consistent with article 49 of the fourth *Geneva Convention* (1949),[147] which forms the basis of the war crimes definition for this conduct but is limited to a situation of occupation.[148] The defendant was charged with deportation or forcible transfer as a crime against humanity on account of allegedly shelling a territory in which civilians were located, thereby causing them to leave, *before* proceeding to occupy it. The question was whether occupation is an element to deportation as a crime against humanity. The ICTY ruled that it is not.[149] The Trial Chamber seemed to presuppose that, by virtue of crimes against humanity and war crimes existing as two categories of crimes in its governing statute, the laws of war are not relevant to interpreting the crime in question irrespective of the existence of an armed conflict.

The point has been made elsewhere that it is futile and dangerous to abstractly fix the relationship between international human rights and humanitarian law and that their interaction with one another must be assessed, for example, on the basis of individual norms.[150] Others have looked to article 31(3)(c) of the *Vienna Convention* (1969) and the corresponding interpretive principle of systemic integration to provide an appropriate starting point for understanding this issue. On its own, article 31(3)(c) offers little guidance except to state that rules of international law, as opposed to policy considerations, '*shall* be taken into account'[151] and that these rules must be both 'relevant' and 'applicable'. These international rules can originate from custom, general principles and, 'where applicable', other treaties.[152] As previously mentioned, there is a distinction between invoking 'relevant' and 'applicable' international rules as interpretive aids to clarify the meaning of text in a treaty and applying those rules directly to the facts in a case. As interpretive aids, international human rights and humanitarian law would provide the 'background' against which articles 6, 7, 8 and 8 *bis* would be interpreted and applied.[153]

---

[147] 75 UNTS 287 (adopted 12 August 1949, entered into force 2 October 1950).

[148] Article 49 provides: 'Individual or mass forcible transfers, as well as deportations of protected persons from occupied territory to the territory of the Occupying Power or to that of any other country, occupied or not, are prohibited, regardless of their motive.'

[149] For a critique of this decision, see P Akhavan, 'Reconciling Crimes against Humanity with the Laws of War: Human Rights, Armed Conflict, and the Limits of Progressive Jurisprudence' (2008) 6:1 J Int'l Crim Justice 21.

[150] See, e.g., R Cryer, 'The Interplay of Human Rights and Humanitarian Law: The Approach of the ICTY' (2010) 14:3 J Conflict & Security L 511, 526–27; A Orakhelashvili, 'The Interaction between Human Rights and Humanitarian Law: Fragmentation, Conflict, Parallelism, or Convergence?' (2008) 19:1 EJIL 161, 182.

[151] Emphasis added.

[152] See Koskenniemi (n. 143) 215, 218ff. for a review of article 31(3)(c) case law.

[153] Ibid. 231; *Case Concerning Oil Platforms (Islamic Republic of Iran v. United States of America)*, Separate Opinion of Judge Kooijmans [2003] ICJ Rep. 161.

Custom can assist the Court with interpreting the Rome Statute where (1) the latter is 'unclear or open-textured and its meaning is determined by reference to a developed body of international law'; or (2) 'the terms used [in the Rome Statute] have a recognized meaning in customary international law to which the parties can therefore be taken to have intended to refer'.[154] This second matter is the focus of a codification study in Chapters 7 and 8. As for general principles, it is thought that the following two presumptions underlie the concept of systemic integration in article 31(3)(c): (1) a positive presumption that parties are taken 'to refer to general principles of international law for all questions which [the treaty] does not itself resolve in express terms or in a different way'; and (2) a negative presumption that Parties ratifying treaties 'intend not to act inconsistently with generally recognized principles of international law or with previous treaty obligations towards third States'.[155] Finally, treaty law can assist with the interpretation of the Rome Statute where (1) the individual is the national of a State that has ratified the relevant treaty; or (2) where a treaty 'can reasonably be considered to express the common intentions or understanding of all members as to the meaning of the . . . term concerned [in the Rome Statute]'.[156] The role of these interpretive aids over time and their relationship to one another are elaborated upon in Chapter 9.

The principle of systemic integration has been usefully described as a 'master-key in a large building':

> Mostly the use of individual keys will suffice to open the door to a particular room. But, in exceptional circumstances, it is necessary to utilize a master-key which permits access to all of the rooms. In the same way, a treaty will normally be capable of interpretation and application according to its own terms and context. But in hard cases, it may be necessary to invoke an express justification for looking outside the four corners of a particular treaty to its place in the broader framework of international law, applying general principles of international law.[157]

While this analogy implies some common architecture – rooms in one building – the limits of this analogy are tested with respect to conflicts between international rules arising from *different* branches of law with overlapping subject matter but distinct purposes or normativities. For example, while the development of international human rights law and international humanitarian law have increasingly converged since the end of the Second World War, their origins are distinct, and the development of both has had an impact on

---

[154] Koskenniemi (n. 143) 235.   [155] Ibid. 234.

[156] Ibid. 238–39 (citing J Pauwelyn, *Conflict of Norms in Public International Law: How WTO Law Relates to Other Rules of International Law* (Cambridge University Press 2003) 257–63).

[157] C McLachlan, 'The Principle of Systemic Integration and Article 31(3)(c) of the Vienna Convention' (2005) 54:2 Int'l Comp LQ 279, 281.

international criminal law, which is arguably beginning to develop a strict legality normativity that is distinct from them. In this sense, are we really talking about rooms in one building or a street block with neighbouring buildings, each containing its own rooms or cluster of treaties that have developed over the years? On this point, systemic integration as an interpretive principle is intended to pre-empt norm conflicts by mandating the interpretation of treaty rules in harmony with background international rules, thereby promoting coherence rather than fragmentation in the international legal system.[158] Further, it has been suggested that international human rights law and international humanitarian law, while distinct, do share some values, which allow for each branch of law to be interpreted in light of the other.[159]

However, in the context of international criminal law, we do not have the Rome Statute being harmonized with one norm but potentially two categories of norms – international human rights and humanitarian law – which may jostle for priority in a particular case. While harmonizing international human rights law and international humanitarian law will often be possible,[160] some areas of potential conflict include targeted killings, preventive security detention, positive obligations during occupation, as well as the permissible use of force during occupation and non-international armed conflicts.[161] To the extent that these debates arise in cases of crimes against humanity, war crimes or aggression before the Court, it remains to be seen what role, if any, article 21(3) will have in their resolution.

In terms of general legal techniques for furthering systemic integration, the rule of *lex specialis* has featured prominently in academic debates but has not fared so well. Its two roles have been described as follows:

> A particular rule may be considered an application of the general rule in a given circumstance. That is to say, it may give instructions on what a general rule requires in the case at hand. Alternatively, a particular rule may be conceived as an exception to the general rule. In this case, the

---

[158] Ibid. 286, 281.

[159] C Droege, 'Elective Affinities? Human Rights and Humanitarian Law' (2008) 90:871 Int'l Rev of the Committee of the Red Cross 501, 505ff.

[160] Ibid. 524.

[161] M Milanovic, 'A Norm Conflict Perspective on the Relationship Between International and Humanitarian Law and Human Rights Law' (2009) 14:3 J Conflict & Security L 459; I Scobbie, 'Principle or Pragmatics? The Relationship between Human Rights Law and the Law of Armed Conflict' (2009) 14:3 J Conflict & Security L 449, 455; S Vité, 'The Interrelation of the Law of Occupation and Economic, Social and Cultural Rights: The Examples of Food, Health and Property' (2008) 90:871 Int'l Rev of the Committee of the Red Cross 629; M Sassòli and LM Olson, 'The Relationship between International Humanitarian and Human Rights Law Where it Matters: Admissible Killing and Internment of Fighters in Non-International Armed Conflicts' (2008) 90:871 Int'l Rev of the Committee of the Red Cross 599; Duffy (n. 137) 581ff.; Droege (n. 159) 525ff.

particular derogates from the general rule. The maxim *lex specialis derogat legi generali* is usually dealt with as a conflict rule. However, it need not be limited to conflict.[162]

While there is support for the idea that whichever branch of law prevails in a given situation, it can be enriched or informed by rules in the other branch,[163] commentators seriously question the usefulness of the *lex specialis* rule in both of its roles – as 'harmonizer' and as 'conflict resolver'.[164] The International Law Commission (ILC) has also expressed the need for caution in its application where it would result in undermining the substantive rights of treaty Parties or third-Party beneficiaries.[165] In particular, it provides no clear guidance on the meaning of special or general, especially where the norms being compared 'belong' to different branches of law.[166] Further, international law does not contain a hierarchy of substantive norms and therefore cannot establish, for example, whether environmental protection is more special than human rights law, the law of the sea or trade law.[167] Because the rule cannot describe in abstract terms the whole relationship between two areas of law, the analysis and interpretation of norms needs to occur on an individual basis, taking into account their purpose and the context in which they would be applied.[168] For example:

> When determining whether to apply international human rights or inter-national humanitarian law, consideration needs to be given to the under-lying object and purposes of these regimes, the former being premised on the use of law-enforcement powers and the latter centred on the battlefield

---

[162] M Koskenniemi, 'Study on the Function and Scope of the Lex Specialis Rule and the Question of "Self Contained Regimes"' (2004) UN Doc. ILC(LVI)/SG/FIL/CRD.1 and Add.1, 4, cited in Droege (n. 159) 524.

[163] N Prud'homme, '*Lex Specialis:* Oversimplifying a More Complex and Multifaceted Rela-tionship?'(2007) 40:2 Israel L Rev 355; L Doswald-Beck, 'The Right to Life in Armed Conflict: Does International Humanitarian Law Provide all the Answers?'(2006) 88:864 Int'l Rev of the Committee of the Red Cross 881; Droege (n. 159) 522–23; Orakhelashvili (n. 150). For opposition to the 'complementarity approach', see, e.g., B Bowring, 'Frag-mentation, Lex Specialis and the Tensions in the Jurisprudence of the European Court of Human Rights' (2009) 14 J Conflict & Security L 485.

[164] See, e.g., A Lindroos, 'Addressing the Norm Conflicts in a Fragmented System: the Doc-trine of *Lex Specialis*' (2005) 74 Nordic J Int'l L 27; Prud'homme, ibid.; C McCarthy, 'Legal Conclusion or Interpretive Process? *Lex Specialis* and the Applicability of International Human Rights Standards' in R Arnold and N Quénivet (eds.), *International Humanitarian Law and Human Rights Law* (Martinus Nijhoff 2008) 101; Schabas (n. 123) 602.

[165] ILC, 'Conclusions of the work of the Study Group on Fragmentation of International Law: Difficulties arising from the Diversification and Expansion of International Law' (2006) II Ybk of the ILC, Conclusions 10 and 26.

[166] Lindroos (n. 164) 41–42.   [167] Ibid.

[168] Prud'homme (n. 163) 355; McCarthy (n. 164); Lindroos (n. 164) 41–42; Doswald-Beck (n. 163) 903.

(with the exception of occupation). To apply international human rights is therefore only realistic if it is feasible to use the means of law enforcement, thus only in operations conducted by security forces with some effective control over the situation. In those cases, international human rights constitute the *lex specialis*. In combat situations, international humanitarian law constitutes the *lex specialis*.[169]

Gradually, the Court may wish to develop a set of criteria it will consider when determining whether to invoke the interpretive aid of international human rights or humanitarian law.[170] Such criteria would avoid abstractly fixing the relationship between these fields of law for purposes of interpretation but at the same time would contribute to legal certainty and methodological reasoning. Going forward, the Court might wish to consider whether article 21(3) mandates it having a role in the harmonization of international humanitarian law and international human rights law. It might also wish to consider whether it would apply article 21(3) as a conflict resolution provision that favours international human rights over humanitarian law where there is a genuine ambiguity as to which should aid the Court in its interpretation of a crime. The Court should, in the author's view, not lightly attribute these functions to this provision.

On the issue of harmonization, while this goal may generally be desirable in an abstract sense, caution must be exercised to ensure that the fruits of this interaction do not affect interpretive reasoning in a manner that is inconsistent with the principle of legality and other criminal justice norms, such as fair labelling. To this end, the text of articles 6, 7, 8 and 8 *bis* should retain their primacy as should the aspirational strict legal normativity of international criminal justice. In the past, while international human rights have taken judges in the direction of protecting the rights of the accused, some have argued that it has more often led them to adopt victim-focused teleological reasoning.[171] With respect to interpreting articles 6, 7, 8 and 8 *bis* of the Rome Statute, such a tendency sits uncomfortably with the principle of legality. Further, in spite of the trend towards complementarity and mutual influence of these branches of law, these areas of law are and should perhaps remain distinct.

On the issue of conflict resolution, it should not be assumed that the invocation of article 21(3) will yield consistent results on the ground in terms of protecting individuals. In fact, there are many rights that are non-derogable under international humanitarian law but derogable under international human

---

[169] Droege (n. 159) 536.
[170] Prud'homme (n. 163) suggests the idea of developing criteria.
[171] Robinson (n. 1) 930.

rights law.[172] Similarly, while international humanitarian law admits limitations to rights based on military necessity,[173] it is not always the case that humanitarian law protection will be lower than that under human rights law.[174]

In light of the systemic integration challenges that are likely to confront the Court in the years to come and the need to determine what role, if any, article 21(3) is to have in addressing these challenges, it seems prudent for international criminal lawyers to join larger debates that could be constructive in shaping their thoughts on this issue. The relationship between international human rights law and international humanitarian law is also a challenge for human rights treaty monitoring bodies,[175] the International Committee of the Red Cross[176] and courts,[177] including the International Court of Justice (ICJ). The ICJ has confirmed that both regimes may be applicable in a given situation but has offered no guidance on how to determine which normative environment is most relevant, seeming to resile from its previous mention of the *lex specialis* rule being of assistance.[178] More generally, courts and the ILC have, in recent years, confronted the issue of how best to operationalize systemic integration as an interpretive principle in article 31(3)(c) of the *Vienna Convention* (1969).[179] Neither doctrine to date has been able to reduce the discretion of judges in this regard, to increase certainty.[180] However, it is hoped that the fruits of these debates can be brought to bear on the work of the Court so as to form a 'coherent and meaningful' part of its interpretive reasoning that reflects realities on the ground.[181]

---

[172] Droege (n. 159) 521.   [173] See, e.g., Pictet (n. 8).

[174] Orakhelashvili (n. 150) 161.   [175] See, e.g., Hampson (n. 137) 549.

[176] H Krieger, 'A Conflict of Norms: The Relationship between Humanitarian Law and Human Rights Law in the ICRC Customary Law Study' (2006) 11 J Conflict & Security 265.

[177] HJ Heintze, 'On the Relationship between Human Rights Law Protection and International Humanitarian Law' (2004) 86:856 Int'l Rev of the Committee of the Red Cross 789; Droege (n. 159) 507ff.

[178] *Legality of the Threat or Use of Nuclear Weapons* (n. 140) 240; *Legal Consequences of the Construction of a Wall in the Occupied Territory* (n. 140) 191–94; *Case Concerning Armed Activities on the Territory of the Congo* (n. 140) 242–43.

[179] See Koskenniemi (n. 143) 40ff., 85ff. for a review of the relevant case law.

[180] d'Aspremont (n. 124) 28–29.   [181] Ibid. 208.

4

Challenges to the principle of legality

4.1 Introduction

In the previous Chapter, the normative tensions underlying international criminal law were described and their appearance in the Rome Statute made plain. It was argued that article 21(3), which obliges judges to interpret and apply the Rome Statute in a manner consistent with internationally recognized human rights, and article 22, which contains a strict legality standard, could be understood as entrenching two (mostly) opposing normativities for the purpose of interpreting crimes in the Statute. Absent any harmonizing methodology, judges favouring the liberal interpretation of crimes could invoke the former provision, and those favouring their strict construction could rely on the latter. A brief review of the ordinary meaning of these provisions in their context and in light of their object and purpose as well as their drafting histories, however, unearthed their potential to be reconciled, and an attempt at such coherence was made. The main thesis advanced was that the legality imperative in article 22 is to be the guiding interpretive principle for crimes in the Rome Statute against a background presumption that the Statute's drafters defined the crimes in a manner that does not violate the internationally recognized human rights of the person investigated, prosecuted or convicted. However, the content of the legality principle for purposes of interpretation was not examined in detail. In the absence of such an inquiry, it is difficult to envision how, in practice, article 22 might assist judges in carrying out their interpretive work. Accordingly, the goal of the next two Chapters is to fully unpack the content of the *nullum crimen sine lege* imperative with a view to achieving the principled 'operationalization' of article 22 for purposes of interpreting the crimes in the Rome Statute.

The principle of legality is 'solidly embedded' in international criminal law, meaning the Court 'may only apply substantive criminal rules that existed at the time of commission of the alleged crime'.[1] In fact, the Appeals Chamber of the Special Tribunal for Lebanon recently held that legality is a

---

[1] A Cassese, *International Criminal Law*, 2nd edn (Oxford University Press 2008) 44. For a discussion of intertemporality and the Rome regime, see Chapter 9, Section 9.3.2.

peremptory norm.[2] In spite of this and advances in international human rights law, it has been observed that international criminal law statutes, as compared to their domestic counterparts, are relatively sparse and vague. While some have argued that this difference is due to the understanding that international criminal law provisions will be domestically enacted and thereby acquire greater specificity, it has also been posited that the 'principal explanation for the deficiency in . . . [these] texts . . . is the lack of technical expertise of the officials who draft them'.[3] In fact, international tribunals have found that the principle of legality at the international level is not as strict as it might be in certain national jurisdictions and that international criminal prohibitions that are not very detailed do not offend the principle of legality at the international level.[4] As well, in light of custom as a source of international criminal law, the legality principle at the international level admits unwritten law, being reformulated as *nullum crimen sine jure*.[5] However, these general descriptions are not particularly fitting for the Rome Statute, which comes closer than any other international criminal statute to resembling its domestic counterparts. As well, this facial difference between national and international texts might be misleading, suggesting that domestic legal systems have achieved perfect concordance with strict legality.

In practice, many domestic legal systems that profess respect for the principle of legality may well admit various exceptions to its application, thereby diluting its actual force and finding a balance between certainty and flexibility. As will be demonstrated, international criminal law is no exception to this trend. In hard cases, where the law has not quite caught up with the impugned and obviously antisocial conduct in question, judges at bottom are confronted with a perfectly unbearable tension between sending a message to society that the relevant conduct is impermissible and the notion that criminal law is limited in its reach to conduct that has previously been defined as criminal.[6] The judge might reason: why should the accused benefit from the limited imagination of the legislator when criminalizing abhorrent conduct and thereby go unpunished for conduct that he or she must have known to be wrong? President and judge Sir David Baragwanath of the Special Tribunal for Lebanon recently wrote:

---

[2] Interlocutory Decision on the Applicable Law: Terrorism, Conspiracy, Homicide Perpetration, Cumulative Charging, STL-11–01/I, 16 February 2011, para. 76.

[3] H Kelsen, *Peace Through Law* (University of North Carolina Press 1944) 116, cited in MC Bassiouni (ed.), 'Principles of Legality in International and Comparative Law' in *International Criminal Law*, vol. I, 3rd edn (Martinus Nijhoff 2008) 73, 100.

[4] See JJ Paust, '*Nullum Crimen* and Related Claims' (1997) 25 Denv J Int'l L & Pol'y 321, fn. 1 for a list of such literature.

[5] B Van Schaack, 'Crimen Sine Lege: Judicial Lawmaking at the Intersection of Law and Morals' (2008) 97 Georgetown LJ 119, 161–62.

[6] HL Packer, *The Limits of Criminal Sanction* (Stanford University Press 1968) 97.

The credibility of the tribunal requires a wise blend of two elements – applying the law and doing justice. A common lawyer must steer between the rock of outmoded precedent and the whirlpool of uncertainty. Equally, a civil law judge of an international tribunal, helped by a lesser concern with *stari* [*sic*] *decisis*, may perhaps bear in mind that the absence of any legislature might warrant a somewhat more expansive approach to judicial law-making than is familiar.[7]

This tension between strict legality and substantive justice cannot therefore be completely excised from international criminal law judgments by reconciling articles 21(3) and 22 of the Rome Statute. Strict legality, as defined in article 22, is an ideal that even national systems have achieved only to varying degrees.[8]

Despite the qualified success of strict legality in liberal criminal justice systems, drafters of the Rome Statute proceeded to embed in article 22 a robust definition of the legality principle, which includes: (1) the principle of non-retroactivity (*nullum crimen, nulla poena sine lege praevia*); (2) the prohibition against analogy (*nullum crimen, nulla poena sine lege stricta*); (3) the principle of certainty (*nullum crimen, nulla poena sine lege certa*); and (4) the prohibition against uncodified criminal provisions (*nullum crimen, nulla poena sine lege scripta*).[9] It is submitted that the last three elements of the legality principle are essentially guards against retroactive application of the law, which is its core preoccupation. Pursuant to article 22, judges have at their disposal certain *devices* to protect legality (non-retroactivity), namely, the limitation of jurisdiction to crimes defined in the Rome Statute at the time the conduct occurred, strict construction, interpretation in favour of the person being investigated, prosecuted or convicted in case of ambiguity and the prohibition against analogy. This Chapter will examine the interests protected by the legality principle and the competing interests that might be invoked to undermine them. The merits of the reasoning advanced in support of these interests will be critiqued for the purpose of developing the second tier of the methodology – arguments that support and undermine the principle of legality. In Chapter 5, the lessons learned from this inquiry will be used to develop the first tier of the methodology – giving principled content to the interpretive devices in article 22 of the Rome Statute in light of articles 31–33 of the *Vienna Convention* (1969).

---

[7] D Baragwanath, 'The Interpretative Challenges of International Adjudication across the Common Law/Civil Law Divide', Paper presented at the Cambridge Conference on Interpretation in International Law', Lauterpacht Centre for International Law (27 August 2013) 7 (on file with author).

[8] EM Wise, 'General Rules of Criminal Law' (1997) 25 Denv J Int'l L & Pol'y 313, fn. 19.

[9] C Kreß, 'Nullum Crimen, Nulla Poena Sine Lege' in R Wolfrum (ed.), *Max Planck Encyclopedia of Public International Law* (2008–), online edition, www.mpepil.com, para. 1, accessed 15 March 2011.

4.2 Interests protected by the legality principle

The purpose of this section is to critically review four interests or values that the principle of legality is intended to protect and to understand how this might occur in the Rome regime. The hope is that by understanding these interests, it will be possible to assess the merits of arguments that dilute application of the legality principle and thereby better delineate the scope and operation of the devices in article 22 that are intended to safeguard these values.

4.2.1 Fair notice

It is often said that the principle of legality ensures that individuals have fair notice or warning that a criminal sanction can attach to certain conduct. Members of society rely on this knowledge and plan their actions accordingly. Fair notice is the elixir to the 'perceived unfairness of punishing conduct not previously defined as criminal'.[10] The relationship between notice and fairness contemplates an innocent person who reasonably and in good faith relies on existing criminal law only to be trapped by an *ex post facto* legal prohibition.[11] Fair notice, however, is considered not to be violated by the *ex post facto* establishment of tribunals so long as the law being applied by the tribunal existed at the time the conduct occurred.[12] As well, article 31(3) of the Rome Statute, like many jurisdictions, empowers judges to consider recognizing justifications and excuses for criminal conduct that are not listed in the Statute. Such provisions do not undermine the fair warning interest because many defences, such as duress, insanity and intoxication, entail a mental state such that the unlawfulness of the act could not be appreciated by the individual and therefore could not guide his or her actions.[13]

The first inquiry that the concept of fair notice invites is to ask what type of notice meets the requirement of 'fair'. Blackstone and others posited that notice of the law is fair if it is knowable to those expected to abide by it. The public nature of the notification is thought to meet the test of knowability:

> [Notification must be] to the people who are to observe it. But the manner in which this notification is made is a matter of very great indifference . . . whatever way is made use of, it is incumbent on the promulgator to do it in the most public and propitious manner; not like Caligula, who

---

[10] JC Jeffries Jr, 'Legality, Vagueness, and the Construction of Penal Statutes' (1985) 71 Virginia L Rev 189, 201.

[11] Ibid. 205.

[12] *Demjanjuk* v. *Petrovsky*, 776 F.2d 571, 582–83 (6th Cir. 1985); *Attorney General of Israel* v. *Eichmann* (1961) 36 ILR 5 (Israel District Court); *Eichmann* v. *Attorney General of Israel* (1962) 36 ILR 277 (Supreme Court of Israel).

[13] K Ambos, 'Defences in International Criminal Law', BS Brown (ed.), *Research Handbook on International Criminal Law* (Elgar 2011) 299, 301.

(according to Dio Cassius) wrote his laws in a very small character and hung them upon high pillars, the more effectively to ensnare the people.[14]

Importantly, therefore, the concept of fair notice contemplates objective knowability and stops short of asking whether the individual charged did in fact know the law that he or she allegedly violated. This understanding is confirmed by briefly considering what happens when notice fails, when an individual did not in fact know the law. The response in many legal systems is to inform the individual that his or her ignorance of the law is no excuse.[15] Article 32(2) of the Rome Statute offers the same response, except where the ignorance of the individual negates the requisite mental element of the offense:

> A mistake of law as to whether a particular type of conduct is a crime within the jurisdiction of the Court shall not be a ground for excluding criminal responsibility. A mistake of law may, however, be a ground for excluding criminal responsibility if it negates the mental element required by such a crime, or as provided for in article 33.[16]

If one contemplates an individual making a fraudulent claim of ignorance, such an outcome might not be troubling. But surely there are situations where a person lacked actual notice and did not intend to engage in criminal conduct. In such cases, Jeffries rightly asks: 'If notice of illegality is an essential prerequisite to the fairness of punishment, how can the law be indifferent to claims of honest and reasonable mistake?'[17] It would appear that other policy considerations are weighed against the notion of fair warning, including giving the public an incentive to know the law.[18] It is here that concern for the honest and reasonable citizen gives way to addressing the clever and malevolent citizen who is trying his or her best to skirt the law.

> [A] person who embarks on obviously wrongful conduct takes his chances on just how seriously the rest of society may view the matter.... That is not to say, of course, that society has no obligation to treat wrongdoers

---

[14] W Blackstone, *Commentaries on the Laws of England*, vols. I–IV (Clarendon Oxford 1765–1769), cited in H Kelsen, 'The Rule Against *Ex Post Facto* Laws and the Prosecution of the Axis War Criminals' (1945) II:3 The Judge Advocate J 8, 9.

[15] Jeffries Jr (n. 10) 208: 'a defense of estoppel bars prosecution [in some jurisdictions] where the government has affirmatively misled the individual, but where the government is not responsible for the error, ignorance of the law is no excuse'.

[16] Article 33 provides: '1. The fact that a crime within the jurisdiction of the Court has been committed by a person pursuant to an order of a Government or of a superior, whether military or civilian, shall not relieve that person of criminal responsibility unless: (a) The person was under a legal obligation to obey orders of the Government or the superior in question; (b) The person did not know that the order was unlawful; and (c) The order was not manifestly unlawful. 2. For the purposes of this article, orders to commit genocide or crimes against humanity are manifestly unlawful.'

[17] Jeffries Jr (n. 10) 209.   [18] Ibid.

fairly, but only that fairness, at least in any sense even roughly congruent with our penal law, does not turn on the wrongdoer's own conception of the legal consequences of his act.[19]

Several courts have confirmed that fair warning does not require absolute legal certainty. For example, the European Court of Human Rights has held that it is possible to draft criminal provisions in general terms or for a criminal prohibition to have a 'penumbra of doubt' so long as the provision 'is sufficiently clear in the large majority of cases'.[20] It has been argued that the legality principle should not shield those who deliberately try to circumvent the law or who knowingly decide to exploit the fringes of criminal law's reach. In England, this has come to be known as the 'thin ice principle', meaning 'people who knowingly "sail close to the wind" should not be surprised if the law is interpreted so as to include their conduct'.[21] Lord Morris described it as follows: 'those who skate on thin ice can hardly expect to find a sign which will denote the precise spot where he [sic] will fall in'.[22] As well, some vagueness is necessary so that the legislature does not have to constantly amend criminal prohibitions to keep pace with changing circumstances.[23]

Thus, after legislators meet the burden of rendering the law objectively knowable, the burden is on the public to become acquainted with the law. Because fair warning is concerned with constructive rather than actual notice, some consider the notion to have an abstract and artificial ring.[24] Indeed, Glaser tried to prove that there is 'no possible justification for the principle, *ignoratia juris nocet*. It is, in particular, irreconcilable with the principle, "no punishment without guilt," the acceptance of which is universal and uncontested.'[25]

A second and related critique of the fair warning justification for the legality principle is mounted after inquiring into the kinds of notice that meet the requirement of knowability. Here, critics question the minimal efforts of legislators to render laws publicly accessible.[26] Is the kind of legal research required to know the content of an obscure criminal law provision in a particular jurisdiction much easier for a layperson to carry out than having to climb a ladder with a magnifying glass to read the laws of Caligula? This naturally leads to revisiting the notion of knowability and whether it is to be facilitated for the

---

[19] Ibid. 231.

[20] App. No. 17862/91, *Cantoni* v. *France*, ECHR, 1996–V, No. 20, para. 32.

[21] A Ashworth, 'Interpreting Criminal Statutes: A Crisis of Legality?' (1991) 107 LQ Rev 419, 443.

[22] *Reg* v. *Knuller (Publishing Printing and Promotions) Ltd* [1973] AC 435, 463–64.

[23] *Cantoni* (n. 20) para. 31.   [24] Jeffries Jr (n. 10) 210.

[25] S Glaser, 'Nullum Crimen Sine Lege' (1942) 24 J Comparative Legis and Int'l L 29, 34–35 (citing Glaser, 'Ignorantia juris dans le Droit pénal' (February 1931) Revue de Droit pénal et de Criminologie); H Kelsen (n. 14) 8, 9).

[26] Jeffries Jr (n. 10) 207–08.

layperson with the assistance of legal counsel. Where a criminal law provision is vague and its content has been clarified through judicial construction, fair warning would require reviewing this case law, which is challenging for a lawyer, no less a person who has no legal training.[27]

The question of knowable law takes on even greater importance in the realm of international criminal law where core crimes have their source in unwritten custom, and the exact content of these prohibitions is elaborated upon in voluminous jurisprudence scattered across the world. For this reason, Robinson rightly observes that '[w]e have yet to identify convincingly the root of what "fair warning" requires in circumstances with no legislature'.[28] While some have taken comfort in the reliance of international criminal tribunals on all sources of law listed in article 38 of the Statute of the International Court of Justice (ICJ Statute) for providing notice to a defendant about the content of international criminal law, one must ask to what extent this approach renders notice to the defendant fair. Is the concept of fair notice in fact a legal fiction? For certain sources of law, Kelsen concluded that it is.

> [The legality principle] is effective only with respect to legislation, not against the creation of law by custom or judicial decisions. Any rule of customary law is retroactive in the first case in which it is applied as a rule of law. Any rule of law created by a precedent is retroactive in the case in which it is first applied. The doctrine that custom is not a creation of law but merely evidence of a pre-existing law is the same fiction as the doctrine that tries to hide the retroactive character of precedent by presenting the judicial decision as an interpretation rather than the creation of law.[29]

Fortunately, whatever the merits of this critique, it holds little currency within the Rome regime, which defines legality so as to limit the Court's jurisdiction only to crimes 'in this Statute'.[30] The interest in fair warning or notice is therefore taken very seriously. As discussed in the previous Chapter, specificity was a guiding consideration for the Rome Statute's drafters.[31]

Third, and unique to the Rome regime, doubt has been expressed as to whether fair warning for individuals was the underlying justification for drafting article 22. It has been asserted that article 22 was motivated by the political concerns of States to ensure that the Court's jurisdiction would be certain and predictable. The concern was one of sovereignty, the 'delineation between national jurisdictions and the International Criminal Court, or the issue of

---

[27] Ibid.
[28] D Robinson, 'Legality and Our Contradictory Commitments: Some Thoughts About How We Think' (2009) 103 ASIL Proceedings 5.
[29] Kelsen (n. 14).   [30] Articles 6, 7, 8 and 8 *bis* Rome Statute.
[31] See Chapter 3, Sections 3.2 and 3.3.

"complementarity".[32] Evidence advanced in support of this claim is that, had the protection of individual rights been the main concern, inclusion of the *nulla poena sine lege* principle would not have occurred so late in the drafting process and attracted so little interest.[33] However, this critique is not particularly convincing, as the argument boils down to States being more preoccupied with fair warning for themselves than for the individual who might be on the hook down the road. Either way, fair warning was a motivating factor.

Finally, it might be argued that it lacks credibility to suggest that those who engage in the conduct prohibited in the Rome Statute would have acted differently if they knew that their conduct was prohibited by it; they know their conduct is wrong. This critique is examined in Section 4.3.2. below. Similarly, it has been argued that in the majority of cases, 'the picture of a citizen relying to his or her detriment on highly technical legal sources is simply not credible'.[34] One might think of rebel fighters in this regard. However, the same might not be said of State officials who have access to the opinions of well-staffed legal departments or of the professional adult soldier who is trained to respect rules of international law. The judicial decisions of international tribunals are becoming increasingly accessible, and those that accurately describe the content of international criminal law are considered by some to provide sufficient notice to defendants about prohibited conduct.[35]

While the notion of fair warning has merit, the 'counter-principle' that ignorance of the law is no excuse renders the concept of fair warning on its own 'overly simplistic' and 'in some ways misleading'.[36] Fair warning might be better seen as 'a thinly disguised version of the second and more sophisticated rationale of the principle of legality, which is [the rule of law,] that it is necessary in order to prevent abuse of official discretion'.[37]

4.2.2 Rule of law

The principle of legality is often justified on the basis of preventing the arbitrary (and sometimes oppressive) exercise of discretion. Examples of arbitrariness include the exercise of discretion in a manner that is socially, racially or

---

[32] M Boot, *Genocide, Crimes Against Humanity, War Crimes: Nullum Crimen Sine Lege and the Subject Matter Jurisdiction of the International Criminal Court* (Intersentia 2002) 362–63; WA Schabas, *The International Criminal Court: A Commentary on the Rome Statute* (Oxford University Press 2010) 407–08; A Pellet, 'Applicable Law' in A Cassese and Others (eds.), *The Rome Statute of the International Criminal Court: A Commentary*, vol. II (Oxford University Press 2002) 1051, 1057.

[33] Boot (n. 32) 362–63; K Ambos, '*Nulla Poena Sine Lege* in International Criminal Law' in R Haveman and O Olusanya (eds.), *Sentencing and Sanctioning in Supranational Criminal Law* (Intersentia 2006) 17.

[34] Jeffries Jr (n. 10) 230.   [35] Van Schaack (n. 5) 170–71.

[36] Packer (n. 6) 80.   [37] Ibid. 85.

otherwise discriminatory,[38] the pursuit of private ends through the misuse of government power,[39] reliance on illegitimate selection criteria,[40] and the satisfaction of immediate political objectives through one's decision-making powers.[41]

The legal formalism that this justification for legality encompasses is most often characterized as an appeal to the 'rule of law'.[42] This concept in the context of criminal law means that 'agencies of official coercion should, to the extent feasible, be guided by rules – that is, by openly acknowledged, relatively stable and generally applicable statements of proscribed conduct'.[43] Underlying these goals is the fundamental premise that each individual, even the worst criminal, has a basic worth and dignity that must be respected through legal procedure and that these values and the benefits to which they give rise are worth protecting, even in difficult cases.[44] Legal certainty is concerned with substantive equality.[45]

A second and equally important premise underpinning the rule of law is legitimacy, which requires that courts are established according to law and that they are independent as well as impartial.[46] Thus, the fact that the law is knowable to the public at the time the conduct occurred promotes the perceived legitimacy of courts and their decisions.[47] Accordingly, individuals are expected to comply with the law not only because of the threat of punishment for violating it but also because they perceive its enactment and the administration of justice to be legitimate.[48] It is perhaps for this reason that the Nuremberg tribunal went to some lengths to reason that the Nuremberg Charter 'is not an arbitrary exercise of power on the part of the victorious nations, but . . . the expression of international law existing at the time of its creation'.[49] Invoking legality as a device to preserve the rule of law is not a foolproof undertaking.[50] In the following paragraphs, three challenges to the rule of law justification for the legality principle will be considered.

The first challenge is the impossibility of absolute legal certainty.[51] Two factors contribute to this, namely, the imperfect medium of the written language and the need for some judicial discretion to be built into a legal

---

[38] Ashworth (n. 21) 442; Jeffries Jr (n. 10) 197.
[39] Jeffries Jr (n. 10) 212.   [40] Ibid.
[41] GP Fletcher, *Basic Concepts of Criminal Law* (Oxford University Press 1998) 207.
[42] Jeffries Jr (n. 10) 212.   [43] Ibid.
[44] J Hall, 'Nulla Poena Sine Lege' (1937) 165 Yale LJ 165, 192.   [45] Jeffries Jr (n. 10) 213.
[46] KS Gallant, *The Principle of Legality in International and Comparative Criminal Law* (Cambridge University Press 2009) 24.
[47] Ibid. 23.   [48] Ibid.
[49] (1946) 22 IMT Judgment 461. Similarly, the Nuremberg indictment cited several international treaties that Germany allegedly violated: (1946) 1 IMT Judgment 84–92 (Appendix C of indictment).
[50] Packer (n. 6) 80.   [51] Hall (n. 44) 181–82.

system. Regarding the latter, judicial discretion facilitates decision making in cases where certain factors are not foreseeable or are particularly complex.[52]

Thus, legislators draft 'indeterminate directives' that guide the future conduct of criminal law agencies, including the police, prosecutors and courts.[53] As well, judicial discretion might be necessary to avoid unjust results and thereby preserve the legitimacy of the legal system in another sense.[54] Classic examples of devices that enable this are proportionality tests and legislative terms that invite judges to make moral judgments, both of which are sometimes required to ensure the fair distribution of criminal liability.[55] In addition, some inherently vague concepts might need to be given precision through judicial interpretation, which might be considered law making but that, in certain degrees, can be tolerated by the principle of legality.[56] It has been cautioned that while there is room for normative judgments in the exercise of judicial discretion where legislatively indicated, care should be taken to not legislate standards that require judges to balance non-intuitive public policy issues.[57] Examples of legislated discretion for normative judgments in the Rome Statute can be found in articles 7(1)(g) ('any other form of sexual violence of a *comparable gravity*') and 7(1)(k) ('other inhumane acts of a *similar character*') for crimes against humanity.[58]

Accordingly, adherence to the rule of law is a matter of degree, as no legal system can consist of absolutely fixed, precise, clear and mechanical rules.[59] The goal is to maximize certainty and to minimize arbitrariness.[60] One doctrine that is invoked in support of achieving these goals is that of the separation of powers or the allocation of law-making and law-applying competences to different bodies.[61] Nevertheless, it is pointed out by some that 'interpretation' of 'existing law' by judges still leaves plenty of room for the exercise of discretion.[62]

---

[52] PH Robinson, 'Legality and Discretion in the Distribution of Criminal Sanctions' (1988) 25 Harv J on Legis 393, 400.

[53] Packer (n. 6) 92–93: 'The fact that courts operate in the open according to a system of reasoning that is subjected to the scrutiny of an interested audience, both professional and lay, militates against any but the most marginal invasions of the values represented by the principle of legality. . . . The principle of legality, then, is important for the allocation of competences not between the legislative and judicial branches, but among those who initiate the criminal process through the largely informal methods of investigation, arrest, interrogation, and charge that characterize the operation of criminal justice.' See also Packer, 88–89.

[54] Robinson, 'Legality and Discretion' (n. 52) 403–04.   [55] Ibid. 403, 413.

[56] G Mettraux, *International Crimes and the Ad Hoc Tribunals* (Oxford University Press 2006) 16.

[57] Robinson (n. 52) 404–05, 430–31.

[58] Emphasis added. See also articles 8(b)(xxii) and (e)(vi) on sexual violence as a war crime.

[59] Jeffries Jr (n. 10) 213.

[60] Hall (n. 44) 182; Jeffries Jr (n. 10) 214.   [61] Packer (n. 6) 85–86.   [62] Ibid.

However, such a critique delusively presupposes the idea that it is possible to perfectly separate the roles of law making and law application.[63] In the administration of law, there is a 'penumbral zone that is of great importance',[64] 'interstitial areas' of the law.[65] In addition to judges, the police and prosecutors are also delegated discretion that they are entrusted to exercise responsibly.[66]

The second challenge to the rule of law justification is that the devices intended to ensure respect for legality are not entirely consistent with this justification. In the Rome Statute, one device is the prohibition against analogical reasoning. However, Packer has asserted that the *use of* analogical reasoning is a means of guarding against discrimination, caprice and hidden bias in the common law tradition:

> Courts operate in the open through what has been described as a process of reasoned elaboration. They have to justify their decisions. It is not enough to say: this man goes to jail because he did something bad. There is an obligation to relate the particular bad thing that this man did to other things that have been treated as criminal in the past. The system of analogical reasoning that we call the common-law method is a very substantial impediment to arbitrary decision-making.[67]

Strict construction is another device in the Rome Statute that is intended to ensure respect for the legality principle. However, like the prohibition against analogy, it has been argued that

> [it bears no] necessary or predictable relation to the concerns suggested by the rule of law. Some instances of exculpatory construction are necessary to avoid dangerous openendedness in the criminal law; others are not. We must therefore recast the constraints surrounding the interpretation of criminal statutes in terms that correspond more exactly to the essential rationale underlying *nulla poena sine lege* ... What is needed, in other words, is a re-examination of the appropriate normative criteria for judicial construction of penal statutes.[68]

---

[63] Ibid. 92.

[64] Ibid. 86–87: 'The idea of a law-making and a law-applying institution is highly atypical in the context of the Anglo-American legal system; and it is not very descriptive of the way in which Anglo-American criminal law has actually evolved. ... The texture of the law of torts, of contracts, and of property contains far more judge-made, retrospective strands than it does legislative, prospective strands. And the same is true of the criminal law, except for the formal differences that *after* centuries of retrospective law-making by judges, the results of their work have been put into prospective odes by legislatures. Thus the process of judicial law-making in the criminal field has, except in the most interstitial kind of way, come to a halt.'

[65] This is a term devised by Justice Holmes of the United States Supreme Court in the realm of private law. Hall (n. 44) 190.

[66] Packer (n. 6) 93.   [67] Packer (n. 6) 88.   [68] Jeffries Jr (n. 10) 219.

Indeed, how the devices to safeguard legality are defined ought to bear some principled correlation to the underlying values ultimately being protected. This matter is considered in the next Chapter.

Third, it has been claimed that in light of the ICTY's and ICTR's interpretive practices and definition of legality, it is unrealistic to expect the principle of legality to adequately constrain the exercise of judicial discretion at the Court.[69] While some think that the Rome Statute 'delimit[s] in great detail any possible exercise of judicial discretion',[70] others are convinced that judicial policymaking is in the Court's future.[71] In support of the latter claim, it is recalled that Judge Shahabuddeen of the ICTY concluded that the principle of legality is not a bar to progressive development of the law and that so long as the relevant conduct is consistent with the 'the fundamental criminality of the crime charged', the principle of legality is respected.[72]

In the face of this challenge (which is also taken up in the next Chapter), and recognizing that judges will ultimately determine the extent to which they check their discretion, it should be recalled that the principle of legality is not the only constraint on the arbitrary exercise of judicial discretion.[73] Other constraints include the consent of States Parties when electing judges; the costs to the Court of States Parties exiting the Rome regime, not cooperating with it and reducing its budget; and direct mechanisms for States Parties to influence interpretation, such as amending the Rome Statute or Elements of Crimes and reacting to the Court's decisions through subsequent law, agreements and practice. Indeed, 'international tribunals risk losing the trust that states have placed in them if they are seen to assume too much discretion when determining what the law is, regardless of what states consider it to be'.[74]

4.2.3 Separation of powers

The separation of powers justification for the principle of legality firmly advances the view that it is for legislators and not judges to criminalize conduct and prescribe its punishment.[75] The rise of parliamentary influence in England contributed to the evolution of the legality principle from a vague

---

[69] J Wessel, 'Judicial Policy-Making at the International Criminal Court: An Institutional Guide to Analyzing International Adjudication' (2006) 44 Columbia J Transnat'l L 377, 414.

[70] WA Schabas, *An Introduction to the International Criminal Court*, 2nd edn (Cambridge University Press 2004) 90.

[71] Wessel (n. 69) 414.

[72] M Shahabuddeen, 'Does the Principle of Legality Stand in the Way of Progressive Development of Law?' (2004) 2 J Int'l Crim Justice 1007.

[73] Hall (n. 44) 180. For other constraints, see T Ginsburg, 'Bounded Discretion in International Judicial Lawmaking' (2005) 45 Virginia J Int'l L 631.

[74] Mettraux (n. 56) 16.

[75] *Prosecutor* v. *Delalić and Others*, Judgment, ICTY-96-21-T, 16 November 1998, para. 408.

maxim into a rule – legislation eventually subordinated the common law, and judges had to develop rules of statutory interpretation.[76] Legislative primacy is thought to rest on popular sovereignty and the 'consequent illegitimacy of judicial innovation'.[77] New laws must originate from the legislature as it is the branch of government that is most directly accountable to the polity, and the criminalization of conduct entails the serious consequence of surrendering individual freedoms.[78] The ideal legislative process is thought to ensure public discussion and accountability.[79] It is certainly arguable that the Rome Diplomatic Conference facilitated public discussion within international civil society as a result of the direct participation of hundreds of non-governmental organizations.

Further, Enlightenment theorists such as Montesquieu and Beccaria argued that liberty is best secured when political power is divided among different branches of government.[80] It has often been observed that, unlike domestic criminal justice systems, the coherent development of a universal corpus of international criminal law is thwarted by the absence of a world legislature that is able to fill interstitial legal gaps, modernize old legal prohibitions and correct problematic legal formulations.[81] While the international community lacks a world legislature, the Rome regime consists of the Court as well as the Assembly of States Parties (ASP), the latter being tantamount to a permanent legislative oversight body that is mandated to make binding decisions regarding the Court. Of course, States Parties can only amend the Statute in accordance with articles 121–123 of the Statute.[82]

The ASP is composed of States Parties who meet annually to discuss Court matters and can convene a Review Conference. It therefore ought to project upon judges a sense of being held democratically accountable for their work every year and offers a forum in which States Parties can regularly consider whether the Rome regime needs to be reformed in some way. If articles 6, 7, 8 and 8 *bis* are lacking in some way, it is for States Parties to decide whether to amend the Court's jurisdiction. For example, States Parties at the first Review Conference of the Rome Statute in 2010 adopted two resolutions: one containing amendments to the Rome Statute that define the crime of aggression

---

[76] Hall (n. 44) 167–68.   [77] Jeffries Jr (n. 10) 201.   [78] Ibid.   [79] Ashworth (n. 21) 442.

[80] C Montesquieu: 'the judges of the nation are only . . . the mouth which pronounces the words of the law, they are only inanimate beings who can neither moderate its force nor its rigour': *De l'esprit des lois* (Barillot 1748) bk. XI, ch. 6; C Beccaria, *Dei delitti e delle pene* (Livorno 1764).

[81] Cassese (n. 1) 42; Van Schaack (n. 5) 137.

[82] B Broomhall, 'Article 22' in O Triffterer (ed.), *Commentary on the Rome Statute of the International Criminal Court*, 2nd edn (CH Beck/Hart/Nomos 2008) 713, 725. See articles 121–23, Rome Statute.

and conditions for activation of the Court's jurisdiction over this crime, and another amending the war crimes provisions.[83]

In some jurisdictions, criminal legislation is so abundant that there are almost no gaps tempting judges to innovate. Some argue that this renders the separation of powers doctrine unhelpful for understanding the content of the legality principle and its operation.[84] However, international criminal law is a relatively young body of law, and, despite the detail in articles 6, 7, 8 and 8 *bis* of the Rome Statute, this doctrine arguably still resonates, not least because of the practices of the ICTY and ICTR. It has been argued that their judicial creativity in identifying the existence of customary international law undermined the principle of legality by paying mere lip service to the separation of powers doctrine:[85] 'An aspiration to fill gaps in the law – to legislate from the bench – is often the only method discernible in the tribunals' efforts to prove the existence of a rule of customary law.'[86] Such practices are said to 'challenge the exclusive power of states to make custom'.[87] But while States retain this power, the legality principle does not bar a court from clarifying or specifying through interpretation the elements of a crime under customary international law.[88] This is why, if strict construction were to be adopted immediately in all cases of ambiguity, it would promote the ASP's absolute supremacy but also undermine powers delegated to the judiciary, which is also problematic for the separation of powers doctrine.[89]

In this section, three challenges to the separation of powers justification for the legality principle will be considered. The first rather serious challenge is that the separation of powers doctrine cannot usefully guide judges when resolving interpretive problems:

> At most, the separation of powers doctrine instructs judges to refrain from assigning meaning to a legislative text that is inconsistent with legislative choice, so a meaning that the text will not bear, that is clearly contradicted by legislative history, or that does unnecessary violence to the policy expressed in some other enactment.[90]

---

[83] First Review Conference of the Rome Statute, Official Records, Resolution on the Crime of Aggression (adopted 11 June 2010) RC/Res.6, www.icc-cpi.int/iccdocs/asp_docs/Resolutions/RC-Res.6-ENG.pdf, accessed 5 November 2013; First Review Conference of the Rome Statute, Official Records, Resolution on Amendments to article 8 of the Rome Statute (adopted 10 June 2010) RC/Res.5, www.icc-cpi.int/iccdocs/asp_docs/Resolutions/RC-Res.5-ENG.pdf, accessed 5 November 2013. In these resolutions, States Parties also amended the Elements of Crimes.

[84] Jeffries Jr (n. 10) 202.   [85] Mettraux (n. 56) 17.

[86] A Zahar and G Sluiter, *International Criminal Law* (Oxford University Press 2008) 99.

[87] Mettraux (n. 56) 17.   [88] Ibid. 17.   [89] Ashworth (n. 21) 439.

[90] Jeffries Jr (n. 10) 205; B Hale, 'Common Law and Convention Law: The Limits to Interpretation' (2011) 16:5 European HR L Rev 534, 535.

The goal is to 'avoid large-scale innovation' so as to steer clear of controversial public policy debates,[91] respect 'considered legislative inaction'[92] and avoid the 'reproach that the tribunal has substituted its own intention for that of the parties'.[93] The difficulty is that many interpretive choices fall short of large-scale innovation while still respecting drafters' choices, and, as between these interpretive outcomes, the separation of powers doctrine offers little guidance because it prohibits none of them.[94] One response to this is for a legislative body, like the ASP, to adopt non-binding and non-exhaustive lists of examples illustrating conduct that does and does not meet certain elements of crimes included in legislation.[95] Where an element requires one to make a complex judgment, the ASP could also devise a description of factors to be taken into account and their relationship to one another.[96] This guidance may take the form of 'interpretive understandings' that judges would be legally required to 'take into account' pursuant to article 31(3)(a) of the *Vienna Convention* (1969).[97] In the resolution that the Review Conference of the Rome Statute adopted on the crime of aggression, seven interpretive Understandings were included to help ensure that judges interpret the definition of this crime in a manner consistent with the intentions of States.

The second challenge is that drafters of a treaty, as with drafters of legislation at the domestic level, implicitly delegate quasi-legislative powers to courts for various reasons, a matter touched upon in the previous section.[98] Thus, courts are tapped to resolve future disputes arising from the terms of a treaty, a concept known as 'downstream coordination', so that States can save on the negotiation costs of enhancing the specificity of a treaty text.[99] As well, vagueness and ambiguity might be deliberate so that States can claim before domestic audiences that a treaty provision supports their preferred meaning, but also before a court in case a dispute arises in the future.[100] Further, the notion of a common legislative intent has rightly been questioned, thereby rendering it doubtful that judges have no delegated law-making power.[101] This perceived fiction becomes harder to ignore as time passes and judges are confronted with fact patterns that drafters of a treaty or statute could not have envisioned.[102] Still, the following distinction is drawn in these situations: 'we are seeking to identify and apply the underlying principles of the law,

---

[91] Hale, ibid.   [92] Ibid.
[93] H Lauterpacht, 'Restrictive Interpretation and the Principle of Effectiveness in the Interpretation of Treaties' (1949) 26 British Ybk Int'l L 48, 74.
[94] Jeffries Jr (n. 10) 205.   [95] Robinson (n. 52) 430–31.   [96] Ibid.
[97] Article 31(3)(a) states: 'There shall be taken into account, together with the context: . . . any subsequent agreement between the parties regarding the interpretation of the treaty or the application of its provisions' (see Chapter 9, Section 9.2.7).
[98] ATH Smith, 'Judicial Law Making in the Criminal Law' (1984) 100 LQ Rev 46, 68; Ginsburg (n. 73) 643.
[99] Ginsburg, ibid. 643–44.   [100] Ibid.   [101] Hall (n. 44) 174–75.   [102] Ibid.

extending and adapting them to meet new situations but not turning them on their head.'[103]

The third challenge is that the 'branches of government' at the international level cannot be compared to those that exist at the national level where corrective law making and amendments can remedy problems unearthed in a court's jurisprudence.[104] In contrast, it is posited that multilateral treaty amendment processes are relatively slow because States are reluctant to revise agreed-upon treaty terms, which entail negotiation costs.[105] It is thought that this state of affairs causes international judges to struggle 'between the "is" and the "ought", between positivism and normativity'.[106] However, international criminal lawyers should be careful not to romanticize the efficiency and responsiveness of domestic legislatures to problems confronting their criminal courts. Criminal law scholars also challenge the parliamentary supremacy doctrine justifying the legality principle by observing that, in practice, legislatures are not terribly responsive or reliable in the criminal law domain.[107] It is possible that the transaction costs for legislatures are also great when contemplating criminal law revisions. Accordingly, pragmatists reason that, if judges do not fill existing gaps, modernize existing laws and fix awkward statutory formulations, the work will not get done.[108] Where the legislature has thoroughly debated the issue and declined to act, however, a criminal court ought to exercise restraint and leave the law as it stands.[109]

Despite the aforementioned challenges, there does seem to be some merit in the separation of powers reasoning insofar as judges should keep in mind that drafters of the Rome Statute had the opportunity to openly debate the possible inclusion of various crimes in the Court's jurisdiction, and judges are legally bound to respect these legislative choices. If they do not, the separation of powers doctrine would be undermined, as would, perhaps, the rule of law and fair warning justifications for the legality principle.

4.2.4 Prior law as the basis for punishment

While the principle of legality for some is a device to ensure the separation of powers, it is for others a necessary ingredient for permitting the Court to impose a punishment on an individual, which can result in a serious deprivation of his or her liberty.[110]

---

[103] Hale (n. 90).   [104] Van Schaack (n. 5) 137.   [105] Ibid.

[106] Ibid. 191–92   [107] Ashworth (n. 21) 439.

[108] Ibid.; WN Eskridge Jr., 'Dynamic Statutory Interpretation' (1987) 135 Univ Pennsylvania LR 1479, 1554–55 (It is appropriate for courts to adapt old norms with little chance of legislative revision).

[109] Ashworth (n. 21) 448.

[110] PJA Ritter von Feuerbach, 'The General Principles of International Criminal Law: The Foundations of Criminal Law and the Nullum Crimen Principle' in *Lehrbuch des gemeinen*

> The purpose of the infliction of punishment is establishing the effectiveness of the statutory threat, insofar as without it that threat would be empty (ineffective). Since the statute should deter all citizens, but enforcement should give effect to the law, the indirect goal (ultimate purpose) of its infliction similarly is merely to deter citizens by the law [as opposed to morality].... The legal basis for infliction of punishment is the prior threat of the law [not morality].... From the above deduction results the following highest principle of penal law: every legal punishment in the State is the legal consequence of a law, justified by the necessity to uphold external rights [äussere Rechte] and threatening breaches of law with physical evil.[111]

This conception of law as the basis for punishment is not concerned with the goals of preventing the accused from future violations of the law, moral retribution, deterring others after the wrongful conduct has occurred or moral reformation of the accused.[112] The goal is to prevent the initial wrongful conduct of all citizens by ensuring that the threat of a criminal sanction precedes the imposition of punishment, by justifying punishment solely on the basis of necessity – not the necessity of preventing further wrongdoing but of rendering the threat of criminal sanction effective.[113] The requirement of a pre-existing criminal sanction, which the principle of legality requires, gives effect to the law's 'purpose of expressing clearly the conduct that is collectively condemned'.[114] This is why legality is the 'fundamental basis of modern criminal legislation'.[115]

Applied to the Rome regime, legality is concerned with ensuring that the power of the international community to punish individuals is limited to violations of law that 'express clearly the conduct that is collectively condemned' so that criminal sanctions in the Statute are effective at deterring (all) acts of aggression, genocide, other crimes against humanity and war crimes before they occur. The obvious criticism of this justification for legality is that the threat of punishment based on a criminal sanction will not deter all persons from engaging in the prohibited conduct. However, as Feuerbach clarifies, the aim is more modest here. It is to render the criminal sanction itself effective, and whether or not someone will nevertheless engage in the wrongful conduct is immaterial.[116] The premise seems to be that the effectiveness of the criminal sanction is a societal good even if it only prevents some, though not all, from engaging in wrongful conduct and because it forms the basis for punishment.

---

in Deutschland gültigen peinlichen Rechts, 11th edn (Heyer 1832) 12–19, translation by IL Fraser in (2007) 5 J Int'l Crim Justice 1005.
[111] Ibid. 16.   [112] Ibid. 17.   [113] Glaser (n. 25) 34.
[114] Van Schaack (n. 5) 121.   [115] Glaser (n. 25) 34.   [116] Ibid. 34.

4.2.5 Conclusions

In sum, the justification of fair warning appears to be a bit of a legal fiction in all jurisdictions, but it is a compelling expression of rule of law considerations underlying legality. The rule of law is a strong justification for the legality principle and is concerned with preserving the human dignity and substantive equality of persons investigated, prosecuted and convicted as well as the legitimacy of the Court itself. The rule of law is not an absolute quantity but exists in degrees in all legal systems, as no criminal prohibitions can be perfectly fixed, precise, clear and mechanically applied. The key is to limit judicial discretion to the 'penumbral zone' or 'interstitial area' so that the law is certain in the great majority of cases. These considerations should help to ensure that the interpretive devices in article 21 are given principled content and are not dogmatically or blindly applied. The separation of powers doctrine is another important interest underlying the principle of legality. It warns judges to 'avoid large-scale innovation' so as to steer clear of controversial public policy debates,[117] respect 'considered legislative inaction'[118] and avoid the 'reproach that the tribunal has substituted its own intention for that of the parties'.[119] Legality is also essential to ensuring the effectiveness of the Court, that is, the criminal prohibitions in articles 6, 7, 8 and 8 *bis* of the Rome Statute and the threat of punishment for their violation. It sends a message to potential perpetrators of atrocities that because the international community has enacted law expressing its collective condemnation of particular conduct, such conduct may be punished.

4.3 Arguments that undermine the legality principle

As important as the values discussed above are, the principle of legality must in all liberal criminal justice systems compete with arguments in support of other interests, namely, the prosecution of individuals who have committed obviously antisocial conduct and the community's understandable interest in condemning and punishing that conduct. These arguments, if successful, often weaken or undermine a robust notion of the legality principle. International criminal justice is no exception to this dynamic. A summary of the methodology of the European Court of Human Rights illustrates this point:

> [W]here juridical developments are consistent with the essence of an offense and could have been reasonably foreseen, the prosecution is not arbitrary or unjust. In particular, the Court will find no violation [of the legality principle] where the basic ingredients of a criminal offense remain unchanged but non-core elements are added, modified, or abandoned. In addition, the Court will also look to changes in society that might render

---

[117] Jeffries Jr (n. 10) 205.   [118] Ibid.   [119] Lauterpacht (n. 93).

an old rule anachronistic. Where there is considerable uncertainty in the law, the Court considers the populace essentially on notice that the law is in flux and could be interpreted adversely to them in the future.[120]

On other occasions, the nature of international law is invoked to justify a weaker understanding of the legality principle being applied by international criminal tribunals:

> [T]he affected State or States must take into account the following factors, *inter alia*: the nature of international law; the absence of international legislative politics and standards; the *ad hoc* processes of technical drafting; and the basic assumption that international criminal law norms will be embodied into the national criminal law of the various States.[121]

In this section, a critical examination will be undertaken of the arguments invoked for diluting robust conceptions of legality in the international criminal law context. This will be done for the purpose of determining their admissibility within a methodology for interpreting crimes defined in the Rome Statute.

4.3.1 Higher order justice

The first argument advanced for the principle of legality giving way to other considerations was made at Nuremberg. After the Second World War, the principle of legality was regarded as not yet a free-standing principle or rule in customary international law but rather a subset of the principle of justice that would have to yield to a 'higher order' principle of justice in cases of conflict.[122] The legal accuracy of this characterization was confirmed in a major study of the legality principle.[123] Judges at Nuremberg were able to identify a principle of justice that ranked higher than legality, namely, the injustice of not punishing Nazis for their clearly immoral conduct.[124] Kelsen commended the Nuremberg judges for their understanding of legality:

---

[120] B Van Schaack, 'Legality and International Criminal Law' (2009) 103 ASIL Proceedings 2.

[121] *Delalić* (n. 75) para. 405.   [122] Kelsen (n. 14) 10–11.   [123] Gallant (n. 46) 9 and ch. 3.

[124] IMT Judgment (1947) 41 AJIL 172, 217. Similarly, in *United States* v. *Altstötter* (1947), the invocation of legality as a defence was rejected on the basis that it does not apply 'to a treaty, a custom, or a common law decision of an international tribunal' (reprinted in 3 Trials of War Criminals Before the Nuremberg Military Tribunal under Control Council Law No. 10 (1951) 954, 974–75). During the Tokyo trial, Justice Röling of the Netherlands held in a separate opinion that the maxim of legality did not bar convictions for this *ex post facto* crime because legality is a policy, not a principle: 'However, this maxim is not a principle of justice but a rule of policy, valid only if expressly adopted . . . This maxim of liberty may, if circumstances necessitate it, be disregarded even by powers victorious in a war fought for freedom.' *United States* v. *Araki and Others*, Separate Opinion of Judge Röling, Trial 44–45A in RJ Pritchard and S Magbanua Zaide (eds.), *The Tokyo Major War Crimes* (Garland 1981) 21, cited in Van Schaack (n. 5).

Justice required the punishment of these men, in spite of the fact that under positive law they were not punishable at the time they performed the acts made punishable with retroactive force. In case two postulates of justice are in conflict with each other, the higher one prevails; and to punish those who were morally responsible for the international crime of the Second World War may certainly be considered as more important than to comply with the rather relative rule against ex post facto laws, open to so many exceptions.[125]

Courts have in recent years taken up 'higher order justice' reasoning.[126] On some occasions, the Martens Clause has been invoked in order to give priority to interpretations that most favour the principles of humanity and the moral standards it embodies.[127] The practice of weighing collective goals such as substantive justice against the principle of legality has been defended by some: 'It is still difficult not to admit that, as in all too urgent situations, the principle of non-retroactivity is set aside under a more pressing social and moral need for punishment. It is perhaps better to admit this than to engage in legal gymnastics of doubtful value.'[128] It has even been suggested that, where the principle of legality is compromised, courts can compensate the defendant for its violation by mitigating his or sentence to reflect a penalty that exists for the same or analogous crime under the law that was applicable to him or her when the crime was committed.[129]

However, such a practice does not overcome the original methodological difficulty. As one scholar aptly put it: 'if we are not convicting them for breaking *law*, then how can we be sure the process is justice? There must be some unstated limit, other than moral intuition, to this [Nuremberg substantive justice] principle.'[130] Otherwise, international criminal law is left to develop in a manner that might be unforeseeable and inaccessible to the person in the dock,

---

[125] H Kelsen, 'Will the Judgment in the Nuremberg Trial Constitute a Precedent in International Law?' (1947) 1:2 Int'l LQ 153, 165. See also Kelsen (n. 14) 11.

[126] *Attorney General of Israel* v. *Eichmann* (n. 12) paras. 22–23; *R* v. *Finta* (1994) 1 SCR 701, 736.

[127] Van Schaack (n. 5) 148. The Martens Clause provides: 'Until a more complete code of the laws of war is issued . . . populations and belligerents remain under the protection and empire of the principles of international law, as they result from the usages established between civilized nations, from the laws of humanity and the requirements of the public conscience.' *Convention Respecting the Laws and Customs of War on Land* (adopted 21 July 1899, entered into force 4 September 1900) 32 Stat. 1803, TS No. 403.

[128] R Kolb, 'The Jurisprudence of the European Court of Human Rights on Detention and Fair Trial in Criminal Matters from 1992 to the End of 1998' (2000) 21 Human Rights LJ 348, cited in B Juratowitch, 'Retroactive Criminal Liability and International Human Rights Law' (2004) 75:1 British Ybk Int'l L 337, 358.

[129] Van Schaack (n. 5) 188.   [130] Robinson (n. 28) 4.

depending on who is sitting in judgment.[131] Fortunately, legality has evolved since the Second World War from a principle of justice that must compete with other notions of substantive justice into a non-derogable internationally recognized human right that admits no limitations.[132] Nevertheless, the content of the principle remains uncertain in international law. The ICTY stated: 'It is not certain to what extent [the principle of legality and its components] have been admitted as part of international legal practice, separate and apart from the existence of the national legal system.'[133] Article 22 of the Rome Statute overcomes some of this uncertainty. And substantive justice considerations might have (in)advertently been built into the definitions of certain crimes, in particular, the residual category of crimes against humanity, which includes 'other inhumane acts *of a similar character*.'[134] Perhaps this formally expressed discretion is unavoidable (and welcome) if the Court's jurisdiction extends to the 'most serious crimes of concern to the international community as a whole'.[135]

4.3.2 Immorality

International criminal tribunals have recalled the immorality of impugned conduct as a justification for not providing defendants with formal notice that their conduct would entail penal consequences. Justice Jackson argued at Nuremberg: 'The refuge of the defendants can be only their hope that International Law will lag so far behind the moral sense of mankind that conduct which is a crime in the moral sense must be regarded as innocent in law.'[136] A modified version of this reasoning continues to be invoked by modern tribunals.[137] For example, the ICTY Appeals Chamber observed:

---

[131] A Cassese, 'Balancing the Prosecution of Crimes against Humanity and Non-Retroactive Criminal Law: The *Kolk and Kislyiy v. Estonia* Case before the ECHR' (2006) 4 J Int'l Crim Justice 410, 416–17.

[132] Gallant (n. 46) 8–9.

[133] *Delalić* (n. 75) para. 403. This reasoning was echoed in *Prosecutor v. Karemera and Others*, Decision on Defense's Preliminary Motions Challenging Jurisdiction: Joint Criminal Enterprise, ICTR-98–44-T, 11 May 2004, para. 43: 'The Chamber holds that, given the specificity of international criminal law, the principle of legality does not apply to international criminal law to the same extent as it applies in certain national legal systems.'

[134] Emphasis added. This is not to say that the principle of legality is unacceptably compromised. See the introduction to crimes against humanity in the Elements of Crimes.

[135] Preambular para. 4, Rome Statute.

[136] RH Jackson, *The Nürnberg Case* (Cooper Square 1947) 94.

[137] Van Schaack (n. 5) 156 (citing *Delalić* (n. 75) para. 313); *Prosecutor v. Delalić and Others*, Judgment, ICTY-96–21-A, 20 February 2001, para. 173; *Prosecutor v. Milutinović and Others*, Decision on Dragoljub Ojdani's Motion Challenging Jurisdiction: Joint Criminal Enterprise, ICTY-99–37-AR72, 21 May 2003, para. 42.

> Although the immorality or appalling character of an act is not a sufficient factor to warrant its criminalization under customary international law, it may in fact play a role in that respect, insofar as it may refute any claim by the Defence that it did not know of the criminal nature of the acts.[138]

Similarly, the European Court of Human Rights recently held that 'where conduct is *malum in se* rather than *malum prohibitum*, such as ... rape ... [the] individual could not have reasonably believed the conduct to be lawful.'[139]

The subsequent criminalization of 'clearly immoral' conduct has attracted academic support on the basis that morals do not change quickly[140] and that social customs and common sense are the real source of fair notice rather than obscure statements of law.[141] However, the conflation of morality and criminality poses several serious problems. First, the morality argument only seeks to defeat the fair warning justification for the legality principle and thereby leaves the rule of law, the separation of powers doctrine and the effectiveness of criminal sanctions interests favouring legality intact.

Second, such an approach could work great injustice where the prevailing morals are inhumane. History bears this out. Consider when the Nazi regime amended article 2 of the German Criminal Code in 1935 to read: 'Anyone shall be punished who commits an act which is declared punishable by statute or which deserves a penalty according to the basic principles of a criminal statute and of the people's sound sense of justice.'[142] There was also the Star Chamber in England, which from 1660 to 1860, without any specific precedent, often punished conduct held to be *contra bonos mores*.[143] Indeed, exceptions to or abolition of the legality principle provide 'a sieve through which can flow not only humanity and science but also repression and stupidity.'[144] Third, it is an open question whether judges are the best actors to be arbiters of what is moral and immoral. If criminal law is going to be conflated with morality, 'the process of criminalisation should arguably be as democratic as possible.'[145]

This leads to the fourth problem, which is that morals or the 'feelings of the people' do not always result in immoral conduct being criminalized. Arguments favouring retroactive application of the law where the conduct is 'clearly immoral'[146] fail to consider this or want the logic of their reasoning to run in only one direction. Many laws do not embody a moral imperative (e.g.,

---

[138] Van Schaack, ibid. (citing *Milutinović*, ibid.).

[139] Van Schaack, ibid. 181 (citing App. No. 20190/92, *CR* v. *United Kingdom*, ECHR (1995) Series A, No. 335-C, para. 42).

[140] Hall (n. 44) 171–72, 175.

[141] Jeffries Jr. (n. 10) 231 (citing Justice Holmes in *Nash* v. *United States*, 229 U.S. 373, 377 (1913)).

[142] Cited in Kelsen (n. 14) 12.   [143] Hall (n. 44) 179.

[144] Ibid. 189.   [145] Smith (n. 98) 58.   [146] Kelsen (n. 14) 9.

some zoning regulations), and many normative rules are often not embodied in criminal sanctions (e.g., prohibition of adultery).[147] Unfortunately, where conduct is considered by the public to be clearly immoral but is not encompassed by an existing criminal sanction, judges worry that an acquittal might be perceived as an endorsement of the impugned conduct.[148] This is a symptom of a larger problem – that criminal law does not distinguish between rules of conduct that are to guide citizens and rules of adjudication that judges are to observe.[149] Just because respect for the principle of legality might result in an acquittal does not mean that a rule prohibiting certain conduct should be perceived as weakened in any way, although this might understandably occur. Nor should an acquittal be considered a stamp of moral approval for the impugned conduct.[150]

Finally, even where normative proscriptions are embodied in criminal sanctions, morals are uncertain and change over time.[151] International criminal law, however, is said to operate in the realm of relatively great moral certainty, and therefore a less strict application of the legality principle can be accommodated.[152] Similarly, it is suggested that legality jurisprudence indicates that the 'gravity of the act charged is a consideration to be borne in mind in interpreting and applying the principle *nullum crimen sine lege*, it being improbable that the law did not previously provide for a grave act to be punishable.'[153] As attractive as these appeals are, such arguments contain echoes of the natural law origins of international criminal law and the contested notion that universal conceptions of morality and justice exist.[154] The reality is that the world is characterized by moral disagreement, especially in borderline cases, which is precisely where legality can be expected to do its most important work.[155]

In the case of *Prosecutor* v. *Norman* (2004) before the Special Court for Sierra Leone, at issue was whether the conscription or enlistment of children under the age of fifteen years into armed forces or groups or using them to participate

---

[147] A Roberts, 'Traditional and Modern Approaches to Customary International Law: A Reconciliation' (2001) 95 AJIL 757, 761.

[148] Ashworth (n. 21) 436–37 (citing DN MacCormick, *Legal Reasoning and Legal Theory* (Oxford University Press 1978) ch. 6).

[149] PH Robinson, 'Rules of Conduct and Rules of Adjudication' (1990) 57 U Chic LR 729; P Alldridge, 'Rules for Courts and Rules for Citizens' (1990) 10 Oxford J Legal Studies 487, cited in Ashworth (n. 21) 438.

[150] T Meron, 'Revival of Customary Humanitarian Law' (2005) 99 AJIL 817, 825.

[151] Hall (n. 44) 178; R Cryer, 'The Doctrinal Foundations of International Criminalization' in MC Bassiouni (ed.) *International Criminal Law*, vol. I, 3rd edn (Martinus Nijhoff 2008) 107, 111–12.

[152] Van Schaack (n. 5) 157.   [153] Shahabuddeen (n. 72).

[154] Van Schaack (n. 5) 157 (citing S Glaser, 'La Méthode d'Interpretation en Droit International Pénal' (1966) 9 Rivista Italiana Di Diretto e Procedura Penale 757, 762–64).

[155] Fletcher (n. 41) 207.

actively in hostilities was a crime under customary international law at the time the defendant was alleged to have engaged in this conduct.[156] The defendant conceded that the conduct was prohibited under international humanitarian law at the relevant time. The majority of the Appeals Chamber concluded, however, that the conduct was also criminal prior to the defendant's conduct even if it took several years for this criminal prohibition to find positive expression in the Rome Statute. Justice Robertson wrote a strong dissenting opinion and asserted that the majority had conflated immorality with criminality. He wrote that 'it is precisely when the acts are abhorrent and deeply shocking that the principle of legality must be most stringently applied, to ensure that the defendant is not convicted out of disgust rather than evidence, or of a non-existent crime'.[157] For this reason, pleas have been made for adopting the traditional practice-based approach to customary international law formation:

> [S]ociety, in particular international society, has not reached full consensus on *a priori* moral precepts, and the best evidence of fundamental principles of behaviour in the world is that which has been accepted as criminal by virtue of the normal process of international law.... As a result, international criminalization must be studied from the empirical/inductive standpoint. To do otherwise, and to attempt to deduce specific crimes from general moral postulates risks allegations of a return to naturalism and its fellow traveller, (neo)colonialism.[158]

For all of these reasons, national and international tribunals have largely rejected conflations of morality and criminality for being inconsistent with the principle of legality.[159] It is hoped that this trend continues. The principle of legality would not, however, exclude the principled consideration of the value harmed or threatened by the prohibited conduct, the mischief that a criminal prohibition seeks to prevent or the principle to be protected.[160]

4.3.3 World order

In addition to substantive justice and the immorality of impugned conduct being invoked to pierce the veil of legality, the collective goals of peace and

---

[156] *Prosecutor v. Norman*, Decision on Preliminary Motion Based on Lack of Jurisdiction (Child Recruitment), SCSL-2004–14-AR72(E), 31 May 2004.

[157] Ibid., Dissenting Opinion of Judge Robertson, paras. 12–13.

[158] Cryer (n. 151) 112–13; Van Schaack (n. 5) 165–66.

[159] Gallant (n. 46) 135, but citing as an exception *Polyukhovich* v. *Australia*, Australian High Court, Opinion of Judge Dawson, 14 August 1991, para. 18. For an early decision rejecting the conflation of morality and criminality, see R Pal, 'Judgment' in BVA Röling and CF Rüter (eds.), *The Tokyo Judgment: The International Military Tribunal for the Far East (IMTFE) 29 April 1946–12 November 1948* (Amsterdam University Press 1977) 579.

[160] Ashworth (n. 21) 447. For example, an attack directed against a civilian population during an armed conflict violates the principle of distinction.

security have also been weighed against providing the person investigated, prosecuted or convicted with fair warning.[161] The development of international law in support of these collective goals and at the expense of legality is believed by some to 'generate a more reliable deterrent effect, contribute to the prevention of abuses in the future, and ensure a more secure public order for all'.[162] However, similar 'law and order' arguments have been advanced at the domestic level[163] and raise serious concerns.

First, if individual rights can be weighed against laudable collective goals such as peace and security, when can the former ever prevail in the context of international criminal law proceedings? The core crimes of aggression, genocide, other crimes against humanity and war crimes by definition pose a threat to these fundamental values.[164] The preamble of the Rome Statute recognizes that crimes within it 'threaten the peace, security and well-being of the world'.[165]

Another concern is that the policy goals of peace and security could easily politicize the international criminal justice enterprise. The political will of some States to see agents of another State prosecuted for certain conduct could lead to declarations of that conduct threatening peace and security, thereby permitting the principle of legality to be diluted or ignored. Such a concern is serious for the emerging international criminal justice system, which is defined by a 'continuous battle with *realpolitik*' in the pursuit of 'accountability, justice, and, in the future, deterrence'.[166]

This leads one to consider a third concern, which is that such politicization would not only result in the unprincipled administration of justice but also that such a state of affairs would ultimately undermine the effectiveness of international criminal law. Contrary to the claim that prosecution at the expense of legality might be necessary to achieve a 'reliable deterrent effect' and thereby ensure peace and security,[167] the opposing view has also been expressed. To achieve the value-oriented goals of prevention through deterrence, the enhancement of peace, providing redress to victims, disclosing the truth and meting out justice, it is thought that international criminal justice processes must be consistently applied, impartial, fair and non-political and must be perceived to be so.[168] It has been argued that a policy-oriented approach to criminal law

---

[161] *Delalić* (n. 75) para 405; Van Schaack (n. 5) 141.   [162] Van Schaack, ibid.

[163] J Bell, *Policy Arguments in Judicial Decisions* (Oxford University Press 1983) 222, cited in Ashworth (n. 21) 441.

[164] O Triffterer, 'Can the "Elements of Crimes" Narrow or Broaden Responsibility for Criminal Behaviour defined in the Rome Statute?' in C Stahn and G Sluiter (eds.), *The Emerging Practice of the International Criminal Court* (Martinus Nijhoff 2009) 381, 399.

[165] Preambular paragraph 3, Rome Statute.

[166] MC Bassiouni, 'The Philosophy and Policy of International Criminal Justice' in LC Vohrah and Others (eds.), *Man's Inhumanity to Man: Essays on International Law in Honour of Antonio Cassese* (Kluwer Law International 2003) 65, 109.

[167] Van Schaack (n. 5) 141.   [168] Bassiouni (n. 166) 103, 125.

would not result in a principled exception to the legality principle but in fact would run contrary to it.[169] It could seriously undermine the rule of law and effectiveness of criminal sanctions.

4.3.4 Illegality

Like immorality, the illegality (as opposed to criminality) of conduct under international law is a proxy that has been advanced for the existence of a (written or unwritten) criminal prohibition. Some have reasoned that international crimes can be incorporated 'by reference' in international instruments and that the latter need not expressly refer to the conduct as a crime.[170]

The earliest examples of this reasoning can be found in the Nuremberg and Tokyo judgments as well as many proceedings following the end of the Second World War.[171] For example, the Nuremberg tribunal held that the conduct prohibited by the *Hague Conventions* (1907) was criminal.[172] As well, when considering whether crimes against peace violate the legality principle, the Nuremberg tribunal pointed to the Kellogg-Briand Pact (1928) and some bilateral treaties on neutrality and non-aggression to make the point that general international law prohibits acts of aggression. Since the Kellogg-Briand Pact contained a 'solemn renunciation of war as an instrument of national policy [, this] necessarily involves the proposition that such a war is illegal in international law; and that those who plan and wage such a war, with its inevitable and terrible consequences, are committing a crime in so doing'.[173]

Decades later, some think that the ICTY Appeals Chamber echoed this logic. In its landmark decision in *Tadić* (1995), it held inter alia that satisfaction of the following four factors results in the existence of a criminal prohibition under article 3 of the ICTY statute in the context of a non-international armed conflict: (1) conduct violating a rule of international humanitarian law; (2) the rule exists under customary international law or is in an applicable treaty; (3) the violation is 'serious', meaning it protects 'important values', and its breach

---

[169] *Prosecutor v. Erdemović*, Judgment, Separate and Dissenting Opinion of Judge Cassese, ICTY-96–22-A, 7 October 1997, para 11.

[170] Paust (n. 4) 323.

[171] Van Schaack (n. 5) 134; Cassese (n. 1) 72. A common refrain of judges was that the legality principle does not apply with the same force to international criminal law as compared to national criminal laws.

[172] 22 IMT Judgment (n. 49) 463.

[173] RR Baxter, 'The Effects of Ill-Conceived Codification and Development of International Law' in *Recueil d'études de droit international en hommage à Paul Guggenheim* (Geneva 1968) 146, 150.

has 'grave consequences for the victim'; and (4) the customary or treaty rule entails individual criminal liability.[174]

In its recognition of crimes in non-international armed conflicts, the ICTY Appeals Chamber has been criticized for conflating the illegality of certain conduct in the *Geneva Conventions* (1949) with individual criminal liability. Consequently, it has been argued that such conflation is particularly prevalent in war crimes jurisprudence, which draws heavily from international human-itarian law treaties that prohibit all kinds of conduct.[175] Some have not found this conflation of illegality and criminality to be objectionable and have even suggested its expansion to include prohibitions in international human rights instruments that are almost universally accepted and have entered the global consciousness, thereby providing defendants with 'fair notice of the possibil-ity of criminal liability for abusive practices'.[176] However, a 'human right is a right held *vis-à-vis* the state, by virtue of being a human being' and it has been recalled that '[t]his basic proposition, and its difference from principles of international criminal law . . . where individuals do have responsibilities under international law, must be kept firmly in mind when considering questions of retroactivity'.[177]

Similarly, the Appeals Chamber of the Special Tribunal for Lebanon recently held that it could interpret Lebanese law on terrorism in accordance with inter-national legal standards contained in the *Arab Convention for the Suppression of Terrorism* (1998) (*Arab Convention*)[178] and customary international law, even though the definition of terrorism in the *Arab Convention* was not intended to replace national definitions of this crime and was meant to operate only for purposes of judicial cooperation among ratifying States:

> [I]t was foreseeable for a Lebanese national or for anybody living in Lebanon that any act designed to spread terror would be punishable, regardless of the kind of instrumentalities used as long as such instrumen-talities were likely to cause a public danger. This proposition is borne out by the fact that neither the Arab Convention nor customary international law, both applicable within the Lebanese legal order, restrict the means used to perpetrate terrorism, and both of these sources of law are binding on Lebanon. Furthermore, Lebanon's legislature has gradually authorised or approved ratification of or accession to a number of international treaties against terrorist action, which likewise do *not* contain any such limitation as to the means to be used for a terrorist act.[179]

---

[174] *Prosecutor* v. *Tadić*, Decision on the Defence Motion for Interlocutory Appeal on Juris-diction, ICTY-94–1-AR72, 2 October 1995, para. 94.

[175] Van Schaack (n. 5) 150.   [176] Ibid. 183.

[177] Juratowitch (n. 128) 351 (citing R Higgins, *Problems and Processes: International Law and How We Use It* (Oxford University Press 1994) 98).

[178] League of Arab States (adopted 22 April 1998, entered into force 7 May 1999).

[179] Interlocutory Decision on the Applicable Law: Terrorism, Conspiracy, Homicide, Perpe-tration, Cumulative Charging, STL-II-0l/I, 16 February 2011, paras. 138–139.

Reasoning that conflates illegality and criminality is not without its weaknesses. First, not all illegal conduct under international law will give rise to individual criminal liability.[180]

> It is a well-established truism in international law that if a given conduct is permitted by general or particular international law, that permissibility deprives the conduct of its criminal character under international criminal law. But if a given conduct is prohibited by general or particular international law it does not mean that it is criminal *ipso iure*. The problem thus lies in distinguishing between prohibited conduct which falls within the legally defined criminal category and that which does not.[181]

The conflation of illegality and criminality offers no guidance on which illegal conduct might become criminal, thereby generating considerable uncertainty in the field of international criminal law. Such a troubling state of affairs undermines the rule of law by leaving great scope for judicial discretion.

A second concern is that the conflation of illegality and criminality might well result in a 'new' law inflicting a greater punishment on an individual than previously contemplated. In *Calder* v. *Bull* (1798), the United States Supreme Court identified four situations in which the prohibition against retroactivity is violated: (1) if an action 'innocent when done' is criminalized under a new law; (2) if a new law 'aggravates a crime'; (3) if a new law 'inflicts a greater punishment'; or (4) if a new law 'alters the legal rules of evidence, and receives less, or different, testimony, than the law required . . . in order to convict the offender'.[182] The Nuremberg reasoning can be supported by the fact that the conduct was not perfectly 'innocent' when committed because an international prohibition existed at the relevant time. However, what about the third situation? Can it not be said that the notion of individual criminal responsibility 'inflicts a greater punishment' on relevant actors than that of State responsibility under international law arising from illegal conduct? Unlike a State, an individual may well be imprisoned for many years as a result of committing a crime under international law. However, this reasoning was rejected by the ICTY in *Prosecutor* v. *Hadžihasanović and Others* (2002), which held that the principle of legality is not violated simply because the penalty is different than what the accused might have thought: 'whether the conduct may lead to criminal responsibility, disciplinary responsibility or other sanctions is not of material importance' so long as the defendant knew that the conduct was condemned, meaning not innocent.[183]

---

[180] Kelsen (n. 3) 116, cited in Bassiouni (n. 3) 89.

[181] MC Bassiouni, *Crimes Against Humanity in International Criminal Law* (Martinus Nijhoff 1992) 113, cited in *Delalić* (n. 75) para. 406.

[182] 3 U.S. (3 Dall.) 385 (1798).

[183] *Prosecutor* v. *Hadžihasanović and Others*, Decision on Joint Challenge to Jurisdiction, ICTY-01–47-PT, 12 November 2002, para. 62.

Third, the conflation of illegality and criminality raises questions about the separation of powers doctrine. If States wanted to criminalize illegal conduct, they could have done this expressly in a treaty, or the illegal norm could have crystallized into a crime under customary law through the accretion of State practice and *opinio juris*.

4.3.5 Reclassification of the offence

Application of the legality principle at the international level has been said to permit fair warning to the accused in the form of national law and therefore retroactive creation of an offence under international law.[184] Another type of reclassification that international tribunals have permitted, which will not be the focus of this section, is where the name of a crime within the international legal system is changed to that of another crime in the same system.[185] Regarding the reclassification of national crimes to international ones, the idea is that the defendant has 'sufficient notice of the wrongfulness and criminality of the underlying conduct, even when the act is prosecuted under an unprecedented international law analog that requires a showing of additional elements, such as the existence of an armed conflict or discriminatory intent'.[186] Such additional elements are considered to be merely 'jurisdictional' or 'aggravating'.[187] So long as the material elements of the original crime are not lessened, it is thought that the principle of non-retroactivity is not violated.[188] Further, the defendant cannot claim that he or she did not know that the conduct in question was criminal, only that prosecution before an international tribunal was unforeseen.[189]

Again, one is able to trace the contemplated reasoning to post-Second World War jurisprudence. Although prosecutors at Nuremberg made the reclassification argument, judges did not comment on it in their final judgment.[190] It did, however, succeed in the *Einsatzgruppen* case (1948) under Control Council Law No. 10:

---

[184] Gallant (n. 46) 130; Van Schaack (n. 5) 168 (citing *Milutinović* (n. 137) paras. 40–41; *Prosecutor* v. *Hadžihasanović and Others*, Interlocutory Appeal on Decision on Joint Challenge to Jurisdiction, ICTY-01–47-PT, 27 November 2002, para. 62; *Prosecutor* v. *Kupreškić and Others*, Judgment, ICTY-95–16-T, 14 January 2000, paras 681–687).

[185] Gallant, ibid. 322. '[T]he core rule of legality, that the act must have been a crime when committed, is met.' Gallant does not think that the principle of fair labelling is threatened by such reclassification (367). As well, the 'jurisprudence of the tribunals also directly refutes any suggestion that the act of labelling a particular act as genocide as opposed to, for example, war crimes, automatically makes a defendant liable for a greater sentence'. T Meron, 'Remarks' (2009) 103 ASIL Proceedings 8.

[186] Van Schaack (n. 5) 168 (citing *Delalić* (n. 75) para. 312).

[187] Ibid.   [188] Gallant (n. 46) 131–32.   [189] Van Schaack (n. 5) 168–69.

[190] Gallant (n. 46) 131–32.

Murder, torture, enslavement and similar crimes which heretofore were enjoined only by the respective nations now fall within the prescription of the family of nations. Thus murder becomes no less murder because directed against a whole race instead of a single person.[191]

Legality so understood requires, at a minimum, that the conduct charged is criminal under some law that is applicable to the defendant.[192] Conversely, French courts admitted the reclassification of international crimes as national crimes following the Second World War.[193] However, not all courts of that era reclassified offences.[194]

With the renaissance of international criminal law in the early 1990s, the reclassification argument was revived and enjoyed limited success.[195] One ICTY Trial Chamber reasoned that the primary issue is 'the conduct, rather than . . . the specific description of the offence in substantive criminal law',[196] and that judges are to ask 'whether the act of the accused was a crime as generally understood at the time of the offense charged'.[197] One example of such reclassification is where the doctrine of 'joint criminal enterprise' was recognized under international criminal law by reclassifying acts of criminal complicity that had previously existed under national laws.[198] However, the ICTY, ICTR and Special Court for Sierra Leone have generally asserted their ability to decide cases without resorting to the retroactive reclassification of offences.[199]

Several concerns about reclassification might be raised. First, it is difficult to reconcile with an important aspect of the theory of international law, which is that crimes exist under it 'whether or not in violation of the domestic laws

---

[191] 4 Trials of War Criminals Before the Nuremberg Military Tribunal under Control Council Law No. 10 (1951) 496.

[192] Gallant (n. 46) 131–32. See also *Altstötter* (n. 124); *United States* v. *Ohlendorf and Others* (1948), cited in C Kreß (n. 9) para. 16.

[193] Gallant (n. 46) 130.

[194] See ibid. 131–32 on the practice of British military courts under Control Council Law No. 10.

[195] Ibid. 134.

[196] *Prosecutor* v. *Hadžihasanović and Others*, Decision on Interlocutory Appeal Challenging Jurisdiction in Relation to Command Responsibility, ICTY-01–47-AR72, 16 July 2003, paras. 62, 165.

[197] Gallant (n. 46) 320–21 (citing *Hadžihasanović and Others*, ibid. para. 34); *Norman* (n. 156) para. 25.

[198] Gallant, ibid. (citing *Milutinović* (n. 137) para. 10).

[199] Gallant, ibid. (citing *Prosecutor* v. *Akayesu*, Judgment, ICTR-96–4-T, 2 September 1998, paras. 611–617; *Prosecutor* v. *Furundžija*, Judgment, ICTY-95–17/1-T, 10 December 1998, paras. 165–169; *Norman* (n. 156) para. 25; *Prosecutor* v. *Delalić and Others*, Judgment, ICTY-96–21-A, 20 February 2001, paras. 178–180).

of the country where perpetrated'.[200] If national law is relied on to provide fair notice of what is criminal under international law, could not the lack of a national prohibition be raised to object to the international criminalization of conduct permissible under national law?

Second, it is questionable whether jurisdictional elements are completely benign. It has been argued that these elements do not go to the 'guilt or innocence of a particular accused'.[201] Nevertheless, some jurisdictional elements are morally material and have to be proven, such as 'knowledge of the attack directed against any civilian population'.[202] Still, it often cannot convincingly be argued that the defendant would have behaved any differently had he or she known that the relevant conduct would be classified as a more, rather than a less, serious offence.[203] Even if this is true, a third concern is that reclassification within the Rome regime may still offend the separation of powers doctrine and be inconsistent with the attendant rule of strict construction.

> A strict construction requires that no case shall fall within a penal statute which does not comprise all the elements which, whether morally material or not, are in fact made to constitute the offence as defined by the statute. In other words, a strict construction requires that an offence is made out in accordance with the statute creating it only when all the essential ingredients, as prescribed by the statute, have been established.[204]

Indeed, legislative bodies bear the burden of defining criminal conduct clearly. This gives rise to a fourth and related concern, which is violating the principle of fair labelling. At the domestic level, concerns of fair labelling might arise, for example, when a person intended to commit manslaughter rather than murder or cause bodily harm rather than grievous bodily harm, and the more serious latter offence is charged.[205] Similarly, it is arguable, for example, that greater stigma attaches to a conviction of a crime against humanity as compared to a conviction for rape or murder. Unlike national crimes, the 'punishability of international crimes rests on the fact that such acts injure the international community in whole or in part and its prevention, control, and repression are not based on the individual victim but on the international community as a whole'.[206] The reclassification argument cannot offer an explanation for violating the principle of fair labelling. Instead, the ICTY has responded to this concern by asserting that violation of this principle must be weighed against 'the

---

[200] Control Council Law No. 10, adopted in Berlin, 20 December 1945, Official Gazette of the Control Council for Germany No. 3, 31 January 1946, reprinted in B Ferencz, *An International Criminal Court: A Step Toward World Peace*, vol. I (Oceana 1980) 488.

[201] LN Sadat and SR Carden, 'The New International Criminal Court: An Uneasy Revolution' (2000) 88 Georgetown LJ 381, 426.

[202] Ibid. 429–31; article 7(1), Rome Statute.   [203] Ashworth (n. 21) 442.

[204] *Delalić* (n. 75) para. 411.

[205] Ashworth (n. 21) 442.   [206] Bassiouni (n. 3) 89.

fundamental principle of protecting human dignity', a potent normative notion that judges have struggled to define.[207] It also does not sit comfortably alongside the ICTY and ICTR's jurisprudence on the *ne bis in idem* doctrine, which seems to take fair labelling quite seriously. The doctrine precludes these tribunals from trying an individual for the same crime prosecuted by a national court but permits the prosecution of conduct that was prosecuted at the national level as an 'ordinary' as opposed to international crime.[208] Such an understanding of the *ne bis in idem* doctrine supports the view that ordinary and international crimes are different in a morally material sense and not distinguishable solely on the basis of jurisdictional elements. Finally, it has been argued that such a practice is 'too easily subject to abuse'[209] and would give rise to serious conflict of jurisdiction problems.[210]

Despite the aforementioned concerns, the reclassification of offences is a practice that has been defended by some who would permit it in very narrow circumstances. For example, it is argued that the principle of legality is not offended where an international tribunal prosecutes an individual for a crime that was not a crime under international law at the relevant time but was a crime under applicable national law when committed.[211] '[T]he core rule of legality, that the act must have been a crime when committed, is met.'[212] The author agrees that if the crime charged (or a sufficiently similar one) existed under applicable national law when the conduct occurred, the principle of legality is not offended if that crime is prosecuted before an (*ex post facto*) international criminal tribunal. And neither is the principle of fair labelling. The national legislature where the defendant resides has the authority and institutional competence to define conduct as criminal in a legally binding manner for the defendant.[213] As well, where an ordinary national crime is reclassified as an international crime and the latter's jurisdictional elements are not morally material, judges should perhaps address in a principled manner how this interpretation does not offend the separation of powers or strict construction doctrines associated with the legality principle.

4.3.6 Criminal law in a changing world

In 1975, the House of Lords stated in *Regina* v. *Withers* that it would no longer seek to exercise the power to create new offences.[214] However, Lord Dilhorne added: 'To say that there is now no power in the judges to declare new offences

---

[207] *Furundžija* (n. 199) para. 184; C McCrudden, 'Human Dignity and Judicial Interpretation of Human Rights' (2005) 19 EJIL 655.

[208] JJ Paust, 'It's No Defense: Nullum Crimen, International Crime and the Gingerbread Man' (1997) 60 Albany L Rev 657, 663.

[209] Gallant (n. 46) 369.   [210] Kreß (n. 9) para. 25.

[211] Gallant (n. 46) 367.   [212] Ibid.

[213] Packer (n. 6) 80; Gallant (n. 46) 368.   [214] [1975] AC 842.

does not, of course, mean that well-established principles are not to be applied to new facts.'[215] Thus, old crimes can be committed in new ways without violating the principle of legality, but the 'difficulty arises in knowing how to identify when a species of wrongdoing is wholly new'.[216] At Nuremberg, the tribunal reasoned that the law of war 'is not static, but by continual adaptation follows the needs of a changing world'.[217] Similarly, the European Court of Human Rights held: 'However clearly drafted a legal provision may be, there is an inevitable element of judicial interpretation. There will always be a need for elucidation of doubtful points and for adaption to changing circumstances.'[218]

But when is a law applied to new facts, and when is a wholly new species of wrongdoing created? The distinction may sometimes be difficult to discern. Consider the following two examples of the law responding to the 'needs of a changing world'. A law criminalizes the use of weapons that cause indiscriminate harm. At the time of the law's enactment, the only weapons that fell into this category were machine guns and bombs. But then, technological advances led to the development of nuclear warfare, biological and chemical warfare and other weapons of mass destruction. Would a judge be violating the principle of legality if he or she concluded that an individual was guilty of this crime for engaging in chemical warfare? No, assuming that the judge was able to take judicial notice of the indiscriminate impact of such warfare. The criminal prohibition is sufficiently broad in its wording that developments in the changing world can be accommodated by it. But what if the criminal prohibition was that no one may use machine guns or bombs? And what if the legislative purpose behind the prohibition was to forbid the use of weapons that cause indiscriminate harm to individuals? Would it violate the principle of legality to interpret this provision broadly to include chemical warfare in order to respond to the needs of a changing world? The answer seems to be yes if one is to apply a strict notion of legality, which would not permit judges to revise the wording of a criminal prohibition.[219] Thus, the needs of a changing world cannot be understood, in and of themselves, as a justification for violating the principle of legality.

In some cases, accommodating such changes will not require the principle to be endangered and, where it is, it is not obvious that the Rome Statute would accept its violation. Article 22(3) clearly provides: 'This article shall not affect the characterization of any conduct as criminal under international

---

[215] Ibid. 859.   [216] Smith (n. 98) 57.   [217] (1946) 1 IMT Judgment 209.

[218] App. No. 24246/94, *Okçuoglu* v. *Turkey*, ECHR (1999) para. 39.

[219] However, see Chapter 5, Section 5.7.1 on analogous reasoning in common and civil law jurisdictions.

law independently of this Statute.'[220] Thus, precisely because drafters of the Rome Statute could not agree unanimously on which crimes to include and exclude from the Court's jurisdiction, it was agreed that, if certain conduct is excluded from the Rome Statute, the principle of legality would result in the exclusion of criminal liability by the Court. Such a ruling is not tantamount to a pronouncement on the legality or criminality of that conduct, which may well be criminal under general international law. As well, judges can request amendments to the Elements of Crimes and thereby signal their concerns about a changing world to the Assembly of States Parties.

In conclusion, it is essential to 'not confuse the deliberate invention of new rules with the relatively unconscious subsumption of unanticipated or even unintended sets of facts under old prescriptions – a process found in both code and common law adjudication, and a phenomenon inseparable from the endless interaction of a growing language and changing socioeconomic institutions'.[221] More is said in Chapter 5 about how to balance respect for the interpretive imperative of strict construction in article 22(2) with the principle of effective interpretation.

4.3.7 Purposive or teleological reasoning

The ICTY has advanced purposive or teleological reasoning to overcome adhering to very strict conceptions of legality. It held that the Security Council's decision to create the ICTY was for the purpose of ensuring that all individuals responsible for serious violations of international humanitarian law on the territory of the former Yugoslavia would be held accountable for their actions and that this goal existed irrespective of whether the conflict was international or not.[222] It further bolstered its position by describing the object and purpose of international humanitarian law in general as 'regulating the means and methods of warfare [, the protection of] persons not actively participating in armed conflict from harm' and 'respect for human dignity'.[223] As mentioned in the previous Chapter, the goal of protecting victims of rights violations gave rise to normative tensions with strict legality, and the former prevailed on several occasions absent examination of the presumed positive relationship between convictions supported by such reasoning and the protection of victims.[224] For example, in *Furundžija* (1998), the ICTY bolstered its finding that forcible oral

---

[220] See Chapter 5, Section 5.8.   [221] Hall (n. 44) 179–80.
[222] *Hadžihasanović* (n 196) paras. 97–101; Boot (n. 32) 389.
[223] Van Schaack (n. 5) 143 (citing *Hadžihasanović* (n. 196) para. 64). In support of this, the ICTY drew inspiration from the 'Preamble of the Second Additional Protocol to the Geneva Conventions, which contains a variant of the Martens Clause'.
[224] Boot (n. 32) 389.

intercourse can be charged as rape and therefore as a war crime by recalling the object and purpose of international humanitarian law:

> The essence of the whole corpus of international humanitarian law as well as human rights law lies in the protection of the human dignity of every person, whatever his or her gender . . . This principle is intended to shield human beings from outrages upon their personal dignity, whether such outrages are carried out by unlawfully attacking the body or by humiliating and debasing the honour, the self-respect or the mental well-being of a person.[225]

Additionally, it is common for legal regimes to have multiple objectives and not offer guidance on their relationship to one another in cases of conflict.[226] Some regimes might indicate that competing interests be 'balanced,' 'blended,' 'accommodated,' 'taken account of' or 'dealt with such that the public interest will be served',[227] which is essentially a delegation of discretion to be exercised in cases of such conflict. The Rome Statute contains no such express guidance or delegation, although it might be implied.

The object and purpose of a treaty are often discussed together even though 'the "object" is . . . about *what* the treaty covers and the "purpose" is about *why* the treaty covers an issue'.[228] For the Rome Statute, it might be useful to step back and decouple the two concepts so as not to stretch the regime beyond its natural limits. One *object* of the Rome Statute is the most serious crimes under international law, *as defined in* articles 6, 7, 8 and 8 *bis* of the Statute. One *purpose* of this Statute is to establish a permanent international criminal court that has jurisdiction over *these* crimes. Judges are entrusted with applying the Rome Statute as it stands, not implementing a general policy to end impunity for serious international crimes. Viewed this way, an interpretation that includes a 'most serious crime' within the jurisdiction of the Court would confirm or justify an interpretation that emerges from other interpretive techniques rather than form an 'independent basis for interpretation', to borrow a phrase from the WTO Appellate Body.[229] By interpreting a treaty in accordance with articles 31–33 of the *Vienna Convention* (1969), the idea of effective interpretation can operate as follows: (1) serve a 'confirming or corrective function' in a negative sense, meaning the interpretation being considered should not be ineffective; (2) remind judges to arrive at interpretations of treaty provisions that, taken together, are 'intellectually coherent' and consider their

---

[225] *Furundžija* (n. 199) para. 179.   [226] Robinson (n. 52) 426–27.   [227] Ibid.

[228] I Van Damme, 'Treaty Interpretation by the WTO Appellate Body' (2010) 21:3 EJIL 605, 631.

[229] Appellate Body Report, Japan – Taxes on Alcoholic Beverages (Japan–Alcoholic Beverages II), WT/DS8/AB/R, WT/DS10/AB/R, WT/DS11/AB/R (adopted 1 November 2006) 106, fn. 20.

'implications for the future development of the treaty regime'; and (3) call for a treaty to be 'interpreted as a whole', meaning provisions are not reduced to having no meaning and are read in a harmonious manner to the extent possible – thereby encouraging cross-referencing.[230]

Unlike the ICTY, article 22(3) of the Rome Statute seems to expressly discourage reasoning of the type seen in *Prosecutor v. Furundžija* (1998) by contemplating that not all crimes under international law will fall within the scope of the Court's jurisdiction and that the acquittal of an individual says nothing about whether he or she is guilty of committing a crime under international law or violating the human dignity of another. Thus, the goal of the Rome regime is not to hold accountable every individual who is responsible under international criminal law for the commission of serious crimes, but rather to exercise the regime's limited jurisdiction effectively, which includes respecting the principle of legality as described in article 22. The question that remains to be answered in the following Chapter, however, is whether the object and purpose of the criminal prohibition in question is interpretive reasoning that can be accommodated within a methodology for which legality is the guiding interpretive principle.

Such an inquiry might be helpful when considering whether a criminal prohibition is intended to apply to particular conduct, classes of persons or circumstances. It is arguable that the legality principle should not be applied in a manner that prevents a criminal prohibition from responding to the mischief it is intended to address. There will always be borderline cases, a penumbra of doubt, and this is where the legality principle is intended to do its work. In the vast majority of cases, however, it should be fairly clear whether a criminal prohibition covers the conduct, class of individuals or circumstances in question. Legality would prevent a criminal prohibition from covering every imaginable conduct that remotely seems to meet the definition contained therein while allowing the latter to be effective in most cases. Effectiveness is therefore a question of degree and not an absolute. And the danger of teleological reasoning that invokes sympathy for the victims of grave violations of human rights, and a protection or ending impunity narrative, is that it could legitimize arguments of absolute effectiveness, which would gut the legality of *its* purpose altogether. Indeed, Sir Humphrey Waldock expressed concern that if the principle of effectiveness was expressly codified in the *Vienna Convention* (1969), it could unintentionally lead to 'extreme functional interpretation which may, in fact, lead to "legislation" or the revision of a treaty'.[231]

---

[230] Van Damme (n. 228) 635, 637–38.
[231] ME Villiger, 'The Rules on Interpretation: Misgivings, Misunderstandings, Miscarriage? The "Crucible" Intended by the International Law Commission' in E Cannizzaro (ed.),

4.3.8 Foreseeability and accessibility

Over the years, a certain refrain has taken hold in the legality jurisprudence of the European Court of Human Rights (ECtHR), the idea that this principle is upheld so long as the legal innovation is reasonably foreseeable and accessible.[232] Perhaps the most famous example of this reasoning can be found in *SW* v. *United Kingdom* (1995). In 1992, the House of Lords had to determine whether a husband could be held criminally liable for raping his wife.[233] The common law stated that he could not, and the Sexual Offences (Amendment) Act of 1976 (Sexual Offences Act) seemed to recognize this common law exception by criminalizing only rape that is 'unlawful'. The House of Lords ruled that the word 'unlawful' in the Sexual Offences Act did not recognize this common law exception. It held that it was not creating a new offence, but rather removing a common law fiction that had become anachronistic and offensive. The appellant appealed that judgment to the ECtHR and challenged the legality of the decision under article 7(1) of the *European Convention on Human Rights (ECHR)* (1950).[234] The ECtHR held that article 7, which prohibits the retroactive application of criminal laws, did not prevent the retroactive application of the criminal law and its clarification through judicial interpretation, provided that the development of the law was clearly defined and 'reasonably foreseeable, with appropriate legal advice, to the applicant'.[235]

Proponents of the progressive development of international criminal law, such as Judge Shahabuddeen, have seized upon this concept.[236] The idea is that the device of strict construction does not prevent a judge from endorsing an interpretation of a criminal prohibition that is not favourable to the accused (compared to other interpretations) so long as the criminal prohibition can tolerate the interpretation, it is consistent with the 'essence' of the offence (a concept to be analysed in the next section) and it is reasonably foreseeable and accessible to the defendant at the time the conduct occurred.[237] This reasoning has been advanced by the ECtHR when confronted with allegations of the legality principle being violated in common law countries and has resulted in the finding that criminal prohibitions can be unwritten and still respect the

---

The Law of Treaties Beyond the Vienna Convention (Oxford University Press 2011) 105, 106–07, 110.

[232] App. No. 18139/91, *Miloslavsky* v. *United Kingdom*, ECHR (1995) Series A, No. 316-B, para. 37; App. No. 45771/99, *Veeber* v. *Estonia*, ECHR (2003), Rep. 2003-I, para. 32; App. No. 6538/74, *Sunday Times* v. *United Kingdom*, ECHR (1979) Series A, No. 30, para. 49.

[233] *R* v. *R* [1992] 1 AC 599.

[234] 213 UNTS 221 (adopted 4 November 1950, entered into force 3 September 1953).

[235] App. No. 20166/92, *SW* v. *United Kingdom*, ECHR (1995) Series A, No. 335-B, para. 40.

[236] Shahabuddeen (n. 72).

[237] App. No. 74613/01, *Jorgić* v. *Germany*, ECHR (2007) para 114. For a case on unforeseeability, see App. No. 40403/02, *Pessino* v. *France*, ECHR (2006) para 36.

principle of legality if the aforementioned conditions are met.[238] If the criminal sanction is foreseeable and accessible, it is thought to be just to punish an individual because he or she had a chance to avoid engaging in conduct expected to be criminal.[239] However, the standard is objective, one of 'reasonable' foreseeability.[240] The ECtHR has held that retroactively applied criminal law innovations can be foreseeable even if this would require obtaining legal advice.[241] It has even posited holding individuals engaged in professional activities to a stricter standard of foreseeability because they can 'be expected to take special care in assessing the risk that such activity entails.'[242] As for accessibility, the test is that the law has a 'publicly available meaning', which is tantamount to fair warning – although not of the law, but of the foreseeable law.[243]

Importantly, customary international law has been held to be accessible.[244] The tests of foreseeability and accessibility are to 'allow the character of a law, its interpretation and application to be assessed against independent criteria'.[245] These standards have been endorsed by the ICTY.[246] However, neither the United Nations Human Rights Committee nor the Inter-American Court of Human Rights has expressly validated them.[247] Perhaps this is because there are concerns that the concept of reasonable foreseeability is not sufficiently robust. It has been cautioned that this doctrine 'must be carefully applied and circumscribed. Otherwise, it may swallow the principle of legality whole' by making it easy for judges to apply criminal laws retroactively simply by stating that the criminal prohibition was foreseeable.[248] One scholar rightly and provocatively queried: 'In light of past trends of ambitious interpretation in ICL [international criminal law], does a "foreseeable innovation" test *exclude* anything?'[249] Whether foreseeability can operate as an effective device to limit

---

[238] Schabas (n. 32) 404.

[239] Kelsen (n. 14) 9; App. No. 25390/94, *Rekvenyi* v. *Hungary*, ECHR (1999) 1999-III, para. 60.

[240] R Higgins, 'Time and Law'(1997) 46 Int'l Comp LQ 501, 508.

[241] B Juratowitch (n. 128) 348 (citing App. No. 14307/88, *Kokkinakis* v. *Greece*, ECHR (1993) Series A, No. 260, para. 52; *SW* (n. 235) para. 35; *Okçuoglu* (n. 218) paras. 36, 39; *Veeber* (n. 232) para. 30; and, on the other hand, *Cantoni* (n. 20) para. 35).

[242] *Parker* v. *Levy*, 417 U.S. 733, 756 (1974) (U.S. Supreme Court indicating that '[f]or the reasons which differentiate military society from civilian society, . . . Congress is permitted to legislate both with greater breadth and with greater flexibility when prescribing the rules by which the former shall be governed than it is when prescribing rules for the latter', cited in Van Schaack (n. 5) 179).

[243] Gallant (n. 46) 366.

[244] Ibid. (citing *Hadžihasanović* (n. 196) para. 34; *Norman* (n. 156) para. 25; *Furundžija* (n. 199); *Delalić* (n. 199) paras. 178–180).

[245] Juratowitch (n. 128) 350.

[246] *Delalić* (n. 75) paras. 311ff.; *Delalić* (n. 199) para. 817, fn. 1400.

[247] Juratowitch (n. 128) 350.   [248] Gallant (n. 46) 364–65.

[249] Robinson (n. 28) 4 (emphasis in original).

the retroactive creation of crimes to exceptional cases depends greatly on the concept being precisely defined and circumscribed. One may also insist not only that retroactively applied criminal prohibitions must be foreseeable but also that methods of interpretation applied by judges must also be foreseeable.

One suggestion is to define foreseeability as requiring that some law applicable to the defendant contain the criminal prohibition at the time the conduct occurred.[250] The consistency of this concept with legality has been endorsed and discussed in a previous section.[251] Another proxy suggested for foreseeability is the conduct not being innocent when it occurred.[252] Accordingly, the ICTY has, on occasion, held that knowledge of conduct not being innocent means that criminalization of the impugned conduct was foreseeable and accessible to the defendant.[253] If lack of innocence is a reference to the conduct being illegal but not criminal under international law, this has been discussed in a previous section, as has the concept of moral innocence or lack thereof.[254] Regarding the immorality of the conduct in question, the foreseeability analysis of the ECtHR has taken into consideration 'changes in society that might render an old rule *offensive, anachronistic,* or presently unworkable.'[255]

Yet another understanding of foreseeability that the European Commission advanced was to say that '[w]here there is considerable uncertainty or movement in the law . . . the populace is essentially on notice that the law is in flux and could be interpreted adversely to future defendants. Contrary judicial opinions or legislative debate can indicate such instability in the law.'[256] However, such an understanding of foreseeability does not sit well with the notion in article 22(2) that, in case of ambiguity, the law must be interpreted in favour of the person being investigated, prosecuted or convicted. This provision places the burden on States Parties to draft laws that are sufficiently clear in the majority of cases and that are interpreted in favour of the defendant in borderline cases.

In conclusion, Blackstone and many after him have identified foreseeability as a bar to injustice.[257] However, the foreseeability argument does pose some problems. As well, another bar to injustice that should be borne in mind is the judicial presumption in some countries that the drafters of laws do not intend to override fundamental rights absent clear and unambiguous statutory language.[258] Unlike the foreseeability argument, this latter bar to injustice gives drafters an appropriate incentive to draft clear laws, which is in the interest

---

[250] Ibid. 364.   [251] See Section 4.2.1.   [252] Blackstone (n. 14) (cited in Kelsen (n. 14) 9).
[253] Van Schaack (n. 5) 142 (citing *Hadžihasanović* (n. 196) para. 62).
[254] See Section 4.3.2.
[255] Van Schaack (n. 5) 178–79 (citing App. No. 20190/92, *CR* (n. 139) paras. 37, 41) (emphasis added).
[256] Ibid. (citing *CR,* ibid. paras. 41, 59).   [257] Blackstone (n. 14).
[258] *R* v. *Home Secretary, ex parte Simms* [1999] 3 WLR 328.

of all members of the international community. It also seems to be more in line with the presumption of innocence, which is the cornerstone of so many criminal justice systems, including the Rome criminal justice system.[259] The foreseeability exception to legality is very tempting, especially given the nature and gravity of some conduct. For the time being, however, there does not seem to be a sufficiently certain way to circumscribe the concept of foreseeability apart from the existence of the same criminal prohibition under applicable national law. Further, article 22(1) of the Rome Statute seems to foreclose the possibility of admitting arguments of foreseeability, as it limits findings of criminal liability to conduct that constitutes '*at the time it takes place*, a crime within the jurisdiction of the Court'.[260]

4.3.9 Essence of the offence

Another concept appearing in the ECtHR's jurisprudence is that of consistency with the 'essence of the offence' as evidence of retroactively applied criminal law not being arbitrary and therefore respectful of the legality principle.[261] Accordingly, the ECtHR held that where the 'prosecution leaves the basic ingredients of a criminal offense unchanged, but modifies or abandons non-core elements – such as attendant or circumstantial elements', the principle of legality is not violated.[262] However, this gives rise to concerns about so-called 'non-core' elements actually being material and concerns about fair labelling, discussed elsewhere.[263] Nevertheless, international criminal tribunals have taken up this reasoning in their jurisprudence.[264] For example, Judge Shahabuddeen reasoned that interpreting the term 'deportation' to cover not just the crossing of a border but also the crossing of a front line, even one that is constantly changing, is consistent with the essence of the offence of deportation as a crime against humanity.[265] It is submitted that the 'essence' of the offence is a concept that may well be invoked for noble reasons but is perhaps too malleable for criminal law and therefore at risk of being abused.[266] It may also not sit well with the

---

[259] Article 66, Rome Statute: '1. Everyone shall be presumed innocent until proved guilty before the Court in accordance with the applicable law. 2. The onus is on the Prosecutor to prove the guilt of the accused. 3. In order to convict the accused, the Court must be convinced of the guilt of the accused beyond reasonable doubt.'

[260] Emphasis added.   [261] Van Schaack (n. 5) 181 (citing *CR* (n. 139) para. 32).

[262] Ibid. 178 (citing App. No. 8710/79, *X Ltd & Y v. United Kingdom*, Eur Comm'n HR (1982) 28 Eur Comm'n HR Dec. & Rep. 77, 81).

[263] See Section 4.3.5.   [264] Van Schaack (n. 5) 173.

[265] *Prosecutor v. Stakić*, Judgment, Partly Dissenting Opinion of Judge Shahabuddeen, ICTY-97–24-A, 22 March 2006, paras. 23ff.

[266] The same has been said about the argument of interpretation consistent with the 'spirit' of a treaty or treaty provision. R Gardiner, *Treaty Interpretation* (Oxford University Press 2008) 197ff.

ban on analogous reasoning in article 22(2) of the Statute: 'The definition of a crime shall be strictly construed and shall not be extended by analogy.'

4.3.10 Interpretive aids

In the previous sections, arguments that might be used to override the express wording of the Rome Statute, and thereby undermine the principle of legality, were examined. However, nothing has been said about how these arguments might be used in the context of invoking aids to interpret the definitions of crimes in the Statute. For example, can a new class of individuals, conduct or circumstances be held by judges to be tolerated by the wording of the Statute on the basis that this is supported by an interpretive aid such as custom, a treaty or general principle of law? The Rome Statute limits the Court's jurisdiction to crimes listed in article 5 as defined in articles 6, 7, 8 and 8 *bis*.[267] But do any sources of law identified in article 38 of the ICJ Statute and article 21 of the Rome Statute violate the principle of legality? Some posit that international criminal tribunals have defined the concept of fair notice as encompassing all sources of law listed in article 38 of the ICJ Statute.[268] The idea is that the principle of legality is satisfied so long as one of the main or subsidiary sources of law in article 38 notifies the defendant that certain conduct is prohibited although not necessarily criminal.[269]

Consequently, article 15 of the *International Covenant on Civil and Political Rights* (1966) *(ICCPR)* provides:

1. No one shall be held guilty of any criminal offence on account of any act or omission which did not constitute a criminal offence, under national or international law, at the time when it was committed. Nor shall a heavier penalty be imposed than the one that was applicable at the time when the criminal offence was committed. If, subsequent to the commission of the offence, provision is made by law for the imposition of the lighter penalty, the offender shall benefit thereby.
2. Nothing in this article shall prejudice the trial and punishment of any person for any act or omission which, at the time when it was committed, was criminal according to the general principles of law recognized by the community of nations.

---

[267] Article 22(1), Rome Statute.
[268] 3 Bevans 1179; 59 Stat. 1031; TS 993 (adopted 26 June 1945, entered into force 24 October 1945).
[269] Van Schaack (n. 5) 158–59; IMT Judgment (n. 49) 463–64; Meron (n. 150) 830 (citing *United States* v. *List and Others* (1948), 11 Trials of War Criminals Before the Nuremberg Military Tribunals under Control Council Law No. 10 (1951) 759, 1239).

Article 21(1)(b) of the Rome Statute refers to 'the principles and rules of international law' as applicable law. This term is considered to be a reference to customary international law,[270] thereby rendering it an authoritative interpretive aid that must be taken into account if relevant.[271] The same is true of treaty law and general principles, which are also mentioned in article 21(1)(b) and (c) of the Statute. Individuals appearing before the Court are therefore on notice that these sources of law are applicable to their case for gap-filling purposes and may be used to interpret (but not modify) the definitions of crimes in the Rome Statute. In light of this, arguments about their use not being foreseeable or accessible or resulting in offences being reclassified or conflated with illegality do not seem persuasive.

As we shall see, the sources of law that can give rise to the criminalization of conduct in international law remains 'hotly contested' at the ICTY.[272] In this section, consideration will be given to this debate and what it says about the use of these sources of law as interpretive aids in the Rome regime and whether their invocation respects the principle of legality.

4.3.10.1 Custom

Decades after the Nuremberg judgment, the UN Secretary-General confirmed 'although not without ambiguity and not without significant exception, that international or internationalized criminal courts shall apply or prefer customary international law.'[273] Although some national jurisdictions define legality so as not to permit the application of customary international criminal law absent a written proscription of this law enacted by the legislature, legality in the international legal context is not so strictly defined as to require that a

---

[270] Pellet (n. 32) 1070–71; Schabas (n. 70) 92. Article 21(1)(b) is thought to generally correspond to the sources of international law listed in article 38 of the ICJ Statute: Schabas 91.

[271] RS Summers and M Taruffo, 'Interpretation and Comparative Analysis' in DN MacCormick and RS Summers (eds.), *Interpreting Statutes: A Comparative Study* (Ashgate 1991) 461, 475–76. This distinction has been acknowledged on occasion by judges at the ICTY: *Delalić* (n. 75) paras. 168–169. However, unlike the judges in *Delalić*, Summers and Taruffo define authoritative aids as including non-binding materials, such as official regulations and similar statutes in other jurisdictions.

[272] Zahar and Sluiter (n. 86) 82.

[273] Ibid. 88. This position has recently been challenged by D Jacobs, 'Positivism and International Criminal Law: The Principle of Legality as a Rule of Conflict of Theories' in J d'Aspremont and J Kammerhofer (eds.), *International Legal Positivism in a Post-Modern World* (Cambridge University Press, forthcoming October 2014) 1, http://papers.ssrn.com/sol3/papers.cfm?abstract_id=2046311, accessed 16 October 2013.

criminal prohibition be written.[274] No international human rights instruments require this.

However, there is considerable disagreement as to whether customary criminal prohibitions are able to adequately limit the discretion of judges, which is a value underpinning legality. In Chapter 2, the alleged judicial creativity of judges of the ICTY and ICTR, under the guise of declaring and interpreting custom, was briefly discussed.[275] Indeed, some argue that judges have rarely rejected charges because they lack a basis in customary international law.[276] An example advanced of this trend is the ICTY's recognition that the doctrine of command responsibility could be applied to internal conflicts under customary international law.[277] However, others have argued that customary international law has more often than not served to limit rather than expand the jurisprudence of the ICTY.[278] In support of this position, they offer the examples of the ICTY finding that a particular form of command responsibility, attacks on civilians without serious result, a broad contemplated definition of deportation, the concept of 'violence to life and person' and the concept of 'indirect co-perpetration' did not find support under customary international law at the relevant time.[279] One judge also maintained the view that the crime of spreading terror among the civilian population did not exist under customary international law at the relevant time.[280] Of course, this debate in the context of the ICTY statute must be distinguished from the relevance of custom as an interpretive aid in the Rome Statute, which is considerably more detailed than its ICTY and ICTR counterparts and is a relatively great constraint on judicial creativity.

4.3.10.2 Treaties

The existence of the Rome Statute is perhaps the most obvious example of support for the proposition that treaty law can criminalize conduct, be a source of international criminal jurisdiction and respect the principle of legality.[281]

---

[274] Kreß (n. 9) para. 21.   [275] See Section 2.3.1.9.

[276] C Tomuschat, *Human Rights: Between Idealism and Realism*, 2nd edn (Oxford University Press 2008) 347.

[277] *Hadžihasanović* (n. 196) para. 179, affirmed by the Appeals Chamber, ICTY-01–47-A, 22 April 2008, para. 31.

[278] Meron, 'Remarks' (n. 185) 9.

[279] *Hadžihasanović* (n. 196) paras. 37ff.; *Prosecutor* v. *Kordić and Čerkez*, Judgment, ICTY-95–14/2-A, 17 December 2004, paras. 67–68; *Prosecutor* v. *Stakić*, Judgment, ICTY-97–24-A, 22 March 2006, paras. 288–303, 320–321; *Prosecutor* v. *Milutinović and Others*, Decision on Ojdanic's Motion Challenging Jurisdiction: Indirect Co-Perpetration, ICTY-05–87-T, 22 March 2006.

[280] *Prosecutor* v. *Galić*, Judgment, Separate and Partly Dissenting Opinion of Judge Schomburg, ICTY-98–29-A, 30 November 2006 with respect to acts and threats of violence intended to spread terror among the civilian population.

[281] Consider as well treaties that criminalize transnational crimes.

The report of the Secretary-General on the establishment of the ICTY states that the 'application of the principle *nullum crimen sine lege* requires that the international tribunal should apply rules of international humanitarian law which are beyond any doubt part of customary law so that the problem of adherence of some but not all States to specific conventions does not arise'.[282] However, the President of the ICTY went on to clarify to the Preparatory Committee drafting the Rome Statute: 'As is clear, this is not a definition of the principle of legality, which is well settled, but an elaboration as to what applicable law, consistent with the principle of *nullum crimen sine lege*, may be applied by the International Tribunal.'[283]

But what if the relevant treaty provision prohibits the relevant conduct but does not expressly criminalize it? This was the issue in *Prosecutor v. Galić* (2006), where the defendant was charged with inflicting terror on the civilian population as a war crime. The ICTY Appeals Chamber inter alia opaquely held that the relevant treaty provisions merely codified the customary principle of distinction and protection in international humanitarian law and therefore did not give rise to any new legal obligations.[284] It then added that even if a relevant treaty provision exists, 'in practice the International Tribunals always ascertain that the treaty provision in question is also declaratory of custom'.[285] In a separate and dissenting opinion, Judge Schomburg found no support for this crime under customary international law and reasoned that although the conduct is prohibited under international humanitarian treaty law, this is not sufficient to give rise to individual criminal responsibility.[286]

Galić (2006) is just one of several decisions that have had to struggle with the ruling in *Prosecutor v. Tadić* (1995) that a treaty prohibition, even if not expressly criminalizing the relevant conduct, can give rise to individual criminal responsibility if binding on the relevant States.[287] Since then, ICTY judges have taken positions in support of[288] and against this finding in *Tadić* (1995).[289] The

---

[282] UNSC, 'Report of the Secretary-General Pursuant to Paragraph 2 of Security Council Resolution 808' (1993), UN Doc. S/25704, para. 34.

[283] A Cassese (President of the ICTY), 'Definition of Crimes and General Principles of Criminal Law as Reflected in the International Tribunal's Jurisprudence', Memo to Members of the Preparatory Committee on the Establishment of an International Criminal Court (22 March 1996), para. 25, www.iccnow.org/documents/Memorandum.pdf, accessed 3 July 2014.

[284] Van Schaack (n. 5) 160.   [285] Meron, 'Remarks' (n. 185) 9.

[286] *Galić* (n. 280) paras. 7ff.

[287] Zahar and Sluiter (n. 86) 89 (citing *Tadić* (n. 174) paras. 94, 143).

[288] Ibid. 90 (citing *Prosecutor v. Kordić and Čerkez*, Judgment, ICTY-95–14/2-T, 26 February 2001, paras 165–169; *Prosecutor v. Galić*, Judgment, ICTY-98–29-T, 5 December 2003, paras 63–138).

[289] Ibid. 90 (citing *Milutinović* (n. 137) para 9; *Hadžihasanović* (n. 196) paras. 35, 51; *Prosecutor v. Blaškić*, Judgment, ICTY-95–14-A, 29 July 2004, para. 141).

appropriateness of this reasoning measured against the principle of legality has been discussed elsewhere.[290] Suffice it to mention that where a treaty prohibits but does not criminalize conduct, it is difficult to argue that the fair notice principle and separation of powers doctrine are respected. However, where the Rome Statute criminalizes conduct that is already criminalized or prohibited in another treaty, legality does not necessarily preclude that treaty from serving as an interpretive aid. This is especially the case where a term from a treaty has been transplanted to the Rome Statute.

4.3.10.3 General Principles

Because article 15(1) of the *ICCPR* (1966) refers to international law and article 38 of the ICJ Statute confirms that general principles of law recognized by the community of nations are a source of international law, it is thought by some that article 15(2) of the *ICCPR* (1966) redundantly states: 'Nothing in this article shall prejudice the trial and punishment of any person for any act or omission which, at the time when it was committed, was criminal according to the general principles of law recognized by the community of nations.' The reference to general principles in article 15(2) has been interpreted to mean that legality is upheld so long as the conduct in question is considered 'fundamentally criminal' by the community of nations.[291] According to the ICTY Trial Chamber in *Prosecutor* v. *Delalić and Others* (1998), article 15(2) was inserted to validate the Nuremberg and Tokyo tribunals' application of prohibitions in the *Hague Conventions* (1907) and *Geneva Conventions* (1929) that had not been expressly criminalized.[292] Such reasoning would categorize treaty prohibitions as reflecting conduct considered to be criminal according to general principles. International criminal tribunals also typically canvas national laws to ascertain general principles.[293]

Can general principles establish international criminal jurisdiction, as suggested by the wording of article 15 of the *ICCPR* (1966)? In fact, the International Law Commission (ILC) asserted, while drafting a statute for a permanent international criminal court, that they were not sufficiently precise to give rise to individual criminal responsibility, an opinion that has recently been revived.[294] This opinion, however, has not prevented tribunals from reasoning that general principles provide a defendant with 'sufficient notice' of novel interpretations of international criminal law.[295] Coherence between the Rome Statute and background general principles can promote 'predictability

---

[290] See Section 4.3.4.   [291] Shahabuddeen (n. 72) 1011.
[292] *Delalić* (n. 75) para. 313.   [293] Van Schaack (n. 5) 167.
[294] Ibid. 167 (citing Boot (n. 32) 330; Jacobs (n. 273) 36).
[295] Ibid. (citing *Tadić* (n. 174) para. 135; *Prosecutor* v. *Tadić*, Sentencing Judgment, ICTY-94–1-T*bis*-R117, 11 November 1999, para. 32).

and legal security.'[296] Such a practice would suggest the use of general principles as an interpretive aid rather than the actual source of criminalization. For example, in *Prosecutor* v. *Furundžija* (1998), the ICTY canvassed general principles of law to determine whether forcible oral intercourse can be charged as the war crime of rape and concluded that it could.[297] Others might characterize this practice as the resort to general principles for the purpose of making rather than interpreting the law.[298] Why is this?

General principles have been described as 'sweeping and loose standards of conduct that can be deduced from treaty and customary rules by extracting and generalizing some of their most significant common points'.[299] They are 'the potent cement that binds together the various and often disparate cogs and wheels of the normative framework of the [international] community'.[300] General principles of law recognized by civilized nations were added to article 38 of the ICJ Statute as a source of law to prevent the possibility of a *non liquet*, meaning the law is not clear and therefore provides no answer to the legal question raised by a case.[301] As such, it has been said that general principles have as their purpose judicial law making or come 'very close' to law creation, especially to respond to new developments and needs.[302] For this reason, it is a matter of debate whether general principles can independently be a source of international crimes.[303] It is the considered view of some that article 15 of the *ICCPR* (1966) and certain national constitutions implementing general principles of law make it clear that a general principle of law can criminalize conduct.[304] It is thought that the ICTY's recognition of contempt of court as a crime under general principles of law is an example of this position.[305]

Article 15 of the *ICCPR* (1966) has also been interpreted by some national courts as permitting the retroactive application of national law to conduct that was criminal under international law at the relevant time.[306] However,

---

[296] M Koskenniemi, 'Fragmentation of International Law: Difficulties Arising from the Diversification and Expansion of International Law: Report of the Study Group of the International Law Commission' (4 April 2006), UN Doc. A/CN.4/L.682, 248.

[297] Ibid. (citing *Furundžija* (n. 199) para. 177).

[298] M Swart, 'Judicial Lawmaking at the Ad Hoc Tribunals: The Creative Use of the Sources of International Law and "Adventurous Interpretation"' (2010) 70 ZaöRV 459, 468.

[299] A Cassese, *International Law*, 2nd edn (Oxford University Press 2004) 151.

[300] Ibid.

[301] H Lauterpacht, *The Functions of Law in the International Community* (Oxford University Press 1933) 205ff. See also C Voigt, 'The Role of General Principles of International Law and their Relationship to Treaty Law' (2008) 2:121 (38) Retfærd Årgang 3, 21; K Kulovesi, 'Legality or Otherwise? Nuclear Weapons and the Strategy of *Non Liquet*' (1999) 10 Finnish Ybk Int'l Law 55.

[302] Swart (n. 298) 468; Cassese (n. 299).   [303] Gallant (n. 46) 373.

[304] Ibid. 368.   [305] Ibid.

[306] Kreß (n. 9) para. 26 (citing *Fédération nationale des déportés et internés résistants et patriotes and others* v. *Barbie*, Cour de Cassation, 20 December 1985, 78 ILR 125, 132; *Polyukohovich* (n. 159) para 18).

this interpretation does not give particular content to article 15(2). A possible interpretation of article 15(2) is to treat it as an exception to non-retroactivity in cases where serious human rights violations have occurred for which there is a duty to prosecute, especially in situations of transitional justice.[307] For example, the German Constitutional Court in the *Border Guards* case (1996) held that criminal law can be retroactively applied exceptionally 'for reasons of substantial justice where a democratic regime has to deal with serious violations of internationally recognized human rights based on the policy of a past oppressive regime'.[308] Others share the view that if the law being applied by an international criminal tribunal goes beyond customary international law, it is retroactive in its effect and should therefore be founded in general principles of law.[309] Appeals to natural law or morality as a justification for retroactivity are to be replaced with arguments of general principles of law that in fact criminalize the relevant conduct at the time that it occurred.[310] General principles rendering an act 'unjust, immoral, or a breach of human rights principles are insufficient'.[311]

While these arguments might be appealing, the drafting history of article 15(2) does not bear out the view that it was intended to be an exception to the principle of non-retroactivity. In fact, a careful review of the drafting history of this provision suggests the opposite. It was intended to 'avoid uncertainty about the prohibition of retroactive crime creation'.[312] Several statements made by delegates during the drafting process confirm that general principles were considered to be a source of international law, consistent with article 38 of the ICJ Statute, which is cited in article 15(1) of the *ICCPR* (1966).[313] Further, the reference in the Nuremberg judgment to criminality under general principles was considered to be consistent with the view that article 15(2) is not an exception to non-retroactivity.[314] Apart from this view possibly being questioned in 1955,[315] from 1960 onwards, the prevailing view was that draft article 15 'prohibited the retroactive application of criminal law. It was pointed out that there could be no offences other than those specified by law, either

---

[307] Kreß, ibid.

[308] Ibid. (citing Bundesverfassungsgericht, 24 October 1996, 2 BvR 1851, 1853, 1875, 1852/94 (BVerfGE 95, 96)).

[309] Juratowitch (n. 128) 340–42 (citing as supporting this view C Tomuschat, 'Crimes Against the Peace and Security of Mankind and the Recalcitrant Third State' in Y Dinstein and M Tabory (eds.), *War Crimes in International Law* (Martinus Nijhoff 1996) 52).

[310] Juratowitch, ibid. 360.   [311] Ibid.   [312] Gallant (n. 46) 191–93.

[313] Ibid. 193–94 (citing UNSC, Draft International Covenant on Human Rights and Measures of Implementation, The General Adequacy of the First Eighteen Articles (Parts I and II), Memorandum by the Secretary-General (2 April 1951), UN Doc. E/CN.4/528, para. 164). 'The 1951 memorandum is an accurate statement of matters as they then stood' (195).

[314] Ibid. 194 (citing UNSC ibid.).   [315] Ibid. 195–98.

national or international.[316] This would suggest that general principles were considered a source of international criminal law. True, concern was expressed that article 15(2) might call into question the legality of the Nuremberg and Tokyo trials.[317] Ultimately, however, the opposite view carried the day, with a final vote overwhelmingly favouring its retention.[318] Accordingly, article 15(2) possesses no special meaning independent from article 15(1) except to emphasize that general principles are a source of international law, and therefore their application by an international criminal court does not violate the absolute prohibition against retroactive crime creation.

Core international crimes, which fall within the province of international criminal tribunals such as the ICTY, are supposed to be criminal under customary international law, as they have attracted the *jus puniendi* of the entire international community.[319] The idea that core crimes can emerge from general principles does not sit well with this theory if their role is to provide answers to legal questions whose answers are not clear at the level of treaty and customary law.

The inclusion of general principles in article 15 of the *ICCPR* (1966) should therefore not be seen as an invitation to prosecute persons for violating those principles that criminalize certain conduct. Rather, the goal should be, as at Nuremberg, to limit their invocation to situations of a possible *non liquet*. In such situations, international criminal law is not technically being applied retroactively – legality is respected – although legal certainty and fair warning are arguably weak.[320] As an aid to interpreting crimes, their role would therefore be subsidiary where a more precise aid exists.

4.3.10.4 Judicial decisions

Some confusion has arisen as to whether judges are criminalizing conduct that was previously innocent when declaring the existence of a crime under international law after the conduct in question occurred. In *Prosecutor* v. *Aleksovski* (2000), the defendant submitted that the ICTY's reliance on a decision declaring certain conduct to be criminal under customary international

---

[316] Ibid. 198 (citing Draft International Covenants on Human Rights, Report of the Third Committee (8 December 1960), UN Doc. A/4625, para 13, Annexes 3, 4).

[317] Ibid. 200.

[318] Ibid. (citing an Argentine amendment to delete it, where the vote in the Third Committee was nineteen for deletion, fifty-one against and ten abstentions: UN Doc. A/C.3/SR.1013, para 47. At para. 50, there was a vote of fifty-three to four, with twenty-two abstentions, in favour of the sentence).

[319] Kreß (n. 9).

[320] Judge Shahabuddeen, however, takes the view that the 'fair demands for specificity are met by proof that the conduct of the accused corresponds to the fundamental criminality of the crime charged [under general principles of law] even though the correspondence is not perfect in every detail'. (n. 72) 1011.

law violated the principle of legality because the decision was made after the relevant conduct occurred. In response, the ICTY Appeals Chamber rightly explained that there is a difference between interpreting and clarifying the content of custom, which judges are mandated to do, and creating custom, which they are not and would indeed violate the principle of legality.[321] Article 15 of the *ICCPR* (1966) does not suggest that judicial decisions can criminalize conduct under international law. However, such decisions are permissible interpretive aids according to article 21(1)(c) and 21(2) of the Rome Statute, as well as article 38 of the ICJ Statute. Although there is no doctrine of precedents in international law, the Court may rely on its previous decisions for guidance. These decisions can provide notice to individuals about the scope and content of international criminal law – substantive and procedural.[322] Indeed, consistency in the jurisprudence of the Court would enhance the rule of law by promoting certainty, predictability and transparency in its reasoning and outcomes.

4.3.10.5 Teachings of publicists

International criminal tribunals have rightly refrained from relying purely on the teachings of publicists as providing fair notice of judicial innovations or as a source of criminalization under international law. However, in *Prosecutor v. Jorgić* (1997), the Higher Court of Düsseldorf (*Oberlandesgericht*) interpreted the definition of genocide in the German criminal code as encompassing 'cultural genocide', even though it is identical to the *Genocide Convention* (1948) definition, whose drafters famously decided to exclude this concept.[323] In doing so, they relied on teachings of publicists in support of this position. It has rightly been observed that such reliance renders the notion of fair notice an even greater legal fiction by assuming 'the defendants' ability to undertake virtually global legal research to determine the scope and content of ICL [international criminal law]'.[324] It is agreed that, even with the assistance of legal counsel, it is perhaps inappropriate to claim respect for legality and the notion of fair warning underlying it by relying *solely* on the teachings of publicists in support of an innovative interpretation that is contraindicated by other interpretive aids. This practice might also undermine the rule of law and separation of powers doctrine. In general, however, teachings of publicists are a useful and permissible aid for confirming and clarifying the scope of crimes in the Rome Statute.

---

[321] *Prosecutor v. Aleksovski*, Judgment, ICTY-95–14/1-A, 24 March 2000, paras. 126ff.

[322] Ibid. paras. 92ff.

[323] Van Schaack (n. 5) 171. The Constitutional Court declined to hear Jorgić's appeal. BVerfG, 12 December 2000, 2 BvR 1290/99, NJW 2001, 1848, www.bverfg.de/entscheidungen/ rk20001212_2bvr129099en.html, accessed 11 November 2013.

[324] Van Schaack (n. 5) 172.

4.3.11 Conclusions

This Chapter considered ten interpretive arguments expected to be made before the Court that might weaken or undermine a robust notion of legality when interpreting crimes within its jurisdiction. The merits of these arguments have been considered with a view to assessing whether they ought to form part of a method of interpretation for crimes in the Rome Statute. The notion of higher order principles of (substantive) justice being able to outweigh the principle of legality is no longer tenable in light of legality evolving into a non-derogable and internationally recognized human right and articles 21(3) and 22 of the Rome Statute treating it as such. To argue, therefore, that it would be unjust not to punish an individual and therefore the prohibition against retroactive creation of the law should be ignored, has no place in an interpretive methodology for the Court. The same is true of any morality argument serving as a proxy for the existence of an applicable criminal prohibition. It is agreed that morality is a 'sieve through which can flow not only humanity but also repression and stupidity'.[325] It is also dubious to structure international criminal justice so that judges are primarily responsible for articulating the moral views of the international community.

Third, arguments of world order – the need to safeguard peace and security – risk politicizing the Court and undermining its effectiveness. All crimes in the Court's jurisdiction implicate peace and security, and it is therefore unreasonable to weigh these considerations against the robust conception of legality that drafters of the Rome Statute nevertheless chose to embed in article 22. It is the primary mandate of the Security Council, not the Court, to work to ensure collective peace and security. Fourth, the conflation of illegality with criminality is tempting but ultimately provides no inherent guidance on which illegal acts will become criminal, a decision that is for States rather than judges to make and undermines all interests protected by the legality principle.

Fifth, as for the practice of reclassifying offences, this argument depends very much on whether the principle of fair labelling is respected. Where an individual is charged with a crime under international law, and a sufficiently similar crime existed under applicable national law when the conduct occurred, reclassifying the offence as an international crime does not seem to offend this principle or legality. The same is true where conduct is charged as one crime under international law and then charged as another under international law, all of these being serious in nature. This might also be the case where an 'ordinary' national crime is reclassified as an international crime, and the additional jurisdictional elements are not material to the guilt or innocence

---

[325] Hall (n. 44) 189.

of the individual. In this situation, however, the argument should address in a principled manner how this interpretation does not offend the separation of powers or strict construction doctrines associated with the legality principle.

Sixth, it may be argued that the world today is very different than that which existed in 1998 when the Rome Statute was drafted and that, to remain effective, the Court must recognize certain conduct that was unforeseen in 1998 as criminal under the Rome Statute. Again, this argument needs to be broken down a bit. The principle of legality is violated if this argument is admitted to modify the wording of the Rome Statute and to recognize a wholly new species of wrongdoing that is not expressly provided for in articles 6, 7, 8 or 8 *bis*. However, where the wording of a criminal prohibition in the Rome Statute can tolerate the meaning proposed, the principle of legality is not necessarily offended when that meaning is ascribed to the provision. More is said in Chapter 5 about how to balance the interpretive imperative of strict construction in article 22(2) with the principle of effective interpretation. Seventh, teleological reasoning about the purpose of the Rome Statute to end impunity or something to that effect is a dangerous argument to accept, as it could swallow the principle of legality whole. Consideration of the purpose of a criminal prohibition in the Rome Statute is not necessarily excluded by the legality principle, a matter that is also taken up in the next Chapter. A limited role for the principle of effective interpretation is perhaps also not excluded.

Eighth, many concerns have been expressed about arguments of foreseeability, and article 22 is considered to prohibit their admission. Similarly, the concept of retroactive application of criminal law consistent with the 'essence' of an existing offence is perhaps too loose a concept and is arguably prohibited by the ban on analogy, discussed in Chapter 5. Finally, article 22(1) of the Rome Statute makes it clear to the Court that legality limits its jurisdiction to crimes defined in it. But custom, treaties and general principles of law and judicial decisions are all authoritative aids to interpretation under article 21 of the Rome Statute. General principles of law are not an exception to the prohibition against retroactivity and are sufficiently consistent with the principle of legality when used in exceptional cases to avoid a *non liquet*. As for teachings of publicists, they are generally useful aids, but care should be taken not to rely solely on the teachings of one publicist in support of an innovative interpretation that is contraindicated by other interpretive aids. Article 21 of the Rome Statute and article 38 of the ICJ Statute respect the rule of law by putting the accused on notice about possible interpretive aids. It is therefore not particularly convincing to argue that interpretations of articles 6, 7, 8 and 8 *bis* of the Rome Statute resulting from the use of these aids are not foreseeable or accessible or based on a reclassification or conflation with illegality.

On balance, the legality principle is 'a powerful barrier against tendencies towards the abuse of justice. It is unquestionably one of the most important safeguards against the worst of all oppressions – that oppression which hides itself under the mask of justice.'[326] It is therefore commendable that articles 21(3) and 22 require that this principle be respected. In the next Chapter, lessons learned from this Chapter will inform efforts to usefully operationalize article 22 so that its content can assist judges and counsel with interpreting crimes in the Court's jurisdiction.

---

[326] Glaser (n. 25) 37.

Operationalizing the principle of legality

5.1 Introduction

In this Chapter, consideration will be given to the different elements of article 22 with a view to assessing their origins, purpose and limits. The references to 'strict interpretation', 'favouring the accused' and the 'prohibition against analogy' will be unpacked. In the final section, a method for the principled operationalization of these devices will be outlined to assist judges and lawyers with the interpretation of crimes in the Rome Statute. By giving meaningful content to these imperatives, the goal is to facilitate reasoning by judges and counsel that is informed, principled and transparent. In the absence of this effort, article 22 may be invoked in a manner that leads to interpretive reasoning and outcomes that are over- or underinclusive in some way.

5.2 Drafting history

Article 22 provides:

1. A person shall not be criminally responsible under this Statute unless the conduct in question constitutes, at the time it takes place, a crime within the jurisdiction of the Court.
2. The definition of a crime shall be strictly construed and shall not be extended by analogy. In case of ambiguity, the definition shall be interpreted in favour of the person being investigated, prosecuted or convicted.
3. This article shall not affect the characterization of any conduct as criminal under international law independently of this Statute.

At the Rome Diplomatic Conference, the legality principle as it appears in article 22 sparked little debate and was adopted with minor changes.[1] In the International Law Commission's 1994 and 1996 Draft Statutes of the Court

---

[1] WA Schabas, *The International Criminal Court: A Commentary on the Rome Statute* (Oxford University Press 2010) 406 (citing for these propositions UN Docs. A/CoNF.183/ C.1/WGGP/L.4, 2, A/CONF.183/C.1/L.76/Add.3, 1 and A/CONF.183/C.1/WGGP/L.1).

(ILC), the principle of legality was defined so as to accommodate the inclusion of crimes under customary international law – the 'core crimes' of aggression, genocide, other crimes against humanity and war crimes – but also treaty crimes, the latter category ultimately not making it into the final Rome Statute.[2] For these 'core crimes', the draft language was limited to a prohibition against retroactive application of international law. Thus, so long as the conduct was criminal under international law at the relevant time, it mattered not that national law applicable to the accused did not criminalize the same conduct.[3]

Rejecting the idea of simply listing categories of criminal prohibitions in the Rome Statute, the Preparatory Committee in 1996 resolved to define the crimes within the Court's jurisdiction with the 'clarity, precision and specificity required for criminal law in accordance with the principle of legality' and agreed that fundamental principles of criminal law should, for the same reason, be set out in the Rome Statute.[4] At this time, three proposals were put forward, which variously modified the content of the ILC proposal to include the prohibition against analogy and apply the more lenient law to the accused if the law changes between the commission of an offence and rendering of the final judgment.[5] It was at the Rome Diplomatic Conference that Per Saland, Chair of the Working Group on General Principles of Criminal Law, recommended adding the requirement of strict construction.[6] As it became increasingly clear that treaty crimes would not be included in the final Statute, the legality requirement for these crimes, that the relevant State have ratified the relevant treaty at the time the conduct occurred, fell away.[7] Accordingly, crimes within the Court's jurisdiction need not be criminalized under a treaty other than the Rome Statute or within the relevant national jurisdiction.

Some critical words have been penned about the 'real motivation' of States for drafting article 22 of the Rome Statute to contain such a robust conception of legality, one that is more rigorous than that which exists under international law.[8] It has been said that article 22 'reflects a most extreme and distorted interpretation of the scope of the rule'.[9] Further, while 'many references to *nullum crimen* and legal certainty at the Rome Conference were often couched in language suggesting this was out of concern for the rights of the accused[,] . . . the exercise seemed to be driven more by the implications this might have for States

---

[2] ILC, '1994 Draft Code of Crimes against the Peace and Security of Mankind' (1994) II (Part Two) Ybk of the ILC 18, 55–56 (article 39).

[3] B Broomhall, 'Article 22' in O Triffterer (ed.), *Commentary on the Rome Statute of the International Criminal Court*, 2nd edn (CH Beck/Hart/Nomos 2008) 714.

[4] Ibid. 715.   [5] Ibid.   [6] Ibid.   [7] Ibid. 716; Schabas (n. 1) 406.

[8] Broomhall (n. 3) 717; C Kreß, 'Nullum Crimen, Nulla Poena Sine Lege' in R Wolfrum (ed.), *Max Planck Encyclopedia of Public International Law* (2008–), online edition, www.mpepil. com, paras. 18, 33, accessed 15 March 2011.

[9] WA Schabas, 'Follow Up to Rome: Preparing for Entry into Force of the International Criminal Court Statute' (1999) 20 Human Rights LJ 157, 163.

themselves, given the nature of most international crimes and their *nexus* with State activity'.[10] Similarly, it has been written:

> The reason invoked most frequently in favour of the approach retained in the Statute is the need to respect the *nullum crimen sine lege* principle. The so-called problem being 'that the elements of the offenses arising out of "general international law" are often too vague'. The result of a veritable brainwashing operation led by criminal lawyers, with the self-interested support of the United States, this argument is unacceptable.[11]

The common thread in these critiques seems to be that the interests of States in fair warning and constraining the law-making competence of judges[12] are weak justifications for insisting on such a strict conception of legality in the Rome Statute. However, these objections are not particularly convincing when one considers that fair warning, the rule of law, the separation of powers doctrine and the effectiveness of the threat of criminal sanctions, are interests underpinning the legality principle. There is nothing objectionable in States pursuing their own interest in legal certainty by insisting that judges perform their functions in a manner that respects a strict notion of legality.

Perhaps another (implicit) cause for dissatisfaction with the legality principle in article 22 is how robust it is in comparison to how this concept was understood at the Nuremberg and Tokyo trials or even by some judges at the ICTY and ICTR. However, a robust conception of legality in the Rome Statute does not undermine respect for legality by the ad hoc tribunals, which are bound by a less strict notion of it under international law. Further, it is perhaps useful to view legality as a concept that has evolved in a principled manner to reflect important developments in international criminal law. It could be argued that, much like the beginning of criminal law jurisprudence in common law jurisdictions, legality was originally conceived of as a flexible concept to allow for critical legal developments, even if they occurred retroactively. As in the common-law tradition, perfect positivism was not and still is not required under general international law as an element of legality.[13] However, once laws became sufficiently detailed in statutes and in judicial decisions, common-law methodology was rejected, and judicial crime creation was thought to be 'unacceptable and unnecessary'.[14]

One could argue that a similar transformation has occurred from the Nuremberg era to the detailed enumeration of crimes in the Rome Statute and

---

[10] Schabas (n. 1) 407–08; Broomhall (n. 3) 717.

[11] A Pellet, 'Applicable Law' in A Cassese and Others (eds.), *The Rome Statute of the International Criminal Court: A Commentary*, vol. II (Oxford University Press 2002) 1051, 1057.

[12] Broomhall (n. 3) 714.   [13] Kreß (n. 8) paras. 10, 21.

[14] JC Jeffries Jr, 'Legality, Vagueness, and the Construction of Penal Statutes' (1985) 71 Virginia L Rev 189, 195.

accompanying Elements of Crimes. Whereas a relatively weak understanding of legality as a principle of justice that can be outweighed by considerations of substantive justice was perhaps essential to the birth of modern international criminal law at the Nuremberg and Tokyo trials (and perhaps even its renaissance under the scant and vaguely worded ICTY and ICTR Statutes), the Rome Statute is sufficiently detailed and comprehensive that it can accommodate a stronger notion of legality. Drafters of the Rome Statute have defined in unprecedented detail the crimes that are within the Court's jurisdiction. Although the principle of legality at the level of general international law may need to remain 'broader and considerably more tolerant of imprecision' than it is in many domestic systems because of the existence of unwritten law and no world legislature, its meaning can be and is relatively strict and rigorous in the Rome Statute.[15] So although the strictest domestic formulations of the legality principle, which would require all criminal laws to be written, cannot be satisfied under general international criminal law, a positivist approach to legality can be accommodated in the Rome regime.

Still, it was not the intention of the drafters to take positivism to the extreme. Legality, as defined in article 22, does not oblige judges to apply the Elements of Crimes. Contrary to the ruling of the Pre-Trial Chamber in *Lubanga* (2009),[16] article 9(1) of the Rome Statute indicates that the Elements 'shall assist' the judges, meaning the Elements *must be considered but may or may not be applied.* This understanding of the role of the Elements does not 'significantly erode' the legality principle in article 22 because this provision does not define the principle of legality so as to render application of the Elements mandatory. If this had been the intent of the drafters, which it decidedly was not, such an important aspect of legality could have been expressly stated.[17]

5.3 Criminal responsibility 'under this Statute'

Article 22(1) of the Rome Statute limits findings of criminal liability to the commission of crimes listed in article 5 and defined in articles 6, 7, 8 and

---

[15] Kreß (n. 8) paras. 18, 33; Broomhall (n. 3) 717.

[16] Schabas (n. 1) 408 (citing *Prosecutor* v. *Al Bashir*, Decision on the Prosecution's Application for a Warrant of Arrest against Omar Hassan Ahmand Al Bashir, ICC-02/05–01/09, 4 March 2009, para. 131).

[17] R Clark, 'Article 9' in O Triffterer (ed.), *Commentary on the Rome Statute of the International Criminal Court*, 2nd edn (CH Beck/Hart/Nomos 2008) 505, 529; D Robinson and H von Hebel, 'Reflections on the Elements of Crimes' in RS Lee (ed.), *The International Criminal Court: Elements of Crimes and Rules of Procedure and Evidence* (Transnational 2001) 219, 231. For a different view, see WK Lietzau, 'Checks and Balances and Elements of Proof: Structural Pillars for the International Criminal Court' (1999) 32 Cornell Int'l LJ 477, 480–81; on the relationship between articles 9(1) and 21(1)(a), see Chapter 7, Section 7.9.

8 *bis*.[18] Prohibited conduct may include acts or omissions (e.g., command responsibility in article 28(1)).[19] And the strict principle of legality in the Rome Statute does not necessarily apply to offences against the administration of justice in article 70.[20] A claim that article 22(1) has been violated can be raised well before a conviction. It could be raised when the Court is determining its jurisdiction or confirming the charges, after an admission of guilt or even after the completion of a full trial.[21] Article 22(1) prohibits judges from expanding the Court's jurisdiction by finding that a crime, although not set out in the Rome Statute, is prohibited under customary international law, in some other applicable treaty or under general principles of law, and therefore falls within its jurisdiction. As well, the Court 'is not required to determine, as a precondition to the exercise of its jurisdiction, that the charges against the accused constituted crimes under customary international law at the time of their alleged commission, even if the Court is likely to examine the issue in particular circumstances'.[22] To be clear, the Rome Statute does not do away with customary international criminal law or its usefulness, but merely creates a regime that is derived from a written treaty.

5.4 Non-retroactivity

Article I(9) of the United States Constitution (1798) prohibits the passage of *ex post facto* laws, which encompasses retroactive crime creation and aggravation, retroactive increases in punishment and retroactive relaxation of the applicable rules of evidence.[23] In the 1970s, the House of Lords definitively adopted the principle of non-retroactivity by abolishing the doctrine of residual judicial discretion to create common-law crimes.[24] It has been argued that the concept of non-retroactive application of the law is a bit of a legal fiction. Whether a judicial decision is inspired by a treaty or custom, it 'reaches back into time and places the authoritative stamp of criminality upon the prior conduct'.[25] Even so, it is a fiction that legal systems around the world choose to retain. A recent study on legality concludes that the most important rules of non-retroactive application of criminal laws and punishment are so widely recognized (albeit to varying degrees) that they bind national and international judges as a matter of customary international law or at least as a general principle of law

---

[18] Broomhall (n. 3) 722.   [19] Ibid.

[20] Ibid. 723. However, this does not mean that legality will not be applied to crimes against the administration of justice by judges.

[21] Ibid.; see articles 19, 61, 65, Rome Statute.   [22] Ibid.

[23] *Calder* v. *Bull*, 3 U.S. 386 (1798).

[24] *Knuller (Publishing, Printing and Promotions), Ltd.* v. *DPP* [1973] AC 435; *R* v. *Withers* [1975] AC 842.

[25] J Hall, 'Nulla Poena Sine Lege', (1937) 47 Yale LJ 165, 171.

recognized by the community of nations.[26] In fact, the Appeals Chamber of the Special Tribunal for Lebanon recently held that legality is a peremptory norm.[27]

Reference to jurisdiction in article 22(1) was inserted 'at a time prior to the agreement on the selection of crimes and their definitions, whether they be only the "core crimes" or also some of the "treaty crimes" such as drug trafficking and terrorism'.[28] However, irrespective of what crimes are in the Rome Statute or are added to it in the future, the Court's jurisdiction is conditional upon the crime being in the Rome Statute at the time that the conduct occurred.

It is the Court that must determine when the conduct occurred, the existence of the relevant criminal prohibition and its applicability to the suspect or accused.[29] This includes determining whether continuing or composite crimes fall within the Court's jurisdiction. It is well known that this question was deliberately left unresolved at Rome. A continuing crime has been defined as one that is 'committed and then maintained', such as enforced disappearance as a crime against humanity.[30] A composite crime takes time to commit because of its nature, such as entailing a pattern of conduct (e.g., genocide, apartheid). Article 11 of the Rome Statute states:

1. The Court has jurisdiction only with respect to crimes committed after the entry into force of this Statute.
2. If a State becomes a Party to this Statute after its entry into force, the Court may exercise its jurisdiction only with respect to crimes committed after the entry into force of this Statute for that State, unless that State has made a declaration under article 12, paragraph 3.

And article 24 provides:

1. No person shall be criminally responsible under this Statute for conduct prior to the entry into force of the Statute.
2. In the event of a change in the law applicable to a given case prior to a final judgement, the law more favourable to the person being investigated, prosecuted or convicted shall apply.

---

[26] KS Gallant, *The Principle of Legality in International and Comparative Criminal Law* (Cambridge University Press 2009) 8–9; R Higgins, 'Time and the Law: International Perspectives on an Old Problem' (1997) 46:3 Int'l Comp LQ 501, 507–08.

[27] Interlocutory Decision on the Applicable Law: Terrorism, Conspiracy, Homicide Perpetration, Cumulative Charging, STL-11–01/I, 16 February 2011, para. 76.

[28] P Saland, 'International Criminal Law Principles' in RS Lee (ed.), *The International Criminal Court: The Making of the Rome Statute – Issues, Negotiations, Results* (Kluwer Law International 1999) 189, 195.

[29] Broomhall (n. 3) 723. On temporal jurisdiction, see also articles 11 and 24, Rome Statute and Chapter 7, Section 7.4.

[30] A Nissel, 'Continuing Crimes in the Rome Statute' (2004) 25 Michigan J Int'l L 653, 654.

There was no single view on the question of continuing crimes according to the coordinator of the negotiations of part III of the Statute, and it boiled down to a choice between using in article 24(1) the verb 'committed' or 'occurred'; both were thought to carry a slightly different meaning in the present context. Ultimately, the conference opted for deliberate ambiguity by deciding not to include any verb to modify the noun 'conduct' in article 24(1).[31] Interestingly, a footnote in the Elements of Crimes for the crime against humanity of enforced disappearance provides that this 'crime falls under the jurisdiction of the Court only if the attack referred to in elements 7 and 8 occurs after the entry into force of the Statute'.

There are those who favour the inclusion of continuing and composite crimes in the Court's jurisdiction on the basis of balancing legality against the goal of ending impunity.[32] However, in light of legality emerging as the guiding interpretive principle for crimes in the Rome Statute, such a balancing exercise seems inapt and suggests that, in any case, this goal must give way to the principle of legality. Accordingly, at the time the criminal prohibition applies, all elements of a crime should be present.[33] For a State referral or investigation initiated by the prosecutor, the Statute must have entered into force for the relevant State Party prior to the criminal conduct occurring. In the case of a Security Council referral or a Non-State Party accepting the jurisdiction of the Court for a particular situation, the conduct must have occurred after 1 July 2002.[34] Of course, this position does not speak at all to the question of admitting evidence of conduct occurring prior to the relevant time period for purposes of proving the historical backdrop against which the impugned criminal conduct occurred.[35]

The definition of crimes in the Rome Statute, the existence of written text, is one means of guarding against retroactive application of the law. However, in the author's view, the imperatives listed in article 22 are all *devices* intended to help judges ensure that their findings do not violate the prohibition against retroactive application of articles 6, 7, 8 and 8 *bis*. It is the use of these interpretive devices that will assist judges in determining whether a criminal prohibition in the Rome Statute covers the person, conduct and circumstances in question. The origins, purposes and limits of these devices are the focus of the remainder of this Chapter.

5.5 Strict construction

There are various historic justifications for strict construction that will be described in this section. As it relates to the principle of legality, however,

---

[31] Saland (n. 28) 196–97.   [32] See, e.g., Nissel (n. 30).

[33] Broomhall (n. 3) 723; M Boot, *Genocide, Crimes Against Humanity, War Crimes: Nullum Crimen Sine Lege and the Subject Matter Jurisdiction of the International Criminal Court* (Intersentia 2002) 362–63, 371.

[34] Articles 12 and 13, Rome Statute.

[35] See, e.g., *Prosecutor* v. *Nahimana*, Judgment, ICTR 96–11-AR72, 5 September 2000.

strict construction is thought to promote the idea that it is the proper role of the legislature, not the judiciary, to resolve complex policy issues arising from criminal laws, and this is especially so when the legislature has recently considered the issue in dispute and chosen not to amend the relevant law that needs to be interpreted.[36] It is a device to keep legality and arguably its underlying interests of the rule of law and separation of powers 'in good repair'.[37] In the author's view, strict construction is more a device intended to guard against judicial law making than to ensure fair warning, although it still promotes legal certainty, which is essential to the latter.[38] A famous American example of strict construction resulting in an acquittal that illustrates this point is the case of *McBoyle* v. *United States* (1931).[39] There, the relevant federal statute criminalized transporting a stolen 'motor vehicle' in interstate commerce. Mr. McBoyle transported a stolen airplane. Justice Holmes, on behalf of a unanimous Supreme Court, wrote the opinion reversing the conviction, reasoning that the 'statute should not be extended to aircraft simply because it may seem to us that a similar policy applies, or upon the speculation that, if the legislature had thought of it, very likely broader words would have been used'.[40] Such reasoning highlights that it is the prerogative of the legislature to enact criminal law but that it must do so in as clear a manner as possible. When this is not done, the accused is to be found not guilty, even if the conduct in question, in this case the theft of an airplane, could hardly be considered 'innocent' from a moral perspective.

5.5.1 National history

There are two narratives that explain the origin of strict construction at the national level, and both predate the modern legality principle. The first dates back to Ulpian and the 'historical peculiarities of *stipulation* in Roman law'.[41] This narrative provides that in a contractual relationship between, for example, a creditor and debtor, the obligations of the debtor should be interpreted restrictively in his or her favour.[42] Even then, however, this restrictive interpretation was invoked as a last resort once all other methods of interpretation failed.[43] Some have claimed that strict construction of the law, considered a modern-day device for preserving the principle of legality, can be understood as a means of ensuring that penal statutes, which are drafted by States, are

---

[36] A Ashworth, 'Interpreting Criminal Statutes: A Crisis of Legality?' (1991) 107 Law Q Rev 419, 448.
[37] HL Packer, *The Limits of Criminal Sanction* (Stanford University Press 1968) 93.
[38] Ibid. 93, 95.   [39] 283 U.S. 25 (1931).   [40] Ibid. 27, cited in Packer (n. 37) 95.
[41] H Lauterpacht, 'Restrictive Interpretation and the Principle of Effectiveness in the Interpretation of Treaties' (1949) 26 British Ybk Int'l L 48, 84.
[42] Ibid. 60.   [43] Ibid.

construed against them, a notion borrowed from contract law.[44] However, this analogy has come under attack for failing to recognize that, unlike a contract between two private individuals, a penal statute is enacted in the public interest, meaning the goal of securing justice between two individuals is inapt.[45]

The second narrative has bloodier origins and dates back to a time in England when the death penalty was imposed for relatively minor criminal offences under the common law. Freedom from the death penalty for such felonies was known as 'benefit of clergy' and grew popular in the second half of the fourteenth century.[46] This doctrine led to so many successful claims that the benefit of clergy started to be expressly excluded in fifteenth-century statutes.[47] During the rule of Henry VIII, numerous such statutes were enacted, and it is estimated that 72,000 subjects were executed.[48] Although Edward VI in 1547 repealed almost all of these statutes, some remained.[49] In the seventeenth century, growing humanitarianism led to the emergence of strict construction as a general rule that was consciously applied by judges to deal with these older statutes that mandated the death penalty.[50] Further, between 1691 and 1765, the benefit of clergy was excluded by the legislature for various crimes to which it formerly applied, thereby creating an even greater rift between the ethos of the legislature and that of judges, juries and prosecutors.[51] In these circumstances, courts applied the doctrine of strict construction irrespective of whether the evidence clearly proved commission of the offence in order to exclude conviction for a 'non-clergyable' charge and sought pleas of guilt for lesser offences *in favorem vitae*.[52] Similarly, excuses or justifications for offences were interpreted broadly to avert the death penalty, which is why the term 'strict interpretation' is rather misleading.[53] 'It was from cases and text writers in the England of this period that the doctrine of strict construction was brought to [the United States].'[54] By the nineteenth century, the death penalty was no longer the chief punishment for serious crimes in England and the United States, but the doctrine that was invented purely as a response to it 'lived, the sole relic of what had once been a veritable conspiracy for administrative nullification'.[55]

Because of the extreme invocation of the doctrine of strict construction to the point of absurdity during this bygone era, reactions against this practice were integral to relegating it to the end of the interpretive sequence.[56] Maxwell in England proposed: 'Where an equivocal word or ambiguous sentence leaves

---

[44] L Hall, 'Strict or Liberal Construction of Penal Statutes' (1935) 48 Harvard L Rev 748, 757.

[45] Ibid.   [46] Ibid. 749 (citing 2 Hale PC 335, Foster CL 357 and 1 Bl Comm 88).

[47] Hall, ibid. 749.   [48] Ibid.   [49] Ibid. 750.   [50] Ibid.; Jeffries Jr (n. 14) 198.

[51] Hall, ibid. 751. The offences included various forms of fraud, embezzlement and aggravated larceny. The legislature was pressured by property owners to deter the aforementioned conduct by imposing the severest possible punishment.

[52] Ibid.   [53] Ibid.   [54] Ibid.   [55] Ibid.   [56] Ibid. 751–52.

reasonable doubt of its meaning which the canons of interpretation fail to resolve, the benefit of the doubt should be given to the subject and against the Legislature which has failed to explain itself.'[57] This reasoning was endorsed in Canada[58] and also espoused by Chief Justice Marshall of the United States Supreme Court: '[T]hough penal laws are to be construed strictly, they are not to be construed so strictly as to defeat the obvious intention of the legislature... The intention of the legislature is to be collected from the words they employ. Where there is no ambiguity in the words, there is no room for construction.'[59]

As was to be expected, relegating strict construction to an interpretive device of last resort and conditional upon the existence of a lingering ambiguity left room for judicial discretion in determining whether such an ambiguity exists.[60] However, most, though not all American courts have followed the rule where they genuinely doubt the construction of a particular penal statute, even if this leads to regrettable consequences (e.g., acquittal of a morally culpable accused).[61] The frustrating results that this rule produced led several legislatures in the United States to partially or completely oust it by introducing express statutory imperatives that penal statutes be liberally construed and interpreted in a manner to carry out the 'true intent and meaning of the legislature' or 'with a view to effecting their objects and promoting justice'.[62] These reforms were largely ineffective, with courts choosing to retain by various means the common law rule of strict construction in cases where a punishment is thought to be disproportionately severe relative to the impugned conduct.[63] For all of these reasons, it is posited that the rule of strict construction survived but has been invoked as a 'makeweight for results that seem right on other grounds than as a consistent policy of statutory interpretation. Citation to the rule is usually pro forma.'[64]

It is not surprising that such a state of affairs has nurtured cynicism in situations where judges invoke strict construction in the criminal law context, leading to questions about whether the doctrine or something else is truly guiding the reasoning of judges.[65] The cynic might ask whether the sporadic invocation of strict construction reasoning is motivated by a judge's personal desire to reach a particular outcome. This state of affairs has also led to scepticism about whether the rule of strict construction really exists.[66] Proponents of the rule often advance one or both of the following justifications for its

---

[57] PB Maxwell, *The Interpretation of Statutes*, 7th edn (GFL Bridgman 1929) 244.
[58] *Bell Express Vu ltd Partnership* v. *Rex* [2002] 2 SCR 559.
[59] Hall (n. 44) 751–52 (quoting *United States* v. *Wiltberger*, 18 U.S. 76, 95–96 (1820)).
[60] Hall, ibid. 752. [61] Ibid. [62] Ibid. 752–54. [63] Ibid. 755–56, 758.
[64] Jeffries Jr (n. 14) 198–99. [65] Ibid.
[66] Ashworth (n. 36) 432 (citing Law Commission No. 177, *Criminal Law: A Criminal Code for England and Wales*, vols. I–II (1989) para. 3.17).

preservation: (1) fair warning; and (2) unelected judges are supposed to interpret and apply the law, not make or amend it, these functions falling properly to elected officials.[67] Because interpretation, if taken too far, can lead to the making or amendment of law, this power, so it is argued, should be exercised cautiously, and strict interpretation in favour of the accused is a device to aid in achieving this end.[68]

5.5.2 International history

Four narratives dot the landscape of international law when trying to understand the origins of strict construction. The first can be traced to the sovereignty concerns of States. In proceedings before the International Court of Justice and its predecessor, the Permanent Court of International Justice, States would oppose the voluntary jurisdiction of one of these courts by arguing that a jurisdictional clause limits the sovereignty of the State, and therefore it should be interpreted restrictively.[69] The Permanent Court 'nominally subscribed' to this argument as it applies to jurisdictional instruments but even then relegated it to an aid of last resort if all other methods of interpretation did not assist it with discerning the intentions of the Parties, which never occurred.[70] The same is true of the International Court of Justice.[71] Perhaps this is because States are understood as voluntarily participating in the development of international law, and international treaties are, by definition, intended to limit State sovereignty in a particular area.[72] The contract law theory of treaties also led to domestic contract law reasoning of *contra proferentem* and favouring the debtor being advanced by States before international courts.[73] This was also minimally successful and 'made dependent upon the double condition of doubt and of the complete absence of any other means of interpretation'.[74]

---

[67] Ibid.   [68] Ibid. 432–33.

[69] IFI Shihata, *The Power of the International Court to Determine Its Own Jurisdiction: Compétence de la Compétence* (Martinus Nijhoff 1965) 189–90; Lauterpacht (n. 41) 58, 60.

[70] Ibid. (citing *Free Zones Case (France v. Switzerland)* (1932) PCIJ Series A/B, No. 46, 138–9; *Phosphates in Morocco Case (Italy v. France)* (1938) PCIJ Series A/B, No. 74, 23–4; *Territorial Jurisdiction of Int'l Comm'n of River Oder (United Kingdom v. Poland)* (1929) PCIJ Series A, No. 23, 26; *Polish Postal Service Case*, Advisory Opinion (1925) PCIJ Series B, No. 2, 39). In other cases, the Permanent Court of International Justice avoided any reference to restrictive interpretation in spite of its invocation by respondents (citations omitted). The principle was, however, applied by some dissenting judges (citations omitted).

[71] Lauterpacht (n. 41) 61–62.

[72] 'The purpose of treaties – and of international law in general – is to limit the sovereignty of states in the particular sphere with which they are concerned.' Lauterpacht, ibid. 60. 'But the right of entering into international engagements is an attribute of State sovereignty.' *The SS Wimbledon Case (United Kingdom, France, Italy and Japan v. Germany)* (1923) PCIJ Series A, No. 1, 16, 25.

[73] Shihata (n. 69) 189–90; Lauterpacht, ibid. 58.   [74] Lauterpacht, ibid. 84.

Over the years, the International Court of Justice has variously endorsed both the principle of restrictive interpretation and the opposite rule of effective interpretation.[75] A leading study of the rule of strict construction, however, concluded that its application by the International Court of Justice 'has been more honoured in the breach than in the observance'.[76] A more recent study similarly concluded that '[t]oday, with few exceptions, the rule is always rejected in international decisions. Nonetheless the maxims are still used [by counsel] to found an interpretation.'[77]

> [I]t is perhaps not necessary to view with alarm the fact that there is an obvious inconsistency between the rule that treaty obligations ought to be interpreted so as to impose the minimum of obligation upon the party bound by it and the principle that provisions of a treaty ought to be construed so as to display a proper – if not the maximum – degree of effectiveness.[78]

The third narrative is that of human rights courts invoking the rule of strict construction or *expressio unius esclusio alterius* to interpret exceptions to a right narrowly, which indirectly promotes a broad interpretation of rights protected by international human rights instruments.[79]

The fourth narrative emerges from the jurisprudence of the European Court of Human Rights (ECtHR) and ICTY. Both have held that strict construction does not prevent a court from judicially clarifying the content of an offence over time.[80] Further, in the case of *Prosecutor v. Delalić and Others* (1998), the ICTY held:

> To put the meaning of the principle of legality beyond doubt, two important corollaries must be accepted. The first of these is that penal statutes must be strictly construed, this being a general rule which has stood the test of time.... The rule of strict construction requires that the language of a particular provision shall be construed such that no cases shall be held to fall within it which do not fall both within the reasonable meaning of its terms and within the spirit and scope of the enactment. In the construction of a criminal statute no violence must be done to its language to include people within it who do not ordinarily fall within its express language.... The paramount object in the construction of a criminal provision, or any other statute, is to ascertain the legislative intent. The rule of strict construction is not violated by giving the expression its full meaning or the alternative meaning which is more consonant with the legislative intent and best effectuates such intent.... The effect of strict construction

---

[75] Ibid. 51.   [76] Ibid. 66–67.

[77] L Crema, 'Disappearance and New Sightings of Restrictive Interpretation(s)' (2010) 21:3 EJIL 681, 682.

[78] Lauterpacht (n. 41) 67 fn. 1.

[79] Crema (n. 77) 692 and accompanying footnotes for ECtHR case law.

[80] App. No. 20166/92, *SW v. United Kingdom*, ECHR (1995) Series A, No. 335-B, para. 34.

of the provisions of a criminal statute is that *where an equivocal word or ambiguous sentence leaves a reasonable doubt of its meaning which the canons of construction fail to solve, the benefit of the doubt should be given to the subject and against the legislature* which has failed to explain itself. This is why ambiguous criminal statutes are to be construed *contra proferentem*.[81]

Accordingly, the ICTY would permit consideration of all canons of interpretation and interpretive aids (including preparatory work) before resorting to strict construction should an ambiguity still linger.[82] However, it is hard to imagine that the canons of interpretation in the *Vienna Convention* (1969) and beyond could produce no result and that an ambiguity would remain.[83] This is borne out by the jurisprudence of the ICTY and ICTR, which has assigned 'little significance' to the rule of strict construction.[84]

Further, it has been argued that the principle of effectiveness might not always be consistent with the subjective intentions of the Parties to a treaty, for they 'often wish their obligation to go so far and no farther. . . . They use language which, in their view, adequately expresses their determination not to concede to the treaty a full measure of realization of all its inherent and potential purposes.'[85] As previously discussed, this is believed by some to be the motivation for the definition of legality in article 22 of the Rome Statute.[86] However, judges have to infer the intention of the Parties to the Rome Statute in an objective manner and therefore assume that, once States Parties ratify it, 'good faith requires that, in the absence of compelling reasons to the contrary, it should not be treated as a non-committal enunciation of principle.'[87]

Indeed, there is a 'vast reservoir of judicial inspiration available in the principle of effectiveness', which is considered to be an aspect of interpreting a treaty in good faith as well as in light of its object and purpose.[88] In the author's view, effectiveness is indeed a matter of degree, and the key is considerably reducing the reservoir it makes available to judges in the Rome regime. This concept is not new. It has been said that 'politicians may re-invent the wheel; judges may

---

[81] *Prosecutor* v. *Delalić*, Judgment, ICTY-96–21-T, 16 November 1998, paras. 408, 410, 412–413 (emphasis added); see also *Prosecutor* v. *Tadić*, Judgment, ICTY-94–1-T, 7 May 1997, para. 713.

[82] See Chapter 2, Section 2.3.1.8; Broomhall (n. 3) 726; A Cassese, *International Criminal Law*, 2nd edn (Oxford University Press 2008) 51.

[83] Lauterpacht (n. 41) 61–62.

[84] Schabas (n. 1) 409–10 (citing *Prosecutor* v. *Tadić*, Judgment, ICTY-94–1-A, 15 July 1999, para. 73; *Prosecutor* v. *Erdemović*, Judgment, Separate and Dissenting Opinion of Judge Cassese, ICTY-96–22-A, 7 October 1997, para. 49; *Prosecutor* v. *Kayishema and Others*, Judgment, ICTR-95–1-T, 21 May 1999, para. 103; *Prosecutor* v. *Akayesu*, Judgment, ICTR-96–4-T, 2 September 1998, para. 319; *Prosecutor* v. *Rutaganda*, Judgment, ICTR-96–3, 6 December 1999, para. 51; *Prosecutor* v. *Musema*, Judgment, ICTR-96–13-T, 27 January 2000, para. 155).

[85] Lauterpacht (n. 41) 73.   [86] Broomhall (n. 3) 725.   [87] Lauterpacht (n. 41) 73–74.

[88] Ibid. 61–62, 83.

not. Law is evolutive. Politics is revolutionary. Law and government both make new lamps; but law, certainly the common law, makes new lamps from old.'[89] With respect to international law, it has been said that 'the judge . . . may change the law but he does so without moving out of the legal framework within which the law requires him to work'.[90]

A criminal law can be more or less effective, depending on how its scope is interpreted. If the effectiveness of the definitions of crimes in the Rome Statute is construed to be conditional upon ending impunity for the most serious crimes under international law, this being the Statute's 'object and purpose', effective interpretation could lead to the inappropriate expansion of the Court's jurisdiction beyond what its drafters intended and in violation of the principle of legality. Ironically, this approach might, in the long term, jeopardize the effectiveness of the Court and the criminal prohibitions in its Statute by undermining fair warning, the rule of law and separation of powers doctrine, something to which Feuerbach alluded.[91] Thus, the principle of effectiveness has to be defined so as to avert the reproach that the judges of the Court are 'acting as legislators in a manner which is outside their legitimate province'.[92] Any residual law-making authority that has been delegated to them by the Rome Statute's drafters is limited to the most interstitial and minimal developments.

Accordingly, if effective interpretation is defined as interpreting the definition of a crime in the Rome Statute in accordance with the mischief it is intended to address (e.g., whether it was intended to cover a particular class of persons, type of conduct or set of circumstances), the interests underlying the principle of legality are arguably not offended. For these reasons, it is a false dichotomy to suggest that restrictive and effective interpretations are mutually exclusive concepts. The two can be reconciled under the umbrella of legality. It is submitted that legality's interpretive device of strict construction is as essential (or more) to the good faith interpretation of the criminal provisions in a detailed international criminal law treaty as interpreting its provisions consistent with the mischief they are intended to address. It is further submitted that expansive and abstract conceptions of effective interpretation (e.g., ending impunity and securing justice for victims) offends the good faith interpretive imperative in light of the express wording of article 22.[93]

---

[89] Lord J Laws, 'The Good Constitution', Sir David Williams Lecture, Cambridge (4 May 2012), 11, http://www.judiciary.gov.uk/Resources/JCO/Documents/Speeches/lj-laws-speech-the-good-constitution.pdf, accessed 18 October 2013.

[90] RY Jennings, Interview in Antonio Cassese, *Five Masters of International Law* (Hart Publishing 2011) 115, 176.

[91] See Chapter 4, Section 4.2.4.   [92] Ibid. 73–74.

[93] Lauterpacht (n. 41) 83 wrote: 'Unlike the rule of restrictive interpretation of international obligations, the principle of effectiveness constitutes a general principle of law and a cogent requirement of good faith.' While this is arguably correct regarding treaties in general, it

It is the intention of the Parties that breathes life into every canon of interpretation, the latter being aids to the former's objective discovery.[94] From this flows the need to ensure that none of these canons – including effectiveness and strict construction – assume 'an existence independent of the intention, express or legitimately implied, of the parties. No rule or principle of interpretation is acceptable unless it proceeds from or acts upon that paramount consideration.'[95] For example, in order to argue that strict construction favours interpreting excuses and justifications for criminal conduct in favour of the accused in case of ambiguity, one might reason that the principle of legality and article 31(3) are indicative of this intent.[96]

At trial, the Court may consider a ground for excluding criminal responsibility other than those referred to in paragraph 1 where such a ground is derived from applicable law as set forth in article 21. The procedures relating to the consideration of such a ground shall be provided for in the Rules of Procedure and Evidence. Article 31(3) suggests that the drafters of the Court wanted to ensure that only those who are legally culpable for prohibited conduct are found guilty.

On balance, the author finds the conclusion of Lauterpacht bold but appropriate: 'To say that the rule as to restrictive interpretation . . . may be relied upon only when the treaty is not clear is to lay down a condition the actual application of which is the result of the process of interpretation and not its starting-point.'[97] The challenge is to 'operationalize' the rule of strict construction, which is a corollary of legality being the guiding interpretive principle for crimes in the Rome Statute, alongside other rules of interpretation in a manner that does not render them 'mutually exclusive and contradictory'.[98] If a sincere effort is not made to fixing the relationship between the rules of strict construction and effective interpretation, there is a danger that judges will be left with ample room for engaging in 'fact-specific, case-by-case criminalization', which would send the prosecutor, States Parties and the Security Council a 'potent message: the limits of official coercion are not fixed; the suggestion box is always open'.[99] Consequently, 'lawmaking devolves to law enforcement,

---

is the author's view that restrictive interpretation is a 'cogent requirement of good faith' in the interpretation of a detailed international criminal law treaty.

[94] On whether the 'intention of the parties' is, in general, the dominating factor in treaty interpretation, see C de Visscher, *Problèmes d'Interprétation Judiciaire en Droit International Public* (Pedone 1963) 50; JF Hogg, 'The International Court: Rules of Treaty Interpretation' (1958) 43 Minn L Rev 369, 372–74; GG Fitzmaurice, 'The Law and Procedure of the International Court of Justice: Treaty Interpretation and Certain Other Treaty Points' (1951) 28 British Ybk Int'l L 1, 6–7; and see a summary of the Court's view on this point in *South-West Africa Cases (Libya and Ethiopia* v. *South Africa)*, Dissenting Opinion of Judge Van Wyk [1962] ICJ Rep. 319, 576–91.

[95] Lauterpacht (n. 41) 73, 74, 83.   [96] *Erdemović* (n. 84) para. 49.

[97] Lauterpacht (n. 41) 51.   [98] Ibid. 52.   [99] Jeffries Jr (n. 14) 223.

and police and prosecutors are invited to play too large a role in deciding what to punish. Obviously, this problem can never be entirely eliminated. But it is also clear that the problem can be made better or worse by the behaviour of judges.'[100] Even those in favour of abandoning the doctrine of strict construction concede that the 'best thing that can be said about strict construction is that, if followed, it would create no incentive for police and prosecutors to proceed in doubtful cases'.[101]

Turning now to the voices of sceptics, there are those who favour weakening or even abandoning the rule of strict construction for various reasons, some of which have been discussed in the previous Chapter as reasons to weaken the principle of legality. For example, it has been argued that strict construction would obstruct the ability of the law to adapt to 'changing conditions of modern civilization, and the growth of scientific knowledge on criminology', and so penal statutes should not be so strictly construed so as to gut their very purpose but not so broadly construed so as to have 'unforeseen consequences'.[102] Two additional arguments remain to be discussed.

The first argument is to abandon strict construction for the interpretation of criminal law except where it can assist in avoiding the following types of injustice: (1) a disproportionate penalty; (2) an honest attempt at compliance; and (3) a change in social and economic policies of a subsequent generation.[103] One might ask to what extent the Rome Statute responds in some way to these concerns. Judges have the power to mitigate sentences, including where an honest attempt at compliance was made, the mistake of fact and law provisions ensure that no one is held criminally liable if they lack a 'guilty mind' and the Assembly of States Parties can respond to changes in social and economic policies of a subsequent generation that warrant the revision of the Rome Statute and Elements of Crimes.[104] Judges can also choose not to apply the Elements of Crimes.[105] Moreover, the origins of the crimes in the Rome Statute can by and large be traced to considerations of humanity rather than social and economic policies. They are perhaps for this reason a bit more impervious to changes in social priorities and preferences.

Second, it has been argued that because the judicial practice of invoking strict construction cannot entirely be explained by concerns of fair notice,[106] liberal construction should become the guiding interpretive principle for criminal law statutes.[107] Livingston Hall provocatively queries: 'Simply because liberal construction might work injustice in some cases is no proper reason for inflicting on the people the rule of strict construction in all cases.'[108] However, such reasoning seems rather extreme. Why must strict construction rely on only one

---

[100] Ibid.   [101] Ibid.   [102] Hall (n. 44) 759.   [103] Ibid. 763–67.
[104] Articles 78, 32, 121 and 9 respectively, Rome Statute.   [105] Article 9, Rome Statute.
[106] Hall (n. 44) 759; Jeffries Jr (n. 14) 206.
[107] Hall, ibid.   [108] Ibid. 759 (quoting Hall (n. 44)).

of several justifications for the legality principle and be categorically dismissed if that one justification cannot explain its invocation by judges? Perhaps judges have failed to articulate that other considerations are guiding their interpretive reasoning and reliance on strict construction. Is it not better then to argue in favour of more transparent and full legal reasoning rather than do away with such a rule?

It is submitted that the rule of strict construction should require judges of the Court to 'interpret crimes in the Statute in a moderate manner', meaning that they are interpreting and applying existing definitions of crimes rather than crafting new ones[109] and favouring the suspect or accused when the intent of the provision as it relates to the interpretive issue before the Court is 'left in doubt'.[110] The general rule of interpretation in article 31 of the *Vienna Convention* (1969) remains applicable, but 'object and purpose' and the idea of effective interpretation are to be read down to exclude considerations of collective goals such as ending impunity or securing peace and world order. Instead, these canons should invite judges to turn their minds to the specific mischief that the relevant criminal prohibitions in the Rome Statute seek to address. Where the ordinary meaning of their words in their context and in light of their object and purpose yield more than one interpretive outcome that could reasonably be thought to reflect the intent of the States Parties, strict construction trumps the canons of effective or purposive interpretation as a tiebreaker for this dilemma. It does not therefore have a fixed place in interpretive reasoning[111] – all canons of interpretation in article 31 of the *Vienna Convention* (1969) may be considered in any order – but must be considered at some stage and, in so doing, regarded as an essential safeguard to the legality principle. In the general rule of interpretation in article 31 of the *Vienna Convention* (1969), strict construction might be seen as logically entailed by the mandate to interpret the definitions of crimes in good faith and in light of their purpose to respect the principles of specificity and legality. It is therefore a part of this general rule and not an afterthought. Strict construction is concerned with the 'proper balance of the distribution of rights within a treaty system'.[112] In the Rome regime, those are the rights of the person investigated, prosecuted or convicted to not have the Statute applied retroactively to conduct, and the right of States Parties to prosecute individuals for crimes in the Rome Statute.

In practice, application of the strict construction rule may raise questions about whether an interpretive outcome expands the scope of the criminal

---

[109] Broomhall (n. 3) 723–24.
[110] A Ashworth, *Principles of Criminal Law*, 4th edn (Oxford University Press 2003) 82.
[111] Ashworth, ibid. 81.
[112] *Iron Rhine Arbitration (Belgium v. The Netherlands)* (2005) para. 53, www.pca-cpa.org, accessed 15 February 2011.

prohibition to include a new category of individuals,[113] a new class of conduct,[114] a new set of contextual circumstances[115] or a new and less rigorous type of mental element,[116] and whether it forecloses an existing defence[117] or does away with an element of a crime.[118] Confronted with these challenges, this rule should invite judges to expressly consider in their judgments how the preferred interpretive outcome avoids usurping the authority of the Assembly of States Parties. This means it is consistent with the express or implied legislative choices of States Parties, avoids threatening unfair surprise for an 'ordinarily law-abiding person in the actor's situation' and renders the law more, rather than less, certain.[119] The legislative choices of States Parties are to be gleaned by applying the rules of interpretation in the *Vienna Convention* (1969).

Regarding the standard of the 'ordinarily law-abiding person in the actor's situation', it is submitted that judges should give consideration to whether the individual, in his or her circumstances, could be expected to have obtained legal advice prior to engaging in the conduct at issue. An individual acting in a professional capacity might, for example, be expected to have done this so that a higher standard of 'lawyer's notice' might be applied to his or her conduct. As well, the leader of a State would be expected to have access to a well-staffed legal department qualified to advise him or her on the legality of contemplated conduct.[120] When considering the certainty that the interpretive

---

[113] *Kenya Situation*, Decision Pursuant to Article 15 of the Rome Statute on the Authorization of an Investigation into the Republic of Kenya, ICC-01/09, 31 March 2010, paras. 115–128 (para. 117 in particular); see also the Dissenting Opinion of Judge Hans-Peter Kaul.

[114] *Nahimana and Others* v. *Prosecutor*, Judgment, ICTR-99–52-A, 28 November 2007, paras. 221–223, 376; DF Orentlicher, 'Criminalizing Hate Speech in the Crucible of Trial: Prosecutor v. Nahimana' (2005) 12 New England J Int'l & Comp L 17.

[115] *Prosecutor* v. *Tadić*, Decision on the Defence Motion for Interlocutory Appeal on Jurisdiction, ICTY-94–1-AR72, 2 October 1995, paras. 77ff.

[116] Schabas, *The International Criminal Court* (n. 1) 410 (citing *Prosecutor* v. *Bemba*, Decision Pursuant to Article 61(7)(a) and (b) of the Rome Statute on the Charges of the Prosecutor Against Jean-Pierre Bemba Gombo, ICC-01/05–01/08, 15 June 2009, para. 369 (rejecting *dolus eventualis* or recklessness as part of the Rome Statute)).

[117] F Jessberger, 'Bad Torture – Good Torture? What International Criminal Lawyers may Learn from the Recent Trial of Police Officers in Germany' (2005) 3 J Int'l Crim Justice 1059 (citing therein for reaching the same conclusion P Gaeta, 'May Necessity be Available as a Defence for Torture in the Interrogation of Suspected Terrorists?' (2004) 2 J Int'l Crim Justice 785).

[118] The war crimes nexus for crimes against humanity was removed in Control Council Law No. 10, adopted by the victorious powers in December 1945; WA Schabas, 'Criminal Responsibility for Violations of Human Rights' in J Symonides (ed.), *Human Rights: International Protection, Monitoring, Enforcement* (UNESCO 2003) 281.

[119] Jeffries Jr (n. 14) 220.

[120] Ashworth (n. 36) 443, making such a comment in respect of a large corporation with a well-staffed legal department that is 'dedicated to circumventing new penal provisions in the sphere of taxation and corporate finance . . .'

outcome might foster in the law, one might ask the following questions: 'Would this interpretation, taken as precedent, constrain future applications? Or would it merely multiply the possibilities? Would the decision resolve the ambiguity in the law, or merely exploit it?'[121] Also, which category of offenders could now expect to be covered by the criminal prohibition? If an interpretive outcome would foster the openendedness of a criminal prohibition rather than rendering its application more predictable (e.g., by providing criteria that the Court will take into consideration or illustrative examples of conduct prohibited by the relevant provision), this should perhaps be avoided because it could lead to abuse in the future.[122]

One deceptive form of open-ended decision making is where the interpretive reasoning of judges in a criminal law case is largely fact-driven, as this 'invites further innovation on other facts' and might cause judges to overlook how the contemplated interpretation would cover a wide population of offenders.[123] Thus, the key is to provide reasoning that promotes predictability by making the considerations of judges transparent and anchored in principles rather than facts.

The strict construction imperative in article 22(2) is arguably also rebutted where the Rome Statute contains deliberately open-textured language signalling the States Parties' intention to delegate a degree of law-making power to judges.[124] In such a case, the suspect or accused is fairly warned by the generality of the wording in the Rome Statute, and there are no concerns about the separation of powers or rule of law. In *Prosecutor* v. *Kupreškić and Others* (2000), the ICTY held that the crime against humanity of 'other inhumane acts' is intended to be a residual category.[125] However, it also went on to express concern that it 'lacks precision and is too general to provide a safe yardstick for the work of the Tribunal, and hence, that it is contrary to the principle of "specificity" of criminal law'.[126] Confronted with this dilemma and not wanting to exhaustively enumerate a list of prohibited conduct for a category that is intended to be residual, the tribunal decided that it should consult international human rights law in order to 'identify a set of basic rights appertaining to human beings, the infringement of which may amount, depending on the accompanying circumstances, to a crime against humanity.'[127] The principle of legality was therefore thought to have been protected.[128] A similar approach has also

---

[121] Jeffries Jr (n. 14) 220–21.   [122] Ibid.   [123] Ibid. 221.
[124] Ashworth (n. 36) 422–23.
[125] *Kupreškić*, Judgment, ICTY-95–16-T, 14 January 2000, para. 563.
[126] Ibid.; see also *Prosecutor* v. *Blagojević*, Judgment, ICTY-02–60-T, 17 January 2005, para. 625.
[127] *Kupreškić*, ibid. para. 566.
[128] B Van Schaack, 'Crimen Sine Lege: Judicial Lawmaking at the Intersection of Law and Morals' (2008) 97 Georgetown LJ 119, 139–40 (citing *Prosecutor* v. *Stakić*, Judgment, ICTY-97–24-A, 22 March 2006, para. 315; *Prosecutor* v. *Vasiljević*, Judgment, ICTY-98–32-T, 29 November 2002, para. 203).

been advocated at the national level to constrain judicial discretion. Arguments have been advanced in favour of legislatures including in statutes non-binding and non-exhaustive lists of conduct captured by various open-textured phrases in legislation.[129] Where this is not done, judges can include in their reasoning illustrative examples of the conduct prohibited as a means of constraining their own discretion in future cases. Wherever such open-textured phrases exist, the focus of judges should be on upholding the rule of law and providing a reasonable degree of legal certainty (without pre-judging later cases) as to who and what may or may not be captured by the prohibition.

Finally, strict construction seems to oblige judges to interpret grounds for excluding criminal liability on which a defendant might have relied, such as self-defence, more liberally (or not more narrowly than a reasonable person could expect) so that the retroactive imposition of criminal responsibility can be avoided.[130] For example, it has been argued that the *ex post facto* removal of the recognized defence of obedience to superior orders in the governing statutes of the Nuremberg and Tokyo trials constituted a 'serious violation' of the legality principle.[131]

5.6 Ambiguity and favouring the accused

The imperative to interpret crimes in the Rome Statute in a manner that is favourable to the person being investigated, prosecuted or convicted in case of ambiguity is a device to avoid retroactive law making. This imperative is considered by some to be a consequence of the rule of strict construction rather than a free-standing imperative and originates from the common law presumption of *in favorem vitae*.[132] In addition, the ICTY and ICTR have invoked the evidentiary rule of *in dubio pro reo* ('when in doubt, in favour of the accused'),[133] normally to resolve differences between French and English versions of the Statutes.[134] For example, this rule was used to justify imposing an intent requirement for killings as genocide.[135] Other judges have rejected *in dubio pro reo* as an interpretive principle or argument.[136]

---

[129] PH Robinson, 'Legality and Discretion in the Distribution of Criminal Sanctions' (1988) 25 Harv J on Legis 393, 430–31.

[130] Broomhall (n. 3) 724; Ashworth (n. 112) 62.

[131] MC Bassiouni, *Crimes against Humanity in International Criminal Law* (Martinus Nijhoff 1992) 130, cited in Broomhall, ibid. 724.

[132] Broomhall, ibid. 724, 726.

[133] *Prosecutor* v. *Tadić*, Decision on Appellant's Motion for the Extension of the Time-Limit and Admission of Additional Evidence, ICTY-94-1-T, 15 October 1998, para. 73.

[134] *Prosecutor* v. *Rutaganda*, Judgment, ICTR-96-3-T, 6 December 1999, para. 50; *Akayesu* (n. 84) para. 501; *Musema* (n. 84) para. 155.

[135] *Blagojević* (n. 126) para. 642, fn. 2057; *Akayesu*, ibid. 501.

[136] Judge Schomburg has taken the position that the rule *in dubio pro reo* applies only to findings of fact and 'legal facts', and not to interpreting the statute and rules of procedure and evidence: *Prosecutor* v. *Limaj and Others*, Judgment, Partially Dissenting and Separate

In the Rome Statute, the imperative in article 22(2) to interpret ambiguities in favour of the person investigated, prosecuted or convicted perhaps more accurately captures the ideas underlying the rule of strict construction, namely, the moderate interpretation of criminal prohibitions and more liberal interpretation of provisions 'relieving or diminishing liability'.[137] Interpretation in favour of the accused in every case of ambiguity would be overreaching in light of the justifications for legality, and such a literal reading therefore seems 'simplistic and wrong'.[138] For example, '[s]eparation of powers might be taken to mean that courts should make law only interstitially, but not that all change must move in one direction'.[139] As well, legal certainty is not unduly compromised if ambiguities are not always resolved in favour of the defendant, as the prohibition against retroactivity is not threatened, the latter being the real concern. Indeed, one Law Commission rightly remarked: 'We do not think it would be acceptable for the Code to provide in effect that wherever some arguable point of doubt arose about the interpretation of an offence the point should automatically be resolved in favour of the accused.'[140]

Like strict construction, perhaps because it is a consequence of it, the notion of interpretation in favour of the accused is thought by some to apply as a 'final step in the interpretive sequence'.[141] The ICTY in the *Prosecutor* v. *Delalić and Others* (1998) held:

> A criminal statute is one in which the legislature intends to have the final result of inflicting suffering upon, or encroaching upon the liberty of, the individual. It is undoubtedly expected that, in such a situation, the intention to do so shall be clearly expressed and without ambiguity. The legislature will not allow such intention to be gathered from doubtful inferences from the words used. It will also not leave its intention to be inferred from unexpressed words. The intention should be manifest.[142]

Thus, there is a presumption *against* ambiguity in criminal statutes – that States Parties did not intend to be ambiguous.[143] However, as at the domestic level, this presumption may not be consistent with reality, because legislators and diplomats sometimes deliberately use ambiguous language in order to bridge substantive differences of opinion.[144] On other occasions, drafters of penal statutes will invoke vague language so that courts have 'considerable power' to interpret certain terms.[145] For example, statutory laws on theft frequently

---

Opinion and Declaration of Judge Schomburg, ICTY-03–66-A, 27 September 2007, paras. 15ff.

[137] Hall (n. 44) 748–49.   [138] Jeffries Jr (n. 14) 219; Kreß (n. 8) para. 31.

[139] Jeffries Jr, ibid. 219.

[140] Ashworth (n. 36) 432 (citing Law Commission No. 177, *Criminal Law: A Criminal Code for England and Wales*, vols. I–II (1989) para. 3.17).

[141] Broomhall (n. 3) 726.   [142] *Delalić* (n. 81) para. 409.   [143] Broomhall (n. 3) 726.

[144] Lietzau (n. 17) 487.   [145] Ibid. 484; Ashworth (n. 36) 422–23.

contain the criminal element of 'dishonesty', and self-defence laws often require the use of force to be 'reasonable'.[146] It is posited that the deliberate use by drafters of open-ended language is a means of 'delegating effective power to the court to decide exactly where the cutting edge of the criminal law is to fall'.[147] This can be achieved when judges provide 'reasoned explanations' as well as 'search for principles, [the] classification of differing factual situations, and so on'.[148]

As previously discussed,[149] vagueness is also often required for normative terms so that punishment can be individualized and justice can be done in an individual case. Examples of normative terms in written criminal prohibitions include 'artfully, insidiously, astutely, fraudulently, maliciously, spitefully, against the public interest, brutally, negligently, against social morality, against decency' and so on.[150] Furthermore, judges themselves might feel compelled to define an element of an offence in a normative manner. In *Prosecutor v. Akayesu* (1998), for example, the Trial Chamber held that the crime of rape 'cannot be captured in a mechanical description of objects and body parts' and that judges need to consider the object of the conduct, which is 'intimidation, degradation, humiliation, control or discrimination'.[151] When such inherently or deliberately vague terms are used to define a criminal prohibition, the drafters of the prohibition must be assumed to have delegated a degree of law-making power to judges, and this does not violate any of the interests protected by the legality principle.

The work of the imperative to resolve ambiguities in favour of the person investigated, prosecuted or convicted is basically the same as the rule of strict construction and can also be accommodated by the reference to 'good faith' in article 31(1) of the *Vienna Convention* (1969). However, the interpretive presumption against redundancy, the idea that every word in a legal text has a distinct meaning, leads to the finding that this imperative might best be regarded as reminding judges of a rebuttable presumption against ambiguity, that States Parties bear the burden of drafting criminal prohibitions using language that is as clear as possible. It can also remind judges that collective goals (e.g., peace, security, justice for victims etc.) are not permitted as justifications for retroactive application of the crimes in the Rome Statute – that the rights of the person on trial trump these legitimate policy goals (assuming one actually thinks that respect for legality endangers these goals).[152] Regarding this

---

[146] Ashworth, ibid. 423.   [147] Ibid.

[148] PS Atiyah, 'Common Law and Statute Law' (1985) 48 Modern L Rev 1, 4, cited in Ashworth, ibid.

[149] See Chapter 4, Section 4.2.2.

[150] S Glaser, 'Nullum Crimen Sine Lege' (1942) 24:1 J Comp Legis & Int'l L 29, 36.

[151] *Akayesu* (n. 84) para. 597.

[152] As Judge Cassese rightly remarked in his Separate and Dissenting Opinion in *Prosecutor v. Erdemović* (n. 84) para. 11: 'a policy-oriented approach in the area of criminal law could run counter to the fundamental customary principle nullum crimen sine

burden of States Parties to draft the definitions of crimes clearly, it has been submitted by some that, in case of a lingering ambiguity – after applying the interpretive imperatives in articles 31 and 33 of the *Vienna Convention* (1969) and Rome Statute – this should be resolved in favour of the accused rather than resorting to the Statute's drafting history.[153] This argument is consistent with the presumption against ambiguity and, if accepted, would, in theory, limit the invocation of article 32 of the *Vienna Convention* (1969) in the Court's decisions. However, it is hard to imagine that, in practice, judges would not take the time to understand the drafting history of a disputed provision.

5.7 Analogous reasoning

The Austrian Code of Joseph II (1787) was the first modern criminal law statute to specifically prohibit analogous reasoning.[154] It is yet another device that is 'directly linked' to the prohibition against retroactivity.[155] In fact, the extension of criminal prohibitions by analogy is forbidden in most legal systems for this reason.[156] Both Feuerbach and Bentham rejected reasoning by analogy.[157] Infamously, this notion was flouted by the Nazi regime in the Act of 28 June 1935:

> Whoever commits an act which the law declares to be punishable or which is deserving of punishment according to the fundamental idea of a penal law and sound perception of the people, shall be punished. If no determinate penal law is directly applicable to the action, it shall be punished according to the law, the basic ideal of which fits it best.[158]

---

lege'. This does not mean, however, that the interests of victims cannot be appropriately taken into consideration when interpreting other provisions of the Rome Statute.

[153] D Akande, 'The Sources of International Criminal Law' in A Cassese (ed.), *The Oxford Companion to International Criminal Justice* (Oxford University Press 2009) 41, 45; D Jacobs, 'Positivism and International Criminal Law: The Principle of Legality as a Rule of Conflict of Theories' in J d'Aspremont and J Kammerhofer (eds.), *International Legal Positivism in a Post-Modern World* (Cambridge University Press, forthcoming October 2014), 1, 32–33, http://papers.ssrn.com/sol3/papers.cfm?abstract_id=2046311, accessed 16 October 2013.

[154] Hall (n. 25) 168.

[155] Kreß (n. 8) para. 28; App. No. 14307/88, *Kokkinakis v. Greece*, ECHR (1994) Series A, No. 260-A, para. 52.

[156] Broomhall (n. 3) 724.   [157] Hall (n. 25) 170.

[158] L Preuss, 'Punishment by Analogy in National Socialist Penal Law' (1936) 26 J Crim L & Criminology 847. Article 16 of the Soviet Code comparably provided that 'if any socially dangerous act is not provided for by the present Code, the basis and limits of responsibility for it shall be determined by application of those articles of the Code which provide for crimes most similar to it in nature'. H German and J Spindler, *Soviet Criminal Law and Procedure: The RSFSR Codes*, 2nd edn (Harvard University Press 1972) 22, cited in DN

Analogous reasoning can result in judges criminalizing conduct that the legislature did not intend to punish.[159] A famous English example of this is *Shaw v. Director of Public Prosecutions* (1961). A statute had been enacted that prohibited London prostitutes from streetwalking. In response, Mr. Shaw decided to publish the 'Ladies' Directory', which contained a list of the names, addresses and telephone numbers of prostitutes in the London area. Mr. Shaw was subsequently convicted of the judge-made offense of 'conspiring to corrupt public morals', a conviction that the House of Lords controversially affirmed.[160]

5.7.1 National history

In the common law tradition, it was permissible to criminalize conduct that was analogous to existing common law crimes.[161] A judge examines the facts before him or her to determine whether they are sufficiently like those in a previous case in legally relevant ways so that the previous case stands as an applicable precedent.[162] This is known as 'reasoning by analogy' and is still practiced today to ensure that the same statutory or common-law rule is applied to cases that are sufficiently similar.[163] In the early years of the common law in England and the United States, this often led to retroactive crime creation.[164] For example, in *State* v. *Buckman* (1836), the accused was charged with having put a dead animal in another person's well. This conduct had not been criminalized, but the court nevertheless convicted the accused by drawing an analogy between this conduct and the common-law offence of selling unwholesome food or poisoning food or drink intended for human consumption.[165] In another case, a defendant dropped the dead body of a child in a river, and although such conduct was not a crime at the relevant time, the individual was nevertheless convicted, with the court drawing an analogy between the accused's conduct and the criminal prohibition that forbids the digging up of dead bodies.[166] Despite these origins, as jurisprudence accumulated in common-law countries and numerous criminal law statutes were enacted, reasoning by analogy proved itself to be a 'very substantial impediment to arbitrary decision-making'.[167]

In the civil law tradition, reasoning by analogy has a different meaning. For example, the Bavarian Code of 1751 provided that cases not covered by the

---

Husak and CA Callender, 'Wilful Ignorance, Knowledge, and the "Equal Culpability" Thesis: A Study of the Deeper Significance of the Principle of Legality' (1994) Wis L Rev 29, 30 fn. 3.
[159] Hall (n. 25) 175–76.   [160] [1962] AC 220.   [161] Hall (n. 25) 725.
[162] Gallant (n. 26) 38.   [163] Ibid.
[164] M Ribeiro, *Limiting Arbitrary Power: The Vagueness Doctrine in Canadian Constitutional Law* (University of British Columbia Press 2005) 20.
[165] 8 NH 203, cited in Ribeiro, ibid.   [166] Ribeiro (n. 164) 20.   [167] Packer (n. 37) 88.

Code should be decided inter alia by analogy.[168] Thus, acts falling outside of a statutory prohibition may be declared criminal because they are similar in legally relevant ways to acts covered by an existing statute.[169] Crime creation by analogy in civil law jurisdictions traditionally involved ascertaining whether the conduct in question closely resembled conduct that was already subject to a codified criminal sanction.[170] Further, the doctrine of precedents is not recognized in the civil law tradition in the same way it is in the common law, meaning the retroactive creation of a crime by analogy in a civil law system would not be a binding precedent for similar cases in the future.[171] Accordingly, if a judge hearing another case subsequently agreed with the reasoning in a previous ruling that was based on reasoning by analogy, the new decision would again be considered an example of retroactive crime creation because the prohibition would not be grounded in the express words of the relevant statute.[172] This approach has its benefits in that bad decisions can remain in the past rather than bind judges in the future, but it can also foster a perception of arbitrary legal reasoning.[173] Though a few cases prior to the Second World War referred to this type of reasoning by analogy as offending the principle of legality, many civil law countries did not prohibit this practice during that era.[174]

As we have seen, a key historic distinction between reasoning by analogy in the common and civil law traditions is that the common law is concerned with the gradual development of binding case law over centuries (although there are exceptions to this trend) as compared to the civil law mandate to make law when necessary in an individual case.[175] However, both remedies rest upon a fiction of sorts. The common-law judge would reason that the law is not new but merely discovered, and the civil law judge might characterize the legal innovation as not law per se, as it is not binding on anyone other than the individual appearing before him or her. Common-law reasoning by analogy would permit the following analysis:

> It being granted that statute or rule R correctly applies to the X situation, the Y situation is subsumed under R by *logical* analogy if Y resembles X in a number of particulars which outweigh known important differences. Thus, under extensive interpretation the same rule is applied to both situations.[176]

The prohibition against analogy in the common law tradition would, however, not operate if the Y situation could not be tolerated by the wording of statute or rule R.[177]

---

[168] Hall (n. 25) 168 (discussion of *ex aequitate et analogia juris*).
[169] Gallant (n. 26) 36, 38.   [170] Ibid. 36.   [171] Ibid. 38.   [172] Ibid.   [173] Ibid.
[174] Ibid. 37.   [175] Hall (n. 25) 174.   [176] Ibid. 172–73.   [177] Ibid.

Where the wording of a criminal prohibition can tolerate situation Y, reasoning by analogy would not seem to be prohibited in either tradition. Where it cannot, the prohibition against analogy would bar the creation of a new crime in many countries.[178] The different forms of reasoning by analogy in the common and civil law traditions are arguably not an indication of respect or lack thereof for legality. Rather, they are best understood as a function of the existing sources of law in both traditions. In most continental systems, statutory law is the exclusive source of law, and legal solutions must accordingly be derived therefrom, including by analogy.[179] In contrast, Anglo-American systems offer judges statutes and common law, and they can rely on the latter to fill legal gaps. Today, however, the traditional distinction described is less sharp so that many 'code' countries have rich jurisprudence that has a function similar to that in common-law countries.[180] As well, limits to arguments of statutory analogy exist to varying degrees in all countries.[181] Most important, statutory analogies are generally not permitted in the realm of criminal law or tax law or in order to extend a statutory exception.[182] However, portions of Islamic criminal justice systems can be very 'flexible' and may even allow for the identification of a criminal prohibition by analogy.[183]

Finally, incremental decision making and packaging decisions as 'self-evident, deductive extensions of pre-existing law' is appealing to judges generally, irrespective of whether they work in a jurisdiction that has a system of binding precedents.[184] Indeed, with the exception of France:

> [t]ogether with the statute applied in order to decide the case, precedents are the most frequently used materials in judicial opinions. This is true not only where precedents *must* be used because they are a source of law and have binding force (as in the UK and USA), but also in the European systems which have no formal rule of *stare decisis*.... [I]f one looks at the actual use of precedents in the opinions of the higher courts in the several countries [studied], it can be observed that there are no great differences in their use between the so-called common law and civil law systems.... [And even where] precedents of the higher courts are binding, this effect may be

---

178 Ibid. 174.
179 RS Summers and M Taruffo, 'Interpretation and Comparative Analysis' in DN MacCormick and RS Summers (eds.), *Interpreting Statutes: A Comparative Study* (Dartmouth Publishing Company Ltd 1991) 461, 471–72; MC Bassiouni, 'Principles of Legality in International and Comparative Law', in *International Criminal Law: Sources, Subjects and Contents*, vol. I (Martinus Nijhoff 2008) 83.
180 Summers and Taruffo, ibid. 471–72.   181 Ibid.   182 Ibid.
183 JJ Paust, 'It's No Defense: Nullum Crimen, International Crime and the Gingerbread Man' (1997) 60 Albany L Rev 657, 675 (citing MC Bassiouni and P Manikas, *The Law of the International Criminal Tribunal for the Former Yugoslavia* (Transnational 1996) 279).
184 T Ginsburg, 'Bounded Discretion in International Judicial Lawmaking' (2005) 45 Va J Int'l L 631, 635–36.

overcome or bypassed in several ways, for example, through distinguishing, overruling or simply not following the precedents. It is of course true that civil law systems generally ascribe only a *persuasive* or *de facto* effect (that is, not formally binding) to precedents. But again this persuasive force is often very strong.[185]

5.7.2 International history

Logical reasoning by analogy within the scope of a criminal prohibition is permitted by the *eiusdem generis* canon of statutory construction.[186] *Eiusdem generis* means that 'general words when following (or sometimes preceding) special words are limited to the genus, if any, indicated by the special words.'[187] However, international tribunals have applied the *eiusdem generis* rule of interpretation in 'a number of cases'.[188] On at least one occasion, the ICTY held that this rule lacked precision and was 'too general to provide a safe yardstick for the work of the Tribunal'.[189] Instead, the rule was thought to be a useful 'supplementary tool, to establish whether certain acts . . . reach the level of gravity required' by a particular provision'.[190]

In practice, reasoning by analogy could, for example, inspire judges to provide reasons for why certain conduct is sufficiently similar (in legally material ways) to other crimes against humanity listed in article 7 of the Rome Statute. Article 7(1)(k) – other inhumane acts of a similar character – is deliberately vague and imprecise.[191] In *Stakić* (2002), the ICTY expressed concern that the category of other inhumane acts as a crime against humanity might be so imprecise as to violate the principle of legality.[192] However, the Rome Statute contains a list of crimes against which comparisons can be made, and the Court has recently held that inhumane acts must be 'serious violations of international customary law and the basic rights pertaining to human beings, drawn from the norms of international human rights law, which are of a similar nature

---

[185] Summers and Taruffo (n. 179) 487. For more on similarities and differences in national jurisdictions in the use of precedents in the interpretive process, see Summers and Taruffo 487–89.

[186] See Chapter 2, Section 2.3.1.2. On reasoning by analogy generally in international law, see S Vöneky, 'Analogy in International Law' in R. Wolfrum (ed.), Max Planck Encyclopedia of Public International Law (2008–), online edition, www.mpepil.com, accessed 4 July 2014.

[187] R Jennings and A Watts, *Oppenheim's International Law*, 9th edn (Longman, Harlow 1992) 1279–80. See also *Delalić* (n. 81) para. 166; *Kupreškić* (n. 125) paras. 564, 620.

[188] Jennings and Watts, ibid.   [189] *Kupreškić* (n. 125) para. 564.

[190] Ibid. para. 620.

[191] Schabas (n. 1) 409 (citing *Kupreškić* (n. 125) para. 563) and see fn. 32 for more case law citations for this proposition.

[192] Ibid. (citing *Prosecutor v. Stakić*, Decision on Rule 98 bis Motion for Judgment of Acquittal, ICTY-97-24-T, 31 October 2002, para. 131).

and gravity to the acts referred to in article 7(1) of the Statute'.[193] Still, concern continues to be expressed that the Rome Statute 'fails to provide an indication, even indirectly, of the legal standards which would allow us to identify the prohibited inhumane acts'.[194]

Perhaps the most famous international criminal law example of reasoning by logical analogy – albeit implicitly – is the *Tadić* jurisdiction decision (1995) in which the ICTY held that the criminal prohibitions in article 3 of its statute extend equally to crimes committed during an international as well as a non-international armed conflict. Reasoning by analogy in the traditional civil law sense was, however, rejected by the ICTY:

> The accepted view is that if the legislature has not used words sufficiently comprehensive to include within its prohibition all the cases which should naturally fall within the mischief intended to be prevented, the interpreter is not competent to extend them. The interpreter of a provision can only determine whether the case is within the intention of a criminal statute by construction of the express language of the provision.[195]

Despite this sensible reasoning,

> it was the perceived willingness of the ICTY to engage in liberal reasoning-by-analogy that contributed, in part, to the adoption of article 22 para. 2. That the ICC States Parties are slow to modify the definition of crimes contained in the Statute, even in the face of pressing international need, does not give the judges the power to supplant the authoritative law-maker. While the scope of crimes at customary or treaty law beyond the realm of the Statute may potentially change, the scope of the Court's *jurisdiction ratione materiae* will not without the deliberate action of the Assembly of States Parties.[196]

As for the doctrine of precedents (stare decisis), this matter was analyzed by the ICTY in *Prosecutor* v. *Aleksovski* (2000):

---

[193] The general introduction to crimes against humanity in the Elements of Crimes echoes this:

> Since article 7 pertains to international criminal law, its provisions, consistent with article 22, must be strictly construed, taking into account that crimes against humanity as defined in article 7 are among the most serious crimes of concern to the international community as a whole, warrant and entail individual criminal responsibility, and require conduct which is impermissible under *generally applicable international law, as recognized by the principal legal systems of the world* (emphasis added).

[194] Schabas (n. 1) 409–10 (citing *Prosecutor* v. *Katanga and Others*, Decision on Confirmation of Charges, ICC-01/04–01/07, 30 September 2008, para. 448; *Kupreškić* (n. 125) para. 565).

[195] *Delalić* (n. 81) para. 410.   [196] Broomhall (n. 3) 725.

> The Appeals Chamber ... concludes that ... [it] should follow its previous decisions, but should be free to depart from them for cogent reasons in the interests of justice.... Instances of [such] situations include cases where the previous decision has been decided on the basis of a wrong legal principle or cases where a previous decision has been given *per incuriam*, that is a judicial decision that has been "wrongly decided, usually because the judge or judges were ill-informed about the applicable law." ... It is necessary to stress that the normal rule is that previous decisions are to be followed, and departure from them is the exception.... What is followed in previous decisions is the legal principle (*ratio decidendi*), and the obligation to follow that principle only applies in similar cases, or substantially similar cases. This means less that the facts are similar or substantially similar, than that the question raised by the facts in the subsequent case is the same as the question decided by the legal principle in the previous decision. There is no obligation to follow previous decisions which may be distinguished for one reason or another from the case before the court. Where, in a case before it, the Appeals Chamber is faced with previous decisions that are conflicting, it is obliged to determine which decision it will follow, or whether to depart from both decisions for cogent reasons in the interests of justice.[197]

In the context of the Rome Statute, the prohibition against analogy can perhaps be understood as prohibiting judges from creating crimes by interpreting a criminal prohibition beyond its express wording.[198] This prohibition is very different from logical reasoning by analogy, which is permissible – because it constrains judicial discretion – and is used to bring the facts of a case within the scope of a treaty or unwritten criminal prohibition by reasoning that they are sufficiently similar to the facts of a case previously held to be captured by the relevant prohibition. Analogy is a 'valid and ... necessary tool ... [that] does not extend to law-making, but is restricted to interpretation. It can thus be used to fill gaps in legislated definitions'.[199] Indeed, it has rightly been observed that the line marking this distinction might be 'thin and porous'.[200] However, it is a distinction that has been confirmed by the European Court of Human Rights (ECtHR). In *Okçuoglu* v. *Turkey* (1999), the ECtHR reviewed a Turkish court's decision to impose a criminal sentence by analogy.[201] The law expressly applied to editors, and the court reasoned by analogy to have it apply to a publisher. The ECtHR held that this finding offends the principle of legality.

Article 21(2) of the Rome Statute reads: 'The Court may apply principles and rules of law as interpreted in its previous decisions.' It is submitted that the Appeals Chamber of the Court and even the Trial Chambers should aspire to follow their previous decisions where appropriate and thereby erect another

---

[197] *Prosecutor* v. *Aleksovski*, Judgment, ICTY-95–14/1-A, 24 March 2000, paras. 97, 107–111.
[198] Kreß (n. 8) para. 28.   [199] Broomhall (n. 3) 725.   [200] Cassese (n. 82) 152.
[201] App. No. 24246/94, ECHR (1999).

pillar in support of legal consistency and certainty.[202] Among other things, gradual reasoning by analogy in the Court's case law enables counsel appearing before the Court to better prepare their arguments. In employing this type of reasoning, however,

> [t]he court must look beyond the present dispute toward the entire class of cases bounded by the statutory phrase. Generalization of the question in this way helps to disentangle the legal issue from the personality of the particular defendant and to prevent individualized, ad hoc declarations of criminality. Perhaps more important, projecting the issue across an entire range of cases pushes the court toward a more rule-like decision, one that resolves rather than exploits the statutory ambiguity and leaves the agencies of law enforcement with definitive guidance for future action.[203]

Wherever the prohibition against analogy exists, it is a tool that calibrates the 'newness' of a crime to a certain degree, barring the finding of a 'substantially new crime'.[204] As such, it is a device for safeguarding the legality principle and can be accommodated in the 'good faith' interpretive imperative in article 31(1) of the *Vienna Convention* (1969). The difference is between interpreting the law and making it, a distinction which is most difficult to discern in hard cases. Which types of analogical reasoning, then, are permitted and prohibited? '[W]here the judicial innovation is smaller, less controversial, [and] consistent with the pattern of legislative action, there is less risk of frustrating considered legislative choice.'[205] In some jurisdictions, an exception to the prohibition against analogy and therefore retroactivity has been foreseeability and fairness; however, such standards would bring with them the entire set of problems attendant with considerations of foreseeability, substantive justice and morality that were discussed in the previous Chapter.[206]

Further, consistent with the major legal systems of the world, the ban on analogy in the Rome Statute should not prohibit the following types of reasoning: (1) exceptionally resorting to general principles of international criminal law or criminal justice, or to 'principles common to the major legal systems of the world', to determine whether the impugned conduct is prohibited under the Rome Statute;[207] (2) analogous reasoning where the wording of the crime itself requires this (e.g., 'other inhumane acts of a similar character');[208] (3) logical reasoning that leads to the invocation of provisions in the Rome Statute to determine whether the impugned conduct is prohibited under general principles of law;[209] or (4) a plain reading of the Rome Statute in light of

---

[202] *London Tramways Co.* v. *London County Council* [1898] AC 375; *Practice Statement (Judicial Precedent)* [1966] 1 WLR 1234.

[203] Jeffries Jr (n. 14) 232. [204] Broomhall (n. 3).

[205] Jeffries Jr. (n. 14) 205; Hall (n. 25) 173–74. [206] Broomhall (n. 3) 725.

[207] Cassese (n. 82) 49. [208] Ibid.; Broomhall (n. 3) 725.

[209] Cassese, ibid. 50. The example Cassese provides is where judges try to determine whether use of a particular weapon offends the general principle prohibiting the use of weapons

its object and purpose revealing a gap that needs to be filled by reference to other articles or paragraphs of the same article.[210] Indeed, the first and final types of reasoning are not even forms of reasoning by analogy. Thus, the ban on analogy does not typically prohibit contextual reasoning inspired by statutory provisions or logical reasoning, or resort to applicable law to fill gaps in a criminal statute. Finally, and in contrast to analogous reasoning, distinguishing two concepts within the Rome Statute from one another can sometimes lead to a better understanding of the ideas that the concept at issue seeks to represent.

5.8 Legality without prejudice

Article 22(3) provides: 'This article shall not affect the characterization of any conduct as criminal under international law independently of this Statute.' This provision is intended to make clear that the effect of the interpretive outcomes resulting from the application of the legality principle as defined in article 22 are limited to the Rome Statute. It thereby 'prevents any misconceptions that might arise as to whether the Statute exclusively codifies or exhausts international criminal prohibitions'.[211] Thus, where application of the interpretive devices in article 22 leads to conduct not being characterized as criminal under the Rome Statute, this finding is without prejudice to the same conduct being characterized as a crime under international law.[212] In this way, article 22(3) serves an important function by reminding observers of the Court's work that mandatory rules of adjudication for the Court, such as the principle of legality in article 22, are distinct from rules of conduct for individuals.[213] Stated differently, the rules of interpretation emerging from article 22, which might in some cases lead to an acquittal or ruling that certain conduct does not fall within the Court's jurisdiction, are rules to be applied to the exercise of adjudication. The application of these rules does not necessarily offer guidance on whether the conduct ruled to be 'not guilty' or excluded from the Court's jurisdiction is criminal under international law.

> that are inherently indiscriminate or cause unnecessary suffering and, in doing so, look at weapons prohibitions in treaties to see which weapons have been prohibited for this reason. Judges may then compare the characteristics of these weapons with the characteristics of the new weapon to determine whether the latter violates the aforementioned general principle.

[210] Broomhall (n. 3) 725. One example of this that Broomhall gives is where the Rome Statute and Elements of Crimes do not clearly define the elements that need to be proven in light of a particular set of facts. Here, other provisions of the Statute and Elements may be consulted to aid the Court in its reasoning.

[211] Ibid. 726.

[212] Ibid. For more on the meaning of articles 10 and 22(3), see Chapter 7, Section 7.7.

[213] P Alldridge, 'Rules for Courts and Rules for Citizens' (1990) 10:4 Oxford J Legal Stud 487.

5.9 Conclusions

In this Chapter, the three interpretive devices intended to safeguard legality, which is concerned with the non-retroactive application of international criminal law, have been examined with a view to giving them useful content for purposes of interpreting the definitions of crimes in the Rome regime. In light of this analysis, it has been suggested that these devices should be subsumed under the 'good faith' imperative in article 31(1) of the *Vienna Convention* (1969) because they serve to ensure respect for the principle of legality. Like the rules of interpretation in the *Vienna Convention* (1969), the imperatives below may be construed as mandatory guidelines for interpreting articles 6, 7, 8, 8 *bis* and, where applicable, the Elements of Crimes, which elaborate the elements of those crimes. Indeed, the first paragraph of the general introduction to the Elements of Crimes states: 'The provisions of the Statute, including article 21 and the general principles set out in Part 3 [which includes legality in article 22], are applicable to the Elements of Crimes.'

Strict Construction

1. Strict construction 'does not prevent a court from interpreting and clarifying the elements of a particular crime'.[214]
2. Judges have been delegated some law-making authority, but this is limited to the most interstitial and minimal developments. Incremental legal developments and moderate interpretive outcomes are to be favoured over expansive interpretations and the recognition of new crimes.[215]
3. Arguments about object and purpose under article 31(1) of the *Vienna Convention* (1969) should, to the greatest extent possible, be limited to commenting about the mischief that the relevant criminal prohibition – as opposed to the Rome regime as a whole – is intended to address. This includes the class of individuals, the type of conduct and the set of circumstances that are covered by it, all while ensuring intellectual and textual coherence. Thus, the principle of effectiveness is limited to this coherence mandate.
4. Where application of the general rule of interpretation in article 31 of the *Vienna Convention* (1969) yields more than one outcome that could reasonably reflect the intent of States Parties, strict construction favours adopting the most modest interpretation – that which is least expansive.

---

[214] *Prosecutor v. Delalić and Others*, Judgment, ICTY-96–21-A, 20 February 2001, para. 173 (citing *Aleksovski* (n. 197)).

[215] *Prosecutor v. Milutinović and Others*, Decision on Dragoljub Ojdanić's Motion Challenging Jurisdiction: Joint Criminal Enterprise, ICTY-99–37-AR72, 21 May 2003, paras. 37–38.

5. The interpretive outcome selected should be one a reasonable and law-abiding individual in the place of the suspect or accused could be expected to have been aware of when reading the relevant provisions of the Rome Statute (perhaps with the aid of legal advice if the conduct was committed in a professional capacity).
6. Interpretive outcomes that enhance certainty should be favoured over those that fail to resolve an ambiguity in the law, exploit it, multiply the possibilities for its application, do not identify which categories of offenders are covered by a criminal prohibition or render the prohibition's application open-ended and less predictable.
7. Interpretive reasoning should be anchored in and guided by principles rather than facts.
8. The strict construction imperative is rebutted where States Parties choose to insert in the Rome Statute open-textured language, thereby signalling the delegation of a greater than normal degree of law-making power to judges.
9. When interpreting open-textured provisions, and where possible, illustrative examples of conduct that is included in or excluded from them, as well as lists of criteria that will be considered in future cases when determining their application, can all enhance legal certainty.
10. Strict construction entails the liberal interpretation of grounds for excluding criminal liability on which a defendant might have relied, such as self-defence (as opposed to intoxication) – or at least that their interpretation not be narrower than a reasonable person could expect.

Favouring the person investigated, prosecuted or convicted in case of ambiguity

1. States bear the burden of drafting international criminal prohibitions using language that is as clear as possible.
2. Accordingly, there is a rebuttable presumption against ambiguity.
3. Where an ambiguity exists and needs to be resolved through interpretation, arguments that favour giving preference to the collective goals of the international community (e.g., ending impunity, ensuring peace, security and world order, punishing morally reprehensible conduct, securing justice for victims and so on)[216] are not permitted as justifications for resolving it. The right of the person being investigated, prosecuted or convicted to respect for the principle of legality trumps these legitimate policy goals when interpreting the definitions of crimes.

---

[216] See Chapter 4 for all of the arguments that might be advanced in favour of weakening the legality principle.

4. If an interpretive finding depends solely on a provision's drafting history and is not supported by any other acceptable interpretive principle, argument or aid, then the ambiguity should be resolved in favour of the accused, as States Parties have not met their burden to define the crime in sufficiently clear terms.

Analogous reasoning

1. Article 22(2) prohibits analogous reasoning that leads to the recognition of substantially new crimes, meaning crimes that cannot be accommodated by the wording of articles 6, 7, 8 and 8 *bis* of the Rome Statute.
2. Article 22(2) does not prohibit logical reasoning by analogy, which is used to bring the facts of a case within the scope of a treaty or unwritten criminal prohibition by reasoning that they are sufficiently similar to the facts of a case previously held to be covered by the relevant law.
3. Article 22(2) does not prohibit previous decisions of the Court from being followed where appropriate, through gradual reasoning by analogy so as to build consistency, certainty and predictability in the Court's interpretation of crimes.
4. Article 22(2) does not prohibit contextual reasoning inspired by provisions in the Rome Statute and Elements of Crimes or resort to applicable law to fill gaps in the Statute or Elements.

6

Custom as an aid to interpretation

6.1 Introduction

In Chapter 3, the normative tensions underlying international criminal law were revealed and their potential recurrence in articles 21(3) and 22 of the Rome Statute exposed. The detrimental impact that this apparent normative conflict might have on a method of interpretation for crimes was discussed, and an attempt was made to reconcile the interpretive imperatives in the Rome Statute. It was concluded that the principle of legality is to be the guiding principle of interpretation, and consistency with internationally recognized human rights a background interpretive principle. In Chapters 4 and 5, consideration was given to the content of legality for purposes of interpretation, which resulted in the discerning of guiding interpretive considerations as well as arguments that are consistent and inconsistent with the legality principle.

To review, a method of interpretation is understood to mean a systemic general approach to reasoning through the resolution of interpretive issues. A fully developed method has three tiers. It offers its users, in this case judges of the Court and counsel appearing before them, the following levels of assistance: (1) a primary interpretive principle to guide their reasoning process when confronted with interpretive issues; (2) arguments or reasons that support (and do not support) this interpretive principle; and (3) a catalogue of materials or aids that must, may and, if applicable, may not be taken into account in support of these arguments.[1]

The purpose of the remainder of this study is to discern which interpretive aids judges and counsel must, may and may not consider in support of their interpretive reasoning with a focus on the aids of customary international law and the Elements of Crimes (Elements). Both aids potentially offer considerable guidance on the content of crimes in the Rome Statute. Regarding the role

---

[1] This definition takes its inspiration from the study in DN MacCormick and RS Summers (eds.), *Interpreting Statutes: A Comparative Study* (Ashgate 1991). A legal methodology may be defined 'as a systemic general approach to the duly purposive and consistent execution of a recurrent type of major task arising in the making or application of law', RS Summers, *Form and Function in a Legal System: A General Study* (Cambridge University Press 2006) 241.

of custom, the Rome Statute does not expressly state whether the crimes contained therein codify customary international law. Accordingly, the purpose of Chapters 6, 7 and 8 is to discern the relationship between the crimes in the Rome Statute and custom and how this relationship could impact a method of interpretation for these crimes. Given that international criminal law grew out of custom,[2] is customary international law to be seen as a mandatory aid to interpreting the crimes of aggression, genocide, other crimes against humanity and war crimes? If so, what does this mean exactly, especially in light of the fact that drafters of the Rome Statute went to the trouble of drafting the Elements of Crimes? Must custom assist the Court, may it assist the Court and, if the Elements and custom diverge on whether a particular material or mental element needs to be proven or articulate the content of an element in different ways, to which aid should judges defer? Did the drafters of the Rome Statute intend to create a self-contained sub-regime of international criminal law that is sealed off from the influence of customary international law, relevant treaty law, as well as general principles of law? The necessity of a codification study under taken in the following Chapters for developing an interpretive methodology is not considered to be self-evident. An explanation is therefore in order.

This Chapter is divided into three main sections. In Section 6.2, an attempt will be made to explain how the relationship of crimes in the Rome Statute to custom is relevant to the task of interpretation. In Section 6.3, the meaning of codification will be examined. In Section 6.4, the benefits and drawbacks of codification will be recalled, and the indicia for discerning a treaty's codification of custom will be identified. In Chapters 7 and 8, these indicia will be applied to the Rome regime. In Chapter 9, materials or aids which must, may and, if applicable, may not be taken into account will be catalogued, including their role over time and relationship to one another.

6.2 Need for a codification study

The need to determine the relationship between the Rome Statute and customary international law can be explained in a variety of ways, some of which will be attempted here. First, it has been suggested that two rules of interpretation specific to international criminal law exist: (1) interpretation in conformity with customary law where appropriate and (2) interpretation in conformity with customary law in case of doubt.[3] These interpretive principles are derived from the decision of the Appeals Chamber in *Prosecutor* v. *Tadić* (1999) in which the drafters of the ICTY statute were held to have intended to remain

---

[2] C Kreß, 'International Criminal Law' in R Wolfrum (ed.), *Max Planck Encyclopedia of Public International Law* (2008–), online edition, www.mpepil.com, paras. 10–18, accessed 15 March 2011.

[3] G Werle, *Principles of International Law* (TMC Asser Press 2005) 55.

within the framework of customary international law wherever they did not indicate in the statute or applicable sources of law an intention to deviate from it.[4] This means that where a term in the ICTY statute could be traced to a customary legal norm, that norm is supposed to govern the interpretation of the statutory term. And where it is unclear which of several definitions of a term should be adopted, that which is most reflective of custom is thought to prevail.[5]

Taking a step back from the *Tadić* (1999) ruling and the subsequent presumptions thought to emerge from it, one realizes that the Appeals Chamber was merely attempting to respect the will of the ICTY statute's drafters, who expressly intended to limit the tribunal's jurisdiction to certain crimes under customary international law.[6] Accordingly, the presumptions could also be seen as products of interpreting the statute in '*good faith* in accordance with the ordinary meaning to be given to the terms of the treaty in their context and *in the light of its object and purpose*'.[7] It is well known that the report of the UN Secretary-General on the establishment of the tribunal expressly stated that it should apply rules of international law that are undoubtedly reflective of custom so as to respect the principle of legality.[8] As a result, the Appeals Chamber in *Tadić* (1995) also recognized the applicability of 'any treaty which: (i) was unquestionably binding on the parties at the time of the alleged offence; and (ii) was not in conflict with or derogating from peremptory norms of international law, as are most customary rules of international humanitarian law'.[9]

Viewed this way, it is hard to take the interpretive presumptions derived from the *Tadić* case (1999) and automatically transpose them to the work of the judges at the Court. No document from the drafters of the Rome Statute akin to the Report of the UN Secretary-General preceded the creation of the Court. Further, the ICTY recognizes that crimes within its jurisdiction can arise from treaty law and not only from custom.[10] On the one hand, if the

---

[4] *Prosecutor* v. *Tadić*, Judgment, ICTY-94–1-A, 15 July 1999, para. 296; *Prosecutor* v. *Milutinović and Others*, Decision on Dragoljub Ojdanić's Motion Challenging Jurisdiction: Joint Criminal Enterprise, ICTY-99-37-AR72, 21 May 2003, paras. 9–10; *Prosecutor* v. *Kordić and Čerkez*, Decision on Joint Defence Motion to Dismiss the Amended Indictment for Lack of Jurisdictional Reach of Articles 2 and 3, ICTY-95–14/2-PT, 2 March 1999, para. 20. In *Prosecutor* v. *Galić*, Judgment, ICTY-98–29-T, 5 December 2003, paras. 63ff., the Trial Chamber relied upon a treaty to find that it had jurisdiction over certain conduct.

[5] Whether the guiding interpretive principle set out in *Tadić* was applied by the ICTY is not relevant to the current inquiry. For the interpretive practices of the ICTY, see Chapter 2.

[6] UNSC, 'Report of the Secretary-General Pursuant to Paragraph 2 of Security Council Resolution 808' (1993), UN Doc. S/25704, para. 34 (ICTY Report).

[7] Article 31(1), *Vienna Convention on the Law of Treaties* (1969) (emphasis added).

[8] ICTY Report (n. 6).

[9] *Prosecutor* v. *Tadić*, Decision on the Defence Motion for Interlocutory Appeal on Jurisdiction, ICTY-94–1-AR72, 2 October 1995, para. 143.

[10] See Chapter 4, Sections 4.3.4 and 4.3.10.2.

drafters of the Rome Statute wanted crimes to be interpreted in accordance with customary law, then why not expressly state this in the treaty? And why go to the trouble of defining the crimes in so much detail, to go so far as to draft not only the most detailed international criminal law treaty in history but also Elements of Crimes? On the other hand, if the drafters did not want customary law to inform the interpretation of the Rome Statute, why would they borrow so many terms whose origins are clearly traceable to customary legal concepts?[11] Article 31(4) of the *Vienna Convention on the Law of Treaties* (1969) (*Vienna Convention*) provides that '[a] special meaning shall be given to a term if it is established that the parties so intended'. Do such terms possess a special meaning? Articles 31–33 of the *Vienna Convention* (1969) are widely thought to reflect customary international law, and the Court has held that they apply to its interpretive work.[12]

A second way to appreciate the centrality of the treaty-custom relationship for purposes of developing an interpretive methodology is to consider three interpretive arguments that are commonly invoked by international judges: (1) *lex specialis derogat legi generali*; (2) *lex posterior derogat legi priori*; and (3) *lex superior derogat legi inferiori*. In their simultaneous application, these arguments generate more questions than answers. With the first, one wonders whether its application would lead to the Elements of Crimes prevailing over customary law in all cases. Invoking the second argument, one wonders whether subsequent custom or treaty law might be able to influence the jurisprudence of the Court by persuading judges to interpret terms in the Statute in accordance with evolving law.[13] With respect to the third argument, one wonders whether customary law should have a greater role in informing the interpretation of crimes in the Rome Statute than the Elements of Crimes. Juxtaposed to one another, one quickly sees that these interpretive arguments have the potential to produce contradictory outcomes.

---

[11] D Robinson and H von Hebel, 'Reflections on the Elements of Crimes' in R.S. Lee and Others (eds.), *The International Criminal Court: Elements of Crimes and Rules of Procedure and Evidence* (Transnational 2001) 219, 224ff.

[12] M Koskenniemi, 'Fragmentation of International Law: Difficulties Arising from the Diversification and Expansion of International Law: Report of the Study Group of the International Law Commission' (4 April 2006), UN Doc. A/CN.4/L.682, 181; G Bitti, 'Article 21 of the Statute of the International Criminal Court and the Treatment of Sources of Law in the Jurisprudence of the ICC' in C Stahn and G Sluiter (eds.) *The Emerging Practice of the International Criminal Court* (Martinus Nijhoff 2009) 281, 295 (citing *Prosecutor v. Lubanga Dyilo*, Judgment on the Prosecutor's Application for Extraordinary Review of the Pre-Trial Chamber I's 31 Mar. 2006 Decision Denying Leave to Appeal, ICC-01/04–168, 13 July 2006, paras. 33–42).

[13] To be clear, the idea here is to give new meaning to a term that can tolerate it (e.g., 'severe') as opposed to modifying the Rome Statute by reading words into it or ignoring words contained in it. Admittedly, the line between interpretation in accordance with subsequent practice and modification can in certain cases be fine.

Does any of this matter? It is well known that the relationship between prior and subsequent law might become entangled with the operation of the *lex specialis* principle in different ways and that it is fruitless to formulate a general rule about what the relationship of priority concerning these interpretive arguments might be.[14] While this may be true as applied to the universe of cases that come before international judges and involve any number of treaties and customary legal issues, such resignation seems less compelling in the context of a treaty regime for a permanent body such as the Court. Here, we have judges who will be repeatedly confronted with the question of the relationship between the definitions of crimes within the Rome Statute, the Elements of Crimes, customary international law, treaties and general principles. Left without an interpretive method that addresses this relationship, judges of the Court might apply the three aforementioned interpretive arguments inconsistently and in a purely fact-driven or outcome-driven manner.

This leads to the third way of understanding the importance of the relationship to be explored in Chapters 6, 7 and 8. Article 31(3)(c) of the *Vienna Convention* (1969) states that '[t]here shall be taken into account, together with the context: . . . any relevant rules of international law applicable in the relations between the parties'. Article 31(3)(c) encompasses the imperative of 'systemic integration'. 'This means that although a tribunal may only have jurisdiction in regard to a particular instrument, it must always *interpret* and *apply* that instrument in its relationship to its normative environment – that is to say, "other" international law'.[15]

> All treaty provisions receive their force and validity from general law, and set up rights and obligations that exist alongside rights and obligations established by other treaty provisions and rules of customary international law. None of such rights or obligations has any *intrinsic* priority against the others. The question of their relationship can only be approached through a process of reasoning that makes them appear as parts of some coherent and meaningful whole.[16]

Thus, the relationship between the definitions of the crimes in the Rome Statute and possible interpretive aids must be fixed only after undertaking a careful process of reasoning 'that makes them appear as parts of some coherent and

---

[14] Koskenniemi (n. 12) 97, 102; CW Jenks, 'The Conflict of Law-Making Treaties' (1953) 30 British Ybk of Int'l L 401, 407; I Sinclair, *The Vienna Convention on the Law of Treaties*, 2nd edn (Manchester University Press 1984) 96; *Mavrommatis Palestine Concessions Case (Greece v. United Kingdom)* (1924) PCIJ Series A, No. 2, 31.

[15] Koskenniemi, ibid. 212–13; AD McNair, *The Law of Treaties* (Oxford University Press 1961) 466.

[16] Koskenniemi, ibid. 208.

meaningful whole'. Custom is directly relevant to the interpretation of a conventional rule, especially if that rule is a codification of custom.[17] Unfortunately, article 31(3)(c) provides little guidance. Although its reference to 'rules of international law' can be taken to include custom, treaties and general principles, it does not offer guidance on which rules of international law are relevant and applicable to the interpretation of a particular treaty. Article 31(3)(c) is also lacking in two additional ways.[18] First, it does not specify whether relevance and applicability require that a treaty being taken into account must have the same Parties to it as the treaty that gives rise to the dispute.[19] Given that the Rome Statute is a multilateral treaty that has been ratified by 122 States at the time of writing, the chances of other seemingly relevant treaties having the same Parties to it are slim.[20] Second, it does not contain any temporal guidance, meaning it is not clear whether the relevant and applicable rules of international law are those that existed when the treaty was concluded or those that exist when a dispute under the treaty arises.[21] Given that customary law evolves over time and that chains or clusters of treaties are drafted on certain topics, the latter problem is especially acute.[22]

A fourth way of understanding the proposed starting point is to return briefly to the notion of drafters' intent. In developing an interpretive methodology, one goal is to help garner legitimacy for the Court by demonstrating that the work of judges is imbued with reason and method. But what legitimacy can the most reasonable interpretive method garner if it is out of step with the nature of the instrument being interpreted and out of step with what the drafters of that instrument intended for that instrument to be? A progressive method of interpretation would not be applied to a domestic tax statute, no matter how coherent and reasonable the former may be. If it were, the legitimacy of the latter would be undermined rather than strengthened. So, too, with the Rome Statute, one yardstick for measuring the success of a method of interpretation must surely be its faithfulness to the law it seeks to interpret. Such faithfulness can only be achieved once the legal system in which it operates is understood so that an eventual method will minimally disturb it.

> Legal interpretation, and thus legal reasoning, builds systemic relationships between rules and principles by envisaging them as parts of some human effort or purpose. Far from being merely an "academic" aspect of the legal craft, systemic thinking penetrates all legal reasoning, including the practice of law-application by judges and administrators. This results

---

[17] ME Villiger, *Customary International Law and Treaties* (Martinus Nijhoff 1985) ch. 8, s. 3; Y Dinstein, 'Interaction between Customary International Law and Treaties' (2006) 322 Recueil des Cours de l'Académie de Droit International 243, 345.

[18] Koskenniemi (n. 12) 180–81.   [19] Ibid.   [20] See Chapter 9, Section 9.2.3.

[21] Koskenniemi (n. 12) 179–81.

[22] On the problems of time and interpretation, see Chapter 9, Section 9.3.

precisely from the "clustered" nature in which legal rules and principles appear. But it may also be rationalized in terms of a *political obligation* on law-appliers to make their decisions cohere with the preferences and expectations of the community whose law they administer.[23]

It is therefore submitted that the relationship between the Rome Statute and custom will profoundly impact the admissibility of interpretive arguments and the respective roles of various interpretive aids. Accordingly, much like determining the relationship between articles 21(3) and 22 of the Rome Statute,[24] it is necessary to fix this relationship before assigning roles to various interpretive aids. And like the relationship between articles 21(3) and 22, it is submitted that this relationship can serve as a measure of the likelihood that a proposed methodology, when applied, will yield outcomes that respect the integrity of the text being interpreted. This relationship is therefore at once a foundation and a yardstick.

Looking at the Rome Statute, some might posit that the relationship sought to be ascertained is clearly stated in the Rome Statute itself. This, however, is unfortunately not the case, which is the fifth way to understand the importance of the present exercise. One might point to article 21, an understandable starting point, as it contains a list of legal sources.[25] Article 21 provides:

1. The Court shall *apply*:
    (a) In the first place, this Statute, Elements of Crimes and its Rules of Procedure and Evidence;
    (b) In the second place, where appropriate, *applicable* treaties and the principles and rules of international law, including the established principles of the international law of armed conflict;
    (c) Failing that, general principles of law derived by the Court from national laws of legal systems of the world including, as appropriate, the national laws of States that would normally exercise jurisdiction over the crime, provided that those principles are not inconsistent with this Statute and with international law and internationally recognized norms and standards.
2. The Court may *apply* principles and rules of law as *interpreted* in its previous decisions.

---

[23] Koskenniemi (n. 12) 20 (citing inter alia on the concept of systematization J Raz, *The Concept of a Legal System* (Oxford University Press 1979), and on the political obligation of law-appliers R Dworkin, *Taking Rights Seriously* (Harvard University Press 1977)) (underlined emphasis added).

[24] See Chapter 3.

[25] A Pellet, 'Applicable Law' in A Cassese and Others (eds.), *The Rome Statute of the International Criminal Court: A Commentary*, vol. II (Oxford University Press 2002) 1051, 1052.

3. The *application* and *interpretation* of law pursuant to this article must be consistent with internationally recognized human rights, and be without any adverse distinction founded on grounds such as gender as defined in article 7, paragraph 3, age, race, colour, language, religion or belief, political or other opinion, national, ethnic or social origin, wealth, birth or other status.

Although article 21 contains a useful list of applicable sources of law, it does not provide the developer of an interpretive methodology with many answers on the interpretive relationship between the Rome Statute and various aids to interpretation. Throughout, it distinguishes between judges *applying* sources of law to the case before them and *interpreting* terms in the Rome Statute. The International Law Commission's 1993[26] and 1994[27] Draft Statutes for the Court listed crimes within the jurisdiction of the Court and applicable sources of law to which the Court should refer in its decisions. Article 21 builds on these draft articles.[28]

While the line between application (gap filling) and interpretation may be fine in hard cases,[29] the drafters of the Rome Statute thought the line sufficiently clear in enough cases to maintain the distinction between these legal tasks. Indeed, the Appeals Chamber of the Court has confirmed that application of article 21(1)(b) and (c) of the Rome Statute is subject to the existence of a gap in the Statute.[30] A gap in the Rome Statute may be defined as follows:

> [A]n "objective" which could be inferred from the context or the object and purpose of the Statute, an objective which would not be given effect by the express provisions of the Statute or the Rules of Procedure and Evidence, thus obliging the judge to resort to the second or third source of law – in that order – to give effect to that objective.[31]

---

[26] ILC, 'Report of the International Law Commission on the Work of its Forty-Fifth Session' (3 May–23 July 1993), UN Doc. A/48/10, 111. The text of article 28, entitled 'Applicable Law', provides: 'The Court shall apply: (a) this Statute; (b) applicable treaties and the rules and principles of general international law; (c) as a subsidiary source, any applicable rule of national law'.

[27] ILC, 'Report of the International Law Commission on the Work of its Forty-Sixth Session' (2 May–22 July 1994), UN Doc. A/49/10, 103. The text of article 33, entitled 'Applicable Law', states: 'The Court shall apply: (a) this Statute; (b) applicable treaties and the principles and rules of general international law; and (c) to the extent applicable, any rule of national law'.

[28] Pellet (n. 25) 1051, 1052.   [29] This point was made in Chapter 1, Section 1.2.2.

[30] *Prosecutor* v. *Lubanga Dyilo*, Judgment on the Appeal of Mr. Thomas Lubanga Dyilo against the Decision on the Defence Challenge to the Jurisdiction of the Court pursuant to Article 19(2)(a) of the Statute of 3 October 2006, ICC-01/04–01/06, 14 December 2006, para. 34.

[31] Bitti (n. 12) 295.

Seen this way, article 21 provides limited guidance on interpreting the Rome Statute insofar as the role of applicable laws as aids to interpretation (as opposed to gap fillers), and their relationship to one another, are not spelled out.[32]

Alternatively, one might point to articles 9(1) and (3) of the Rome Statute:

> 1. Elements of Crimes shall assist the Court in the interpretation and application of articles 6, 7, 8 and 8 *bis*. They shall be adopted by a two-thirds majority of the members of the Assembly of States Parties....
>
> 3. The Elements of Crimes and amendments thereto shall be consistent with this Statute.

While this provision states that the Elements are to assist the Court with interpreting the definitions of crimes within its jurisdiction and that the Elements must conform to the definitions in the Rome Statute, they say nothing about custom's relationship to these statutory definitions or to the Elements. In fact, the Elements themselves add a complicating twist to this issue. Article 30(1) of the Rome Statute states: '*Unless otherwise provided*, a person shall be criminally responsible and liable for punishment for a crime within the jurisdiction of the Court only if the material elements are committed with intent and knowledge.'[33] Paragraph two of the general introduction to the Elements of Crimes then states:

> 2. As stated in article 30, unless otherwise provided, a person shall be criminally responsible and liable for punishment for a crime within the jurisdiction of the Court only if the material elements are committed with intent and knowledge. Where no reference is made in the Elements of Crimes to a mental element for any particular conduct, consequence or circumstance listed, it is understood that the relevant mental element, i.e., intent, knowledge or both, set out in article 30 applies. *Exceptions to the article 30 standard, based on the Statute, including applicable law under its relevant provisions, are indicated below.*[34]

Just as soon as one thinks that custom is irrelevant and there is only the Rome Statute and the Elements of Crimes to deal with, there appears a statement that seems to turn this notion on its head. The general introduction to the Elements suggests that exceptions it contains to the mental states in article 30 are derived from not only the words in the Statute but also applicable law. If this is a reference to the applicable law set out in article 21 of the Rome Statute, then

---

[32] On the meaning of article 21(3) for purposes of interpreting crimes in the Rome Statute, see Chapter 3.

[33] Emphasis added.   [34] Emphasis added.

it is a reference inter alia to customary law.[35] However, if article 9(3) states that the Elements of Crimes are to be consistent with the Statute, and the Elements contain customary law elements, does this not mean that an intimate relationship exists between the definitions of crimes in the Rome Statute and customary law? If not, then would not the drafters of the Elements be taking an enormous risk that their entire project would be aborted by the judges of the Court for failing to strictly conform to the Rome Statute? Alternatively, does consistency with the Statute mean that all applicable law, including the Elements on their own, can 'otherwise provide' a mental element for purposes of article 30?

Surely the decision of the drafters of the Elements to draw inspiration from customary international law was taken with the article 9(3) imperative in mind. Perhaps the drafters noted the categories of crimes within the jurisdiction of the Court as well as the preamble to the Rome Statute, which refers to the 'most serious crimes of concern to the international community as a whole'. Seeing this, they might have concluded that the crimes within the jurisdiction of the Court are also crimes under customary international law. Indeed, the categories of crimes in the Rome Statute – aggression, genocide, other crimes against humanity and war crimes – amount to crimes under customary international law, and such prohibitions are *jus cogens* norms from which no derogation is permitted.[36] What is less clear, however, is the degree to which the *definitions of crimes falling under these broad categories* conform to customary international law.

A sixth way to appreciate the uncertainty surrounding this relationship is to take a closer look at article 31(3) of the *Vienna Convention* (1969). Recall that article 31(1) states that '[a] treaty shall be interpreted in good faith in accordance with the ordinary meaning to be given to the terms of the treaty in their context and in the light of its object and purpose.' Article 31(3) provides:

3. There shall be taken into account, together with the context:
   (a) *any subsequent agreement between the parties* regarding the interpretation of the treaty or the application of its provisions;
   (b) any subsequent practice in the application of the treaty which establishes the agreement of the parties regarding its interpretation;
   (c) *any relevant rules of international law* applicable in the relations between the parties.[37]

Three points need to be made here. First, the Elements of Crimes constitute a subsequent agreement between States Parties regarding the interpretation of the Rome Statute and the application of its provisions. Second, article 31(3) is

---

[35] Article 21(1)(b) makes reference to 'principles and rules of international law', which is widely understood to be a reference to customary international law. Pellet (n. 25) 1051, 1070–71.

[36] Koskenniemi (n. 12) 188–89.   [37] Emphasis added.

mandatory in that judges are obliged to take the three aids listed into account.[38] Third, the three aids listed are not ranked in order of priority. Thus, both the Elements of Crimes and (relevant and applicable) custom must be taken into account when interpreting crimes in the Rome Statute, but one does not know which has priority in cases of conflict.

A seventh way to understand the significance of what this part of the study seeks to ascertain is to attempt an answer to the question posed by Brierly in 1931: 'Does it matter that when we try to reduce international law to systematic form we find that we shall be driven to legislate and not merely to codify? Why not accept the different conditions and proceed with the work?'[39] With this question, Brierly provocatively asks us to consider whether there are any practical implications for finding that a treaty codifies customary international law or 'makes new law'. Concerning the Rome Statute, there are at least two very important practical implications that turn on this distinction. First, to the extent that the definitions of crimes in the Statute reflect customary international law, they are binding on a national of a Non-State Party who commits a crime on the territory of a Non-State Party. Recall that the jurisdiction of the Court extends to nationals of Non-States Parties who commit crimes on the territory of States Parties but also to such nationals committing crimes on the territory of a Non-State Party. For example, the UN Security Council may refer situations to the Court involving the latter form of conduct in accordance with its powers under Chapter VII of the Charter of the United Nations and article 13(b) of the Rome Statute.[40]

Jus cogens norms aside, since treaties may derogate from general customary law,[41] the question becomes whether all crimes (as opposed to categories of crimes) within the Rome Statute, as well as all elements of these crimes, conform to customary international law. If not, then how can the aforementioned jurisdiction of the Court be understood? In such a situation, would not the consent of the relevant States to be bound to the Rome Statute be lacking and the customary jurisdictional heads of nationality and territoriality be inapplicable? Or else, would not the non-customary parts of definitions of crimes in the Rome Statute be applied retroactively to the conduct of the accused, thus

---

[38] In making this point, Koskenniemi (n. 12) 180 compares article 31(3) to article 32, which makes recourse to preparatory works discretionary and conditional.

[39] JL Brierly, 'The Future of Codification' (1921) 12 British Ybk Int'l L 1, 3.

[40] Article 13(b) provides: 'The Court may exercise its jurisdiction with respect to a crime referred to in article 5 in accordance with the provisions of this Statute if... [a] situation in which one or more of such crimes appears to have been committed is referred to the Prosecutor by the Security Council acting under Chapter VII of the Charter of the United Nations...'

[41] HWA Thirlway, 'The Law and Procedure of the International Court of Justice 1960–1989' (1989) 60 British Ybk Int'l L 1, 147.

compromising the principle of legality? Second, there is a legal policy issue to consider. If the Rome Statute creates a self-contained regime disconnected from custom, the work of the Court, which is a permanent institution, may contribute to fragmentation within international criminal law. Article 10 of the Statute provides: 'Nothing in this Part shall be interpreted as limiting or prejudicing in any way existing or developing rules of international law for purposes other than this Statute.'

For all of the aforementioned reasons, the next two Chapters are dedicated to determining the relationship between crimes in the Rome Statute and custom so that the latter's role in relation to other interpretive aids can be understood.

6.3 Codification

Towards the end of the eighteenth century, Bentham proposed that all public international law – not necessarily only existing law – be written down in a code, which he thought would be integral to securing eternal peace among nations.[42] Bentham's ideas, which were likely influenced by the Code Napoleon, soon gave rise to a codification movement, with the first major effort to codify public international law culminating in the Congress of Vienna in 1815.[43] Subsequently, several non-governmental organizations, such as the Institut de Droit International and the International Law Association, made important contributions by drafting several codes and proposals.[44] One motivation for this early codification movement was 'the desire to put at the disposal of international tribunals a body of ascertained and agreed rules and thus, it was thought, to stimulate the willingness of states to submit disputes to judicial determination.'[45]

---

[42] J Bentham, 'Principles of International Law' in *The Works of Jeremy Bentham*, vol. II (published under the Superintendence of his Executor J Bowring (W Tait 1838–1843)) 535. For more on the history of codification, see S Rosenne, 'Codification of International Law' (1984) 7 Max Planck Encyclopedia of Public Int'l L 34, 36; B Simma, 'The General Assembly: Function and Powers' in B Simma and Others (eds.), *The Charter of the United Nations: A Commentary*, vol. I, 2nd edn (Oxford University Press 2002) 257, 299.

[43] RY Jennings, 'The Progressive Development of International Law' (1947) 24 British Ybk Int'l L 301 (citing a historical survey by the Division of Development and Codification of International Law of the United Nations Secretariat, which was reprinted in (1947) 41 AJIL, No. 4, Supp. 29). For more on the codification of international law, see RY Jennings and A Watts (eds.), *Oppenheim's International Law*, vol. I, 9th edn (Longman, Harlow 1992) 96–115.

[44] Both organizations were founded in 1873. See 'Note on the Private Codification of Public International Law' (16 May 1947), UN Doc. A/AC.10/25 reprinted in (1947) 41 AJIL, No. 4, Supp. 138. Individuals have also attempted to draft codes. Villiger (n. 17) 141.

[45] Jennings and Watts (n. 43) 97, 101.

On 22 September 1924, the Assembly of the League of Nations passed a resolution to create a permanent body known as the Committee of Experts for the Progressive Codification of International Law. This Committee was to represent 'the main forms of civilization and the principal legal systems of the world' and comprised seventeen experts who were to prepare lists of subjects for codification.[46] This first worldwide intergovernmental effort to codify and develop rules in entire fields of international law was not particularly successful. The Committee selected three topics for codification at a diplomatic conference – nationality, territorial waters and the responsibility of States for damage done in their territory to the person or property of foreigners. The codification conference convened in The Hague for a month in 1930. In the end, the delegates from forty-seven governments could agree only to the drafting of a convention on nationality, and it took another seven years for this convention to obtain the requisite ten ratifications in order for it to enter into force.

In October 1945, the UN Charter entered into force and provided that the 'General Assembly shall initiate studies and make recommendations for the purpose of . . . encouraging the progressive development of international law and its codification'.[47] Accordingly, the General Assembly adopted a resolution on 21 November 1947 establishing the International Law Commission (ILC), which began its work two years later.[48] The mandate of the ILC is the 'promotion of the progressive development of international law and its codification'.[49] It consists of thirty-four members who 'shall be persons of recognized competence in international law'.[50]

The ILC plays a preeminent role in codification, which is thought to result in international law being clear, precise and based on express consent.[51] Usually, a codification effort will begin with a series of preparatory stages, conducted by 'experts with regular facilities for controlled political input by governments as work on the topic is initiated and progresses', which is then followed by a 'decision-making phase conducted on the diplomatic level'.[52] Since 1946, the UN General Assembly has, in one form or another, discussed codification

---

[46] Records of the Assembly and of its Committees (1920–1946), League of Nations Official Journal, Special Supp. 21, 9–10.

[47] Article 13(1)(a), UN Charter.　　[48] UNGA Res. 174 (II) (21 November 1947) as amended.

[49] UNGA, Statute of the International Law Commission (adopted and entered into force 21 November 1947) article 1 (ILC Statute).

[50] Article 2(1), ILC Statute. To reflect increased membership in the UN and meet the need to reflect the main forms of civilization and the principle legal systems, the ILC Statute has been amended three times to increase the membership of the Commission from fifteen to twenty-one (1956), twenty-one to twenty-five (1961) and twenty-five to thirty-four (1981). See respectively UNGA Res. 1103 (XI) (18 December 1956), UNGA Res. 1647 (XVI) (6 November 1961) and UNGA Res. 36/39 (18 November 1981).

[51] O Schachter, International Law in Theory and Practice (Martinus Nijhoff 1991) 66.

[52] Rosenne (n. 42) 39.

issues at each of its sessions.[53] An early example of this can be found at the General Assembly's first session, at which it unanimously affirmed the principles of the Nuremberg judgment.[54] In 1948, it adopted the *Genocide Convention* (1948) and two years later commissioned studies on a code of offences under international law.[55]

Codification is defined in article 15 of the Statute of the International Law Commission (ILC Statute) as 'the more precise formulation and systematization of rules of international law in fields where there already has been extensive State practice, precedent and doctrine'.[56] Codification of international law is therefore distinct from setting forth internal legal rules for the conduct of foreign relations and the publication of digests of national practice.[57] However, the definition of codification in the ILC Statute might be seen as overlooking the second ingredient to the formation of custom, *opinio juris*, and for suggesting by its reference to 'more precise' that a code is more than a pure restatement of the law.[58] Indeed, regarding this latter point, article 20(b) of the ILC Statute, which falls under the heading 'Codification', instructs the ILC to mention the following in its commentaries: '(i) The *extent of agreement* on each point in the practice of States and in doctrine; (ii) *Divergences and disagreements* which exist, as well as arguments invoked in favour of one or another solution.'[59]

These articles are thought to 'offer the legal foundation for some degree of innovation and reform and presuppose a certain selective, structuring function of codification'.[60] From this understanding arises the difficulty of 'delimiting such codification *sensu non strictissimo* from progressive development (and its equivalent, codification *sensu lato*)'.[61] Progressive development is defined in article 15 of the ILC Statute to mean 'the preparation of draft conventions on subjects which have not yet been regulated by international law or in regard to which the law has not yet been sufficiently developed in the practice of States'. The definition of progressive development clearly encompasses innovation, that is, *lex ferenda*. It is the '*writing down of new rules*', which may or may not evolve into custom.[62]

Perhaps owing to the definitions of codification and progressive development in the ILC Statute, the early codification work at the United Nations in the 1950s gave rise to 'sharp differences' as to whether the task of codification should be a scientific or political undertaking.[63] In practice, codification efforts initiated by the UN have not been purely scientific but rather a diplomatic effort driven

---

[53] Ibid. 36. Although this statement was made in 1984, it likely still holds true in light of efforts to draft a code of crimes against the peace and security of mankind.
[54] UNGA Res. 95 (I) (11 December 1946). [55] Simma (n. 42) 314.
[56] Article 15, ILC Statute. See also articles 3 and 8 of the ILC Statute.
[57] Rosenne (n. 42) 35 contains a list of examples as well.
[58] Villiger (n. 17) 123. [59] Emphasis added. [60] Villiger (n. 17) 123. [61] Ibid.
[62] Ibid. 124 and fns. 62, 64. [63] Schachter (n. 51) 66–67.

by the General Assembly.[64] The ILC and governments realized that enduring codification requires existing law to be supplemented and to some degree modified in light of current conditions and political views, and that it is the product of bargaining and negotiation at a diplomatic conference.[65] Fortunately, the expansion of UN membership and consequently ILC membership has resulted in codification efforts no longer being Euro-centric.[66]

Although the ILC Statute distinguishes between subjects of international law to codify and progressively develop, the ILC in practice has selected topics that contain elements of both, with the balance between these varying from topic to topic.[67] The ILC recognized that even the codification of customary law inevitably requires governments to make policy choices.[68] The difference between codification and progressive development as defined in article 15 seems to be between 'minor and major changes of the law, respectively'.[69] Accordingly, the ILC's early attempts to distinguish between codification and progressive development have 'largely been abandoned over the years'.[70] The concepts are not mutually exclusive.[71] Nevertheless, a leading treatise on international law continues to assert that it 'is desirable that in each case the codifying agency should leave no doubt as to the proportion in which rules formulated by it amount to a statement of the existing law or a change thereof'.[72] The reason for this encouragement will be considered below. Thirlway concludes that there is not much to be gained by attempting to distinguish between a codification that merely restates existing law and codification that contains elements of innovation, opaquely suggesting that it might 'sometimes be convenient' to distinguish between restatements and instruments that contain a considerable amount of new law.[73] Villiger maintains, however, that such a distinction is of 'central importance in the context of sources'.[74] In this regard, it is important to recall that a code is not a formal source of international law or obligation on its own.[75]

In his writings, Jennings supported the view that the 'the difference between codification and development, if it exists at all, is one of degree rather than

---

[64] Simma (n. 42) 300.   [65] Schachter (n. 51) 66–67.   [66] Rosenne (n. 42) 39.

[67] ILC, 'Review of the Multilateral Treaty-Making Process' (1979) II (Part One) Ybk of the ILC 183, 210; ILC, 'Report of the International Law Commission on the Work of its Forty-Eighth Session (6 May–26 July 1996)' (1996) II (Part Two) Ybk of the ILC 1, 84, 86.

[68] S Rosenne, 'Relations between the International Law Commission and Governments' (1965) Ybk of World Affairs 183.

[69] Villiger (n. 17) 126.

[70] Dinstein (n. 17) 370; Jennings and Watts (n. 43) 110; Villiger (n. 17) 126.

[71] Simma (n. 42) 302.   [72] Jennings and Watts (n. 43) 111.

[73] HWA Thirlway, International Customary Law and Codification (Sijthoff 1972) 27–28.

[74] ME Villiger, Customary International Law and Treaties (Kluwer Law International 1997) 279.

[75] Villiger (n. 17) 122.

kind'.[76] A treaty, he reminds us, does not affect the law that applies to States that do not become Parties to it.[77] He also recalled that there is no process of true legislation available for international law because there is no authoritative body that can lay down general norms applicable to all States without obtaining their consent.[78] He rejected a strict definition of codification that limits the task to 'the writing down of already existing rules of law', which 'may also involve the making of a few minor changes in the law'.[79] This definition of codification in Jennings view 'can have little place in a comparatively undeveloped system like international law'.[80] He asserted that the purpose of codifying international law is precisely to 'resolve differences and to fill in the gaps'.[81] Jennings therefore described codification as follows:

> [A]ny systematic statement of the whole or part of the law in written form, and that it does not necessarily imply a process which leaves the main substance of the law unchanged, even though this may be true of some cases. In other words, codification properly conceived is itself a method for the progressive development of the law. It is not denied, of course, that the task of codifying an existing and consistent body of law is very different from the task of creating a code where the existing law is fragmentary and requires the devising of new rules to fill the gaps or resolve discrepancies or even where the draftsman starts with a *tabula rasa*. But the essential differences between the processes involved depend not upon the object in view but on the differences in the materials available for the task. The end in view – a systematic statement of the law – is the same in either case. A man who sets himself to build a house may start from the ground or he may start with an existing building which is to be modified to suit his requirements but the finished article is in either case properly called a house.[82]

In 1955, Lauterpacht published an article aimed at assessing the 'achievements and prospects of the codification of international law within the United Nations in the light of the experience of the first five years of the activity of the International Law Commission'.[83] Lauterpacht commented on the absence of an agreed-upon definition of the concept of codification. He noted that if the definition of codification is that contained in article 15 of the ILC Statute, then there 'is very little to codify':

> For, once we approach at close quarters practically any branch of international law, we are driven, amidst some feeling of incredulity, to the conclusion that although there is as a rule a consensus of opinion on

---

[76] RY Jennings, 'The Progress of International Law' (1958) 34 British Ybk Int'l L 334, 345, 381.

[77] Jennings (n. 43) 303.   [78] Ibid.   [79] Ibid. 301.

[80] Ibid. 302.   [81] Ibid.   [82] Ibid. 301–03.

[83] H Lauterpacht, 'Codification and Development of International Law' (1955) 49 AJIL 16.

broad principle – even this may be an overestimate in some cases – there is no semblance of agreement in relation to specific rules and problems.[84]

After citing numerous examples of this phenomenon, Lauterpacht concluded that if the concept of codification is to mean anything under international law, it should be understood primarily as the task of 'bringing about an agreed body of rules rather than introducing systematic order and precision into legal rules already covered by customary or conventional agreement of states. At present the areas of such agreement is small in the extreme.'[85] Lauterpacht's comments, while ringing true in some respects even today, must be read in light of the state of international law in 1955. In the field of international criminal law alone, one can see an enormous growth in both custom and treaty law since that time. Such growth makes the distinction between codification and progressive development perhaps less difficult to draw.

Lauterpacht also drew attention to assumptions underlying the definitions of codification and progressive development in article 15 of the ILC Statute that might not be true in all cases. The definition of codification seems to assume that the existence of long practice, precedent and doctrine means that there is agreement on the content of legal rules. As well, the definition of progressive development seems to assume the existence of large legal gaps that need to be filled. However, both conceptions are limiting. First, there may be practice but no agreement. Second, laws might exist that are 'agreed, undisputed, and amply covered by precedent and doctrine, but in which a change – a development – is felt to be called for by considerations of progress, of mutuality of enlightened economic interest, of international interdependence, of good faith, of morality, of the rights of man'.[86] Lauterpacht in fact concluded that, given the limited degree of concurrence on the content of international law, codification of this field 'must be substantially legislative in nature', meaning States would be accepting new law as opposed to existing custom.

In 1958, Brierly identified another cause for confusion surrounding the term codification in the context of international law. He pointed out to international lawyers that the term has a different meaning for British and American lawyers than it has for continental lawyers. In the common-law world, codification is a term that relates primarily to the law being in written form:

> When we codify, we do not regard the task as one of improving the sub-
> stance of the law, but as one of collecting the existing rules and stating them
> concisely and clearly. It is true that, even so, the work must involve some
> elements of law-creating, for when we examine the materials on which
> we have to work, the customary rules, the judicial precedents, the partic-
> ular statutes or conventions, we inevitably come across points on which
> no authority exists, or on which the existing authorities are conflicting,

---

[84] Ibid. 17.   [85] Ibid. 22.   [86] Ibid. 27, 29.

and it would be pedantic to insist that, because codification is concerned only with the form of the law, these defects should be reproduced in the finished code. Where the authorities are in conflict, therefore, the codifier must choose the rule which seems the most desirable. Where there are gaps in the existing law, he must suggest a new rule to fill them. To that extent codifiers must legislate. But it is only to a limited extent. In the main, the work is not one of legislation, but of careful drafting.[87]

Continental codifications, on the other hand, are not an exercise in tidying up the existing law. Rather, they are concerned with unifying the law:

> France started the fashion in 1804 with the Code of Napoleon, not because Frenchman had discovered that codified is superior to uncodified law, but because up to that time there had been different kinds of law in different parts of the country, and this was an inconvenient state of things and out of touch with the growing strength of national feelings. Other nations have followed the French example, partly no doubt because of the great prestige that France has always held in intellectual matters, but many of them, too, had the same need to create a unified national system of law.[88]

The Polish codification after the First World War is an example of a continental code that was intended to unify the diverging laws that had emerged in the Russian, Prussian and Austrian parts of the country. Looking at codification from the viewpoint of a domestic lawyer, the first question about codifying international law must be to ask what kind of codification is contemplated – one of simply improving the form of international law or securing the agreement among States about the substance of international law. Brierly and others observe that the goal is clearly the latter and analogous to concerns that motivated the drafting of continental codes.[89] This sharp distinction between common law and continental codifications is useful but should not be taken too far. It should be recalled that, also in common-law systems, legislation may 'codify, partly codify, add to, change or contradict the common law'.[90] In addition, others have cautioned that a 'true codification treaty must be declaratory of customary international law: it should not be muddled up with treaties that, say, bring about the unification and harmonization of domestic laws'.[91] Thus, resolving divergent practices should be with a view to settling the

---

[87] JL Brierly, 'The Codification of International Law' in H Lauterpacht and CHM Waldock (eds.), *The Basis of Obligation in International Law and Other Papers by the Late James Leslie Brierly* (Clarendon Press 1958) 338.

[88] Ibid. 339.

[89] Ibid. 340; C de Visscher, *Theory and Reality in International Law*, P Corbett (trans.), rev. edn (Princeton University Press 1968) 150.

[90] R Sullivan, *Sullivan and Driedger on the Construction of Statutes*, 4th edn (Butterworths 2002) 339.

[91] Dinstein (n. 17) 347 (citing Rosenne, 'Codification of International Law' (n. 42)).

content of a customary rule of international law. Unlike domestic statutes, a code of international law is not an independent source of law.[92] Rather, a code of international law 'derives its force from the fact that it either expresses in convenient and systematic form existing rules of general international law, or is contained in a treaty, and has therefore the force of *droit conventionnel* as between the parties to the treaty.'[93]

When defining the concept of codification, it is also important to bear in mind that, generally, customary rules are less detailed than rules articulated in treaties, the latter resulting from complex negotiations, and that it therefore might not be possible to prove the customary status of every last detail in a treaty rule that seeks to codify existing law.[94] Law creation is inevitable when moving from an abstract rule describing current practice to a prescriptive rule that is sufficiently precise to be able to direct future practice.[95] For example, consider the detailed description of the principle of distinction in articles 48–52 of the first *Additional Protocol* (1977) to the *Geneva Conventions* (1949) and the short statement of the International Court of Justice recognizing it to be a 'cardinal' and 'intransgressible' principle of international customary law.[96] As well, details that emerge from the codification exercise may be the result of understanding and formulating a long-standing customary rule in light of present-day realities.[97] The movement from less to more detail as a legitimate part of the codification exercise is not considered troubling: 'It is only natural for successful codification to give the original picture better definition and higher resolution; illuminating points that used to be obscure while the law was unwritten; removing trifle inner contradictions; and polishing off edges by couching the norms in a more calibrated language.'[98]

A variation on this theme is the observation that a treaty can be declaratory of customary law at varying levels of abstraction.[99] A treaty may be 'generally declaratory', meaning 'conformity with existing law could be found only on a relatively high level of abstraction'.[100] For example, the *Convention on the High Seas* (1958) states that it is 'generally declaratory of established principles of international law'.[101] Another example is a study of customary international humanitarian law carried out by the International Committee of the Red Cross

---

[92] Thirlway (n. 73) 24–25.   [93] Ibid. 25.   [94] Dinstein (n. 17) 366.

[95] A Roberts, 'Traditional and Modern Approaches to Customary International Law: A Reconciliation' (2001) 95 AJIL 757, 761.

[96] *Legality of the Threat or Use of Nuclear Weapons*, Advisory Opinion [1996] ICJ Rep. 226, 257.

[97] M Virally, 'The Sources of International Law' in M Sørensen (ed.), *Manual of Public International Law* (MacMillan 1968) 116.

[98] Dinstein (n. 17) 366.

[99] RR Baxter, 'Treaties and Custom' (1970–I) 129 Recueil des Cours de l'Académie de Droit International 31, 41–42.

[100] Ibid.   [101] 450 UNTS 82 (adopted 29 April 1958, entered into force 30 September 1962).

in 2005, which has been variously described as a photograph and a 'great impressionist painting'.[102] It is possible, therefore, that the categories of crimes in the Rome Statute – aggression, genocide, other crimes against humanity and war crimes – embody *jus cogens* customary prohibitions,[103] but that the list of crimes subsumed under these categories and, or, certain elements of crimes for them are not or are only partly reflective of custom.

In 1969, the International Court of Justice decided the *North Sea Continental Shelf Cases*[104] and consequently shed more light on the concept of codification. Denmark and the Netherlands unsuccessfully argued that article 6 of the *Convention on the Continental Shelf* (1958) had crystallized into custom when the convention was adopted by States.[105] The Court's analysis confirmed that a 'norm-creating' treaty provision can crystallize into custom when a treaty is adopted at a diplomatic conference or at a later date.[106] For example, the four *Geneva Conventions* (1949)[107] on the laws of war are considered by many to have crystallized into customary international humanitarian law.[108] Codification has subsequently been defined as encompassing such crystallization.[109] Others retain a distinction and state that a treaty can be part codifying and part crystallizing.[110]

The idea that certain provisions of a treaty can be declaratory of custom while others are not has also been endorsed.[111] Even subclauses in a treaty can

---

[102] R Cryer, 'Of Custom, Treaties, Scholars and the Gavel: The Influence of the International Criminal Tribunals on the ICRC Customary Law Study' (2006) 11 J Conflict & Security L 239, 241.

[103] *Jus cogens* is a 'norm accepted and recognized by the international community of States as a whole ... from which no derogation is permitted'. M Akehurst, 'Hierarchy of Sources' (1974–1975) 47 British Ybk Int'l L 273, 275–76.

[104] *North Sea Continental Shelf Cases (Germany v. Denmark; Germany v. The Netherlands)* [1969] ICJ Rep. 3.

[105] Ibid. 38. Article 2 of the *Convention*, 499 UNTS 311 (adopted 29 April 1958, entered into force 10 June 1964), was held to be such a provision (40).

[106] Ibid. 41–42.

[107] *Convention (I) for the Amelioration of the Condition of the Wounded and Sick in Armed Forces in the Field*, 75 UNTS 31; *Convention (II) for the Amelioration of the Condition of Wounded, Sick and Shipwrecked Members of Armed Forces at Sea*, 75 UNTS 85; *Convention (III) relative to the Treatment of Prisoners of War*, 75 UNTS 135; *Convention (IV) relative to the Protection of Civilian Persons in Time of War*, 75 UNTS 287 (all adopted 12 August 1949, all entered into force 2 October 1950).

[108] Schachter (n. 51) 69.

[109] A D'Amato, 'Manifest Intent and the Generation by Treaty of Customary Rules of International Law' (1970) 64 AJIL 892, 895; Villiger (n. 17) 125; Roberts (n. 95) 763.

[110] HWA Thirlway, 'The Law and Procedure of the International Court of Justice: 1960–1989 (Part Two)' (1990) 61:1 British Ybk Int'l L 1, 99; HWA Thirlway, 'Reflections on *Lex Ferenda*' (2001) 32 Netherlands Ybk Int'l L 3, 10.

[111] Dinstein (n. 17) 372; *North Sea Continental Shelf Cases* (n. 104) 41–42. In *Case Concerning Military and Paramilitary Activities in and against Nicaragua (Nicaragua v. United States of*

be partly declaratory of customary international law and partly constitutive.[112] Nevertheless, while treaty provisions that are not declaratory of custom remain 'fuses for treaty-generated custom', it is necessary to always 'keep in mind that an artificial separation between the components of the instrument may disrupt an inner equilibrium. The entire text of the treaty may be the product of a delicate balance – a "package deal" struck by the framers against the background of stiff bargaining resulting in mutual concessions – and on stipulations may form a *quid pro quo* for another.'[113] This point is especially important in respect of the Rome Statute, as it is well known that the final text was the product of a package deal prepared by the Bureau of the conference and accepted by the delegates at the eleventh hour.[114] Thus, one must be careful not to disaggregate too much and perhaps artificially the definitional contents of the Rome Statute.

Treaty provisions that are reflective of custom do not displace custom, which continues to exist alongside codifying treaty provisions.[115] As confirmed by the International Court of Justice in the *Nicaragua* v. *United States of America* judgment (1986), a codifying treaty provision would bind not only Parties to the treaty but also third States qua customary law.[116] In discussing how to distinguish between treaty and customary rules that possess identical content, the Court stated:

> There are a number of reasons for considering that, even if two norms belonging to two sources of international law appear identical in content, and even if the States in question are bound by these rules both on the level of treaty-law and on that of customary international law, these norms retain a separate existence. This is so from the standpoint of their applicability.... [I]f the two rules in question also exist as rules of customary international law, the failure of the one State to apply the one rule does not justify the other State in declining to apply the other rule.[117]

America) [1986] ICJ Rep. 14, 94, 99 the ICJ held that articles 2(4) and 51 of the UN Charter are reflective of custom. In the *Tehran* case (1980), the ICJ held that the obligations to protect the inviolability of diplomatic and consular agents, their premises, archives, etc. in two different conventions are not 'merely contractual' but 'also obligations under general international law' (*Case concerning United States Diplomatic and Consular Staff in Tehran (United States of America* v. *Iran)* [1980] ICJ Rep. 3, 30–31).

[112] Dinstein, ibid. 356 (citing as an example article 31(1) of the *Vienna Convention on Diplomatic Relations* (1961)).

[113] Ibid. 373 (citing O Schachter, 'Recent Trends in International Law-Making' (1992) 12 Australian Ybk Int'l L 1, 9).

[114] P Kirsch and JT Holmes, 'The Birth of the International Criminal Court: The 1998 Rome Conference' (1998) 36 Canadian Ybk Int'l L 3, 38.

[115] ILC, 'Report of the International Law Commission covering its Second Session, 5 June–29 July' (1950) II Ybk of the ILC 364, 368. The idea that customary law may parallel a conventional rule can also be found in articles 3(b) and 4 of the *Vienna Convention* (1969) according to Villiger (n. 17) 157.

[116] *Nicaragua* (n. 111) 96.   [117] Ibid. 95–96.

Articles 38 and 43 of the *Vienna Convention* (1969) are 'saving provisions' that affirm the distinction between custom and a treaty provision that might codify custom.[118] Article 38 provides: 'Nothing in articles 34 to 37 precludes a rule set forth in a treaty from becoming binding upon a third State as a customary rule of international law, recognized as such.' Article 43 provides:

> The invalidity, termination or denunciation of a treaty, the withdrawal of a party from it, or the suspension of its operation, as a result of the application of the present Convention or of the provisions of the treaty, shall not in any way impair the duty of any State to fulfil any obligation embodied in the treaty to which it would be subject under international law independently of the treaty.

The International Court of Justice in the *Nicaragua* judgment (1986) stated but did not explain that, though they may be equal sources of law, an identical rule under custom and in a treaty may be subject to different methods of interpretation and application.[119] The Institut de Droit International posits that a 'norm deriving from one of these two sources may have an impact upon the content and interpretation of norms deriving from the other source.'[120] Indeed, regarding the interpretation of a treaty provision that codifies a customary rule, article 31(3)(c) of the *Vienna Convention* (1969) provides: 'There shall be taken into account, together with the context: ... any relevant rules of international law applicable in the relations between the parties.'[121] To further complicate the relationship between treaties and custom, a treaty might alter customary law through the crystallization of a draft convention or a treaty that is in force.[122]

A review of the leading debates about the meaning of codification discloses the rejection of a strict definition of codification in the field of international law, that being 'the writing down of already existing rules of law' with only a few minor changes in the law.[123] To be a worthwhile undertaking, the codification process will involve the crystallization of custom as States bargain to achieve consensus and avoid yielding lowest common denominator results.[124] Further, compared with domestic codification efforts, the content of customary international law is regarded as less detailed.[125] Thus, every codification of

---

[118] Baxter (n. 99) 32. [119] *Nicaragua* (n. 111) 95–96.

[120] Institut de Droit International, 'Problems Arising from a Succession of Codification Conventions on a Particular Subject' (Lisbon Session 1995) 66-I Annuaire de l'Institut de Droit International 39, conclusion 10 (concerning the relationship between treaty and custom).

[121] See also Rosenne (n. 42) 34–35; Villiger (n. 17) 16.

[122] Villiger, ibid. 122. [123] Jennings (n. 43) 301.

[124] Schachter (n. 51) 66–68; H von Hebel and D Robinson, 'Crimes within the Jurisdiction of the Court' in RS Lee (ed.), *The International Criminal Court: The Making of the Rome Statute* (Kluwer Law International 1999) 79, 122; Jennings and Watts (n. 43) 113.

[125] Lauterpacht (n. 83) 17. On the different meanings of codification in common and civil law traditions, see Brierly (n. 87) 338–39.

international law involves an element of innovation, meaning the difference between codification of custom and progressive development of the law is a matter of degree – 'between minor and major changes of the law, respectively'[126] or between a 'few nuances' in relation to prior custom and going 'substantially beyond' that law.[127] Stated differently, 'when a process is qualified as "codification" or "development" [,] in fact only the prevailing one is meant'.[128]

> If the written rule's innovative or reformatory elements outnumber and outweigh the typical components of the original customary rule, and they appear on the whole as two separate entities, the written norm constitutes progressive development, and "it becomes misleading to describe the process as one of codification at all".[129]

Further, a customary rule codified in a treaty continues to exist alongside its articulation in a treaty, thereby continuing to bind all States qua customary law and not just Parties to the codifying treaty.[130] It is submitted that the distinction between codification and progressive development is germane to the issue of relevant interpretive aids.[131] A customary rule is codified if one of the following three conditions is met: (1) the treaty rule is declaratory of an existing customary rule; (2) the treaty rule has crystallized into custom during the process of its formation and adoption; or (3) the treaty rule has generated new customary law subsequent to its adoption.[132] For the codification study undertaken in Chapters 7 and 8, codification is understood as satisfying one of the first two conditions. However, whatever the outcome of that study, it is possible for the status of all provisions in the Rome Statute to evolve into custom over time, depending on how well they are received by States Parties and Non-States Parties. Although it happens infrequently, a treaty formulated to be declaratory of custom can lose this standing due to changes arising from the subsequent practice and *opinio juris* of States.[133] Finally, a treaty can be declaratory of custom at varying levels of abstraction,[134] and certain provisions,

---

[126] Villiger (n. 17) 126.   [127] Thirlway (n. 73) 28; Dinstein (n. 17) 366.

[128] K Wolfke, 'Can Codification of International Law be Harmful?' in J Makarczyk (ed.), *Essays in International Law in Honour of Judge Manfred Lachs* (Martinus Nijhoff 1984) 313, 314.

[129] Villiger (n. 17) 248 (citing Brierly (n. 39) 3).

[130] *Nicaragua* (n. 111) 85; Baxter (n. 99) 32; articles 38, 43 of the *Vienna Convention* (1969).

[131] Villiger (n. 17) 126: this distinction is of 'central importance in the context of sources'.

[132] *North Sea Continental Shelf Cases* (n. 104) 37–46; O Schachter, 'Entangled Treaty and Custom' in Y Dinstein (ed.), *International Law at a Time of Perplexity: Essays in Honour of Shabtai Rosenne* (Springer 1989) 717–18; Thirlway, 'The Law and Procedure of the International Court of Justice' (n. 110) 94.

[133] Dinstein (n. 17) 352.   [134] Baxter (n. 99) 41–42.

or parts of provisions, may be declaratory of custom while others are not,[135] which is often the case.[136]

6.4 Codification benefits, drawbacks and indicia

Codifying customary international criminal law offers certain benefits, including improvements in 'legal clarity and certainty, systematization of the law, coherence, consistency and perhaps the reform of pre-existing deficient law'.[137] It also enables States to 'bring about a rapid reform of international law and to adapt it to the new needs of the international community'.[138] It allows them to speak with 'one voice' instead of through 'conflicting, ambiguous and multi-temporal evidence that might be amassed through an examination of the practice of each of the individual States'.[139]

In practice, a myth of congruence between a treaty and custom might take hold, given the attraction for practical reasons to written law.[140] It might also be more politically attractive to rely on a treaty as opposed to custom, because the former is a negotiated text resulting from a democratic and inclusive process and acquires certain legitimacy by obtaining the requisite number of ratifications in order to enter into force.[141] By becoming Parties to a treaty, States fully realize the legal obligations they are assuming.[142] A codification resulting from a conference involving all States is also perceived as 'settling' customary law.[143] The decision to ratify such a treaty might even accelerate the process of a non-customary provision crystallizing into custom.[144] It is not surprising, therefore, that third States may also find it convenient to rely on treaty provisions to understand their obligations under customary law.[145] A code can also result in a clearer line being drawn between the role of lawmakers and judges.[146] And for the practising lawyer, a code means that jurisprudence is used to illustrate or explain the codified rule rather than deduce it.[147]

However, there are at least four perceived drawbacks to purporting that a treaty codifies an area of law. First, a 'colourable case against a long-established

[135] *North Sea Continental Shelf Cases* (n. 104) 37–46; Dinstein (n. 17) 355–56.
[136] Dinstein, ibid.
[137] Baxter (n. 99) 36–37; Schachter (n. 51) 66; Villiger (n. 17) 271; A Ashworth, 'Interpreting Criminal Statutes: A Crisis of Legality?' (1991) 107 L Quart Rev 419, 420.
[138] R Pisillo-Mazzeschi, 'Treaty and Custom: Reflections on the Codification of International Law' (1997) 23 Commonwealth L Bull 549, 550–51.
[139] RR Baxter, 'Multilateral Treaties as Evidence of Customary International Law' (1965–66) 41 British Ybk Int'l L 275, 278.
[140] Schachter (n. 132) 722.   [141] Ibid. 722; Pisillo-Mazzeschi (n. 138).
[142] Baxter (n. 99) 38.   [143] Schachter (n. 51) 68–69.
[144] Thirlway (n. 73) 114–16; Pisillo-Mazzeschi (n. 138) 550–52.
[145] Dinstein (n. 17) 351; Villiger (n. 17) 270.   [146] Ashworth (n. 137) 420.
[147] Brierly (n. 87) 338.

rule of customary law' may be made 'on the ground that it was not expressly stated in the convention'.[148] Thus, if the Rome Statute is referred to as a code of crimes under international law, it might erroneously be argued that conduct expressly excluded from the Rome Statute is not criminal under international law.[149] Second, evidence of a 'negative *opinio juris*' may be asserted if many States decline to ratify a 'codifying' treaty or challenge the customary nature of a particular rule, thereby weakening its claim to be reflective of custom and rendering the law less certain.[150] If the Rome Statute expressly stated that it was a code of crimes and few States proceeded to ratify it, the criminality of the codified conduct might be called into question.[151]

Third, a codifying treaty may have the effect of inadvertently freezing the development of customary international law by 'photographing' the law at a moment in time but 'speaking' in present terms when it is applied to cases.[152] By calling the Rome Statute a code, the natural growth of international criminal law may be stifled at a critical phase in its development.[153] Fourth, there was perhaps a fear that if custom were recognized as the direct source of law for the Court's jurisdiction, the perceived judicial creativity of ICTY and ICTR judges might repeat itself with judges of the Court.[154]

The Rome Statute does not state whether the crimes in articles 6, 7, 8 and 8 *bis* are declaratory of custom. Accordingly, where the character of a treaty is not expressed in the text itself, this point may be made implicit in the text of the treaty or gathered from the *travaux préparatoires*.[155] The following considerations and statements in the following materials have been identified as having probative value for purposes of ascertaining whether a treaty codifies

---

[148] Jennings (n. 43) 305.

[149] Consider in this regard exclusion of the prohibition against the use of weapons of mass destruction.

[150] Thirlway (n. 73) 114–16; Dinstein (n. 17) 367, referring to this as a 'decodifying effect'; RR Baxter, 'The Effects of Ill-Conceived Codification and Development of International Law' in *Recueil d'études de droit International en hommage à Paul Guggenheim* (Geneva 1968) 146; Lauterpacht (n. 83) 33.

[151] Thirlway cautions that this logic should not be taken too far as there may be other reasons for deciding not to ratify a treaty (n. 73) 115.

[152] Baxter (n. 139) 299; Thirlway, ibid. 125.

[153] Jennings (n. 43) 305; A Cassese, 'The Statute of the International Criminal Court: Some Preliminary Reflections' (1999) 10 EJIL 144, 158 (concerned about retrograde elements freezing legal development); Amnesty International, *International Criminal Court: The Failure of States to Enact Effective Implementing Legislation* (30 August 2004) Index No. IOR 40/019/2004.

[154] WA Schabas, 'Customary Law or "Judge-Made" Law: Judicial Creativity at the UN Criminal Tribunals' in J Doria, H-P Gasser and MC Bassiouni (eds.), *The Legal Regime of the International Criminal Court: Essays in Honour of Professor Igor Blishchenko* (Martinus Nijhoff 2009) 75, 77.

[155] Baxter (n. 99) 42–43 (citing *North Sea Continental Shelf Cases* (n. 104) 36–47 in support of this); Dinstein (n. 17) 361.

custom:[156] whether an area of law is ripe for codification prior to the drafting of a treaty; materials preceding the work of the ILC; ILC materials; UN General Assembly Sixth Committee statements; diplomatic conference *travaux préparatoires*; the adoption of a provision 'without a dissenting voice'; widespread and representative drafting participation by States; adoption of a convention by 'an overwhelming majority of States'; the final act of the diplomatic conference; the text of the treaty, including its preamble; ratifications, reservations, denunciations and revisions; subsequent practice by States and Non-States Parties; statements by States and Non-States Parties;[157] mention of the same conventional rules in subsequent legal texts; case law;[158] doctrinal writings; and the nature of the rules in the treaty, their norm-creating character.[159] Although the definitions of crimes will be briefly examined in the next Chapter, limiting oneself to doing this would defeat the purpose of drafting a codifying treaty, which is to fix a particular relationship between custom and a treaty, a relationship that also needs to be fixed in a method of interpretation for crimes in the Rome Statute.[160]

Not surprisingly, scholars disagree about the relative weight to be given to the aforementioned considerations and materials, with some focussing on elements internal to the treaty and others on practice and *opinio juris* external to it.[161] Accordingly, all of the aforementioned elements will be considered, which is the predominant approach taken in international jurisprudence.[162] In the next Chapter, mainly objective considerations emerging from the text of the Rome Statute will be considered. Chapter 9 examines predominantly subjective elements or elements external to the Rome Statute.

---

[156] See, e.g., Baxter, ibid.; Baxter (n. 139) 277–78, 287; Thirlway, 'The Law and Procedure of the International Court of Justice' (n. 110) 99–101; Thirlway (n. 73) 21; Villiger (n. 17) 158–59, 239–44, 247; Schachter (n. 132) 735; Wolfke (n. 128) 314; Pisillo-Mazzeschi (n. 138) 553. These indicia are variously identified as having probative value.

[157] The behaviour of States is subject to the Baxter paradox, 'Treaties and Custom' (n. 99) 64, 73: 'as the number of parties to a treaty increases, it becomes more difficult to demonstrate what is the state of customary international law dehors the treaty. . . . As the express acceptance of the treaty increases, the number of states not parties whose practice is relevant diminishes.'

[158] See, e.g., *Prosecutor v. Furundžija*, Judgment, ICTY-95–17/1-T, 10 December 1998, para. 227; *Prosecutor v. Kupreškić and Others*, Judgment, ICTY-95–16-T, 14 January 2000, para. 50.

[159] Schachter (n. 132) 732–35.   [160] Baxter (n. 99) 56; Baxter (n. 139) 287.

[161] See, e.g., Pisillo-Mazzeschi (n. 138) 556ff.; Villiger (n. 17) 244, 247; Dinstein (n. 17) 362–63.

[162] Pisillo-Mazzeschi, ibid. 559.

Internal indicia of codification

7.1 Introduction

In Chapter 6, an attempt was made to explain why, in order to develop a method of interpretation for crimes in the Rome Statute, the relationship between the Statute and custom must be understood. The nature of this relationship is essential to determining custom's role as an aid to interpretation and the relationship of this aid to other interpretive aids, especially the Elements of Crimes. The codification study that follows is guided by indicia of codification identified in the previous Chapter. The goal in this and the following Chapter is to determine whether the definitions of crimes in the Rome Statute are more of a codification of custom or a progressive development of international criminal law. Codification experts disagree on the relative weight to be given to indicia of codification in the text of a treaty and those external to it (e.g., *travaux préparatoires*).[1] Accordingly, all indicia will be considered. In this Chapter, consideration will be given to the provisions of the Rome Statute on the following issues and the clues they offer about the relationship between the Statute and custom: material, personal and temporal jurisdiction; legality; applicable law; the Rome Statute's relationship to existing and developing international law; definitions of crimes; Elements of Crimes; and mental elements of crimes. In the next Chapter, indicia of codification external to the Rome Statute will be examined.

7.2 Material jurisdiction (article 5)

According to the preamble of the Rome Statute, crimes within its jurisdiction are 'grave' and 'threaten the peace, security and well-being of the world'.[2] They are the 'most serious crimes of concern to the international community as a whole' and 'must not go unpunished'.[3] This notion of seriousness is expressly reiterated in articles 1 and 5 of the Rome Statute and in the Elements of

---

[1] See Chapter 6, Section 6.2.   [2] Preambular para. 3, Rome Statute.
[3] Preambular para. 4 and article 1, Rome Statute.

Crimes.[4] Article 8(1) of the Rome Statute also emphasizes to the Court and prosecutor that their focus should be on the most egregious war crimes: 'The Court shall have jurisdiction in respect of war crimes in particular when committed as part of a plan or policy or as part of a large-scale commission of such crimes.' What does this general gravity threshold suggest about the nature of the crimes within the Court's jurisdiction? It has been posited that consideration must be given to the magnitude and widespread nature of the conduct, the heinousness of the offence and whether the individual charged is a 'major' offender.[5]

Article 5 lists the crimes of aggression, genocide, other crimes against humanity and war crimes as falling within the Court's jurisdiction. One indication of a treaty reflecting custom is the norm-creating nature of its subject matter. For example, international humanitarian law and human rights treaties are said to be norm-creating because they give rise to an objective (as opposed to synallagmatic) regime, meaning their direct beneficiaries are individuals as opposed to States.[6] As well, a norm-creating treaty provision is one that has a character that would form 'the basis of a general rule of law',[7] a task that is typically accomplished through the drafting of multilateral treaties.[8] A synallagmatic treaty, one that is reciprocal in character, is suggestive of a treaty that is not declaratory of custom and therefore not binding on Non-Parties.[9] While normative treaties are thought to have a greater potential of reflecting customary international law and thereby binding Non-States Parties, their objective nature is thought to frustrate the traditional custom formation process because they do not generate State practice in the relations between States and often mainly require States or individuals to refrain (rather than engage) in certain conduct.[10] However, the drafting of a normative treaty is variously considered by scholars to amount to State practice or evidence of *opinio juris*.[11]

---

[4] See the first introductory paragraphs for crimes against humanity and war crimes in the Elements of Crimes.

[5] LN Sadat and SR Carden, 'The New International Criminal Court: An Uneasy Revolution' (2000) 88 Geo LJ 381, 419; MM de Guzman, '*Gravity and the Legitimacy of the International Criminal Court*' (2008) 32 Fordham Int'l LJ 1400.

[6] M Mendelson, 'Remarks: Disentangling Treaty and Customary International Law' (1987) 81 ASIL Proceedings 157, 162–63; O Schachter, 'Entangled Treaty and Custom' in Y Dinstein (ed.), *International Law at a Time of Perplexity: Essays in Honour of Shabtai Rosenne* (Martinus Nijhoff 1989) 717, 735.

[7] *North Sea Continental Shelf Cases (Germany v. Denmark; Germany v. The Netherlands)* [1969] ICJ Rep. 3, 41–42.

[8] BB Jia, 'The Relations between Treaties and Custom' (2010) 9 Chinese J Int'l L 81, 92. See also ME Villiger, *Customary International Law and Treaties* (Kluwer Law International 1997).

[9] Schachter (n. 6) 735; Villiger, ibid.   [10] Mendelson (n. 6) 162–63.

[11] Schachter (n. 6) 732 (making this point in respect of developments on the law of the sea, namely, extension of the territorial sea and the establishment of exclusive economic zones).

The aforementioned crimes are considered to be classic examples of norm-creating subject matter in a treaty and are thought to even have the status of *jus cogens* or a normativity that is higher than that of other international rules.[12] The concept of *jus cogens* usefully recalls the traditional relationship between custom and these crimes. Customary international law has played a central role in the field of international criminal law.[13] Beginning with the concept of crimes under international law, it has long been understood that the aforementioned crimes bind all individuals under general international law and that their prohibition are *jus cogens* norms from which no derogation by States is permitted through any source of law listed in article 38 of the Statute of the International Court of Justice without the same status.[14] These crimes consist of violations of international customary rules, including treaty provisions that codify these rules or have crystallized into custom:[15]

> International criminal law *stricto sensu* establishes individual criminal responsibility directly under international law. . . . [It] may be articulated in international treaties to correspond with the principle of legality in its most stringent form. Ultimately, however, it must be rooted in general international law because of its inextricable connection with fundamental values of the international legal community as whole.[16]

In *Re List and Others (Hostages Trial)* (1948), a US military tribunal affirmed that an international crime is an 'act universally recognized as criminal, which is considered a grave matter of international concern and for some valid reason cannot be left within the exclusive jurisdiction of the State that would have control over it under ordinary circumstances'.[17] It is the view of some that the categories of crimes currently listed in article 5 of the Rome Statute have the 'status of custom and even of jus cogens obligations'.[18] The views of scholars

---

[12] Ibid. 734 (citing inter alia *Legal Consequences for States of the Continued Presence of South Africa in Namibia (South West Africa) notwithstanding Security Council Resolution 276 (1970)*, Advisory Opinion [1971] ICJ Rep. 16, 31–32; *Filártiga v. Peña-Irala*, 630 F.2d 876 (2d Cir. 1980)).

[13] IMT Judgment (1947) 41 AJIL 172; ICJ, *Reservations to the Convention on Prevention and Punishment of Genocide*, Advisory Opinion [1951] ICJ Rep. 15.

[14] *Prosecutor v. Furundžija*, Judgment, ICTY-95–17/1-T, 10 December 1998, para. 153.

[15] A Cassese, *International Criminal Law*, 2nd edn (Oxford University Press 2008) 11–12; K Kittichaisaree, *International Criminal Law* (Oxford University Press 2001) 3.

[16] C Kreß, 'International Criminal Law' in R Wolfrum (ed.), *Max Planck Encyclopedia of Public International Law* (2008–), online edition, www.mpepil.com, paras. 10–11, accessed 15 March 2011.

[17] (1953) 15 Annual Digest 632, 636.

[18] M Koskenniemi, 'Fragmentation of International Law: Difficulties Arising from the Diversification and Expansion of International Law: Report of the Study Group of the International Law Commission' (4 April 2006), UN Doc. A/CN.4/L.682, paras. 188–189; Sadat and Carden (n. 5) 409–10.

are provided in the sections below dealing with each category of crime and in the next Chapter.[19] Even if these categories of crimes are reflective of *jus cogens* obligations, this does not say anything about the crimes listed in the Rome Statute under each category and the definitions of their elements in the Elements of Crimes. As well, the Nuremberg judgment[20] and some decisions of the ICTY and ICTR suggest that treaties can also be a source of these crimes, a position endorsed by some observers.[21]

The International Court of Justice has posited that the obligations to which the crimes in the Rome Statute give rise are generally *erga omnes* in nature.[22] Obligations *erga omnes* are also evidence of obligations that are norm-creating and therefore not solely limited to relations between contracting Parties.[23] The Statute's preamble states that 'their effective prosecution must be ensured by taking measures at the national level and by enhancing international cooperation,' and that it is the 'duty of every State to exercise its criminal jurisdiction over those responsible for international crimes'.[24] Whereas the *jus cogens* status of a rule relates to its hierarchy in the international normative order, its *erga omnes* status is related to its enforcement.[25]

> [O]bligations *erga omnes* designate the *scope of application* of the relevant law, and the procedural consequences that follow from this. A norm which is creative of obligations *erga omnes* is owed to the "international community as a whole" and all States – irrespective of their particular interest in the matter – are entitled to invoke State responsibility in case of breach. The *erga omnes* nature of an obligation, however, indicates no clear superiority of that obligation over other obligations. Although in practice norms recognised as having an *erga omnes* validity set up undoubtedly important obligations, this importance does not translate into a hierarchical superiority similar to that of . . . *jus cogens*.[26]

---

[19] See Chapter 8, Section 8.6.   [20] See Chapter 4, Sections 4.3.4 and 4.3.10.2.

[21] Ibid.; R Cryer, 'The Doctrinal Foundations of International Criminalization' in MC Bassiouni (ed.), *International Criminal Law*, vol. I, 3rd edn (Martinus Nijhoff 2008) 107, 108 (citing case law in favour of this position: *Prosecutor v. Tadić*, Decision on the Defence Motion for Interlocutory Appeal on Jurisdiction, ICTY-94-1-AR72, 2 October 1995, para. 94; *Prosecutor v. Kordić and Čerkez*, Judgment, ICTY-95-14/2-A, 17 December 2004, paras. 40–46; and case law rejecting this position: *Prosecutor v. Vasiljević*, Judgment, ICTY-98-32-T, 29 November 2002, para. 26; *Prosecutor v. Galić*, Judgment, Separate and Partially Dissenting of Judge Nieto-Navia, ICTY-98-29-T, 5 December 2003, paras. 109–112).

[22] *Case concerning the Barcelona Traction, Light and Power Company, Limited (Belgium v. Spain) (Second Phase)* [1970] ICJ Rep. 3, 32.

[23] Y Dinstein, 'Interaction Between Customary International Law and Treaties' (2006) 322 Recueil des Cours de l'Académie de Droit International 243, 361.

[24] Preambular paras. 4 and 6, Rome Statute.

[25] *Furundžija* (n. 14).   [26] Koskenniemi (n. 18) 162.

The concept of *erga omnes* is also not conclusive for the present inquiry, as an *erga omnes* obligation can arise from treaty law and not only custom.[27] In sum, the *jus cogens* nature of the categories of offences in the Rome Statute and the gravity threshold for the Court's jurisdiction suggest that articles 6, 7, 8 and 8 *bis* may well be reflective of custom. In fact, the tendency at the Rome Diplomatic Conference was that if States could decide on a case-by-case basis to accede to the Court's jurisdiction, they were willing to have a more expansive list of crimes. If not, they wanted a narrow list of crimes, narrower definitions and higher thresholds.[28] Article 5 of the Rome Statute and the gravity threshold mentioned throughout the Statute and the Elements of Crimes is indicative that the latter model prevailed.

7.3 Personal jurisdiction (articles 12 and 13)

The Court's jurisdiction is limited to natural persons who are at least eighteen years old at the time they allegedly commit a crime.[29] During the drafting of the Rome Statute, States that strongly support the Court lost in their efforts to extend its jurisdiction under the principle of universal jurisdiction to all crimes under international law regardless of where, by whom or against whom they were committed.[30] Had the universal jurisdiction model prevailed, this would have lent support to the idea that crimes within the Court's jurisdiction reflect custom. The compromise position, however, was for the Court's jurisdiction to respect the jurisdictional rules of territoriality and nationality, with some exceptions that will be examined.[31] The jurisdictional model is therefore mainly consent-based. The Court's jurisdiction can be triggered by a State Party referring a situation involving one or more crimes to the Court, by the Security Council making such a referral under Chapter VII of the Charter of the United Nations and pursuant to article 13(b) of the Rome Statute, or by the prosecutor initiating an investigation into a crime (*proprio motu*).[32] However, in order

---

[27] Institut de Droit International (IDI), 'Obligations and Rights Erga Omnes in International Law' (Krakow Session 2005) 71-II Annuaire de l'Institut de Droit International 289, article 1; Institut de Droit International (IDI), 'The Protection of Human Rights and the Principle of Non-Intervention in Internal Affairs of States' (Santiago de Compostela Session 1989) 3-II Annuaire de l'Institut de Droit International 341, article 1.

[28] P Kirsch and JT Holmes, 'The Birth of the International Criminal Court: The 1998 Rome Conference' (1998) 36 Canadian Ybk Int'l L 3, 18.

[29] Articles 1, 23, 26, Rome Statute. Persons over the age of fifteen are considered lawful combatants and may be tried by national courts. M Frulli, 'Jurisdiction *Ratione Personae*' in A Cassese and Others (eds.), *The Rome Statute of the International Criminal Court: A Commentary*, vol. I (Oxford University Press 2002) 527, 534–35.

[30] G Werle, *Principles of International Criminal Law* (TMC Asser Press 2005) 21.

[31] Ibid.   [32] See articles 12(2), 13, Rome Statute; Frulli (n. 29) 535.

for a State Party to refer a situation or the prosecutor to initiate an investigation into a crime, one of the following two conditions in article 12(2) must be met:

> [T]he Court may exercise its jurisdiction if one or more of the following States are Parties to this Statute or have accepted the jurisdiction of the Court in accordance with paragraph 3 [by lodging a declaration with the Registrar accepting the Court's jurisdiction]:
>
> (a) The State on the territory of which the conduct in question occurred or, if the crime was committed on board a vessel or aircraft, the State of registration of that vessel or aircraft;
> (b) The State of which the person accused of the crime is a national.

Accordingly, the Court has jurisdiction over nationals of States Parties to the Rome Statute, irrespective of where they perpetrate crimes (nationality) and crimes committed on the territory of any State Party irrespective of who perpetrated the crime (territoriality). Nationality and territoriality are accepted heads of jurisdiction under international law.[33] However, there are three situations where the consent of the relevant State at the relevant time will be lacking, two involving a national of a Non-State Party who commits a crime on the territory of a Non-State Party to the Rome Statute. In this scenario, the relevant State has not ratified the Rome Statute at the time the conduct occurred, and the jurisdictional rules of nationality and territoriality are not satisfied. Nevertheless, the Court may exercise jurisdiction over such an individual if the Security Council refers the relevant situation to it pursuant to article 13(b) of the Rome Statute or if the State with personal or territorial jurisdiction subsequently lodges a declaration with the Court's Registrar pursuant to article 12(3) consenting to its jurisdiction. In the third scenario, the Security Council may refer to the Court a situation involving conduct that occurred on the territory of a State Party or that was allegedly committed by a national of a State Party prior to that Party's ratification of the Statute.

The difficulty with Security Council referrals in these situations as well as declarations lodged by a relevant State after the conduct in question occurred is that the principle of legality is offended. The relevant State has not ratified the Rome Statute at the time the conduct occurred, thereby resulting in the Rome Statute's retroactive application to an individual.[34] One way to overcome this legality concern is for the crimes in the Rome Statute to be reflective of

---

[33] *The Case of the SS Lotus (France v. Turkey)* (1927) PCIJ Series A, No. 10, 18–19; D Akande, 'The Jurisdiction of the International Criminal Court over Nationals of Non-Parties: Legal Basis and Limits' (2003) 1 J Int'l Crim Justice 618, 621–34; KS Gallant, 'Jurisdiction to Adjudicate and Jurisdiction to Prescribe in International Criminal Courts' (2003) 48 Vill L Rev 763, 821.

[34] Gallant, ibid. 817–18.

custom.[35] That way, the individual of or in the relevant State(s) would be bound by the definitions of crimes in the Rome Statute qua customary international law.[36]

If a treaty rule is not reflective of custom, the *Vienna Convention* (1969) confirms that it cannot impose obligations or rights on a third State without its consent.[37] Article 35(1) requires that for a Non-State Party to be bound by obligations in the Rome Statute, States Parties to the Statute must have intended to impose obligations on a Non-State Party, and the latter must agree in writing to be bound by these obligations.[38] Article 36(1) clarifies that where a treaty confers a right on a Non-State Party, it is presumed, unless the treaty provides otherwise, that the latter assents to this right so long as it does not express a contrary view.[39] Opinions diverge on whether a Non-State Party must actively accept the right conferred on it or whether the right is created immediately unless and until the Non-State Party disclaims it.[40] However, it is generally agreed that if a treaty provision deviates from custom, this is a ground for ruling it inapplicable to a Non-State Party that has not consented to its application.[41]

One argument advanced to overcome this difficulty, at least with respect to Security Council referrals, is that the Security Council has the competence to legislate for members of the United Nations. Counter-terrorism resolutions 1373 and 1540, adopted by the Security Council, are pointed to in support of this claim.[42] However, even if this is the case, the precedential value and import of these resolutions when defining the Security Council's powers in general as concerns UN member States remains contested.[43] Article 25 of the Charter

---

[35] Ibid. 821, 824; B Broomhall, 'Article 22' in O Triffterer (ed.), *Commentary on the Rome Statute of the International Criminal Court*, 2nd edn (CH Beck/Hart/Nomos 2008) 720. For a different explanation, see Sadat and Carden (n. 5) 406ff.; LN Sadat, 'Custom, Codification and Some Thoughts about the Relationship Between the Two: Article 10 of the ICC Statute' (2000) 49 DePaul L Rev 909, 919–20, 923. In both situations, 'the Court would have a rare opportunity to clarify the customary law status of the particular provisions'. T Meron, 'Revival of Customary International Humanitarian Law' (2005) 99:4 AJIL 817, 832.

[36] Article 48, *Vienna Convention* (1969); R Jennings and A Watts, *Oppenheim's International Law*, vol. II, 9th edn (Longman, Harlow 1992) 1260–61; RF Roxburgh, *International Conventions and Third States* (Longmans, Green and Co. 1917) 112.

[37] Jennings and Watts, ibid.; Roxburgh, ibid. 29, 111; Dinstein (n. 23) 340 (acceptance of an obligation must be in writing).

[38] Article 35, *Vienna Convention* (1969); *Free Zones Case (France* v. *Switzerland)* (1929) PCIJ Series A, No. 22, 17–18.

[39] Jennings and Watts (n. 36) 1262.

[40] Ibid.; M Fitzmaurice, 'Third Parties and the Law of Treaties' (2002) 6 Max Planck Ybk of UN Law 37, 48ff.

[41] Dinstein (n. 23) 357.

[42] UNSC Res. 1373 (28 September 2001); UNSC Res. 1540 (28 April 2004).

[43] E de Wet, 'The Security Council as a Law Maker: The Adoption of (Quasi)-Judicial Decisions' in R Wolfrum and V Röben (eds.), *Developments in International Law in Treaty Making* (Springer 2005) 183, 198–99.

of the United Nations empowers it to adopt decisions that are binding on member States, and the International Court of Justice held in its advisory opinion on *Namibia* (1971) that article 25 is not limited to decisions taken under Chapter VII of the Charter.[44] However, the Security Council has not claimed that it is empowered to legislate generally.[45] Further, it is not at all clear that the Security Council is empowered to enact offences.[46]

Another argument advanced to explain the Court's jurisdiction in such situations is that the Rome Diplomatic Conference 'functioned in a quasi-legislative manner, and prescribed international norms of universal application. Thus, the adoption of the Rome Statute was revolutionary in that it transformed jurisdictional principles concerning "which State" may exercise its authority over particular cases into norms establishing the circumstances under which the international community may prescribe rules of international criminal law and may punish those who breach those rules.'[47] Understood this way, the Rome conference was a 'quietly revolutionary, quasi-legislative event that produced a criminal code for the world'.[48] However, this view has yet to garner much support, and it arguably strains credibility that such a revolutionary event would be quiet.

Finally, a brief discussion of the crime of aggression is necessary. Article 5 of the Rome Statute reflects a delicate compromise that was struck in 1998. It was agreed at that time to include the crime of aggression in the Court's jurisdiction but to make the exercise of this jurisdiction conditional on a provision being 'adopted in accordance with articles 121 and 123 defining the crime and setting out the conditions under which the Court shall exercise jurisdiction with respect to this crime'.[49] The Final Act of the Rome Conference designated the task of preparing proposals on the crime of aggression to the Preparatory

---

[44] *Namibia* (n. 12) 52–53.   [45] Dinstein (n. 23) 421.

[46] *Prosecutor* v. *Delalić and Others*, Judgment, ICTY-96-21-T, 16 November 1998, para. 417; Gallant (n. 33) 826. See also B Swart, 'International Crimes: Present Situation and Future Development' (2004) 19 Nouvelles études pénales 201; C Szasz, 'The Security Council Starts Legislating' (2002) 96 AJIL 901; N Tsagourias, 'Security Council Legislation, Article 2(7) of the UN Charter, and the Principle of Subsidiarity' (2004) 24:3 LJIL 539; S Talmon, 'The Security Council as World Legislator' (2005) 99 AJIL 175; E Rosand, 'The Security Council as "Global Legislator": Ultra Vires or Ultra Innovative?' (2004) 28:3 Fordham Int'l LJ 542; J Wouters and J Odermatt, 'Quis Custodiet Consilium Securitatis? Reflections on the Lawmaking Powers of the Security Council', Working Paper No. 109, Leuven Centre for Global Governance Studies (June 2013), http://papers.ssrn.com/sol3/papers.cfm?abstract id=2286208, accessed 3 July 2014.

[47] Sadat (n. 35) 919.   [48] Ibid. 923.

[49] Article 121 contains a series of rules for amending the Rome Statute, and article 123 requires the convening of a Review Conference to consider amendments to the Rome Statute seven years after its entry into force. On the controversial inclusion of the crime of aggression in the Rome Statute, see A Zimmermann, 'Article 5' in O Triffterer (ed.), *Commentary on the Rome Statute of the International Criminal Court*, 2nd edn (CH Beck/Hart/Nomos 2008) 129, 136–37.

Commission for the Court, which was tasked inter alia with preparing draft Rules of Procedure and Evidence, Elements of Crimes and a host of agreements, rules and regulations.[50]

The Preparatory Commission was able to facilitate a preliminary discussion of the crime of aggression and concluded this work in July 2002.[51] It recommended that work on aggression be continued by a Special Working Group on the Crime of Aggression (Special Working Group). The Special Working Group was established by the Assembly of States Parties (ASP) at its first session on 9 September 2002.[52] On 13 February 2009, the Special Working Group adopted by consensus a set of 'proposals for a provision on aggression' and submitted it to the ASP.[53] This text, which consisted of six draft amendments to the Rome Statute, was forwarded by the ASP to the first Review Conference of the Rome Statute held in Kampala, Uganda, in June 2010[54] and was the product of five and a half years of multilateral negotiations that were open to all States on an equal footing.[55] On 11 June 2010, the Review Conference adopted by consensus a comprehensive package of amendments on the crime of aggression, including a definition.[56]

In order for the amendments to be activated, a decision needs to be taken in support of this after 1 January 2017 by at least two-thirds of all States Parties if consensus cannot be reached.[57] As well, at least thirty States Parties need to ratify the amendments.[58] Once the activation decision is taken *and* one year after thirty States Parties have ratified or accepted the amendments on the crime

---

[50] Resolution F of the Final Act of the Rome Conference (17 July 1998), UN Doc. A/CONF.183/10, paras. 5, 7.

[51] Within the Preparatory Commission proposals and documents relating to the crime of aggression in PCNICC/2002/2/Add.2. See also RS Clark, 'Rethinking Aggression as a Crime and Formulating its Elements: the Final Work-Product of the Preparatory Commission for the International Criminal Court' (2002) 15 LJIL 859; SA Fernández de Gurmendi, 'The Process of Negotiations' in RS Lee (ed.), *The International Criminal Court: The Making of the Rome Statute* (Kluwer Law International 1999) 217.

[52] ICC-ASP/1/Res.1.

[53] Report of the Special Working Group on the Crime of Aggression, ICC-ASP/7/20/Add.1, Annex II, Appendix I (Proposals for a provision on Aggression elaborated by the Special Working Group on the Crime of Aggression, Draft Resolution (to be adopted by the Review Conference)).

[54] First Review Conference of the Rome Statute, Official Records, Resolution on the Crime of Aggression (adopted 11 June 2010) RC/Res.6, www.icc-cpi.int/iccdocs/asp_docs/Resolutions/RC-Res.6-ENG.pdf, accessed 5 November 2013 (Aggression Resolution).

[55] The drafting history of the Special Working Group is fully documented elsewhere. S Barriga, W Danspeckgruber and C Wenaweser (eds.), *The Princeton Process on the Crime of Aggression: Materials of the Special Working Group on the Crime of Aggression, 2003–2009* (Princeton University: Liechtenstein Institute on Self-Determination, 2009); S Barriga and C Kreß, *The Travaux Préparatoires of the Crime of Aggression* (Cambridge University Press 2012).

[56] Aggression Resolution (n. 54).   [57] Articles 15 *bis*(3), 15 *ter*(3), ibid.

[58] Articles 15 *bis*(2), 15 *ter*(2), ibid.

of aggression,[59] whichever is later, the Court's jurisdiction over this crime will be activated and will operate prospectively. The preamble to the resolution on aggression adopted at the Review Conference provides that States Parties are 'resolved to activate the Court's jurisdiction over the crime of aggression as early as possible'.[60]

The amendments on aggression distinguish between the Court's jurisdiction being triggered by either a State Party referral or the prosecutor initiating an investigation on the one hand (articles 13(a) and (c), Rome Statute), and the Security Council referring a situation to the Court on the other hand (article 13(b), Rome Statute). Article 15 *bis* adopted by the Review Conference deals with the first two jurisdictional triggers and article 15 *ter* with the Security Council trigger. However, both require the two aforementioned conditions to be met in order to activate the Court's jurisdiction over this crime.

Article 15 *bis*(4) provides:

> The Court may, in accordance with article 12, exercise jurisdiction over a crime of aggression, arising from an act of aggression committed by a State Party, unless that State Party has previously declared that it does not accept such jurisdiction by lodging a declaration with the Registrar.[61]

Accordingly, the Court would lack jurisdiction in cases where the amendment has not entered into force for the alleged aggressor State. The regime therefore provides consent-based jurisdiction in that it allows any State Party to declare prospectively that it does not accept the Court's jurisdiction over the crime of aggression.[62]

---

[59] Understanding 3, ibid.; The reference in articles 15 *bis*(2) and 15 *ter*(2), ibid., to 'amendments' strongly suggests that the amendments are to be ratified or accepted as a package, which is consistent with the negotiating principle that 'nothing is agreed until everything is agreed'. See also operative para. 5: '*Calls upon* all States Parties to ratify or accept the *amendments* contained in annex I' (emphasis added)

[60] Emphasis in original.   [61] Article 15 *bis*(2) and (4), ibid.

[62] 'As the final package does not contain an explicit understanding on the question whether a nonratifying state party that has allegedly aggressed, but not opted out, may be subject to the Court's jurisdiction under Article 15 *bis*, divergent interpretations on the issue have emerged after Kampala. The approach that Ambassador Wenaweser presented to the plenary on the morning of Thursday, June 10, 2010, was strongly based on Article 12(1) of the Statute, under which states parties have already accepted jurisdiction over the crime of aggression. Consequently, nonratifying and allegedly aggressing states parties that do not accept the Court's jurisdiction under Article 15 *bis* would have to submit an opt-out declaration to prevent the Court from exercising jurisdiction. . . . Those opposing this view maintain that the second sentence of Article 121(5) already precludes the Court from exercising jurisdiction with respect to nationals or the territory of nonratifying states parties. . . . In essence, both views coincide in that Article 15 *bis* is a consent-based regime, though opinions diverge as to whether active consent is required by the alleged aggressor state (that is, ratification) or passive consent only (that is, not to submit an opt-out declaration).' S Barriga and L Grover, 'A Historic Breakthrough on the Crime of Aggression' (2011) 105 AJIL 517, fn. 38.

Importantly, under no circumstances can nationals of Non-States Parties become subject to the regime in article 15 *bis* – even if a State Party is a victim of aggression and even if a Non-State Party has been aggressed by a State Party.[63] To be clear, Non-States Parties are unable to lodge a declaration under article 12(3) of the Rome Statute consenting to the Court's jurisdiction over the crime of aggression. The reason for absolutely cutting Non-States Parties out of the regime established under article 15 *bis* is twofold. First, Non-States Parties strongly felt that being subject to the Court's jurisdiction over the crime of aggression should be based on the consent of the relevant State(s) and that, if States Parties can choose not to be subject to this regime, the principle of equality would require that Non-States Parties also have the right to make the same choice. As for certain States Parties, the view was expressed that if they consent to being subject to the regime created by the amendments on aggression, and their foes choose to remain outside of the Rome regime, it is not fair to allow the latter to benefit from the protection of the Rome regime (e.g., by lodging an article 12(3) declaration) but free them from all of its attending responsibilities – to be immune from prosecution. Accordingly, article 15 *bis* is an exception to the jurisdictional regime created by articles 12(2) and (3), which govern all other crimes in the Rome Statute. The exclusion of Non-States Parties from the aggression regime under the Rome Statute might suggest that the definition of the crime that was adopted is not reflective of customary law. It might also, however, be motivated solely by the aforementioned practical considerations.

As for article 15 *ter*, which governs Security Council referrals, it too applies prospectively once a decision is taken after 1 January 2017 *and* one year after the thirtieth ratification is deposited, whichever is later.[64] Unlike article 15 *bis*, however, article 15 *ter* recognizes the competence of the Security Council to refer any and all situations involving aggression to the Court, even if they involve a non-consenting State Party or a Non-State Party.[65] Article 15 *ter* is consistent with the existing mechanism for Security Council referrals of situations pursuant to article 13(b) of the Rome Statute involving other crimes within the Court's Statute. This aspect of the Court's jurisdiction would suggest that the definition of the crime of aggression is consistent with existing custom.

7.4 Temporal jurisdiction (articles 11 and 24)

Article 11 of the Rome Statute provides:

1. The Court has jurisdiction only with respect to crimes committed after the entry into force of this Statute.

---

[63] Article 15 *bis*(5), Aggression Resolution (n. 54).
[64] Understanding 1, ibid.   [65] Article 15 *ter*(2) and (3), ibid.

2. If a State becomes a Party to this Statute after its entry into force, the Court may exercise its jurisdiction only with respect to crimes committed after the entry into force of this Statute for that State, unless that State has made a declaration under article 12, paragraph 3.

Similarly, article 24(1) provides: 'No person shall be criminally responsible under this Statute for conduct prior to the entry into force of the Statute.' It is often said that the Court's jurisdiction is 'strictly prospective'[66] in contrast to several ad hoc international criminal tribunals (e.g., Nuremberg, Tokyo, ICTY and ICTR). Whereas ad hoc tribunals have had statutes that apply to conduct occurring prior to their establishment, the Rome Statute is said to apply only to conduct committed after the Statute enters into force for the relevant State.[67] However, this is an oversimplification of the Court's temporal jurisdiction.

Temporal jurisdiction is substantively linked to the principle of legality as defined in article 22 of the Rome Statute. Article 22(1) provides that no person may be held criminally responsible under the Statute 'unless the conduct in question constitutes, at the time it takes place, a crime within the jurisdiction of the Court'. For States Parties that ratified the Statute prior to its entry into force, the Court's jurisdiction is limited to crimes committed by its nationals or on its territory after the entry into force of the Statute on 1 July 2002 (article 11(1)). For States that become Parties to the Rome Statute after its entry into force, the Court's jurisdiction is limited to crimes committed by its nationals or on its territory after the entry into force of the Statute for that State (article 11(2)). For both groups of States, this prospective jurisdiction applies to investigations arising from a normal State Party referral or those initiated by the prosecutor (*proprio motu*).[68] So, if the Security Council refers a situation involving a State Party, it may concern conduct that occurred prior to that State ratifying the Rome Statute, thereby violating the principle of legality.

If jurisdiction cannot be established based on State Party nationality or territoriality, an individual may only be tried by the Court if the relevant situation is referred to it by the Security Council in accordance with article 13(b) or if a Non-State Party with one of these jurisdictional links lodges a declaration with the Registrar accepting the Court's jurisdiction with respect to the crime in question (articles 11(2) and 12(3)).[69] For example, the Security Council in 2005 referred the situation in Darfur, Sudan, to the Court.[70] At the time of this writing, two declarations have been lodged by Non-States Parties:

---

[66] S Bourgon, 'Jurisdiction *Ratione Temporis*' in A Cassese and Others (eds.), *The Rome Statute of the International Criminal Court: A Commentary*, vol. I (Oxford University Press 2002) 545.

[67] Article 11, Rome Statute.   [68] Article 13(a) and (c), Rome Statute.

[69] Article 12(3), Rome Statute.

[70] UNSC Res. 1593 (31 March 2005); article 13(b), Rome Statute.

Côte d'Ivoire and Palestine.[71] The only temporal limitation for a Security Council referral or the acquisition of jurisdiction vis-à-vis the lodging of a declaration is that the conduct in question occurred after the entry into force of the Statute.[72] In both of these situations, as discussed in the previous section, there is the problem that the Court's jurisdiction over a national of a Non-State Party for conduct committed on the territory of a Non-State Party is exercised retroactively without State consent (Security Council referral) or retroactively with such consent (declaration). The same is true regarding Security Council referrals of situations involving the crime of aggression.

It has been suggested that there are limits to the temporal jurisdiction of the Court. The first is the Security Council's power to adopt a resolution under Chapter VII of the Charter of the United Nations requesting deferral of the Court's proceedings for a period of twelve months.[73] This request is renewable.[74] The second is the opt-out mechanism in article 124 of the Statute, which allows for States Parties to declare that for a period of seven years after the entry into force of the Statute for that State, it does not accept the jurisdiction of the Court with respect to war crimes.[75] However, the Security Council's deferral of proceedings does not seem to limit the temporal jurisdiction of the Court but rather prevents it from continuing its work. The Court would still have jurisdiction over the crime and the person(s) involved, meaning conduct occurring after the entry into force of the Statute for the relevant State could still be the subject of an indictment, also when this conduct occurs during the deferral period. Nothing in the Statute suggests that temporal jurisdiction is affected by article 16 (Security Council referral) – that conduct occurring before or during the deferral period is no longer within the Court's temporal jurisdiction or becomes excluded.

As for the war crimes opt-out mechanism, this is perhaps best seen as an exception to the temporal jurisdiction rules set out above, similar to the Security Council referral and declaration exceptions. Whereas these can render the temporal jurisdiction retroactive to when the Statute entered into force, the war crimes opt-out mechanism – in cases of a State Party referral or a *proprio motu* investigation – is an exception that pushes the temporal jurisdiction of

---

[71] The former was declared to be admissible and the latter inadmissible. The negative decision concerning Palestine, however, may be revisited in light of the United Nations General Assembly's vote on 29 November 2012 to accord it the status of non-member State observer.

[72] See articles 11, 12(3), 13(b) and 24, Rome Statute; N White and R Cryer, 'The ICC and the Security Council: An Uncomfortable Relationship' in J Doria, H-P Gasser and MC Bassiouni (eds.), *The Legal Regime of the International Criminal Court: Essays in Honour of Professor Igor Blishchenko* (Martinus Nijhoff 2009) 455, 463–64.

[73] Article 16, Rome Statute.   [74] Ibid.

[75] A shorter period can be designated, and also the opt-out can be unilaterally terminated. A Zimmermann, 'Article 124' in O Triffterer (ed.), *Commentary on the Rome Statute of the International Criminal Court*, 2nd edn (CH Beck/Hart/Nomos 2008) 1767, 1769.

the Court forward by seven years after the entry into force of the Statute for the relevant State.[76] An open question is whether the Security Council may refer a situation involving war crimes to the Court, which implicates a State Party that has made a declaration under the war crimes opt-out mechanism.

It has been suggested that such a referral would be contrary to the relevant State Party's intentions and thus *ultra vires* the Statute.[77] If accepted, however, such reasoning would lead to the unfair consequence that Non-States Parties' nationals and, or, any crimes occurring on their territory could be subject to the jurisdiction of the Court vis-à-vis a Security Council referral but that a State Party to the Statute could fully shield its nationals and crimes occurring on its territory from such jurisdiction by making a declaration under the opt-out mechanism. This assumption produces unjust results, and nothing in the Statute suggests that it was intended. Rather, the power of the Security Council to refer situations to the Court seems boundless, applying equally to crimes occurring on the territory of States Parties and Non-States Parties, as well as involving nationals of any country, irrespective of whether or when that country has ratified the Statute. This interpretation is consistent with article 12(2), which expressly applies the nationality and territoriality requirements to State Party referrals and *proprio motu* investigations of the prosecutor, but not to Security Council referrals. Once the seven-year period lapses, the Court would be able to prosecute war crimes situations referred to it by States Parties or the prosecutor.[78]

7.5 Legality (article 22(1))

Over the years, ad hoc tribunals established post-conflict have relied on the customary nature of crimes in their jurisdiction as the basis for respecting the principle of legality, which prohibits the retroactive application of criminal law. At Nuremberg, defendants submitted that Germany and persons acting on its behalf were not bound to respect the *Hague Convention (IV) Respecting the Laws and Customs of War on Land* (1907)[79] because it is applicable only if all the belligerents to a conflict have ratified it, which was not the case during the Second World War.[80] To overcome this difficulty, the Nuremberg tribunal

---

[76] The declaration to opt out of the war crimes regime for seven years may be withdrawn at any time, and the provision was reviewed at the Review Conference in June 2010 (article 124). Ultimately, the Review Conference decided to retain this provision. RC/Res.4 (10 June 2010).

[77] Bourgon (n. 66) 556.

[78] Zimmermann (n. 75) 1770. For a contrary view, see Bourgon (n. 66) 556.

[79] 35 Stat 2277, TS 539, 1 Bevans 631 (adopted 18 October 1907, entered into force 26 January 1910).

[80] RR Baxter, 'Multilateral Treaties as Evidence of Customary International Law' (1965–1966) 41 British Ybk Int'l L 274, 280.

held that 'by 1939 these rules laid down in the Convention were recognised by all civilised nations, and were regarded as being declaratory of the laws and customs of war which were referred to in Article 6(b) of the Charter'.[81] In *Von Leeb and Others (High Command* case) (1948),[82] the accused were charged inter alia with violations of the *Geneva Convention Relative to the Treatment of Prisoners of War* (1929),[83] and the same type of legality objection was made. Again, it was held that certain provisions of the *Geneva Convention* (1929) are 'clearly an expression of the accepted views of civilized nations and binding upon Germany and the defendants on trial before us in the conduct of the war against Russia'.[84] A similar defence was raised and rejected at Nuremberg regarding this convention.[85] The Tokyo tribunal also engaged in the practice of determining whether crimes listed in its Charter were reflective of customary law and relied on treaties as one source of such evidence.[86]

Legality concerns were also reflected in the Report of the UN Secretary-General on the ICTY:

> In the view of the Secretary-General, the application of the principle *nullum crimen sine lege* requires that the international tribunal should apply rules of international humanitarian law which are beyond any doubt part of customary law so that the problem of adherence of some but not all States to specific conventions does not arise. This would appear to be particularly important in the context of an international tribunal prosecuting persons responsible for serious violations of international humanitarian law.[87]

Judges at the ICTY and ICTR have repeatedly professed their respect for the principle of legality and consequent adherence to customary international law.[88] In the field of international humanitarian law, there exists what has been described by Waldock as 'chains of multilateral treaties dealing with

---

[81] Judgment of the International Military Tribunal for the Trial of German Major War Criminals, Nuremberg (1946), Cmd 6964, 65.

[82] II Trials of War Criminals before the Nuremberg Military Tribunals under Control Council Law No. 10 (1950) 1327, 1340.

[83] 5 UNTS 135 (adopted 27 July 1929, entered into force 21 October 1950).

[84] Baxter (n. 80) 274, 281. Interestingly, the tribunal identified nineteen paragraphs of the *Convention* (as opposed to all of it) as reflective of customary international law. However, explanations were not provided as to why certain provisions and not others were reflective of custom.

[85] Ibid. fn. 5.

[86] Ibid. 283 (citing Judgment of the International Military Tribunal for the Far East (1948) Annual Digest 356, 366).

[87] UNSC, 'Report of the Secretary-General Pursuant to Paragraph 2 of Security Council Resolution 808' (1993), UN Doc. S/25704, para. 34.

[88] *Prosecutor* v. *Delalić and Others*, Judgment, ICTY-96–21-T, 16 November 1998, para. 417; *Prosecutor* v. *Jelisić*, Judgment, ICTY-95–10-T, 14 December 1999, para. 61.

the same subject-matter'.[89] Within such a cluster of treaties or the regime it creates, judges have asked which of these treaty provisions is reflective of customary international law. However, in *Tadić* (1995), the Appeals Chamber of the ICTY held that the legality principle is also respected where the relevant State has ratified the treaty applied by the tribunal prior to the impugned conduct occurring – and that the tribunal accordingly has jurisdiction over this conduct, a position that has been accepted by some judges at the ICTY and challenged by others.[90]

In light of this jurisprudence, how the legality principle is formulated in the Rome Statute is likely relevant to understanding the Court's material jurisdiction. Article 22(1) reads: 'A person shall not be criminally responsible under this Statute unless the conduct in question constitutes, at the time it takes place, a crime within the jurisdiction of the Court.' How can the retroactive exercises of jurisdiction discussed in the previous section be reconciled with delegates' legality concerns when drafting the Rome Statute? Absent relevant national criminal law prohibiting the impugned conduct when it occurred, the Court's jurisdiction would have to be established on the basis of the relevant crimes forming a part of customary international law,[91] thereby binding *all* individuals.[92]

In his commentary on article 22, Broomhall identified an important silence that is germane to this point. He contrasted the formulation of the legality principle in the 1994 Draft Statute prepared by the ILC with its present formulation in article 22. Article 39(b) of the 1994 Draft Statute adapted the principle of legality for treaty crimes by requiring that no accused could be found guilty of a treaty crime 'unless the treaty in question was applicable to the conduct of the accused . . . at the time the act or omission occurred'.[93] Others have remarked that a pragmatic reason for limiting the Rome Statute's jurisdiction to crimes under international law and not extending it to include treaty crimes 'was that becoming a party to the Statute would not be contingent on the acceptance of legal instruments defining the substance of such crimes'.[94] The absence of such a provision in the Rome Statute is notable as it suggests that the crimes within

---

[89] H Waldock, 'Third Report on the Law of Treaties' (1964) II Ybk of the ILC 5, 43.

[90] On the controversy surrounding this position, see Chapter 4, Sections 4.3.4 and 4.3.10.2.

[91] Broomhall (n. 35) 720; Gallant (n. 33) 821, 826. For a different explanation, see Sadat and Carden (n. 5) 406ff.; Sadat (n. 35) 919–20, 923.

[92] Article 38, *Vienna Convention* (1969).

[93] ILC, 'Draft Statute for an International Criminal Court', 1994 Draft Statute, UN Doc. A/49/10, 43, article 39.

[94] H von Hebel and D Robinson, 'Crimes within the Jurisdiction of the Court' in RS Lee (ed.), *The International Criminal Court: The Making of the Rome Statute* (Kluwer Law International 1999) 79, 122. Accordingly, articles 12(2) and 13(b) of the Rome Statute result in the Court having jurisdiction over 'core crimes' committed anywhere in the world irrespective of any relevant treaty being ratified.

the Court's jurisdiction are limited to 'core' crimes under international law or international criminal law *sensu stricto*.[95] If 'treaty crimes' were to be added to the Court's jurisdiction one day,[96] Broomhall reasons that the legality principle in article 22 would have to be amended to reflect this.[97] Alternatively, the jurisdiction of the Court could be revised so that it is always limited to conduct occurring after the relevant State has ratified the Statute. Thus, the principle of legality's formulation in the Rome Statute is consistent with treating articles 6, 7, 8 and 8 *bis* as largely reflective of customary international law. To the extent that they are not, individuals in the aforementioned circumstances may challenge the Court's jurisdiction over them.[98]

7.6 Applicable law (article 21)

Applicable law is set out hierarchically in article 21(1) of the Rome Statute:

1. The Court shall apply:
    (a) *In the first place*, this Statute, Elements of Crimes and its Rules of Procedure and Evidence;
    (b) *In the second place*, where appropriate, applicable treaties and the principles and rules of international law, including the established principles of the international law of armed conflict . . . [99]

This ordering might give rise to questions about whether the Rome Statute is reflective of custom. If it is, then why would Elements of Crimes have priority over custom, and why would treaty law have the same ranking as custom? Article 21(1), the ranking of sources therein, is addressed to the legal task of gap filling, not interpretation. When judges are confronted with a legal issue, they must first apply the Statute, as required by article 21(1). If, however, the Statute is ambiguous in some way, judges must interpret the impugned provision to resolve the ambiguity. If the interpreted words do not resolve all of the legal issues before the Court and if there are legal issues arising in the case on which the Statute is silent, then judges must also engage in the further task of gap filling. If the gap pertains to the definitions of crimes, judges are required by articles 21(1)(a) and 9 to ascertain if the Elements of Crimes can assist them with formulating an answer. If the Elements are not helpful, then judges must apply treaty and customary law in an attempt to fill the gap in the Statute. Read this way, one sees that article 21 is silent on the issue of whether

---

[95] Broomhall (n. 35) 729.
[96] On this possibility, see Final Act of the Rome Conference (n. 50) Annex I, Res. E.
[97] Broomhall (n. 35) 729.
[98] For a slightly different view, see KS Gallant, *The Principle of Legality in International Comparative Criminal Law* (Cambridge University Press 2008) 339–40.
[99] Emphasis added.

custom should or should not be a primary aid for judges engaged in the task of interpreting crimes in the Statute. It is equally silent on whether the Elements of Crimes or other applicable sources of law should be the primary interpretive aid used by judges.

The distinction between interpretation and gap filling was not always clear in the jurisprudence of the ICTY and ICTR but has become clearer at the International Criminal Court. Not only has this distinction been entrenched in article 21 of the Rome Statute, which makes alternating references to 'interpretation' and 'application' of the Rome Statute, but judges of the Court have also distinguished between these legal tasks.[100] Gap filling has been defined as 'an "objective" which could be inferred from the context or the object and purpose of the Statute, an objective which would not be given effect by the express provisions of the Statute or the Rules of Procedure and Evidence, thus obliging the judge to resort to the second or third source of law [in article 21(1)] – in that order – to give effect to that objective'.[101] Accordingly, article 21(1) is a bit of a red herring for those trying to understand the status of the applicable sources of law as aids to interpreting crimes in the Rome Statute. At most, it confirms that custom and the Elements, by virtue of having the status of applicable law, are at least authoritative interpretive aids, meaning their consideration is mandatory if relevant.[102] However, article 21 does not clarify the relationship between these aids.

7.7 The Rome Statute's relationship to international law (articles 10 and 22(3) and Understanding 4)

A key consideration for the present inquiry is article 10. Located in part II of the Rome Statute, which deals with jurisdiction, admissibility and applicable law, and the only provision in the Statute that does not have a heading, it reads: 'Nothing in this Part shall be interpreted as limiting or prejudicing in any way existing or developing rules of international law for purposes other than this

---

[100] *Prosecutor* v. *Lubanga Dyilo*, Judgment on the Appeal of Mr Thomas Lubanga Dyilo against the Decision on the Defence Challenge to the Jurisdiction of the Court pursuant to Article 19(2)(a) of the Statute of 3 October 2006, ICC-01/04–01/06–772, 14 December 2006, para. 34.

[101] G Bitti, 'Article 21 of the Statute of the International Criminal Court and the Treatment of Sources of Law in the Jurisprudence of the ICC' in C Stahn and G Sluiter (eds.), *The Emerging Practice of the International Criminal Court* (Brill 2008) 285, 295 (citing *Democratic Republic of Congo Situation*, Judgment on the Prosecutor's Application for Extraordinary Review of the Pre-Trial Chamber I's 31 March 2006 Decision Denying Leave to Appeal, ICC-01/04–168, 13 July 2006, para. 39).

[102] RS Summers and M Taruffo, 'Interpretation and Comparative Analysis' in DN MacCormick and RS Summers (eds.), *Interpreting Statutes: A Comparative Study* (Ashgate 1991) 461, 475–76.

Statute.' This provision was introduced during the Preparatory Committee sessions[103] and was not discussed much at Rome.[104] Article 10 was proposed by Professor Bassiouni of Egypt to allay concerns about the codification of some but not all international crimes in the Rome Statute.[105] Originally, the draft provision was intended to speak only to the definitions of war crimes in the Statute.[106] At Rome, several delegations supported draft article 10, and the International Committee of the Red Cross (ICRC) stated that it was of 'critical importance' for two reasons: 'It is essential that the Statute of the Court indicates that it in no way affects existing international humanitarian law nor impede its development.'[107] The ICRC also pointed out that the list of war crimes was underinclusive and that the status of excluded war crimes under customary international law should not thereby be called into question.[108]

Although it has been analogized to a reservation[109] or 'without prejudice' clause in other treaties, there is no exact precedent for the wording used in article 10.[110] Absent its inclusion, there are at least two ways in which the Rome Statute might mistakenly be construed as limiting or prejudicing existing or developing international criminal law. First, definitions of crimes in the Rome Statute might be retrogressive relative to existing law or might go beyond it (substantive legal departure). Second, the absence in the Statute of all crimes under customary international law might give the Court jurisdiction in some but not all cases (jurisdictional departure). The goal of article 10 was therefore to ensure that these substantive and jurisdictional departures 'would not negatively impact either the existing customary international framework or the development of new customary law'.[111] Article 10 thus 'underscores the framers' wish to preserve the role of custom in the development of normative standards of conduct in the area of international criminal justice'.[112] As has rightly been pointed out, this role of custom as an independent source of international criminal law outside the Rome Statute is already an accepted legal principle.[113]

---

[103] Article 10 was originally referred to as article Y and read: 'Without prejudice to the application of the provisions of the Statute, nothing in this part of the Statute shall be interpreted as limiting or prejudicing in any way existing or developing rules of international law.' Preparatory Committee, Draft Statute for the International Criminal Court (1998), UN Doc. A/CONF.183/2/Add.1, 2, 25.

[104] Von Hebel and Robinson (n. 94) 88.   [105] Sadat (n. 35) 910–11.

[106] WA Schabas, *The International Criminal Court: A Commentary on the Rome Statute* (Oxford University Press 2010) 269.

[107] International Committee of the Red Cross, 'Statement of 8 July 1998 Relating to the Bureau Discussion Paper in Document A/CONF.183/C.1/L.53', UN Doc. A/CONF.183/INF/10, para. 4.

[108] Ibid.

[109] O Triffterer, 'Article 10' in O Triffterer (ed.), *Commentary on the Rome Statute of the International Criminal Court*, 2nd edn (CH Beck/Hart/Nomos 2008) 531, 533.

[110] Sadat (n. 35) 917.   [111] Ibid. 910–11.   [112] Ibid. 912.

[113] Triffterer (n. 109) 534 (citing *Case Concerning Military and Paramilitary Activities in and Against Nicaragua (Nicaragua v. United States of America)* [1986] ICJ Rep. 14, 95–96).

Was the role of article 10 merely to reinforce this principle in the Rome regime? One theory posits that 'without prejudice' may in reality 'be an open admission of a failure to resolve salient matters of substance in the negotiations leading to the treaty'.[114] This could very well be true of the Rome Statute. Delegates at Rome were acutely aware that developments in the field of international criminal law are occurring at a fast pace, and they experienced many difficulties in reaching consensus on the inclusion and definitions of certain crimes. Accordingly, they did not want the language in the Rome Statute to negatively influence the progressive development of the law in this area:[115]

> [T]he mere fact that there was dispute over which of these crimes should fall under the jurisdiction of the court and that a compromise may limit them to "the most serious crimes of international concern", should not bar their progressive development towards new crimes within this category nor raise the impression that absence of an agreement about an international jurisdiction for certain crimes would mean that such crimes and their punishability directly under international law do not exist.[116]

Indeed, the Preparatory Committee at an early stage decided that 'it was more important to identify opportunities for compromise than to strive for a perfect solution in one or the other direction'.[117] As well, when the General Assembly convened the Diplomatic Conference in Rome, it recognized 'the importance of concluding the work of the conference through the promotion of general agreement on matters of substance'.[118] Relying on these facts and analogizing article 10 to a reservations clause, it has been suggested that the definitions of crimes in the Rome Statute are restricted to the work of the Court and have no binding effect on States Parties (e.g., for national prosecutions on behalf of the international community and when conducting trials pursuant to the principle of complementarity)[119] or ad hoc tribunals.[120] Similarly, it has been suggested that a strong form of State practice for ascertaining custom is a widely accepted multilateral treaty, and so article 10 acts as a bar to arguments that 'much of the substantive law in the Statute was essentially a codification of the customary international law outside the Statute'.[121] In fact, it 'had been agreed during the Preparatory Committee negotiations that the *Rome Statute* would not constitute a codification of international criminal law'.[122] Instead, the exercise in relation to substantive crimes at the Rome Diplomatic Conference was to negotiate the material jurisdiction of the new Court, which would

---

[114] Dinstein (n. 23) 383.   [115] Triffterer (n. 109) 533.   [116] Ibid. 531.

[117] Ibid. 532, 533.   [118] UNGA Res. 52/160 (15 December 1997).

[119] Triffterer (n. 109) 533.   [120] Ibid. 535.

[121] Sadat (n. 35) 918. See also WA Schabas, *An Introduction to the International Criminal Court*, 2nd edn (Cambridge University Press 2004) 28.

[122] TLH McCormack and S Robertson 'Jurisdictional Aspects of the Rome Statute for the New International Criminal Court' (1999) 23 Melb U L Rev 635, 653.

only ever deal with 'the most serious crimes of concern to the international community'.[123]

Some of these views seem to go too far. Article 10 is not a denial that the definitions of crimes in the Rome Statute are reflective of customary international law. The better legal view seems to be that article 10 is merely analogous to a 'without prejudice clause'. It thereby acknowledges that some definitions might fall short of custom or go beyond it and that some crimes under customary international law are not included in the Rome Statute at all. A classic 'without prejudice' clause can be found in article 4 of the *Vienna Convention on the Law of Treaties* (1969): 'Without prejudice to the application of any rules set forth in the present Convention to which treaties would be subject under international law independently of the Convention, the Convention applies only to treaties which are concluded by States after the entry into force of the present Convention with regard to such States.' Similarly, article 10 'was intended to emphasize that the inclusion or non-inclusion in the ICC Statute of certain norms would not prejudice the positions of States on the customary status of such norms, would not prejudice existing norms or future development of international law, and would not authorize the ICC to apply existing or new norms omitted deliberately in the ICC Statute'.[124]

Thus, article 10 does not foreclose assertions that the definitions of crimes in the Rome Statute are reflective of customary law.[125] And to the extent that the definitions of crimes in the Rome Statute are reflective of customary international law, they are binding on *all* individuals acting anywhere, not just nationals of States Parties or those engaging in criminal conduct on their territory. To assert otherwise would be to ignore the continued existence of custom.[126]

Another nuance in the literature on article 10 is the suggestion that it speaks only to definitions of crimes in the Rome Statute that fall short of custom and not to definitions that go beyond it.[127] It is argued that drafters intended for the latter departures from custom to crystallize into custom:[128] 'Certainly article 10 was not intended to provide China with a basis upon which to argue that the internal armed conflict provisions were not now (if they were not already) agreed-upon norms of customary international law.'[129] While many have suggested that these provisions did crystallize into

---

[123] Ibid.   [124] Kittichaisaree (n. 15) 52.

[125] Sadat and Carden (n. 5) 423 argue that article 10 does foreclose such assertions but will not operate effectively.

[126] Articles 38 and 43, *Vienna Convention* (1969).

[127] Dinstein (n. 23) 390; Sadat (n. 35) 918; R Cryer, *Prosecuting International Crimes: Selectivity and the International Criminal Law Regime* (Cambridge University Press 2005) 174–75.

[128] Sadat, ibid.   [129] Ibid.

custom upon their inclusion in the Rome Statute,[130] the aforementioned understanding of article 10 does not seem to be supported by its wording.

Although article 10 lacks clarity,[131] it does refer to both 'limiting' as well as 'prejudicing', which suggests that the two words should be given distinct meanings. The reference to 'limiting' might be to the exclusion of some crimes under customary international law or retrogressive definitions of crimes in the Rome Statute. The reference to 'prejudicing' might also refer to these concepts, but it could refer to the idea that progressive definitions of crimes in the Rome Statute are not automatically assumed by the States Parties as being reflective of custom. As previously mentioned, consensus was lacking on the customary status of every aspect of every definition. Accordingly, the better legal view is that article 10 'cuts both ways':

> Those who argue that customary law goes beyond the Statute . . . can rely on this provision. It will become more and more important in the future, because customary law should evolve and the Statute may not be able to keep pace with it. . . . But, of course, the logic of Article 10 cuts both ways. To those who claim that the Statute sets a new minimum standard, . . . conservative jurists will plead Article 10 and stress the differences between the texts in the Statute and their less prolix ancestors.[132]

This view has also found support among judges at the ICTY:

> [N]otwithstanding article 10 of the Statute, . . . resort may be had . . . to these provisions [of the Rome Statute] to help elucidate customary international law. Depending on the matter at issue, the Rome Statute may be taken to restate, reflect or clarify customary rules or crystallise them, whereas in some areas it creates new law or modifies existing law.[133]

Seen this way, in order for the definition of a crime to be applied to a national or territory of a State that has not consented to this at the relevant time, a judge needs to be satisfied that any seemingly retrogressive *or* progressive aspect of that definition is reflective of customary international law. Article 10 cannot be read to affirm perfect correspondence between custom and the definitions of crimes and thereby relieve a judge of this concern.

Article 22(3), like article 10, confirms that the exclusion of certain crimes from the Rome Statute 'shall not affect the characterization of any conduct

---

[130] C Kreß, 'War Crimes Committed in Non-International Armed Conflict and the Emerging System of International Criminal Justice' (2000) 30 Israel Ybk Human Rights 103.

[131] Von Hebel and Robinson (n. 94) 88.

[132] Schabas (n. 121) 28. More recently, Schabas has taken the view that '[t]he best approach would be to read article 10 narrowly, and to confine its scope to the definitions of war crimes to the extent possible.' Schabas (n. 106) 272, 409.

[133] *Furundžija* (n. 14) para. 227. This holding was confirmed by the ICTY Appeals Chamber in *Prosecutor v. Tadić*, Judgment, ICTY-94–1-A, 15 July 1999, para. 223. See also *Prosecutor v. Kupreškić and Others*, Judgment, ICTY-95–16-T, 14 January 2000, para. 580.

as criminal under international law independently of this Statute'. A treaty can partially codify an area of law.[134] In addition, article 22(3) clarifies that application of the legality principle in article 22, which might result in a ruling that certain conduct is *ultra vires* the Court's jurisdiction, does not mean that the conduct is not criminal under international law. Accordingly, article 22(3) also ensures that individual criminal responsibility arising under customary international law will continue to exist and develop external to the Rome Statute and that the application of article 22 by the Court will in no way undermine this or determinations by national courts and international tribunals.[135] Legality is an adjudicative tool, meaning that the outcomes it produces do not speak to whether conduct is condemned or not by the international community.[136]

Interestingly, courts and tribunals have 'largely ignored' article 10 and used definitions of crimes in the Rome Statute to interpret other treaties, regarding the former as reflective of custom.[137] Despite the existence of article 10, 'the *Rome Statute* is one of the major international instruments of our time, most of whose principles represent a consensus reached by a large number of States following a lengthy and complex drafting process. Its provisions will inevitably influence the evolution of international law'.[138]

The Court's jurisdiction is derived from the Rome Statute, which is the first applicable source of law identified in article 21. Thus, articles 6, 7, 8 and 8 *bis* bind only the Court and are not intended to create a universally binding criminal code for the international community.[139] They aim to define the Court's jurisdiction and not 'to codify, or restate, or contribute to the development of customary international law'.[140] Further, article 10 reminds one of the general international rule that customary law continues to exist and develop alongside treaty law even where the two contain identical rules.[141] It therefore guards against 'the danger of an "encrustation" of international criminal law'.[142] Similarly, article 22(3) operates to 'prevent the perception that the Statute would rob general international law of its power to criminalize behaviour, or would narrow the scope of any such criminalization outside the ICC regime, such that non-States parties could then claim a greater degree of impunity than would be the case had the Statute not been adopted at all'.[143]

Articles 10 and 22(3) are therefore intended to contain the influence of the Rome Statute on the development of custom – even if this objective has been 'largely ignored' – but not necessarily the influence of custom on the

---

[134] See Chapter 6, Section 6.3.
[135] Broomhall (n. 35) 726.   [136] See Chapter 4, Section 4.3.2.
[137] Schabas (n. 106) 271. See article 31(3)(c), *Vienna Convention* (1969).
[138] Schabas, ibid.   [139] Cassese (n. 15) 14, 56.   [140] Ibid.
[141] *Nicaragua* (n. 113) 95; Triffterer (n. 109) 533–34.
[142] Werle (n. 30) 45.   [143] Broomhall (n. 35) 726–27.

Rome Statute for purposes of interpretation. The recognition of custom as an interpretive aid would not undermine the purpose of these provisions or require the Court to treat articles 6, 7, 8 and 8 *bis* as codifying international criminal law. Article 10 ensures that States can continue to take positions on the (non-)customary status of certain norms[144] by distinguishing between the Rome regime and general international law.[145]

Finally, it is worth noting that interpretive Understanding 4 in annex III to the resolution on aggression adopted by the Review Conference states:

> 4. It is understood that the amendments that address the definition of the act of aggression and the crime of aggression do so for the purpose of this Statute only. The amendments shall, in accordance with article 10 of the Rome Statute, not be interpreted as limiting or prejudicing in any way existing or developing rules of international law for purposes other than this Statute.

At the Review Conference, the United States expressed concern about the definitions of the crime and act of aggression in the resolution not being reflective of custom and therefore sought the adoption of an understanding that the amendments 'shall not be interpreted as constituting a statement of the definition of "crime of aggression" or "act of aggression" under customary international law'.[146] Further, a leading member of the American delegation at the Review Conference stated that the definition of aggression in article 8 *bis* 'does not truly reflect customary international law'.[147] However, there was 'virtually no support for this proposal', according to the focal point for the bilateral negotiations on this matter, and so the aforementioned Understanding was adopted.[148] The negotiation background of Understanding 4 lends support to the proposed interpretation of article 10.

7.8 Definitions of crimes (articles 5–8 *bis*)

The prohibition of aggression, genocide, other crimes against humanity and violations of basic rules of humanitarian law are among the most frequently cited international norms to have the status of *jus cogens*.[149] As categories of

---

[144] Von Hebel and Robinson (n. 94) 88.   [145] Cassese (n. 15) 157.

[146] United States, 'Proposed "Understandings"', circulated informally at the Review Conference of the Rome Statute of the International Criminal Court, 6 June 2010 (on file with author).

[147] Harold Hongju Koh, Legal Adviser, U.S. Department of State, Statement at the Review Conference of the International Criminal Court, 4 June 2010, www.state.gov/s/l/releases/remarks/142665.htm, accessed 2 November 2013.

[148] C Kreß, 'Harmony and Dissonance in International Law' (2011) 105 ASIL Proceedings 160, 161.

[149] Koskenniemi (n. 18) 158–59.

crimes under international law, their customary legal status is not terribly controversial. Also, these prohibitions are considered to give rise to *erga omnes* obligations, meaning obligations that are owed to the international community as a whole.[150] In spite of the normative status and scope of these categories of crimes, it must be recalled that each category contains within it a list of individual crimes, and each of these crimes consists of material and mental elements. Such details are in the Rome Statute and accompanying Elements of Crimes[151] and beg the question whether custom is reflected at these deeper levels or whether major departures from custom are discernible. In this section, scholarly commentary on the customary status of the crimes listed in the Rome Statute will briefly be surveyed. For the crime of aggression, such commentary is generally lacking, given that a definition for this crime under the Rome Statute was not adopted until very recently.

7.8.1 'For the purpose of this Statute'

The definitions of crimes in articles 6, 7, 8 and 8 *bis* all begin with the words 'For the purpose of this Statute'. It has been suggested that this phrase serves the same function as article 10 by indicating that the drafters did not intend for the Rome Statute to be mistaken for a complete codification of international criminal law[152] and that any modification of custom in the Rome Statute is without prejudice to its development and States Parties' positions on its content.[153]

As well, such language can prevent the falling into desuetude of these conventional definitions should customary definitions upon which they are based subsequently be modified to such an extent (and thereby fall into desuetude) that they cannot be accommodated by the wording of the definitions in the Rome Statute.[154] Further, should treaty crimes be added to the Rome Statute (or already exist in the Rome Statute, according to the opinion of some),[155]

---

[150] See, e.g., *Case concerning the Barcelona Traction, Light and Power Company, Limited (Belgium* v. *Spain) (Second Phase)* [1970] ICJ Rep. 3, 32; *Furundžija* (n. 14) paras. 151, 153; Koskenniemi (n. 18) 162; IDI, Obligations and Rights (n. 27); IDI, The Protection of Human Rights (n. 27).

[151] For the crime of aggression, this information is in the Aggression Resolution (n. 54), which includes elements for this crime.

[152] Schabas (n. 121) 28, fn. 7.

[153] M Boot, R Dixon and CK Hall (revised by CK Hall), 'Article 7' in O Triffterer (ed.), *Commentary on the Rome Statute of the International Criminal Court*, 2nd edn (CH Beck/Hart/Nomos 2008) 159, 170.

[154] ME Villiger, *Customary International Law and Treaties* (Martinus Nijhoff 1985) 216–17: 'The original customary rule will pass out of use for lack of widespread practice and *opinio juris*.'

[155] An example of this is the crime of apartheid as a crime against humanity. Cassese (n. 15) 126.

this wording also resolves problems arising from subsequent treaties (e.g., in statutes of ad hoc tribunals) dealing with the same subject matter and any conflict between them and the definitions of treaty crimes in the Rome Statute.[156] It does away with the need to include a conflict clause in the Rome Statute. A conflict clause can either prohibit the application of incompatible subsequent conventional definitions of crimes or expressly permit them, providing they are 'compatible' with the existing definitions in the Rome Statute.[157] A conflict clause can also provide that the Rome Statute is not to be considered incompatible with later treaty definitions of crimes, meaning subsequent treaty definitions would prevail.[158] The absence of any conflict clause and the phrase 'For the purpose of this Statute' suggest that the Rome Statute was conceived of as a self-contained regime with the definitions contained therein at the top of the legal hierarchy.

7.8.2 Aggression

The definition in article 8 *bis*(1) of the individual act of aggression is based on the Nuremberg, Tokyo and Control Council Law No. 10 precedents, and the State act of aggression is based on General Assembly Resolution 3314 (XXIX). As these are the main written reflections of State practice and *opinio juris* on the subject, it is difficult to argue that the Special Working Group was not interested in aligning the definition of the crime and State act of aggression in the Rome Statute with their counterparts under general international law. Concerning Nuremberg, the UN General Assembly in 1946 affirmed 'the principles of international law recognized by the Charter of the Nuremberg Tribunal and the judgment of the Tribunal',[159] thereby evidencing the *opinio juris* of the international community.[160] As for General Assembly Resolution 3314 (XXIX), which contains a definition of aggression for the purpose of article 39 of the Charter of the United Nations, it was adopted by consensus, and the International Court of Justice has affirmed that it is at least partly reflective of custom.[161] Some have alleged that the definition of aggression departs

---

[156] For the International Law Commission's commentary on the problem of conflicting treaties, see Waldock (n. 89) 34ff.

[157] Koskenniemi (n. 18) 115.

[158] See article 30(2), *Vienna Convention* (1969). On the possible role of subsequent developments in international law in the interpretation of crimes in the Rome Statute, see Chapter 9, Section 9.3 on time and the law.

[159] UNGA, 'Affirmation of the Principles of International Law Recognized by the Charter of the Nürnberg Tribunal' (1946), UN Doc. Res. 95 (I).

[160] MD Öberg, 'The Legal Effects of Resolutions of the Security Council and General Assembly in the Jurisprudence of the ICJ' (2006) 16 EJIL 879, 898–900.

[161] In fact, the International Court of Justice decided that the provision in article 3(g) of the definition reflects customary international law. *Nicaragua* (n. 113) para. 3; see also

from that found in post-Second World War precedents and General Assembly Resolution 3314 (XXIX) in places.

Two departures from precedents have been observed. First, it has been argued that these precedents created a leadership standard that is lower than that reflected in article 8 *bis*(1) by criminalizing the conduct of persons who could 'shape and influence' national policy, not only those who are 'in a position to effectively exercise control over or to direct the military action of a State.'[162] This difference in language is thought to exclude the prosecution of non-governmental actors (e.g., industrialists, arms dealers) who are instrumental in carrying out an act of aggression, as well as third States who lend critical support to the aggressing State.[163] This difficult issue cannot be resolved in a cursory manner. The preparatory works of the Special Working Group evidence, however, that its members did not necessarily intend by using this language to categorically exclude non-governmental actors from the Rome regime.[164] Further, article 8 *bis* does not expressly exclude the possibility of the leader of a third State lending support to an aggressing State and thereby being subject to prosecution – in fact, article 8 *bis*(2)(f) and (g) contemplates exactly this: 'The action of a State in allowing its territory, which it has placed at the disposal of another State, to be used by that other State for perpetrating an act of aggression against a third State'; and '[t]he sending by *or on behalf of a State* of armed bands, groups, irregulars or mercenaries, which carry out acts of armed force against another State of such gravity as to amount to the acts listed above, or its substantial involvement therein'.[165]

Second, scholars have noted that article 8 *bis*(1) does not expressly mention that the perpetrator must be aware of a special collective intent that was considered to be an element of the crime of aggression – the State act requirement specifically – in some of the post-Second World War jurisprudence; an intent

---

Armed Activities on the Territory of the Congo (Democratic Republic of the Congo v. Uganda) [2005] ICJ Rep. 168.

[162] T Weigend, '"In General a Principle of Justice" – The Debate on the 'Crime against Peace' in the Wake of the Nuremberg Judgment' (2012) 10 J Int'l Crim Justice 41, 57.

[163] KJ Heller, 'Retreat from Nuremberg – the Leadership Requirement in the Crime of Aggression' (2007) 18 EJIL 477, 479–88. For a summary of the profiles of individuals tried following the Second World War for the crime of aggression, see Preparatory Commission, Working Group on the Crime of Aggression (Secretariat), 'Historical Review of Developments relating to Aggression', Part I (18 January 2002), UN Doc. PCNICC/2002/WGCA/L.1/Add.1, 32–45 (Historical Review). Allied Control Council Law No. 10 specifically provided that both private economic actors and complicit third-State officials could be convicted of crimes against peace. 15 Trials of War Criminals Before the Nürnberg Military Tribunals Under Control Council Law No. 10 (1951) art. II, para. 2(f), 20 December 1945.

[164] See Coalition for the International Criminal Court, *Report of the CICC Team on the Crime of Aggression* (2005) 30–31.

[165] Emphasis added.

to conquer and subjugate another State.[166] Whether this intent is a customary element of the crime cannot be explored in any detail here, except to note that several post-Second World War cases did not consider this to be an element of the crime;[167] the Special Working Group apparently could not agree on how to define this intent;[168] and the 'manifest' threshold in article 8 *bis*(1) was a 'more modest' attempt to deal with this issue.[169]

If this intent does exist under customary international law but cannot be accommodated by the wording of article 8 *bis* it has been suggested that the definition of the crime of aggression may depart 'slightly' from custom, that this departure might merely be a function of clarifying and transposing unwritten and imprecise custom into proscriptive written rules and that this departure may well have crystallized or, in the future, may crystallize into custom.[170]

As for General Assembly Resolution 3314 (XXIX), its customary legal status has been called into question by some.[171] Others have pointed to the Nuremberg Charter criminalizing only a 'war' of aggression, followed by Control Council Law No. 10 criminalizing 'invasions'.[172] However, on the latter point, it is interesting to note that following the Second World War, judges

> considered the nature and characteristics of a war of aggression in deter-
> mining the charges of crimes against peace in relation to the specific facts
> and circumstances of the cases that were before them. Thus, the judge-
> ments of the tribunals provide further guidance as to the type of conduct
> by a State which may constitute a war of aggression depending on the stage
> of the military operations, including the threat of force, *an armed attack,
> invasion, occupation, annexation or incorporation, and war.*[173]

The distinction drawn between this jurisprudence and the definition in article 8 *bis*(2) may therefore not be as great as initially thought when merely reading the definitions in the governing statutes.

On balance, what the amendments adopted at the Review Conference suggest is an attempt to limit the Court's jurisdiction to the 'clearest' cases of aggression under customary international law.[174] This is evidenced by the definitions closely mirroring legal precedents on aggression, limiting the crime to a leadership offence and requiring the act of aggression manifestly to violate the Charter of the United Nations. To the extent that elements of this offence

---

[166] M Milanovic, 'Aggression and Legality: Custom in Kampala' (2012) 10 J Int'l Crim Justice 165.

[167] Historical Review (n. 163) 60–62.

[168] C Kreß, 'Time for Decision: Some Thoughts on the Immediate Future of the Crime of Aggression: A Reply to Andreas Paulus' (2009) 20 EJIL 1139, 1139–40.

[169] Ibid. 1140.   [170] Kreß (n. 168) 1140.

[171] See, e.g., *Uganda* (n. 161) Separate Opinion of Judge Kooijmans, 306, para. 63.

[172] Historical Review (n. 163); Preparatory Commission, Working Group on the Crime of Aggression (Secretariat), 'Historical Review of Developments relating to Aggression', pt. II (24 January 2002), UN Doc. PCNICC/2002/WGCA/L.1/Add.1.

[173] Historical Review (n. 163) 8 (emphasis added).   [174] Barriga and Grover (n. 54) 532.

are considered to depart from custom, they might well crystallize into custom in the coming years as States ratify the amendments on aggression and take a decision in 2017 or later to activate the Court's jurisdiction over this crime.

7.8.3 Genocide

Although not perfect,[175] States were hesitant to alter the definition of genocide in the *Convention on the Prevention and Punishment of the Crime of Genocide* (1948) (*Genocide Convention*),[176] as it is widely regarded as reflective of custom:[177]

> It was argued that a modified definition would have questionable status under customary international law and might produce conflicting obligations for States Parties to the Statute when incorporating the crime in their national legislation. Notwithstanding this clear trend, a few proposals to expand the definitions were made during the 1996 sessions of the Preparatory Committee. However, none of these suggestions were included in the text.[178]

Indeed, there was 'overwhelming support' for not debating a revised definition of genocide.[179] The goal of building consensus in this case was consistent with adopting the customary legal definition of this category of crime. The Rome Statute is widely regarded as codifying the customary definition of genocide.[180] But it is not regarded as a complete codification by some. Cassese points out that, unlike article III of the *Genocide Convention* (1948), the Rome Statute does not prohibit 'conspiracy to commit genocide', the crime of planning and organizing genocide without actually perpetrating it.[181] However, a treaty may partially codify custom. In addition, even though States agreed to use the definition of genocide in the *Genocide Convention* (1948), the footnotes accompanying the draft text reflect different interpretations of this crime.[182]

---

[175] McCormack and Robertson (n. 122) 635.

[176] 78 UNTS 277 (adopted 9 December 1948, entered into force 12 January 1951).

[177] See, e.g., *Reservations to the Convention on the Prevention and Punishment of the Crime of Genocide*, Advisory Opinion [1951] ICJ Rep. 15, 23.

[178] See Von Hebel and Robinson (n. 94) 89 for details of these proposals. See also Sadat and Carden (n. 5) 425.

[179] McCormack and Robertson (n. 122) 635.

[180] See, e.g., GM Danilenko, 'The Statute of the International Criminal Court and Third States' (1999–2000) 21 Mich J Int'l L 445, 482; UNSC, 'Report of the Secretary-General Pursuant to Paragraph 5 of Security Council Resolution 955' (1994), UN Doc. S/1995/134, para. 45.

[181] Cassese (n. 15) 146.   [182] (14 February 1997), UN Doc. A/AC.249/1997/WG.1/CRP.1.

7.8.4 Crimes against humanity

The category of crimes against humanity has been recognized repeatedly since the end of the Second World War under international law, and while definitions for it have varied somewhat over the years, 'considerable consistency' in respect of certain elements is discernible.[183] However, unlike other crimes in the Rome Statute, drafting the definition of crimes against humanity was not aided by a conventional definition that had attracted a lot of support. Instead, drafters had to draw inspiration from a number of sources, including the Nuremberg and Tokyo Charters, Control Council Law No. 10, the ILC Draft Codes, the ICTY and ICTR statutes and relevant jurisprudence.[184] Although all of these instruments contain lists of acts amounting to crimes against humanity, important differences exist between them,[185] and none of them are the product of a large multilateral negotiation,[186] thus giving rise to diverging views and difficult negotiations.[187] Indeed, two weeks of negotiations were needed for this category of crime during the five-week conference in Rome.[188]

In 1998, States were concerned about distinguishing crimes against humanity from 'ordinary' crimes under domestic law and 'determining which acts are punishable under international law as a matter of individual criminal liability, as opposed to State responsibility for violations of human rights'.[189] Thus, negotiating the threshold or chapeau provision for this category of crime was a difficult and delicate process.[190] The resulting threshold contains three important elements.

First, although States were divided on whether a crime against humanity is a distinct crime or must be committed as part of an armed conflict, delegates finally agreed that this nexus is no longer required under customary international law (if it ever was), a position that is consistent with the majority of the legal authorities.[191] Second, States were able to agree that a crime against humanity occurs as part of a widespread *or* systematic attack against a civilian population, which is consistent with the ICTY and ICTR jurisprudence as well as other authorities thought to be reflective of customary international

---

[183] Boot, Dixon and Hall (n. 153) 159, 167.

[184] D Robinson, 'The Elements of Crimes Against Humanity' in RS Lee (ed.), *The International Criminal Court: Elements of Crimes and Rules of Procedure and Evidence* (Transnational 2001) 58.

[185] Danilenko (n. 180) 483–84; Robinson, ibid. 62.

[186] McCormack and Robertson (n. 122) 635.

[187] GM Danilenko, 'ICC Statute and Third States' in A Cassese and Others (eds.), *The Rome Statute of the International Criminal Court: A Commentary*, vol. II (Oxford University Press 2002) 1871, 1892 (citing (1994) II Ybk of the ILC 40).

[188] McCormack and Robertson (n. 122) 635.

[189] Sadat and Carden (n. 5) 427.   [190] Robinson (n. 184) 62.

[191] Ibid. 58; McCormack and Robertson (n. 122) 635.

law.[192] This requirement helps to exclude isolated crimes from the definition of crimes against humanity.[193] Third, States were divided about whether all crimes against humanity must be committed with a discriminatory intent or whether such intent is limited to the crime of persecution as a crime against humanity.[194] France and a few other delegations asserted that a discriminatory intent on the basis of national, political, ethnic, racial or religious grounds must exist, as is reflected in the ICTR statute.[195] Consistent with the bulk of authorities, a large majority of States rejected this requirement, finding that it is not required by customary international law for all crimes against humanity, just the crime of persecution.[196]

One threshold requirement articulated in the Elements of Crimes has sparked controversy. According to article 7(2)(a) and the Elements of Crimes, an 'attack directed against a civilian population' is understood to mean an attack 'pursuant to or in furtherance of a State or organizational policy to commit such attack. . . . It is understood that "policy to commit such attack" requires that the State or organization actively promote or encourage such an attack against a civilian population.'[197] The customary legal status of this requirement has been called into question, and it has been suggested that it might be sufficient that the attack was 'accepted, or tolerated, or acquiesced in by the state or the organization . . .'[198] Indeed, a footnote in the Elements to this policy requirement suggests this, which reflects the views of the majority of delegations.[199]

Regarding the list of crimes against humanity, some have had their customary legal status questioned while others have been accepted, but the customary legal status of certain elements of these crimes has been called into question. Beginning with extermination as a crime against humanity, some have disputed whether extermination can occur if a person kills only one person, as suggested in the Elements of Crimes.[200] As well, while torture as a crime against humanity

---

[192] Robinson, ibid.; von Hebel and Robinson (n. 94) 94. Cassese observes that article 7 falls short of custom by referring to the victim or target of a crime against humanity as 'any civilian population', thereby possibly excluding non-civilians (e.g., military). However, if read to include belligerents *hors de combat*, this would bring it more in line with custom. Cassese (n. 15) 125.

[193] Robinson, ibid. The requirement in the Elements of Crimes that the accused have knowledge of the attack is also considered to be consistent with customary international law. Cassese, ibid. 123–24.

[194] Robinson, ibid. 62; von Hebel and Robinson (n. 94) 123.

[195] von Hebel and Robinson, ibid. 93–94.   [196] Ibid. 93–94, 123.

[197] Article 7, introduction, para. 3, Elements of Crimes.   [198] Cassese (n. 15) 125.

[199] Robinson (n. 184) 78. It provides that such a policy 'may, in exceptional circumstances, be implemented by a deliberate failure to take action, which is consciously aimed at encouraging such attack. The existence of such a policy cannot be inferred solely from the absence of government or organizational action.' Article 7, fn. 6, Elements of Crimes.

[200] Article 7(1)(b), element 1, Elements of Crimes.

is also not doubted, some have questioned whether torture can be committed by a person who is not acting in an official capacity, a notion implied in the Rome Statute and Elements of Crimes.[201] Others think that the definition of torture as a crime against humanity is correct in this regard by being broader than the definition of torture *simpliciter* as a crime under customary international law.[202] Another example is the absence of a requirement that the act of torture as a crime against humanity be carried out for a specific purpose.[203] There is simply no reference to purpose at all.[204]

Article 7(1)(g) of the Rome Statute criminalizes as crimes against humanity '[r]ape, sexual slavery, enforced prostitution, forced pregnancy, enforced sterilization, or any other form of sexual violence of comparable gravity'. Some have suggested that the inclusion of forced pregnancy broadens the definition of crimes against humanity but might crystallize into custom over time.[205] It has also been suggested that the drafters did not regard this provision as expanding the definition of crimes against humanity but rather as making explicit acts that are considered 'inhumane' by the international community.[206] Recall that a residual category of crimes against humanity is '[o]ther inhumane acts of a similar character intentionally causing great suffering, or serious injury to body or to mental or physical health'.[207] A similar 'catch-all' provision appeared in the Nuremberg and Tokyo Charters and in the ICTY and ICTR statutes. One may therefore conclude that in respect of crimes against humanity at least, such a residual clause has acquired customary legal status.[208]

Persecution as a crime against humanity under customary international law is not contested. However, the definition of this crime in article 7(1)(h) of the Rome Statute is thought by some to go beyond custom in its long list of grounds of persecution, which have or may eventually crystallize into custom.[209] As well, since delegates could not agree on whether this list should be exhaustive or not, they ultimately decided to leave it open but limited to 'other grounds that are universally recognized as impermissible under international law'.[210] It has been suggested that this phrase should be interpreted to mean 'widely recognized'.[211] However, article 21(3) refers to 'internationally recognized human rights', and it is curious that article 7(1)(h) uses the term

---

[201] Article 7(1)(f), Elements of Crimes.

[202] Cassese (n. 15) 124.   [203] Danilenko (n. 180) 487.

[204] Article 7(2)(e), Rome Statute; article 7(I)(f), Elements of Crimes.

[205] Cassese (n. 15) 126.

[206] Robinson (n. 184) 58; von Hebel and Robinson (n. 94) 99–100; UNGA (n. 159).

[207] Article 7(1)(k), Rome Statute.   [208] McCormack and Robertson (n. 122) 635.

[209] Grounds of persecution include political, racial, national, ethnic, cultural, religious and gender grounds. Cassese (n. 15) 126; Boot, Dixon and Hall (n. 153) 159, 218; Danilenko (n. 180) 487.

[210] von Hebel and Robinson (n. 94) 101.   [211] Boot, Dixon and Hall (n. 153) 159, 220.

'universally recognized' grounds of persecution, the latter suggesting a stricter standard. Persecution as a crime against humanity must occur 'in connection with any act [crime against humanity] referred to in this paragraph or any crime within the jurisdiction of the Court'.[212] Again, owing to conflicting law on this point,[213] delegates were divided as to whether this link to another crime is required under customary law.[214] In spite of the compromise reached by delegates on this point, the customary legal status of this requirement continues to be questioned.[215]

Doubts have been raised about the customary legal status of enforced disappearance and apartheid as crimes against humanity.[216] Although these crimes did not expressly appear in precedents on crimes against humanity, a majority of States sought their explicit recognition as being similar in character and gravity to other 'inhumane acts' acknowledged to be crimes against humanity and therefore customary in nature.[217] Some have asserted that the prohibition on apartheid is a *jus cogens* norm.[218] Even if these assertions are incorrect, these crimes may have crystallized (or will in the future) into custom as a result of being included in the Rome Statute.[219]

As previously mentioned, the definition of crimes against humanity in the Rome Statute contains the following residual clause: 'Other inhumane acts of a similar character intentionally causing great suffering, or serious injury to body or to mental or physical health.'[220] Judges will have to give meaning to the phrase 'of a similar character'. In this regard, it is worth noting that proposals to include economic embargoes, terrorism and mass starvation as crimes against humanity did not obtain widespread support because it was argued that they are not crimes under customary international law.[221] Others suggested that mass starvation is covered by the crimes of 'murder', 'extermination' or 'other inhumane acts' and was not included separately because, unlike enforced disappearance and apartheid, it was not expressly recognized in any other international instrument.[222] These omissions suggest that 'of a similar character' might impose a requirement of recognition of the crime under

---

[212] Article 7(1)(h), Rome Statute.
[213] The connection required was set out in the Nuremberg and Tokyo Charters but not in Control Council Law No. 10, the ILC Draft Codes or the ICTY or ICTR Statutes.
[214] von Hebel and Robinson (n. 94) 101.
[215] Cassese (n. 15) 125–26. Cassese suggests that persecution under customary international law can be acts resulting in 'egregious violations of fundamental human rights' that 'are part of a widespread or systematic practice' and 'are committed with a discriminatory intent'. *Kupreškić and Others* (n. 133) para. 580.
[216] Articles 7(1)(i) and (j), Rome Statute; Cassese (n. 15) 126; Danilenko (n. 180) 487.
[217] von Hebel and Robinson (n. 94) 102.
[218] M Byers, *Custom, Power and the Power of Rules* (Cambridge University Press 1999) 186.
[219] Cassese (n. 15) 13, 126.   [220] Article 7(1)(k), Rome Statute.
[221] von Hebel and Robinson (n. 94) 102–03.   [222] Ibid.

customary international law. Such an interpretation is supported by the strongly worded introduction to crimes against humanity in the Elements of Crimes:

> Since article 7 pertains to international criminal law, its provisions, consistent with article 22, must be strictly construed, taking into account that crimes against humanity as defined in article 7 are among the most serious crimes of concern to the international community as a whole, warrant and entail individual criminal responsibility, and require conduct which is impermissible under *generally applicable international law, as recognized by the principal legal systems of the world.*[223]

It has been asserted that the definition of crimes against humanity is based largely on an elaboration and clarification of customary international law[224] and conforms to 'the bulk of authorities on each of the major issues'.[225] Departures from the latter do, however, exist,[226] in part because there was a strong group of like-minded States seeking to ensure that the definition of this category of crimes was broad enough to crystallize recent legal developments.[227]

7.8.5 War crimes

International humanitarian law has been codified in a number of treaties to which many States have acceded, as well as denunciation clauses that have not been used. The result is a corpus of treaty rules, the great majority of which are customary, reflecting the most universally recognized humanitarian principles.[228]

A war crime is a violation of international humanitarian law that has been criminalized under international law.[229] Article 8 of the Rome Statute lists approximately fifty war crimes. The gravity of these crimes was a significant consideration for delineating the Court's jurisdiction. Consequently, article 8(1) contains the following compromise language: 'The Court shall have jurisdiction in respect of war crimes *in particular* when committed as part of a plan or policy or as part of a large-scale commission of such crimes.'[230] The words 'in particular' emphasize a subcategory of these crimes while not excluding the Court's jurisdiction over the commission of a single war crime listed in

---

[223] Introduction, para. 1, article 7, Elements of Crimes (emphasis added).
[224] Cassese (n. 15) 123.   [225] von Hebel and Robinson (n. 94) 123.
[226] Cassese (n. 15) 123; von Hebel and Robinson (n. 94) 123; Danilenko (n. 187) 1894–95.
[227] von Hebel and Robinson (n. 94) 91.
[228] *Legality of the Threat or Use of Nuclear Weapons*, Advisory Opinion [1996] ICJ Rep. 226, 258.
[229] M Cottier, 'Article 8' in O Triffterer (ed.), *Commentary on the Rome Statute of the International Criminal Court*, 2nd edn (CH Beck/Hart/Nomos 2008) 275, 283. This definition applies to international law, and definitions in national jurisdictions may vary.
[230] Emphasis added.

article 8.[231] More than considerations of gravity, the status of norms under customary international law played a prominent role in war crimes negotiations at Rome.[232] There was a firm intention to remain within the realm of customary law.[233] This naturally influenced discussions of whether to include in the Statute norms applicable to internal armed conflicts.[234] Negotiations were centred on the customary legal status of norms found in several major international humanitarian law treaties: the two *Hague Conventions and Regulations* (1899 and 1907) (Hague law),[235] the four *Geneva Conventions* (1949) and two *Additional Protocols* (1977) to it.[236]

While delegates agreed that Hague law and the four *Geneva Conventions* (1949) reflect customary norms that give rise to individual criminal responsibility,[237] strong and diverging views emerged regarding the customary nature of the two *Additional Protocols* (1977).[238] A large majority of States considered the first *Additional Protocol* (1977) to reflect custom in light of the fact

---

[231] MH Arsanjani, 'The Rome Statute of the International Criminal Court' (1999) 93 AJIL 22, 32.

[232] von Hebel and Robinson (n. 124) 103–04 (citing 1995 Ad Hoc Committee Report, para. 74).

[233] A Zimmermann, 'Israel and the International Criminal Court – an Outsider's Perspective' (2006) 36 Israel Ybk of Human Rights 231.

[234] McCormack and Robertson (n. 122) 635.

[235] *Convention (II) with Respect to the Laws and Customs of War on Land and its Annex: Regulations concerning the Laws and Customs of War on Land* 32 Stat. 1803, 1 Bevans 247, 187 TS 429; (adopted 29 July 1899, entered into force 4 September 1900), *Convention (IV) respecting the Laws and Customs of War on Land and its Annex: Regulations concerning the Laws and Customs of War on Land* 36 Stat. 2277, 1 Bevans 631, 205 TS 277 (adopted 18 October 1907, entered into force 26 January 1910).

[236] *Convention (I) for the Amelioration of the Condition of the Wounded and Sick in Armed Forces in the Field*, 75 UNTS 31; *Convention (II) for the Amelioration of the Condition of Wounded, Sick and Shipwrecked Members of Armed Forces at Sea*, 75 UNTS 85; *Convention (III) relative to the Treatment of Prisoners of War*, 75 UNTS 135; *Convention (IV) relative to the Protection of Civilian Persons in Time of War*, 75 UNTS 287 (all adopted 12 August 1949, all entered into force 2 October 1950); *Protocol Additional to the Geneva Conventions of 12 August 1949, and relating to the Protection of Victims of International Armed Conflicts* (first *Additional Protocol*), 1125 UNTS 3; *Protocol Additional to the Geneva Conventions of 12 August 1949, and relating to the Protection of Victims of Non-International Armed Conflicts* (second *Additional Protocol*) 1125 UNTS 609 (both adopted 8 June 1977, both entered into force 7 December 1978).

[237] McCormack and Robertson (n. 122) 635. See also K Dörmann, 'Article 8' in O Triffterer (ed.), *Commentary on the Rome Statute of the International Criminal Court*, 2nd edn (CH Beck/Hart/Nomos 2008) 275, 301.

[238] It is noteworthy, however, that, according to the commentary on article 20 of the International Law Commission's Draft Code of Crimes against the Peace and Security of Mankind (1996), it was based on violations of these Protocols. (1996) II (Part Two) Ybk of the ILC 17, 53ff.

that it has been ratified by a large number of States.[239] Others viewed most but not all of its provisions in this manner.[240] In respect of the second *Additional Protocol* (1977), which regulates conduct in internal armed conflicts, a majority of delegates opined that some of its provisions were reflective of custom.[241] In support of this position, delegates pointed to the ICTR statute and a decision of the ICTY Appeals Chamber in *Prosecutor* v. *Tadić* (1995).[242] Interestingly, almost as many States at the beginning of 1998 had ratified both *Protocols* (1977).[243]

It is the diverging views that arose in respect of war crimes in particular that gave rise to the Egyptian proposal for a 'without prejudice' clause to preserve all divergent views – now article 10 of the Rome Statute.[244] In addition, wherever language could be taken from Hague law rather than the *Additional Protocols* (1977), the former was chosen, as its customary status was not contested.[245]

Article 8 divides war crimes into four subcategories: (1) grave breaches of the *Geneva Conventions* (1949);[246] (2) '[o]ther serious violations of the laws and customs applicable to international armed conflict, within the established framework of international law';[247] (3) serious violations of article 3 common to the *Geneva Conventions* (1949); and (4) '[o]ther serious violations of the laws

---

[239] von Hebel and Robinson (n. 94) 103–04 (citing 1995 Ad Hoc Committee Report, para. 74). A similar discussion took place within the Preparatory Committee on whether all provisions in the first *Additional Protocol* (1977) are part of customary law. (1996) I PrepCom Report, para. 81.

[240] Ibid.   [241] Ibid. 105.

[242] Danilenko (n. 187) 1891–1893; *Tadić* (n. 21) para. 134. As well, three permanent members of the Security Council, including the United States, considered violations of the *Additional Protocols* (1977) to be within the Yugoslavia Tribunal's jurisdiction, which is limited to crimes under customary law. Danilenko, 'The Statute of the International Criminal Court and Third States' (n. 180) 486–87.

[243] As of 28 January 1998, 150 states had ratified the first *Additional Protocol* (1977), and 142 had ratified the second *Additional Protocol* (1977). McCormack and Robertson (n. 122) 635.

[244] von Hebel and Robinson (n. 94) 88, fn. 30; see Section 7.7 of this Chapter.

[245] von Hebel and Robinson, ibid. 124; Zimmermann (n. 233); T Graditzky, 'War Crimes Issues Before the Rome Diplomatic Conference on the Establishment of an International Criminal Court' (1999) 5 UC Davis J Int'l Law and Policy 199, 204–05. France and the United Kingdom were not Parties to the first *Additional Protocol* (1977) at the time of the negotiations.

[246] This repeats the definition of grave breaches contained in the four *Geneva Conventions* (1949) (articles 50 GC I, 51 GC II, 130 GC III and 147 GC IV).

[247] Of the twenty-six offences listed here, about ten are based on the 1907 Hague Regulations, four on the grave breaches provisions of the first *Additional Protocol* (1977), six on other provisions of it or the *Geneva Conventions* (1949), three on the wording of other international instruments and three from a mixture of international instruments. Dörmann, 'Article 8' (n. 237) 323.

and customs applicable in armed conflicts not of an international character, within the established framework of international law'.[248] It is widely accepted that categories one and three are reflective of customary international law.[249] Thus, references in these chapeau provisions to the *Geneva Conventions* (1949) are references to custom. How then can the chapeau references to 'within the established framework of international law' in categories two and four be understood? One possible interpretation is that the offences listed under these chapeaus 'are to be considered as war crimes only if they are so classified by *customary international law*'.[250]

> In other words, while in respect of the other classes of war crimes (or, for that matter, crimes against humanity and genocide) the Statute confines itself to setting out the content of the prohibited conduct, and the relevant provision can thus be directly and immediately applied by the court, it would be otherwise in the case of the two provisions under consideration. The Court might find that the conduct envisaged in these provisions amounted to a war crime *only if and to the extent that* general international law already regarded the offences as a war crime.[251]

Cassese rejected this possible interpretation because it runs counter to the principle of specificity, which guided the drafters.[252] Indeed, the drafters attempted 'to set out in detail all the classes of crimes falling under the jurisdiction of the Court, so as to have a *lex scripta* laying down the substantive criminal rules to be applied by the ICC'.[253] Accordingly, Cassese suggests the following way to understand these chapeau provisions:

> [T]he expression at issue is intended to convey the notion that for the authors of the Statute the various classes of war crimes specified in Article 8(2)(b) and (e) are already part of the "established framework of international law". In other words, by the use of that expression the draughtsmen aimed at making it clear that these two provisions were declaratory of customary international law, as much as the provisions of Article 8(2)(a), concerning "grave breaches", and Article 8(2)(c), concerning common Article 3. Since no one contests that these two last provisions refer to war crimes already firmly established in customary law, whereas for the other two categories doubts might arise, the framers of the Rome Statute aimed at dispelling such doubts by making reference to the 'established framework of international law'.[254]

---

[248] About half of these provisions mirror exactly provisions in article 8(2)(b), dealing with international armed conflict. A Zimmermann, 'Article 8' in O Triffterer (ed.), *Commentary on the Rome Statute of the International Criminal Court*, 2nd edn (CH Beck/Hart/Nomos 2008) 275, 477.

[249] A Cassese, 'The Statute of the International Criminal Court: Some Preliminary Reflections' (1999) 10 EJIL 144, 152.

[250] Ibid. 151.   [251] Ibid.   [252] Ibid. 152.   [253] Ibid.   [254] Ibid. 152.

This certainly appears to be the better legal view and finds support among those who helped draft this provision.[255] Article 10 in this context might best be understood as emphasizing that the list of war crimes might not be exhaustive of custom. That these definitions, perhaps more than any other in the Rome Statute, are derived from a patchwork of legal sources also supports the view advanced by Cassese – that it was important for the drafters to expressly state their view that these crimes are reflective of custom. Indeed, thirty-five offences listed under article 8(2)(b), some of which expressly refer to the *Geneva Conventions* (1949),[256] are derived from several international instruments.[257] The same is true of the twenty-one offences listed under article 8(2)(e) of the Statute.[258]

> Rather than legislating and creating new war crimes, only war crimes *reflecting well established international law* should be included under the Draft Statute. Delegations informally came to broadly agree on *two cumulative criteria to select and define the war crimes* to be included under the Draft Statute: First, the conduct concerned must amount to a *violation of customary international humanitarian law*. Secondly, the violation of humanitarian law concerned must be *criminalized under customary international law.*[259]

While these intentions support the view that the definitions of war crimes are reflective of customary international law, such a view does not shield these provisions from judicial scrutiny. Certainly judges are entitled to satisfy themselves that these offences are reflective of custom should a party to the proceedings raise this issue. Indeed, it has been pointed out that aspects of the war crimes listed in article 8 are retrograde, and others go beyond established custom.

Provisions alleged to be retrograde include certain distinctions drawn between international and internal armed conflict. For example, article 8(2)(c), which deals with crimes perpetrated against combatants *hors de combat* contains a different threshold for armed conflict (a lower one) than that which must be met for crimes committed in combat in an internal conflict under article 8(2)(f).[260] Further, article 8(2)(b)(iv) on intentionally launching an attack causing loss of life to civilians or civilian objects is thought to be retrograde

---

[255] Most drafters of article 8(2)(e) agree that the goal was to limit this provision to crimes under customary international law. D Scheffer, 'The United States and the International Criminal Court' (1999) 93 AJIL 12, 16.

[256] See Articles 8(2)(b)(vii), (xxii), (xxiv) and (xxv), Rome Statute.

[257] Dörmann (n. 237): References to the *Geneva Conventions* (1949) can be found in articles 8(2)(e)(ii) and (vi) of the Rome Statute.

[258] These are based largely on the two *Additional Protocols* (1977) and Hague law. Zimmerman, 'Article 8' (n. 248) 475, 493ff.

[259] M Cottier, 'Article 8' in O Triffterer (ed.), *Commentary on the Rome Statute of the International Criminal Court*, 2nd edn (CH Beck/Hart/Nomos 2008) 275, 283, 287–88.

[260] Cassese (n. 15) 96.

insofar as the crime requires such loss to be 'clearly excessive'. This provision is an amalgam of three provisions in the first *Additional Protocol* (1977), one that deals with collateral damage[261] and two that deal with damage to the environment.[262] By combining these provisions, the proportionality criterion for collateral damage – 'clearly excessive' – becomes applicable to damage to the environment as well, for which the only relevant criterion in the *Protocol* (1977) is whether the environmental damage is 'widespread, long-term and severe'.[263]

War crimes included in the Rome Statute that are regarded by some as going beyond customary international law include the criminalization of acts against personnel of the UN and humanitarian organizations, attacks against buildings dedicated to education, the conscription or enlistment of children under fifteen years of age into the national armed forces or active participation in hostilities,[264] and indirect transfer by an occupying power of its civilian population to an occupied territory.[265] However, these crimes might well have crystallized into custom shortly after the Rome Statute was adopted.[266] Others have suggested that the crime of attacking UN and other personnel is merely symbolic, as it falls under the customary legal prohibition against attacking civilians.[267] As for the crime of conscripting child soldiers, a majority of delegates, over the objections of the United States, strongly supported its inclusion, considering it to be reflective of customary international law.[268]

The legal threshold for war crimes committed in the course of an internal armed conflict is also regarded as being substantially lower than the threshold set forth in the second *Additional Protocol* (1977) in two respects. First, the *Protocol* (1977) applies only to internal armed conflict in which governmental authorities are at least one of the participants. Pursuant to article 8(2)(f), however, conflicts between armed groups *inter se* are also covered by the Rome

---

[261] Article 85(3)(b), first *Additional Protocol* (1977).

[262] Articles 35(3) and 55(1), first *Additional Protocol* (1977).

[263] von Hebel and Robinson (n. 94) 111–12; Cassese (n. 15) 96.

[264] *Prosecutor* v. *Norman*, Decision on Preliminary Motion Based on Lack of Jurisdiction (Child Recruitment), Dissenting Opinion of Judge Robertson, SCSL-2004–14-AR72(E), 31 May 2004.

[265] Danilenko (n. 187) 1895; Zimmermann (n. 233) 241–43; McCormack and Robertson (n. 122) 635.

[266] T Meron, 'Crimes under the Jurisdiction of the International Criminal Court' in H von Hebel, JG Lammers and J Schukking (eds.), *Reflections on the International Criminal Court: Essays in Honour of Adriaan Bos* (TMC Asser Press 1999) 47, 48–49.

[267] von Hebel and Robinson (n. 94) 110.

[268] Ibid. 118. A few delegations suggested raising the relevant age from fifteen to eighteen, but this was rejected because there was not adequate support for this in customary international law. Ibid.

Statute.[269] Second, the *Protocol* (1977) requires that the dissident armed forces or other organized armed groups 'exercise such control over a part of the territory as to enable them to carry out sustained and concerted military operations'. It also requires that such forces or groups act 'under responsible command' and be able to implement obligations under the *Protocol* (1977). In contrast, article 8(2)(f) imposes a much lower threshold by merely requiring a 'protracted armed conflict'.[270] This approach is thought to go some way towards correcting certain asymmetries for how the same conduct committed in international and internal armed conflicts might nevertheless be treated differently in terms of criminalization[271] and is consistent with attaching individual criminal responsibility to serious violations of international humanitarian law.[272]

It has also been pointed out that the list of war crimes in the Rome Statute is not exhaustive because it does not adequately or consistently address the issue of weapons whose use is prohibited under customary law and excludes the customary legal prohibition on the use of all weapons of mass destruction.[273] The Rome Statute does not give the Court jurisdiction to try persons for the use of weapons that cause superfluous injury and unnecessary suffering, or weapons that are inherently indiscriminate, even though their use is widely regarded as constituting an infringement of customary international law.[274] There was considerable support for including nuclear weapons and landmines in the list of prohibited weapons, but there was also strong resistance, especially by permanent members of the Security Council, on the grounds that the threat or use of such weapons is not prohibited under existing international law.[275] Ultimately, this intractable debate led delegates to exclude all weapons of mass destruction from the Statute for now and not refer to the general prohibition on causing superfluous injury or unnecessary suffering.[276] Article 8(2)(b)(xx) does, however, enable States Parties to list in an annex to the Statute select weapons that cause superfluous injury or unnecessary suffering (or are inherently indiscriminate) *and* are also the subject of a comprehensive prohibition. However, this provision applies only to international armed conflicts and not to internal armed conflicts, with this distinction being regarded as inconsistent with customary international law.[277] At the first Review Conference of the

---

[269] Ibid. 120–21. See also Zimmermann (n. 248) 477; Kreß (n. 130) 104–09.
[270] von Hebel and Robinson (n. 94) 120–21. They point out that the requirement for a protracted armed conflict was taken from *Tadić* (n. 21).
[271] Kreß (n. 130) 103, 104–09; Zimmermann (n. 248) 476.
[272] von Hebel and Robinson (n. 94) 125; Dinstein (n. 23) 345.
[273] von Hebel and Robinson, ibid. 113–14; McCormack and Robertson (n. 122) 635.
[274] Cassese (n. 15) 95.
[275] Kirsch and Holmes (n. 28) 24.
[276] McCormack and Robertson (n. 122) 635.   [277] Cassese (n. 15) 97.

Rome Statute, delegates adopted a resolution to partially remedy this asymmetry by adopting article 8(2)(e), giving the Court jurisdiction over the war crime of employing certain poisonous weapons and expanding bullets, asphyxiating or poisonous gases, and all analogous liquids, materials and devices, when committed in armed conflicts not of an international character.[278]

It has been said that codification has little merit if the lowest common denominator is the decisive factor in negotiations.[279] The negotiations on war crimes reveal that delegates agreed upon and pushed hard for a list of crimes that is largely consistent with customary law although not entirely exhaustive or reflective of it. Indeed, the goal of delegates was to balance strong support for the Court with strong definitions of crimes. Those progressive definitional aspects that have not already crystallized into custom may do so in the near future.[280] And for those doubting the customary status of war crimes committed as part of an internal armed conflict, it is interesting to note that of the 161 rules of customary international humanitarian law identified by the International Committee of the Red Cross in its 2005 study of this body of law, 147 were determined to be applicable in *any* armed conflict.[281]

The attempt of drafters to define war crimes in the Court's jurisdiction was understandably a politically sensitive matter. However, codification is concerned with exposing political differences and bridging them with the emergence of a legal rule.[282] Finally, it is noteworthy that article 124 of the Statute permits a State Party to opt out of the war crimes regime for a period of seven years; this is taken up in the next Chapter.

7.9 Elements of Crimes (article 9)

At the end of the Rome Diplomatic Conference, States resolved to establish a Preparatory Commission mandated to draft inter alia Elements of Crimes (Elements).[283] The drafting process has been described as 'one of the first times the international community had to work as a quasi-legislative body in

---

[278] Review Conference, RC/Res.5 (10 June 2010) (Article 8 Resolution).

[279] H Lauterpacht, 'Codification and Development of International Law' (1995) 49 AJIL 16, 35.

[280] *Prosecutor* v. *Kordić and Čerkez*, Decision on the Joint Defence Motion to Dismiss the Amended Indictment for Lack of Jurisdiction Based on the Limited Jurisdictional Reach of Articles 2 and 3, ICTY-95–14/29-T, 9 March 1999, paras. 23–28, 30, 32; Meron (n. 266) 48–49.

[281] JM Henckaerts, 'The ICRC Study on Customary International Humanitarian Law – An Assessment' in L Maybee and B Chakka (eds.), *Custom as a Source of International Humanitarian Law* (International Committee of the Red Cross 2006) 43, 49–50.

[282] Lauterpacht (n. 279) 25.

[283] Resolution F of the Final Act of the Rome Conference, para. 5(b) (n. 50).

elaborating and agreeing upon a partial code of international criminal law'.[284] The Elements were adopted by consensus and without discussion at the first session of the Assembly of States Parties (ASP) on 9 September 2002 and precisely detail the material and mental elements of each crime in the Rome Statute, thereby serving as a critical tool for the prosecution and adjudication of these crimes.[285] All States participated in the Preparatory Commission, and the first president of the Court (also president of the conference in Rome) has said that the Elements 'clearly reflect the *opinio juris* of the international community, further supporting the customary nature of crimes within the court's jurisdiction.'[286]

Article 9 of the Rome Statute provides that the Elements 'shall be consistent with' the Statute and 'shall assist the Court in the interpretation and application of articles 6, 7, 8 and 8 *bis*'.[287] Accordingly, the Elements of Crimes is a 'subsidiary source of law' that is not legally binding on judges and must be consistent with the Statute.[288] Article 9 was proposed at Rome to allay the concerns of some delegates about the need to strictly construe the crimes in the Rome Statute and sufficiently clarify their elements.[289] Despite the clear wording of article 9, article 21(1)(a) of the Statute is notorious for giving rise to some ambiguity on the non-binding nature of the Elements of Crimes by providing that the Court 'shall apply' them. It is well known, however, that delegates at Rome ultimately rejected the United States' proposal to make the Elements legally binding on the Court, a decision that is confirmed by commentaries recording the drafting process:

> In light of the negotiating history, this argument [that the Elements are binding] is not tenable. Throughout the negotiations, there was never a majority in favour of binding elements. Only by formulating article 9 as it now states, specifying that the instrument is only of assistance to the Court and has to be consistent with the Statute, did the inclusion of a provision on the Elements of Crimes become acceptable to all delegations. Article 21 of the Statute lays down what the applicable law is and merely

---

[284] Resolution F, para. 2, ibid.; von Hebel and Robinson, 'Reflections on the Elements of Crimes' in RS Lee (ed.), *The International Criminal Court: The Making of the Rome Statute* (Kluwer Law International 1999) 219, 220.

[285] ICC-ASP/1/3.

[286] P Kirsch, 'Customary International Humanitarian Law, its Enforcement, and the Role of the International Criminal Court' in L Maybee and B Chakka (eds.) (n. 281) 79, 80.

[287] Articles 9(3) and 9(1) respectively, Rome Statute.

[288] K Ambos, 'Some Preliminary Reflections on the Mens Rea Requirements of the Crimes in the ICC Statute and the Elements of Crimes' in LC Vohrah and Others (eds.), *Man's Inhumanity to Man: Essays on International Law in Honour of Antonio Cassese* (Kluwer Law International 2003) 11, 12.

[289] O Triffterer, 'Can the "Elements of Crimes" Narrow or Broaden Responsibility for Criminal Behaviour defined in the Rome Statute?' in C Stahn and G Sluiter (eds.), *The Emerging Practice of the International Criminal Court* (Martinus Nijhoff 2009) 381, 386.

enumerates the sources of law, which the Court shall apply. It makes no determination on the status of such sources. That status, as far as necessary, is regulated elsewhere, such as in article 9 regarding the Elements of Crimes. Of course, while the Elements are not binding *per se*, they will undoubtedly have persuasive force, reflecting the consensus view of the international community; ultimately, however, the judges will have to reach their own understanding of the Statute.[290]

In addition to this drafting history, it has been suggested that, as between article 21(1)(a) and article 9, any perceived inconsistency should be resolved in favour of the latter provision on the basis of the *lex specialis* rule.[291] It has also been argued that the Elements are unable to bind the Court because the Assembly of States Parties, which adopted this instrument, has no legislative power to enact substantive international criminal law.[292]

The consequence of article 9 is that the relationship between the Statute and Elements is embodied in the rule *lex superior derogat legi inferiori*, so that if there is a conflict between them, the Statute prevails.[293] This relationship does not conform to the interpretive rule of *lex posterior derogat legi priori*, which 'cannot be applied where the later rule is derived from a lower source than the earlier rule, unless the authority which created the earlier rule expressly provides for this'.[294] It also does not conform to the *lex specialis derogat lex generalis* rule, which is merely a presumption that can be rebutted where proof of a contrary intention is proffered.[295] Further, if the Elements of Crimes are considered to be a 'subsequent agreement' for purposes of interpreting the Statute,[296] the Elements must still be consistent with the latter. Thus, article 31(3)(a) of the *Vienna Convention* (1969) may not be used as a back door to undermine the consistency requirement that is expressly provided for in article 9(3) of the Statute.

---

[290] H von Hebel, 'The Decision to Include Elements of Crimes in the Rome Statute' in RS Lee and Others (eds.), *The International Criminal Court: Elements of Crimes and Rules of Procedure and Evidence* (Transnational 2001) 3, 8; Triffterer, ibid. 384, 387–88; MC Bassiouni, *The Legitimacy of the International Criminal Court*, vol. 1 (Transnational 2005) 163; P Kirsch, 'The Work of the Preparatory Commission' in RS Lee and Others (eds.), ibid. xlv, xlvii; A Pellet, 'Applicable Law' in A Cassese and Others (eds.), *The Rome Statute of the International Criminal Court: A Commentary*, vol. II (Oxford University Press 2002) 1051, 1058.

[291] Bassiouni, ibid.   [292] Triffterer, 'Elements of Crimes' (n. 289) 381, 384.

[293] RS Clark, 'Article 9' in O Triffterer (ed.), *Commentary on the Rome Statute of the International Criminal Court*, 2nd edn (CH Beck/Hart/Nomos 2008) 505, 528.

[294] M Akehurst 'The Hierarchy of the Sources of International Law' (1974–1975) 47 British Ybk Int'l L 273.

[295] Ibid.

[296] Article 31(3)(a) provides: 'There shall be taken into account, together with the context: (a) any subsequent agreement between the parties regarding the interpretation of the treaty or the application of its provisions.'

Of course, to the extent that the Elements of Crimes are consistent with the Statute, the Court will rightly exhibit 'substantial deference' to them, as they reflect 'conclusions of the Preparatory Commission and the Assembly of States Parties' on the elements that need to be proven for each crime in the Statute.[297] Ultimately, however, the Court arguably has the power and duty to satisfy itself in each case that the elements it applies, which are guidelines, are compliant with article 9(3).[298] Unfortunately, not all judges at the Court have adopted this view.

A primary argument advanced in support of the Elements was that they were needed to satisfy the principle of legality and to give the latter concept 'teeth'.[299] At Rome, the United States and others suggested that the definitions of crimes in the Rome Statute are too vague.[300] However, this position is difficult to reconcile with the fact that the Rome Statute is the most detailed statute ever enacted for an international criminal tribunal and that judges have, in the past, been able to elaborate definitions of crimes in their jurisprudence.[301] Importantly, article 22 on legality does not mention the Elements at all, let alone suggest that its mandatory application is essential to legality as defined in this provision. Nevertheless, the Pre-Trial Chamber of the Court in Al Bashir (2009) incorrectly made this link and treated the Elements as mandatory: 'had the application of the Elements of Crimes been fully discretionary for the competent Chamber, the safeguards provided for by the article 22 *nullum crimen sine lege* principle would be significantly eroded'.[302] This ruling is most unfortunate and confirms the fears of two international judges who early on articulated the possibility of the Elements improperly usurping the judicial function.[303]

Any State Party, an absolute majority of judges or the prosecutor may propose amendments to the Elements, which must then be adopted by a two-thirds

---

[297] Clark (n. 293) 529; von Hebel and Robinson (n. 94) 231.

[298] Clark, ibid.; von Hebel and Robinson, ibid.; K Dörmann, 'Contributions by the Ad Hoc Tribunals for the Former Yugoslavia and Rwanda to the Ongoing Work on Elements of Crimes in the Context of the ICC' (2000) 94 ASIL Proceedings 284, 286; Triffterer(n. 289) 381, 387–88.

[299] Pellet (n. 290) 1060 (citing US Reference Paper: Elements of Offenses for the International Criminal Court, submitted to Preparatory Committee, 27 March 1998).

[300] WK Lietzau, 'Checks and Balances and Elements of Proof: Structural Pillars for the International Criminal Court' (1999) 32 Cornell Int'l LJ 477, 480–81.

[301] von Hebel and Robinson (n. 284) 223–24.

[302] *Prosecutor* v. *Al Bashir*, Decision on the Prosecution's Application for a Warrant of Arrest against Omar Hassan Ahmand Al Bashir, ICC-02/05–01/09, 4 March 2009, para. 131.

[303] R Higgins, 'The Relationship between the International Criminal Court and the International Court of Justice' in H von Hebel, JG Lammers and J Schukking (eds.), *Reflections on the International Criminal Court: Essays in Honour of Adriaan Bos* (TMC Asser Press 1999) 163, 168–69; D Hunt, 'The International Criminal Court – High Hopes, 'Creative Ambiguity' and an Unfortunate Mistrust in International Judges' (2004) 2:1 J Int'l Crim Justice 56.

majority of the members of the ASP in order to take effect.[304] By involving judges and the prosecutor in the amendment process, the drafters of the Statute support a dialogue between the Court and the Assembly of States Parties rather than a one-directional hierarchical relationship.[305] Such a relationship is consistent with the non-binding nature of the Elements. It must also be borne in mind that if the Court were to apply the Elements of Crimes in the face of an inconsistency with the Statute, any subsequent amendment correcting this inconsistency would be made too late, after being applied to an actual case, thereby raising serious legal concerns.[306] To date, no amendments to the Elements have been proposed other than to reflect the definition of the crime of aggression and the addition of article 8(2)(e).[307]

The consistency requirement in the Rome Statute has been described as an important 'safety valve' to ensure that the Elements truly assist rather than hinder judges in carrying out their work.[308] It is at this juncture, however, where our analysis does not end but rather begins. The fundamental question that begs an answer is: How does one define 'consistent'? If the drafting process teaches one anything, it is that consistency is in the eye of the beholder:

> [A]ll delegations agreed that the Elements must be consistent with the Statute. Of course, this still left latitude for disagreement, since different readers of the Statute may obviously have a very different understanding of what the various terms of the Statute were intended to signify. For this reason, no one can authoritatively say whether the Elements as a whole restrict the Statute, expand the Statute, or are exactly co-extensive with the Statute. It all depends on what one believed or hoped that the statutory provisions meant in the first place.[309]

Ensuring consistency with the Statute was supported by States that wanted to leave no room for judges to interpret and apply the Statute in unintended ways, to preserve the delicate package of compromises reflected in the Statute and to produce a coherent and complementary legal tool that accords with

---

[304] Article 9(2) is somewhat ambiguously worded, suggesting that the ASP must, rather than may, adopt whatever amendments are proposed: 'Such amendments *shall* be adopted by a two-thirds majority of the members of the Assembly of States Parties.' (emphasis added). However, such a reading would lead to absurd results, as it would allow the prosecutor or any State Party on its own to amend the Elements. In addition, nothing in the drafting history of this provision suggests that this was the intention of the drafters.

[305] von Hebel and Robinson, 'Reflections on the Elements of Crimes' (n. 284) 224 and, for more details, 229.

[306] Pellet (n. 290) 1062.   [307] Article 8 Resolution (n. 278).

[308] von Hebel and Robinson, 'Reflections on the Elements of Crimes' (n. 284) 229–30.

[309] Ibid. 221–22.

fundamental principles of justice.[310] In spite of the fact that many States initially did not think that Elements of Crimes were necessary, their usefulness has become apparent.[311] Two aspects of their usefulness go to the issue of whether the Elements are consistent with the Statute. The first is the Elements' function as a 'decoder' of archaic language in the Statute, and the second is its function as a 'detail filler' of vague or ambiguous terminology. In performing both of these functions, the Elements must be consistent with the Statute. Although many issues had been resolved in the Statute, there remained a continued interest in balancing strong elements with strong State support for the Court.[312]

In terms of decoding, the Elements take the sometimes archaic language in the Statute, which may be a 'patchwork' of language taken from different treaties drafted over the years, and explain its ordinary meaning.[313] The use of language derived from such treaties in the Statute was borne out of a desire on the part of delegates to include in the Statute existing law and not legislate new crimes.[314] Thus, in taking outdated language that is reflective of customary international law (e.g., the war crime of killing 'treacherously'), care had to be taken to give it an ordinary meaning, taking into account modern warfare but without legislating a new crime.[315]

Second, the function of adding detail to vague or ambiguous phrases in the Statute also required drafters of the Elements to take care in ensuring that the added details were consistent with the Statute and did not expand or restrict the crimes stated therein. Indeed, some States Parties (and most NGOs)[316] were interested in the Elements facilitating prosecution while others approached the drafting exercise with the goal of preserving State sovereignty and the rights of the accused.[317] In both cases, however, States had to be willing to accept law considered reflective of 'applicable' law, meaning law consistent with the Rome Statute.[318]

Concern has been expressed that the Elements instrument 'underlines that it will be what States will agree to as "elements of these crimes" that the new Court will be authorized to apply and not necessarily what is the general international law on the matter'.[319] For others who point to customary international law as the culprit for progressive and improperly expansive interpretations of international criminal law, this is a welcome constraint.[320] However, the

---

[310] RS Lee, 'Introduction' in RS Lee (ed.), *The International Criminal Court: Elements of Crimes and Rules of Procedure and Evidence* (Transnational 2001) lv, lvii–lviii.
[311] von Hebel and Robinson (n. 284) 224.   [312] Ibid. 222–23.   [313] Ibid. 224–25.
[314] Ibid.   [315] Ibid.   [316] Hunt (n. 303) 56.   [317] von Hebel and Robinson (n. 284) 221.
[318] Ibid. 222–23.   [319] Higgins (n. 303) 168–69.
[320] J Wessel, 'Judicial Policy-Making at the International Criminal Court: An Institutional Guide to Analyzing International Adjudication' (2006) 44 Columbia J Transnat'l L 377, 412–13.

latter reasoning presupposes that the Elements themselves do not improperly expand the definitions of crimes in the Rome Statute.

In recent years, it has been claimed that the Elements in places do precisely this and, moreover, seek in other places to improperly constrain judges through elements that are unduly restrictive relative to the Rome Statute. Both charges lead to a claim of inconsistency with the Rome Statute. Examples of seemingly expansive elements include the elements for the crime of enforced disappearance, which embraces persons involved at various stages of carrying out the disappearance;[321] some elements of sexual violence crimes,[322] which are not restricted to 'protected persons' under the *Geneva Conventions* (1949)[323] and 'only' require 'gravity *comparable to* that of a grave breach';[324] and the definition of extermination as a crime against humanity, which includes a single killing if it is knowingly committed in the course of a widespread or systematic attack directed against a civilian population, and it took place as part of a mass killing of members of that civilian population.[325] Objections of expansiveness have also been raised regarding the definition of 'forcibly' with respect to certain crimes, the 'should have known' knowledge standard for the age of recruited child soldiers and the diminished knowledge requirements inter alia for crimes against humanity.[326]

Examples of allegedly restrictive imperatives in the Elements of Crimes include the suggestion that crimes against humanity can be committed only if State or organizational 'action' is involved and such action is required to prove the policy element mentioned in the Statute.[327] Furthermore, the requirement that crimes against humanity must be committed as a result of or in connection with a 'policy' has also been described as an 'insidious and less obvious' limitation in the Elements to limit the 'scope of the Court's inquiry'.[328] The accompanying knowledge element for certain contextual elements – knowledge of the existence of an armed conflict for war crimes and knowledge of the surrounding genocide for the latter crime – has also been described by some as too restrictive.[329] For the war crime of 'denying quarter', change in the wording of this crime from 'declaring that no quarter *will be given*' in article 8(2)(b)(xii) of the Rome Statute to 'declared or ordered that there *shall be no survivors*' in the Elements has also been challenged on these grounds.[330]

---

[321] von Hebel and Robinson (n. 284) 222, 226–27; article 7(1)(i), Elements of Crimes.

[322] von Hebel and Robinson, ibid. 222; articles 7(1)(g)-6, 8(2)(b)(xxii)-6 and 8(2)(e)(vi)-6, Elements of Crimes.

[323] *Geneva Conventions* (1949) (n. 236).

[324] von Hebel and Robinson (n. 284) 227; article 8(2)(b)(xxii), Elements of Crimes (emphasis added).

[325] Hunt (n. 303) (56); article 7(1)(b), Elements of Crimes.

[326] von Hebel and Robinson (n. 284) 222.

[327] Robinson (n. 184) 67.   [328] Hunt (n. 303) 56.

[329] von Hebel and Robinson (n. 284) 222.   [330] Triffterer(n. 289) 381, 383.

In other situations, it is deliberately not clear whether the resulting elements are consistent with the Statute. Consider, for example, the controversial war crime of an occupying power's direct or indirect transfer of all or parts of its population in the territory it occupies, or deportation or transfer of all or parts of the population of the occupied territory within or outside this territory.[331] Israeli fears about the 'indirect' transfer reference in the Statute and the opinion of many States that indirect transfers are prohibited under customary international law led to compromise language being inserted in a footnote to the Elements stating that the 'term "transfer" needs to be interpreted in accordance with the relevant provisions of international humanitarian law'.[332] As well, the *travaux préparatoires* for the *Genocide Convention* (1948), which forms the basis of the definition of genocide in the Statute, does not clarify whether systematic expulsion from homes amounts to genocide. Accordingly, drafters of the Elements of Crimes inserted in a footnote that such conduct may be covered by the crime of genocide caused by deliberately inflicting conditions of life calculated to bring about physical destruction.[333] Similarly, the Elements suggest that the war crime of torture can occur without the involvement of a State official, something that is required by the *Convention against Torture and Other Cruel, Inhuman or Degrading Treatment or Punishment* (1984).[334] The Elements deliberately excluded this requirement to signal to judges that it might no longer be required.[335]

Finally, the Elements also contain guidance about entire categories of crimes, emphasizing the seriousness of the conduct that falls within the Court's jurisdiction. For example, genocide does not encompass 'isolated hate crimes' or individual criminal acts, and crimes against humanity are not intended to cover all human rights violations.[336]

In light of the foregoing, addressing opposing fears that the Elements might unduly restrict or expand the definitions of crimes in the Rome Statute by requiring that the Elements be consistent with the Statute leaves 'latitude for disagreement, since different readers of the Statute may obviously have a very

---

[331] Article 8(2)(b)(viii), Rome Statute.

[332] Fn. 44, Elements of Crimes; Zimmermann (n. 233) 200; see also von Hebel (n. 290) 159, 161.

[333] Fn. 4, Elements of Crimes: 'The term "conditions of life" may include, but is not necessarily restricted to, deliberate deprivation of resources indispensable for survival, such as food or medical services, or systematic expulsion from homes'; von Hebel and Robinson (n. 284) 227, fn. 24.

[334] 1465 UNTS 85 (adopted 10 December 1984, entered into force 26 June 1987).

[335] von Hebel and Robinson (n. 284) 227, fn. 23; articles 8(2)(a)(ii)-1 and 8(2)(c)(i)-4, Elements of Crimes. Also, unlike the *Torture Convention* (1984), torture as a crime against humanity does not require proof of a specific purpose motivating the torture. See articles 7(1)(f) and 7(2)(e) of the Rome Statute as well as fn. 14 of the Elements of Crimes.

[336] von Hebel and Robinson, ibid. 228.

different understanding of what the various terms of the Statute were intended to signify'.[337] Beyond this disagreement, there is the matter of whether reliance in the Elements on general international law is consistent with the Statute. In the view of the author and others, it is, to the extent that this reliance is consistent with the origins of the crimes in the Rome Statute, be they customary, treaty or other law:

> Elements of crimes are "consistent" with the Statute, if they correspond to the elements, which are *expressly or silently mentioned in the relevant definitions* contained in Articles 6, 7 and 8 [and now 8 *bis*], irrespective of whether they concern the material or the mental side.... The task of the elements is primarily to provide clarification in cases in which definitions are not sufficiently transparent or understandable, or to confirm the material or mental requirements of crimes, which are not described in a completely satisfactory fashion in Articles 6, 7 or 8 [or 8 *bis*].[338]

More generally, it has been said that regulations internal to an international criminal tribunal, such as rules of procedure and evidence, must not 'conflict *either* with the primary (or "secondary") legislation governing the same matter (the Statute of the ICTY, the ICTR, the ICC, the SCSL, or the STL) *or with rules and principles laid down in customary law*. In case of inconsistency, a court should refrain from applying the relevant regulation or rule of procedure, *or else it must construe and apply them in such a manner that they prove consonant with the overriding rules*.'[339]

Indeed, the Preparatory Commission was assisted in preparing the Elements by a study of relevant case law conducted by the International Committee of the Red Cross spanning the trials at Leipzig after the First World War, trials following the Second World War, national jurisprudence and judgments of the ICTY and ICTR.[340] The goal of the drafters of the Elements was 'properly reflecting the state of existing law without prejudicing its future development'.[341] As such, they are an obvious starting point for understanding the definition of a crime in the Rome Statute but should also be consistent with the law they are intended to reflect. And because custom is notorious for being vague and lacking in detail, it will not very often be the case that a perfectly clear mental or material element is discerned in customary international law that contradicts that which is contained in the Elements of Crimes.[342]

---

[337] Ibid. 221.   [338] Triffterer(n. 289) 381, 387–88 (emphasis added).
[339] Cassese (n. 15) 26 (emphasis added).   [340] Dörmann (n. 298) 284.
[341] Ibid.   [342] Lietzau (n. 300) 477, 482.

7.10 Mental elements of crimes (article 30)

Material elements of a crime may be acts or omissions.[343] Article 30(2) and (3) differentiates between three types of material elements: conduct, consequences and circumstances.[344] Conduct must be carried out with intent, meaning the person 'means to engage in that conduct'. A consequence may occur with intent or knowledge, meaning the person 'means to cause the consequence or is aware that it will occur in the ordinary course of events'. And a circumstance must be known, meaning that the perpetrator is aware that it exists.

Article 30(1) of the Rome Statute is a default rule that states: '*Unless otherwise provided*, a person shall be criminally responsible and liable for punishment for a crime within the jurisdiction of the Court only if the material elements are committed with intent and knowledge.'[345] For example, it has been said that articles 6, 7 and 8 of the Rome Statute 'otherwise provide' mental elements including intent[346] and wilfulness,[347] as well as behaviour conducted 'wantonly'[348] or 'treacherously'.[349] Drafters of the Elements treated only the latter two – 'wantonly' and 'treacherously' – as otherwise providing and regarded references in the Rome Statute to intent and wilfulness as consistent with the default rule in article 30.[350] Other parts of the Rome Statute contain references such as 'should have known'[351] and 'for the purpose of'.[352]

Paragraph 2 of the general introduction to the Elements seems to contemplate that law and instruments *other* than the Rome Statute may 'otherwise provide' a mental element for crimes in articles 6, 7, 8 and 8 *bis*:

---

[343] Article 30 covers acts and omissions. *Prosecutor* v. *Lubanga Dyilo*, Decision on Confirmation of Charges, ICC-01/04–01/06–803, 29 January 2007, paras. 351, 355.

[344] von Hebel (n. 290) 3, 15.

[345] DK Piragoff and D Robinson, 'Article 30' in O Triffterer (ed.), *Commentary on the Rome Statute of the International Criminal Court*, 2nd edn (CH Beck/Hart/Nomos 2008) 849, 856 (emphasis added). On reading 'and' as 'or', see Cassese (n. 15) 74.

[346] Articles 6, 7(1)(k), 7(2)(b), 7(2)(e), 7(2)(f), 7(2)(h), 7(2)(i), 8(2)(b)(i), (ii), (iii), (iv), (ix), (xxiv), (xxv), as well as 8(2)(e)(i), (ii), (iii), and (iv), Rome Statute.

[347] Article 8(2)(a)(i), (iii), (vi) and (b)(xxv), Rome Statute.

[348] Article 8(2)(a)(iv), Rome Statute.

[349] Article 8(2)(b)(xi) and (e)(ix), Rome Statute, all cited in Werle (n. 30) 106–07.

[350] I am grateful to Roger Clark for this point. Wantonly is not defined, but the concept of treachery is.

[351] Article 28(a)(i), Rome Statute; O Triffterer, 'The New International Criminal Law – its General Principles Establishing Individual Criminal Responsibility' (2003) 32 Thesaurus Acroasium 633, 699; O Triffterer, 'Command Responsibility, Article 28 Rome Statute, an Extension of Individual Criminal Responsibility for Crimes within the Jurisdiction of the Court – Compatible with Article 22, Nullum Crimen Sine Lege?' in O Triffterer (ed.), *Gedächtnisschrift für Theo Vogler* (CF Müller 2004) 213.

[352] Article 25(3)(c), Rome Statute.

As stated in article 30, unless otherwise provided, a person shall be criminally responsible and liable for punishment for a crime within the jurisdiction of the Court only if the material elements are committed with
intent and knowledge. Where no reference is made in the Elements of
Crimes to a mental element for any particular conduct, consequence or
circumstance listed, it is understood that the relevant mental element, i.e.,
intent, knowledge or both, set out in article 30 applies. Exceptions to the
article 30 standard, based on the Statute, *including applicable law under its
relevant provisions*, are indicated below.[353]

Read together, article 30 and the General Introduction suggest that exceptions to the default mental elements of knowledge and intent may be derived
not only from the words in the Rome Statute but also from 'applicable law
under its relevant provisions'. If this is a reference to the applicable law set
out in article 21 of the Rome Statute, then it is a reference inter alia to the
Elements of Crimes, treaty law, customary law and general principles of law.[354]
Scholars have taken different views on the meaning of 'otherwise provided' in
article 30. Interestingly though, none have suggested that national law, which
is listed in article 21(1)(c) as applicable law, can 'otherwise provide'. Some
think that departures from the mental elements in article 30 can be provided
for in the Statute as well as in applicable treaties, customary law and general
principles of law in accordance with article 21.[355] Others go even further and
take the view that, in addition to these sources, the Elements of Crimes can,
on their own, otherwise provide for a mental element.[356] In fact, the meaning of 'otherwise provided' in article 30 was not agreed upon at the Rome
Conference:

> An issue that was not settled at the Rome Conference was whether only the
> Rome Statute could "otherwise provide", or whether other sources such as
> the Elements of Crimes, could also provide for a deviation. This debate

---

[353] Emphasis added.
[354] Article 21(1)(a) and (b), Rome Statute. Article 21(1)(b) makes reference to 'principles
and rules of international law', which is understood to be a reference to customary
international law. Pellet (n. 290) 1070–71; Schabas (n. 121) 92. Article 21(1)(b) is thought
to generally correspond to the sources of international law listed in article 38 of the ICJ
Statute. Schabas (n. 121) 91.
[355] RS Clark, 'The Mental Element in International Criminal Law' (2001) 12 Crim L Forum
291, 321; M Kelt and H von Hebel, 'General Principles of Criminal Law and Elements of
Crimes' in RS Lee (ed.), *The International Criminal Court: Elements of Crimes and Rules
of Procedure and Evidence* (Transnational 2001) 19, 29; M Politi, 'Elements of Crimes'
in A Cassese and Others (eds.), *The Rome Statute of the International Criminal Court: A
Commentary*, vol. 1 (Oxford University Press 2002) 443, 461.
[356] G Werle and F Jessberger, 'Unless Otherwise Provided: Article 30 of the ICC Statute and
the Mental Element of Crimes under International Criminal Law' (2005) 3 J Int'l Crim
Justice 35, 45–46.

continued during the negotiation of the Elements. Some delegations were of the view that the Elements could not call for a deviation from article 30, as the Elements document is subsidiary to the Statute. Other delegations, while conceding that the Elements could not override the Statute, argued that some deviations were necessary to make the crimes workable and to faithfully reflect the intent of the Statute as well as the jurisprudence. The latter view was eventually accepted . . . This formulation recognized the primacy of the Statute and indicates that exceptions must directly or indirectly flow from the Statute, but also recognized that the Statute itself, through article 21 (applicable law), allows reliance on the other sources, including treaties, general principles and the Elements. Thus, the approach seems to avoid suggesting that States parties could *legislate* a deviation through the Elements, but allows them to *codify* a deviation where necessary to reflect their intent when drafting the Statute or to reflect the relevant treaties and jurisprudence.[357]

This view is not shared by everyone, and it is not clear what if any difference there is between a 'legislated' deviation and a 'codified' one. Some think that while the Statute can definitely 'otherwise provide' a mental element for purposes of article 30, the Elements of Crimes, on their own, cannot.[358]

It would seem to be going too far to suggest that the Article 30 standard in the Statute could be amended if an exception is provided for in the Elements, yet this is precisely what is done when the Elements refer to a crime committed against a person who the offender "should have known" was under age, or in cases where he or she "should have known" of the prohibited use of a flag of truce or the Red Cross emblem and similar insignia.[359]

Indeed, some go further in this direction and think that only the Statute can 'otherwise provide' a mental element and that this element can be expressly provided for in the Statute or 'deduced from the definitions of the crimes or

---

[357] Piragoff and Robinson (n. 345) 856.

[358] Schabas (n. 121) 109, 158; C Kreß, 'The Crime of Genocide under International Law' (2006) 6 Int'l Comp L Rev 461, 485; KJ Heller, 'Mistake of Legal Element, the Common Law, and Article 32 of the Rome Statute: A Critical Analysis' (2008) 6 J Int'l Crim Justice 419, 435–36; Triffterer, 'Command Responsibility' (n. 351) 225, 226: 'The words "otherwise provided" in Article 30 can only mean in the Statute.' In an earlier publication, Triffterer hinted at these words having a wider scope. 'The New International Criminal Law' (n. 351).

[359] Schabas (n. 121) 109 (citing articles 6(e), para. 6; 8(2)(b)(xxvi), para. 3; and 8(2)(e)(vii), para. 3 in the Elements of Crimes ('should have known' individual was underage) as well as article 8(2)(b)(vii), para. 3 in the Elements of Crimes ('should have known' standard in respect of prohibited flag use)).

the description of their appearances, as listed' in the Statute.[360] Such statutory provisions include article 25, which addresses modes of individual liability and article 28, which pertains to the responsibility of commanders and other superiors.[361] For example, article 28(a)(i) provides that a military commander is criminally liable for crimes committed by his subordinates if he 'knew or, owing to the circumstances at the time, *should have known* that the forces were committing or about to commit such crimes'.[362] Under this understanding, the Elements 'as helpful as they may be, represent only an opinion of the Assembly of States Parties and, thus, offer a deviation of Article 30, *not* "otherwise provided" in the Statute'.[363]

The Elements instrument plays an important role in respect of the mental elements for crimes in the Rome Statute. It offers a common conceptual framework in which to situate these elements as well as consistent terminology and a consistent drafting approach.[364] For example, many provisions of articles 6, 7, 8 and 8 *bis* specifically use the term 'intentionally', whereas others do not. Express inclusion of the qualifier 'intentionally' in some provisions was not meant to introduce a stricter mental element relative to the default standard, nor was the absence of such a reference in other provisions supposed to imply that there is no mental element for that crime. Rather, express references to intent haphazardly appear in the Statute where they happened to appear in the precedent instruments or out of an abundance of caution.[365] In this regard, it is important to recall that diplomats, many of whom are not lawyers, negotiated the content of articles 6, 7, 8 and 8 *bis*. The Elements document helps to ameliorate these apparent inconsistencies and provides a more systematic framework for recurring issues.[366]

Views also diverge on the customary legal status of the default elements of intent and knowledge for crimes in the Rome Statute. It has been asserted that there is 'no customary rule setting out a *general definition* of the various categories of mens rea (such as intent, recklessness, or negligence)' and that it is 'doubtful' that article 30 reflects custom.[367] It applies only to the crimes in the Rome Statute and does not seek to reflect or codify custom.[368] Others suggest the opposite – that the default rule in article 30 is 'hardly necessary

---

[360] Triffterer, 'The New International Law' (n. 351) 699; Triffterer, 'Command Responsibility' (n. 351) 213, 226, 229, 245; Cassese (n. 15) 74 (although his commentary might be read to include modification of the mental element through customary law); Heller (n. 358) 435; Ambos (n. 288) 17–18, 26–27, 32; T Weigend, 'Intent, Mistake of Law and Co-perpetration in the Lubanga Decision on Confirmation of Charges' (2008) 6 J Int'l Crim Justice 471, 473.

[361] Triffterer, 'The New International Criminal Law' (n. 351); Triffterer, 'Command Responsibility' (n. 351).

[362] Emphasis added.   [363] Triffterer, 'Command Responsibility' (n. 351) 229.

[364] von Hebel and Robinson (n. 284) 224–25.   [365] Ibid.

[366] Ibid. 225.   [367] Cassese (n. 15) 56.   [368] Ibid. 60.

for most of the crimes listed in the Rome Statute, because the definitions have their own built-in *mens rea* requirement'.[369] If most of these crimes are also customary, this position would suggest that their built-in mental elements are also customary in nature.[370] Indeed, it has been suggested that article 30 and the 'unless otherwise provided' proviso 'enables the Statute to absorb the corresponding rules of international humanitarian law (the definition of war crimes under article 8) without having to modify the definitions of these crimes. It also enables the Statute to adopt *verbatim* the definitions of the crimes of genocide, as defined in the 1948 Genocide Convention, without having to change any of its subjective elements'.[371] To the extent that the mental elements of intent and knowledge are not customary, article 10 does not prevent article 30 from having crystallized into custom or doing so in the future.

Importantly, a close reading of the Elements of Crimes reveals that its drafters drew inspiration from sources other than the Statute in at least two respects. First, the elements for crimes against humanity open with the following introduction:

> Since article 7 pertains to international criminal law, its provisions, consistent with article 22, must be strictly construed, taking into account that crimes against humanity as defined in article 7 are among the most serious crimes of concern to the international community as a whole, warrant and entail individual criminal responsibility, and require conduct which is impermissible *under generally applicable international law, as recognized by the principal legal systems of the world.*[372]

As previously mentioned, the reference to generally applicable law appears to be a reference to customary international law. Accordingly, forced pregnancy as a crime against humanity must be carried out 'with the intent of affecting the ethnic composition of any population or carrying out other grave violations of international law'.[373] Similarly, persecution as a crime against humanity requires a severe deprivation of fundamental rights 'contrary to international law' and targeting on grounds 'universally recognized as impermissible under international law'.[374]

---

[369] Schabas (n. 121) 108.   [370] See Werle (n. 30) 107–08.

[371] ME Badar, 'The Mental Element in the Rome Statute of the International Criminal Court: A Commentary from a Comparative Perspective' (2008) 19 Crim L Forum 473, 500.

[372] Article 7, introduction, para. 1, Elements of Crimes (emphasis added).

[373] Article 7(1)(g)-4, element 1, Elements of Crimes. This accords with the wording of article 7(2)(f) of the Statute and is the same requirement for forced pregnancy as a war crime as part of an international armed conflict and non-international armed conflict. See element 1 of articles 8(2)(b)(xxii)-4 and 8(2)(e)(vi)-4 respectively, Elements of Crimes.

[374] Article 7(1)(h), elements 1 and 3, Elements of Crimes.

Further, the introduction to the elements for war crimes states:

> [War crimes defined in the Statute] shall be interpreted within the *established framework of the international law of armed conflict* including, as appropriate, the international law of armed conflict applicable to armed conflict at sea.[375]

Accordingly, the definitions of war crimes in the Rome Statute seem to be based on international law outside of the Statute. In fact, the elements for war crimes contain numerous references to the protected person status 'under one or more of the Geneva Conventions',[376] 'relevant provisions of international humanitarian law',[377] the protection of persons and property under the 'rules of international law applicable to armed conflict'[378] and conduct that violates the 'international law of armed conflict'.[379] Similarly, the war crime of sexual violence must constitute a 'grave breach of the Geneva Conventions' or 'a serious violation of article 3 common to the four Geneva Conventions'.[380] There are two other types of references that are noteworthy. First, an element for the war crime of attacking personnel or objects involved in a humanitarian assistance or peacekeeping mission requires that the mission be 'in accordance with the Charter of the United Nations'.[381] As well, sexual slavery as a crime against humanity and as a war crime includes the element of deprivation of liberty, which 'may, in some circumstances, include exacting forced labour or otherwise reducing a person to a servile status as defined in the Supplementary Convention on the Abolition of Slavery, the Slave Trade, and Institutions and Practices Similar to Slavery of 1956'.[382]

In conclusion, it is submitted that, because the Elements must be consistent with articles 6, 7, 8 and 8 *bis* of the Rome Statute in accordance with article 9(3),

---

[375] Article 8, introduction, Elements of Crimes (emphasis added)

[376] See elements for war crimes under articles 8(2)(a), 8(2)(b)(vii) and 8(2)(b)(ix). See also elements for articles 8(2)(b)(xxiv) and 8(2)(e)(ii) – the war crime of attacking objects or persons using, 'in conformity with international law', the distinctive emblems of the *Geneva Conventions* (1949), thereby indicating protection under these conventions.

[377] Article 8(2)(b)(viii), fn. 44, Elements of Crimes: 'The term "transfer" [of a civilian population] needs to be interpreted in accordance with the relevant provisions of international humanitarian law.'

[378] See, e.g., elements of crimes for articles 8(2)(b)(xi), 8(2)(b)(xiii), 8(2)(b)(xxiii), 8(2)(e)(iii), 8(2)(e)(iv), 8(2)(e)(ix) and 8(2)(e)(xii), Elements of Crimes.

[379] Article 8(2)(b)(xix), element 2, Elements of Crimes.

[380] Article 8(2)(b)(xxii)-6, element 2 and article 8(2)(e)(vi)-6, element 2 respectively, Elements of Crimes, which mirror the wording of these provisions in the Statute.

[381] See elements of crimes for articles 8(2)(b)(iii) and 8(2)(e)(iii), Elements of Crimes, which mirror this requirement in the Statute.

[382] See elements of crimes for articles 7(1)(g)-2, fn. 18, 8(2)(b)(xxii)-2, fn. 53 and 8(2)(e)(vi)-2, fn. 65, Elements of Crimes.

departures in the Elements from the intent and knowledge elements mentioned in article 30 must be based on wording found in the Statute or the legal origin of a crime – be it customary, treaty or other law.[383] In other words, the Elements cannot legislate on their own or 'otherwise provide' a mental element because this would violate the consistency requirement in article 9(3) – or at least render it meaningless – and offend the status of the Statute being superior to the Elements. An example may be useful.

In the *Lubanga* Decision on Confirmation of Charges (2007),[384] Pre-Trial Chamber I accepted the mental element of negligence indicated in the Elements for the war crime of conscripting and enlisting children under the age of fifteen.[385] This mental element is clearly a departure from the default elements of intent and knowledge in article 30 of the Rome Statute. Accordingly, it is submitted that the Pre-Trial Chamber should have provided reasons for how this element is consistent with the Rome Statute by pointing either to the definition of this crime in the Rome Statute or to the customary, treaty or other law it reflects.[386] Where neither the Rome Statute nor the law it reflects indicates a mental element, the default mental elements in article 30 would apply, as the Elements should not be able to provide otherwise.[387] Curiously, the Chamber may have introduced a presumption of consistency between the Statute and the Elements and a corresponding obligation to apply the Elements:

> [T]he Majority considers that the Elements of Crimes and the Rules must be applied unless the competent Chamber finds an irreconcilable contradiction between these documents on the one hand, and the Statute on the other hand. If such irreconcilable contradiction is found, the provisions contained in the Statute must prevail.[388]

7.11 Conclusions

On balance, the jurisdiction of the Court, the Rome Statute's articulation of the legality principle and applicable law, the Statute's relationship to

---

[383] Hinting at this possibility is Badar (n. 371) 473, 500. It is not clear whether Cassese (n. 15) 74 and Triffterer, 'The New International Criminal Law' (n. 351) 699, also hint at this possibility.

[384] *Lubanga Dyilo* (n. 343) paras. 356–359.   [385] Article 8(2)(b)(xxvi), Rome Statute.

[386] Weigend (n. 360) 471, 474.

[387] Clark asserts that Werle and Jessberger (n. 356) 'grossly misstate the position of the drafters of both the Statute and the Elements when they conclude that "[i]n most cases, the mental element is 'otherwise provided'". RS Clark, 'Elements of Crimes in Early Confirmation Decisions of Pre-Trial Chambers of the International Criminal Court' (2008) 6 New Zealand Ybk Int'l L 209, 213, fn. 14.

[388] *Al Bashir* (n. 302) para. 128.

existing and developing law, the definitions of crimes including their mental elements and the Elements of Crimes lend support to the idea that the crimes in the Rome Statute are generally or largely reflective of custom. Departures may be discerned that are progressive and retrogressive relative to custom, and the Statute may not reflect all crimes that exist under customary international law.

External indicia of codification

8.1 Introduction

In the previous Chapter, codification indicia that are largely internal to the Rome Statute were examined in order to discern whether crimes in the Statute are reflective of custom. This codification study is motivated by the need to determine the role that custom should play as an aid to interpreting these crimes. To the extent that the definitions of these crimes are reflective of custom, it can be argued that custom is an aid that must be considered when interpreting them. This inquiry is also undertaken to assist in determining what the relationship might be between custom and the Elements of Crimes as aids to interpretation, the latter being essential. Recall that judges must consider the Elements pursuant to article 9(1) of the Rome Statute when interpreting articles 6, 7, 8 and 8 *bis*. In this Chapter, the codification study will be completed by analyzing the following indicia: drafting history of the Rome Statute and Final Act of the Rome Conference; ratifications, reservations, denunciations and revisions; the conduct of States and Non-States Parties; jurisprudence on the (non-)codificatory nature of crimes in the Rome Statute; and doctrinal writings on this matter. Broadly speaking, these indicia may be characterized as external to the Rome Statute.

8.2 Drafting history

In this section, the *travaux préparatoires* of the International Law Commission (ILC), the pre-Rome drafting bodies and the Rome Diplomatic Conference will be combed for evidence of the nature of the Rome Statute and whether drafters intended for it to reflect customary international law. In doing so, the following two streams of legal development will be canvassed: (1) efforts to codify international crimes and (2) efforts to establish an international criminal court. Although these efforts seem to converge with the drafting of the Rome Statute, they were previously treated by those involved as two distinct legal tasks, as will be explained below. This section is written chronologically while trying to maintain a distinction between these two streams of development. And since this history is well rehearsed in many other places,[1] the focus of this section is really to extract from that material that which is relevant to the question of the relationship between the Rome Statute and customary international law.

On 11 December 1946, the UN General Assembly adopted two significant resolutions. It first affirmed 'the principles of international law recognized by the Charter of the Nürnberg Tribunal and the judgment of the Tribunal'. It also directed the Committee on the Codification of International Law (the precursor to the ILC) to 'treat as a matter of primary importance plans for the formulation, in the context of a general codification of offences against the peace and security of mankind, or of an International Criminal Code, of the principles recognized in the Charter of the Nürnberg Tribunal and in the judgment of the Tribunal'.[2] The second resolution affirmed that 'genocide is a crime under international law'.[3] Genocide is a type of crime against humanity, and while the latter category of crime was mentioned in the Nuremberg Charter, genocide as a subclass of crimes was not specifically mentioned. Accordingly, the resolution of the General Assembly on genocide was an important recognition of this crime's customary legal nature.

In 1947, the General Assembly directed the ILC to 'formulate the principles of international law recognized in the Charter of the Nürnberg Tribunal and in the judgment of the Tribunal, and . . . [p]repare a draft code of offences against the peace and security of mankind, indicating clearly the place to be accorded to the principles . . . '[4] In 1948, discussion within the General Assembly on the *Convention on the Prevention and Punishment of the Crime of Genocide* (1948)[5] gave rise to questions about the trial by an international criminal tribunal of persons perpetrating these and similar acts. Consequently, the General Assembly invited the ILC 'to study the desirability and possibility of establishing an international judicial organ for the trial of persons charged with genocide or other crimes over which jurisdiction will be conferred upon that organ by international conventions'.[6] Discussion of a draft code

---

[1] See, e.g., A Cassese, 'From Nuremberg to Rome: International Military Tribunals to the International Criminal Court' in A Cassese and Others (eds.), *The Rome Statute of the International Criminal Court: A Commentary*, vol. I (Oxford University Press 2002) 3; J Crawford, 'The Work of the International Law Commission' in A Cassese and Others (eds.), ibid. 23; A Bos, 'From the International Law Commission to the Rome Conference (1994–1998)' in A Cassese and Others (eds.), ibid. 35; P Kirsch and D Robinson, 'Reaching Agreement at the Rome Conference' in A Cassese and Others (eds.), ibid. 67; LS Sunga, *The Emerging System of International Criminal Law: Developments in Codification and Implementation* (Kluwer Law International 1997) 9.

[2] UNGA Res. 95 (I) (11 December 1946).   [3] UNGA Res. 96 (I) (11 December 1946).

[4] UNGA Res. 177 (II) (21 November 1947).

[5] 78 UNTS 277 (adopted 9 December 1948, entered into force 12 January 1951).

[6] UNGA Res. 260 (III) (9 December 1948). The first such proposal was made by the NGO community in 1874, and governments started discussing the idea in earnest in 1899. CK

and the creation of an international criminal court began to proceed on two tracks.[7]

The ILC formulated the Nuremberg principles in 1950[8] and a first draft code of offences against the peace and security of mankind in 1951 (Draft Code).[9] The Nuremberg principles recognized crimes against peace, war crimes and crimes against humanity as crimes under international law, meaning irrespective of the content of internal law or the ratification of a particular treaty.[10] The Draft Code of 1951 was limited inter alia to acts of aggression, the violation of treaty obligations 'designed to ensure international peace and security', genocide, crimes against humanity and violations of the laws or customs of war.[11] Like the crimes listed in the Nuremberg principles, this list of crimes largely resembled the core list of crimes under customary international law, although definitions for these crimes differed from their modern counterparts. This was not the first attempt to codify the customary law of warfare; private and semiprivate organizations as well as States had previously undertaken this effort.[12]

Also in 1950, the General Assembly established the Committee on International Criminal Jurisdiction to draft a statute for a permanent international criminal court.[13] In 1951, the Committee presented its first draft (Draft Statute) to the General Assembly.[14] The Draft Statute had as its purpose the trial of persons accused of crimes under international criminal law 'as may be provided in conventions or special agreements among States parties to the present Statute'.[15] In 1952, as a result of discussions in the Sixth (Legal) Committee, the General Assembly adopted a resolution calling for the further study of the Draft Statute by a new Committee (1953 Committee on International Criminal Jurisdiction).[16] The Committee met in the summer of 1953 and produced a revised Draft Statute that it submitted to the General Assembly in 1954.[17]

Hall, 'Première proposition de création d'une cour criminelle international permanente' (1998) 80: 829 Int'l Rev of the Committee of the Red Cross 59, 61, 75; Sunga (n. 1) 9.

[7] A Cassese, 'From Nuremberg to Rome' (n. 1) 9.

[8] ILC, 'Formulation of the Nuremberg Principles' (1950) II Ybk of the ILC 181.

[9] ILC, 'Draft Code of Offences Against the Peace and Security of Mankind' (1951) II Ybk of the ILC 58 (1951 Draft Code).

[10] UNGA (n. 3); ILC (n. 8).   [11] 1951 Draft Code (n. 9) article 1.

[12] A Cassese, International Criminal Law (Oxford University Press 2008) 28–29, mentioning the Lieber Code of 1863, the adoption by the Institut de Droit International of the important Oxford Manual in 1880 and the Hague codification (1899–1907).

[13] UNGA Res. 489 (V) (12 December 1950).

[14] UNGA, Official Records of the General Assembly, Seventh Session, Supp. No. 11 (A/2136), reproduced in (1952) 46 AJIL Supp.: Official Documents, 1–11.

[15] 1951 Draft Code (n. 9) article 1.   [16] UNGA Res. 687 (VII) (5 December 1952).

[17] UNGA, Official Records of the General Assembly, Ninth Session, Supp. No. 12 (A/2645) (1954); YL Liang, 'The Establishment of an International Criminal Jurisdiction: The Second Phase' (1953) 47 AJIL 638.

The Draft Statute of 1953 revised the purpose of the international criminal court to the trial of persons accused of crimes 'generally recognized under international criminal law', as opposed to 'as may be provided in conventions or special agreements among States parties to the present Statute'.[18] While this revision might suggest a movement towards jurisdiction limited to crimes under customary international law, the opposite is in fact true. The Israeli member of the Committee proposed this language because the term 'generally recognized' 'implied that international criminal law could not be invoked against a State which did not recognize that particular part of international law' and that the previous reference to conventions and agreements to which a State is Party could be deleted, as it duplicates the meaning of 'generally recognized'.[19]

In 1954, the ILC adopted a revised Draft Code with commentary that took into account comments received by governments.[20] It contained the same categories of crimes as the 1951 Draft Code and, because of the ILC's understanding of the term 'offences against the peace and security of mankind', excluded all crimes that do not 'endanger or disturb the maintenance of international peace and security' (e.g., piracy, drug trafficking, counterfeiting currency, etc.).[21] Later that year, however, the General Assembly decided to shelve this project as well as the ILC's work on drafting a statute for a permanent international criminal court until a clear definition of aggression could be drafted by a Special Committee on this topic and taken up by the General Assembly.[22]

The Cold War impeded the work of all United Nations organs, including that of the Special Committee on defining aggression.[23] Indeed, it was not until 1977 that the General Assembly adopted a definition.[24] In spite of this development, the General Assembly did not invite the ILC to resume its work on a Draft Code until 1981[25] and its work on establishing the Court until 1989.[26] What followed were two more Draft Codes (1991 and 1996), three more Draft Statutes (1991, 1993 and 1994) and the establishment of two pre-Rome bodies (the Ad Hoc Committee and the Preparatory Committee) to carry forward the ILC's work on drafting a statute for a permanent international criminal court.

The 1991 Draft Code (and accompanying Draft Statute) was not particularly well received, as it was considered to be overly broad.[27] It included

---

[18] Revised Draft Statute for an International Criminal Court (Annex to the Report of the 1953 Committee on International Criminal Jurisdiction on its Session held from 27 July to 20 August 1953) reprinted in UNGA, Official Records of the General Assembly (n. 17).

[19] Liang (n. 17) 646.   [20] (1954) I Ybk of the ILC 123, 133–37.   [21] Ibid. 134.

[22] UNGA Res. 897(IX) (4 December 1954) and 898(IX) (14 December 1954).

[23] A Cassese, 'From Nuremberg to Rome' (n. 1) 9–10.

[24] UNGA Res. 3314(XXIX) (14 December 1974).

[25] UNGA Res. 36/106 (10 December 1981).   [26] UNGA Res. 44/39 (4 December 1989).

[27] J Crawford (n. 1) 24. Article 1 of the accompanying Draft Code provided: 'The Court shall try individuals accused of the crimes defined in the code of crimes against the peace and security of mankind [accused of crimes defined in the annex to the present statute] in

the crimes of aggression; threat of aggression; intervention in the affairs of another State; colonial domination and other forms of alien domination; genocide; apartheid; systematic or mass violations of human rights; exceptionally serious war crimes; the recruitment, use, financing and training of mercenaries; international terrorism; illicit traffic in narcotic drugs; and wilful and severe damage to the environment.[28] The breadth of the Draft Code is due in part to the instructions of the General Assembly to the ILC to resume its work, taking into account the progressive development of the law in this field since 1954.[29] Thus, crimes thought to arise from various international treaties found their way into the Draft Code. Another complicating factor was the lack of consensus within the Sixth (Legal) Committee of the General Assembly on whether the Draft Code should contain an exhaustive list of crimes.[30] There was a proposal to have an exhaustive list but then allow for the addition over time of new crimes defined in international instruments.[31]

The 1993 Draft Statute proposed by the ILC limited jurisdiction to crimes defined by agreements between States Parties in 'special treaties' or in a 'unilateral instrument of a State'.[32] The explanation for this was that discussions within the ILC 'have not made it possible to define offences within the jurisdiction *ratione materiae* of the court, with the exception of genocide and possibly apartheid' and that the list of crimes 'should be limited to a few offences about which the international community is in broad agreement'.[33]

In 1994, the ILC adopted a revised Draft Statute for an international criminal court.[34] The Draft Statute took into account the comments of States, non-governmental organizations (NGOs) and several experts,[35] as well as the ICTY statute.[36] Article 20 of the Draft Statute limits itself to existing international law and treaties[37] by listing the following crimes over which the Court would have jurisdiction: genocide, aggression, serious violations of the laws and customs applicable in armed conflict, crimes against humanity and crimes

---

respect of which the State or States in which the crime is alleged to have been committed has or have conferred jurisdiction upon it.' Both the 1991 Draft Code and Statute can be found in UN Doc.A/CN.4/435 & Corr.1 and Add.1 & Corr.1.
[28] 1991 Draft Code, ibid.   [29] UNGA Res. 36/106 (10 December 1981).
[30] ILC, 'Topical Summary of the Discussion held in the Sixth Committee of the General Assembly during its Forty-Fifth Session' (1991), UN Doc. A/CN.4/L.456, para. 24; ILC, 'Ninth Report on the Draft Code of Crimes against the Peace and Security of Mankind' (1991), UN Doc. A/CN.4/435/Add.1 in which Special Rapporteur Doudou Thiam proposed two versions for delimitation of competence *ratione materiae*.
[31] Sunga (n. 1) 13.
[32] ILC, 1993 Draft Statute, UN Doc. A/CN.4/449 and Corr.1, article 5(3).
[33] Ibid. 111, 116. For commentary on the content of the 1993 Draft Statute, see J Crawford, 'The ILC's Draft Statute for an International Criminal Tribunal' (1984) 88 AJIL 140.
[34] ILC, 1994 Draft Statute, UN Doc. A/49/10, 20.
[35] UN Doc. A/CN.4/L.491/Rev.2/Adds.1&2.
[36] Sunga (n. 1) 20.   [37] 1994 Draft Statute (n. 34) 21.

'established under or pursuant to the treaty provisions listed in the Annex, which, having regard to the conduct alleged, constitute exceptionally serious crimes of international concern'.[38] Thus, with the exception of the final category of 'treaty crimes', the list was limited to 'core crimes', meaning crimes under customary international law.[39] Interestingly, the legality principle as set out in the Draft Statute distinguishes between the first four categories of crimes (requiring that the act or omission in question must have constituted a crime under international law at the relevant time) and the fifth category of treaty crimes (requiring that the treaty in question be applicable to the conduct of the accused at the relevant time).[40] There seems to be an awareness of the differences in the types of crimes that are within the Court's jurisdiction and that this distinction has an impact on how to respect the principle of legality.

The list of treaty crimes in the annex to the 1994 Draft Statute is curious insofar as it contains a mix of crimes, some of which would today be considered reflective of customary law (e.g., grave breaches of the *Geneva Conventions* (1949)). The other 'treaty' crimes are as follows: the unlawful seizure of aircraft,[41] crimes defined in article 1 of the *Convention for the Suppression of Unlawful Acts against the Safety of Civil Aviation* (1971),[42] apartheid,[43] crimes defined in article 2 of the *Convention on the Prevention and Punishment of Crimes against Internationally Protected Persons, including Diplomatic Agents* (1973),[44] hostage-taking,[45] torture, crimes defined in article 3 of the *Convention for the Suppression of Unlawful Acts against the Safety of Maritime Navigation* (1988),[46] crimes defined in article 2 of the *Protocol for the Suppression of Unlawful Acts against the Safety of Fixed Platforms located on the Continental Shelf* (1988)[47] and drug trafficking.[48] The decision to list crimes within the Court's

---

[38] Ibid. 38.

[39] H von Hebel and D Robinson, 'Crimes within the Jurisdiction of the Court' in RS Lee and Others (eds.), *The International Criminal Court: The Making of the Rome Statute* (Kluwer Law International 1999) 79, 80.

[40] 1994 Draft Statute (n. 34) 55, article 39.

[41] As defined in article 1 of the *Convention for the Suppression of Unlawful Seizure of Aircraft*, 860 UNTS 105 (adopted 16 December 1970, entered into force 14 October 1971).

[42] 974 UNTS 178 (adopted 23 September 1971, entered into force 26 January 1973).

[43] As defined in article II of the *International Convention on the Suppression and Punishment of the Crime of Apartheid*, 1015 UNTS 243 (adopted 30 November 1973, entered into force 18 July 1976).

[44] 1035 UNTS 167 (adopted 14 December 1973, entered into force 20 February 1977).

[45] As defined in article 1 of the *International Convention against the Taking of Hostages*, 1316 UNTS 205 (adopted 17 December 1979, entered into force 3 June 1983).

[46] 1678 UNTS 221 (adopted 10 March 1988, entered into force 1 March 1992).

[47] 1678 UNTS I-29004 (adopted 10 March 1988, entered into force 1 March 1992).

[48] *United Nations Convention against Illicit Traffic in Narcotic Drugs and Psychotropic Substances*, 1582 UNTS 95 (adopted 20 December 1988, entered into force 11 November 1990).

jurisdiction and merely refer the reader to applicable treaties was motivated by the ILC's considered view that it is not the Draft Statute's 'function to define new crimes. Nor is it the function of the Statute authoritatively to codify crimes under general international law. With respect to certain of these crimes, this is the purpose of the Draft Code of Crimes against the Peace and Security of Mankind, although the Draft Code is not intended to deal with all crimes under general international law.'[49] Thus, the 1994 Draft Statute was regarded by the ILC as 'primarily an adjectival and procedural instrument'.[50] As well, the ILC sought to draft a modest Statute, that is, one without definitions of crimes, because it did not want to 'scare potential and influential States'.[51]

In response to the 1994 Draft Statute, the UN General Assembly created an Ad Hoc Committee on the Establishment of an International Criminal Court and requested it to 'review the major substantive and administrative issues arising out of the draft statute prepared by the International Law Commission and, in light of that review, to consider arrangements for the convening of an international conference of plenipotentiaries'.[52] Treaties drafted by the ILC are normally finalized by either the UN General Assembly or by a special intergovernmental conference convened for this purpose.[53] The final text produced by the ILC is usually accompanied by a detailed commentary that serves as 'an invaluable aid, in fact indispensable to understanding the thrust and the purport of any given provision'.[54] However, the ILC commentaries generally 'refrain from expressing a clear opinion on the question whether any particular draft article represents, in whole or in part, a rule of customary international law'.[55]

In its 1995 report, the Ad Hoc Committee commented on the first four crimes listed in the 1994 Draft Statute as representing 'a common core of agreement in the [International Law] Commission, and [as being] without prejudice to the identification and application of the concept of crimes under general international law for other purposes'.[56] Thus, the Ad Hoc Committee was careful to point out that the list of crimes was exhaustive for the purposes of the Statute but not necessarily reflective of all crimes that exist under general international

---

[49] Commentary on article 20(4), 1994 Draft Statute (n. 34) 38.   [50] Ibid. 26, 38.

[51] Crawford (n. 1).   [52] UNGA Res. 49/53 (9 December 1994).

[53] Y Dinstein, 'Interaction Between Customary International Law and Treaties' (2006) 322 Recueil des Cours de l'Académie de Droit International 243, 247, 370.

[54] Ibid. (citing S Rosenne, 'Codification Revisited after 50 Years' (1998) 2 Max Planck Ybk of UN Law 1, 13).

[55] Dinstein (n. 53) (quoting A Watts, 'The International Court and the Continuing Customary International Law of Treaties' in N Ando, E McWhinney and R Wolfrum (eds.), *Liber Amicorum Judge Shigeru Oda*, vol. I (Kluwer Law International 2002) 251, 255).

[56] UNGA, 'Report of the Ad Hoc Committee on the Establishment of an International Criminal Court' (1995), UN Doc. A/50/22 Supp. 22, 71 (1995 Ad Hoc Committee Report).

law. The Ad Hoc Committee also proposed eliminating the distinction between establishing international criminal jurisdiction and drafting a code of international crimes.[57] Going forward, the Court's jurisdiction and the definitions of crimes would be contained in a single document.

According to the Chair of the Ad Hoc Committee, two clear tendencies emerged from the very first discussions of the Committee:

> [The first was to] limit the scope of the subject-matter jurisdiction of the Court to the most serious crimes, which are of concern to the international community as a whole. This meant limiting the crimes to those mentioned in Article 20(a) to (d) of the [1994] ILC Draft, i.e. genocide, crimes of aggression, serious violations of the laws and customs applicable in armed conflict, and crimes against humanity, although opinions were divided with regard to the inclusion of the crime of aggression.[58]

Delegates expressed the view that the Ad Hoc Committee was not mandated to progressively develop the law in this field and 'should, therefore, concentrate on these core crimes, being crimes under international customary law'.[59] This meant that treaty crimes were excluded.[60]

The second was a clear tendency to define the crimes within the Statute.[61] It was thought that there was sufficient legal material to assist with the drafting of such definitions, that the principle of legality required definitions to be included in the Statute and that the inclusion of definitions would allay concerns about unchecked prosecutorial and judicial discretion.[62] These views suggest that the jurisdiction of the Court was to be limited to crimes existing under customary international law and that custom was sufficiently detailed or 'ripe' to inform the definitions of crimes to be included in the Statute. It would appear, therefore, that the Ad Hoc Committee did envision codifying customary definitions of these crimes in the Rome Statute.

While the Ad Hoc Committee was working on the Draft Statute for the Court, the ILC adopted a revised Draft Code in 1996.[63] It was much more modest than its 1991 counterpart but more expansive than the 1993 Draft Statute and limited the list of crimes to aggression, genocide, crimes against humanity, crimes against United Nations and associated personnel and war crimes.[64] The reduced number of crimes within the 1996 Draft Code was in response to comments received from several governments and some members of the ILC.[65] As well, though article 13 of the Draft Code prohibited the conviction of

---

[57] Ibid. [58] Bos (n. 1) 41. [59] Ibid. [60] Ibid. [61] Ibid. 42.

[62] Ibid. 42–43. See also 1995 Ad Hoc Committee Report (n. 56) para. 57.

[63] 1996 Draft Code, UN Doc. A/CN.4/L.522.

[64] Articles 16–20, ibid.; N Boister, 'The Exclusion of Treaty Crimes from the Jurisdiction for the Proposed International Criminal Court: Law, Pragmatism, Politics' (1998) 3 J Conflict & Security Law 27, 27–28.

[65] ILC, 'Comments and Observations of Governments on the Draft Code of Crimes against the Peace and Security of Mankind adopted on First Reading by the International Law Commission at its Forty-Third Session' (1 March 1993), UN Doc. A/CN.4/448.

a person under the Code prior to its entry into force, it did not preclude such conviction if the act in question was criminal at the time it was committed 'in accordance with international law or national law'.[66] Implicit in this provision is an acknowledgement that not all of the crimes contained in the Draft Code were 'new' crimes or 'treaty' crimes and that their criminality stemmed from existing customary international law. This evolution from the 1991 to the 1996 Draft Code has been described as 'the "hard core" of relatively well-established international criminal law norms' being 'discerned from a "softer" normative periphery'.[67] In spite of this progress, the Draft Code was 'not thought to be susceptible of application by the Court, whether by the Rome Conference, the Preparatory Committee or even, in truth, the ILC itself'.[68] Thus, work on defining the crimes within the jurisdiction of the Court would continue to be done by those working on drafting a Statute for the Court. Fortunately, the Ad Hoc Committee experienced little difficulty in identifying texts defining the elements for the crimes of aggression, genocide, other crimes against humanity and war crimes that are widely recognized and accepted.[69] In sum then, treaty crimes were included in all of the ILC's Draft Codes and Statutes until being dropped from the 1996 Draft Code.

After the Ad Hoc Committee submitted its report to the General Assembly, the latter established a Preparatory Committee to carry on the work of drafting a Statute.[70] The Preparatory Committee met for a total of fifteen weeks between March 1996 and April 1998. Its mandate included 'preparing a *widely acceptable* consolidated text of a convention for an international criminal court'.[71] Thus, the negotiations had reached a point where consensus-building was paramount.[72]

According to the chair of the Preparatory Committee, the debates were serious, and international law and criminal law experts were encouraged to participate.[73] Consensus was reached that the core crimes of genocide, other crimes against humanity and war crimes should be included in the Statute.[74] On the inclusion of the crime of aggression, diverging views were expressed.[75] Further, while the 1996 Preparatory Committee debates were reported on, the Committee recommended to the UN General Assembly that such reporting not be required for the 1997 and 1998 debates, because this was thought to

---

[66] 1996 Draft Code (n. 63). [67] Sunga (n. 1) 14.

[68] A Pellet, 'Applicable Law' in A Cassese and Others (eds.), *The Rome Statute of the International Criminal Court: A Commentary*, vol. II (Oxford University Press 2002) 1051, 1056.

[69] WA Schabas, *The International Criminal Court: A Commentary on the Rome Statute* (Oxford University Press 2010) 405.

[70] UNGA Res. 50/46 (11 December 1995); Bos (n. 1) 51–52.

[71] UNGA, ibid. (emphasis added).

[72] H Lauterpacht, 'Codification and Development of International Law' (1955) 49 AJIL 16, 31.

[73] Bos (n. 1) 46. [74] Ibid. 48. [75] Ibid.

take time away from drafting and discussing the text of the Statute.[76] The general view was that the changes to the text would be clear from reading the draft texts circulated.[77] The historic record is therefore somewhat compromised.

Still, a couple of findings relevant to the present study are well documented. First, the Preparatory Committee sought to limit the Court's jurisdiction to crimes established under customary international law so as to attract the widest possible consensus.[78] Second, in response to the concerns of the Ad Hoc Committee, it decided that the crimes should be defined in the Statute so as to respect the principle of legality.[79] Indeed, some delegations argued strongly for a code-based international criminal court.[80] For example, the United States suggested during the Preparatory Committee debates that elements for the crimes should be elaborated in the Statute, while a clear majority resisted the idea.[81] The majority argued inter alia that drafting such elements was not necessary because the definitions in the Draft Statute were sufficiently precise to respect the principle of legality,[82] the general principles of criminal law adequately covered the subject matter[83] and such a text would unduly bind the judges, who are best situated to discern such elements.[84] Most relevant to the present inquiry is that the majority of delegates considered existing general international law to be sufficiently detailed to inform the content of the Rome Statute and do away with any perceived need to draft Elements of Crimes.

From 15 June until 17 July 1998, delegates from 160 countries convened in Rome for a Diplomatic Conference that resulted in the adoption of the Rome Statute. The Preparatory Committee forwarded to the conference a

---

[76] Ibid. 51.

[77] Ibid.; 1997 Preparatory Committee Report, UN Doc. A/AC.249/1997/L.9/Rev.1; 1998 Preparatory Committee Report, UN Doc. A/CONF.183/2.

[78] 1996 Preparatory Committee Report, UN Doc. A/51/22, vol. I, 78; M Kelt and H von Hebel, 'The Making of the Elements of Crimes: What are Elements of Crimes?' in RS Lee (ed.), *The International Criminal Court: Elements of Crimes and Rules of Procedure and Evidence* (Transnational 2001) 13; TLH McCormack and S Robertson, 'Jurisdictional Aspects of the Rome Statute for the New International Criminal Court' (1999) 23 Melbourne Univ L Rev 25.

[79] 1996 Preparatory Committee Report (n. 78).

[80] MC Bassiouni, *A Draft International Criminal Court and Draft Statute for an International Criminal Tribunal* (Martinus Nijhoff 1987) 9–10; EM Wise, 'General Rules of Criminal Law' (1997) 25 Denver J Int'l L & Pol 313, 317–19.

[81] Bos (n. 1) 56; H von Hebel, 'The Decision to Include Elements of Crimes in the Rome Statute' in RS Lee (ed.), *The International Criminal Court: Elements of Crimes and Rules of Procedure and Evidence* (Transnational 2001) 3, 5–6. Note that the United States' idea to draft Elements of Crimes does not appear in the Preparatory Committee's Draft Statute. 1998 Preparatory Committee Report (n. 77) Add.1.

[82] von Hebel, ibid.   [83] Bos (n. 1) 56.   [84] Ibid.

Draft Statute containing approximately 1,400 square brackets.[85] Politically sensitive issues were intertwined. For example, if the Court's jurisdiction over each crime was based on the consent of the relevant State(s), the latter were prepared to entertain the idea of the Court having jurisdiction over a broad range of crimes, including treaty crimes, such as drug trafficking and terrorism.[86] Equally, if jurisdiction was universal or automatic upon ratification, then some delegations favoured the Court having jurisdiction over a limited number of crimes, defined narrowly and accompanied by high jurisdictional thresholds.[87] States' jurisdictional preferences were also influenced by the issue of whether reservations to the Court's jurisdiction could be lodged.[88]

The topic of customary international law and its relationship to the Rome Statute surfaced in at least four ways at Rome. First, delegates relied on this relationship to argue for the exclusion from the Court's jurisdiction of what were considered treaty crimes (e.g., drug trafficking).[89] Second, delegates relied on this relationship to argue for the inclusion of certain crimes in the Rome Statute, such as aggression, war crimes committed during internal armed conflict and certain crimes against humanity.[90] Finally, the relationship was invoked as an argument for either narrowing[91] or broadening[92] the definition of a crime to bring it in line with custom. The importance of this relationship should not, however, be overstated. Practical concerns were ever present, including the need to attract the widest possible consensus.[93] For example, while it was understood that the Rome Statute should be limited to existing crimes under international law and it was widely regarded that several treaty provisions prohibiting the use of certain weapons were reflective of customary international law, their inclusion in the Rome Statute hinged on a major controversy as to whether the use of nuclear weapons and land mines should be listed as a war crime.[94] Agreement could not be reached on whether the threat or use of these weapons was prohibited under international law.[95]

The Rome Diplomatic Conference has been described as the closest that States have come to drafting a general code of international criminal law.[96] The

---

[85] P Kirsch and JT Holmes, 'The Rome Conference on an International Criminal Court: The Negotiating Process' (1999) 93 AJIL 2.
[86] Ibid. 6 and fn. 19.   [87] Ibid. fn. 19.   [88] Ibid.
[89] See, e.g., the discussion in P Kirsch and D Robinson (n. 1) 69.
[90] Ibid. 79, 81.   [91] See article 7(2)(e), Rome Statute.
[92] See article 8(2)(b)(iv), Rome Statute ('clearly excessive').
[93] See, e.g., the discussion on war crimes in von Hebel (n. 81) 5.
[94] Kirsch and Robinson (n. 1) 79–80; Kirsch and Holmes (n. 85) 6.
[95] Kirsch and Robinson, ibid.; Kirsch and Holmes, ibid. 7.
[96] R Cryer, 'The Doctrinal Foundations of International Criminalization' in MC Bassiouni (ed.), *International Criminal Law*, vol. I (Martinus Nijhoff 2008) 107, 118.

American representative to the UN General Assembly described the approach of most States at Rome as follows:

> This Court should not ... be in the business of deciding even what is a crime. This is not the place for progressive development of the law into uncertain areas, or for the elaboration of new and uncertain international criminal law. The Court must concern itself with those atrocities which are universally recognized as wrongful and condemned.[97]

This intention of drafters to limit the Court's jurisdiction to crimes existing under customary international law is confirmed by a number of experts and scholars.[98]

> In elaborating the definitions, one of the major guiding principles was that the definitions should be reflective of customary international law. It was understood that the Court should operate only for crimes that are of concern to the international community as a whole, which meant the inclusion only of crimes which are universally recognized. An additional pragmatic reason was that becoming a party to the Statute would not be contingent on the acceptance of legal instruments defining the substance of such crimes.[99]

However, not everyone agrees with this characterization,[100] and States did disagree at times about whether certain crimes were part of customary international law.[101] This concern was the impetus prior to Rome for not referring to it as a codification conference lest a decodifying effect take hold should many States reject the Rome Statute or register reservations to the definitions of crimes therein.[102] This and the potential that not all crimes under customary international law would find their way into the Rome Statute was the motivation for including article 10 in the Statute.[103] Nevertheless, the Final Act of the Rome Conference reiterates (perhaps inadvertently) the limited scope of articles 6, 7 and 8 by providing that the addition of 'treaty crimes' to the Rome

---

[97] 'US Rep to the GA Assembly 23 October 1997 (Agenda Item 150)', cited in Cryer, ibid.

[98] R Clark, 'Article 9' in O Triffterer (ed.), *Commentary on the Rome Statute of the International Criminal Court*, 2nd edn (Beck/Hart/Nomos 2008) 505, 508; R Cryer, 'Of Custom, Treaties, Scholars and the Gavel: The Influence of the International Criminal Tribunals on the ICRC Customary Law Study' (2006) 11 J Conflict & Security L 239, 251; GM Danilenko, 'ICC Statute and Third States' in A Cassese and Others (eds.), *The Rome Statute of the International Criminal Court: A Commentary*, vol. I (Oxford University Press 2002) 1871, 1891.

[99] von Hebel and Robinson (n. 39) 122.

[100] Triffterer notes that during the drafting process, there was little agreement as to whether a codification of international law 'should merely declare and systematize existing rules or also include "progressive development"' of international law. O Triffterer, 'Article 10' in O Triffterer (ed.), *Commentary on the Rome Statute of the International Criminal Court*, 1st edn (Beck/Hart/Nomos 1999) 315, 316.

[101] R Clark (n. 98) 508.   [102] Dinstein (n. 53) 367.   [103] Cryer (n. 96).

regime is a matter that may be considered at the first Review Conference for the Statute.[104]

An indicator of codification that is related to a treaty's drafting history is whether custom in the relevant field of law was 'ripe' for codification prior to the treaty being drafted and whether it was sufficiently developed and coherent to take the form of a written code.[105] Where the development of law in a particular area has stalled, is characterized by too many diverse practices, is too generic, is too nascent or contains rules that are considered undesirable, States may try to draft a treaty that departs from custom.[106] On the complex development of international criminal law, the following has been observed:

> The manner in which international criminal law has developed – through States meeting under UN auspices, with the Security Council acting (or, more specifically, a small group of States operating through the Security Council at times with the assistance of the OLA), meeting alone, or with the ICRC – has led to a body of international criminal law which is characterised by "overlaps, gaps and ambiguities."[107]

While jurisprudence of the ICTY and ICTR certainly helped to overcome overlaps, gaps and ambiguities, some contend that international criminal law continues to lack uniformity with respect to the application of legal sources and that problems of comprehensiveness, coherence and clarity remain.[108] However, these are problems of degree, and it is difficult to assess the extent to which these problems presented real obstacles to codifying crimes under international criminal law in the Rome Statute. Further, such problems might have led to a partial codification of crimes, but a codification nevertheless, or the use of creative ambiguities during the drafting process, thereby codifying existing ambiguities. When the General Assembly convened the Diplomatic Conference in Rome, emphasis was placed not on resolving all outstanding problems in the field of international criminal law but on drafting provisions that would attract the consensus needed for work on the Rome Statute to be successfully concluded.[109] The Preparatory Committee similarly concluded that 'it was more important to identify opportunities for compromise than to strive for a perfect solution in one or the other direction'.[110] Most important, the goal of reaching consensus at Rome seems largely to have corresponded with including in the Statute only crimes that exist under customary international

---

[104] Final Act of the Rome Conference (17 July 1998), UN Doc. A/CONF.183/10, para. 26 and Resolution E.
[105] See Chapter 6, Section 6.4.   [106] Dinstein (n. 53) 348–50.   [107] Cryer (n. 96) 119.
[108] Sunga (n. 1) 2–3, 6.   [109] UNGA Res. 52/160 (15 December 1997).
[110] O Triffterer, 'Article 10' in O Triffterer (ed.), *Commentary on the Rome Statute of the International Criminal Court*, 2nd edn (Beck/Hart/Nomos 2008) 531, 532–33.

law. However, this goal was not always achieved.[111] And, even after the Rome Statute was drafted, a leading scholar described international criminal law as a 'very rudimentary branch of law'.[112]

> Given these characteristics of the evolution of ICL, it should not be surprising that even the recent addition of the sets of written rules referred to above has not proved sufficient to build a coherent legal system, as is shown by the heavy reliance by the newly created *international* courts upon customary rules or unwritten general principles.[113]

But this close relationship to custom and general principles is arguably necessary for all fields of international law. The international legal system has been described as being in 'large part an unsystematic accumulation, accretion, and incremental development of norms, institutions, practices, and processes, whose evolution lacks the characteristics of linearity, consistency, or predictability'.[114]

After Rome, the Preparatory Commission met for fourteen weeks and adopted by consensus the Elements of Crimes on 30 June 2000. 'As with all documents that are adopted by general agreement, the outcome reflects compromises, some of which were difficult to reach or to accept.'[115] Further, the Elements of Crimes were an exercise in giving detail to customary norms that are in some cases too vague or imprecise for the purpose of effectively prosecuting an individual.[116] The Working Group on Elements of Crimes met in formal sessions, which were open to the public, and informal sessions, which took place behind closed doors.[117] The formal meetings were interpreted into six official languages[118] but 'were mainly held for the purpose of assigning tasks, reporting on progress, adopting reports, and taking decisions. Most serious negotiations were conducted in working groups or through informal meetings, consultations or contacts, which were closed to the public and without official

---

[111] Y Dinstein, 'Crimes against Humanity and the Rome Statute of the International Criminal Court', Paper presented at the Universality of Human Rights Conference (German Innovation Center/IDC Herzliya and the Science Center of North Rhine-Westphalia 2005).

[112] Cassese (n. 12) 4.   [113] Ibid. 5.

[114] MC Bassiouni, 'The Philosophy and Policy of International Criminal Justice' in LC Vohrah and Others (eds.), *Man's Inhumanity to Man: Essays on International Law in Honour of Antonio Cassese* (Kluwer Law International 2003) 65, 66.

[115] P Kirsch, 'The Work of the Preparatory Commission' in RS Lee (ed.), *The International Criminal Court: Elements of Crimes and Rules of Procedure and Evidence* (Transnational 2001) xlv.

[116] WK Lietzau, 'Checks and Balances and Elements of Proof: Structural Pillars for the International Criminal Court' (1999) 32 Cornell Int'l LJ 477, 482, fn. 25.

[117] von Hebel (n. 81) 8.

[118] RS Lee, 'Introduction' in RS Lee (ed.), *The International Criminal Court: Elements of Crimes and Rules of Procedure and Evidence* (Transnational 2001) lvii.

records.'[119] However, twenty-nine diplomats and jurists 'who played a central role in the preparation of the Elements, many of whom chaired or coordinated negotiations on a particular subject or subjects published a collective analysis of the legislative history.'[120]

Finally, unlike other core international crimes, whose definitions have legally evolved and matured since the Second World War the crime of aggression, with the exception of the adoption of United Nations General Assembly Resolution 3314 (XXIX) in 1974, has remained underdeveloped. The exact scope of the elements of this crime under customary law are therefore 'difficult to ascertain'.[121]

This absence of State practice renders unclear the extent to which the drafters of the definition of the crime of aggression could be guided by existing custom. However, a few things are clear. First, the Preparatory Commission for the International Criminal Court, which was initially tasked with drafting a definition for the crime of aggression (a task later carried forward by the Special Working Group on the Crime of Aggression (Special Working Group)), prepared two major studies in which it reviewed in painstaking detail the historical legal developments on the crime of aggression.[122] This suggests that the drafters of the definition were hardly interested in departing from existing legal precedents. Second, the Special Working Group was determined to embed the definition of the crime of aggression as seamlessly as possible within the Rome Statute, which was drafted with a view to departing as little as necessary from existing custom.[123] Third, the negotiations on aggression were open to all States until their conclusion, and the amendments were ultimately adopted without a dissenting voice breaking the consensus reached – which is also suggestive of the codificatory potential of the definition adopted.[124]

---

[119] Ibid.

[120] Ibid. vii. See also K. Dörmann, *Elements of War Crimes under the Rome Statute of the International Criminal Court* (Cambridge University Press 2003).

[121] C Kreß and L von Holtzendorff, 'The Kampala Compromise on the Crime of Aggression' (2010) 8 J Int'l Crim Justice 1179, 1188.

[122] Preparatory Commission, Working Group on the Crime of Aggression (Secretariat), 'Historical Review of Developments relating to Aggression' Parts I and II (18 and 24 January 2002), UN Doc. PCNICC/2002/WGCA/L.1/Add.1.

[123] S Barriga, 'Negotiating the Amendments on the Crime of Aggression' in S Barriga and C Kreß (eds.), *The Travaux Préparatoires of the Crime of Aggression* (Cambridge University Press 2012) 3, 18.

[124] First Review Conference of the Rome Statute, Official Records, Resolution on the Crime of Aggression (adopted 11 June 2010) RC/Res.6, www.icc-cpi.int/iccdocs/asp_docs/Resolutions/RC-Res.6-ENG.pdf, accessed 5 November 2013 (Aggression Resolution); although, see the statements made by some States, including the United States, following the adoption of the resolution. Barriga and Kreß, ibid. item 156 ('Explanations

8.3 Ratifications, reservations, denunciations and revisions

Departing from the prior rule of unanimity, article 9(2) of the *Vienna Convention* (1969) provides that a two-thirds majority is required for the adoption of a treaty at an international conference, unless the same majority of attending States decides otherwise.[125]

> The scope of conventions adopted, even if only by a two-thirds majority vote, after such preparatory procedures have been followed is likely to become enlarged as the result of subsequent accession. The very fact of their continued validity among large groups of states cannot fail to exercise considerable influence, quite apart from the possibility of the convention giving rise to rules of customary international law.[126]

The Rome Statute was adopted by a non-recorded vote of 120 in favour, 7 against and 21 abstentions. On 9 September 2002, the Assembly of States Parties adopted by consensus the draft Elements of Crimes prepared by the Preparatory Commission.

> In fact, an almost universal participation to the treaty tends to strengthen the evidence that such a treaty reflects customary law; but this can never act as decisive proof of such, since even a treaty that tends towards a progressive development of the law can still obtain notable success together with the participation of many States. Similarly, the fact that the treaty has entered into force tends to strengthen the evidence that the treaty reflects customary law; but it is also true that nothing impedes a treaty not yet in force to correspond, entirely or in part, to customary law.[127]

In the following sections, consideration will be given to the idea of participation in the Rome regime and what this tells us about the nature of the crimes defined in the Rome Statute. Ratifications, reservations, denunciations and revisions relating to the Statute will be considered in turn as well as the significance, if any, that should be ascribed to these practices.

8.3.1 Ratifications

In the *North Sea Continental Shelf* cases (1969), the International Court of Justice (ICJ) stated in its dictum that to prove that a treaty rule also exists

---

of Position' in *Review Conference Official Records* (2010), RC/11, Annexes VII–IX, 122, para. F).

[125] R Jennings and A Watts, *Oppenheim's International Law*, vol. I, 9th edn (Longman, Harlow 1992) 111–12.

[126] Ibid. 113.

[127] R Pissillo-Mazzeschi, 'Treaty and Custom: Reflections on the Codification of International Law' (1997) Commonwealth L Bull 549, 555.

under customary international law, 'a very widespread and representative participation in the convention might suffice of itself, provided it included that of States whose interests were specially affected'.[128] In rejecting the customary status of the impugned provision, the ICJ noted that the thirty-nine ratifications it received were 'hardly sufficient' to meet the threshold of 'widespread and representative'.[129] In its *Nuclear Weapons* advisory opinion (1996), the ICJ also opaquely referred to the 'broad accession' and 'extent of accession' to the treaties under consideration.[130] Consequently, scholars have turned their attention to what weight, if any, should be given to ratifications of a treaty when attempting to discern the customary legal status of its provisions.

It has been suggested that where a treaty expressly states that it is intended to codify custom, fifty ratifications of it 'has the same persuasive force as would evidence of the State practice of fifty individual States.'[131] However, the inexplicable absence of such ratification might offer evidence of a 'negative *opinio juris*', a belief that the treaty is not reflective of custom.[132] It has been cautioned that such reasoning should not be taken too far, as there may be many reasons that a State chooses not to ratify a treaty, quite apart from whether it reflects custom.[133]

However, the validity of the aforementioned reasoning is doubtful where a treaty that seems to codify customary law makes no mention in its text that it has done so.[134] Here, it is not clear whether ratification is indicative of a State's intent to be bound to a treaty – to assume obligations towards other States Parties – or its *opinio juris* for the purpose of establishing customary international law, meaning the assumption of obligations that are owed equally to States and Non-States Parties.[135] While a treaty can be reflective of custom or eventually crystallize into custom, it 'cannot pull itself by its own metaphorical bootstraps, and turn into custom'.[136] More is required, such as general State practice and communal *opinio juris*. On this point, drafters of a treaty might intend to crystallize a rule into custom, and ratifications of the relevant treaty in this case may validly be considered relevant State practice.[137]

---

[128] *North Sea Continental Shelf Cases (Germany v. Denmark; Germany v. The Netherlands)* [1969] ICJ Rep. 3, 42.

[129] Ibid.

[130] *Legality of the Threat or Use of Nuclear Weapons*, Advisory Opinion [1996] ICJ Rep 226, 257–58.

[131] RR Baxter, 'Multilateral Treaties as Evidence of Customary International Law' (1965–1966) 41 British Ybk Int'l L 275, 277–78; RR Baxter, 'Treaties and Custom' (1970) 129 Recueil des Cours de l'Académie de Droit International 25, 55.

[132] HWA Thirlway, *International Customary Law and Codification* (Sijthoff 1972) 115.

[133] Ibid.   [134] Baxter, 'Treaties and Custom' (n. 131) 38.

[135] Ibid. 64.   [136] Dinstein (n. 53) 375.

[137] O Schachter, 'Entangled Treaty and Custom' in Y Dinstein (ed.), *International Law at a Time of Perplexity: Essays in Honour of Shabtai Rosenne* (Martinus Nijhoff 1989) 717, 725.

Insofar as aspects of articles 6, 7 and 8 of the Rome Statute were not reflective of custom in 1998, the Statute's ratification by 122 countries at the time of writing may, along with communal *opinio juris*, suggest that these elements have been or will soon be considered to have crystallized into custom. To date, the amendments on the crime of aggression have been ratified by thirteen States.[138] Further, '[t]o the extent that the Statute is widely ratified . . . even the inclusion of article 10 will not prevent States from eventually arguing that the Statute's definitions represent customary international law.'[139]

8.3.2 Reservations

In the *North Sea Continental Shelf* cases (1969), the ICJ gave weight to the permissibility of reservations as evidence of the non-customary nature of certain treaty provisions.

> [S]peaking generally, it is a characteristic of purely conventional rules and obligations that, in regard to them, some faculty of making unilateral reservations may, within certain limits, be admitted – whereas this cannot be so in the case of general or customary law rules and obligations which, by their very nature, must have equal force for all members of the international community, and cannot therefore be the subject of any right of unilateral exclusion exercisable at will by any one of them in its own favour. Consequently, it is to be expected that when, for whatever reason, rules or obligations of this order are embodied, or are intended to be reflected in certain provisions of a convention, such provisions will figure amongst those in respect of which a right of unilateral reservation is not conferred or is excluded.[140]

A couple of judges dissented from this reasoning, pointing out that custom and treaty have equal status as sources of law, that the latter may therefore depart from the former[141] and that the power to make reservations to a treaty

---

[138] Report of the International Criminal Court to the UN General Assembly (13 August 2013), UN Doc. A/68/314, 2, 4; The Global Campaign for Ratification and Implementation of the Kampala Amendments on the Crime of Aggression, 'Status of Ratification and Implementation', http://crimeofaggression.info, accessed 5 November 2013.

[139] LN Sadat and SR Carden, 'The New International Criminal Court: An Uneasy Revolution' (2000) 88 Georgetown LJ 381, 423.

[140] *North Sea Continental Shelf Cases* (n. 128) 38–39. In General Comment No. 24 (1994), UN Doc. CCPR/C/21/Rev.1/Add.6, para. 8, the UN Human Rights Committee stated that 'provisions in the Covenant [on Civil and Political Rights] that represent customary international law . . . may not be the subject of reservations'. See also *Reservations to the Convention on the Prevention and Punishment of the Crime of Genocide*, Advisory Opinion [1951] ICJ Rep. 15.

[141] *North Sea Continental Shelf Cases* (n. 128) Dissenting Opinion of Judge Sørensen 242, 248.

is not incompatible with it codifying custom.[142] This view is shared by some scholars, as is the idea that the impermissibility of reservations is not solely determinative of the opposite finding.[143] The two are not mutually exclusive ideas, and while weight should be attached to the reservation, the rest of the treaty may still reflect the views of all States Parties on the content of custom.[144] As well, the reservation of one State is silent on how other States view the same issue.[145]

In its Guidelines on Reservations to a Provision Reflecting a Customary Norm (2007), the International Law Commission stated in Guideline 3.1.8:

1. The fact that a treaty provision reflects a customary norm is a pertinent factor in assessing the validity of a reservation although it does not in itself constitute an obstacle to the formulation of the reservation to that provision.
2. A reservation to a treaty provision which reflects a customary norm does not affect the binding nature of that customary norm which shall continue to apply as such between the reserving State . . . and other States . . . .which are bound by that norm.[146]

It has further been suggested that if many States enter a reservation to a particular treaty provision, this may indirectly and negatively affect the underlying customary rule over time.[147] Indeed, where a treaty is intended to codify custom, one commentator has observed that it 'makes no sense to go through the process . . . if the results are going to be counter-productive, weakening custom instead of reinvigorating it. . . . [A] reservation to a codification treaty should be deemed "incompatible with the object and purpose of the treaty"'.[148] However, some allegedly declaratory conventions have more reservations to them than conventions that are regarded as being largely *lege ferenda*.[149] The *North Sea Continental Shelf* judgment (1969) seems to imply two further fallacies. First, it appears to ignore the important distinction between *jus dispositivum* and *jus cogens*, the former category of rules being freely varied or excluded by agreement in the relations between two or more States, provided the position of a third State is not prejudiced.[150] Second, it incorrectly characterizes reservations as being purely unilateral acts; their legal effect on multilateral treaties

---

[142] Ibid., Dissenting Opinion of Judge Morelli, 198, 199.
[143] Baxter, 'Treaties and Custom' (n. 131) 50; ME Villiger, *Commentary on the 1969 Vienna Convention on the Law of Treaties* (Martinus Nijhoff 2009) 15.
[144] Baxter, ibid.   [145] Baxter (n. 131) 50.
[146] (2007) II (Part Two) Ybk of the ILC 88ff.
[147] Villiger (n. 143).
[148] Dinstein (n. 53) 364–65 (in which case it is disallowed under article 19(c) of the *Vienna Convention* (1969)).
[149] Ibid. 51.   [150] Thirlway (n. 132) 120–21.

is subject to the consent of States in accordance with article 20 of the *Vienna Convention* (1969).[151] For all of these reasons, the *dictum* of the Court should not be read too broadly.[152]

Article 20(3) of the *Vienna Convention* (1969) provides: 'When a treaty is a constituent instrument of an international organization and unless it otherwise provides, a reservation requires the acceptance of the competent organ of that organization.' Because of this provision and anticipating that the Rome Statute would be adopted as a package of delicate and interrelated compromises, the International Law Commission initially sought in its draft statutes to limit or exclude reservations:

> The draft statute has been constructed as an overall scheme, incorporating important balances and qualifications in relation to the working of the court: it is intended to operate as a whole. These considerations tend to support the view that reservations to the statute and its accompanying treaty should either not be permitted, or should be limited in scope. This is of course a matter for States Parties to consider in the context of negotiations for the conclusion of the statute and its accompanying treaty.[153]

It is important to recall that the International Law Commission made this proposal at a time when it and NGOs contemplated that States would opt into the Rome regime for each crime, an approach that was ultimately rejected for genocide and other crimes against humanity but accepted for war crimes.[154]

Article 120 of the Rome Statute provides: 'No reservations may be made to this Statute.' In the 'Updated Siracusa Draft' of 1996, which was the product of expert and NGO discussions that were chaired by Professor Bassiouni, it was contemplated that reservations are permissible 'with respect to existing international obligations and with respect to any crime defined in the special part of the International Criminal Code'.[155] The language in article 120 appeared

---

[151] Ibid. Perhaps this is owing to the definition of reservations in article 2(1)(d) of the *Vienna Convention* (1969): 'a unilateral statement, however phrased or named, made by a State, when signing, ratifying, accepting, approving or acceding to a treaty, whereby it purports to exclude or to modify the legal effect of certain provisions of the treaty in their application to that State'.

[152] Thirlway (n. 132) 119–20.   [153] 1994 Draft Statute (n. 34) 29.

[154] G Hafner, 'Article 120' in O Triffterer (ed.), *Commentary on the Rome Statute of the International Criminal Court*, 2nd edn (Beck/Hart/Nomos 2008) 1737, 1741.

[155] Committee of Experts on International Criminal Law, Draft Statute for an International Criminal Court – Alternative to the ILC Statute (15 March 1996) (Updated Siracusa Draft) 119.

for the first time in a proposal made by the Secretariat in December 1997[156] and was based on a suggestion made during discussions in the Preparatory Committee in 1996 in order to retain the integrity of the text as a whole.[157] It was then carried over into the Zutphen text.[158]

The Preparatory Committee in March 1998 had the first full discussion of reservations, which resulted in a new text containing three options: (1) prohibit all reservations; (2) list articles to which reservations were permissible; or (3) have no provision on reservations so that the *de facto Vienna Convention* (1969) regime would apply.[159] In the 'Draft Statute for the International Criminal Court', a fourth option was inserted: list articles to which reservations are not permissible.[160] At Rome, the matter was only briefly discussed in a group coordinated by Ambassador Sloane (Samoa) before the first option, prohibition of reservations, was adopted.[161] The provision 'preserves the integrity of the text which is infringed only by the transitional provision of article 124'.[162] This decision was supported by several NGOs in Rome that were concerned that reservations could weaken the nature of the obligations in the Statute and its moral authority.[163]

States may try to circumvent article 120 by lodging 'interpretive declarations' in which they claim to 'clarify the meaning or scope' of a treaty provision.[164] Such a declaration 'shall be presumed not to constitute a reservation except when it purports to exclude or modify the legal effect of certain provisions of the treaty or of the treaty as a whole with respect to certain specific aspects in their application to its author'.[165] To the extent that a declaration in substance seeks to exclude or modify articles 6 or 7 of the Rome Statute, it would be inadmissible in light of article 120.[166] A declaration that modifies article 8 would be similarly inadmissible.

---

[156] 'Draft Text relating to Final Clauses, Final Act and Establishment of a Preparatory Commission' (1998), UN Doc. A/AC.249/1998/L.11, 2, article B.

[157] 1996 Preparatory Committee Report (n. 78) 9.

[158] Preparatory Committee, 'Report of the Inter-Sessional Meeting from 19 to 30 January 1998 in Zutphen, The Netherlands' (4 February 1998), UN Doc. A/AC.249/1998/L.13, 169, article 92(B).

[159] UN Doc. A/AC.249/1998/CRP.4.

[160] 1998 Preparatory Committee Report, Draft Statute and Draft Final Act (1998), UN Doc. A/Conf.183/2/Add.1, article 109.

[161] Hafner (n. 154) 1740.   [162] Ibid.   [163] Ibid. 1741.

[164] A Pellet, 'Third Report on Reservations to Treaties' (30 April 1998), UN Doc. A/CN.4/491/Add.4, 33 and confirmed by the ILC in guideline 1.2, 'Report of the International Law Commission on the Work of its Fifty-Third Session' (2001), UN Doc. A/56/10, 457.

[165] ILC, ibid. 458, guideline 1.3.3.

[166] Hafner (n. 154) 1744; App. No. 10328/83, *Belilos* v. *Switzerland*, ECHR (1988) Series A, No. 132, 22.

However, article 124 is titled 'Transitional Provision' and provides:

> [A] State, on becoming a party to this Statute, may declare that, for a
> period of seven years after the entry into force of this Statute for the
> State concerned, it does not accept the jurisdiction of the Court with
> respect to the category of crimes referred to in article 8 [war crimes]
> when a crime is alleged to have been committed by its nationals or on its
> territory. A declaration under this article may be withdrawn at any time.
> The provisions of this article shall be reviewed at the Review Conference
> convened in accordance with article 123, paragraph 1.

To date, only France and Colombia have lodged declarations pursuant to this
provision, which amounts to a reservation.[167] France withdrew its declaration
in 2008, and Colombia's declaration has meanwhile expired. At the Review
Conference in 2010, it was decided that this provision would be retained for
the time being in order to allow new States Parties to the Rome Statute the same
consideration that was afforded to States that joined the regime prior to 2010.[168]

While some may find it tempting to rely on article 124 as evidence of the
definitions of genocide and other crimes against humanity in articles 6 and 7 of
the Rome Statute being declarative of custom and article 8 not, the impetus for
article 124 does not support this hypothesis. Article 124 is based on a German
proposal[169] that was made two days before the end of the Rome Diplomatic
Conference in response to a proposal supported by all five members of the
Security Council. The latter proposal envisioned States having the option to
ratify an optional protocol that would exclude their nationals from the Court's
jurisdiction in respect of war crimes and crimes against humanity.[170] This
protocol was to be in force for ten years and renewable by a simple majority
vote within the Assembly of States Parties.[171] Article 124 was drafted to secure
the acceptance of the Statute by certain States, in particular, France.[172] In
fact, following private discussions with a restricted number of countries, many
delegations learned about the existence of article 124 only near the end of the
conference, in the Bureau's final attempt to secure the greatest possible support
for the Rome Statute.[173]

---

[167] This was true as of June 2010; see also A Cassese, 'The Statute of the International Criminal
Court: Some Preliminary Reflections' (1999) 10 EJIL 144, 146.

[168] Review Conference, Resolution RC/Res.4 (adopted 10 June 2010).

[169] Unlike article 124, the German proposal contemplated the declaration being valid for a
non-renewable period of three rather than seven years.

[170] A Zimmermann, 'Article 124' in Otto Triffterer (ed.), *Commentary on the Rome Statute
of the International Criminal Court*, 2nd edn (Beck/Hart/Nomos 2008) 1767, 1768.

[171] Ibid. 1740.   [172] Ibid. 1767.

[173] T Graditzky, 'War Crimes Issues Before the Rome Diplomatic Conference on the Establishment of an International Criminal Court' (1999) 5 UC Davis J Int'l Law and Policy
200, 212.

It has been argued that article 120, the general prohibition on reservations, is supposed to apply to future amendments such as those concerning the crime of aggression and any other crimes added to the Rome regime, unless another provision provides otherwise.[174] In fact, the amendments on the crime of aggression envision the Court's jurisdiction over this crime being subject to an opt-out regime for States Parties.[175] To date, no States Parties have lodged such an opt-out declaration.

8.3.3 Denunciations

States can respond to the growing difference between a codifying treaty and actual custom in the following four ways: (1) amend the treaty to narrow or close the gap between the treaty and actual custom; (2) terminate the treaty by consent of all States Parties; (3) allow the treaty to fall into desuetude through the subsequent practice of States Parties; or (4) tolerate indefinite divergence with the possibility that States Parties and Non-States Parties might eventually start to denounce the treaty or consider it no longer binding for the reason that it is outdated and no longer reflective of custom.[176] In its *Nuclear Weapons* advisory opinion (1996), the International Court of Justice noted that the denunciation clauses in the relevant treaties had never been used, a factor it seemed to consider relevant for determining whether the obligations in these treaties are reflective of custom.[177] It has been suggested that provisions on denunciation and revision should be given the same weight as those on reservations as evidence of a treaty not reflecting custom.[178] The Rome Statute does not contain a denunciation provision, and, to date, no State has formally denounced it or the amendments on the crime of aggression that were adopted at the first Review Conference for the Rome Statute. However, if the denunciation of a treaty were accepted as evidence of the non-customary nature of the obligations within it, this reasoning would sit uncomfortably with article 43 of the *Vienna Convention* (1969):

> The invalidity, termination or denunciation of a treaty, the withdrawal of a party from it, or the suspension of its operation, as a result of the application of the present Convention or of the provisions of the treaty, shall not in any way impair the duty of any State to fulfil any obligation

---

[174] Hafner (n. 154) 1742.

[175] Review Conference, Resolution RC/Res.6 (adopted 10 June 2010) (Aggression Resolution) article 15 *bis* (4).

[176] Dinstein (n. 53) 366–67.

[177] *Nuclear Weapons* (n. 130) 258; R Clark, 'Treaty and Custom' in L Boisson de Chazournes and P Sands (eds.), *International Law, the International Court of Justice and Nuclear Weapons* (Cambridge University Press 1999) 171, 175.

[178] Baxter, 'Treaties and Custom' (n. 131) 52.

embodied in the treaty to which it would be subject under international
law independently of the treaty.[179]

In practice, a denunciation might be evidence only that a State is motivated
by practical considerations or has had a change of heart about how a rule of
international law is formulated in a particular provision.[180]

8.3.4 Revisions

The existence of a revision provision also does not point in one direction or the
other.[181] This is perhaps because of the aforementioned distinction between
jus dispositivum and *jus cogens*, the former category of rules being freely varied
or excluded by agreement in the relations between two or more States, provided
the position of a third State is not prejudiced.[182] The effort of one or more States
to revise a treaty does indicate dissatisfaction with its current content, perhaps
because it is no longer considered reflective of custom, it is deficient in some
respect or because there is a desire to create new legal norms *de lege ferenda*.[183]
Crimes within the jurisdiction of the Court are subject to the amendment
procedure in article 121(5) of the Rome Statute:

> Any amendment to articles 5, 6, 7 and 8 of this Statute shall enter into force
> for those States Parties which have accepted the amendment one year after
> the deposit of their instruments of ratification or acceptance. In respect
> of a State Party which has not accepted the amendment, the Court shall
> not exercise its jurisdiction regarding a crime covered by the amendment
> when committed by that State Party's nationals or on its territory.

Article 121(5) imposes a consent-based model on States Parties for amending
the crimes of genocide, other crimes against humanity and war crimes. If a
State Party does not accept the proposed amendment, the amended crime
when committed on its territory or by its nationals can no longer be tried by
the Court, which is an exception to the jurisdictional regime established by
article 12(2) for State Party referrals and *proprio motu* investigations by the
prosecutor. Article 121(5) is silent on the matter of Security Council referrals,
which would continue to allow for all situations involving amended crimes to
come before the Court, irrespective of the relevant State Party's consent to an
amendment.[184] As previously discussed, this aspect of the Court's jurisdiction
would indicate that the crimes in its jurisdiction are generally reflective of
custom.[185] However, an amendment to articles 6, 7, 8 and eventually 8 *bis*

---

[179] Ibid.   [180] Ibid.   [181] Ibid.   [182] Thirlway (n. 132) 120–21.
[183] Baxter, 'Treaties and Custom' (n. 131) 51–52.
[184] Articles 12 and 13(b), Rome Statute.   [185] See Chapter 7, Section 7.3.

may well depart from custom, thereby giving rise to objections about their retrospective application in certain cases.

Confusing as well and arguably unfair is that the second sentence of article 121(5) refers only to States Parties that have not consented to the relevant amendment, meaning Non-States Parties are nevertheless subject to it even if the crime involves one of their nationals or occurred on their territory Stated differently, article 12(2) continues to apply in situations involving a Non-State Party. It would appear, therefore, that article 121(5) was not drafted with a view to considering the (non-)customary nature of crimes in the Rome Statute. What is perhaps more telling in this regard is article 121(4), which governs the addition of new crimes to the Rome Statute:

> Except as provided in paragraph 5, an amendment shall enter into force for all States Parties one year after instruments of ratification or acceptance have been deposited with the Secretary-General of the United Nations by seven-eighths of them.

Accordingly, in order for a new crime not falling within articles 6, 7 or 8 of the Rome Statute to become subject to the Court's jurisdiction (e.g., drug trafficking), seven-eighths of all States Parties must accept the amendment.[186] A State Party that does not accept such an amendment may withdraw from the Rome Statute up to one year after the amendment enters into force. Such a large number of ratifications may be indicative of consent to be bound by the Rome treaty regime for the crime in question or suggest the crystallization of a crime into custom. As discussed above in respect of ratifications, more is needed by way of *opinio juris* and State practice to conclude that the new crime in the Rome regime is reflective of custom.

At the Review Conference, two amendments concerning crimes within the Court's jurisdiction were adopted. The first was an amendment to article 8, which would add an article 8(2)(e) giving the Court jurisdiction over the war crime of employing certain poisonous weapons and expanding bullets, asphyxiating or poisonous gases, and all analogous liquids, materials and devices, when committed in armed conflicts not of an international character.[187] This amendment is subject to the procedure outlined in article 121(5).[188] Second, the Review Conference adopted by consensus a package of amendments on the crime of aggression. Alongside the wording of article 5(2), articles

---

[186] Article 121(6), Rome Statute. At the time of writing, article 121 was silent on how to amend the amendments on aggression (e.g., article 8 *bis*), which have yet to be activated.

[187] Review Conference, Resolution RC/Res.5 (10 June 2010).

[188] Ibid., preambular para. 2.

121(4) and (5) are ambiguous in respect of which provision applies to amendments concerning this crime.[189] Ultimately, the Review Conference adopted a consent-based amendment procedure for the aggressor State in accordance with article 121(5), and Non-States Parties are not subject to the Rome regime in respect of aggression.[190]

8.4 Conduct of States

In the *North Sea Continental Shelf* cases (1969), the International Court of Justice decided against considering the conduct of States Parties to the relevant convention in order to determine whether the impugned provision had crystallised into customary international law. It reasoned that States Parties were 'acting actually or potentially in the application of the Convention', and so '[f]rom their action no inference could legitimately be drawn as to the existence' of a rule of customary international law generated by a treaty'.[191] The Court opted instead to look at the practice of Non-States Parties with a view to ascertaining whether an 'inference could justifiably be drawn that they believed themselves to be applying a mandatory rule of customary international law'.[192]

This reasoning of the Court has given rise to a paradox famously identified by Baxter:

> [A]s the number of parties to a treaty increases, it becomes more difficult to demonstrate what is the state of customary international law dehors the treaty.... As the express acceptance of the treaty increases, the number of states not parties whose practice is relevant diminishes.[193]

Two views have emerged in scholarly discourse on the Baxter paradox. The majority view holds that proof of custom requires 'adequate proof of State

---

[189] Article 5(2) provides: 'The Court shall exercise jurisdiction over the crime of aggression once a provision is adopted in accordance with articles 121 and 123 defining the crime and setting out the conditions under which the Court shall exercise jurisdiction with respect to this crime.' Article 121(4) provides: 'Except as provided in paragraph 5, an amendment shall enter into force for all States Parties one year after instruments of ratification or acceptance have been deposited with the Secretary-General of the United Nations by seven-eighths of them.' Article 121(5) states: 'Any amendment to articles 5, 6, 7 and 8 of this Statute shall enter into force for those States Parties which have accepted the amendment one year after the deposit of their instruments of ratification or acceptance. In respect of a State Party which has not accepted the amendment, the Court shall not exercise its jurisdiction regarding a crime covered by the amendment when committed by that State Party's nationals or on its territory.'

[190] Aggression Resolution (n. 124) article 15 *bis*.

[191] *North Sea Continental Shelf* (n. 128) 43.

[192] Ibid. 43–44.   [193] Baxter, 'Treaties and Custom' (n. 131) 64, 73.

practice and *opino juris* outside of the application of the treaty in question'.[194] The Institut de Droit International confirmed that the conduct of States Parties should be taken into account, but 'the significance of the practice will be substantially enhanced if it is established that the State concerned acted in the conviction that the practice was required by a rule of customary international law independently of the applicability of the convention'.[195] The minority view is that, in some circumstances, the 'act of adopting the treaty and the ratifications and adherences of States constitute State practice and evidence of *opinio juris* for purposes of customary law. This would hold particularly for treaties of a declaratory character, but not only for them.'[196]

Assuming it is worthwhile to inquire into the practice of States Parties and Non-States Parties alike, the question becomes: Which practice? For example, it has been argued that '[w]hat practise of what States is relevant turns on the subject-matter of the agreement. The practice of States particularly affected by the treaty must count heavily.'[197] Others have suggested that State practice includes domestic legislation and judicial decisions and that, should a State incorporate the treaty provisions as an integral part of its domestic law, this will suffice as a manifestation of its practice.[198] This reasoning necessitates recalling the distinction between monist and dualist legal regimes, the former generally allowing for the automatic application of custom (but not treaty law) by domestic courts despite the absence of domestic implementing legislation and the latter usually requiring exactly this.[199] However, it should also be recalled that a monist domestic legal system may nevertheless enact implementing legislation for a treaty that is reflective of custom for reasons unrelated to its customary status.[200]

8.4.1 States Parties

The Rome Statute does not expressly require or urge States Parties to enact domestic implementing legislation for crimes within its jurisdiction. This

---

[194] Schachter (n. 137) 718.

[195] Institut de Droit International, Problems Arising from a Succession of Codification Conventions on a Particular Subject (Lisbon Session 1995) 66-I Annuaire de l'Institut de Droit International 39, conclusion 13.

[196] Meaning treaties that expressly declare that they are reflective of custom; Schachter (n. 137) 718–19.

[197] Baxter, 'Treaties and Custom' (n. 131) 66.   [198] Dinstein (n. 53) 379.

[199] Ibid. 347. Of course the relationship between international and domestic law is far more complex and nuanced. D Shelton, 'Introduction' in D Shelton (ed.), *International Law and Domestic Legal Systems: Incorporation, Transformation, and Persuasion* (Oxford University Press 2011) 1, 2.

[200] H Keller and A Stone Sweet, 'Assessing the Impact of the ECHR on National Legal Systems' in H Keller and A Stone Sweet (eds.), *A Europe of Rights* (Oxford University Press 2008) 677, 683–86.

silence is noteworthy given that the Rome regime contemplates the Court being a court of 'last resort'; national courts will have primary jurisdiction to try the crimes defined in the Statute.[201] The preamble does, however, recall that 'it is the duty of every State to exercise its criminal jurisdiction over those responsible for international crimes'. In light of both monist and dualist domestic legal regimes requiring treaty law that is not reflective of custom to be implemented in national legislation before a domestic court may apply it, this silence is suggestive of the crimes possessing customary status. However, it might have also been an oversight on the part of drafters or it might reflect the view of drafters that most States already have national legislation in force criminalizing the crimes within the Court's jurisdiction.

Despite the Rome Statute's neutrality on the matter of domestic implementing legislation, non-governmental organizations have encouraged States Parties to enact legislation implementing their obligations under the Rome Statute. A study carried out by Amnesty International in August 2004 indicated that thirty-six States Parties enacted such legislation or were in the process of drafting such legislation.[202] An updated 2010 report by Amnesty International indicated that currently only thirty-two States Parties have yet to draft implementing legislation, meaning the remainder have either enacted such legislation or have at least drafted it.[203] Of these States, several enacted legislation exactly mirroring the definitions of crimes in the Rome Statute while others variously modified these definitions in retrogressive and progressive ways.[204] In the category of retrogressive legislation, there are States Parties that fail to enact definitions for all of the crimes listed in the Rome Statute as well as States Parties that adopt 'weaker' definitions.[205]

For the crime of genocide, several States Parties have adopted the exact definition in the Rome Statute, which reflects the definition in article II of the *Genocide Convention* (1948).[206] Other States Parties have adopted broader

---

[201] Paragraph 10 of the preamble to the Rome Statute states: 'Emphasizing that the International Criminal Court established under this Statute shall be complementary to national criminal jurisdictions'. Article 17(1)(a) of the Rome Statute provides: 'Having regard to paragraph 10 of the Preamble and article 1, the Court shall determine that a case is inadmissible where: . . . The case is being investigated or prosecuted by a State which has jurisdiction over it, unless the State is unwilling or unable genuinely to carry out the investigation or prosecution.'

[202] Amnesty International, *International Criminal Court: The Failure of States to Enact Effective Implementing Legislation* (30 August 2004) Index No. IOR 40/019/2004, 1.

[203] Amnesty International, *International Criminal Court: Rome Statute Implementation Report Card, Part One* (1 May 2010) Index No. IOR 53/011/2010, 10.

[204] Amnesty International (2004) (n. 202) 6.   [205] Ibid. 6, 43–48.

[206] Amnesty International, ibid. 8 (Argentina, Ireland, New Zealand, Uganda, the United Kingdom, Uruguay, Belgium, Canada, Mali, Malta and South Africa). For States that

definitions of genocide by increasing the number of protected groups,[207] increasing the scope of prohibited conduct,[208] or broadening the requisite mental element for genocide.[209] One State Party has adopted a narrower definition of genocide, which omits mention of conduct causing serious mental harm to members of the group.[210] Amnesty International also criticized States for not enacting definitions of genocide that include all modes of liability listed in article III of the *Genocide Convention* (1948), namely, conspiracy to commit genocide, incitement to commit genocide, attempt to commit genocide and complicity in genocide, all of which it considers reflective of custom.[211] Relying on article 10, Amnesty International recalled that the Rome Statute does not contain an exhaustive list of crimes under customary international law and thus called on States to enact implementing legislation for all customary crimes.[212]

For other crimes against humanity, several States Parties adopted the definitions of crimes in article 7 of the Rome Statute,[213] while others excluded some of them from their domestic legislation (e.g., rape and other crimes of sexual violence, enslavement, persecution and apartheid).[214] As well, some of the definitions of rape, sexual violence and extermination are weaker than the definitions in the Rome Statute.[215] Conversely, other countries lowered the threshold for exercising jurisdiction over crimes against humanity[216] or adopted broader definitions of conduct amounting to such a crime.[217]

As for war crimes, Amnesty International criticized certain States Parties for adopting definitions of war crimes in the Rome Statute as opposed to broader

---

have not done this, see ibid. 7 and schedule 1, part 1 for relevant legislation from these countries.

[207] Ibid. 8 and schedule 1 for more details (Ecuador, Estonia, Finland, Panama and the Republic of the Congo, all in different ways).

[208] Ibid. (Belgium, Colombia, Democratic Republic of the Congo, Estonia, Finland, Panama, Portugal and Spain).

[209] Ibid. (Spain and Germany).

[210] Ibid. 7 (Portugal and perhaps also Estonia, although this is not clear).

[211] Ibid.   [212] Ibid. 6.

[213] Ibid. 12 (Argentina, Costa Rica, Ireland, New Zealand, Uruguay, Uganda, the United Kingdom, Malta, South Africa and Canada). However, Belgium and the Republic of the Congo omit definitions of certain crimes against humanity in article 7(2) of the Rome Statute, leaving it unclear whether these are incorporated into national law or not.

[214] Ibid. 9 (Brazil, Estonia, Georgia, Germany, Panama, Peru, Spain and Finland).

[215] Ibid. 10–12 (Bosnia-Herzegovina, Brazil, Portugal, Estonia, Republic of Congo, Finland, Malta and South Africa).

[216] Ibid. 12–13 (Canada).

[217] Ibid. 13 (Democratic Republic of the Congo, Estonia, the Republic of the Congo, Brazil, Portugal and Panama).

definitions of the same crimes found in the first *Additional Protocol* (1977) to the *Geneva Conventions* (1949).[218] As well, it criticized States Parties for adopting the definition of the crime of recruiting child soldiers in the Rome Statute, which applies to children under the age of fifteen rather than eighteen.[219] Some States Parties were singled out for omitting from national legislation war crimes that are not expressly mentioned in the Rome Statute, such as mass starvation during a non-international armed conflict,[220] unjustified delay in repatriating prisoners of war after hostilities have ceased[221] and attacking a demilitarized zone.[222] Other States included all war crimes under customary international law in their domestic legislation.[223] Most States mirror the Rome Statute by maintaining in their legislation a distinction between war crimes committed during an international armed conflict and a non-international armed conflict.[224] Some States Parties have broadened their definitions of war crimes in certain respects,[225] and others have even added torture, extrajudicial execution and, or, enforced disappearance as individual crimes in their domestic legislation.[226]

---

[218] Ibid. 15 (Democratic Republic of the Congo, Ecuador, Germany, Ireland, Mali, Malta, South Africa, Uganda and the United Kingdom). Countries that have adopted definitions preferred by Amnesty International in the first *Additional Protocol* (1977) include Australia, Belgium, Brazil, Finland, the Netherlands and Portugal. Ibid. 15–16.

[219] Ibid. 16 (Australia, Belgium, Canada, Germany, Ireland, Mali, Malta, the Netherlands, New Zealand, South Africa, Uruguay and Uganda). The age of fifteen is consistent with article 38 of the *Convention on the Rights of the Child*, 1577 UNTS 3 (adopted 20 November 1989, entered into force 2 September 1990) but not with the *Optional Protocol on the Involvement of Children in Armed Conflict*, 2173 UNTS 222 (adopted 25 May 2000, entered into force 12 February 2002), which sets the age at eighteen. Countries that have defined the crime using the age of eighteen include Argentina, Brazil, Democratic Republic of the Congo, Ecuador, Panama and Portugal. Ibid. 16–17.

[220] Some countries, however, have included this in their domestic legislation: Argentina, Belgium, Brazil, Bosnia-Herzegovina, Germany, Panama and Portugal. Ibid. 17–18.

[221] States that recognize this war crime include Australia, Belgium, Estonia, Georgia, Germany, the Netherlands, Panama, Spain, Bosnia-Herzegovina (in part), Brazil (in part) and Portugal (in part). Ibid. 18.

[222] States that recognize this war crime in their domestic legislation include Australia, Belgium, Bosnia-Herzegovina, Estonia, Georgia, Germany, the Netherlands, Panama and Spain. Ibid.

[223] Bosnia-Herzegovina, Canada, the Netherlands, the Republic of the Congo and Finland (although it is not clear). Countries that have only included war crimes derived from treaties they have ratified include Costa Rica, Panama and Spain. Ibid. 17–18.

[224] States that include a single conflict standard for all war crimes include Bosnia-Herzegovina, Costa Rica, Georgia, Panama, Spain, Argentina (for some crimes), Brazil (for some crimes) and Portugal (for some crimes). Ibid. 18–19.

[225] Ibid. 19 (Belgium and Democratic Republic of the Congo).

[226] Ibid. (Bosnia-Herzegovina, Ecuador and Mali).

There are also countries that adopted the definitions of crimes in the Rome Statute wholesale, such as Australia, the Netherlands and New Zealand, the latter two also going beyond the Rome Statute in places.[227] As for the Elements, which are thought by some to help with the domestic implementation of the Rome Statute as well as assist national judges and prosecutors,[228] a few States have included this instrument in their domestic legislation but have expressed caution that this instrument should play only a subsidiary role,[229] consistent with article 9 of the Rome Statute, as it is thought to contain departures from customary law.[230] Finally, to date, four States have incorporated the definition of aggression in the Rome Statute into domestic legislation.

8.4.2 Non-States Parties

Non-States Parties to a treaty can indicate by their conduct that the entire treaty or part of it is not declaratory of customary international law.[231] This disagreement on its own does not displace the need for a factual inquiry where doubts are raised about whether a particular treaty provision reflects custom.[232] However, a significant group of dissenting States at a conference could cast serious doubt as to whether a multilateral treaty is reflective of custom, while some isolated objections would be less disconcerting.[233] At the Rome Diplomatic Conference, the vote was unrecorded, but those present recall that only 7 of the 160 countries in attendance voted against the Rome Statute: China, Iraq, Israel, Libya, Qatar, the United States and Yemen.[234]

If Non-States Parties do consider a treaty to be reflective of custom, it will be of interest to them as reflecting their obligations.[235] The Permanent Court of International Justice has acknowledged on several occasions that treaties may

---

[227] G Boas, 'An Overview of Implementation by Australia of the Statute of the International Criminal Court' (2004) 2 J Int'l Crim Justice 179, 186; G Sluiter, 'Implementation of the ICC Statute in the Dutch Legal Order' (2004) 2 J Int'l Crim Justice 158, 174; J Hay, 'Implementing the ICC Statute in New Zealand' (2004) 2 J Int'l Crim Justice 191, 195, 196. For an account of inconsistent legislation, see M Roscini, 'Great Expectations: The Implementation of the Rome Statute in Italy' (2007) 5 J Int'l Crim Justice 493.

[228] D Robinson and H von Hebel, 'Reflections on the Elements of Crimes' in RS Lee (ed.), *The International Criminal Court: Elements of Crimes and Rules of Procedure and Evidence* (Transnational 2001) 219, 224, 230.

[229] Hay (n. 227) 199: New Zealand courts are required 'to have regard to any elements of crimes adopted or amended in accordance with Article 9'.

[230] Amnesty International (n. 202) 6.

[231] O Schachter, *International Law in Theory and Practice* (Martinus Nijhoff 1991) 70–71.

[232] Ibid. 72.   [233] Ibid.

[234] M Scharf, 'Results of the Rome Conference for an International Criminal Court' (August 1998) ASIL Insight 1

[235] Villiger (n. 143) 21.

not bind third States absent their consent.[236] Article 34 of the *Vienna Convention* (1969) codifies this customary rule.[237] However, as with all multilateral treaties, the Rome Statute's existence will for many serve as 'an agreed starting point – an attractive force to which non-party practice will be drawn like iron filings to a magnet'.[238]

> If certain treaties both bind the parties and form evidence of customary international law, they will be the instruments of harmonization of the law on a widespread basis. The very existence of multi-lateral treaties declaratory or constitutive of law will induce even the non-parties to conform their conduct to some, if not all, of the rules of the treaty. The simplicity of the use of a treaty rule and its widespread acceptance by others make it a convenient short-cut for non-parties.... [I]t becomes difficult for the non-party to justify resort to older treaties or customary law, especially since the treaty has already crowded out customary international law to a large extent.[239]

Further, different interpretations of a legal rule or principle that is both customary and contained in a treaty can give rise to 'uncertainty and confusion' with respect to its actual content.[240]

Evidence of Non-States Parties endorsing the customary nature of crimes in the Rome Statute predates its drafting. It has been pointed out that all five permanent Security Council members acknowledged the customary status of crimes in the ICTY statute, which contains many substantive legal provisions that are similar to those contained in the Rome Statute.[241] Further, referral of the Darfur situation to the Court by the Security Council in 2005 evidences that its members consider the Court's jurisdiction to be consistent with customary international law.[242] The same has been said of replicating the Rome Statute provisions for establishing the Iraqi Special Tribunal and the East Timor special

---

[236] *German Interests in Polish Upper Silesia (Germany* v. *Polish Republic)* (1926) PCIJ Series A, No. 7, 29; *Nationality Decrees Issues in Tunis and Morocco (French Zone)* (1923) PCIJ Series B, No. 5, 27–8; *Territorial Jurisdiction of the International Commission of the River Oder (United Kingdom, Czechoslovakia, Denmark, France, Germany, Sweden* v. *Poland)* (1929) PCIJ Series A, No. 23, 19–22; *Free Zones of Upper Savoy and the District of Gex (France* v. *Switzerland)* (1932) PCIJ Series A/B, No. 46, 141, cited by GM Danilenko, 'The Statute of the International Criminal Court and Third States' (1999–2000) 21 Mich J Int'l L 445, 447.

[237] 1155 UNTS 331 (adopted 23 May 1969, entered into force 27 January 1980): A 'treaty does not create either obligations or rights for a third state without its consent'.

[238] Baxter, 'Treaties and Custom' (n. 131) 73.

[239] Ibid. 102–03. The Baxter paradox was also identified by the ICTY in *Prosecutor* v. *Delalić and Others*, Judgment, ICTY-96–21-T, 16 November 1998, para. 302.

[240] Schachter (n. 137) 728–29.   [241] Danilenko (n. 236) 486.

[242] A Zimmermann, 'Israel and the International Criminal Court – an Outsider's Perspective' (2006) 36 Israel Ybk on Human Rights 231, 235.

panels for the punishment of serious crimes.[243] The former was created by the Coalition Provisional Authority – the United States and United Kingdom as occupying powers – and the latter by the United Nations, also acting as a transitional administrative authority.This replication, especially by Non-States Parties, suggests that various provisions of the Rome Statute are considered by them to be reflective of customary international law.[244]

There remains the matter of the impact of a codifying treaty on a State that objects to its characterization of customary law:

> The position of dissentient States which are in a small minority may . . . be made more difficult by the conclusion of a codifying treaty setting out rules with which they disagree. . . . [T]he dissentient State will be deprived of the opportunity of maintaining open and consistent protest, and may find it difficult to resist the application of the general rule to its own interests at a subsequent date. It would appear that a dissentient State which participates in the work of a codification conference can at least be expected to make its views known.[245]

A State may also be able to show that a particular rule never applied to it because of its consistent and open dissent during the formation of the rule and prior to its crystallization.[246] Indeed, it is the view of some that Israel is a candidate for persistent objector status because it sharply disagrees with the list of war crimes and some aspects of crimes against humanity in the Rome Statute.[247]

Finally, the conduct of the United States, a Non-State Party, deserves to be briefly reviewed as American practice is the most extensive of any Non-State Party to date. The United States signed the Rome Statute but decided not to ratify it. In July 2002, it unsuccessfully threatened to use its veto in the UN Security Council to block the renewal of many UN peacekeeping missions unless the Council agreed to permanently exclude US nationals from the jurisdiction of the Court.[248] It then unsuccessfully tried to convince the Security Council to adopt an approach whereby personnel on UN peacekeeping missions could be prosecuted only by their country of nationality.[249] Subsequently, the United States tried to invoke article 16 of the Rome Statute in order to suspend for one year the Court's exercise of jurisdiction over its nationals working as UN peacekeepers and further tried to have the renewal of this request every year made automatic unless a Security Council resolution ceasing such automatic

---

[243] Ibid. 235–36.   [244] Danilenko (n. 236) 482.   [245] Thirlway (n. 132) 116–17.

[246] Schachter (n. 231) 72.   [247] Dinstein (n. 111); Danilenko (n. 98) 1895.

[248] C Stahn, 'The Ambiguities of Security Council Resolution 1422 (2002)' (2003) 14 EJIL 85.

[249] SD Murphy, 'Efforts to Obtain Immunity from ICC for US Peacekeepers' (2002) 96 AJIL 725.

renewal was adopted.[250] Concerned about the future of UN peacekeeping missions around the world, a compromise was struck whereby the Security Council invoked article 16 for a period of one year to exclude UN peacekeepers from the Court's jurisdiction.[251] In 2003, the Security Council agreed to another resolution to exempt all citizens of the United States from the Court's jurisdiction[252] but then refused to renew this exemption in 2004 after pictures of American troops abusing Iraqi prisoners emerged.[253]

In addition to these efforts within the Security Council, the United States has to date concluded nearly 100 bilateral immunity agreements with States Parties and Non-States Parties that have come to be known as 'article 98' agreements.[254] Article 98(1) of the Rome Statute provides:

> The Court may not proceed with a request for surrender or assistance which would require the requested State to act inconsistently with its obligations under international law with respect to the State or diplomatic immunity of a person or property of a third State, unless the Court can first obtain the cooperation of that third State for the waiver of the immunity.

States that refuse to sign article 98 agreements may be subject to a suspension of American military and development assistance (unless an exception is made, e.g., for NATO members and other American allies), and those that do sign are often handsomely rewarded financially.[255]

The period just described has been characterized by a current legal adviser to the United States Department of State as one of 'outright hostility' towards the Court.[256] However, in recent years, the United States has entered a phase of positive engagement with the Court, which includes referral of the Darfur situation to the Court by the Security Council, public diplomacy to encourage the arrest of individuals against whom the Court has issued warrants and financial support of the Court. Most recently, this engagement led to the presence and participation of a large American observer delegation at meetings

---

[250] UNSC, 'Security Council Requests One-Year Extension of UN Peacekeeper Immunity from International Criminal Court' (12 June 2003) Press Release SC/7789.

[251] UNSC Res. 1422 (12 July 2002).   [252] UNSC Res. 1487 (12 June 2003).

[253] BBC News, 'Q&A: International Criminal Court' (last updated 11 March 2013), www.bbc.co.uk/news/world-11809908, accessed 1 May 2014.

[254] As of December 2009, the United States had concluded these agreements with ninety-five States: Georgetown Law Library, *International Criminal Court: Article 98 Agreements Research Guide*, www.law.georgetown.edu/library/research/guides/article_98.cfm, accessed 1 May 2014.

[255] Coalition for the International Criminal Court, 'Questions & Answers: US Bilateral Immunity Agreements or So-Called "Article 98" Agreements', www.iccnow.org/documents/FS-BIAs_Q&A_current.pdf, accessed 1 May 2014.

[256] HH Koh, US Department of State, 'Remarks', Panel Discussion at NYU Center For Global Affairs, (27 October 2010), www.state.gov/s/l/releases/remarks/150497.htm, accessed 5 November 2013.

of the Assembly of States Parties to the Rome Statute and at the first Review Conference of the Statute in Kampala, Uganda, in June 2010. The delegation was especially active in negotiations on defining the crime of aggression.[257] In light of these developments, which are expected to continue, it will arguably become more difficult for the United States to claim *persistent* objector status, especially for the definitions of crimes in the Rome Statute.

8.5 Jurisprudence

Courts are often the first to identify the existence of a rule or norm of customary international law on the basis of *opinio juris* and State practice, and therefore their decisions 'can be utilized as authoritative statements of the state of customary international law at the time'.[258] In this section, a summary will be provided of the surveys carried out by Schabas on international jurisprudence that comments on the customary nature (or not) of crimes defined in the Rome Statute.[259]

Beginning with the ICTY and ICTR, resort to the Rome Statute has been limited due to the fact that crimes within the jurisdiction of these ad hoc tribunals must have been committed prior to 1998, when the Rome Statute was drafted.[260] Given these divergences in time periods, statements by the ICTY and ICTR about the non-customary nature of particular crimes may be outdated, and statements on the content of custom may have been overtaken by subsequent legal developments.[261] Further, different chambers of these tribunals have adopted different positions on the content of the Rome Statute.[262]

In *Prosecutor v. Furundžija* (1998), an ICTY Trial Chamber found evidence of *opinio juris* in the Rome Statute:

> In many areas the [Rome] Statute may be regarded as indicative of the legal views, i.e. *opinio juris* of a great number of States. Notwithstanding article 10 of the Statute, the purpose of which is to ensure that existing or developing law is not 'limited' or 'prejudiced' by the Statute's provisions, resort may be had cum grano salis to these provisions to help elucidate customary international law. Depending on the matter at issue, the Rome

---

[257] Ibid.

[258] T Ginsburg, 'Bounded Discretion in International Judicial Lawmaking' (2005) 45 Virginia J Int'l L 631, 639.

[259] Schabas (n. 69) 271, 409–10; WA Schabas, 'Customary Law or "Judge-Made" Law: Judicial Creativity at the UN Criminal Tribunals' in J Doria, H-P Gasser and MC Bassiouni (eds.), *The Legal Regime of the International Criminal Court: Essays in Honour of Professor Igor Blishchenko* (Brill 2009) 77. Constraints of time and space do not permit the author to research the jurisprudence of all domestic courts.

[260] G Mettraux, *International Crimes and the Ad Hoc Tribunals* (Oxford University Press 2005) 9–10, fn. 19.

[261] Ibid.   [262] Schabas, 'Customary Law or "Judge-Made" Law' (n. 259).

Statute may be taken to restate, reflect or clarify customary rules or crystallise them, whereas in some areas it creates new law or modifies existing law. At any event, the Rome Statute by and large may be taken as constituting an authoritative expression of the legal views of a great number of States.[263]

Subsequently, this view was endorsed by the Appeals Chamber of the ICTY in *Prosecutor* v. *Tadić* (1999), which stated that the Rome Statute 'is supported by a great number of States and may be taken to express the legal position i.e. opinio juris of those States'.[264] While these decisions treat States' ratification of the Rome Statute as *opinio juris*, this and State Practice are sometimes referred to together without distinction.[265] On another occasion, the ICTY referred to the Rome Statute reflecting State practice.[266]

Certain provisions of the Rome Statute have also been identified as departing from custom. In *Prosecutor* v. *Kupreškić and Others* (2000), an ICTY Trial Chamber stated: 'although the Statute of the ICC may be indicative of the *opinio juris* of many States, Article 7(1)(h) [on persecution as a crime against humanity] is not consonant with customary international law', holding as being too narrow the requirement that this crime be connected with a crime within the Court's jurisdiction.[267] Further, the Rome Statute has been implicitly treated by at least one ICTY judge as reflective of custom and the absence of a crime within the Court's jurisdiction as evidence of that crime not existing under customary international law. In *Prosecutor* v. *Galić* (2006), Judge Schomburg in a dissenting opinion wrote: 'even though I am fully aware of Article 10' of the Rome Statute, 'it should be pointed out that the Rome Statute does not have a provision referring to terrorization against a civilian population. If indeed this crime was beyond doubt part of customary international law, in 1998 (!) states would undoubtedly have included it in the relevant provision of the Statute or in their domestic legislation implementing the Statute.'[268]

In the jurisprudence of the European Court of Human Rights (ECtHR), judges have commented at times on the customary nature of certain crimes in the Rome Statute. In *Korbely* v. *Hungary* (2008), Judge Louca in a dissenting opinion wrote: 'As regards the elements of crimes against humanity, one may

---

[263] *Prosecutor* v. *Furundžija*, Judgment, ICTY-95–17/I-T, 10 December 1998, para 227.

[264] *Prosecutor* v. *Tadić*, Judgment, ICTY-94–1-A, 15 July 1999, para. 223.

[265] Schabas, 'Customary Law or "Judge-Made" Law' (n. 259) 82–83.

[266] See *Prosecutor* v. *Krnojelac*, Judgment, ICTY-97–25-A, 17 September 2003, para 221: 'recent state practice, as reflected in the Rome Statute, which provides that displacements both within a state and across national borders can constitute a crime against humanity and a war crime'.

[267] *Prosecutor* v. *Kupreškić and Others*, Judgment, ICTY-96–16-T, 14 January 2000, paras. 579–581.

[268] *Prosecutor* v. *Galić*, Judgment, Separate and Partially Dissenting Opinion of Judge Schomburg, ICTY-98–29-A, 30 November 2006, para. 20 (references omitted).

take the recent Rome Statute of the International Criminal Court as declaratory of the definition in international law of this crime.'[269] In *C* v. *Bulgaria* (2003), the ECtHR referred to the definition of rape in the Rome Statute as 'evidence of the evolving international law concerning the definition of this crime'.[270] Similarly, the Inter-American Court of Human Rights (IACtHR) has repeatedly cited the crime of enforced disappearance in articles 7(1)(i) and 7(2)(i) of the Rome Statute as evidencing the international community's condemnation of this practice.[271] The United Nations Human Rights Committee has said the same in respect of this crime.[272] The IACtHR has also referred to the crime against humanity of torture in the Rome Statute as 'evidence of an evolving prohibition of international law'.[273]

Finally, Pre-Trial Chamber I of the International Criminal Court in *Prosecutor and Others* v. *Katanga* (2008) referred to the crime against humanity of 'other inhumane acts' in article 7(1)(k) as 'serious violations of international customary law and the basic rights pertaining to human beings, drawn from the norms of international human rights law, which are of a similar nature and gravity to the acts referred to in article 7(1) of the Statute'.[274]

8.6 Doctrinal writings

When translating unwritten custom into written rules, it is often difficult to retain a clear line between strict codification of existing law and progressively developing this law.[275] This codification study concludes with a review of what experts and scholars have said to date about the relationship between custom and articles 6, 7 and 8 of the Rome Statute.

A large overlap of custom and these articles is first indicated in the statements of key players involved in their drafting. Adrian Bos, who, from 1995 to 1998, chaired the Ad Hoc and Preparatory Committees that preceded the Rome Diplomatic Conference, considers them to be reflective of customary international law:

---

[269] App. No. 9174/02, *Korbely* v. *Hungary*, Dissenting Opinion of Judge Loucaidis, ECHR, 19 September 2008; App. Nos. 34044/96, 35532/97 and 44801/98, *Streletz, Kessler and Krenz* v. *Germany*, Concurring Opinion of Judge Loucaidis, ECHR, 22 March 2001.

[270] *C* v. *Bulgaria*, ECHR, 4 December 2003, para. 128.

[271] App. No. 39272/98, *Goiburú and Others* v. *Paraguay*, 22 September 2006, Inter-American Court of Human Rights Series C 153, para 82.

[272] *Sarma* v. *Sri Lanka* (2003) 8 Selected Decisions of the Human Rights Committee 210 (Communication No. 950/2000), para. 9.3.

[273] *Castro* v. *Peru*, 25 November 2006, Inter-American Court of Human Rights Series C 202, para. 402, fn. 205.

[274] The Court's decision was *Prosecutor* v. *Katanga and Others*, Decision on the Confirmation of Charges, ICC-01/04–01/07, 30 September 2008, para. 448.

[275] Danilenko (n. 98) 1891.

> [The Rome Statute's] provisions serve to reflect prevailing law and at the same time they can be used as examples to help States implement the Rome Statute in their own national legislation. The Rome Statute deals with crimes under international law. Provisions of national legislation will not always correspond to the definitions in the Rome Statute. Where they do not, the Rome Statute's provisions must prevail, because the offenses in question constitute crimes under international law. It may therefore be assumed that the very existence of the Rome Statute can contribute to the harmonization of national provisions.[276]

Philippe Kirsch, who chaired the Committee of the Whole at Rome and was the Court's first president, stated more than once that States intended and generally agreed that 'the definitions of crimes in the ICC Statute were to reflect existing customary international law, and not create new law . . . [and that the] Rome Statute is thus, in this respect, a codification of customary norms'.[277] The result achieved was definitions that are 'broadly based on existing international law'.[278] As for the outcome, Kirsch admits that although the Rome Statute 'contains uneasy technical solutions, awkward formulations, [and] difficult compromises that fully satisfied no one',[279] it and the Elements of Crimes 'clearly reflect the *opinio juris* of the international community, further supporting the customary nature of crimes within the Court's jurisdiction'.[280]

Herman von Hebel, who chaired the Working Group on the Elements of Crimes, stated that '[i]n elaborating the definitions [of crimes], one of the major guiding principles was that the definitions should be reflective of customary international law. It was understood that the Court should operate only for crimes that are of concern to the international community as a whole, which meant the inclusion only of crimes which are universally recognized.'[281] He further stated that, on balance, 'the crimes as defined in the Rome Statute will give the Court a broad subject-matter jurisdiction consistent with customary

---

[276] A Bos, 'The International Criminal Court: A Perspective' in RS Lee and Others (eds.), *The International Criminal Court: The Making of the Rome Statute* (Kluwer Law International 1999) 469.

[277] P Kirsch, 'Foreword' in Knut Dörmann, *Elements of War Crimes under the Rome Statute of the International Criminal Court* (Cambridge University Press 2003) xiii; P Kirsch, 'Customary International Humanitarian Law, its Enforcement, and the Role of the International Criminal Court' in L Maybee and B Chakka (eds.), *Custom as a Source of International Humanitarian Law* (International Committee of the Red Cross 2006) 79, 80, 83.

[278] P Kirsch, 'The Development of the Rome Statute' in RS Lee and Others (eds.), *The International Criminal Court: The Making of the Rome Statute* (Kluwer Law International 1999) 451, 458.

[279] P Kirsch and JT Holmes, 'The Birth of the International Criminal Court: The 1998 Rome Conference' (1998) 36 Canadian Ybk Int'l L 3, 38.

[280] P Kirsch, 'Customary International Humanitarian Law' (n. 277).

[281] von Hebel and Robinson (n. 39) 122.

international law and, at the same time, lend support to current developments', thereby suggesting the crystallization of certain norms.[282] Roy S. Lee, executive secretary to the Rome Diplomatic Conference and to the Preparatory Committee prior to the conference, wrote: 'the definitions of crimes contained in the Statute reflect existing practices and affirm current developments in international law'.[283]

Scholars have also cautiously and variously described the Rome Statute as roughly congruent with custom. Cassese stated that the definitions of crimes in the Rome Statute 'are not couched as provisions of a criminal code. Furthermore, they are not intended to codify, or restate, or contribute to the development of customary international law. Their legal value is therefore limited (although, of course, they may gradually have a bearing on, and bring about a change in, existing law).'[284] He asserted that two regimes of international criminal law will exist: 'one established by the Statute and the other laid down in general international criminal law. The Statute also seems to presuppose the partial coincidence of these two bodies of law: *they will probably be similar or identical to a very large extent*, but there will be areas of discrepancy.'[285] Accordingly, 'as the Statute is not intended to codify international customary law, one ought always to take it with a pinch of salt, for in some cases it may go beyond existing law, whereas in other instances it is narrower in scope than current rules of customary international law'.[286] 'This conclusion does not of course detract from the importance of the ICC Statute as a set of rules that clarify many points in ICL [international criminal law] and which, in this respect, may also prove useful to consider by other courts.'[287]

Meron asserted that the 'Rome Statute of the International Criminal Court codifies many rules and principles of IHL [international humanitarian law] as customary criminal law.'[288] He further wrote: 'Articles 6 to 8 . . . will take on a life of their own as an authoritative and largely customary statement of international humanitarian and criminal law, and may thus become a model for national laws to be enforced under the principle of universality of jurisdiction. . . . [T]he Statute is largely reflective of customary law. *Largely, but not completely.*'[289]

[282] Ibid. 126.
[283] RS Lee, 'Introduction' in RS Lee and Others (eds.), *The International Criminal Court: The Making of the Rome Statute* (Kluwer Law International 1999) 26, 38.
[284] Cassese (n. 12) 56.   [285] Cassese (n. 167) 157 (emphasis added).
[286] Cassese (n. 12) 43   [287] Ibid. 14.
[288] T Meron, 'Customary Law' in R Dworkin, R Gutman and D Rieff (eds.), *Crimes of War 2.0: What the Public Should Know*, revised and expanded edn (WW Norton 2008).
[289] T Meron, 'Crimes under the Jurisdiction of the International Criminal Court' in H von Hebel, JG Lammers and J Schukking (eds.), *Reflections on the International Criminal Court: Essays in Honour of Adriaan Bos* (TMC Asser 1999) 47, 48–49 (emphasis added).

Schabas observed that the Rome Statute is not an exhaustive codification of international law because it contains serious gaps.[290] 'Although the Rome Conference was a most open, transparent and democratic attempt at codification, it generated a verbose text that is riddled with inconsistencies, compromises, lacunae and "constructive ambiguities".'[291] It 'appears to deviate from custom in a number of areas, including its inadequate codification of prohibited weapons and its failure to incorporate the prohibition on conspiracy to commit genocide, set out in article III of the 1948 Genocide Convention'.[292] He concluded, however, that the definitions of crimes in the Rome Statute and Elements 'correspond in a general sense to the state of customary international law. The three categories of crimes are drawn from existing definitions and use familiar terminology.... Nevertheless, *while the correspondence with customary international law is close, it is far from perfect.*'[293]

Interestingly, the 2005 study of the International Committee of the Red Cross on customary rules of international humanitarian law relies on the crimes in the ICTY statute and Rome Statute more than 170 times.[294] Further, Henckaerts and Doswald-Beck stated that 'the negotiation of the [Rome] Statute of the ICC was based on the premise that, to amount to a war crime to be included in the Statute, the conduct had to amount to a violation of a customary rule of international law'.[295]

Cryer concluded that the Rome Statute is 'a base-level of what customary law is'.[296] Gallant wrote: 'Most of the war crimes in the ICC Statute are clearly crimes under customary international law already, including those crimes which may be committed in non-international armed conflicts. The same can be said of genocide and crimes against humanity.'[297] Dinstein recognized that although the intention of the drafters was to reflect custom in the definitions of crimes in the Rome Statute, this effort was not always successful.[298] Zimmermann may well have disagreed to some extent.[299] Sadat and Carden wrote that the Rome Statute 'in no way represented codification in the civil law sense ... First, each crime is defined only "for the purpose of this Statute". Thus, the Statute

---

[290] Schabas (n. 69) 270.
[291] Schabas, 'Customary Law or "Judge-Made" Law' (n. 259) 101.   [292] Ibid. 81–82.
[293] W Schabas, *An Introduction to the International Criminal Court*, 2nd edn (Cambridge University Press 2004) 28 (emphasis added).
[294] R Cryer, 'Of Custom, Treaties, Scholars and the Gavel: The Influence of the International Criminal Tribunals on the ICRC Customary Law Study' (2006) 11 J Conflict & Security L 239, 240.
[295] J-M Henckaerts and L Doswald-Beck, *Customary International Humanitarian Law* (Cambridge University Press 2005) 572.
[296] Cryer (n. 294) 251.
[297] KS Gallant, *The Principle of Legality in International and Comparative Criminal Law* (Cambridge University Press 2009) 369.
[298] Dinstein (n. 111).   [299] Zimmermann (n. 242).

does not, by its terms, purport to be a codification of international criminal or international humanitarian law, although the definitions largely reflect existing law and will be universally applied through Security Council referrals to the Court.'[300] Werle wrote: 'It is true that the Statute essentially embodies customary law, but it does not exhaust it; customary international criminal law goes beyond the Statute, especially in the criminalization of violations of international humanitarian law.'[301] Danilenko asserted: 'The majority of States participating in the drafting of the Rome Statute agreed that the substantive criminal law of the Rome Statute essentially restates the existing law.'[302] Simma observed that the Rome Diplomatic Conference was a codification conference but that the resulting Statute contains elements of codification and progressive development without indicating which is prevalent.[303] Further, Hunt wrote:

> The drafters of the Statute and the Elements do appear to have attempted in many cases to stick as closely as possible to customary international law, wherever it could be identified. The numerous compromises which were made in order to obtain agreement have, however, caused the Statute and the Elements to diverge substantially from the actual content of customary international law as it existed at the time. This also obliged the drafters at times to have recourse to the extraordinary concept of 'creative ambiguity' in the Statute, so as not to have to deal with an issue upon which agreement would have proved difficult if not impossible to obtain.[304]

Finally, the vast majority of scholars agree that aggression is a crime under customary international law,[305] but whether the definition of this crime in the Rome Statute is reflective of custom will continue to be debated in the years to come.[306]

8.7 Conclusions

On balance, there is evidence in the drafting history of the Rome Statute, including the Final Act of the Rome Conference, State practice of ratifications, reservations, denunciations and revisions, other conduct of States and

---

[300] Sadat and Carden (n. 139) 422.

[301] G Werle, *Principles of International Criminal Law* (TMC Asser Press 2005) Preface, v.

[302] Danilenko (n. 236) 486.

[303] B Simma, 'Codification and Progressive Development' in B Simma and Others (eds.), *The Charter of the United Nations: A Commentary*, vol. I, 2nd edn (Oxford University Press 2002) 304–05.

[304] D Hunt, 'The International Criminal Court – High Hopes, 'Creative Ambiguity' and an Unfortunate Mistrust in International Judges' (2004) 2 J Int'l Crim Justice 5.

[305] C Kreß, 'The Crime of Aggression before the First Review of the ICC Statute' (2007) 20 LJIL 851, 853 fn. 9.

[306] The definition adopted does align itself very closely with existing precedents. See Chapter 7, Section 7.8.2.

Non-States Parties, jurisprudence and doctrinal writings that is suggestive of the crimes in the Rome Statute being generally or largely consistent with custom. As such, the definitions of crimes may be retrogressive or progressive in places and the Statute is perhaps not exhaustive of all crimes under customary international law. One of the tasks undertaken in the following Chapter is to reflect this important reality in a methodology for interpreting these crimes – to appropriately account for the Rome regime not being wholly self-contained.

The *Vienna Convention* (1969) and aids to interpretation

9.1 Introduction

In Chapters 7 and 8, a codification study was undertaken with a view to determining the relationship between custom and the definitions of crimes in the Rome Statute. It was concluded that these definitions are generally or largely consistent with customary international law.[1] In this Chapter, the consequent role, over time, of custom and other aids to interpreting these crimes – as well as their relationship to one another – will be considered within the framework of articles 31(3), 31(4), 32, 33(3) and 33(4) of the *Vienna Convention on the Law of Treaties* (1969) (*Vienna Convention*), which provide:

Article 31

General rule of interpretation

. . .

3. There shall be taken into account, together with the context:
   (a) any subsequent agreement between the parties regarding the interpretation of the treaty or the application of its provisions;
   (b) any subsequent practice in the application of the treaty which establishes the agreement of the parties regarding its interpretation;
   (c) any relevant rules of international law applicable in the relations between the parties.
4. A special meaning shall be given to a term if it is established that the parties so intended.

Article 32

Supplementary means of interpretation

Recourse may be had to supplementary means of interpretation, including the preparatory work of the treaty and the circumstances of its conclusion,

---

[1] The amendments to the Rome Statute on the crime of aggression have yet to be activated.

in order to confirm the meaning resulting from the application of article 31, or to determine the meaning when the interpretation according to article 31:

(a) leaves the meaning ambiguous or obscure; or
(b) leads to a result which is manifestly absurd or unreasonable.

Article 33

Interpretation of treaties authenticated in two or more languages

. . .

3. The terms of the treaty are presumed to have the same meaning in each authentic text.
4. Except where a particular text prevails in accordance with paragraph 1, when a comparison of the authentic texts discloses a difference of meaning which the application of articles 31 and 32 does not remove, the meaning which best reconciles the texts, having regard to the object and purpose of the treaty, shall be adopted.

9.2 Articles 31(3)(a) and (c) and relevant and applicable aids to interpretation

The subparagraphs of article 31(3) share three characteristics.[2] First, all three pertain to relevant prior and subsequent agreements among Parties to a treaty influencing the interpretation of a treaty, including as expressed in applicable law. Second, all of these sources of agreement are extrinsic to the treaty being interpreted. Third, consideration of all of these agreements is obligatory and therefore may not be regarded as 'norms of interpretation in any way inferior to those which precede them' in article 31, which is to be applied as one general rule.[3] In the following sections, the content of article 31(3)(a) and (c) will be considered, in reverse order, as applied to crimes in the Rome Statute.

When interpreting the crimes of aggression, genocide, other crimes against humanity and war crimes, article 31(3)(c) of the *Vienna Convention* (1969) obliges judges of the Court to take into account 'any relevant rules of international law applicable in the relations between the parties'. The backdrop of international law as an aid to treaty interpretation has a long history.[4] Until

---

[2] R Gardiner, *Treaty Interpretation* (Oxford University Press 2008) 202–04.
[3] Ibid. 204 (citing ILC (1966) II Ybk of the ILC, 220, para. 9).
[4] Ibid. (citing *Case Relating to the Territorial Jurisdiction of the International Commission of the River Oder (United Kingdom, Czechoslovakia, Denmark, France, Germany, Sweden v. Poland)* (1929) PCIJ Series A, No. 23; *Admission of a State to the United Nations (Article 4 of the Charter)*, Dissenting Opinion of Judges Basdevant, Winiarski, McNair and Read [1948] ICJ Rep. 57, 82; *Case Concerning Right of Passage over Indian Territory (Portugal v. India)*

recently, however, courts have not referred very much to this provision, even though they often take account of law external to treaties they interpret.[5] Article 31(3)(c) has two main functions, namely, to put into play the interpretive principle of systemic integration, which was introduced in Chapter 3,[6] and the intertemporal rule of interpretation.[7] The former concerns interpreting a treaty consistent with the international legal system in which it is situated. The latter regulates whether this consistency requirement pertains to the system as it existed when a treaty term was adopted or when a dispute regarding that term arises. Judges interpreting crimes in the Rome Statute will be confronted with both of these challenging issues, which will be discussed in turn below.

In Chapter 3, the principle of systemic integration was introduced to highlight potential regime conflicts between international human rights and humanitarian law and how this might pose problems when interpreting crimes in the Rome Statute. In this Chapter, the principle is intended to frame a discussion of sources of international law and their relationship to crimes in the Rome Statute. Pursuant to article 31(3)(c), account must be taken of 'any relevant rules of international law not only as constituting the background against which the treaty's provisions must be viewed, but in the *presumption* that the parties intend something *not inconsistent* with generally recognised principles of international law, or with previous treaty obligations towards third states'.[8] Like all presumptions, that of a treaty not conflicting with existing

---

[1957] ICJ Rep. 125; *Case Concerning Rights of Nationals of the United States of America in Morocco (France v. United States of America)* [1952] ICJ Rep. 176; *Arbitral Award (Guinea-Bissau v. Senegal)* [1991] ICJ Rep. 53; Institut de Droit International, 'Resolution on the Interpretation of Treaties' (Granada Session 1956) 46-II Annuaire de l'Institut de Droit International 364, article 1: 'the terms of the provisions of the treaty should be interpreted ... in the light of the principles of international law').

[5] For an excellent survey of this case law, see M Koskenniemi, 'Fragmentation of International Law: Difficulties Arising from the Diversification and Expansion of International Law: Report of the Study Group of the International Law Commission' (4 April 2006), UN Doc. A/CN.4/L.682, 183–96.

[6] See, e.g., C McLachlan, 'The Principle of Systemic Integration and Article 31(3)(c) of the Vienna Convention' (2005) 54 Int'l Comp L Quart 279.

[7] Gardiner (n. 2) 276 (citing *Arbitration regarding the Iron Rhine Railway (Belgium v. Netherlands)*, Award of 24 May 2005, 36).

[8] R Jennings and A Watts, *Oppenheim's International Law*, 9th edn (Longman, Harlow 1992) 1275 (citing *Case Concerning Right of Passage over Indian Territory (Portugal v. India)* [1957] ICJ Rep. 125, 141) (emphasis added). The ICJ recalled at 141 that 'it is a rule of interpretation that a text emanating from a Government must, in principle, be interpreted as producing and as intended to produce effects in accordance with existing law and not in violation of it'. See also *Reparations Case for Injuries Suffered in the Service of the United Nations*, Advisory Opinion [1949] ICJ Rep. 174, 182; H Lauterpacht, *The Development of International Law by the International Court* (Praeger 1958) 26–31; *Case Concerning Oil Platforms (Islamic Republic of Iran v. United States of America)*, Separate Opinion of Judge Kooijmans [2003] ICJ Rep. 161, 246, 253–54 (*Oil Platforms Case*).

international law is rebuttable and similar to the presumption in many common law systems that a statute is not inconsistent with unwritten common law.[9]

Perhaps the most famous (or notorious) recent example of international judges resorting to general international law to interpret a treaty is the *Oil Platforms* case (2003) decided by the International Court of Justice.[10] The majority of judges claimed to resort to the general law on the use of force to interpret the term 'necessity' in the *Treaty of Amity Economic Relations and Consular Rights (Article II)* (1955) between Iran and the United States.[11] It was therefore an attempt to give meaning to a *lex specialis* by drawing from *lex generalis*:

> The relationship between the special regime and the general law – that is to say, the degree to which a regime is self-contained in the first place – will be predominantly a matter of interpreting the treaties that form the regime. To what extent does a general law come in to fill the gaps or to assist in the interpretation or application – that is, in the administration – of the regime? Once it is clear that no regime is completely isolated from general law, the question emerges as to their relationship *inter se*.[12]

As the number of special regimes mushrooms, courts invoke two techniques for applying the presumption of a particular legal regime not being inconsistent with general international law: (1) trying to harmonize seemingly conflicting norms by interpreting them to have compatible meanings; and (2) where this is not possible or desirable, stating that general international law remains in the 'background' but a norm in the special regime has to be given priority in a particular case.[13] Article 31(3)(c) of the *Vienna Convention* (1969) is of use to judges seeking to support their interpretation of a legal provision by referring to a general rule of international law but also reminds judges of the gap-filling function of international law where a matter 'comes within the general scheme of a treaty but is not covered by its terms, or not fully covered'.[14] For the latter exercise, which is not the subject of the present study, article 21 of the Rome Statute provides judges with a hierarchy of gap-filling aids. For the former, it remains to be seen which of these aids or rules of international law are 'relevant' and 'applicable' under article 31(3)(c) in light of the definitions of crimes in the Rome Statute.

---

[9] M Akehurst, 'The Hierarchy of the Sources of International Law' (1974–1975) 47 British Ybk Int'l L 273, 275–76. In common law jurisdictions, there is also the phenomenon whereby the common law is resorted to where legislation offers an 'inadequate' solution. R Sullivan, *Sullivan and Driedger on the Construction of Statutes*, 4th edn (Butterworths 2002) 354.

[10] *Oil Platforms Case* (n. 8).

[11] 284 UNTS 93 (adopted 15 August 1955, entered into force 16 June 1957).

[12] Koskenniemi (n. 5) 71.   [13] Ibid. 174.   [14] Gardiner (n. 2) 284–85.

Generally, relevant rules 'must be those which can aid the quest for the meaning of a treaty provision, not those applying to a situation generally.[15] These rules may not 'override or limit the scope or effect of a provision'.[16] However, the work of the International Law Commission suggests that article 31(3)(c) was not merely intended to create a presumption of a treaty not being inconsistent with 'relevant rules' of international law but rather that the interpretation adopted by a court 'was to conform, as far as possible' to these rules so that minor differences between treaties and custom could be reconciled.[17]

9.2.1 Customary law

The International Court of Justice has occasionally relied on custom as an aid to interpreting a treaty term, to assign it a meaning that was not readily apparent from the treaty text or confirm that meaning.[18] As well, the ICTY in its initial judgments made 'abundant references' to customary law.[19] Importantly, in contrast to the general presumption that treaties are not inconsistent with general international law, a treaty that codifies custom contains terms that 'have a recognised meaning in customary international law' and so 'the parties can therefore be taken to have intended to refer' to this meaning.[20] Accordingly, a rule of consistency could be said to emerge between the underlying custom and the codifying treaty. The fine and difficult distinction between a presumption of 'not inconsistent with' and 'consistent with' can begin to be understood by considering a simple example. If one were asked to list words that are not inconsistent with the meaning of the word 'dog', one might readily come up with a long list of words such as: poodle, puppy, Dalmatian, Golden Retriever, St. Bernard, animal, mammal and so forth. If one were again given the word

---

[15] Ibid. 266.

[16] A Orakhelashvili, 'Restrictive Interpretation of Human Rights Treaties in the Recent Jurisprudence of the European Court of Human Rights' (2003) 14 EJIL 529, 537.

[17] M Villiger, *Customary International Law and Treaties* (Martinus Nijhoff 1985) 268–69.

[18] Ibid. 269–70 (citing *Continental Shelf Arbitration (France v. United Kingdom)* [1979] 54 ILR 6, 75; *Case Concerning Military and Paramilitary Activities in and Against Nicaragua (Nicaragua v. United States of America)* [1986] ICJ Rep. 14, 94).

[19] W Schabas, 'Customary Law or "Judge-Made" Law: Judicial Creativity at the UN Criminal Tribunals' in J Doria, H-P Gasser and M Bassiouni (eds.), *The Legal Regime of the International Criminal Court: Essays in Honour of Professor Igor Blishchenko* (Brill 2009) 77–78.

[20] Koskenniemi (n. 5) 198; O Schachter, *International Law in Theory and Practice* (Martinus Nijhoff 1991) 71–72 (stating more mildly that custom is important 'since a codification treaty will give rise to differences that may well require examination of the prior customary law to throw light on the new text'); R Baxter, 'Treaties and Custom' (1970) 129 Recueil des Cours de l'Académie de Droit International 31, 103.

'dog' and asked to list words that are consistent with its meaning, one would perhaps offer up a shorter list of words, including: canine, hound and such.

9.2.2 The Rome Statute customary law presumption

An attempt was made in Chapters 7 and 8 to determine the importance of custom as an aid to interpreting crimes in the Rome Statute by assessing whether the Statute is supposed to be reflective of crimes under customary international law. This codification study was undertaken not least because the ICTY has referred in its case law to a presumption of interpreting crimes within its jurisdiction in accordance with custom. However, unlike the statutes governing other international criminal tribunals, the Rome Statute contains deliberately detailed definitions of crimes that are supplemented by the Elements of Crimes, which are even more detailed and, in accordance with article 9 of the Statute, 'shall assist' judges with interpreting crimes in the Court's jurisdiction. These characteristics might point in the direction of a self-contained regime in which custom has no place.[21]

The conclusions reached at the end of the codification study were that crimes defined in the Rome Statute are generally or largely reflective of custom (containing retrogressive and progressive elements in places) and that not all crimes under custom fall within the Court's jurisdiction. Further, while the intent of the Statute's drafters was to limit the Court's jurisdiction to crimes under international law, they were careful not to claim that the Rome Statute is a code of these crimes, precisely because of the aforementioned conclusions and perception of possible drawbacks to codification, which were discussed in Chapter 6. Thus, while the terms 'code' and 'codification' are inapt, custom does have an important role to play in the Rome regime:

> The gravamen of future pleadings in the ICC will be interpretation of the Statute, not its customary law underpinnings. However, because of the high level of generality of the Statute, when the Court interprets it in accordance with the principle of interpretation contained in the Vienna Convention on the Law of Treaties, it will inevitably have to resort to customary law to construe and apply the crimes that the Statute enumerates. The Elements of Crimes will provide some, but not all, the answers. Moreover, Article 21 of the Statute, which concerns applicable law, opens the door wide to

---

[21] Indeed, Jacobs rejects a role for custom as an interpretive aid owing to the specificity and comprehensiveness of the Rome Statute and Elements of Crimes, the alleged closed nature of the lists of crimes in the Rome Statute, the hierarchy of applicable law in article 21 and the fact that article 21 contains no express reference to 'custom'. D Jacobs, 'Positivism and International Criminal Law: The Principle of Legality as a Rule of Conflict of Theories' in J d'Aspremont and J Kammerhofer (eds.), *International Legal Positivism in a Post-Modern World* (Cambridge University Press, forthcoming October 2014), http://papers.ssrn.com/sol3/papers.cfm?abstract_id=2046311, accessed 16 October 2013.

such additional sources of international law as "principles and rules of international law, including the established principles of international law of armed conflict", as well as "general principles of law derived by the Court from national laws of legal systems of the world."[22]

In light of the results of the codification study, it is submitted that judges should recognize a rebuttable presumption of interpretation consistent with custom for crimes in the Rome Statute.[23] This recognition avoids 'throwing the baby out with the bathwater', something which may result if article 10 is interpreted as foreclosing the influence of custom on the Rome Statute and entailing a hermetically sealed regime in which the Elements of Crimes in all cases reign supreme.

> If ... it would be unwise to give conclusive effect as evidence of the law to the purportedly declaratory treaty, it is still not necessary to swing to the opposite extreme by confining the effect of the treaty wholly to its actual parties. A suitable middle course would be to give *presumptive effect* as evidence of customary law to the treaty purporting to declare the law while allowing the State or individual against whom the treaty is proffered the right to demonstrate that the particular treaty provision invoked does not correctly express the law. If the objecting party fails to sustain that burden, the presumption created by the treaty is not overcome.[24]

A legal presumption is an inference that stands until refuted.[25] It is a form of reasoning that fills a gap and requires that, in the absence of better information, a particular conclusion be drawn.[26] A legal presumption is a *provisional* truth that can be displaced by evidence disproving its validity in a particular case.[27] For example, the presumption of innocence is not tantamount to actual innocence, and proof of guilt can displace this presumption. Every presumption is, by definition, defeasible.[28] The strength of a presumption need not be grounded in fact.[29] For example, the presumption of innocence is not

---

[22] T Meron, 'Revival of Customary International Humanitarian Law' (2005) 99 AJIL 817, 832.

[23] It remains to be seen whether the amendments on aggression will be activated in 2017.

[24] R Baxter, 'Multilateral Treaties as Evidence of Customary International Law' (1965–66) 41 British Ybk Int'l L 275, 290 (emphasis added); Villiger (n. 17) 246; HWA Thirlway, *International Customary Law and Codification* (Sijthoff 1972) 28, 99–100. See also Y Dinstein, 'Interaction between Customary International Law and Treaties' (2006) 322 Recueil des Cours de l'Académie de Droit International 243. This presumption of Baxter's was conceived of as a way to address situations where a treaty that purportedly is mostly declaratory of custom is applied to a Non-State Party. However, it appears to be equally useful as an interpretive presumption in the present context.

[25] N Rescher, *Presumption and the Practices of Tentative Cognition* (Cambridge University Press 2006) 1.

[26] Ibid.   [27] Ibid. 4, 7.   [28] Ibid. 5.   [29] Ibid. 6.

dependent on the majority of accused being innocent. Rather, it is a means by which the law, for whatever reason, chooses to take a matter for granted and closes a gap that would otherwise impede the legal process in some way.[30] The requisite standard of proof for rebutting a presumption varies. For the presumption of innocence, proof of guilt beyond a reasonable doubt may be required.[31] Other presumptions may be rebutted on a balance of probabilities. A legal presumption may not be defeated at a general level. Rather, its application to a particular case can be rebutted.[32]

The concept of a rebuttable presumption that a treaty is declaratory of custom was introduced by Baxter[33] and endorsed by Thirlway.[34] In practice, attempts to rebut such a presumption are rare, and 'the new law tends to be observed and accepted'.[35] However, it should be noted that practice to date is limited to treaties that do not create an international criminal jurisdiction. Indeed, drafters of the Rome Statute had the right to depart from the meaning of certain customary legal terms, but this intention must be express or implied.[36] It is therefore expected that where the exercise of the Court's jurisdiction is retroactive on its face, an individual may challenge such a presumption, which judges of the Court would have to seriously consider in respect of the crime charged. This situation may arise in the context of Security Council referrals, including referrals involving acts of aggression, as well as article 12(3) declarations.

Today, most common-law countries have statutory definitions of crimes, but certain concepts of crimes or elements of their definitions might continue to be embedded in the common law, which guides the interpretation of criminal statutes.[37] Unlike a criminal statute in a common-law jurisdiction, however, the Rome Statute is supplemented by the Elements of Crimes. In Section 9.2.6 below, the relationship between custom and the Elements of Crimes in cases of conflict will be examined.

The presumption proposed would result in an interpretive relationship between the Rome Statute and custom that is theoretically coherent, consistent with the existing legal framework established by the Rome Statute, reconcilable with alternative conclusions justifiably reached in specific cases (e.g., where a definition of a crime is based on a constitutive treaty rather than custom) and useful as an intellectual technique for resolving conflicts between the Elements

---

[30] Ibid.   [31] Ibid.   [32] Ibid. 7.

[33] Baxter (n. 24) 290.   [34] Thirlway (n. 24).

[35] O Schachter, 'Entangled Treaty and Custom' in Y Dinstein (ed.), *International Law at a Time of Perplexity: Essays in Honour of Shabtai Rosenne* (Martinus Nijhoff 1989) 717, 722.

[36] This point is made by Sullivan in respect of a common-law concept and legislation. (n. 9) 343–44.

[37] K Gallant, *The Principle of Legality in International and Comparative Criminal Law* (Cambridge University Press 2009) 3.

and custom, a matter discussed below.[38] The presumption contemplated is not only legally accurate, as evidenced by the codification study carried out, but also is good legal policy. International criminal law is recognized as a special regime,[39] and the absence of such a presumption would result in a sub-regime within this regime, thereby resulting in a permanent judicial organ for a field of international law persistently contributing to its fragmentation.

In light of the jurisprudence of international courts alleged to have invoked custom as a means of engaging in judicial policymaking, concern has been voiced about custom's prominent placement in article 21 of the Rome Statute.[40] However, unlike other statutes for international criminal tribunals, the Rome Statute is relatively detailed, and crimes contained therein must be interpreted in accordance with the strict and operationalized guiding principle of legality in article 22. Accordingly, the methodology developed in this study and those applying it would respect the distinction between interpretation and modification of a treaty text, a distinction that is difficult to respect in hard cases but must arguably be.[41] The purpose of referring to rules of international law external to the Rome Statute may be to seek clarification of what a provision means or to embed the Court's reasoning in the wider international legal order, thereby promoting coherence within it.[42] These are permissible ends. Modification under the guise of clarification is not.[43] As two judges of the International Court of Justice remarked, 'substantive rules of international law cannot be brought into ... litigation through the back door', and one may not 'invoke the concept of treaty interpretation to displace the applicable law'.[44]

Customary international criminal law has been described as 'still in its infancy, or at least adolescence: consequently, many of its rules still suffer from their loose content'.[45] This assessment calls into question the usefulness of custom as an aid to interpreting crimes in the Rome Statute. However, custom varies in its level of detail, taking on greater detail where it is reflected in a treaty. For example, it has been suggested that article 147 of the third *Geneva*

---

[38] H Chodosh, 'An Interpretive Theory of International Law: The Distinction Between Treaty and Customary Law' (1995) 28 Vanderbilt J Transnat'l L 973, 1001–02.

[39] Koskenniemi (n. 5) 71.

[40] J Wessel, 'Judicial Policy-Making at the International Criminal Court: An Institutional Guide to Analyzing International Adjudication' (2006) 44 Columbia J Transnat'l L 377, 415–16.

[41] See Section 9.3.5.

[42] D French, 'Treaty Interpretation and the Incorporation of Extraneous Legal Rules' (2006) 55 Int'l Comp L Quart 281, 282–83.

[43] Ibid.

[44] *Oil Platforms Case* (n. 8) Separate Opinion of Judge Buergenthal, 270, 281; Separate Opinion of Judge Higgins, 225, 237–38; Gardiner (n. 2) 278.

[45] A Cassese, *International Criminal Law*, 2nd edn (Oxford University Press 2008) 17.

Convention (1949) plays a 'key role' in interpreting the war crime of wilful killing in article 8(2)(a)(i) of the Rome Statute.[46] Further, the presumption of consistency with custom in the Rome regime could play an integral role in the evolution of the definitions of crimes contained therein under customary law and in their transition from adolescence to adulthood. The practice of the Court interpreting crimes in the Rome Statute consistent with their customary counterparts itself contributes to the clarification of those customary elements.[47] The principle of complementarity in the Rome Statute means that national courts will also increasingly contribute to this clarification, thereby enhancing custom's detail.[48]

Where the Rome Statute does mirror a customary legal term or a treaty term reflective of custom, this concurrence ought not to be mistaken for a hierarchy: 'All that transpires is that the authors of a given treaty deem fit to apply their text (in whole or in part) in a manner consistent with a normative matrix *dehors* the instrument.'[49] Such consistency can be said to exist only where a customary meaning can be reasonably accommodated by the actual words in the Rome Statute. However, such a statement begs consideration of when custom can and cannot be 'accommodated' by the Rome Statute. Stated differently, when does the presumption of consistency with custom stand, and under what circumstances may one conclude that it has been successfully rebutted? Although it is futile to attempt a full answer to this question without knowing which customary law and which statutory provision are under consideration, a few general observations can be offered.

When a treaty replicates a term derived from custom or prior treaty law considered to be reflective of custom, it is necessary to carefully consider whether the subsequent treaty must exactly reproduce the relevant legal term in order for the presumption to apply. In places, the Rome Statute contains 'literal incorporation of "parent norms" into the Statute. The terms are absorptions of corresponding rules of IHL [international humanitarian law, for example,] to allow recourse to "parent norms" such as those in the Geneva Conventions, although sometimes noteworthy textual differences may emerge.'[50] On the one hand, it is arguable that so long as the Rome Statute uses language that is apt to refer to the relevant principle or concept, the presumption applies. When the Rome Statute does not reproduce exactly the relevant terminology, the Court must discern whether the words chosen by the drafters were meant to modify the relevant concept. Four considerations may be useful for this exercise.

First, judges should consider whether the modification may be intended to significantly narrow or broaden a concept in scope – resulting in retrograde or progressive crimes or elements thereof. Indeed, it is legally permissible for States to revise or redefine customary legal concepts that are not *jus cogens*

---

[46] G Werle, *Principles of International Criminal Law* (TMC Asser 2005) 108–09.
[47] Schachter (n. 20) 71–72.   [48] Discussed in Chapter 2, Section 2.4.4.
[49] Dinstein (n. 24) 392.   [50] Werle (n. 46) 107.

norms in whole or in part through treaties. Where drafters of the Rome Statute have drafted a change to custom or treaty law for purposes of their relations, it is important for the Court not to undermine this purpose by reintroducing the customary or treaty rule or principle through interpretation. It is not permissible to invoke the presumption to recognize new crimes in the Court's jurisdiction, especially those that were deliberately excluded from the Rome regime.[51]

Second, judges might apply the rule of *expressio unius exclusio alterius* by considering whether the impugned provision or other provisions in the Rome Statute suggest the exclusion of a crime or element under custom. The *expressio unius* rule of interpretation supports the view that 'with the express statement of a new rule in a text, the drafting body implicitly intended to exclude other, incompatible customary rules on the same subject-matter'.[52] Consider, for example, the definition of torture as a crime against humanity in article 7(2)(e) of the Rome Statute and the definition of torture in article 1(1) of the *Convention against Torture and Other Cruel, Inhuman or Degrading Treatment or Punishment* (1984), which is considered to be reflective of custom.[53] Whereas the former definition does not require torture to have occurred at the hand of a public or other official, the latter does. Customary rules on subject matter not covered by the provisions in the Rome Statute are not weakened by the Rome Statute and remain applicable so long as the customary law requirements of State practice and *opinio juris* are met.[54] In addition, customary law arising before or after the adoption of the Rome Statute continues to exist.[55]

Third, judges should consider that 'the step from unwritten custom to written codification is not a small one. The very act of generalizing, systematizing and removing inconsistencies and gaps produces a text that is qualitatively different from unwritten law.'[56] Accordingly, thought might be given to whether the imperfect replication of custom was perhaps merely a function of transitioning from unwritten to written law or from varying and disparate sources of written law to one coherent text (e.g., crimes against humanity).[57] Finally, where custom is particularly 'confused, rudimentary or otherwise unsatisfactory', the Court 'may infer that the legislation [Rome Statute] was intended to substitute a coherent legislative regime for the deficient customary law'.[58] For example, those who consider the definition of the crime of aggression to be materially lacking under customary international law might argue against the influence of

---

[51] Cassese (n. 45).   [52] Villiger (n. 17) 161.
[53] See, e.g., *Prosecutor* v. *Furundžija*, Judgment, ICTY-95–17/1-T, 10 December 1998, paras. 159–160.
[54] Villiger (n. 17) 162.   [55] Ibid. 163.
[56] Schachter (n. 20) 70.   [57] See Chapter 6, Section 6.3.
[58] Sullivan (n. 9) 353 makes this point concerning the relationship between legislation and the common law.

aids suggestive of its customary definition.[59] Thus, it becomes readily apparent that a determination of whether a crime in the Rome Statute is consistent with its customary counterpart is itself an exercise in interpretation and that it is difficult to distinguish an assessment of consistency, as a preliminary step, from subsequent interpretation.[60]

As discussed in Chapter 5, the imperatives in article 22(2) of the Rome Statute cannot generally be used to thwart the ordinary interpretive process of which the proposed interpretive presumption would form a part under article 31(3)(c) of the *Vienna Convention* (1969).[61] Further, the presumption of consistency with custom for crimes in the Rome Statute respects the principle of legality, including its underlying justifications, by respecting the text of the Statute. Is also does not prejudice or undermine the legal force of article 10 of the Rome Statute or the domestic legislation that States choose to enact, even where that legislation departs in some way from the definitions of crimes in the Statute.[62] While the Rome Statute may create a sub-regime of international criminal law, crimes defined therein should, to the greatest extent possible, be interpreted in a manner that is consistent with custom. If the interpretive presumption proposed were recognized, this would, of course, lend momentum to revived interest in custom's interpretation as well as the 'existential' issues of its formation and aids to its interpretation.[63] However, these issues fall outside the scope of this study.

---

[59]   14 December 1994.   [60]   Koskenniemi (n. 5) 174.

[61]   Chapter 5, Sections 5.5.2 and 5.9.

[62]   Perhaps if enough States enacted a particular definition for a crime in the Rome Statute that departed in some way from the Elements of Crimes, it might be argued that a new State practice or *opinio juris* emerged on the content of the elements of that crime under customary international law.

[63]   Meron (n. 22) 832; AE Roberts, 'Traditional and Modern Approaches to Customary International Law: A Reconciliation' (2001) 95 AJIL 757; A Seibert-Fohr, 'Modern Concepts of Customary International Law as a Manifestation of a Value-Based International Order' in A Zimmermann and R Hofmann (eds.), *Unity and Diversity in International Law* (Duncker & Humblot 2006) 257; A Orakhelashvili, *The Interpretation of Acts and Rules of Public International Law* (Oxford University Press 2008) 496ff.; J-M Henckaerts, 'Assessing the Laws and Customs of War: The Publication of Customary International Humanitarian Law' (2006) Human Rights Brief 8. Not all, however, would agree: 'Indeed, although space does not permit a full treatment of the issue here, another of Rome's revolutionary contributions is its chipping away at the authoritativeness and continuing relevance of customary international law as a source of international law.' L Sadat and SR Carden, 'The New International Criminal Court: An Uneasy Revolution' (2000) 88 Georgetown LJ 381, 423. See also ILC, 'Report of the International Law Commission covering its Second Session' (1950) II Ybk of the ILC 364, 367–74 (on how to make evidence of custom more readily available). On the existential nature of these issues, see D Hollis, 'The Existential Function of Interpretation in International Law', Temple University Legal Studies Research Paper No. 2013-43 (24 September 2013), 1, 16–23, http://papers.ssrn.com/sol3/papers.cfm?abstract_id=2330642, accessed 18 October 2013.

It has been said that, in practice, 'the Rome Statute is one of the major international instruments of our time, most of whose principles represent a consensus reached by a large number of States following a lengthy and complex drafting process. Its provisions will inevitably influence the evolution of international law.'[64] Because the rules for interpreting a treaty and ascertaining custom are different, the Court's interpretation of a crime in the Rome Statute may invoke notions of the relevant provision's object and purpose, a concept that is not necessarily relevant to ascertaining custom, and thereby develop the definition of that crime 'in a different direction than the customary rule'.[65] If this happens, and the customary and Rome Statute definitions of a crime are no longer consistent with one another, custom loses much of its function as an aid to interpreting that crime in the Statute.[66] Accordingly, the presumption of consistency with custom can play an important role in discouraging, where appropriate, the Court's reliance on certain arguments of object and purpose to develop the definitions of crimes in the Rome Statute beyond their customary parallels, thereby also discouraging judicial policymaking. Such a view contemplates a new relationship between custom and the fear of judicial activism where the former is not seen as a gateway to the latter, but rather a stop valve for it.

Similarly, account needs to be taken of the distinct possibility that a crime under customary international law that is included in the Court's jurisdiction, once identical, will continue to develop through the *opinio juris* and practice of States, perhaps resulting in its counterpart in the Rome regime being superseded at the customary level.[67] Again, the presumption of consistency with custom can help to prevent this from happening. It can discourage the desuetude of the crimes in the Rome Statute and therefore safeguard their binding nature on nationals and territory subject to the Rome regime absent the consent of the relevant State at the relevant time. Finally, the presumption of consistency with custom must be carefully balanced against the concern for internal coherence within the Rome Statute. Because legality is the guiding interpretive principle for crimes in the Rome Statute, textual primacy and coherence take precedence over the over-importation of custom or other law into the Statute.

9.2.3 Treaty law

The records of the International Law Commission and international jurisprudence confirm that 'any relevant rules of international law applicable in the

---

[64] W Schabas, *The International Criminal Court: A Commentary on the Rome Statute* (Oxford University Press 2010) 271.

[65] Villiger (n. 17) 270; Schachter (n. 20) 70.   [66] Villiger, ibid.

[67] P Weil, 'Towards Relative Normativity in International Law?' (1983) 77 AJIL 413, 438; Schachter (n. 35) 720.

relations between the parties' in article 31(3)(c) includes treaty law.[68] But this provision is silent on what makes a treaty relevant and applicable to a given interpretive exercise. With respect to the Rome Statute, at least a couple of issues arise. First, are treaties relevant to interpreting crimes in the Rome Statute only if they reflect crimes under customary law? Second, in order to aid in the interpretation of crimes in the Rome Statute, must all Parties to the Statute ratify a treaty in order for it to be 'applicable', or only States implicated in the case before the Court? On the first issue, it has already been pointed out that the Rome Statute is generally, but certainly not perfectly, consistent with custom. Accordingly, some crimes in the Rome regime may be traceable to provisions in treaties that do not have customary status. Where words in articles 6, 7, 8 and 8 *bis* can be traced to such treaties, certainly that treaty is a 'relevant' aid to interpreting these words. Is it, however, 'applicable' within the meaning of article 31(3)(c)?

This second issue is harder to address. There are at least three ways to define 'applicable' in article 31(3)(c) in the face of a treaty that is relevant to crimes in the Rome Statute but not reflective of custom: (1) the relevant treaty must have been ratified by all Parties to the Rome Statute; (2) only States implicated in the case before the Court need to have ratified the relevant treaty; or (3) the relevant treaty must have been 'implicitly accepted or tolerated by all parties to the treaty under interpretation',[69] thereby expressing possibly a shared understanding.[70] The first approach is the strictest and may risk precluding consideration of a relevant treaty text.[71]

The second approach is far more relaxed but has not found support in international jurisprudence in respect of multilateral treaties.[72] The third approach has been described as requiring that the relevant treaty provision have the status of customary law or be 'sufficiently accepted to constitute an interpretive agreement' under article 31(3)(a) of the *Vienna Convention* (1969).[73] This matter has not been resolved by the International Law Commission or by

---

[68] Gardiner (n. 2) 262–63 (quoting Jiménez de Aréchaga (1966) I (Part Two) Ybk of the ILC 190, para. 70). Cases in which treaty law is considered and reference is made to article 31(3)(c) include: *Pope & Talbot* v. *Canada (Damages Phase)*, Arbitration under Chapter Eleven of NAFTA (Award in respect of Damages) (2002) 41 ILM 1347; *Pope & Talbot* v. *Canada (Interim Award)*, 26 June 2000, paras. 65–68; *Biotech Case, European Communities – Measures Affecting the Approval and Marketing of Biotech Products*, Reports of the Panel, 29 September 2006, WT/DS291–3/R; App. No. 4451/70, *Golder* v. *the United Kingdom*, ECHR (1975) Series A, No. 18, para. 35.

[69] McLachlan (n. 6) 314–15.

[70] Koskenniemi (n. 5) 201 (citing J Pauwelyn, *Conflict of Norms in Public International Law: How WTO Law Relates to Other Rules of International Law* (Cambridge University Press 2003) 257–63).

[71] Gardiner (n. 2) 271.   [72] Ibid. 273.   [73] Ibid. 275.

international courts, although the former offered the following guidance in a 2006 report:

> [Article 31(3)(c)] requires the interpreter to consider other treaty-based rules so as to arrive at a consistent meaning. Such other rules are of particular relevance where parties to the treaty under interpretation are also parties to the other treaty, where the treaty rule has passed into or expresses customary international law or where they provide evidence of the common understanding of the parties as to the object and purpose of the treaty under interpretation or as to the meaning of a particular term.[74]

Indeed, '[e]ach state brings to the negotiating table a lexicon which is derived from prior treaties (bilateral or multilateral) into which it has entered with other states. The resulting text in each case may be different. It is, after all, the product of a specific negotiation. But it will inevitably share common elements with what has gone before.'[75] In practice, international and national courts do not hesitate to invoke the aid of treaty provisions to interpret a treaty applicable to the case, treating it as an accepted and established practice that does not need to be justified.[76] Courts and tribunals also refer to treaties to describe the evolution of the relevant law and seldom indicate the function in the *Vienna Convention* (1969) framework that a treaty has in aiding the interpretation of an applicable treaty.[77] At the same time, they have cautioned that, although two treaties may contain identical or similar provisions, the result of a transplant, they may be interpreted differently if: (1) they are situated in regimes that have different objects and purposes; (2) there are contextual differences; (3) subsequent practice by Parties to one or both of the treaties varies in content; or (4) the relevant *travaux préparatoires* contemplate different meanings.[78] For example, as discussed in Chapter 3, international human rights, international humanitarian law and international criminal law have different objects and purposes, meaning similar treaty provisions in these regimes may well be subject to different interpretations.

As for the relationship between treaty law that is not reflective of custom and the Elements of Crimes in cases of conflict, a couple of observations are in order. First, where the parent treaty norm actually criminalizes conduct that is also criminalized in the Rome Statute, and the latter incorporates the language

---

[74] Ibid. 275 (citing ILC, 'Report of the International Law Commission on the Work of its Fifty-Eighth Session', GAOR, 61st Session (2006) Supp. No. 10 (A/61/10) 414–15, para. 21).

[75] Ibid. 282 (citing McLachlan (n. 6) 283).

[76] Ibid.   [77] Ibid. 283.

[78] Ibid. 284 (citing *The MOX Plant Case (Ireland* v. *United Kingdom)* [2001] ITLOS, para. 51, available at http://www.itlos.org, accessed 15 February 2011).

used in the former, it is submitted that drafters of the Rome Statute should be presumed to have intended (unless proven otherwise) these definitions to be consistent with one another. Why else mirror the language? This means that conflicts between the treaty definition and the Elements of Crimes should be resolved in favour of the treaty aid, even though the Elements of Crimes is the more recent legal instrument. The latter must be consistent with the Rome Statute. Where the treaty inspiring the definition of a crime in the Rome Statute does not itself criminalize the relevant conduct – perhaps it just prohibits it – the Elements of Crimes should be presumed (unless proven otherwise) to be more faithful to the Rome Statute definition than the relevant treaty. This is because drafters of the Elements were likely cognisant of the need to articulate elements for a crime derived from a treaty that did not previously express the conduct as criminal.

9.2.4 General principles of law

That article 31(3)(c) includes the aid of general principles of law is not controversial.[79] Article 38(1)(c) of the ICJ Statute refers to 'general principles of law recognized by civilized nations'. Two presumptions relevant to this source of law, one positive and one negative, operate at the international level: (1) parties are taken 'to refer to general principles of international law for all questions which [the treaty] does not itself resolve in express terms or in a different way';[80] and (2) States Parties to a treaty 'intend something not inconsistent with generally recognised principles of international law'.[81] As discussed in Chapter 4, Section 4.3.10.3, and in accordance with the first presumption, general principles of law do not really compete with the interpretive aids of treaty and custom, coming into play more to avoid a possible *non liquet*.

Whereas the ICTY and ICTR had to determine on their own whether general principles may be relevant and applicable to their work,[82] part III of the Rome Statute expressly lists general principles of criminal law applicable to the work of the Court. Where these principles do not assist the Court with interpreting the crimes defined therein, judges may survey general principles of international law as well as national laws in order to glean a general principle of law recognized by the community of nations to assist it in interpreting a crime. When doing the latter, the following should be kept in mind:

> (i) unless indicated by an international rule, reference should not be made to one national legal system only, say that of common law or that of civil-law

---

[79] *Golder* (n. 68).   [80] Koskenniemi (n. 5) 234.
[81] Jennings and Watts (n. 8) 1275; Pauwelyn (n. 70) 240–44; Koskenniemi (n. 5) 21.
[82] Chapter 1, Section 1.3.2.

States. Rather, international courts must draw upon the general concepts and legal institutions common to all the major legal systems of the world. This presupposes a process of identification of common denominators in these legal systems so as to pinpoint the basic notions they share; (ii) since "international trials exhibit a number of features that differentiate them from national criminal proceedings", (Para. 5, Separate and Dissenting Opinion of Judge Cassese, Prosecutor v. Drazan Erdemovic, Judgment, Case No. IT-96–22-A, 7 Oct. 1997.) account must be taken of the specificity of international criminal proceedings when utilising national law notions. In this way a mechanical importation or transposition from national law into international criminal proceedings is avoided, as well as the attendant distortions of the unique traits of such proceedings.[83]

Article 21(1)(c) of the Rome Statute recognizes 'general principles of law derived by the Court from national laws of legal systems of the world including, as appropriate, the national laws of States that would normally exercise jurisdiction over the crime, provided that those principles are not inconsistent with this Statute and with international law and internationally recognized norms and standards'. Accordingly, both general principles of international law and general principles of law are authoritative interpretive aids, making their consideration mandatory if relevant.

9.2.5 Judicial decisions and teachings of publicists

Article 31(3)(c) indeed encompasses all of article 38 of the ICJ Statute, including 'judicial decisions and the teachings of the most highly qualified publicists of the various nations, as subsidiary means for the determination of rules of law'.[84] Courts freely enlist the help of these subsidiary aids to interpret treaty provisions 'without apparently seeing any need to find a specific justification in the Vienna rules'.[85] Importantly, subsidiary means are not sources of international law per se, but rather aids to identifying its content, meaning the content of custom, treaty law and general principles. Article 21 of the Rome Statute confirms that judicial decisions include national decisions and the Court's own decisions.[86] Teachings of publicists may include not only journal articles and books but also commentaries to relevant treaties and interpretive aids prepared by expert bodies such as the International Law Commission and International Committee of the Red Cross. Whether international law in article 31(3)(c) includes soft law instruments not listed in article 38 of the ICJ Statute is the subject of

---

[83] *Furundžija* (n. 53), paras. 178, 183.
[84] Article 38(1)(d), ICJ Statute; Gardiner (n. 2) 268.
[85] Gardiner, ibid.; *Golder* (n. 68).   [86] Article 21(1)(c) and 21(2), Rome Statute.

some debate.[87] As previously discussed, for purposes of interpreting crimes in the Rome Statute, article 21(3) of the Rome Statute likely excludes soft law international human rights instruments.[88]

It is important to recall that, unlike the common-law tradition, international criminal law does not adhere to a doctrine of binding precedents.[89] Jurisprudence is therefore merely a permissible aid to interpreting crimes in the Rome Statute. However, jurisprudential consistency does promote the rule of law, which underlies the principle of legality. Given the wealth of ICTY case law, the interpretive presumption of consistency with custom that ICTY judges purport to apply and the large number of lawyers and judges at the Court who have prior experience working at the ICTY, it is expected that the jurisprudence of this ad hoc tribunal will serve as an attractive aid to interpreting crimes in the Rome Statute.

Among its many accomplishments, the ICTY has expounded on the elements of crimes for grave breaches of the *Geneva Conventions* (1949) and defined the test for 'overall control' as well as 'international armed conflict' and the meaning of 'protected persons'. It has also developed definitions of crimes involving sexual violence during wartime; the elements of the crime of genocide, including the target of this crime (a group or part of a group); the scope of crimes against humanity; the definitions of enslavement and persecution as crimes against humanity; and the doctrine of command responsibility, including the requisite knowledge of the superior. However, it must be recalled that international case law is not a source of custom and that judges of the ICTY, like judges at the Court, attempt to discern the existence, scope and content of custom. These judicial pronouncements on the content of a customary rule or absence thereof may be accurate when they were made but may be disproven by the subsequent development of custom.[90] Accordingly, the Court has rightly expressed caution about automatically invoking the jurisprudence of the ICTY.[91] The same caution should be exercised in respect of national case law when examining it for the content of custom or a general principle of law.

As well, findings reached by judicial bodies that carried out their interpretive work in a context that is altogether different from that of the Court need to be carefully scrutinized for their relevance. For example, the 'case law from the

---

[87] Gardiner (n. 2) 268.   [88] See Chapter 3, Section 3.5.   [89] Cassese (n. 45) 18.

[90] Institut de Droit International, 'Problems Arising from a Succession of Codification Conventions on a Particular Subject' (Lisbon Session 1995) 66-I Annuaire de l'Institut de Droit International 39, conclusion 14.

[91] See, e.g., *Prosecutor* v. *Kony and Others*, Decision on the Prosecutor's Position on the Decision of Pre-Trial Chamber II to Redact Factual Descriptions of Crimes in the Warrants of Arrest, Motion for Reconsideration, and Motion for Clarification, ICC-02/04–01/05–60, 28 October 2005, para. 19, cited in G Bitti, 'Article 21 of the Statute of the ICC and the Treatment of Sources of Law in the Jurisprudence of the ICC' in C Stahn and G Sluiter (eds.), *The Emerging Practice of the International Criminal Court* (Martinus Nijhoff 2009) 281, 297.

British military courts for the trials of war criminals whose jurisdiction was based on the rules and procedure of the domestic military courts were less helpful in establishing rules of international law than case law of tribunals set up to apply international law'.[92] Similarly, the ICTY rightly remarked: 'the influence of domestic criminal law practice on the work of the International Tribunal must take due account of the very real differences between a domestic criminal jurisdiction and the system administered by the International Tribunal'.[93] And, as discussed in Chapter 3, the interpretation of international human rights and humanitarian law may well occur in contexts that differ from that in which the Court carries out its work.[94]

9.2.6 Elements of Crimes

Article 31(3)(a) requires judges of the Court to take account of 'any subsequent agreement between the parties regarding the interpretation of the treaty or the application of its provisions'. The Elements of Crimes (Elements), adopted in 2000 by the Assembly of States Parties, is arguably such a subsequent agreement and 'shall assist the Court in the interpretation and application of articles 6, 7, 8 and 8 bis'.[95] Some may choose to treat the Elements as an agreement made in connection with the conclusion of the Rome Statute under article 31(2) of the *Vienna Convention* (1969). This preference, however, would not alter the relationship proposed between the Elements and custom, as no hierarchy exists within article 31. It is submitted that, where the presumption of consistency with custom stands, a provision can accommodate the content of custom but also the Elements, and where these two interpretive aids conflict, custom should prevail. One way to understand this dynamic is to recall that the Elements must be 'consistent' with the definitions of crimes in the Rome Statute.[96] If these provisions are presumed to be consistent with custom, a conflict between custom and the Elements would suggest that the Elements are somehow inconsistent with article 6, 7, 8 or 8 bis. An example may be useful to illustrate this point.

In the *Al Bashir* Arrest Decision (2009), Pre-Trial Chamber I used the Elements of Crimes to interpret the crime of genocide in article 6 of the Rome Statute.[97] The Elements include a requirement that the relevant conduct 'took place in the context of a manifest pattern of similar conduct directed against that group or was conduct that could itself effect such destruction'. The customary status of this element is controversial, but the Pre-Trial Chamber accepted

---

[92] K Kittichaisaree, *International Criminal Law* (Oxford University Press 2001) 50.

[93] *Prosecutor* v. *Kvočka and Others*, Decision on the Defence Preliminary Motions on the Form of the Indictment, ICTY-98–30/1, 12 April 1999, para. 16.

[94] See article 21(1)(c), Rome Statute.   [95] Article 9(1), Rome Statute.

[96] Article 9(3), Rome Statute.

[97] *Prosecutor* v. *Al Bashir*, Decision on the Prosecution's Application for a Warrant of Arrest against Omar Hassan Ahmad Al Bashir, ICC-02/05–01/09, 4 March 2009.

the element in question and seemed to assume that it is required to do so even if it is incompatible with custom:

> [A]ccording to article 21(1)(a) of the Statute, the Court must apply "in the first place" the Statute, the Elements of Crimes and the Rules . . . [T]hose other sources of law provided for in paragraphs (1)(b) and (1)(c) of article 21 of the Statute, can only be applied when the following two conditions are met: (i) there is a *lacuna* in the written law contained in the Statute, the Elements of Crimes and the Rules; and (ii) such *lacuna* cannot be filled by the application of the criteria provided for in articles 31 and 32 of the *Vienna Convention on the Law of Treaties* and article 21(3) of the Statute.[98]

There are a number of difficulties with the cited passage, but only four need to be mentioned for present purposes. First, the Pre-Trial Chamber seemed to treat the hierarchy of applicable law set out in article 21 as the same hierarchy that is to exist when these sources are used as interpretive aids rather than law applied to fill gaps, a distinction the International Court of Justice has struggled with but recognized.[99] Second, the Pre-Trial Chamber seemed to give no consideration to the requirement in article 9(3) of the Rome Statute that the Elements for the crime of genocide must be consistent with its definition in article 6, which was taken directly from the *Convention on the Prevention and Punishment of the Crime of Genocide* (1948)[100] and is itself reflective of custom.[101] Third, the Pre-Trial Chamber seemed to assert that the *Vienna Convention* (1969)

---

[98] Ibid. para. 126.   [99] *Oil Platforms Case* (n. 8); Koskenniemi (n. 5) 228–32.

[100] 78 UNTS 277 (adopted 9 December 1948, entered into force 12 January 1951).

[101] On the convergence and divergence of the definition of genocide in the Rome Statute and customary international law, see, for example, H von Hebel and D Robinson, 'Crimes within the Jurisdiction of the Court' in R Lee (ed.), *The International Criminal Court: The Making of the Rome Statute* (Transnational 1999) 79; TH McCormack and D Robertson, 'Jurisdictional Aspects of the Rome Statute for the New International Criminal Court' (1999) 23 Melbourne Univ LR 25; GM Danilenko, 'The ICC Statute and Third States' in A Cassese and Others (eds.), *The Rome Statute of the International Criminal Court: A Commentary*, vol. II (Oxford University Press 2002) 1871; Cassese (n. 45) 146–47. For the same regarding crimes against humanity, see, for example, M Boot, R Dixon and CK Hall (revised by CK Hall), 'Article 7' in O Triffterer (ed.), *Commentary on the Rome Statute of the International Criminal Court*, 2nd edn (CH Beck/Hart/Nomos 2008) 159, 167; Danilenko, ibid.; D Robinson, 'The Elements for Crimes Against Humanity' in RS Lee and Others (eds.), *The International Criminal Court: Elements of Crimes and Rules of Procedure and Evidence* (Transnational 2001) 57; McCormack and Robertson, ibid.; Cassese, *International Criminal Law* (n. 45) 123ff.; von Hebel and Robinson, ibid. For the same regarding war crimes see Cassese (n. 45) 94–97; R Arnold and Others, 'Article 8' in Triffterer, ibid. 275, including 287 (M Cottier) and 323 (K Dörmann); A Cassese, 'The Statute of the International Criminal Court: Some Preliminary Reflections' (1999) 10 EJIL 144, 152 (on articles 8(2)(b) and (e)); P Gaeta, 'The Defence of Superior Orders: The Statute of the International Criminal Court versus Customary International Law' (1999) 10 EJIL 172, 190; C Kreß, 'War Crimes Committed in Non-International Armed Conflict and the Emerging System of International Criminal Justice' (2000) 30 Israel Ybk Human Rights 103; C Kreß, 'The Crime of Genocide and Contextual Elements' (2009) 7 J Int'l Crim Justice 297.

comes into play only if there continues to be a gap after the Rome Statute and Elements have been 'applied' in accordance with article 21(1)(a).[102] Such an approach incorrectly treats the Elements as binding applicable law rather than an authoritative non-binding aid to interpreting crimes in the Rome Statute.[103] Fourth, and as a result of the third problem, the Pre-Trial Chamber did not seem to acknowledge the effect of article 31(3) of the *Vienna Convention* (1969), which *requires* it to consider as interpretive aids both the Elements of Crimes, which is a 'subsequent agreement between the parties', and custom, which contains relevant and applicable rules of international law.

Article 31(3) contains no hierarchy and clearly does not give the Court any discretion to take only one interpretive aid into account.[104] Where a customary rule of international law is relevant, both it and the Elements must be taken into account. Applied to this case, article 31(3) and the presumption of interpretation consistent with custom would have required consideration of the customary status of the aforementioned element for genocide and, if such an element were found to be inconsistent with custom, would favour a finding that this element in the Elements of Crimes is inconsistent with the definition of genocide in article 6 of the Rome Statute.[105] Further, it is submitted that favouring custom as an interpretive aid would not 'significantly erode' the principle of legality as defined in article 22(2) as it does not mention the Elements of Crimes, or article 9, which requires that the Elements be consistent with the Rome Statute.[106] Article 22(2) contemplates that the suspect or accused has fair notice by virtue of the detail in the Rome Statute, and article 9 permits judges not to apply the Elements in a given case. Further, the separation of powers doctrine that is protected by the principle of legality is not undermined by the Elements aiding but not binding judges, because interpretation of the law is a legitimate judicial function that is recognized in the Rome Statute.[107] As for the effectiveness of criminal law sanctions in the Statute, this continues to be respected, as the presumption is consistent with the Statute, and, although judges may reject the Elements on occasion, the definitions of crimes in the Statute remain intact. For the same reasons, the rule of law interest underlying legality is also respected.

---

[102] I am grateful to Thomas Weigend for this observation.

[103] Article 9(1) of the Rome Statute provides: 'Elements of Crimes shall *assist* the Court in the interpretation and application of articles 6, 7, 8 and 8 *bis*' (emphasis added).

[104] Koskenniemi (n. 5) 214; P Sands, 'Treaty, Custom and the Cross-fertilization of International Law' (1998) 1 Yale Human Rights & Development LJ 85, 103; D French, 'Treaty Interpretation and the Incorporation of Extraneous Legal Rules' (2006) 55 Int'l Comp LQ 281, 301.

[105] For a discussion of this case and policy arguments favouring the consideration of custom, see R Cryer, 'Royalism and the King: Article 21 of the Rome Statute and the Politics of Sources' (2009) 12 New Crim L Rev 390.

[106] *Al Bashir* (n. 97) para. 131; Cryer (n. 105) 402–03.

[107] Articles 21 and 22, Rome Statute.

Most important, and to be abundantly clear, the Elements should not be ignored lightly, as they do contain evidence of the *opinio juris* of the international community and were intended to reflect existing customary international law consistent with articles 6, 7, 8 and 8 *bis* of the Rome Statute.[108] They are therefore an obvious starting point and expected to be a principal aid for understanding the definitions of crimes in the Rome Statute. As well, because custom is sometimes criticized for being vague and lacking in detail, it will not very often be the case that a perfectly clear mental or material element is discerned in customary international law that conflicts with a provision in the Elements of Crimes.[109] As international criminal law continues to mature, it is hoped that this will change. In the meantime, it might be the case that the Elements fail to include an element for a crime that exists under custom (thereby improperly broadening the Rome Statute), or impose a requirement that does not exist under custom (thereby improperly narrowing it).

Accordingly, while the Rome Statute may create a sub-regime of international criminal law, articles 6, 7, 8 and 8 *bis* should, to the greatest extent possible, be interpreted in a manner that is consistent with custom. In addition, care must be taken that the experience of judges at the ICTY and ICTR under different circumstances does not cause the pendulum to swing too far in the opposite direction so that judges consider self-containedness and exclusive reliance on the Elements as 'safe' and openness of the Rome regime as well as the interpretive assistance of custom as 'dangerous'. The picture is not so clear-cut, not least because it is already being suggested that the Elements are inconsistent with the Rome Statute in places by expanding or restricting the scope of crimes defined therein.[110] To conclude, the Elements' will undoubtedly have persuasive force, reflecting the consensus view of the international community; ultimately, however, the judges will have to reach their own understanding of the Statute'.[111]

9.2.7 Interpretive Understandings

Three annexes to the resolution on aggression adopted at the Review Conference of the Rome Statute respectively contain the amendments to the Statute,

---

[108] P Kirsch, 'Foreword' in K Dörmann, *Elements of War Crimes under the Rome Statute of the International Criminal Court* (Cambridge University Press 2003) xiii, xiii–xiv.

[109] W Lietzau, 'Checks and Balances and Elements of Proof: Structural Pillars for the International Criminal Court' (1999) 32 Cornell Int'l LJ 477, 482.

[110] O Triffterer, 'Can the "Elements of Crimes" Narrow or Broaden Responsibility for Criminal Behaviour Defined in the Rome Statute?' in C Stahn and G Sluiter (eds.), *The Emerging Practice of the International Criminal Court* (Brill 2009) 381, 383.

[111] H von Hebel, 'The Making of the Elements of Crimes' in R Lee and Others (eds.), *The International Criminal Court: Elements of Crimes and Rules of Procedure and Evidence* (Transnational 2001) 3, 8.

amendments to the Elements of Crimes and the following seven interpretive[112] Understandings:

Referrals by the Security Council

1. It is understood that the Court may exercise jurisdiction on the basis of a Security Council referral in accordance with article 13, paragraph (b), of the Statute only with respect to crimes of aggression committed after a decision in accordance with article 15 ter, paragraph 3, is taken, and one year after the ratification or acceptance of the amendments by thirty States Parties, whichever is later.

2. It is understood that the Court shall exercise jurisdiction over the crime of aggression on the basis of a Security Council referral in accordance with article 13, paragraph (b), of the Statute irrespective of whether the State concerned has accepted the Court's jurisdiction in this regard.

Jurisdiction ratione temporis

3. It is understood that in case of article 13, paragraph (a) or (c), the Court may exercise its jurisdiction only with respect to crimes of aggression committed after a decision in accordance with article 15 bis, paragraph 3, is taken, and one year after the ratification or acceptance of the amendments by thirty States Parties, whichever is later.

Domestic jurisdiction over the crime of aggression

4. It is understood that the amendments that address the definition of the act of aggression and the crime of aggression do so for the purpose of this Statute only. The amendments shall, in accordance with article 10 of the Rome Statute, not be interpreted as limiting or prejudicing in any way existing or developing rules of international law for purposes other than this Statute.

5. It is understood that the amendments shall not be interpreted as creating the right or obligation to exercise domestic jurisdiction with respect to an act of aggression committed by another State.

Other understandings

6. It is understood that aggression is the most serious and dangerous form of the illegal use of force; and that a determination whether an act of aggression has been committed requires consideration of all the circumstances of each particular case, including the gravity of the acts concerned and their consequences, in accordance with the Charter of the United Nations.

7. It is understood that in establishing whether an act of aggression constitutes a manifest violation of the Charter of the United Nations, the three

---

[112] The author prefers to use the term 'interpretive' rather than 'interpretative', the latter being more commonly used in the relevant literature. However, this preference is not intended to connote any difference in meaning.

components of character, gravity and scale must be sufficient to justify a "manifest" determination. No one component can be significant
enough to satisfy the manifest standard by itself.[113]

Operative paragraph 3 of the resolution on aggression states that the Review
Conference 'decides to adopt the understandings regarding the interpretation
of the above-mentioned amendments contained in annex III of the present
resolution'. For the most part, the Understandings deal with the interpretation of the amendments themselves, as stated in operative paragraph 3. Some
Understandings, however, also imply how States Parties present at the Review
Conference interpret certain provisions of the original Rome Statute as they
relate to aspects of the amendments. Understanding 2, for example, states that
in case of Security Council referrals, the consent of the States concerned is
not necessary for the Court's exercise of jurisdiction. This implies that the
Review Conference was of the view that the second sentence of article 121(5)
of the Statute (which, on its face, seems to state the opposite) does not apply
to Security Council referrals.

The idea to draft Understandings was inspired by the annex to the *United
Nations Convention on Jurisdictional Immunities of States and their Property*
(2004)[114] and dates back to the last meeting of the Special Working Group
on the Crime of Aggression in February 2009.[115] Initially intended to deal
with jurisdictional matters only, non-jurisdictional Understandings were subsequently added to address concerns expressed by the US delegation so that
consensus might ultimately be achieved at the Review Conference.[116] During
the negotiations, discussions centred on the substance of the draft Understandings, and their status as interpretive aids within the *Vienna Convention on the
Law of Treaties* (1969) framework was not debated.[117] In this section, it will
be argued that the Understandings constitute a subsequent agreement under
article 31(3)(a) of the *Vienna Convention* (1969) that the Court *must* consider if
relevant and that they reflect authentic or common understandings on various
issues of interpretation.

Like the amendments themselves,[118] all seven Understandings were adopted
by consensus at the Review Conference, which is a special sitting of the Assembly

---

[113] Review Conference, Resolution on the Crime of Aggression, RC/Res.6 (adopted 10 June
2010), Annex III.
[114] UN Doc. A/RES/59/38, Annex (adopted 2 December 2004, not in force).
[115] On the drafting history of the Understandings, see C Kreß, S Barriga, L Grover and L von
Holtzendorff, 'Negotiating the Understandings on the Crime of Aggression' in S Barriga
and Claus Kreß (eds.), *Travaux Préparatoires of the Crime of Aggression* (Cambridge
University Press 2011) 81.
[116] Ibid.   [117] Ibid. 83.
[118] Article 121(3) enables the ASP to adopt substantive amendments to the Rome Statute by
consensus or by a two-thirds majority of all States Parties.

of States Parties (ASP), the Court's legislative body. This was done in accordance with article 112(7) of the Rome Statute, which provides:

> Each State Party shall have one vote. Every effort shall be made to reach decisions by consensus in the Assembly and in the Bureau. If consensus cannot be reached, except as otherwise provided in the Statute: (a) Decisions on matters of substance must be approved by a two-thirds majority of those present and voting provided that an absolute majority of States Parties constitutes the quorum for voting; (b) Decisions on matters of procedure shall be taken by a simple majority of States Parties present and voting.[119]

Interpretive understandings or declarations[120] have been defined by the International Law Commission as follows: 'a unilateral statement, however phrased or named, made by a State or an international organization, whereby that State or that organization purports to specify or clarify the meaning or scope of a treaty or of certain of its provisions'.[121] One or more Parties to a treaty may formulate an interpretive understanding. However, the ILC maintains that '[t]he joint formulation of an interpretative declaration by several states or international organizations does not affect the unilateral character of that interpretative declaration'.[122] Although the term 'unilateral' is perhaps not the most suitable for statements adopted by a legislative body such as the ASP, it is submitted that each of the seven Understandings meets the ILC's definition of a jointly formulated interpretive understanding:[123]

---

[119] As well, the Elements of Crimes, the Agreement between the International Criminal Court and the United Nations, the Headquarters Agreement with the Host State, the Rules of Procedure and Evidence, the Code of Professional Conduct for Counsel, the Code of Judicial Ethics, the Staff Rules of the International Criminal Court, the Staff Regulations, the Financial Regulations and Rules and the Agreement on the Privileges and Immunities of the International Criminal Court were all adopted by consensus of the ASP in accordance with article 112(7) of the Statute. For a different view on the authority of the Review Conference to adopt the interpretive Understandings as well as their status as interpretive aids, see KJ Heller, 'The Uncertain Legal Status of the Aggression Understandings' (2012) 10 J Int'l Crim Justice 229.

[120] 'Understandings' is one of several terms used in English-speaking countries, especially the United States, to refer to interpretive declarations. ILC, 'Guide to Practice on Reservations to Treaties with Commentaries' (2011) II (Part Two) Ybk of the ILC 1, 38.

[121] Ibid. 1.2. The ILC Guide clarifies that there are other types of unilateral statements, the most well known being reservations, which modify or exclude the legal effect of a treaty or treaty provision.

[122] Ibid. 1.2.1.

[123] Ibid. 1.7.2: 'In order to specify or clarify the meaning or scope of a treaty or certain of its provisions, States or international organizations may also have recourse to procedures other than interpretative declarations, such as: the insertion in the treaty of provisions purporting to interpret the treaty; the conclusion of a supplementary agreement to the same end, simultaneously or subsequently to the conclusion of the treaty.' It is arguable that, like the Elements of Crimes, the Understandings are a 'supplementary agreement'.

> [T]here have also been truly joint declarations, formulated in a single instrument, by "the European Community [now the European Union] and its Member States" or by the latter alone [for example].... The Commission ... considered whether there might be reason to envisage the possibility of all of the contracting States or contracting organizations formulating an interpretative declaration jointly, and whether in such a situation the proposed interpretation would not lose the character of a unilateral act and become a genuinely collective act. The Commission concluded that this is not the case.[124]

And while interpretive understandings typically accompany a State's consent to be bound by a treaty, this is not always the case, and the ILC expressly rejects this requirement.[125]

Rather than concluding that all interpretive understandings fall under a particular subsection of either article 31 or article 32 of the *Vienna Convention* (1969), the ILC has consistently asserted that this determination 'depends on the context of the declaration and the assent of the other States Parties.'[126] It is ultimately up to the Court to determine the role and correctness of the interpretive Understandings by applying the relevant rules of interpretation in the Rome Statute and *Vienna Convention* (1969).[127]

With respect to article 31(2)(a) and (b) of the *Vienna Convention* (1969), these provisions present a temporal hurdle that is difficult to overcome, because it is not plausible to argue that the Understandings were drafted in connection with the conclusion of the Rome Statute – although the aggression amendments might be considered by some to complete that treaty. The better legal view seems to be that the aggression amendments and corresponding Understandings are not sufficiently connected to the conclusion of the Rome Statute for purposes of categorizing the Understandings under article 31(2) of the *Vienna Convention* (1969). This leads one to consider article 31(3). In the author's view, the Understandings are best understood as forming a subsequent agreement under article 31(3)(a) of the *Vienna Convention* (1969).[128]

> However, in that case, the Understandings could simply have been amendments to the Elements of Crimes instead of comprising a separate annex to the resolution on aggression and being termed 'Understandings'.

[124] ILC (n. 120) 73–74.

[125] Ibid. 2.4.4: 'Without prejudice to the provisions of guidelines 1.4 and 2.4.7, an interpretative declaration may be formulated at any time.'

[126] ILC, 'Fourth Report on the Law of Treaties' (1965) II Ybk of the ILC 49, para. 2; ILC, 'Report on the Work of its Sixty-Third Session (26 April to 3 June and 4 July to 12 August 2011)' GAOR Supp. No. 10 (A/66/10 and Add.1) 553; ibid. 4.7.1.

[127] M. Benatar, 'From Probative Value to Authentic Interpretation: The Legal Effects of Interpretative Declarations' (2011) 44 Revue Belge de Droit International 170, 194–95.

[128] For a study of subsequent agreements and practice, see the three reports prepared by G Nolte, Special Rapporteur to the International Law Commission in G Nolte (ed.), *Treaties and Subsequent Practice* (Oxford University Press 2013) 169, 210, 307.

As early as 1966 and as recently as 2011, the ILC confirmed that a subsequent agreement under article 31(3)(a) of the *Vienna Convention* (1969) need not be made by all of the Parties to a treaty: 'the parties, *or some of them*, may conclude an agreement for the purposes of interpreting a treaty previously concluded between them'.[129] An analysis of the structure of article 31(2) and (3), which divides aids to interpretation mainly on temporal grounds,[130] is also revealing when interpreting article 31(3)(a). Article 31(2) contains two subsections, one dealing with agreements made between all the Parties and the other with instruments made by one or more Parties and accepted by the other Parties. In contrast, article 31(3) contains three subsections, the first dealing with *any* subsequent agreement between the Parties, the second with subsequent practice and the third with relevant and applicable rules of international law. Seen this way, one could argue that article 31(3)(a) is intended to mirror article 31(2) in its entirety, to include subsequent agreements made by all but also fewer than all States Parties. This argument considers all of article 31, which is consistent with the 'crucible approach' of its drafters who did not intend to create any hierarchy within article 31 – as well as the views of commentators.[131] As Special Rapporteur Waldock stated, an interpretive agreement under article 31(3)(a) is 'on the same level as the "context" and ... is to be taken into account as if it were part of the treaty';[132] it 'represents an authentic interpretation by the parties'.[133]

Because the Understandings adopted by the Review Conference conform to the procedure set out in the Rome Statute for taking such decisions, one might conclude that they are already 'approved' by all States Parties, similar to the manner in which the Elements of Crimes were adopted.[134] Alternatively, one might argue that States Parties not present in Kampala retain the right to express their approval or opposition to the interpretive Understandings or, more doubtfully, that approval is tied to the amendments entering into force.[135] If approval at the Review Conference does not suffice to establish common understandings, what form of approval may States Parties not present

---

[129] ILC (n. 120) 1.7.2 (emphasis added). For a different view, see Heller (n. 119) 229, 240.

[130] O Dörr, 'General Rule of Interpretation' in O Dörr and K Schmalenbach (eds.), *Vienna Convention on the Law of Treaties: A Commentary* (Springer 2012) 521, 553.

[131] ILC, 'Reports of the International Law Commission on the Second Part of its Seventeenth Session and on its Eighteenth Session' (1966) II Ybk of the ILC 169, 219–20; Gardiner (n. 2) 206–07; ME Villiger, *Commentary on the 1969 Vienna Convention on the Law of Treaties* (Martinus Nijhoff Publishers 2009) 435–36.

[132] H Waldock, 'Sixth Report on the Law of Treaties' (1966) II Ybk of the ILC 51, 95, para. 6.

[133] ILC, 'Reports of the International Law Commission on the Second Part of its Seventeenth Session and on its Eighteenth Session' (1966) II Ybk of the ILC 169, 221, para. 14.

[134] ILC (n. 120) 4.7.3: 'An interpretative declaration that has been approved by all the contracting States and contracting organizations may constitute an agreement regarding the interpretation of the treaty.'

[135] Ibid. 2.4.6: 'An interpretative declaration formulated when signing a treaty does not require subsequent confirmation when a State or an international organization expresses its consent to be bound by the treaty.'

in Kampala express before such understandings are reached? Must it be explicit, or may it also be tacit?

According to Special Rapporteur Waldock, approval by the other States Parties may take the form of acquiescence, meaning tacit or implied consent:

> [I]n the case of a document emanating from a group of the parties to a multilateral treaty, principle would seem to indicate that the relevance of the document in connection with the treaty must be *acquiesced* in by the other parties. Whether a "unilateral" or a "group" document forms part of the context *depends on the particular circumstances of each case*, and the Special Rapporteur does not think it advisable that the Commission should try to do more than state the essential point of the principle – *the need for express or implied assent.*[136]

If one accepts that interpretive understandings to which all States Parties have acquiesced constitute a subsequent agreement under article 31(3)(a) of the *Vienna Convention* (1969), these understandings become mandatory, non-binding aids under article 31 rather than discretionary ones under article 32, thereby considerably elevating their status in the interpretive process. Stated differently, they constitute authentic interpretations[137] that *must* be taken into account when interpreting the relevant treaty provision(s).[138] An authentic interpretation of a treaty provision carries great probative value, as it reflects a high degree of approval by States Parties.[139] On this point, it is important to note that general consensus is an accepted formula for the creation of subsequent agreements that fall under article 31(3)(a).[140] Accordingly, the Court should be reluctant to depart from the Understandings when seeking the common intentions of the Parties in the interpretive process.

The adoption by consensus of the interpretive Understandings at the Review Conference might not prevent any State Party from expressing opposition to them, if they wish; such opposition would impact the probative value that judges assign to the Understandings. However, such expression is not necessarily advisable, given that the Understandings are the product of following a procedure in the Rome Statute to which all States Parties consented. Since Kampala, some States Parties have ratified the amendments on aggression and enacted corresponding domestic legislation, perhaps assuming that the Understandings

---

[136] H Waldock, 'Sixth Report on the Law of Treaties' (1966) II Ybk of the ILC 51, 98, para. 16, cited in ILC, ibid. 4.7.1.

[137] On the concept of 'authentic interpretation', see generally Benatar (n. 127).

[138] ILC (n. 120) 4.7.1. For a different understanding of the drafting history of article 31(3), see Heller (n. 119) 240–41.

[139] ILC (n. 120) 4.7.1; DM McRae, 'The Legal Effect of Interpretative Declarations' (1978) 49 British Ybk Int'l L 155, 169–70.

[140] Dörr (n. 130) 549–50.

reflect the consensus of all States Parties.[141] The ASP is a legislative body and meets annually to deal with matters related to the Court.[142] Should a State Party (or several) seek to voice dissent, the forum and opportunity exist. As well, States Parties are aware that an activation decision concerning the aggression amendments can be taken as early as 2017, meaning they are aware that a distinct window of opportunity exists for when it would be most prudent to express any concerns they may have about the accompanying Understandings, after which an assumption of acquiescence may be appropriate.[143] Ultimately, though, it is the Court's interpretation of the amended Rome Statute to which States Parties are bound, irrespective of their approval or opposition to the Understandings.[144] On this point, it is important to recall that the latter cannot modify the former.

As for any conflicts that may arise between the Understandings and the Elements of Crimes or General Assembly Resolution 3314 (XXIX) of 1974 (discussed below in Section 9.3.4), it is submitted that the Elements should be favoured but that these Understandings should be favoured over the Resolution. With respect to the Elements, this instrument is more of an authoritative aid than the Understandings, as it is listed as applicable law under article 21(1)(a) of the Rome Statute. And, unlike the Resolution, it was drafted specifically to aid judges working in an international criminal law context. However, as between these Understandings and the Resolution, the former should be favoured because, in the author's view, they were intended in part to delimit the influence of the latter, to circumscribe the extent to which it is to be imported into the Rome regime.[145]

9.3 Articles 31(3) and (4) and time

In the introduction to the study of article 31(3)(c) of the *Vienna Convention* (1969), two of its functions were identified: putting into play the interpretive principle of systemic integration and the intertemporal rule. Up until now, only the first of these two functions has been examined. In the following sections,

---

[141] ILC (n. 120) 557: 'It does not matter whether or not this phenomenon is called estoppel; in any case it is a corollary of the principle of good faith in its international relations, a State cannot blow hot and cold. It cannot declare that it interprets a given provision of the treaty in one way and then take the opposite position.'

[142] See ICC, Assembly of States Parties, http://www.icc-cpi.int/en_menus/asp/assembly/Pages/assembly.aspx, accessed 13 March 2014.

[143] It has been argued that even if a party to a treaty expresses approval of an interpretive declaration, it is not necessarily precluded from rejecting this interpretation at a later date. McRae (n. 139) 166–69.

[144] ILC (n. 120) 549.

[145] Compare to the negotiated outcome the proposed Understandings: United States, '2012 Non-Paper of the United States' in Barriga and Kreß (n. 115) 751–52.

the relationship between time and aids to interpretation will be considered, namely, the relationship between the Rome Statute and how relevant prior and subsequent agreements external to it, including sources of international law, may or may not influence the interpretation of crimes defined therein. As a permanent Court, judges will, over time, be confronted with the issue of whether crimes in the Rome Statute are frozen or subject to evolution.

9.3.1 Crystallization

Before considering the intertemporal rule of interpretation, it is useful to call attention to how the passage of time can affect the application of the presumption of consistency with custom. In the *North Sea Continental Shelf* cases (1969), the International Court of Justice (ICJ) recognized the possibility that a treaty provision previously not reflective of custom could, over time, crystallize into custom.[146] Crystallization is the 'moment at which, in consequence, the rule becomes binding, or passes from being a rule *in posse* to a [customary] rule *in esse*'.[147] Such crystallization may occur not only after a treaty enters into force but also at a diplomatic conference to conclude a treaty[148] or even through a draft convention.[149] In *North Sea* (1969), the ICJ confirmed that not a lot of time needs to pass for a rule to crystallize into custom:

> Although the passage of only a short period of time is not necessarily, or of itself, a bar to the formation of a new rule of customary international law on the basis of what was originally a purely conventional rule, an indispensable requirement would be that within the period in question, short though it might be, State practice, including that of States whose interests are specially affected, should have been both extensive and virtually uniform in the sense of the provision invoked; – and should moreover have occurred in such a way as to show a general recognition that a rule of law or legal obligation is involved.[150]

Though it has not further elaborated on the process, the ICJ confirmed the concept of crystallization in subsequent judgments.[151] This concept completes

---

[146] *North Sea Continental Shelf Cases (Germany v. Denmark; Germany v. the Netherlands)* [1969] ICJ Rep. 3, 43.

[147] H Thirlway, 'The Law and Procedure of the International Court of Justice: 1960–1989 (Part Two)' (1990) 61(1) British Ybk Int'l L 1, 94.

[148] See, e.g., *Fisheries Jurisdiction Cases (United Kingdom v. Iceland* [1974] ICJ Rep. 3, 23.

[149] *Continental Shelf Case (Tunisia v. Libya)* [1982] ICJ Rep. 38, 43.

[150] *North Sea Continental Shelf Cases* (n. 146).

[151] R Clark, 'Treaty and Custom' in L Boisson de Chazournes and P Sands (eds.), *International Law, the International Court of Justice and Nuclear Weapons* (Cambridge University Press 1999) 171, 172 (citing *Case of the SS Lotus (France v. Turkey)* (1927) PCIJ Series A, No. 10; *Nottebohm Case, Second Phase (Liechtenstein v. Guatemala)* [1955] ICJ Rep. 4; *North Sea Continental Shelf Cases* (n. 146); *Nicaragua* (n. 18)).

the circle of treaty and customary law's entanglement. A treaty may be reflective of custom, and, likewise, a convention may generate custom and even crystallize into it. This relationship has been described as 'interdependent' and especially close where a treaty essentially codifies custom.[152] Treaties that are generally or largely reflective of custom 'cannot help but insert themselves into the whole of the elements of the practice and *opinio juris* of the States that serve to ascertain customary law' and thereby contribute to the crystallization of its non-customary elements.[153] It has already been observed that although the Rome Statute does not claim to be a complete code of international criminal law, 'it should not be ruled out that, particularly after the ICC begins its juridical activity proper, some of the Statute's provisions may gradually turn [crystallize] into customary international law as a result of other international courts and tribunals broadly accepting and applying these provisions as encapsulating the world community's *opinio juris* on the matter.... If this were to happen, the relevant provisions in the ICC Statute would become binding as universal norms.'[154] It would also mean that the presumption of interpretation consistent with custom, if rebutted in a previous judgment, may stand for a short time later, post-crystallization, once the provision is considered to be reflective of custom. For example, the *Hague Convention* (1907), whose drafters described it as only partly reflective of custom, was held by the Nuremberg tribunal to be reflective of custom by 1939.[155]

9.3.2 Intertemporality[156]

If crimes in the Rome Statute are generally or largely reflective of custom as it existed when the Statute was adopted, does this mean that they are to be interpreted by taking into account relevant and applicable law as it existed in 1998? In fact, concerns have been expressed that the Rome Statute has 'frozen customary definitions in a process of rapid evolution'.[157] Others have expressed concern that the definitions of crimes may negatively interfere with the natural growth of custom in this field.[158] As one commentator put it, 'the

---

[152] R Pissillo-Mazzeschi, 'Treaty and Custom: Reflections on the Codification of International Law' (January and April 1997) Commonwealth L Bull 549, 551.

[153] Ibid. 552.

[154] Cassese (n. 45) 17.   [155] IMT Judgment (1947) 41 AJIL 172, 248–49.

[156] In the literature, the terms contemporaneity and inter-temporality (or intertemporality) are often used interchangeably, although a distinction has on occasion been drawn between the two concepts. M Fitzmaurice, 'Dynamic (Evolutive) Interpretation of Treaties' (2008) 21 Hague Ybk Int'l L 101, 104.

[157] A Pellet, 'Applicable Law' in A Cassese and Others (eds.), *The Rome Statute of the International Criminal Court: A Commentary*, vol. II (Oxford University Press 2002) 1051, 1056; Baxter (n. 24) 299; Thirlway (n. 24) 125.

[158] Cassese and Others, *The Rome Statute of the International Criminal Court* (n. 101) 45.

content of international law changes and develops continuously – it provides a constantly shifting canvas against which individual acts, including treaties, fall to be judged. Any approach to interpretation has to find a means of dealing with this dynamism.'[159] In this section, consideration will be given to how the intertemporal rule might inform interpretation of the crimes in the Rome Statute. Indeed, it has already been suggested that some of the Elements of Crimes have been 'overtaken' by developments in international criminal law.[160]

The intertemporal rule dates back to the *Island of Palmas* arbitration (1928) and Judge Huber's famous two-part dictum: (1) '[a] juridical fact must be appreciated in the light of the law contemporary with it, and not of the law in force at the time such a dispute in regard to it arises or falls to be settled'; and (2) '[t]he existence of the right, in other words, its continued manifestation, shall follow the conditions required by the evolution of the law'.[161] In a dispute arising between the United States and the Netherlands over title to the Island of Palmas, Judge Huber had to determine whether Spain's sovereign title to the island obtained through discovery of it in 1648 could be maintained absent effective occupation since that time. Discovery, while valid in 1648 as a means of obtaining legal title to property, was no longer recognized as such under international law when the dispute arose. At the same time, international law had evolved since 1648 so as to require effective occupation of land in order to maintain sovereign title to it. While accepting that the law of discovery was valid for creating Spain's legal title to the island in 1648, Judge Huber applied the 'new' law to determine the continued existence of this right and concluded that Spain's title had been lost for failing effectively to occupy the island.

Applying this dictum to the law of treaties,[162] commentators have been able to agree that the adoption of a treaty is a juridical fact, but unable to agree on whether Judge Huber's dictum mandates interpretation of a treaty in light of the law contemporary with it at the time of its adoption or whether interpretation is required to reflect evolution of the law up to the point when a dispute arises. Indeed, the second branch of the dictum can be read as wiping out the legal effect of the first branch.[163] In practice, application of the intertemporal rule has, on occasion, resulted in treaty terms being interpreted consonant with the

---

[159] McLachlan (n. 6) 282.

[160] D Hunt, 'The International Criminal Court – High Hopes, "Creative Ambiguity" and an Unfortunate Mistrust in International Judges' (2004) 2 J Int'l Crim Justice 56 (commenting on the definition of rape).

[161] *Island of Palmas Case (the Netherlands* v. *United States)* (1928) 2 RIAA 831, 845.

[162] Rousseau pointed out that Huber's statement was not in principle limited to territorial disputes. C Rousseau, *Principes généraux de droit international public*, vol. I (Pédone 1944) 498.

[163] R Higgins, 'Some Observations on the Inter-Temporal Rule in International Law' in J Makarczyk (ed.), *Theory of International Law at the Threshold of the 21st Century: Essays in Honour of Krzysztof Skubiszewski* (Kluwer Law International 1996) 173, 174.

law at the time the treaty was adopted[164] and on other occasions in conformity with the law that existed when the dispute arose between the parties.[165] In addition to these two moments in time, the International Court of Justice in the *Aerial Incident* case (1959) identified a third salient point in time: 'If a state accedes later to a treaty, its terms will be applied to that state in the light of the circumstances prevailing at the date of its accession and not of those at the time when the treaty was concluded.'[166]

When the International Law Commission (ILC) was drafting the *Vienna Convention* (1969), Sir Humphrey Waldock proposed recognizing both parts of Judge Huber's dictum as applying to the interpretation of treaties.[167] However, members of the ILC were unable to agree on their meaning.[168] Ultimately, the issue could not be resolved, and article 31(3)(c) was adopted. It provides, 'There shall be taken into account, together with the context: ... any relevant rules of international law applicable in the relations between the parties.' Thus, while the provision admits that issues of crystallization and intertemporality affect the task of interpretation, it deliberately avoids providing a one-size-fits-all solution to either of these problems, perhaps because none exists. On the intertemporal rule and Judge Huber's dictum, Jiminéz de Aréchaga of the ILC said it best:

> The intention of the parties should be controlling, and there seemed to be two possibilities as far as that intention was concerned: either they had meant to incorporate in the treaty some legal concepts that would remain unchanged, or, if they had no such intention, the legal concepts might be subject to change and would then have to be interpreted not only in the context of the instrument, but also within the framework of the entire legal order to which they belonged.[169]

---

[164] *Rights of Passage over Indian Territory (Portugal v. India)* [1960] ICJ Rep. 6, 37; *The Grisbadarna Case (Norway v. Sweden)* (1909) 11 RIAA 147, 159–60; *North Atlantic Coast Fisheries Case (Great Britain v. United States)* (1910) 11 RIAA 167, 196; *Abu Dhabi Arbitration* [1951] ICJ Rep. 144; *Rights of Nationals of the United States of America in Morocco (France v. United States of America)* [1952] ICJ Rep. 176, 185–87.

[165] *Legal Consequences for States of the Continued Presence of South Africa in Namibia (South West Africa) Notwithstanding Security Council Resolution 276*, Advisory Opinion [1971] ICJ Rep. 16, 31; *Gabćíkovo-Nagymaros Project (Hungary v. Slovakia)* [1997] ICJ Rep. 7, 64, 67; *Aegean Sea Continental Shelf Case (Greece v. Turkey)* [1978] ICJ Rep. 3, 33–34; *Dispute Regarding Navigational and Related Rights (Costa Rica v. Nicaragua)* [2009] paras. 63–70, http://www.icj-cij.org/docket/files/133/15321.pdf, accessed 20 October 2013.

[166] *Aerial Incident Case (Israel v. Bulgaria)* [1959] ICJ Rep. 127, 142–45.

[167] H Waldock, 'Third Report on the Law of Treaties' (1964) II Ybk of the ILC 5, 8ff. (draft article 56): '1. A treaty is to be interpreted in the light of the law in force at the time when the treaty was drawn up. 2. Subject to paragraph 12, the application of a treaty shall be governed by the rules of international law in force at the time when the treaty is applied.' See also Koskenniemi (n. 5) 182.

[168] ILC, 'Summary Records of the Sixteenth Session' (1964) I Ybk of the ILC 1, 33 (and an interesting ensuing discussion).

[169] Ibid. 34, para. 10. See also ibid., Mr Pal's comments at 35, para. 4.

Special Rapporteur Sir Humphrey Waldock concurred: 'The question whether the terms used [in a treaty] were intended to have a fixed content or to change in meaning with the evolution of the law could be decided only by interpreting the intention of the parties.'[170] Indeed, although not all are in agreement,[171] this has emerged as the prevailing view in the literature on intertemporality. It is perhaps the best way to make sense of the jurisprudence on this matter – that it is the intention of the Parties that is key to determining whether a treaty term should follow the development of the law.[172] This intent is discerned by examining the text of the treaty and having recourse to the 'usual methods of interpretation', as confirmed by the ILC in 2006.[173]

> *Inter-temporality.* International law is a dynamic legal system. A treaty may convey whether in applying article 31(3)(c) the interpreter should refer only to rules of international law in force at the time of the conclusion of the treaty or may also take into account subsequent changes in the law. Moreover, the meaning of the treaty provision may also be affected by subsequent developments, especially where there are subsequent developments in customary law and general principles of law.[174]

The intertemporal rule is therefore 'only adjective law – it is a technique for applying the appropriate law to the facts, not itself a rule of substantive law'.[175] To be clear, the present discussion of intertemporality is not concerned with conflicts between the Rome Statute and any law external to it for purposes of interpreting crimes in articles 6, 7, 8 and 8 *bis*. These provisions open with the phrase, 'For the purpose of this Statute', indicating textual primacy, and their interpretation is governed by the guiding interpretive principle of legality in

---

[170] H Waldock, '872nd Meeting: The Law of Treaties' (1966) I (Part Two) Ybk of the ILC 198, 199.

[171] See Pauwelyn (n. 70) 264–65 with respect to the WTO Agreement; P Jessup, 'The Palmas Island Arbitration' (1928) 22 AJIL 739 (pointing out that an evolutive approach would undermine legal certainty).

[172] Thirlway (n. 147) 135–43; HWA Thirlway, 'The Law and Procedure of the International Court of Justice: 1954–1989 (Part Three)' (1991) 62:1 British Ybk Int'l L 1, 57; GG Fitzmaurice, 'The Law and Procedure of the International Court of Justice 1951–1954: Treaty Interpretation and Other Treaty Points' (1957) 33 British Ybk Int'l L 203, 222; Higgins (n. 163) 173; R Higgins, 'Time and the Law: International Perspectives on an Old Problem' (1997) 46 Int'l Comp L Quart 501, 515–19; Fitzmaurice (n. 156) 111; A D'Amato, 'International Law, Intertemporal Problems' (1992) Encyclopedia of Public Int'l L 1234.

[173] Institut de Droit International, 'The Intertemporal Problem in Public International Law' (Wiesbaden Session 1975) 56:I Annuaire de l'Institut de Droit International 536, para. 4.

[174] ILC 'Conclusions of the Work of the Study Group on the Fragmentation of International Law: Difficulties arising from the Diversification and Expansion of International Law' (2006) II (Part Two) Ybk of the ILC, para. 22.

[175] HWA Thirlway, 'The Law and Procedure of the International Court of Justice: 1960–1989 (Part One)' (1989) 60:1 British Ybk Int'l L 1, 130.

article 22. So, if custom evolves beyond a treaty provision based on custom, and this evolution cannot be accommodated by the treaty term, the treaty must be applied as it stands, not inadvertently amended.[176]

Application of the intertemporal rule requires that 'concrete evidence' of the Parties' intentions must be found when interpreting a treaty provision in accordance with articles 31–33 of the *Vienna Convention* (1969).[177] It has been suggested that courts should be slow and cautious in recognizing a change in custom that affects the interpretation of a treaty provision so as to avoid contriving an intent that States never had for a problem that never occurred to them.[178] Indeed, the ILC considered that the interpretive exercise to determine the temporal element for article 31(3)(c) be carried out in good faith, in accordance with article 31(1) of the *Vienna Convention* (1969).[179] The intertemporal rule lies at the intersection of two goals: a stable treaty regime and recognition of the evolution of law relevant to the relations between Parties to it.[180]

Based on the relevant case law, the ILC has posited that where a treaty term is 'not static but evolutionary', or 'generic', it may reasonably be inferred that States Parties intended its meaning to evolve over time.[181] For example, in *Prosecutor* v. *Tadić* (1997), the ICTY held that it had to interpret the concept of crimes against humanity in light of customary law as it existed at the time the offence was allegedly committed, not in light of custom as it existed after the Second World War.[182] As well, the object and purpose of the treaty regime might shed light on the issue of time. For example, human rights provisions, because of the intent of States inferred from the object and purpose of these regimes, have often been subject to evolutive interpretation.[183] It has even been suggested that foreseeability may be relevant to determining whether States Parties were aware that the relevant and applicable law might evolve over time and impact the interpretation of a treaty provision.[184] In the following section, the Rome Statute's provisions will be examined with a view to discerning the intent of its drafters concerning intertemporality.

---

[176] N Kontou, *The Termination and Revision of Treaties in the Light of New Customary International Law* (Oxford University Press 1994) 18–19.

[177] McLachlan (n. 6) 317 (citing relevant case law).

[178] TO Elias, *The International Court of Justice and Some Contemporary Problems* (Brill 1983) 127–29; Thirlway (n. 175) 143.

[179] Elias, ibid. 142–43 (citing ILC (n. 127) 222).   [180] Elias, ibid. 145.

[181] Koskenniemi (n. 5) 203–04. Some have suggested that the existence of a generic treaty term that is inherently evolutive is presumptively to be interpreted in light of subsequent custom unless a contrary intent of the Parties to it is proven. Kontou (n. 176) 16–17.

[182] *Prosecutor* v. *Tadić*, Judgment, ICTY-94–1-T, 7 May 1997, para. 654.

[183] Higgins (n. 163) 181 (pointing out that the interpretation of human rights provisions in an evolutive manner is not an exception to the intertemporal principle but is an application of it, consistent with the intention of Parties).

[184] *Gabčíkovo-Nagymaros Project* (n. 165).

9.3.3 Crimes in the Rome Statute

A word is not a crystal, transparent and unchangeable, it is the skin of a living thought, and may vary greatly in color and content according to the circumstances and the time in which it is used.

Oliver Wendell Holmes, Jr[185]

On balance, it is submitted that States Parties should be presumed to have intended that crimes in the Rome Statute, to the extent possible and without violating the principle of legality, be interpreted in light of relevant and applicable law as it existed when the crime is alleged to have been committed. The principle of legality is 'solidly embedded' in the Rome Statute, and so the Court 'may only apply substantive criminal rules that existed at the time of commission of the alleged crime'.[186] Article 31(3)(c) of the *Vienna Convention* (1969) should therefore be invoked by judges in this manner. In fact, article 22(1) provides that no person may be held criminally responsible under the Statute 'unless the conduct in question constitutes, *at the time it takes place*, a crime within the jurisdiction of the Court'.[187] Similarly, article 24(2) contemplates changes in applicable law having an impact on the Court's decisions: 'In the event of a change in the law applicable to a given case prior to a final judgement, the law more favourable to the person being investigated, prosecuted or convicted shall apply.' Implicit in this provision is that all changes in applicable law may be taken into account when interpreting crimes in the Rome Statute so long as these changes predate the alleged commission of the crime. To be clear, while these provisions will usually be invoked in the event of an amendment to the Rome Statute, article 22(1) may also be cited where a term in the Rome Statute, such as 'rape', is not defined and the definition of this crime changes after 1998.[188] Where a term such as 'deportation' is defined in the Rome Statute, the principle of legality and article 22(3) would bar changes to this term under international humanitarian law, for example, from altering its definition in the Rome Statute, unless the wording of the definition could accommodate these changes.[189]

The reference in article 21(3) to consistency with internationally recognized human rights has also been taken to suggest that the 'Statute is not locked into the prevailing values at the time of its adoption. International human rights law continues to evolve inexorably, and the reference to it in the Statute is full of promise for innovative interpretation in future years.'[190] Further, articles 10 and 22(3) contemplate custom evolving, and article 21(1)(b) renders

---

[185] Justice Holmes in *Towne* v. *Eisner* 245 U.S. 425 (1918).
[186] Cassese (n. 45) 44.   [187] Emphasis added.
[188] See article 7(1)(g), Rome Statute.   [189] See articles 7(1)(d) and (2)(d), Rome Statute.
[190] WA Schabas, *An Introduction to the International Criminal Court*, 2nd edn (Cambridge University Press 2004) 93.

custom and treaty law authoritative interpretive aids. Accordingly, 'assuming that a new custom has evolved *dehors* the Statute, how can the Court fail to take that development into account'?[191] In interpreting articles 6, 7, 8 and 8 *bis* in light of relevant and applicable law that existed at the time the alleged crime was committed, article 22 serves as a reminder that where the Rome Statute cannot be reconciled with subsequent law, the definitions of crimes in the Statute prevail. Such an approach respects the principle of legality by ensuring that rules are 'fixed, knowable, and certain' (because the wording in the Statute does not change).[192] And it remains for the ASP to determine whether and when a new crime should be added to the Court's jurisdiction.[193]

As for the Elements of Crimes, it should be recalled that during their drafting, France proposed the addition of a 'commentary' following the text of the Elements, which would have included references to case law.[194] This idea received some support but generally was resisted due inter alia to the 'concern that such commentaries would inadvertently freeze interpretations and principles of law in time'.[195] Ultimately, States agreed to draft a small number of succinct comments for possible inclusion, which now appear as footnotes in the Elements but do not refer to case law. This approach is consistent with the discretion of judges, pursuant to article 9, not to apply the Elements in a particular case and even to propose amendments to the Elements, perhaps because they have been 'overtaken' by legal developments.[196] Judges should therefore be mindful of changes in customary international law and should not hesitate to alert the ASP to these developments, suggesting appropriate amendments to the Elements of Crimes. If the Rome Statute were to be interpreted and applied in accordance with the law as it existed in 1998, States would arguably not have hesitated to insert relevant references to case law in the Elements of Crimes.

The presumption contemplated means that a term in article 6, 7, 8 or 8 *bis* may be assigned different meanings over time. This approach injects a suitable degree of flexibility into the Statute, which governs the work of a permanent international criminal court. It also overcomes concerns that the Rome Statute freezes the definitions of crimes and that this will lead to the Court's 'stagnation, if not decline'.[197] Those customary developments that

---

[191] Dinstein (n. 24) 390; MC Bassiouni, *The Legitimacy of the International Criminal Court*, vol. I (Transnational 2005) 163–64.

[192] J Raz, *The Authority of Law* (Oxford University Press 1979) 214–15.

[193] S Lamb, 'Nullum Crimen, Nulla Poena Sine Lege in International Criminal Law' in A Cassese and Others (eds.), *The Rome Statute of the International Criminal Court: A Commentary*, vol. I (Oxford University Press 2002) 733, 753.

[194] V Oosterveld, 'The Elements of Genocide' in RS Lee and Others (eds.), *The International Criminal Court: Elements of Crimes and Rules of Procedure and Evidence* (Transnational 2001) 41, 43.

[195] Ibid.   [196] Hunt (n. 160).   [197] Pellet (n. 157) 1056, 1084.

can be accommodated by the words of the Rome Statute can inform their interpretation, and those that cannot continue to exist alongside it. In this regard, it is interesting to note that some domestic courts also interpret and apply criminal law in a manner that is not frozen.[198] Accordingly, while prior custom will aid in understanding the content of the Statute, the subsequent practice of States interpreting and applying the definitions of crimes therein in domestic proceedings and vis-à-vis ad hoc international criminal tribunals they might establish will contribute to the evolution of this prior custom alongside the definitions of crimes in the Statute.[199] Where possible, this can help to prevent the Rome Statute's definitions from falling into desuetude under customary law.

Concerning the possible addition of treaty crimes to the Rome regime, or to the extent that some of the crimes therein are not yet customary, the intent remains the same: to interpret the crimes in light of relevant applicable international law existing at the time the crime was allegedly committed. Where more than one treaty is invoked as an aid to interpreting a crime in the Rome Statute, neither has customary status and they offer conflicting guidance on the interpretation of a crime, priority between them must be determined by discerning the intent of Parties to them and the Rome Statute – neither can claim automatic preference.[200]

In light of the approach outlined in this section, the next two sections will consider how the evolving meaning of ordinary words, as opposed to legal terms, and the existence of subsequent practice might aid in interpreting crimes in the Rome Statute.

9.3.4 Article 31(4) and special meanings of 'ordinary' words

Article 31(4) forms part of the general rule of interpretation in the *Vienna Convention* (1969) and obliges judges of the Rome Statute to give a 'special meaning . . . to a term if it is established that the parties so intended'. Words with special meanings can be divided into two groups: words that have a unique meaning in 'a particular area of human endeavour' and words that have been assigned a special meaning by an individual who uses the term in a manner different than its common understanding.[201] The intent of the Parties regarding the first group can be discerned from the context in which the term is used – and here is where expert commentaries can be very useful – but the second group's special meaning must be indicated by the individual assigning it a meaning that departs from its common use.[202]

---

[198] A Ashworth and J Horder, *Principles of Criminal Law*, 7th edn (Oxford University Press 2013) 80.

[199] Schachter (n. 20) 71–72.   [200] Koskenniemi (n. 5) 139.   [201] Gardiner (n. 2) 291.

[202] Ibid.

This provision speaks more to the second category of words with special meanings, although it may be read to encompass the first group as well, which is also covered by the reference to context in article 31(1) of the *Vienna Convention* (1969).[203] The main purpose of article 31(4) is to clarify that the party claiming a special meaning has the burden of proof.[204] This proof of intention, not surprisingly, can be demonstrated using the rule of interpretation in article 31 of the *Vienna Convention* (1969), meaning emphasis is placed on the treaty text rather than supplementary means of interpretation in article 32.[205] Examples of treaty terms that parties to a dispute have tried to prove have a special meaning to them include 'Greenland', 'Near East' and 'month'.[206] Courts mostly reject arguments made pursuant to article 31(4), preferring to support their interpretations as reflective of the 'ordinary' meanings of the impugned words.[207] As the number of specialized legal regimes in international law flourishes, however, it is arguable that article 31(4) might take on increased significance. In practice, evidence of a special meaning will have to be fairly explicit, such as the inclusion of a definition in a treaty. When this is not the case, reliance should be placed on authoritative interpretive aids that express the intent of the Parties. As a last resort, preparatory works may be consulted for this purpose.[208]

One example of special meaning in the definitions of crimes in the Rome Statute can be found in article 8 *bis* (2), which defines the State act of aggression. This provision contains a list of acts amounting to aggression that replicates the list contained in article 3 of General Assembly Resolution 3314 (XXIX) of 1974.[209] This resolution may be said to fall under article 31(4) of the *Vienna Convention* (1969), as article 8 *bis* (2) provides: 'Any of the following acts, regardless of a declaration of war, shall, *in accordance with* United Nations General Assembly resolution 3314 (XXIX) of 14 December 1974, qualify as an act of aggression...'[210] The words 'in accordance with' arguably suggest that a special meaning was intended.

Although General Assembly resolutions are not a source of international law according to article 38 of the Statute of the International Court of Justice,

---

[203] Ibid.   [204] Ibid. 292, 295.

[205] Waldock (n. 129) 94; Gardiner (n. 2) 294. See also E Bjorge, *The Evolutionary Interpretation of Treaties* (Oxford University Press 2014).

[206] Gardiner, ibid. 294 (citing, respectively, *Legal Status of Eastern Greenland Case* (1933) PCIJ Series A/B, No. 53, 49; *Air Transport Services Agreement Arbitration (USA* v. *France)* [1963] 38 ILR 182, 230ff.; *Athanassiadis* v. *Government of Greece* [1969] 3 All ER 293).

[207] Ibid. (citing (1964) I Ybk of the ILC 309, para. 6).

[208] Ibid. 296–97: 'Where a special meaning is recorded in the preparatory work, its effect on interpretation is probably no different from that of other statements or declarations in preparatory work, but confirmation of this is not readily found.'

[209] UNGA, 'Definition of Aggression' (1974), UN Doc. Res. 3314 (XXIX).

[210] Emphasis added.

such resolutions may provide evidence of the *opinio juris* of the international community.[211] However, is the *opinio juris* of the international community as concerns the acts of aggression listed in article 8 *bis* (2) frozen to its members' understanding of them in 1974? Or may this provision reflect the evolution of their understanding of these terms over time? In light of the discussion on intertemporality above, judges should consider the extent to which the *opinio juris* of the international community concerning acts of aggression has evolved since 1974.

While General Assembly Resolution 3314 (XXIX) may contain special meanings of terms that could aid in the interpretation of article 8 *bis* (2), it may come to pass that these special meanings conflict with customary international law or the Elements of Crimes instrument, the latter two themselves authoritative[212] interpretive aids that must be considered (but may be rejected) under article 31(3)(c) and (a) of the *Vienna Convention* (1969) respectively. What if custom or the Elements instrument is invoked, however, under article 31(4) of the *Vienna Convention* (1969) as evidence of a special meaning, and, as between them and General Assembly Resolution 3314 (XXIX), it is not clear which aid was intended to conclusively settle the meaning to be given to a term in article 8 *bis* of the Rome Statute?

It is submitted that as between this Resolution and custom, the latter should prevail, and as between it and the Elements instrument, again the latter should prevail. In the author's view, where a reasonable doubt exists about the intent of States Parties, the meaning of a term under customary international law should be favoured over a meaning derived for the same term from General Assembly Resolution 3314 (XXIX). While this Resolution is an important expression of the *opinio juris* of the international community, custom consists of both *opinio juris* and State practice, thereby offering a stronger expression of intent. As for favouring the Elements instrument over this Resolution, it is submitted that this should be done because, unlike the latter, the former was drafted specifically for the Rome Statute, an international criminal law statute. It also contains a more recent expression of the *opinio juris* of the international community on the crime of aggression than anything that might be expressly or implicitly conveyed in General Assembly Resolution 3314 (XXIX).

Another dynamic that might best be incorporated into the second definition of 'special meaning' in article 31(4) is the intent of Parties to assign certain 'ordinary' words a meaning that is reflective of the values of the day. In *Tryer* v. *United Kingdom* (1978), the European Court of Human Rights stated:

---

[211] MD Öberg, 'The Legal Effects of Resolutions of the Security Council and General Assembly in the Jurisprudence of the ICJ' (2006) 16 EJIL 879, 898–900.

[212] The reference in article 21(1)(b) of the Rome Statute to 'principles and rules of international law' is to customary international law. Pellet (n. 157) 1070–71.

[T]he Convention is a living instrument which ... must be interpreted in the light of present-day conditions. In the case now before it the Court cannot but be influenced by the developments and commonly accepted standards in the penal policy of the member States of the Council of Europe in this field.[213]

Unlike the *European Convention on Human Rights* (1955), however, definitions of crimes in the Rome Statute are not in a living constitutional instrument. Accordingly, the reasoning in *Tryer* (1978) cannot be adopted wholesale. However, certain words in the Rome Statute are inherently normative, inviting judges to make moral judgments. And it is arguably fair to assume that, here, drafters of the Rome Statute intend for judges to make these normative judgments in light of the values of the day when the crime was alleged to have been committed. For example, as psychiatric research unearths new understandings of human behaviour, the meaning of the term 'persons of unsound mind' might well evolve.[214] Similarly, the meanings of the following crimes against humanity might also evolve:

Rape, sexual slavery, enforced prostitution, forced pregnancy, enforced sterilization, or any other form of sexual violence *of comparable gravity*;
...

Other inhumane acts *of a similar character* intentionally causing great suffering, or serious injury to body or to mental or physical health....

"Torture" means the intentional infliction *of severe pain or suffering* ...[215]

Baroness Hale, President of the Supreme Court of the United Kingdom, cited the terms 'bodily harm', 'violence' and 'family' as terms whose meaning, according to the House of Lords, has evolved over time and states: 'In all of these examples, the court is seeking to further the purpose of the legislation in the social world as it now is rather than as it was when the statute was passed, but to do so in a principled and predictable way which will not offend against either the intention of Parliament or the principle of legal certainty.'[216] But what are the limits of evolutive interpretation, especially when States Parties to a treaty have engaged in subsequent practice that limits the scope of a treaty term that would otherwise be assigned an expansive evolutive interpretation? With respect to the European Court of Human Rights, Baroness Hale mentions the following factors to consider: (1) not contradicting the 'express language of the Convention';

---

[213] App. No. 5856/72, *Tryer* v. *United Kingdom*, ECHR (1978) Series A, No. 26, para. 31 (concerned judicial corporal punishment for a youth).

[214] Higgins (n. 163) 176 (citing App. No. 6301/73, *Winterwerp* v. *Netherlands*, ECHR (1979) Series A, No. 33, para. 37).

[215] Articles 7(1)(g), 7(1)(k) and 7(2)(e), Rome Statute (emphasis added).

[216] B Hale, 'Common Law and Convention Law: The Limits to Interpretation' (2011) 16:5 European HR L Rev 534, 536.

(2) consistency with the 'established principles of Convention jurisprudence'; (3) consistency with 'standards set in other international instruments relevant to the subject-matter in hand'; and (4) striking a 'fair balance' between the Convention values and democratic legislative choices of member States.[217]

The International Law Commission has also chimed in, stating that a treaty term has an evolutive character where

> (a) The concept is one which implies taking into account subsequent technical, economic or legal developments; (b) the concept sets up an obligation for further progressive development for the parties; or (c) the concept has a very general nature or is expressed in such general terms that it must take into account changing circumstances.[218]

To be clear, judges may assign to a treaty term a different special meaning over time on the basis of evolutive meaning or subsequent practice, for example. And what happens if the subsequent practice of States conflicts with an evolutive interpretation of a treaty term? The dilemma may be summarized as follows:

> [I]n terms of immediate effects it would appear that subsequent practice has the potential to permit greater treaty development in theory, but in many empirical situations, as in *Costa Rica* v. *Nicaragua* [decided by the International Court of Justice], the available evidence of subsequent practice will support less expansion than would be permissible by an evolutive interpretation. Yet irrespective of which technique has the broader expansive potential in any particular instance of interpretation, evolutive interpretation has more lingering effects on a treaty in the long term. Regarding vertical effects, once a term or a treaty is considered evolutive, i.e. inherently susceptible of dynamic interpretation, it is to be reinterpreted in light of the circumstances contemporary to *every successive application* [or in the case of the Rome Statute, contemporary to *every alleged act of criminal conduct*]. A reinterpretation based on subsequent practice, by contrast, implies nothing as to further reinterpretations – future interpretations on this basis would depend upon further conduct meeting the criteria for relevant subsequent practice (except, perhaps, in a case where the subsequent practice concerns the evolutive nature of the treaty – either establishing, expanding, or reducing it).[219]

This matter is taken up in the next section.

---

[217] Ibid. 543.   [218] ILC (n. 174) para. 23 (internal citations omitted).

[219] J Arato, 'Subsequent Practice and Evolutive Interpretation: Techniques of Treaty Interpretation over Time and their Diverse Consequences' (2010) 9:3 *The Law & Practice of International Courts and Tribunals* 443, 493–94; see also G Nolte, 'Jurisprudence of the International Court of Justice and Arbitral Tribunals of Ad Hoc Jurisdiction Relating to Subsequent Agreements and Subsequent Practice: Introductory Report for the ILC Study Group on Treaties over Time' in G Nolte (ed.), *Treaties and Subsequent Practice* (Oxford University Press 2013) 169, 189ff.

9.3.5 *Article 31(3)(b) and subsequent practice*

When interpreting crimes in the Rome Statute, article 31(3)(b) of the *Vienna Convention* (1969) obliges judges to take into account 'any subsequent practice in the application of the treaty which establishes the agreement of the parties regarding its interpretation'. In light of the discussion of intertemporality and the principle of legality, this practice cannot have occurred beyond the date on which the relevant crime was allegedly committed. As well, not all practice is meaningful, only practice involving the 'application of the treaty' and evidencing *agreement* of all the Parties on the interpretation of a treaty term.[220] The subject matter of the treaty, here the Rome Statute, will influence the Court's understanding of subsequent practice, although it must in any case be practice that is 'systematic', 'repetitive' or 'concordant, common, and consistent' in terms of the Statute's application.[221] Most international tribunals have accepted that even in the case of a multilateral treaty, the silence of one or more Parties can contribute to a finding of consensus among all of the Parties to the treaty.[222]

As for the origins of this practice, it may be executive, legislative (including trends), judicial (e.g., speeches, laws, court decisions) or military, as confirmed by the practice of the ICTY, ICTR and International Criminal Court.[223] It can even be the adoption of a subsequent treaty that confirms or elaborates the meaning of a term in the treaty being interpreted. Such a treaty would, however, also find a home in article 31(3)(c). To be clear though, practice interpreting that subsequent treaty may not count as practice in the application of the treaty being interpreted.[224] For example, a UN-backed ad hoc tribunal established after the Court might have a governing statute that contains the same definitions of crimes in the Rome Statute and goes on to give them further content. However, interpretation of that statute is not subsequent practice for purposes of interpreting crimes in the Rome Statute. It might, however, be relevant to ascertaining the content of custom under article 31(3)(c) of the *Vienna Convention* (1969). As to the degree of consensus that must exist among Parties to the Rome Statute in order to give rise to subsequent practice establishing agreement, the practice of States need not be identical but fairly close so as to evidence true agreement.[225] Concerning the volume of practice, it need

---

[220] Dinstein (n. 24) 408; Gardiner (n. 2) 226.

[221] Gardiner (n. 2) 226–28; I Sinclair, *The Vienna Convention on the Law of Treaties*, 2nd edn (Manchester University Press 1984) 137–38.

[222] G Nolte, 'Second Report for the ILC Study Group on Treaties over Time: Jurisprudence under Special Regimes relating to Subsequent Agreements and Subsequent Practice' in G Nolte (ed.), *Treaties and Subsequent Practice* (Oxford University Press 2013) 210.

[223] Ibid. ss. 2.4.1 and 2.5; Gardiner (n. 2) 228–30.

[224] Gardiner, ibid. 234 (citing for this proposition *Land, Island and Maritime Frontier Dispute (El Salvador v. Honduras: Nicaragua Intervening)* [1992] ICJ Rep. 351).

[225] Gardiner (n. 2) 239.

not be abundant, but it 'cannot in general be established by one isolated fact or act, or even by several individual applications'.[226] And if the authors of the practice are only a few States, there must be 'good evidence' that other States Parties knowingly endorsed this practice through acquiescence or express acceptance.[227]

The notion of subsequent practice raises interesting issues in the context of the Rome Statute about the extent to which judges' interpretation of the crimes therein can be counted as such practice, especially if the Assembly of States Parties to the Statute endorses these. Article 31(3)(b) of the *Vienna Convention* (1969) does not bar States from acting collectively, but it does contemplate the practice of States and not of international organizations.[228] However, where States empower judges to interpret the crimes in the Rome Statute, the outcomes they reach are arguably subsequent practice if the agreement of States Parties can be established.[229] Article 21(2) of the Rome Statute treats the jurisprudence of the Court as subsequent practice that judges may but are not obliged to take into account: 'The Court may apply principles and rules of law as interpreted in its previous decisions.' It is important to recall that judges of the Court are obliged to take subsequent practice into account but remain free to reject the interpretation endorsed in this practice. It is wise, though to offer good reasons for this, as subsequent practice is practice that is agreed to by States Parties.

Having attempted a definition of subsequent practice, it is perhaps useful to add two observations about what it is *not*. First, subsequent practice is not necessarily custom, the latter being potentially universally binding and requiring for its formation *opinio juris* in addition to State practice. As well, whereas subsequent practice requires agreement, custom does allow for a small number of persistent objections.[230] Second, subsequent practice ought not to be confused with evolutive interpretation.[231] Whereas the intent for evolutive interpretation must be located in the treaty itself, the intent underlying subsequent interpretive practice can be discerned from material external to the Rome Statute. Further, evolutive interpretation does not require systematic, repetitive or concordant practice by States.[232]

To round out the discussion of subsequent practice, it seems useful to offer an example of it. Article 118 of the third *Geneva Convention* (1949) requires the

---

[226] Ibid. 230 (citing Sinclair (n. 221) 137).

[227] Ibid. 356–57 (citing (1966) II Ybk of the ILC 222).   [228] Ibid. 246.

[229] Ibid.; International Law Association, Committee on International Human Rights Law and Practice, 'Final Report on the Impact of the Findings of the United Nations Human Rights Treaty Bodies', Berlin Conference (2004) 6–7.

[230] Villiger (n. 17) 220.

[231] Gardiner (n. 2) 242 (citing App. No. 8562/79, *Feldbrugge* v. *Netherlands*, Joint Dissenting Opinion, ECHR (1986) Series A, No. 124 A, paras. 23–24). See Section 9.3.4 on special meaning.

[232] Gardiner (n. 2) 243.

release and repatriation of prisoners of war without delay after active hostilities have ceased. When the *Convention* (1949) was drafted, the idea to make repatriation optional was rejected by a large majority. In the wake of the Korean War, masses of North Korean and Chinese prisoners refused to return to their country of nationality. In 1953, the Parties to the conflict agreed that prisoners not wishing to return to their homeland would be assisted in gaining access to other countries. This precedent was followed in the Gulf War in 1991 and today represents an authoritative interpretation of article 118. The agreement of other States regarding this interpretation is derived from this interpretation existing under customary international law without the existence of persistent objections.[233] In this example, therefore, subsequent practice was established through the interpretation of article 118 by a few States and the agreement of all other States, evidenced by the emergence of a customary rule.[234] If this custom had not existed, some other evidence of States Parties endorsing this interpretation of article 118 would have to be proffered.

When the *Vienna Convention* (1969) was being drafted, the following two ideas were considered and rejected: permitting a treaty to be modified by subsequent practice in its application establishing agreement of the relevant Parties; and modification of a treaty as a result of the emergence of a new rule of custom.[235] What survived was article 64: 'If a new *peremptory norm* of general international law emerges, any existing treaty which is in conflict with that norm becomes void and terminates.'[236] In spite of this drafting history, rulings of the International Court of Justice (ICJ) and the conduct of States suggest that when sufficiently pressed, both are willing to blur the line between subsequent practice that interprets a treaty provision and that which modifies it.[237] In its advisory opinion on *Namibia* (1971), the ICJ recognized the subsequent practice of Security Council members in 'interpreting' article 27(3) of the Charter of the United Nations.[238] This provision requires that non-procedural decisions of the Security Council be made by a special majority, 'including the concurring votes' of the five permanent members of the Council. Consistent with the practice of Security Council members, the Court recognized that only a negative vote, not merely abstention from voting, indicates a lack of concurrence. Article 27(3) can arguably be read to require a positive vote by all five permanent members of the Council.

In its advisory opinion on *Certain Expenses of the United Nations* (1962), the ICJ was asked to interpret the phrase 'expenses of the Organization' in article

---

[233] Dinstein (n. 24) 410–11.   [234] Villiger (n. 17) 221.

[235] ILC, 'Report of the International Law Commission on the Work of its Eighteenth Session' (1966) II Ybk of the ILC 163, 172, 182, 163–69, 220–22 and 266–67.

[236] Emphasis added.

[237] M Byers, *Custom, Power and the Power of Rules* (Cambridge University Press 1999) 172–74.

[238] *Namibia* (n. 165) 16.

17(2) of the Charter of the United Nations.[239] The (then) USSR, France and other member States refused to pay certain peacekeeping costs for missions in the Middle East and Congo because they considered the formation of the peacekeeping forces to be in violation of the Charter. However, article 17(2) of the Charter provides that '[t]he expenses of the Organization shall be borne by the Members as apportioned by the General Assembly', and article 19 provides that if a member State is in arrears, it 'shall have no vote in the General Assembly if arrears are not due to circumstances beyond the control of the member and their amount equals or exceeds the amount of the contributions due from it for the preceding two full years'. However, non-payment was within the control of the defaulting States. The ICJ held that 'regular expenses' in article 17(2) includes all those approved by the General Assembly. Once the two-year condition in article 19 was met, the issue became whether these countries would lose their vote. Under threat of the (then) USSR leaving the United Nations, an exception was made by member States on the basis of 'strong and compelling reasons', and it was agreed that the General Assembly would continue with its work without addressing the matter of arrears.

Some scholars argue in favour of subsequent practice revising, modifying or amending treaty provisions in 'good faith' and on the basis inter alia of consent and legitimate expectations, especially where: (1) amendment of the treaty is extremely difficult and that treaty is intended to codify customary rules, thereby making them more accessible to States; and (2) a rule of custom is deeply entrenched so that amendment of a treaty does not seem necessary.[240] However, not all are in agreement.[241] For purposes of crimes in the Rome Statute, the guiding interpretive principle of legality, the subject matter of articles 6, 7, 8 and 8 *bis* of the Statute and the amendment procedures set out in article 121 all point to a rejection of this position. Subsequent practice for purposes of aiding in the interpretation of crimes in the Rome Statute must be limited to interpreting and not surreptitiously modifying, revising or amending these definitions.

As to the dilemma of when to accept an evolutive interpretation argument in favour of one about subsequent practice, it has been argued that the *nature of the treaty norm* at issue and the contemplated interpretation's respect for a treaty's object and purpose are both germane considerations.[242] As opposed to

---

[239] *Certain Expenses of the United Nations (Article 17, paragraph 2, of the Charter)*, Advisory Opinion [1962] ICJ Rep. 151.

[240] Byers (n. 237) 175–77; Villiger (n. 17) 224.   [241] Orakhelashvili (n. 63) 356.

[242] J Arato, 'Accounting for Difference in Treaty Interpretation over Time', Draft Paper prepared for the Cambridge Conference on Interpretation in International Law, Lauterpacht Centre for International Law (27 August 2013) 43 (on file with author); Arato (n. 219) fn. 122.

reciprocal norms, whereby States 'agree to a pseudo-contractual exchange of rights and duties, which may be enforced or sanctioned by retaliatory suspension or termination (respectively), integral norms are those where states agree to create obligations [*erga omnes inter partes* or *erga* omnes] meant *to withstand violations and the changing whims of the parties*'.[243] Arato's analysis leads him to argue that '[f]or the purposes of interpretation, the integral nature of a norm would seem to weigh against an interpretation on the basis of subsequent practice that *cuts against* the object and purpose of a treaty'.[244] The relevance of the object and purpose of a treaty to the weight given to subsequent practice is evident in the practice of various international judicial bodies.[245] Assuming that integral rather than reciprocal norms underlie the definitions of crimes in the Rome Statute, where subsequent practice limits the scope of a crime defined therein, consideration should be given to whether this limitation is in accordance with the object and purpose of the impugned criminal provision.

Finally, there is the issue of international courts assigning greater weight to subsequent agreements than subsequent practice as interpretive aids. Nolte has usefully explained the distinction as follows:

> Article 31 (3) VCLT distinguishes between "subsequent agreement" (para. 3 (a)) and "subsequent practice" (para. 3 (b)). The Commission did not intend this distinction to denote a difference concerning their possible substantive effect. The Report describes "subsequent agreement" as representing "an authentic interpretation by the parties which must be read into the treaty for purposes of its interpretation", and states that "subsequent practice" "similarly" "constitutes objective evidence of the understanding of the parties as to the meaning of the treaty". The relevant legal difference between the two concepts seems to lie in the fact that a "subsequent agreement regarding the interpretation of the treaty" *ipso facto* has the effect of constituting an authentic interpretation of the treaty, whereas "subsequent practice" only has this effect if it "shows the common understanding of the parties as to the meaning of the terms." This means that there is a difference between the two concepts with respect to the evidentiary value which a "subsequent agreement" or a "subsequent practice" may have for constituting an agreement between the parties regarding the interpretation of a particular treaty. This evidentiary value is higher in the case of a "subsequent agreement" than in the case of "subsequent practice".[246]

In conclusion, the integral nature of the norms in the Rome Statute as well as the difficulty of proving agreement among States Parties regarding a particular

---

[243] Arato, 'Accounting for Difference in Treaty Interpretation over Time', ibid.
[244] Ibid. 48.   [245] Nolte (n. 222).   [246] Nolte (n. 219) 173.

practice on how to interpret these norms suggest that such practice might not figure prominently as an aid to interpreting crimes in the Statute.

9.4 Article 32 and supplementary means of interpretation

This Chapter closes with a brief examination of articles 32 and 33 of the *Vienna Convention* (1969), beginning with how supplementary interpretive aids might assist the Court. As mentioned in Chapter 1, the present study is intended to complement rather than rehearse the general literature on articles 31–33 of the *Vienna Convention* (1969), indicating how these provisions might come into play within the Rome regime and be affected by the method developed in this study. Unlike article 31, which is mandatory, article 32 is discretionary and provides:

> Recourse *may* be had to supplementary means of interpretation, including the preparatory work of the treaty and the circumstances of its conclusion, *in order to confirm* the meaning resulting from the application of article 31, *or to determine* the meaning when the interpretation according to article 31:
>
> (a) leaves the meaning ambiguous or obscure; or
> (b) leads to a result which is manifestly absurd or unreasonable.[247]

There are two entry points for accessing supplementary means of interpretation through article 32, and courts often (but not always) indicate which of these entry points is being used.[248] On the first point of entry – confirming an interpretation arrived at by applying the general rule in article 31 – the meaning of a term might *not* be confirmed and then revisited.[249] It might also lead to the detection of an ambiguity not previously perceived.[250]

On the second entry point – determining the meaning of a treaty term – its invocation is 'inherently flexible' because discerning the existence of an ambiguity (paragraph a) is a fairly subjective exercise.[251] This is borne out by the fact that, in nearly every case where the interpretation of a treaty is in dispute, one, some or all parties rely on preparatory work.[252] This practice is consistent with the intention of the International Law Commission, which sought to confirm the appropriateness of consulting the preparatory work of a treaty whenever a question of its interpretation is raised.[253] One useful limit on the meaning of ambiguity in article 32 is that it is concerned with residual

---

[247] Emphasis added.   [248] Gardiner (n. 2) 312–13.   [249] Ibid. 308–10.
[250] Ibid. 309–10.   [251] Waldock (n. 129) 99.
[252] AD McNair, *The Law of Treaties*, 2nd edn (Oxford University Press 1961) 412.
[253] Gardiner (n. 2) 302, 316 (citing *Maritime Delimitation and Territorial Questions between Qatar and Bahrain (Qatar v. Bahrain)*, Jurisdiction and Admissibility [1995] ICJ Rep. 6).

ambiguity – uncertainty that remains *after* the general rule in article 31 of the *Vienna Convention* (1969) has been applied.[254] A party may not merely point to multiple dictionary definitions for a treaty term as conclusive evidence of an ambiguity, although this may be suggestive of one.[255] An ambiguity has also been usefully defined as follows:

> It is . . . not sufficient in itself that a text is *capable* of bearing more than one meaning. These meanings must be equally valued meanings, or at any rate, even if one may appear more possible and likely than the other, both must attain a reasonable degree of possibility and probability, not only grammatically but as a matter of substance and sense.[256]

It is worth mentioning that the textual primacy entailed by the legality principle may lead to an interpretation that stands in opposition to the intentions of States Parties, as evidenced in the Statute's *travaux préparatoires*. Further, the wording of the Statute, because of the values underlying the principle of legality, would be presumed to best reflect the intentions of the Parties to the Statute. And, owing to the burden of States to manifest their intentions clearly in the Statute, an ambiguity that can be resolved only by resorting to the drafting history of the Statute should be resolved in favour of the accused. This does not prevent judges from consulting the drafting history of the Statute as well as that of treaties from which terms have been transplanted to the Statute. Rather, the point is narrower. If an interpretive finding depends solely on a provision's drafting history and is not supported by any other acceptable interpretive principle, argument or aid, then the ambiguity should be resolved in favour of the accused, as States Parties have not met their burden to define the crime in sufficiently clear terms.[257]

As for the meanings of absurdity and unreasonableness in article 32(b), examples of their proper use are difficult to find. On occasion, however, this provision has been incorrectly cited in support of rejecting an interpretive argument that is thought to produce an unreasonable outcome.[258] Reasonable disagreement can exist about what is absurd or unreasonable. The qualifier of manifest offers the potential to constrain this debate somewhat. Article 46(2) of the *Vienna Convention* (1969), a provision on internal law dealing with the

---

[254] Gardiner (n. 2) 328.   [255] Ibid.   [256] Fitzmaurice (n. 172) 216.

[257] D Akande, 'The Sources of International Criminal Law' in A Cassese (ed.), *The Oxford Companion to International Criminal Justice* (Oxford University Press 2009) 41, 45; D Jacobs, 'Positivism and International Criminal Law: The Principle of Legality as a Rule of Conflict of Theories' in J d'Aspremont and J Kammerhofer (eds.), *International Legal Positivism in a Post-Modern World* (Cambridge University Press, forthcoming October 2014), 1, 32–3, http://papers.ssrn.com/sol3/papers.cfm?abstract_id=2046311, accessed 16 October 2013.

[258] Gardiner (n. 2) 329.

competence of States to conclude treaties, defines a manifest violation of that law as if 'it would be *objectively evident to any State* conducting itself in the matter in accordance with normal practice and in good faith'.[259] What is also important to note is that whereas article 32(a) refers to the *meaning* of a treaty term being ambiguous or obscure, article 32(b) permits reliance on supplementary means of interpretation where interpretation in accordance with article 31 would lead to an *outcome* that is manifestly absurd or unreasonable. For example, if the Court's application of article 31 were to yield an interpretive finding that private actors lacking State-like power cannot commit crimes against humanity, a judge might find this *interpretation* manifestly unreasonable but not necessarily think that the *outcome*, perhaps the acquittal of the accused, is manifestly unreasonable. The opposite might also be true. Interpretive reasoning pursuant to article 31 of the *Vienna Convention* (1969) might lead to a perfectly reasonable interpretation but a manifestly absurd or unreasonable outcome on the facts of the case – such as an objectively grave injustice. Here, judges might take their cues from supplementary means of interpretation, such as preparatory work, to avoid reaching such an outcome. At the same time, care should be taken not to allow article 32(b) to serve as an indirect way for admitting arguments that fundamentally undermine the importance of the legality principle in the interpretation of crimes in the Rome Statute.

There remains the matter of defining what constitutes supplementary means for purposes of article 32, which is careful to not list these means exhaustively. Article 32 is clear about the concept including preparatory work, which is 'an omnibus expression which is used rather loosely to indicate all documents, such as memoranda, minutes of conferences, and drafts of the treaty under negotiation'.[260] A supplement completes a work, reinforces it or adds something to it to address a deficiency.[261] It has been argued that in the context of article 32, 'supplementary means' are 'material or substantive matters to be taken under consideration, rather than general interpretative principles of an analytical kind such as lawyers are accustomed to apply [e.g., *ejusdem generis* principle, *expressio unius exclusio alterius* or *a contrario*]'.[262] These principles might find a better home in some part of article 31.

The incompleteness of the preparatory work for the Rome Statute has already been discussed in Chapter 2, Section 2.4.1. However, some official records do exist, and they are complemented by many commentaries on the drafting history of the Rome Statute written by experts who attended the negotiations in Rome. As well, the work of the ASP Special Working Group on the Crime of Aggression (and the Working Group on the Crime of Aggression at the Review Conference) is carefully summarized in official reports that were adopted by

---

[259] Emphasis added.   [260] Gardiner (n. 2) 302 (citing McNair (n. 252) 411–23).
[261] Ibid. 311.   [262] Ibid. 311–12.

consensus at the conclusion of each meeting and are in the public domain.[263] Additionally, the International Committee of the Red Cross prepared a commentary to the Elements of Crimes, which sets out the *travaux préparatoires* or understandings of the Preparatory Commission during the drafting process and relevant legal sources pertaining to each crime. How might the Court use this preparatory work when interpreting crimes in the Rome Statute? Courts typically use such work in more ways than are contemplated in article 32. Beyond relying on it to confirm or determine the meaning of a treaty provision, preparatory work might be mentioned in a judgment as part of a description of the historical development of a legal concept or treaty provision[264] or to reinforce or underscore that the interpretation preferred is consistent with the intention of the Parties.[265] Used in these ways, the requirements in article 32 do not need to be satisfied.[266] The Court might also incidentally cite commentaries on the drafting of the Rome Statute and the analysis contained therein.[267] While judges cannot prevent parties from arguing that certain material constitutes supplementary means, they are free to reject these claims, with reasons, and not consider this material.[268]

Finally, there is the matter of what weight is to be given to supplementary means, especially preparatory work, as an aid to interpreting crimes in the Rome Statute and its relationship to other interpretive aids. Because preparatory work is an attractive starting point for any interpretive exercise, it is likely that a judge will have the interpretation in this work in his or her mind when applying article 31 of the *Vienna Convention* (1969).[269] Article 32 does not comment on the issue of weight, probably because supplementary means is a category that might include several different types of materials of varying relevance.[270] At the very least, however, it can be said that the guiding interpretive principle of legality for crimes in the Rome Statute bars supplementary means from modifying their definitions in the Statute. Furthermore, given the outcome of applying the intertemporal rule to the Rome Statute, it would appear that where older supplementary means exist, such as preparatory work, and this conflicts with an equally relevant interpretive aid existing at the time the crime was allegedly committed, such as custom, the contemporary aids should perhaps prevail. As for the weight to be given to preparatory work for a treaty whose terms have been transplanted into the Rome regime, careful consideration should be given to the context, object and purpose of both treaty regimes and the provisions in question.

---

[263] S Barriga, W Danspeckgruber and C Wenaweser (eds.), *The Princeton Process on the Crime of Aggression: Materials of the Special Working Group on the Crime of Aggression, 2003 – 2009* (Liechtenstein Institute on Self-Determination 2009). An updated compilation of the *travaux préparatoires* for the crime of aggression was recently published. Barriga and Kreß (n. 113).

[264] Gardiner (n. 2) 316.   [265] Ibid. 324–28.   [266] Ibid. 316.   [267] Ibid.

[268] Ibid.   [269] Ibid. 322–23.   [270] Ibid. 331.

9.5 Article 33 and treaties authenticated in two or more languages

Article 128 of the Rome Statute states that it is authenticated in Arabic, Chinese, English, French, Russian and Spanish and that these texts are equally authentic. Articles 33(3) and (4) of the *Vienna Convention* (1969) provide:

3. The terms of the treaty are presumed to have the same meaning in each authentic text.
4. Except where a particular text prevails in accordance with paragraph 1, when a comparison of the authentic texts discloses a difference of meaning which the application of articles 31 and 32 does not remove, the meaning which best reconciles the texts, having regard to the object and purpose of the treaty, shall be adopted.

While the official languages of the Court are English and French, it is important that this rule for multilingual treaties is respected. Complicating communication is the fact that individuals working at the Court speak different languages and were trained in different legal traditions. As well, for the benefit of witnesses, suspects, accused and their legal counsel, proceedings at the Court are often translated into languages that are not authentic.

Despite the best efforts of the ICTY to accommodate different languages and legal cultures, it has been observed that a legal and linguistic imbalance exists in favour of Anglo-Saxon legal culture and language.[271] This asymmetry works to the detriment of the civil law tradition and the French language.[272] In French, there is a lack of equivalents for everyday common-law terms and concepts, such as allegations, cross-examination, pretrial, to plead guilty or not guilty, beyond any reasonable doubt and balance of probability.[273] As well, concepts such as appeal, charges and objection possess different meanings in French and English.[274] Legal and cultural asymmetry forces staff members not trained in the dominant legal culture and language to adapt and adjust.[275]

One reaction to this asymmetry has been the emergence at the ICTY of a hybrid language for some concepts,[276] which might not be understandable to outsiders and newcomers.[277] The International Criminal Court is ripe for having the same experience, especially since the Rome Statute deliberately avoids using terminology that is clearly traceable to just one legal tradition. The

---

[271] L Stern, 'Interpreting Legal Language at the International Criminal Tribunal for the Former Yugoslavia: Overcoming the Lack of Lexical Equivalents' (2007) 2 J Specialised Translation 63.

[272] Ibid. 65.   [273] Ibid.   [274] Ibid.

[275] Ibid. 73: 'Despite these limitations, however, there is no evidence of immediate damage having been done to ICTY cases, or of a miscarriage of justice; furthermore, the high level of awareness by ICTY legal and judicial staff of issues in cross-cultural communication has helped to resolve interpreting and other communication problems as they arise.'

[276] Ibid. 66.   [277] Ibid. 72.

existence of an interpretive methodology can help reduce the risk of misunderstandings and asymmetries of the kind described from emerging in chambers. In addition, the professionalism of judges can contribute to no particular legal culture and its concepts dominating interpretive exercises, especially given that there are six authentic versions of the Rome Statute. Ultimately, judges will have to assign meanings to treaty terms that are consistent with all of these versions, even if these are not favourable to the accused, as legality favours textual primacy and coherence, which benefits all persons who may appear before the Court.

10

Conclusions

10.1 Introduction

The method of interpretation developed in this study is for crimes defined in the Rome Statute and attempts to offer its users the following levels of assistance: (1) a primary interpretive principle to guide their reasoning process when confronted with interpretive issues; (2) arguments or reasons that support (and undermine) this interpretive principle; and (3) a catalogue of materials or aids that must, may and, if applicable, may not be taken into account in support of these arguments.[1] In this final Chapter, the methodology is summarized in the form of mandatory guidelines that are grafted onto articles 31–33 of the *Vienna Convention* (1969). This effort at integration is motivated by the familiarity of these articles to most readers but comes at the price of disassembling the aforementioned three tiers and their content in order to fit this into the *Vienna Convention* (1969) framework. To be clear, what follows is not an explanation of how articles 31–33 operate in general, but rather a summary of the relationship between these provisions and the method developed. Like the rules of interpretation in the *Vienna Convention* (1969), the guidelines that follow must be taken into account if relevant to a particular interpretive exercise. Where a better understanding of the impetus for or operation of a particular guideline is desired, the relevant sections of this book should be consulted.

10.2 Article 31(1) and legality

The general rule of interpretation in article 31(1) of the *Vienna Convention* (1969) provides: 'A treaty shall be interpreted in good faith in accordance with the ordinary meaning to be given to the terms of the treaty in their context and in the light of its object and purpose.' This rule, specifically the requirement of 'good faith', is to be read in light of legality in article 22 of the Rome Statute serving as the guiding interpretive principle for crimes defined therein. The

---

[1] Z Bankowski, DN MacCormick, RS Summers and J Wróblewski, 'On Method and Methodology' in DN MacCormick and RS Summers (eds.), *Interpreting Statutes: A Comparative Study* (Ashgate 1991) 9.

result is that textual primacy and coherence – as opposed to drafters' intent or object and purpose approaches to interpretation – are imperative to ensuring that the law is not applied retroactively to persons investigated, prosecuted or convicted. Textual primacy means the following:

> First, it seems to be generally recognized that an interpretation that does not emerge from the text cannot be accepted, however plausible it may be in view of the circumstance, unless failure to do so would lead to an obviously unreasonable result. Accordingly, tribunals have usually rejected otherwise reasonable interpretations because to accept them would have been tantamount to rephrasing or otherwise altering the actual text. Second, interpretations suggested by means of interpretation not derived from the text cannot be justified by referring to general custom, usage, or even recognized rules of international law unless sufficiently supported by the text. Last, when two or more reasonable interpretations exist, all of which are consistent with the text, the one that appears to be the most compatible with the text should prevail in the absence of persuasive evidence in support of another interpretation.[2]

Considerations of context, object and purpose as well as interpretive aids such as the Elements of Crimes and *travaux préparatoires* cannot be invoked to modify the plain meaning of these articles, to inappropriately restrict or broaden them or to create textual incoherence. To be clear, textual primacy is not incompatible with the 'crucible' approach to interpretation. In practice, a dictionary definition without consideration of a treaty's context, a provision's purpose or any number of relevant and applicable interpretive arguments and aids would prove rather unhelpful.

There are various justifications for the legality principle, including fair warning, the rule of law, the separation of powers doctrine and ensuring the effectiveness of criminal prohibitions in the Rome Statute. The justification of fair warning appears to be a bit of a legal fiction in all jurisdictions but is a compelling expression of rule of law considerations underlying legality. The rule of law is a strong justification for the legality principle and is concerned with preserving the human dignity of persons investigated, prosecuted and convicted as well as the legitimacy of the Court itself. The rule of law is not an absolute quantity but exists in degrees in all legal systems, as no criminal prohibitions can be perfectly fixed, precise, clear and mechanically applied. The key is to limit judicial discretion to the 'penumbral zone' or 'interstitial areas' so that the law is certain in the great majority of cases. The separation of powers doctrine is equally important and warns judges to 'avoid large-scale innovation',

---

[2] R Gardiner, *Treaty Interpretation* (Oxford University Press 2008) 145 (citing RH Berglin, 'Treaty Interpretation and the Impact of Contractual Choice of Forum Clauses on the Jurisdiction of International Tribunals: the Iranian Forum Clause Decisions of the Iran-United States Claims Tribunal' (1986) 21 Tex Int'l LJ 39, 44) (footnotes omitted).

steer clear of controversial public policy debates,[3] respect 'considered legislative inaction'[4] and avoid the 'reproach that the tribunal has substituted its own intention for that of the parties' as expressed in the Statute.[5]

10.3 Article 31(1) and interpretive devices for safeguarding legality

Article 22(2) of the Rome Statute articulates three interpretive devices for preserving legality: 'The definition of a crime shall be strictly construed and shall not be extended by analogy. In case of ambiguity, the definition shall be interpreted in favour of the person being investigated, prosecuted or convicted.' Given their relationship to the principle of legality, these interpretive devices form part of the imperative in article 31(1) of the *Vienna Convention* (1969) to interpret a treaty in 'good faith'. These devices offer the following guidance for interpreting articles 6, 7, 8 and 8 *bis* of the Rome Statute and, where applicable, the Elements of Crimes (Elements).

Strict construction

1. Strict construction 'does not prevent a court from interpreting and clarifying the elements of a particular crime'.[6]
2. Judges have been delegated some law-making authority, but this is limited to the most interstitial and minimal developments. Incremental legal developments and moderate interpretive outcomes are to be favoured over expansive interpretations and the recognition of new crimes.[7]
3. Arguments about object and purpose under article 31(1) of the *Vienna Convention* (1969) should, to the greatest extent possible, be limited to commenting about the mischief that the relevant criminal prohibition – as opposed to the Rome regime as a whole – is intended to address. This includes the class of individuals, the type of conduct and the set of circumstances that are covered by it, all while ensuring intellectual and textual coherence. Thus, the principle of effectiveness is limited to this coherence mandate.
4. Where application of the general rule of interpretation in article 31 of the *Vienna Convention* (1969) yields more than one outcome that could reasonably reflect the intent of States Parties, strict construction favours adopting the most modest interpretation – that which is least expansive.

---

[3] JC Jeffries Jr, 'Legality, Vagueness, and the Construction of Penal Statutes' (1985) 71 Virginia L Rev 189, 205.

[4] Ibid.

[5] H Lauterpacht, 'Restrictive Interpretation and the Principle of Effectiveness in the Interpretation of Treaties' (1949) 26 British Ybk Int'l L 48, 74.

[6] *Prosecutor* v. *Delalić and Others*, Judgment, ICTY-96–21-A, 20 February 2001, para. 173 (citing *Prosecutor* v. *Aleksovski*, Judgment, ICTY-95–14/1-A, 24 March 2000, paras. 97, 107–111).

[7] *Prosecutor* v. *Milutinović and Others*, Decision on Dragoljub Ojdanic's Motion Challenging Jurisdiction: Joint Criminal Enterprise, ICTY-99–37-AR72, 21 May 2003, paras. 37–38.

5. The interpretive outcome selected should be one that a reasonable and law-abiding individual in the place of the suspect or accused could be expected to have been aware when reading the relevant provisions of the Rome Statute (perhaps with the aid of legal advice if the conduct was committed in a professional capacity).

6. Interpretive outcomes that enhance certainty should be favoured over those that fail to resolve an ambiguity in the law, exploit it, multiply the possibilities for its application, do not identify which categories of offenders are covered by a criminal prohibition or render the prohibition's application open-ended and less predictable.

7. Interpretive reasoning should be anchored in and guided by principles rather than facts.

8. The strict construction imperative is rebutted where States choose to insert in the Rome Statute open-textured language, thereby signalling the delegation of a greater than normal degree of law-making power to judges.

9. When interpreting open-textured provisions and where possible, illustrative examples of conduct that is included in or excluded from them, as well as lists of criteria that will be considered in future cases when determining their application, can all enhance legal certainty.

10. Strict construction entails the liberal interpretation of grounds for excluding criminal liability on which a defendant might have relied, such as self-defence (as opposed to intoxication) – or at least that their interpretation not be narrower than a reasonable person could expect.

Favouring the person investigated, prosecuted or convicted in case of ambiguity

1. States bear the burden of drafting international criminal prohibitions using language that is as clear as possible.

2. Accordingly, there is a rebuttable presumption against ambiguity.

3. Where an ambiguity exists and needs to be resolved through interpretation, arguments that favour giving preference to the collective goals of the international community (e.g., ending impunity, ensuring peace, security and world order, punishing morally reprehensible conduct, securing justice for victims, and so on) are not permitted as justifications for resolving it. The right of the person being investigated, prosecuted or convicted to respect for the principle of legality trumps these legitimate policy goals when interpreting the definitions of crimes.

4. If an interpretive finding depends solely on a provision's drafting history and is not supported by any other acceptable interpretive principle, argument or aid, then the ambiguity should be resolved in favour of the accused, as States Parties have not met their burden to define the crime in sufficiently clear terms.

Analogous reasoning

1. Article 22(2) prohibits analogous reasoning that leads to the recognition of substantially new crimes, meaning crimes that cannot be accommodated by the wording of articles 6, 7, 8 and 8 *bis* of the Rome Statute.
2. Article 22(2) does not prohibit logical reasoning by analogy, which is used to bring the facts of a case within the scope of a treaty or unwritten criminal prohibition by reasoning that they are sufficiently similar to the facts of a case previously held to be covered by the relevant law.
3. Article 22(2) does not prohibit previous decisions of the Court from being followed where appropriate, through gradual reasoning by analogy so as to build consistency, certainty and predictability in the Court's interpretation of crimes.
4. Article 22(2) does not prohibit contextual reasoning inspired by provisions in the Rome Statute and Elements of Crimes or resort to applicable law to fill gaps in the Statute or Elements.

Accordingly, arguments consistent with the above guidelines and the aforementioned justifications underlying the principle of legality support legality's role as the guiding interpretive principle for crimes in the Rome Statute. Arguments that undermine the principle of legality include the following:

1. The notion of higher order principles of (substantive) justice being able to outweigh the principle of legality is no longer tenable in light of legality evolving into a non-derogable and internationally recognized human right and articles 21(3) and 22 of the Rome Statute treating it as such. To argue, therefore, that a criminal prohibition should be applied retroactively because it would be unjust not to punish an individual, should have no place in an interpretive methodology for the Court.
2. Any morality argument serving as a proxy for the existence of an applicable criminal prohibition should not be accepted. Morality is a 'sieve through which can flow not only humanity but also repression'.[8] It is also dubious to structure international criminal justice so that judges are primarily responsible for articulating the moral views of the international community.
3. Arguments about world order – the need to safeguard peace and security – risk politicizing the Court and undermining its effectiveness. All crimes in the Court's jurisdiction implicate peace and security, and it is therefore unreasonable to weigh these considerations against the robust conception of legality that drafters of the Rome Statute nevertheless chose to embed

---

[8] J Hall, 'Nulla Poena Sine Lege' (1937) 165 Yale LJ 165, 189.

in article 22. It is not the primary mandate of the Court to work to ensure collective peace and security.

4. Arguments that conflate illegality with criminality are tempting but ultimately provide no inherent guidance on which illegal acts will become criminal, a decision that is for States rather than judges to make and undermines all interests protected by the legality principle.

5. As for the practice of reclassifying offences, this argument depends very much on whether the principle of fair labelling is respected. Where an individual is charged with a crime under international law and a sufficiently similar crime existed under applicable national law when the conduct occurred, reclassifying the offence as an international crime does not seem to offend this principle or legality. The same is true where conduct is charged as one crime under international law and then charged as another under international law, all of these being comparably serious in nature. This might also be the case where an 'ordinary' national crime is reclassified as an international crime and the additional jurisdictional elements are not material to the guilt or innocence of the individual. In this situation, however, the argument should additionally address in a principled manner how this interpretation does not offend the separation of powers or strict construction doctrines associated with the legality principle.

6. It may be argued that the world of today is very different than that which existed in 1998 when the Rome Statute was drafted and that, to remain effective, the Court must recognize certain conduct that was unforeseen in 1998 as criminal under the Rome Statute. Again, this argument needs to be broken down a bit. The principle of legality is violated if this argument is admitted to modify the wording of the Rome Statute and to recognize a wholly new species of wrongdoing that is not expressly provided for in articles 6, 7, 8 or 8 *bis*. However, where the wording of a criminal prohibition in the Rome Statute can tolerate the meaning proposed, the principle of legality is not necessarily offended when that meaning is ascribed to the provision.

7. Teleological reasoning about the purpose of the Rome Statute being to end impunity or something to that effect is a dangerous argument to accept, as it could swallow the principle of legality whole. That said, consideration of the purpose of a criminal prohibition in the Rome Statute is not excluded by the legality principle, nor is a limited role for the principle of effectiveness.

8. Many concerns have been expressed about arguments of foreseeability, and article 22 is considered to prohibit their admission. The concept of retroactive application of criminal law consistent with the 'essence' of an existing offence also seems too loose a concept and is arguably disallowed by the prohibition against analogy in article 22(2). Finally, article 22(1) of the Statute makes it clear to the Court that legality limits its jurisdiction to crimes defined in the Rome Statute.

10.4 Article 31(2) and context

Article 31(2) of the *Vienna Convention* (1969) is not affected by the methodology developed in this study and provides as follows:

2. The context for the purpose of the interpretation of a treaty shall comprise, in addition to the text, including its preamble and annexes:

(a) any agreement relating to the treaty which was made between all the parties in connection with the conclusion of the treaty;
(b) any instrument which was made by one or more parties in connection with the conclusion of the treaty and accepted by the other parties as an instrument related to the treaty.

10.5 Article 31(3)(a), the Elements of Crimes and the interpretive Understandings

Article 31(3)(a) of the *Vienna Convention* (1969) *obliges* judges of the Court to take into account 'any subsequent agreement between the parties regarding the interpretation of the treaty or the application of its provisions'. The Elements of Crimes is such a subsequent agreement that 'shall assist the Court in the interpretation and application of articles 6, 7, 8 and 8 *bis*'.[9] Where a customary rule of international law is relevant, both it and the Elements must be taken into account. It is submitted that where articles 6, 7, 8 and 8 *bis* can accommodate the content of custom, but also the Elements and these two interpretive aids conflict, custom should prevail. One way to understand this dynamic is to recall that the Elements must be 'consistent' with articles 6, 7, 8 and 8 *bis* of the Rome Statute.[10] If these provisions were presumed to be consistent with custom (see below), a conflict between custom and the Elements would suggest that the Elements are somehow inconsistent with article 6, 7, 8 or 8 *bis*.

Most important and to be abundantly clear, the Elements should not lightly be ignored as they do contain evidence of the *opinio juris* of the international community and were intended to reflect existing customary international law in the Rome Statute.[11] They are therefore an obvious starting point for interpretive issues and expected to be a principal aid for understanding the definitions of crimes in the Rome Statute. Ultimately though, 'judges will have to reach their own understanding of the Statute'.[12] As well, because custom is notorious for being vague and lacking in detail, it will not very often be the case that a

---

[9] Article 9(1), Rome Statute.　　　[10] Article 9(3), Rome Statute.
[11] P Kirsch, 'Foreword' in K Dörmann, *Elements of War Crimes under the Rome Statute of the International Criminal Court* (Cambridge University Press 2003) xiii, xiii–xiv.
[12] H von Hebel, 'The Making of the Elements of Crimes' in R Lee and Others (eds.), *The International Criminal Court: Elements of Crimes and Rules of Procedure and Evidence* (Transnational 2001) 3, 8.

perfectly clear mental or material element is discerned in customary international law that conflicts with a provision in the Elements of Crimes.[13] As international criminal law continues to mature, it is hoped that this will change. In the meantime, it might be the case that the Elements fail to include an element for a crime in the Statute that exists under custom (thereby improperly broadening it), or impose a requirement that does not exist under custom (thereby improperly narrowing it).

In addition to the Elements, the seven interpretive Understandings on the crime of aggression that were adopted by the Review Conference in 2010 also form a subsequent agreement under article 31(3)(a) of the *Vienna Convention* (1969). They therefore must also be taken into consideration where relevant. As for any conflicts that may arise between the Understandings and the Elements of Crimes or General Assembly Resolution 3314 (XXIX) of 1974, it is submitted that the Elements should be favoured but that these Understandings should be favoured over the Resolution. With respect to the Elements, this instrument is more of an authoritative aid than the Understandings as it is listed as applicable law under article 21 of the Rome Statute. And, unlike the Resolution, it was drafted specifically to aid judges working in an international criminal law context. However, as between these Understandings and the Resolution, the former should be favoured because, in the author's view, they were intended in part to delimit the influence of the latter, to circumscribe the extent to which it is to be imported into the Rome regime.[14]

10.6 Article 31(3)(b) and subsequent practice

Article 31(3)(b) of the *Vienna Convention* (1969) *obliges* judges to take into account 'any subsequent practice in the application of the treaty which establishes the agreement of the parties regarding its interpretation'. Owing to the principle of legality and application of the rule of intertemporality to the Rome Statute, this practice cannot have occurred beyond the date on which the relevant crime was allegedly committed. As well, not all practice is meaningful – only practice involving the 'application of the treaty' and evidencing *agreement* of the Parties on the interpretation of a treaty term.[15] The subject matter of the treaty, here the Rome Statute, will influence the Court's understanding of subsequent practice, although it must in any case be practice that is 'systematic', 'repetitive' or 'concordant, common, and consistent' in terms of the Statute's

---

[13] W Lietzau, 'Checks and Balances and Elements of Proof: Structural Pillars for the International Criminal Court' (1999) 32 Cornell Int'l LJ 477, 482.

[14] Compare with the negotiated outcome the proposed understandings. '2012 Non-Paper of the United States' in S Barriga and C Kreß (eds.), *The Travaux Préparatoires of the Crime of Aggression* (Cambridge University Press 2012) 751–52.

[15] Y Dinstein, 'Interaction between Customary International Law and Treaties' (2006) 322 Recueil des Cours de l'Académie de Droit International 243, 408; Gardiner (n. 2) 226.

application.[16] This practice may be executive, legislative (including trends), judicial (e.g., speeches, laws, court decisions) or military, as confirmed by the practice of the ICTY, ICTR and International Criminal Court.[17] It can even be the adoption of a subsequent treaty that clarifies the meaning of a crime in the Rome Statute. Such a treaty, however, would also find a home in article 31(3)(c) (see below).

Subsequent practice is not custom, although the latter can establish the former. Unlike subsequent practice establishing agreement amongst parties to a treaty, custom can be universally binding and requires for its formation *opinio juris* in addition to State practice. Whereas subsequent practice requires agreement, custom does allow for a small number of persistent objections.[18] In addition, subsequent practice ought not to be confused with evolutive interpretation.[19] Whereas the intent for evolutive interpretation must be located in the treaty itself, the intent underlying subsequent practice can be discerned from material external to the Rome Statute. Further, evolutive interpretation does not require systematic, repetitive or concordant practice by States.[20] And, as opposed to evolutive interpretation, which can call for a treaty term to be expansively interpreted anew indefinitely, subsequent practice may expand or limit the interpretation of a treaty term in an individual case and would not necessarily require the term to be reinterpreted in future cases absent new practice.[21]

Judges are obliged to take subsequent practice by States Parties into account but remain free to reject the interpretation endorsed in this practice. However, it is wise to offer good reasons for this. To the extent that the wording of the Rome Statute cannot accommodate the interpretation contemplated, the practice might cross over into the impermissible terrain of modifying the Statute. The guiding interpretive principle of legality, the subject matter of articles 6, 7, 8 and 8 *bis* of the Statute and the amendment procedures set out in article 121 all point to subsequent practice for crimes in the Statute being limited to interpreting and not surreptitiously modifying, revising or amending these definitions. Further, given the integral (as opposed to reciprocal) nature of the obligations in the Rome Statute, if a subsequent practice limits the

---

[16] Gardiner, ibid. 226–28; I Sinclair, *The Vienna Convention on the Law of Treaties*, 2nd edn (Manchester University Press 1984) 137–38.

[17] G Nolte, 'Second Report for the ILC Study Group on Treaties over Time: Jurisprudence under Special Regimes relating to Subsequent Agreements and Subsequent Practice' in G Nolte (ed.), *Treaties and Subsequent Practice* (Oxford University Press 2013) 210, pt. IV, s. 2; Gardiner (n. 2) 228–30.

[18] M Villiger, *Customary International Law and Treaties* (Martinus Nijhoff 1985) 220.

[19] Gardiner (n. 2) 242 (citing App. No. 8562/79, *Feldbrugge* v. *Netherlands*, Joint Dissenting Opinion, ECHR (1986) Series A, No. 124 A, paras. 23–24). See Chapter 9, Section 9.3.4 on special meaning.

[20] Gardiner (n. 2) 243.

[21] On the distinction between evolutive interpretation and subsequent practice, see Chapter 9, Sections 9.3.4 and 9.3.5.

definition of a crime, consideration should be given to whether this offends the object and purpose of the impugned criminal provision and, if so, whether this practice should be permitted to affect its interpretation.

10.7 Article 31(3)(c) and relevant and applicable rules of international law

Article 31(3)(c) *obliges* judges to take into account 'any relevant rules of international law applicable in the relations between the parties'. In accordance with article 38 of the Statute of the International Court of Justice, sources of international law include custom, treaties and general principles of law; judicial decisions and teachings of highly qualified publicists aid in their ascertainment. With the exception of teachings of publicists, article 21 of the Rome Statute refers to all of these sources of applicable law. Nothing about the principle of legality itself bars judges from relying on custom, treaties and general principles of law as aids to interpreting crimes in the Rome Statute. However, except in the case of a possible *non liquet*, the rule of law interest underlying the principle of legality tends to discourage the use of vague general principles to definitively settle interpretive issues arising from a criminal prohibition.

Owing to the legality principle and application of the rule of intertemporality to the Rome Statute, the Court 'may only apply substantive criminal rules [and use interpretive aids] that existed at the time of commission of the alleged crime'.[22] Article 31(3)(c) of the *Vienna Convention* (1969) should therefore be invoked by judges in this manner. This approach injects a suitable degree of flexibility into the Statute, which governs the work of a permanent international criminal court. It also overcomes concerns that the Statute freezes the definitions of crimes and that this could lead to the Court's 'stagnation, if not decline'.[23] Those customary developments that can be accommodated by the words of the Rome Statute can inform their interpretation, and those that cannot continue to exist alongside it. Accordingly, although prior custom will aid in understanding the content of the Rome Statute, the subsequent practice of States and evolving *opinio juris* will contribute to that custom's development.[24] Where relevant and applicable to the interpretive exercise, this evolving custom can help to prevent the Rome Statute's definitions from falling into desuetude.

10.7.1 Custom

In light of the results of the codification study carried out in Chapters 7 and 8, judges should recognize a rebuttable presumption of interpretation

---

[22] A Cassese, *International Criminal Law*, 2nd edn (Oxford University Press 2008) 44.

[23] A Pellet, 'Applicable Law' in A Cassese and Others (eds.), *The Rome Statute of the International Criminal Court: A Commentary*, vol. II (Oxford University Press 2002) 1056, 1084.

[24] O Schachter, *International Law in Theory and Practice* (Martinus Nijhoff 1991) 71–72.

consistent with custom for crimes in the Rome Statute.[25] A legal presumption may not be defeated at a general level. Rather, its application to a particular case can be rebutted.[26]

Where the Rome Statute does mirror a customary legal term or a treaty term reflective of custom, this concurrence ought not to be mistaken for a hierarchy: 'All that transpires is that the authors of a given treaty deem fit to apply their text (in whole or in part) in a manner consistent with a normative matrix *dehors* the instrument.'[27] Such consistency can be said to exist only where a customary meaning can be reasonably accommodated by the actual words in the Rome Statute. The presumption of consistency with custom cannot be invoked to oust legality's concern with textual primacy and coherence. When ascertaining whether the presumption stands and under which circumstances one may conclude that it has been successfully rebutted in a particular case, consideration may be given to the following:

1. Whether the Rome Statute must exactly reproduce the relevant legal term in order for the presumption to apply. On the one hand, it is arguable that as long as the Rome Statute uses language that is suitable for referring to the relevant customary principle or concept, the presumption applies. When the Rome Statute does not reproduce exactly the relevant terminology, the Court must discern whether the words chosen by the drafters were meant to modify the relevant concept.

2. Whether the modification may be intended to significantly narrow or broaden in scope a concept – resulting in retrograde or progressive crimes or elements thereof. Indeed, it is legally permissible for States to revise or redefine customary legal concepts that are not *jus cogens* norms in whole or in part through treaties. Where drafters of the Rome Statute have drafted a change to custom or treaty law for purposes of their relations, it is important for the Court not to undermine this purpose by reintroducing the customary or treaty rule or principle through interpretation. It is impermissible to invoke the presumption to recognize new crimes in the Court's jurisdiction, especially those that were deliberately excluded from the Rome regime.[28]

3. The rule of *expressio unius exclusio alterius*, whether the impugned provision or other provisions in the Rome Statute suggest the exclusion of a crime or element under custom. The *expressio unius* rule of interpretation supports the view that 'with the express statement of a new rule in a text, the drafting body implicitly intended to exclude other, incompatible customary rules on the same subject-matter'.[29]

---

[25] It remains to be seen whether the amendments on aggression will be activated in 2017.
[26] Ibid. 7.   [27] Dinstein (n. 15) 392.   [28] Cassese (n. 22) 17.   [29] Villiger (n. 18) 161.

4. The 'step from unwritten custom to written codification is not a small one. The very act of generalizing, systematizing and removing inconsistences and gaps produces a text that is qualitatively different from unwritten law'.[30] Accordingly, thought might be given to whether the imperfect replication of custom was perhaps merely a function of transitioning from unwritten to written law or from varying and disparate sources of written law to one coherent text (e.g., crimes against humanity).

5. Where custom is particularly 'confused, rudimentary or otherwise unsatisfactory', the Court 'may infer that the legislation [Rome Statute] was intended to substitute a coherent legislative regime for the deficient customary law'.[31]

Thus, it becomes readily apparent that a determination of whether a crime in the Rome Statute is consistent with its customary counterpart is itself an exercise in interpretation and that it is difficult to distinguish an assessment of consistency, as a preliminary step, from subsequent interpretation.[32] The presumption of consistency with custom can play an important role in discouraging, where possible, the Court's reliance on arguments of object and purpose to develop the definitions of crimes in the Rome Statute beyond their customary parallels, thereby also discouraging judicial policymaking. Such a view contemplates a new relationship between custom and the fear of judicial activism, where the former is not seen as a gateway to the latter but rather a stop valve for it.

A crime in the Rome Statute, or element thereof, may at a moment in time not reflect custom but then later crystallize into custom. Accordingly, the presumption of consistency with custom may be rebutted in one case and then stand in a later case. As well, account needs to be taken of the distinct possibility that a crime under customary international law that is included in the Court's jurisdiction, once identical, will continue to develop through the *opinio juris* and practice of States, perhaps resulting in its counterpart in the Rome regime being superseded at the customary level.[33] Again, because the rule of intertemporality calls for crimes in the Rome Statute to be interpreted in light of custom as it exists when a crime is alleged to have been committed, the presumption of consistency with custom can help to prevent

---

[30] Schachter (n. 24) 70.

[31] R Sullivan, *Sullivan and Driedger on the Construction of Statutes*, 4th edn (Butterworths 2002) 353 makes this point concerning the relationship between legislation and the common law.

[32] M Koskenniemi, 'Fragmentation of International Law: Difficulties Arising from the Diversification and Expansion of International Law: Report of the Study Group of the International Law Commission' (4 April 2006), UN Doc. A/CN.4/L.682, 174.

[33] P Weil, 'Towards Relative Normativity in International Law?' (1983) 77 AJIL 413, 438; O Schachter, 'Entangled Treaty and Custom' in Y Dinstein (ed.), *International Law at a Time of Perplexity: Essays in Honour of Shabtai Rosenne* (Martinus Nijhoff 1989) 720.

this from happening and guard against the desuetude of the crimes in the Rome Statute. It also helps preserve the ability of the Court to receive a case through a UN Security Council situation referral or article 12(3) declaration where the relevant (Non-)State Party did not consent to the Court's jurisdiction prior to the alleged criminal conduct occurring.

10.7.2 Treaty law

In terms of treaties aiding the interpretion of crimes in the Rome Statute, consideration should be given to the following:

> [Article 31(3)(c)] requires the interpreter to consider other treaty-based rules so as to arrive at a consistent meaning. Such other rules are of particular relevance where parties to the treaty under interpretation are also parties to the other treaty, where the treaty rule has passed into or expresses customary international law or where they provide evidence of the common understanding of the parties as to the object and purpose of the treaty under interpretation or as to the meaning of a particular term.[34]

Given the different normativities of international criminal law, international human rights and humanitarian law, it should be borne in mind that while two treaties may contain identical or similar provisions, they may be interpreted differently if they are situated in regimes that have different objects and purposes, if there are important contextual differences, if subsequent agreements or practice by Parties to one or both of the treaties varies in content or the relevant *travaux préparatoires* contemplate different meanings.[35]

As for the relationship between treaty law that is not reflective of custom and the Elements of Crimes in cases of conflict, a couple of observations are in order. First, where the parent treaty norm actually criminalizes the conduct that is also criminalized in the Rome Statute, it may be presumed (unless proven otherwise) that drafters of the Rome Statute intended for these definitions to be consistent with one another, meaning conflicting elements in the Elements of Crimes should give way to the treaty aid. However, where the treaty inspiring the definition of a crime in the Rome Statute does not itself criminalize the relevant conduct – perhaps it just prohibits it – the Elements of Crimes should be presumed (unless proven otherwise) to be more faithful to the Rome Statute definition than the relevant treaty. This is because drafters of the Elements were likely cognisant of the need to articulate elements for a crime derived from a treaty that does not define the conduct as criminal.

---

[34] Gardiner (n. 2) 275 (citing ILC, 'Report of the International Law Commission on the Work of its Fifty-Eighth Session' (2006), UN Doc. A/61/10, 414–5, para. 21).

[35] Ibid., Gardiner 284 (citing *The MOX Plant Case (Ireland v. United Kingdom)* [2001] ITLOS, para. 51, available at http://www.itlos.org, accessed 15 February 2011).

10.7.3 General principles

Two presumptions relevant to this source of law, one positive and one negative, operate at the international level: (1) parties are taken 'to refer to general principles of international law for all questions which [the treaty] does not itself resolve in express terms or in a different way';[36] and (2) States Parties to a treaty 'intend something not inconsistent with generally recognised principles of international law'.[37] Apart from the general principles of criminal law found in part III of the Rome Statute, general principles do not really compete with the interpretive aids of treaty and custom, coming into play more to avoid a possible *non liquet*.

In addition to general principles of international law, article 21(1)(c) of the Rome Statute recognizes 'general principles of law derived by the Court from national laws of legal systems of the world including, as appropriate, the national laws of States that would normally exercise jurisdiction over the crime, provided that those principles are not inconsistent with this Statute and with international law and internationally recognized norms and standards'. Accordingly, both general principles of international law and general principles of law are authoritative interpretive aids, meaning their consideration is mandatory if relevant. However, care must be taken not to mechanically invoke these aids when interpreting the definition of an international crime.

10.7.4 Judicial decisions and teachings of publicists

Judicial decisions and teachings of publicists are not sources of international law per se, but rather *permissible* aids to identifying its content, meaning the content of custom, treaty law (e.g., crimes in the Rome Statute) and general principles. Article 21 of the Rome Statute confirms that judicial decisions include national decisions and the Court's own decisions.[38] Teachings of publicists may include not only journal articles and books but also commentaries to relevant treaties and interpretive aids prepared by expert bodies such as the International Law Commission and International Committee of the Red Cross. As useful as this expert commentary may be, interests underlying the principle of legality suggest that care should be taken not to rely solely on the teachings of one publicist in support of an innovative interpretation that is contraindicated by other interpretive aids.

---

[36] Koskenniemi (n. 32) 234.
[37] R Jennings and A Watts, *Oppenheim's International Law*, 9th edn (Longman, Harlow 1992) 1275; J Pauwelyn, *Conflict of Norms in Public International Law: How WTO Law Relates to Other Rules of International Law* (Cambridge University Press 2003) 240–44; Koskenniemi (n. 32) 21.
[38] Articles 21(1)(c) and 21(2), Rome Statute.

It is important to recall that, unlike the common-law tradition, international criminal law does not adhere to a doctrine of binding precedents.[39] However, jurisprudential consistency does promote the rule of law, which underlies the principle of legality. Given the wealth of ICTY case law, the interpretive presumption of consistency with custom that ICTY judges purport to apply and the large number of lawyers and judges at the Court who have prior experience working at the ICTY, it is expected that the jurisprudence of this ad hoc tribunal will serve as an attractive aid to interpreting crimes in the Rome Statute.

However, it must be recalled that international case law is not a source of custom and that judges of the ICTY, like judges of the Court, attempt to discern its existence, scope and content. These judicial pronouncements on the content of a customary rule or absence thereof may be accurate when they are made but may be disproven by the subsequent development of custom.[40] Accordingly, the Court has rightly expressed caution about automatically invoking the jurisprudence of the ICTY.[41] The same caution should be exercised in respect of national case law when examining it for the content of custom, a criminal prohibition in the Rome Statute or a general principle of law. More generally, findings reached by judicial bodies that carried out their interpretive work in a context that is altogether different from that of the Court need to be carefully scrutinized for their relevance.

10.7.5 Internationally recognized human rights

Where a provision in the Rome Statute conflicts with a *jus cogens* norm, it thereby becomes inapplicable or void.[42] Additionally, article 21(3) of the Rome Statute calls for the interpretation of crimes therein to be consistent with internationally recognized human rights. The obligation in article 21(3) is a background rule of international law that is both 'relevant and applicable' to the interpretation of these crimes pursuant to article 31(3)(c) of the *Vienna Convention* (1969). The imperative in article 21(3) gives the person being investigated, prosecuted or convicted the right to challenge interpretations

---

[39] Cassese (n. 22) 18.

[40] Institut de Droit International, 'Problems Arising from a Succession of Codification Conventions on a Particular Subject' (Lisbon Session 1995) 66-I Annuaire de l'Institut de Droit International 39, conclusion 14.

[41] See, e.g., *Prosecutor* v. *Kony and Others*, Decision on the Prosecutor's Position on the Decision of Pre-Trial Chamber II to Redact Factual Descriptions of Crimes in the Warrants of Arrest, Motion for Reconsideration, and Motion for Clarification, ICC-02/04–01/05–60, 28 October 2005, para. 19, cited in G Bitti, 'Article 21 of the Statute of the ICC and the Treatment of Sources of Law in the Jurisprudence of the ICC' in C Stahn and G Sluiter (eds.), *The Emerging Practice of the International Criminal Court* (Martinus Nijhoff 2009) 281, 297.

[42] Article 53, *Vienna Convention* (1969); Jennings and Watts (n. 37) 1282.

and applications of crimes in the Rome Statute that conflict with his or her internationally recognized human rights.

For example, were the Court to interpret the crime of directly and publicly inciting others to commit genocide to include hate speech, the suspect or accused could perhaps rely on article 21(3) to argue that the Court's interpretation conflicts with his or her right to freedom of expression, assuming that this right is protected under customary international law, a treaty ratified by the relevant State or a general principle of law and that the hate speech had not been criminalized under international law.[43] Here, international human rights norms would be invoked in a manner consistent with the principle of legality, as there would be no concerns about retroactive application of the law. As well, if States Parties were to add to the Court's jurisdiction a panoply of terrorism-related offences that violated the suspect's or accused's right to liberty or freedom of association, again assuming these were protected by custom, an applicable treaty or general principle, article 21(3) could be invoked to argue that the Court cannot apply these provisions to the extent that they are inconsistent with internationally recognized human rights.

The role contemplated for article 21(3) would roughly resemble that which constitutional rights and freedoms or human rights play in domestic criminal justice systems by virtue of their character as background individual rights, their status as relevant and applicable norms, and the presumption that the 'legislature' would not enact laws that are inconsistent with these norms.[44] It is

---

[43] Article 19(3), *ICCPR* (1966) provides: 'The exercise of the rights provided for in paragraph 2 of this article [which includes freedom of expression] carries with it special duties and responsibilities. It may therefore be subject to certain restrictions, but these shall only be such as are *provided by law* and are necessary: (a) For respect of the rights or reputations of others; (b) For the protection of national security or of public order (ordre public), or of public health or morals' (emphasis added). On this point, it is interesting to note that the *travaux préparatoires* for the *Genocide Convention* (1948) reveal a clear intent to exclude hate speech from the definition of this crime and that the ICTR Appeals Chamber stopped short of holding that there is no norm under customary international law criminalizing hate speech. *Nahimana and Others* v. *Prosecutor*, Judgment, ICTR-99–52-A, 28 November 2007, paras. 692ff., 985; D Orentlicher, 'Criminalizing Hate Speech in the Crucible of Trial: Prosecutor v. Nahimana' (2005) 12 New England J Int'l & Comp L 17. See also A Cassese, 'The Influence of the European Court of Human Rights on International Criminal Tribunals – Some Methodological Remarks' in M Bergsmo (ed.), *Human Rights and Criminal Justice for the Downtrodden: Essays in Honour of Asbjørn Eide* (Martinus Nijhoff 2003) 157.

[44] A Ashworth, B Emmerson and A Macdonald, *Human Rights and Criminal Justice*, 2nd edn (Sweet & Maxwell 2007); R Clayton and H Tomlinson, *The Law of Human Rights*, vol. I, 2nd edn (Oxford University Press 2009) ss. 4.05–4.20. For example, it is not dissimilar to the role of fundamental human rights guarantees in the interpretation and application of criminal law in England. The *Human Rights Act* (1998) (HRA) incorporates the *EHCR* into domestic law. Article 3 of the HRA requires judges to 'interpret statutory provisions, so far as is possible, in such a way as is compatible with Convention rights', something

therefore fundamental. As for the requirement that the right be internationally recognized, this may well exclude sole reliance on one regional human rights treaty or soft law for the purpose of interpreting crimes in the Rome Statute.

The presumption that articles 6, 7, 8 and 8 *bis* are interpreted and applied in a manner that does not offend the international human rights of the individual investigated, prosecuted or convicted and does not adversely distinguish on prohibited grounds would place the evidentiary burden on the person claiming otherwise. As in domestic criminal justice systems, it is expected that this issue is likely to arise in respect of the 'outer edges' of crimes defined in the Rome Statute, whether they implicate protected freedoms or not.[45] These will be the hard cases.

With legality as a guiding interpretive principle for crimes in the Rome Statute, the interpretive principles prevalent in international human rights jurisprudence (e.g., effective, dynamic and progressive interpretation) would lose much of their currency or could not convincingly be advanced solely by relying on the wording of article 21(3), an argument that implicitly asks one to ignore the wording of article 22(2). The role proposed for article 21(3) should also not be understood as empowering judges to frustrate the intent of the Rome Statute's drafters or amenders to impose legally permissible limits on international human rights within it. Lastly, article 21 of the Rome Statute does not appear to address or resolve the issue of which background legal regime – international human rights or international humanitarian law – should be favoured when both appear to be relevant and applicable to an interpretive issue. It is submitted that article 21(3) was not necessarily intended to create a permanent hierarchy between these background regimes and that judges can enhance the rule of law by stating in their decisions the criteria they considered when determining this issue in a particular case.

10.8 Article 31(4) and terms with special meanings

Article 31(4) forms part of the general rule of interpretation in the *Vienna Convention* (1969) and *obliges* judges of the Rome Statute to assign a 'special meaning . . . to a term if it is established that the parties so intended'. Words with special meanings can be divided into two groups: words that have a unique meaning in 'a particular area of human endeavour' and words that have been assigned a special meaning by an individual who uses the term in a manner different than its common understanding.[46] Whereas the intent of States Parties

---

that domestic judges in other jurisdictions have also had to do against the backdrop of their constitutions or bills of rights. Such mandates pose unique challenges in the realm of criminal law where judges take seriously respect for the principle of legality.

[45] Jeffries Jr (n. 3) 196.   [46] Gardiner (n. 2) 291.

regarding the first group can be discerned from the context in which the term is used – here is where expert commentaries may prove to be especially helpful – the second group's special meaning must be indicated by the individual assigning it a meaning that departs from its common use.[47]

This provision speaks more to the second category of words with special meanings, although it may be read to encompass the first group as well, which is also covered by the reference to context in article 31(1) of the *Vienna Convention* (1969).[48] The main purpose of article 31(4) is to clarify that the party claiming a special meaning has the burden of proof.[49] This proof of intention, not surprisingly, can be demonstrated using the rules of interpretation in article 31 of the *Vienna Convention* (1969), meaning emphasis is placed on treaty text rather than supplementary means of interpretation in article 32.[50] When evidence of a special meaning is not discernible in the text of a treaty, reliance should be placed on authoritative interpretive aids that express the intent of the States Parties.[51]

One example of special meaning in the definitions of crimes in the Rome Statute can be found in article 8 *bis*(2), which defines the State act of aggression. This provision contains a list of acts amounting to aggression that replicates the list contained in article 3 of General Assembly Resolution 3314 (XXIX) of 1974.[52] Article 8 *bis*(2) provides: '[a]ny of the following acts, regardless of a declaration of war, shall, in accordance with United Nations General Assembly resolution 3314 (XXIX) of 14 December 1974, qualify as an act of aggression . . .' The words 'in accordance with' arguably suggest that a special meaning was intended.

Although General Assembly resolutions are not a source of international law according to article 38 of the Statute of the International Court of Justice, such resolutions may provide evidence of the *opinio juris* of the international community.[53] However, the *opinio juris* of the international community is not frozen and should be considered as it exists at the time that the alleged conduct in question occurred.

While General Assembly Resolution 3314 (XXIX) may contain special meanings of terms that could aid in the interpretation of article 8 *bis*(2), it may come to pass that these special meanings conflict with customary international law or the Elements of Crimes instrument, the latter two themselves

---

[47] Ibid.   [48] Ibid.   [49] Ibid. 292, 295.
[50] H Waldock, 'Sixth Report on the Law of Treaties' (1966) II Ybk of the ILC 51, 94; Gardiner (n. 2) 294.
[51] Gardiner, ibid. 296–97.
[52] UNGA, 'Definition of Aggression' (1974), UN Doc. Res. 3314 (XXIX).
[53] MD Öberg, 'The Legal Effects of Resolutions of the Security Council and General Assembly in the Jurisprudence of the ICJ' (2006) 16 EJIL 879, 898–900.

authoritative[54] interpretive aids that must be considered (but may be rejected) under articles 31(3)(c) and (a) of the *Vienna Convention* (1969) respectively. What if custom or the Elements instrument is invoked, however, under article 31(4) of the *Vienna Convention* (1969) as evidence of a special meaning, and, as between them and General Assembly Resolution 3314 (XXIX), it is not clear which aid was intended to conclusively settle the meaning to be given to a term in article 8 *bis* of the Rome Statute?

It is submitted that as between this Resolution and custom, the latter should prevail, and as between it and the Elements instrument, again the latter should prevail. In the author's view, where a reasonable doubt exists about the intent of States Parties, the meaning of a term under customary international law should be favoured over a meaning derived for the same term from General Assembly Resolution 3314 (XXIX). While this Resolution is an important expression of the *opinio juris* of the international community, custom consists of both *opinio juris* and State practice, thereby offering a stronger expression of intent. As for favouring the Elements instrument over this Resolution, it is submitted that this should be done because, unlike the latter, the former was drafted specifically for the Rome Statute, an international criminal law statute. It also contains a more recent expression of the *opinio juris* of the international community on the crime of aggression than anything that might be expressly or implicitly conveyed in General Assembly Resolution 3314 (XXIX).

Further, certain words in the Rome Statute are inherently normative, inviting judges to make moral judgments. It is arguably fair to assume that, here, drafters of the Rome Statute intended for judges to make these normative judgments in light of the values of the day when the crime was alleged to have been committed. Examples of words with possible special meanings that may evolve in the Rome Statute include 'comparable gravity', 'similar character' and 'severe pain or suffering'.[55] Evolutive interpretation under article 31(4) is distinct from subsequent practice under article 31(3)(b) and may lead to conflicting interpretations.

10.9 Article 32 and preparatory work

Article 32 of the *Vienna Convention* (1969) on the use of preparatory work and other supplementary means of interpretation is *discretionary*. Affecting the use of preparatory work, however, will be its incompleteness. Fortunately, some

---

[54] The reference in article 21(1)(b) of the Rome Statute to 'principles and rules of international law' means customary international law. A Pellet, 'Applicable Law' in A Cassese and Others (eds.), *The Rome Statute of the International Criminal Court: A Commentary*, vol. II (Oxford University Press 2002) 1051, 1070–71.

[55] Articles 7(1)(g), (1)(k) and (2)(e), Rome Statute.

official records do exist,[56] and they are complemented by many commentaries on the drafting history of the Rome Statute and Elements of Crimes written by experts who attended the negotiations. As well, the work of the ASP Special Working Group on the Crime of Aggression (and Working Group on the Crime of Aggression at the Review Conference) is carefully summarized in official reports that were adopted at the conclusion of each meeting and that are in the public domain.[57]

Courts typically use such work in more ways than are contemplated in article 32:

> Recourse may be had to supplementary means of interpretation, including the preparatory work of the treaty and the circumstances of its conclusion, in order to confirm the meaning resulting from the application of article 31, or to determine the meaning when the interpretation according to article 31:
>
> (a) leaves the meaning ambiguous or obscure; or
> (b) leads to a result which is manifestly absurd or unreasonable.

Beyond relying on it to confirm or determine the meaning of a treaty provision, preparatory work might be mentioned in a judgment as part of a description of the historical development of a legal concept or treaty provision[58] or to reinforce or underscore that the preferred interpretation is consistent with the intention of the Parties.[59] Used in these ways, the requirements in article 32 do not need to be satisfied.[60] The Court might also incidentally cite commentaries on the drafting of the Rome Statute and the analysis contained therein.[61] Although judges cannot prevent parties from arguing that certain material constitutes supplementary means, they are free to reject these claims, with reasons, and not consider this material.[62] As for article 32(a), its invocation is not triggered by just any textual ambiguity; it must arise from the existence of more than one reasonably possible and probable meaning.[63] Similarly, in article 32(b) – which speaks to an interpretive result rather than meaning – the reference to

---

[56] See, e.g., the Legal Tools Project on the website of the International Criminal Court, www. legal-tools.org/en/what-are-the-icc-legal-tools/, accessed 1 May 2014.

[57] S Barriga, W Danspeckgruber and C Wenaweser (eds.), *The Princeton Process on the Crime of Aggression: Materials of the Special Working Group on the Crime of Aggression, 2003– 2009* (Liechtenstein Institute on Self-Determination 2009). An updated compilation of the *travaux préparatoires* for the crime of aggression was recently published. S Barriga and C Kreß (eds.), *Travaux Préparatoires of the Crime of Aggression* (Cambridge University Press 2011).

[58] Gardiner (n. 2) 316.   [59] Ibid. 324–28.   [60] Ibid. 316.   [61] Ibid.   [62] Ibid.

[63] GG Fitzmaurice, 'The Law and Procedure of the International Court of Justice 1951– 1954: Treaty Interpretation and Other Treaty Points' (1957) 33 British Ybk Int'l L 203, 216.

manifest means that the absurdity or unreasonableness of the outcome should be 'objectively evident to any State'.[64]

There is also the matter of what weight is to be given to supplementary means, especially preparatory work, as an aid to interpreting crimes in the Rome Statute and their relationship to other interpretive aids. At the very least it can be said that the guiding interpretive principle of legality bars supplementary means from modifying the definitions of crimes in the Statute and the use of article 32(b) as a back door for admitting arguments that fundamentally undermine legality's primacy. As well, given the outcome of applying the intertemporal rule to the Rome Statute, it would appear that where older supplementary means, such as preparatory work, conflict with an equally relevant aid existing at the time the crime was allegedly committed, such as custom, the contemporary aid should perhaps prevail. As for the weight to be given to preparatory works for a treaty whose terms have been transplanted into the Rome regime, careful consideration should be given to the context, object and purpose of both treaty regimes and the provisions in question.

Finally, recall that the imperative in article 22(2) of the Rome Statute to favour the person investigated, prosecuted or convicted in case of ambiguity requires the following: if an interpretive finding depends solely on a provision's drafting history and is not supported by any other acceptable interpretive principle, argument or aid, then the ambiguity should be resolved in favour of the accused, as States Parties have not met their burden to define the crime in the Rome Statute in sufficiently clear terms.[65]

10.10 Article 33 and differences in authenticated texts

Article 128 of the Rome Statute states that it is authenticated in Arabic, Chinese, English, French, Russian and Spanish and that these texts are equally authentic. Articles 33(3) and (4) of the *Vienna Convention* (1969) provide:

3. The terms of the treaty are presumed to have the same meaning in each authentic text.
4. Except where a particular text prevails in accordance with paragraph 1, when a comparison of the authentic texts discloses a difference of meaning which the application of articles 31 and 32 does not remove, the meaning which best reconciles the texts, having regard to the object and purpose of the treaty, shall be adopted.

---

[64] Article 46(2), *Vienna Convention* (1969).

[65] D Akande, 'The Sources of International Criminal Law' in A Cassese (ed.), *The Oxford Companion to International Criminal Justice* (Oxford University Press 2009) 41, 45; D Jacobs, 'Positivism and International Criminal Law: The Principle of Legality as a Rule of Conflict of Theories' in J d'Aspremont and J Kammerhofer (eds.), *International Legal Positivism in a Post-Modern World* (Cambridge University Press, forthcoming October 2014), 1, 32–3, http://papers.ssrn.com/sol3/papers.cfm?abstract_id=2046311, accessed 16 October 2013.

While the official languages of the Court are English and French, it is important that this rule for multilingual treaties is respected. Ultimately, judges will have to assign meanings to treaty terms that are consistent with all of these versions, even if these are not favourable to the accused. Legality favours textual primacy and coherence, which enhances the rule of law and thereby benefits all persons who may appear before the Court.

10.11 Conclusions

It is hoped that the mandatory guidelines developed in this study offer some assistance[66] to those grappling with the following sources of interpretive problems, which were introduced in the first Chapter: (1) linguistic; (2) background principles; (3) internal structure; (4) inadequate design; (5) value conflicts; (6) methodology; (7) special features of the case; (8) inherent indefiniteness; (9) the Elements of Crimes; (10) inter-treaty relationships; (11) the relationship between a constitutive statute or treaty and customary international law; and (12) subsequent agreements, practice and law. As discussed in Chapter 2, Section 2.4.2, drafting errors are to be corrected by States Parties. These guidelines are meant to create a common umbrella under which principled decisions can be made and reasonable disagreement expressed. In the future, it might be worthwhile to test the functionality of the method of interpretation developed in this study on a representative sample of the jurisprudence emerging from the Court. Such an exercise would help to unearth its shortcomings and rectify them.

Implicit in the effort underlying this study is a measure of optimism that international criminal law is entering its adolescence and can thus start developing certain 'secondary law' attributes[67] that will help ease its transition into a mature and increasingly respected field of international law. This field's contours and content, though difficult to perceive at its birth, have become more visible in the definitions of crimes in the Rome Statute.

> First he would find it easiest to look at shadows, next at the reflections of men and other objects in water, and later on at the objects themselves. After that he would find it easier to observe the heavenly bodies and the sky itself at night, and to look at the light of the moon and stars, rather than at the sun and its light by day. The thing he would be able to do last would be to look directly at the sun itself, and gaze at it without using reflections in water or any other medium, but as it is in itself.
>
> Plato[68]

---

[66] This study has not sought to promote 'excessive formalism': I Van Damme, 'Treaty Interpretation by the WTO Appellate Body' (2010) 21:3 EJIL 605, 641–42; J Tobin, 'Seeking to Persuade: A Constructive Approach to Human Rights Treaty Interpretation' (2010) 23 Harvard HR J 1.

[67] HLA Hart, *The Concept of Law* (Oxford University Press 1961).

[68] Plato, *The Republic*, 2nd edn (Penguin Books 1987) 319.

Going forward, the most ardent supporters of international criminal law will likely continue to closely monitor how judges look at and interpret these crimes, hoping that this complex and challenging work contributes to the ultimate success of the Court. For other reasons, detractors may do the same.

BIBLIOGRAPHY

Ad Hoc Committee, 'Report of the Ad Hoc Committee on the Establishment of an International Criminal Court' 1995 UN Doc. A/50/22.

Ajevski, P, 'Interpretation and the Constraints on International Courts', www.jus.uio.no/pluricourts/english/projects/multirights/docs/p-ajevski-intepretation-constraints.pdf, accessed 20 October 2013.

Akande, D, 'The Sources of International Criminal Law' in A Cassese (ed.), *The Oxford Companion to International Criminal Justice* (Oxford University Press 2009) 41.

'The Jurisdiction of the International Criminal Court over Nationals of Non-Parties: Legal Basis and Limits' (2003) 1 J Int'l Crim Justice 618.

Akehurst, M, 'The Hierarchy of the Sources of International Law' (1974–1975) 47 British Ybk Int'l L 273.

Akhavan, P, 'Reconciling Crimes against Humanity with the Laws of War: Human Rights, Armed Conflict, and the Limits of Progressive Jurisprudence' (2008) 6:1 J Int'l Crim Justice 21.

Alldridge, P, 'Rules for Courts and Rules for Citizens' (1990) 10:4 Oxford J Legal Stud 487.

Allott, P, 'The Concept of International Law' (1999) 10 EJIL 31.

Ambos, K, 'Defences in International Criminal Law' in BS Brown (ed.), *Research Handbook on International Criminal Law* (Elgar 2011) 299.

'Nulla Poena Sine Lege in International Criminal Law' in R Haveman and O Olusanya (eds.), *Sentencing and Sanctioning in Supranational Criminal Law* (Intersentia 2006) 17.

'Some Preliminary Reflections on the Mens Rea Requirements of the Crimes in the ICC Statute and the Elements of Crimes' in LC Vohrah and Others (eds.), *Man's Inhumanity to Man: Essays on International Law in Honour of Antonio Cassese* (Kluwer Law International 2003) 11.

Amnesty International, *International Criminal Court: Rome Statute Implementation Report Card, Part One* (1 May 2010) Index No. IOR 53/011/2010.

International Criminal Court: The Failure of States to Enact Effective Implementing Legislation (30 August 2004) Index No. IOR 40/019/2004.

Arato, J, 'Accounting for Difference in Treaty Interpretation over Time', Draft Paper prepared for the Cambridge Conference on Interpretation in International

Law, Lauterpacht Centre for International Law (27 August 2013) (on file with author).

'Subsequent Practice and Evolutive Interpretation: Techniques of Treaty Interpretation over Time and their Diverse Consequences' (2010) 9:3 The Law & Practice of Int'l Courts and Trib 443.

Arnold, R and Others, 'Article 8' in O Triffterer (ed.), *Commentary on the Rome Statute of the International Criminal Court*, 2nd edn (CH Beck/Hart/Nomos 2008) 275.

Arsanjani, MH, 'The Rome Statute of the International Criminal Court' (1999) 93 AJIL 22.

Ashworth, A, *Principles of Criminal Law*, 4th edn (Oxford University Press 2003).

Ashworth, A, 'Interpreting Criminal Statutes: a Crisis of Legality?' (1991) 107 LQR 419.

Ashworth, A, Emmerson, B, and Macdonald, A, *Human Rights and Criminal Justice*, 2nd edn (Sweet & Maxwell 2007).

Ashworth, A, and Horder, J, *Principles of Criminal Law*, 7th edn (Oxford University Press 2013).

Atiyah, PS, 'Common Law and Statute Law' (1985) 48 Modern L Rev 1.

Aust, A, *Modern Treaty Law and Practice* (Cambridge University Press 2000).

Badar, ME, 'The Mental Element in the Rome Statute of the International Criminal Court: A Commentary from a Comparative Perspective' (2008) 19 Crim L Forum 473.

Bankowski, Z, MacCormick, DN, Summers, RS, and Wróblewski, J, 'On Method and Methodology' in DN MacCormick and RS Summers (eds.), *Interpreting Statutes: A Comparative Study* (Ashgate 1991) 9.

Baragwanath, D, 'The Interpretative Challenges of International Adjudication across the Common Law/Civil Law Divide', Paper presented at the Cambridge Conference on Interpretation in International Law, Lauterpacht Centre for International Law (27 August 2013) (on file with author).

Barriga, S, Danspeckgruber, W, and Wenaweser, C (eds.), *The Princeton Process on the Crime of Aggression: Materials of the Special Working Group on the Crime of Aggression, 2003–2009* (Princeton University: Liechtenstein Institute on Self-Determination 2009).

Barriga, S, and Grover, L, 'A Historic Breakthrough on the Crime of Aggression' (2011) 105 AJIL 517.

Barriga, S, and Kreß, C (eds.), *Travaux Préparatoires of the Crime of Aggression* (Cambridge University Press 2012).

Bassiouni, MC, 'Principles of Legality in International and Comparative Law' in MC Bassiouni (ed.), *International Criminal Law: Sources, Subjects and Contents*, vol. I, 3rd edn (Martinus Nijhoff 2008) 83.

'Principles of Legality in International and Comparative Criminal Law' in MC Bassiouni (ed.), *International Criminal Law: Sources, Subjects and Contents*, vol. II, 3rd edn (Martinus Nijhoff 2008) 73.

The Legislative History of the International Criminal Court: Introduction, Analysis, and Integrated Text (Transnational Publishers 2005).

The Legitimacy of the International Criminal Court, vol. I (Transnational Publishers 2005).

'The Philosophy and Policy of International Criminal Justice' in LC Vohrah and Others (eds.), *Man's Inhumanity to Man: Essays on International Law in Honour of Antonio Cassese* (Kluwer Law International 2003) 65.

Baxter, R, 'Treaties and Custom' (1970–I) 129 Recueil des Cours de l'Académie de Droit International 31.

Baxter, RR, 'The Effects of Ill-Conceived Codification and Development of International Law' in *Recueil d'études de droit international en hommage à Paul Guggenheim* (Geneva 1968) 146.

'Multilateral Treaties as Evidence of Customary International Law' (1965–1966) 41 British Ybk Int'l L 275.

Beccaria, C, *Dei delitti e delle pene* (Livorno 1764).

Beckett, E, 'Comments on the Report of Sir Hersch Lauterpacht' (1950) 43(I) Annuaire de l'Institut de Droit International 435.

Benatar, M, 'From Probative Value to Authentic Interpretation: The Legal Effects of Interpretative Declarations' (2011) 44 Revue Belge de Droit International 170.

Bentham, J, 'Principles of International Law' in *The Works of Jeremy Bentham*, vol. II (published under the superintendence of his executor J Bowring [W Tait 1838–1843]) 535.

Bernhardt, R, 'Evolutive Treaty Interpretation, Especially of the European Convention on Human Rights' (1999) 42 German Ybk Int'l L 11.

Bianchi, A, 'Textual Interpretation and (International) Law Reading: The Myth of (In)determinacy and the Genealogy of Meaning' in *Making Transnational Law Work in the Global Economy: Essays in Honour of Detlev Vagts* (Cambridge University Press 2010) 34.

Bitti, G, 'Article 21 of the Statute of the International Criminal Court and the Treatment of Sources of Law in the Jurisprudence of the ICC' in C Stahn and G Sluiter (eds.), *The Emerging Practice of the International Criminal Court* (Brill 2009) 281.

Bjorge, E, *The Evolutionary Interpretation of Treaties* (Oxford University Press 2014).

Blackstone, W, *Commentaries on the Laws of England*, vols. 1–4 (Clarendon Oxford 1765–1769).

Boas, G, 'An Overview of Implementation by Australia of the Statute of the International Criminal Court' (2004) 2 J Int'l Crim Justice 179.

Boister, N, 'The Exclusion of Treaty Crimes from the Jurisdiction for the Proposed International Criminal Court: Law, Pragmatism, Politics' (1998) 3 J Conflict & Security Law 27.

Bolton, JR, Former Under Secretary for Arms Control and International Security, 'The United States and the International Criminal Court', Remarks to the

Federalist Society in Washington, DC, 2002, www.iccnow.org/documents/ USBoltonFedSociety14Nov02.pdf, accessed 2 November 2013.

Boot, M, *Genocide, Crimes Against Humanity, War Crimes: Nullum Crimen Sine Lege and the Subject Matter Jurisdiction of the International Criminal Court* (Intersentia 2002).

Boot, M, Dixon, R, and Hall, H (revised by C Hall), 'Article 7' in O Triffterer (ed.), *Commentary on the Rome Statute of the International Criminal Court*, 2nd edn (CH Beck/Hart/Nomos 2008) 159.

Bos, A, 'From the International Law Commission to the Rome Conference (1994–1999)' in A Cassese and Others (eds.), *The Rome Statute of the International Criminal Court: A Commentary*, vol. I (Oxford University Press 2002) 35.

 'The International Criminal Court: A Perspective' in RS Lee and Others (eds.), *The International Criminal Court: The Making of the Rome Statute* (Kluwer Law International 1999) 463.

Bos, M, 'Theory and Practice of Treaty Interpretation', (1980) 27 Netherlands Int'l L Rev 3, 135.

Bourgon, S, 'Jurisdiction Ratione Temporis' in A Cassese and Others (eds.), *The Rome Statute of the International Criminal Court: A Commentary*, vol. I (Oxford University Press 2002) 545.

Bowring, B, 'Fragmentation, Lex Specialis and the Tensions in the Jurisprudence of the European Court of Human Rights' (2009) 14 J Conflict & Security L 485.

Brierly, JL, 'The Codification of International Law' in H Lauterpacht and CHM Waldock (eds.), *The Basis of Obligation in International Law and Other Papers by the Late James Leslie Brierly* (Clarendon Press 1958) 338.

 'The Future of Codification' (1921) 12 British Ybk Int'l L 1.

Broomhall, B, 'Article 22' in O Triffterer (ed.), *Commentary on the Rome Statute of the International Criminal Court*, 2nd edn (CH Beck/Hart/Nomos 2008) 713.

Brownlie, I, *Principles of Public International Law*, 6th edn (Oxford University Press 2003).

Byers, M, *Custom, Power and the Power of Rules* (Cambridge University Press 1999).

Cassese, A, *International Criminal Law*, 2nd edn (Oxford University Press 2008).

 'Balancing the Prosecution of Crimes against Humanity and Non-Retroactive Criminal Law: The Kolk and Kislyiy v. Estonia Case before the ECHR' (2006) 4 J Int'l Crim Justice 410.

 International Law, 2nd edn (Oxford University Press 2004).

 'The Influence of the European Court of Human Rights on International Criminal Tribunals – Some Methodological Remarks' in M Bergsmo (ed.), *Human Rights and Criminal Justice for the Downtrodden: Essays in Honour of Asbjørn Eide* (Martinus Nijhoff 2003) 157.

 'From Nuremberg to Rome: International Military Tribunals to the International Criminal Court' in A Cassese and Others (eds.), *The Rome Statute of the International Criminal Court: A Commentary*, vol. I (Oxford University Press 2002) 3.

'The Statute of the International Criminal Court: Some Preliminary Reflections' (1999) 10 EJIL 144.

'Definition of Crimes and General Principles of Criminal Law as Reflected in the International Tribunal's Jurisprudence', Memo to Members of the Preparatory Committee on the Establishment of an International Criminal Court (22 March 1996), www.iccnow.org/documents/Memorandum.pdf, accessed 3 July 2014.

Center for International Policy, '"Article 98" Agreements and the International Criminal Court' (4 June 2007), http://ciponline.org/facts/art98.htm, accessed 9 March 2011.

Chodosh, H, 'An Interpretive Theory of International Law: The Distinction Between Treaty and Customary Law' (1995) 28 Vanderbilt J Transnat'l L 973.

Christoffersen, J, 'Impact on General Principles of Treaty Interpretation' in MT Kamminga and M Scheinin (eds.), The Impact of Human Rights Law on General International Law (Oxford University Press 2009) 37.

Clark, R, 'Article 9' in O Triffterer (ed.), Commentary on the Rome Statute of the International Criminal Court, 2nd edn (CH Beck/Hart/Nomos 2008) 505.

'Article 106' in O Triffterer (ed.), Commentary on the Rome Statute of the International Criminal Court, 2nd edn (CH Beck/Hart/Nomos 2008) 1663.

'Article 121' in O Triffterer (ed.), Commentary on the Rome Statute of the International Criminal Court, 2nd edn (CH Beck/Hart/Nomos 2008) 1751.

'Elements of Crimes in Early Confirmation Decisions of Pre-Trial Chambers of the International Criminal Court' (2008) 6 New Zealand Ybk Int'l L 209.

'Rethinking Aggression as a Crime and Formulating its Elements: the Final Work-Product of the Preparatory Commission for the International Criminal Court' (2002) 15 LJIL 859.

'The Mental Element in International Criminal Law' (2001) 12 Criminal Law Forum 291.

'Article 119' in O Triffterer (ed.), Commentary on the Rome Statute of the International Criminal Court, 1st edn (NVG Baden-Baden 1999) 1241.

'Treaty and Custom' in L Boisson de Chazournes and P Sands (eds.), International Law, the International Court of Justice and Nuclear Weapons (Cambridge University Press 1999) 171.

Clayton, R, and Tomlinson, H, The Law of Human Rights, vol. I, 2nd edn (Oxford University Press 2009).

Coalition for the International Criminal Court, Report of the CICC Team on the Crime of Aggression (2005).

Corten, O, and Klein, E (eds.), The Vienna Conventions on the Law of Treaties: A Commentary (Oxford University Press 2011).

Cottier, M, 'Article 8' in O Triffterer (ed.), Commentary on the Rome Statute of the International Criminal Court, 2nd edn (CH Beck/Hart/Nomos 2008) 275.

Crawford, J, The International Law Commission's Articles on State Responsibility: Introduction, Text and Commentaries (Cambridge University Press 2002).

'The Work of the International Law Commission' in A Cassese and Others (eds.), *The Rome Statute of the International Criminal Court: A Commentary*, vol. I (Oxford University Press 2002) 23.

'The ILC's Draft Statute for an International Criminal Tribunal' (1984) 88 AJIL 140.

Crema, L, 'Disappearance and New Sightings of Restrictive Interpretation(s)' (2010) 21:3 EJIL 681.

Cryer, R, 'The Interplay of Human Rights and Humanitarian Law: The Approach of the ICTY' (2010) 14:3 J Conflict & Security L 511.

'Royalism and the King: Article 21 of the Rome Statute and the Politics of Sources' (2009) 12 New Crim L Rev 390.

'The Doctrinal Foundations of International Criminalization' in MC Bassiouni (ed.), *International Criminal Law*, vol. I, 3rd edn (Martinus Nijhoff 2008) 107.

'Of Custom, Treaties, Scholars and the Gavel: The Influence of the International Criminal Tribunals on the ICRC Customary Law Study' (2006) 11 J Conflict & Security L 239.

Prosecuting International Crimes: Selectivity and the International Criminal Law Regime (Cambridge University Press 2005).

D'Amato, A, 'International Law, Intertemporal Problems' (1992) Encyclopedia of Public Int'l L 1234.

'Manifest Intent and the Generation by Treaty of Customary Rules of International Law' (1970) 64 AJIL 892.

Danilenko, GM, 'ICC Statute and Third States' in A Cassese and Others (eds.), *The Rome Statute of the International Criminal Court: A Commentary*, vol. II (Oxford University Press 2002) 1871.

'The Statute of the International Criminal Court and Third States' (1999–2000) 21 Mich J Int'l L 445.

Danner, AM, and Martinez, JS, 'Guilty Associations: Joint Criminal Enterprise, Command Responsibility, and the Development of International Criminal Law' (2005) 93 California L Rev 75.

d'Aspremont, J, 'Articulating International Human Rights and International Humanitarian Law: Conciliatory Interpretation under the Guise of Conflict of Norms-Resolution' in M Fitzmaurice and P Merkouris (eds.), *The Interpretation and Application of the European Convention on Human Rights: Legal and Practical Implications* (Martinus Nijhoff Publishers 2013) 4.

de Guzman, MM, 'Article 21' in O Triffterer (ed.), *Commentary on the Rome Statute of the International Criminal Court*, 2nd edn (CH Beck/Hart/Nomos 2008) 701.

'Gravity and the Legitimacy of the International Criminal Court' (2008) 32 Fordham Int'l LJ 1400.

Dennis, MJ, 'Application of Human Rights Treaties Extraterritorially in Times of Armed Conflict and Military Occupation' (2005) 99 AJIL 119.

de Visscher, C, *Theory and Reality in International Law*, P Corbett (trans.), rev. edn (Princeton University Press 1968).

Problèmes d'Interpretation Judiciaire en Droit International Public (Pedone 1963).

de Wet, E, 'The Security Council as a Law Maker: The Adoption of (Quasi)-Judicial Decisions' in R Wolfrum and V Röben (eds.), *Developments in International Law in Treaty Making* (Springer 2005) 183.

Dinstein, Y, 'Interaction Between Customary International Law and Treaties' (2006) 322 Recueil des Cours de l'Académie de Droit International 243.

'Crimes against Humanity and the Rome Statute of the International Criminal Court', Paper presented at the Universality of Human Rights Conference (German Innovation Center/IDC Herzliya and the Science Center of North Rhine-Westphalia 2005).

Dörmann, K, 'Article 8' in O Triffterer (ed.), *Commentary on the Rome Statute of the International Criminal Court*, 2nd edn (CH Beck/Hart/Nomos 2008) 275.

International Committee of the Red Cross, Elements of War Crimes under the Rome Statute of the International Criminal Court: Sources and Commentary (Cambridge University Press 2003).

'Contributions by the Ad Hoc Tribunals for the Former Yugoslavia and Rwanda to the Ongoing Work on Elements of Crimes in the Context of the ICC' (2000) 94 ASIL Proceedings 284.

Dörr, O, 'General Rule of Interpretation' in O Dörr and K Schmalenbach (eds.), *Vienna Convention on the Law of Treaties: A Commentary* (Springer 2012) 521.

Doherty, TA, 'The Application of Human Rights Treaties in the Development of Domestic and International Law: A Personal Perspective' (2009) 22:4 LJIL 753.

Doswald-Beck, L, 'The Right to Life in Armed Conflict: Does International Humanitarian Law Provide all the Answers?' (2006) 88:864 Int'l Rev of the Committee of the Red Cross 881.

Droege, C, 'Elective Affinities? Human Rights and Humanitarian Law' (2008) 90:871 Int'l Rev of the Committee of the Red Cross 501.

Duffy, H, 'Human Rights Litigation and the 'War on Terror'' (2008) 90:871 Int'l Rev of the Committee of the Red Cross 573.

Eide, A, Rosas, A, and Meron, T, 'Combating Lawlessness in Gray Zone Conflicts Through Minimum Humanitarian Standards' (1995) 89 AJIL 215.

Elias, TO, *The International Court of Justice and Some Contemporary Problems* (Brill 1983).

The Modern Law of Treaties (Oceana 1974).

Eser, A, 'Article 31' in O Triffterer (ed.), *Commentary on the Rome Statute of the International Criminal Court*, 2nd edn (CH Beck/Hart/Nomos 2008) 863.

Eskridge Jr., WN, 'Dynamic Statutory Interpretation' (1987) 135 Univ Pennsylvania LR 1479.

Fernández de Gurmendi, SA, 'The Process of Negotiations' in RS Lee (ed.), *The International Criminal Court: The Making of the Rome Statute* (Kluwer Law International 1999) 217.

Fish, S, *Is There a Text in This Class? The Authority of Interpretive Communities* (Harvard University Press 1980).

Fitzmaurice, GG, 'The Law and Procedure of the International Court of Justice 1951–1954: Treaty Interpretation and Other Treaty Points' (1957) 33 British Ybk Int'l L 203.

'The Law and Procedure of the International Court of Justice: Treaty Interpretation and Certain Other Treaty Points' (1951) 28 British Ybk Int'l L 1.

Fitzmaurice, M, 'Dynamic (Evolutive) Interpretation of Treaties' (2008) 21 Hague Ybk Int'l L 101.

'Third Parties and the Law of Treaties' (2002) 6 Max Planck Ybk of UN L 37.

Fitzmaurice, M, Elias, O, and Merkouris, P, *Treaty Interpretation and the Vienna Convention on the Law of Treaties: 30 Years On* (Martinus Nijhoff 2010).

Fletcher, G, *Basic Concepts of Criminal Law* (Oxford University Press 1998).

Rethinking Criminal Law (Little, Brown 1978).

French, D, 'Treaty Interpretation and the Incorporation of Extraneous Legal Rules' (2006) 55 Int'l Comp L Quart 281.

Frulli, M, 'Jurisdiction Ratione Personae' in A Cassese and Others (eds.), *The Rome Statute of the International Criminal Court: A Commentary*, vol. I (Oxford University Press 2002) 527.

Gaeta, P, 'The Defence of Superior Orders: The Statute of the International Criminal Court versus Customary International Law' (1999) 10 EJIL 172.

Gallant, KS, *The Principle of Legality in International and Comparative Criminal Law* (Cambridge University Press 2009).

'Jurisdiction to Adjudicate and Jurisdiction to Prescribe in International Criminal Courts' (2003) 48 Vill L Rev 763.

'Individual Human Rights in a New International Organization: The Rome Statute of the International Criminal Court' in MC Bassiouni (ed.), *International Criminal Law*, 2nd edn (Transnational Publishers 1999) 693.

Gardiner, R, *Treaty Interpretation* (Oxford University Press 2008).

Geddes, RS, 'Purpose and Context in Statutory Interpretation' (2005) 2 Univ of New England LJ 5.

Ginsburg, T, 'Bounded Discretion in International Judicial Lawmaking' (2005) 45 Virginia J Int'l L 631.

Glaser, S, 'Nullum Crimen Sine Lege' (1942) 24 J Comp Legis & Int'l L 29.

Graditzky, T, 'War Crimes Issues Before the Rome Diplomatic Conference on the Establishment of an International Criminal Court' (1999) 5 UC Davis J Int'l Law and Policy 199.

Hafner, G, 'Article 120' in O Triffterer (ed.), *Commentary on the Rome Statute of the International Criminal Court*, 2nd edn (Beck/Hart/Nomos 2008) 1737.

Hafner, G, and Binder, C, 'The Interpretation of Article 21(3) ICC Statute Opinion Reviewed' (2004) 9 Austrian Rev Int'l and Eur L 163.

Hale, B, 'Common Law and Convention Law: The Limits to Interpretation' (2011) 16:5 European HR L Rev 534.

Hall, CK, 'Première proposition de creation d'une cour criminelle international permanente' (1998) 80:829 Int'l Rev of the Committee of the Red Cross 59.

Hall, J, 'Nulla Poena Sine Lege' (1937) 47 Yale LJ 165.

Hall, L, 'Strict or Liberal Construction of Penal Statutes' (1935) 48 Harvard L Rev 748.

Hampson, FJ, 'The Relationship between International Humanitarian Law and Human Rights Law from the Perspective of a Human Rights Treaty Body' (2009) 90:871 Int'l Rev of the Committee of the Red Cross 549.

Hart, HLA, *The Concept of Law* (Oxford University Press 1961).

Haveman, R, 'The Principle of Legality' in R Haveman, O Kavran and J Nicholls (eds.), *Supranational Criminal Law: A System Sui Generis* (Intersentia 2003) 39.

Hay, J, 'Implementing the ICC Statute in New Zealand' (2004) 2 J Int'l Crim Justice 191.

Heintze, HJ, 'On the Relationship between Human Rights Law Protection and International Humanitarian Law' (2004) 86:856 Int'l Rev of the Committee of the Red Cross 789.

Heller, KJ, 'The Uncertain Legal Status of the Aggression Understandings' (2012) 10 J Int'l Crim Justice 229.

'Mistake of Legal Element, the Common Law, and Article 32 of the Rome Statute: A Critical Analysis' (2008) 6 J Int'l Crim Justice 419.

'Retreat from Nuremberg – the Leadership Requirement in the Crime of Aggression' (2007) 18 EJIL 477.

Henckaerts, J-M, 'Assessing the Laws and Customs of War: The Publication of Customary International Humanitarian Law' (2006) Human Rights Brief 8.

'The ICRC Study on Customary International Humanitarian Law – An Assessment' in L Maybee and B Chakka (eds.), *Custom as a Source of International Humanitarian Law* (International Committee of the Red Cross 2006) 43.

Henckearts, J-M, and Doswald-Beck, L, *Customary International Humanitarian Law* (Cambridge University Press 2005).

Higgins, R, 'The Relationship between the International Criminal Court and the International Court of Justice' in H von Hebel, JG Lammers and J Schukking (eds.), *Reflections on the International Criminal Court: Essays in Honour of Adriaan Bos* (TMC Asser Press 1999) 163.

'Time and the Law: International Perspectives on an Old Problem' (1997) 46:3 Int'l Comp LQ 501.

'Some Observations on the Inter-Temporal Rule in International Law' in J Makarczyk (ed.), *Theory of International Law at the Threshold of the 21st Century: Essays in Honour of Krzysztof Skubiszewski* (Kluwer Law International 1996) 173.

Hobbes, T, *Leviathan* (JM Dent & Sons Ltd 1970).

Hogg, JF, 'The International Court: Rules of Treaty Interpretation' (1958) 43 Minn L Rev 369.

Hollis, H, 'The Existential Function of Interpretation in International Law', Paper presented at the Cambridge Conference on Interpretation in International Law, Lauterpacht Centre for International Law (27 August 2013), http://papers.ssrn.com/sol3/papers.cfm?abstract_id=2330642, accessed 18 October 2013.

Hunt, D, 'The International Criminal Court – High Hopes, 'Creative Ambiguity' and an Unfortunate Mistrust in International Judges' (2004) 2:1 J Int'l Crim Justice 56.

Husak, DN, and Callender, CA, 'Wilful Ignorance, Knowledge, and the "Equal Culpability" Thesis: A Study of the Deeper Significance of the Principle of Legality' (1994) Wis L Rev 29.

Institut de Droit International, 'Obligations and Rights Erga Omnes in International Law' (Krakow Session 2005) 71-II Annuaire de l'Institut de Droit International 289.

'Problems Arising from a Succession of Codification Conventions on a Particular Subject' (Lisbon Session 1995) 66-I Annuaire de l'Institut de Droit International 39.

'The Protection of Human Rights and the Principle of Non-Intervention in Internal Affairs of States' (Santiago de Compostela Session 1989) 63-II Annuaire de l'Institut de Droit International 341.

'The Intertemporal Problem in Public International Law' (Wiesbaden Session 1975) 56:I Annuaire de l'Institut de Droit International 536.

International Criminal Court, Report of the International Criminal Court to the UN General Assembly, 13 August 2013, UN Doc. A/68/314.

International Law Association, Committee on International Human Rights Law and Practice, Final Report on the Impact of the Findings of the United Nations Human Rights Treaty Bodies, Berlin Conference (2004).

International Law Commission, 'Guide to Practice on Reservations to Treaties with Commentaries' (2011) II (Part Two) Ybk of the ILC 1.

'Report of the International Law Commission on the Work of its Sixty-Third Session (26 April to 3 June and 4 July to 12 August 2011)', UN Doc. A/66/10 and Add.1, 553.

'Guidelines on Reservations to a Provision Reflecting a Customary Norm' (2007) II (Part Two) Ybk of the ILC 88.

'Conclusions of the Work of the Study Group on the Fragmentation of International Law: Difficulties arising from the Diversification and Expansion of International Law' (2006) II (Part Two) Ybk of the ILC.

'Report of the International Law Commission on the Work of its Fifty-Third Session' (2001), UN Doc. A/56/10.

'Draft Code of Crimes against the Peace and Security of Mankind' (1996), UN Doc. A/CN.4/L.522.

'Report of the International Law Commission on the work of its Forty-Eighth Session (6 May–26 July 1996)' (1996) II (Part Two) Ybk of the ILC 1.

'Draft Code of Crimes against the Peace and Security of Mankind' (1994) II (Part Two) Ybk of the ILC 18.

'Draft Statute for an International Criminal Court' (1994), UN Doc. A/49/10.

'Report of the International Law Commission on the Work of its Forty-Sixth Session (2 May–22 July 1994)', UN Doc. A/49/10.

'Comments and Observations of Governments on the Draft Code of Crimes against the Peace and Security of Mankind adopted on First Reading by the

International Law Commission at its Forty-Third Session' (1993), UN Doc. A/CN.4/448.

'Eleventh Report on the Draft Code of Crimes against the Peace and Security of Mankind' (1993), UN Doc. A/CN.4/449 and Corr.1.

'Report of the International Law Commission on the Work of its Forty-Fifth Session (3 May–23 July 1993)', UN Doc. A/48/10.

'Ninth Report on the Draft Code of Crimes against the Peace and Security of Mankind' (1991), UN Doc. A/CN.4/435 & Corr.1 and Add.1 & Corr.1.

'Topical Summary of the Discussion held in the Sixth Committee of the General Assembly during its Forty-Fifth Session' (1991), UN Doc. A/CN.4/L.456.

'Review of the Multilateral Treaty-Making Process' (1979) II Ybk of the ILC 183.

'Reports of the International Law Commission on the Second Part of its Seventeenth Session and on its Eighteenth Session' (1966) II Ybk of the ILC 169.

'Summary Records of the Sixteenth Session' (1964) I Ybk of the ILC 1.

'Draft Code of Offences against the Peace and Security of Mankind' (1954) I Ybk of the ILC 123.

'Draft Code of Offences Against the Peace and Security of Mankind' (1951) II Ybk of the ILC 58.

'Formulation of the Nuremberg Principles' (1950) II Ybk of the ILC 181.

'Report of the International Law Commission covering its Second Session' (1950) II Ybk of the ILC 364.

International Committee of the Red Cross, 'Statement of 8 July 1998 Relating to the Bureau Discussion Paper in Document A/CONF.183/C.1/L.53', UN Doc. A/CONF.183/INF/10.

Jackson, RH, *The Nürnberg Case* (Cooper Square 1947).

Jacobs, D, 'Positivism and International Criminal Law: The Principle of Legality as a Rule of Conflict of Theories' in J d'Aspremont and J Kammerhofer (eds.), *International Legal Positivism in a Post-Modern World* (Cambridge University Press, forthcoming October 2014), http://papers.ssrn.com/sol3/papers.cfm?abstract_id=2046311, accessed 16 October 2013.

Jeffries Jr, JC, 'Legality, Vagueness, and the Construction of Penal Statutes' (1985) 71 Virginia L Rev 189.

Jenks, CW, 'The Conflict of Law-Making Treaties' (1953) 30 British Ybk Int'l L 401.

Jennings, RY, Interview in Antonio Cassese, *Five Masters of International Law* (Hart Publishing 2011) 115.

'Amendment and Modification of Treaties' (1967) 121 Recueil des Cours de l'Académie de Droit International 544.

'The Progress of International Law' (1958) 34 British Ybk Int'l L 334.

'The Progressive Development of International Law' (1947) 24 British Ybk Int'l L 301.

Jennings, R, and Watts, A, *Oppenheim's International Law*, 9th edn (Longman Harlow 1992).

Jessberger, F, 'Bad Torture – Good Torture? What International Criminal Lawyers May Learn from the Recent Trial of Police Officers in Germany' (2005) 3 J Int'l Crim Justice 1059.

Jessup, P, 'The Palmas Island Arbitration' (1928) 22 AJIL 739.

Jia, BB, 'The Relations between Treaties and Custom' (2010) 9 Chinese J Int'l L 81.

Jones, JRWD, 'Composition of the Court' in A Cassese and Others (eds.), *The Rome Statute of the International Criminal Court: A Commentary*, vol. I (Oxford University Press 2002) 235.

Juratowitch, B, 'Retroactive Criminal Liability and International Human Rights Law' (2004) 75:1 British Ybk Int'l L 337.

Kälin, W, and Künzli, J, *The Law of International Human Rights Protection* (Oxford University Press 2009).

Kamminga, MT, 'Final Report on the Impact of International Human Rights Law on General International Law' in MT Kamminga and M Scheinin (eds.), *The Impact of Human Rights Law on General International Law* (Oxford University Press 2009) 1.

Keller, H, and Stone Sweet, A, 'Assessing the Impact of the ECHR on National Legal Systems' in H Keller and A Stone Sweet (eds.), *A Europe of Rights* (Oxford University Press 2008) 677.

Kelsen, H, 'Will the Judgment in the Nuremberg Trial Constitute a Precedent in International Law?' (1947) 1:2 Int'l LQ 153.

'The Rule Against Ex Post Facto Laws and the Prosecution of the Axis War Criminals' (1945) II:3 The Judge Advocate J 8.

Kelt, M and von Hebel, H, 'The Making of the Elements of Crimes: What are Elements of Crimes?' in R Lee and Others (eds.), *The International Criminal Court: Elements of Crimes and Rules of Procedure and Evidence* (Transnational 2001) 13.

Kirsch, P, 'Customary International Humanitarian Law, its Enforcement, and the Role of the International Criminal Court' in L Maybee and B Chakka (eds.), *Custom as a Source of International Humanitarian Law* (ICRC 2006) 79.

'Foreword' in K Dörmann, *Elements of War Crimes under the Rome Statute of the International Criminal Court* (Cambridge University Press 2003) xiii.

'The Work of the Preparatory Commission' in RS Lee (ed.), *The International Criminal Court: Elements of Crimes and Rules of Procedure and Evidence* (Transnational 2001) xlv.

'The Development of the Rome Statute' in RS Lee and Others (eds.), *The International Criminal Court: The Making of the Rome Statute* (Kluwer Law International 1999) 451.

Kirsch, P, and Holmes, JT, 'The Rome Conference on an International Criminal Court: The Negotiating Process' (1999) 93 AJIL 2.

'The Birth of the International Criminal Court: The 1998 Rome Conference' (1998) 36 Canadian Ybk Int'l L 3.

Kirsch, P, and Oosterveld, V, 'The Post-Rome Conference Preparatory Commission' in A Cassese and Others (eds.), *The Rome Statute of the International Criminal Court: A Commentary*, vol. I (Oxford University Press 2002) 94.

Kirsch, P, and Robinson, D, 'Reaching Agreement at the Rome Conference' in A Cassese and Others (eds.), *The Rome Statute of the International Criminal Court: A Commentary*, vol. I (Oxford University Press 2002) 67.

Kitichaiseree, K, *International Criminal Law* (Oxford University Press 2001).

Koh, HH, US Department of State, 'Remarks', Panel Discussion at the NYU Center For Global Affairs (27 October 2010), www.state.gov/s/l/releases/remarks/150497.htm, accessed 5 November 2013.

Kolb, R, *Interprétation et Création du Droit International: Equisse d'une herméneutique juridique modern pour le droit international public* (Bruylant 2006).

Kontou, N, *The Termination and Revision of Treaties in the Light of New Customary International Law* (Oxford University Press 1994).

Koskenniemi, M, 'Fragmentation of International Law: Difficulties Arising from the Diversification and Expansion of International Law: Report of the Study Group of the International Law Commission' (4 April 2006), UN Doc. A/CN.4/L.682.

From Apology to Utopia: The Structure of International Legal Argument (Cambridge University Press 2006).

'Study on the Function and Scope of the Lex Specialis Rule and the Question of "Self Contained Regimes"' (2004), UN Doc. ILC(LVI)/SG/FIL/CRD.1 and Add.1.

Kreß, C, 'Harmony and Dissonance in International Law' (2011) 105 ASIL Proceedings 160.

'The Crime of Genocide and Contextual Elements' (2009) 7 J Int'l Crim Justice 297.

'Time for Decision: Some Thoughts on the Immediate Future of the Crime of Aggression: A Reply to Andreas Paulus' (2009) 20 EJIL 1139.

'International Criminal Law' in R Wolfrum (ed.), *The Max Planck Encyclopedia of Public International Law (2008–)*, online edition, www.mpepil.com, accessed 15 March 2011.

'Nullum Crimen, Nulla Poena Sine Lege' in R Wolfrum (ed.), *The Max Planck Encyclopedia of Public International Law (2008–)*, online edition, www.mpepil.com, accessed 15 March 2011.

'The Crime of Genocide under International Law' (2006) 6 Int'l Comp L Rev 461.

'War Crimes Committed in Non-International Armed Conflict and the Emerging System of International Criminal Justice' (2000) 30 Israel Ybk Human Rights 103.

Kreß, C, Barriga, S, Grover, L and von Holtzendorff, L, 'Negotiating the Understandings on the Crime of Aggression' in S Barriga and C Kreß (eds.), *Travaux Préparatoires of the Crime of Aggression* (Cambridge University Press 2012) 81.

Kreß, C, and von Holtzendorff, L, 'The Kampala Compromise on the Crime of Aggression' (2010) 8 J Int'l Crim Justice 1179.

Kretzmer, D, 'Rethinking Application of IHL in Non-International Armed Conflicts' (2009) 42 Israel L Rev 32.

Krieger, H, 'A Conflict of Norms: The Relationship between Humanitarian Law and
    Human Rights Law in the ICRC Customary Law Study' (2006) 11 J Conflict
    & Security 265.

Kulovesi, K, 'Legality or Otherwise? Nuclear Weapons and the Strategy of Non
    Liquet' (1999) 10 Finnish Ybk Int'l Law 55.

Lamb, S, 'Nullum Crimen, Nulla Poena Sine Lege in International Criminal Law' in
    A Cassese and Others (eds.), *The Rome Statute of the International Criminal
    Court: A Commentary*, vol. I (Oxford University Press 2002) 733.

Lauterpacht, H, *The Development of International Law by the International Court*
    (Praeger 1958).
    'Codification and Development of International Law' (1955) 49 AJIL 16.
    'Restrictive Interpretation and the Principle of Effectiveness in the Interpretation
    of Treaties' (1949) 26 British Ybk Int'l L 48.
    The Function of Law in the International Community (Oxford University Press
    1933).

Laws, Lord J, 'The Good Constitution', Sir David Williams Lecture, Cambridge
    (4 May 2012), www.judiciary.gov.uk/Resources/JCO/Documents/Speeches/
    lj-laws-speech-the-good-constitution.pdf, accessed 18 October 2013.

Lee, RS, 'Introduction' in RS Lee (ed.), *The International Criminal Court: Elements
    of Crimes and Rules of Procedure and Evidence* (Transnational 2001) Iv.
    'Introduction' in RS Lee and Others (eds.), *The International Criminal Court:
    The Making of the Rome Statute* (Kluwer Law International 1999) 1.

Liang, YL, 'The Establishment of an International Criminal Jurisdiction: The Sec-
    ond Phase' (1953) 47 AJIL 638.

Lietzau, WK, 'Checks and Balances and Elements of Proof: Structural Pillars for
    the International Criminal Court' (1999) 32 Cornell Int'l LJ 477.

Linderfalk, U, *On the Interpretation of Treaties: the Modern International Law as
    Expressed in the 1969 Vienna Convention on the Law of Treaties* (Springer
    2007)

Lindroos, A, 'Addressing the Norm Conflicts in a Fragmented System: the Doctrine
    of Lex Specialis' (2005) 74 Nordic J Int'l L 27.

MacCormick, DN, and Summers, RS (eds.), *Interpreting Statutes: A Comparative
    Study* (Ashgate 1991).

Maxwell, PB, *The Interpretation of Statutes*, 7th edn (GFL Bridgman 1929).

McCarthy, C, 'Legal Conclusion or Interpretive Process? Lex Specialis and the
    Applicability of International Human Rights Standards' in R Arnold and
    N Quénivet (eds.), *International Humanitarian Law and Human Rights Law*
    (Martinus Nijhoff 2008) 101.

McCormack, TLH, and Robertson, S, 'Jurisdictional Aspects of the Rome Statute
    for the New International Criminal Court' (1999) 23 Melb U L Rev 635.

McCrudden, C, 'Human Dignity and Judicial Interpretation of Human Rights'
    (2008) 19 EJIL 655.

McDougal, MS, 'The International Law Commission's Draft Articles Upon Inter-
    pretation: Textuality Redivivus' (1967) 61 AJIL 992.

McLachlan, C, 'The Principle of Systemic Integration and Article 31(3)(c) of the Vienna Convention' (2005) 54:2 Int'l Comp LQ 279.

McLachlin, B, 'Judging in a Democratic State', Speech (3 June 2004), www.cjc-ccm.gc.ca/cmslib/general/Matlow_Docs/Authorities/Book%20of%20Authorities%20-%20Tab%20E%20Rt.%20Hon.%20Beverley%20Mclachlin%20article%20-%20Judging%20in%20a%20Democratic%20State.pdf, accessed 23 April 2014.

McNair, AD, The Law of Treaties (Oxford University Press 1961).
    'The Functions and Differing Legal Character of Treaties' (1930) 11 British Ybk Int'l L 100.

McRae, DM, 'Approaches to the Interpretation of Treaties: the European Court of Human Rights and the WTO Appellate Body' in S Breitenmoser and Others (eds.), Human Rights, Democracy and the Rule of Law: Liber amicorum Luzius Wildhaber (Nomos 2007) 1407.
    'The Legal Effect of Interpretative Declarations' (1978) 49 British Ybk Int'l L 155.

Mendelson, M, 'Remarks: Disentangling Treaty and Customary International Law' (1987) 81 ASIL Proceedings 157.

Meron, T, 'Remarks' (2009) 103 ASIL Proceedings 8.
    'Customary Law' in R Dworkin, R Gutman and D Rieff (eds.), Crimes of War 2.0: What the Public Should Know, rev. and expanded edn (WW Norton 2008).
    'Revival of Customary International Humanitarian Law' (2005) 99 AJIL 817.
    'International Law in the Age of Human Rights' (2003) 301 Recueil des Cours de l'Académie de Droit International 9.
    'The Humanization of Humanitarian Law' (2000) 94 AJIL 239.
    'Crimes under the Jurisdiction of the International Criminal Court' in H von Hebel, JG Lammers and J Schukking (eds.), Reflections on the International Criminal Court: Essays in Honour of Adriaan Bos (TMC Asser Press 1999) 47.

Mettraux, G, International Crimes and the Ad Hoc Tribunals (Oxford University Press 2005).

Meyer, RV, 'Following Historical Precedent: An Argument for the Continued Use of Military Professionals as Triers of Fact in Some Humanitarian Law Tribunals' (2009) 7 J Int'l Crim Justice 43.

Milanovic, M, 'A Norm Conflict Perspective on the Relationship Between International and Humanitarian Law and Human Rights Law' (2009) 14:3 J Conflict & Security L 459.

Mokhtar, A, 'Nullum Crimen, Nulla Poena Sine Lege: Aspects and Prospects' (2005) 26 Statute L Rev 41.

Montesquieu, C, De l'esprit des lois (Barillot 1748).

Møse, E, 'Impact of Human Rights Conventions on the Two Ad Hoc Tribunals' in M Bergsmo (ed.), Human Rights and Criminal Justice for the Downtrodden: Essays in Honour of Asbjørn Eide (Martinus Nijhoff 2003) 179.

Murphy, SD, 'Efforts to Obtain Immunity from ICC for US Peacekeepers' (2002) 96 AJIL 725.

Nissel, A, 'Continuing Crimes in the Rome Statute' (2004) 25 Michigan J Int'l L 653.

Nolte, G, 'Jurisprudence of the International Court of Justice and Arbitral Tribunals of Ad Hoc Jurisdiction Relating to Subsequent Agreements and Subsequent Practice: Introductory Report for the ILC Study Group on Treaties over Time' in G Nolte (ed.), *Treaties and Subsequent Practice* (Oxford University Press 2013) 169.

'Second Report for the ILC Study Group on Treaties over Time: Jurisprudence under Special Regimes Relating to Subsequent Agreements and Subsequent Practice' in G Nolte (ed.), *Treaties and Subsequent Practice* (Oxford University Press 2013) 210.

Öberg, MD, 'The Legal Effects of Resolutions of the Security Council and General Assembly in the Jurisprudence of the ICJ' (2006) 16 EJIL 879.

Oosterveld, V, 'The Elements of Genocide' in RS Lee and Others (eds.), *The International Criminal Court: Elements of Crimes and Rules of Procedure and Evidence* (Transnational 2001) 41.

Orakhelashvili, A, 'The Interaction between Human Rights and Humanitarian Law: Fragmentation, Conflict, Parallelism, or Convergence?' (2008) 19:1 EJIL 161.

The Interpretation of Acts and Public Rules in Public International Law (Oxford University Press 2008).

'Restrictive Interpretation of Human Rights Treaties in the Recent Jurisprudence of the European Court of Human Rights' (2003) 14 EJIL 529.

Orentlicher, D, 'Criminalizing Hate Speech in the Crucible of Trial: Prosecutor v. Nahimana' (2005) 12 New England J Int'l & Comp L 17.

Pace, WR, and Schense, J, 'The Role of Non-Governmental Organizations' in A Cassese and Others (eds.), *The Rome Statute of the International Criminal Court: A Commentary*, vol. I (Oxford University Press 2002) 105.

Pace, WR, and Thieroff, M, 'Participation of Non-governmental Organizations' in RS Lee (ed.), *The International Criminal Court: The Making of the Rome Statute: Issues, Negotiations, Results* (Kluwer Law International 1999) 391.

Packer, HL, *The Limits of the Criminal Sanction* (Stanford University Press 1968).

Pal, R, 'Judgment' in BVA Röling and CF Rüter (eds.), *The Tokyo Judgment: The International Military Tribunal for the Far East (IMTFE) 29 April 1946– 12 November 1948* (Amsterdam University Press 1977) 579.

Paust, JJ, 'It's No Defense: Nullum Crimen, International Crime and the Ginger-bread Man' (1997) 60 Albany L Rev 657.

'Nullum Crimen and Related Claims' (1997) 25 Denver J Int'l L & Policy 321.

Pauwelyn, J, *Conflict of Norms in Public International Law: How WTO Law Relates to Other Rules of International Law* (Cambridge University Press 2003).

Pauwelyn, J, and Elsig, M, 'The Politics of Treaty Interpretation: Variations and Explanations Across International Tribunals' (3 October 2011), http://ssrn.com/abstract=1938618, accessed 16 October 2013.

Pellet, A, 'Applicable Law' in A Cassese and Others (eds.), *The Rome Statute of the International Criminal Court: A Commentary*, vol. II (Oxford University Press 2002) 1051.

'Third Report on Reservations to Treaties' (30 April 1998), UN Doc. A/CN.4/491/Add 4.

Perrin, B, 'Searching for Law While Seeking Justice: The Difficulties of Enforcing International Humanitarian Law in International Criminal Trials' (2008) 39 Ottawa L Rev 367.

Pictet, J, *Development and Principles of International Humanitarian Law* (Martinus Nijhoff 1985).

Piragoff, DK, 'Article 69' in O Triffterer (ed.), *Commentary on the Rome Statute of the International Criminal Court*, 2nd edn (CH Beck/Hart/Nomos 2008) 1301.

Piragoff, DK, and Robinson, D, 'Article 30' in O Triffterer (ed.), *Commentary on the Rome Statute of the International Criminal Court*, 2nd edn (CH Beck/Hart/Nomos 2008) 849.

Pissillo-Mazzeschi, R, 'Treaty and Custom: Reflections on the Codification of International Law' (January and April 1997) Commonwealth L Bull 549.

Plato, *The Republic*, 2nd edn (Penguin Books 1987).

Politi, M, 'Elements of Crimes' in A Cassese and Others (eds.), *The Rome Statute of the International Criminal Court: A Commentary*, vol. I (Oxford University Press 2002) 443.

Powderly, J, 'Judicial Interpretation at the Ad Hoc Tribunals: Method from Chaos' in S Darcy and J Powderly (eds.), *Judicial Creativity at the International Criminal Tribunals* (Oxford University Press 2010) 17.

Preparatory Commission, Working Group on the Crime of Aggression (Secretariat), 'Historical Review of Developments relating to Aggression', Part II (24 January 2002), UN Doc. PCNICC/2002/WGCA/L.1/Add.1.

Working Group on the Crime of Aggression (Secretariat), 'Historical Review of Developments relating to Aggression', Part I (18 January 2002), UN Doc. PCNICC/2002/WGCA/L.1/Add.1.

Preparatory Committee, 'Report of the Inter-Sessional Meeting from 19 to 30 January 1998 in Zutphen, The Netherlands' (1998), UN Doc. A/AC.249/1998/L.13.

'Report of the Preparatory Committee on the Establishment of an International Criminal Court' (1998), UN Doc. A/CONF.183/2/Add.1.

'Decisions taken by the Preparatory Committee at its Session held in New York 1 to 12 December 1997' (1997) UN Doc. A/AC.249/1997/L.9/Rev.1.

'Report of the Preparatory Committee on the Establishment of an International Criminal Court', vols. I-II (1996) UN Doc. A/51/22.

Preuss, L, 'Punishment by Analogy in National Socialist Penal Law' (1936) 26 J Crim L & Criminology 847.

Provost, R, *International Human Rights and Humanitarian Law* (Cambridge University Press 2002).

Prud'homme, N, 'Lex Specialis: Oversimplifying a More Complex and Multifaceted Relationship?'(2007) 40:2 Israel L Rev 355.

Ratner, SR, 'The Schizophrenias of International Criminal Law' (1998) 33 Texas Int'l LJ 237.

Rawls, J, *Justice as Fairness* (Belknap 2001).

'Public Reason Revisited' (1997) 64 U Chi L Rev 765.

Raz, J, *The Authority of Law* (Oxford University Press 1979).

Rescher, N, *Presumption and the Practices of Tentative Cognition* (Cambridge University Press 2006).

Research in International Law of the Harvard Law School, 'Harvard Draft Convention on the Law of Treaties' (1935) 29 AJIL, Supp. 657.

Ribeiro, M, *Limiting Arbitrary Power: The Vagueness Doctrine in Canadian Constitutional Law* (University of British Columbia Press 2005).

Roberts, A, 'Traditional and Modern Approaches to Customary International Law: A Reconciliation' (2001) 95 AJIL 757.

Robinson, D, 'Legality and Our Contradictory Commitments: Some Thoughts About How We Think' (2009) 103 ASIL Proceedings 5.

'The Identity Crisis of International Criminal Law' (2008) 21 LJIL 925.

'The Elements for Crimes Against Humanity' in RS Lee and Others (eds.), *The International Criminal Court: Elements of Crimes and Rules of Procedure and Evidence* (Transnational 2001) 57.

'Defining "Crimes against Humanity" at the Rome Conference' (1999) 93 AJIL 43.

Robinson, D, and von Hebel, H, 'Reflections on the Elements of Crimes' in RS Lee (ed.), *The International Criminal Court: Elements of Crimes and Rules of Procedure and Evidence* (Transnational 2001) 219.

Robinson, PH, 'Rules of Conduct and Rules of Adjudication' (1990) 57 U Chic LR 729.

'Legality and Discretion in the Distribution of Criminal Sanctions' (1988) 25 Harv J on Legis 393.

Roht-Arriaza, N, Letter to the Office of the Prosecutor on the meaning of Article 21(3), (14 December 2004) (on file with author).

Rosand, E, 'The Security Council as "Global Legislator": Ultra Vires or Ultra Innovative?' (2004) 28:3 Fordham Int'l LJ 542.

Roscini, M, 'Great Expectations: The Implementation of the Rome Statute in Italy' (2007) 5 J Int'l Crim Justice 493.

Rosenne, S, 'Codification of International Law' (1984) 7 Max Planck Encyclopedia of Public Int'l L 34.

'Relations between the International Law Commission and Governments' (1965) Ybk of World Affairs 183.

Rousseau, C, *Principes généraux de droit international public*, vol. I (Pédone 1944).

Roxburgh, RF, *International Conventions and Third States* (Longmans, Green and Co. 1917).

Sadat, LN, 'Custom, Codification and Some Thoughts about the Relationship Between the Two: Article 10 of the ICC Statute' (2000) 49 DePaul L Rev 909.

Sadat, LN, and Carden, SR, 'The New International Criminal Court: An Uneasy Revolution' (2000) 88 Georgetown LJ 381.

Safferling, C, *International Criminal Procedure* (Oxford University Press 2012).

Saland, P, 'International Criminal Law Principles' in RS Lee (ed.), *The International Criminal Court: The Making of the Rome Statute – Issues, Negotiations, Results* (Kluwer Law International 1999) 189.

Sands, P, 'Treaty, Custom and the Cross-fertilization of International Law' (1998) 1 Yale Human Rights & Development LJ 85.

Sassòli, M, and Olson, LM, 'The Relationship between International Humanitarian and Human Rights Law Where it Matters: Admissible Killing and Internment of Fighters in Non-International Armed Conflicts' (2008) 90:871 Int'l Rev of the Committee of the Red Cross 599.

Schabas, WA, *The International Criminal Court: A Commentary on the Rome Statute* (Oxford University Press 2010).

'Customary Law or "Judge-Made" Law: Judicial Creativity at the UN Criminal Tribunals' in J Doria, H-P Gasser and MC Bassiouni (eds.), *The Legal Regime of the International Criminal Court: Essays in Honour of Professor Igor Blishchenko* (Martinus Nijhoff 2009) 77.

'Lex Specialis? Belt and Suspenders? The Parallel Operation of Human Rights Law and the Law of Armed Conflict, and the Conundrum of Jus ad Bellum' (2007) 40:2 Israel L Rev 592.

An Introduction to the International Criminal Court, 2nd edn (Cambridge University Press 2004).

'Criminal Responsibility for Violations of Human Rights' in J Symonides (ed.), *Human Rights: International Protection, Monitoring, Enforcement* (UNESCO 2003) 281.

'Interpreting the Statutes of the Ad Hoc Tribunals' in LC Vohrah (ed.), *Man's Inhumanity to Man: Essays on International Law in Honour of Antonio Cassese* (Kluwer Law International 2003) 847.

'Follow Up to Rome: Preparing for Entry into Force of the International Criminal Court Statute' (1999) 20 Human Rights LJ 157.

Schachter, O, *International Law in Theory and Practice* (Martinus Nijhoff 1991).

'Entangled Treaty and Custom' in Y Dinstein (ed.), *International Law at a Time of Perplexity: Essays in Honour of Shabtai Rosenne* (Martinus Nijhoff 1989) 717.

Scharf, M, 'Results of the Rome Conference for an International Criminal Court' (August 1998) ASIL Insight 1.

Scheffer, D, 'The United States and the International Criminal Court' (1999) 93 AJIL 12.

Schwarzenberger, G, 'Myths and Realities of Treaty Interpretation: Articles 31–33 of the Vienna Convention on the Law of Treaties' in G Schwarzenberger, *International Law and Order* (Stevens & Sons 1971) 110.

Scobbie, I, 'Principle or Pragmatics? The Relationship between Human Rights Law and the Law of Armed Conflict' (2009) 14:3 J Conflict & Security L 449.

Seibert-Fohr, A, 'Modern Concepts of Customary International Law as a Manifestation of a Value-Based International Order' in A Zimmermann and R Hofmann (eds.), *Unity and Diversity in International Law* (Duncker & Humblot 2006) 257.

Shahabuddeen, M, 'Does the Principle of Legality Stand in the Way of Progressive Development of Law?' (2004) 2 J Int'l Crim Justice 1007.

Shelton, D, 'Introduction' in D Shelton (ed.), *International Law and Domestic Legal Systems: Incorporation, Transformation, and Persuasion* (Oxford University Press 2011) 1.

Sheppard, D, 'The International Criminal Court and "Internationally Recognized Human Rights": Understanding Article 21(3) of the Rome Statute' (2010) 10 Int'l Crim L Rev 43.

Shihata, IFI, *The Power of the International Court to Determine its own Jurisdiction: Compétence de la Compétence* (Martinus Nijhoff 1965).

Simma, B, 'The General Assembly: Function and Powers' in B Simma and Others (eds.), *The Charter of the United Nations: A Commentary*, vol. I, 2nd edn (Oxford University Press 2002) 257.

   'From Bilateralism to Community Interest in International Law' (1994) 250 Recueil des Cours de l'Académie de Droit International 217.

Simma, B, and Alston, P, 'The Sources of Human Rights Law: Custom, Jus Cogens, and General Principles' (1988–1989) 12 Australian Ybk Int'l L 82.

Sinclair, I, *The Vienna Convention on the Law of Treaties*, 2nd edn (Manchester University Press 1984).

Sluiter, G, 'Human Rights Protection in the ICC Pre-Trial Phase' in C Stahn and G Sluiter (eds.), *The Emerging Practice of the International Criminal Court* (Brill 2009) 459.

   'Implementation of the ICC Statute in the Dutch Legal Order' (2004) 2 J Int'l Crim Justice 158.

Smith, ATH, 'Judicial Law Making in the Criminal Law' (1984) 100 LQ Rev 46.

Special Working Group on the Crime of Aggression, Report (2009), ICC-ASP/7/20/Add.1, Annex II, Appendix I.

Stahn, C, 'The Ambiguities of Security Council Resolution 1422 (2002)' (2003) 14 EJIL 85.

Stern, L, 'Interpreting Legal Language at the International Criminal Tribunal for the Former Yugoslavia: Overcoming the Lack of Lexical Equivalents' (2007) 2 J Specialised Translation 63.

Sullivan, R, 'The Plain Meaning Rule and Other Ways to Cheat at Statutory Interpretation', http://aix1.uottawa.ca/~resulliv/legdr/pmr.html, accessed 5 November 2013.

   Sullivan and Driedger on the Construction of Statutes, 4th edn (Butterworths 2002).

Summers, RS, *Form and Function in a Legal System: A General Study* (Cambridge University Press 2006).

   'Statutory Interpretation in the United States' in DN MacCormick and RS Summers (eds.), *Interpreting Statutes: A Comparative Study* (Ashgate 1991) 407.

Summers, RS, and Taruffo, M, 'Interpretation and Comparative Analysis' in DN MacCormick and RS Summers (eds.), *Interpreting Statutes: A Comparative Study* (Ashgate 1991) 461.

Sunga, LS, *The Emerging System of International Criminal Law: Developments in Codification and Implementation* (Kluwer Law International 1997).

Swart, B, 'International Crimes: Present Situation and Future Development' (2004) 19 Nouvelles études pénales 201.

Swart, M, 'Judicial Lawmaking at the Ad Hoc Tribunals: The Creative Use of the Sources of International Law and "Adventurous Interpretation"' (2010) 70 ZaöRV 459.

Szasz, C, 'The Security Council Starts Legislating' (2002) 96 AJIL 901.

Talmon, S, 'The Security Council as World Legislator' (2005) 99 AJIL 175.

Terris, D, Romano, CPR and Swigart, L, *The International Judge – An Introduction to the Men and Women Who Decide the World's Cases* (Brandeis University Press 2007).

Thirlway, HWA, 'Reflections on Lex Ferenda' (2001) 32 Netherlands Ybk Int'l L 3.

'The Law and Procedure of the International Court of Justice: 1960–1989 (Part Three)' (1991) 62:1 British Ybk Int'l L 1.

'The Law and Procedure of the International Court of Justice: 1960–1989 (Part Two)' (1990) 61:1 British Ybk Int'l L 1.

'The Law and Procedure of the International Court of Justice: 1960–1989 (Part One)' (1989) 60:1 British Ybk Int'l L 1.

International Customary Law and Codification (Sijthoff 1972).

Tobin, J, 'Seeking to Persuade: A Constructive Approach to Human Rights Treaty Interpretation' (2010) 23 Harvard HR J 1.

Tomuschat, C, *Human Rights: Between Idealism and Realism*, 2nd edn (Oxford University Press 2008).

Trechsel, S, *Human Rights in Criminal Proceedings* (Oxford University Press 2005).

Triffterer, O, 'Can the "Elements of Crimes" Narrow or Broaden Responsibility for Criminal Behaviour defined in the Rome Statute?' in C Stahn and G Sluiter (eds.), *The Emerging Practice of the International Criminal Court* (Martinus Nijhoff 2009) 381.

'Article 10' in O Triffterer (ed.), *Commentary on the Rome Statute of the International Criminal Court*, 2nd edn (CH Beck/Hart/Nomos 2008) 531.

'Command Responsibility, Article 28 Rome Statute, an Extension of Individual Criminal Responsibility for Crimes within the Jurisdiction of the Court – Compatible with Article 22, Nullum Crimen Sine Lege?' in O Triffterer (ed.), *Gedächtnisschrift für Theo Vogler* (CF Müller 2004) 213.

'The New International Criminal Law – its General Principles Establishing Individual Criminal Responsibility' (2003) 32 Thesaurus Acroasium 633.

'Article 10' in O Triffterer (ed.), *Commentary on the Rome Statute of the International Criminal Court*, 1st edn (Beck/Hart/Nomos 1999) 315.

Tsagourias, N, 'Security Council Legislation, Article 2(7) of the UN Charter, and the Principle of Subsidiarity' (2004) 24:3 LJIL 539.

'Draft Statute for an International Criminal Court' (1954) UN Doc. A/2645.

'Draft Statute for an International Criminal Court' (1950) UN Doc. A/2136.

'Note on the Private Codification of Public International Law' (1947) UN Doc. A/AC.10/25.

UNHRC, 'General Comment No. 32' (2007) UN Doc. CCPR/C/GC/32.
'General Comment No. 24' (1994) UN Doc. CCPR/C/21/Rev.1/Add.6.
'General Comment No. 20' (1992) UN Doc. HRI/GEN/1/Rev.6, 151 (2003).
'General Comment No. 7' (1982) UN Doc. HRI/GEN/1/Rev.6, 129 (2003).
UNSC, 'Security Council Requests One-Year Extension of UN Peacekeeper Immunity from International Criminal Court' (12 June 2003) Press Release SC/7789.
'Report of the Secretary-General on the Establishment of a Special Court for Sierra Leone' (2000) UN Doc. S/2000/915.
'Comprehensive Report of the Secretary-General on Practical Arrangements for the Effective Functioning of the International Criminal Tribunal for Rwanda, Recommending Arusha as the Seat of the Tribunal' (1995) UN Doc. S/1995/134.
'Report of the Secretary-General Pursuant to Paragraph 5 of Security Council Resolution 955' (1994) UN Doc. S/1995/134.
'Report of the Secretary-General Pursuant to Paragraph 2 of Security Council Resolution 808' (1993) UN Doc. S/25704.
Van Damme, I, 'Treaty Interpretation by the WTO Appellate Body' (2010) 21:3 EJIL 605.
Treaty Interpretation by the WTO Appellate Body (Oxford University Press 2009).
Van Schaack, B, 'Legality and International Criminal Law' (2009) 103 ASIL Proceedings 2.
'Crimen Sine Lege: Judicial Lawmaking at the Intersection of Law and Morals' (2008) 97 Georgetown LJ 119.
Verhoeven, J, 'Article 21 of the Rome Statute and the Ambiguities of Applicable Law' (2002) 33 Netherlands Ybk Int'l L 3.
Villalpando, S, 'The Legal Dimension of the International Community: How Community Interests are Protected in International Law' (2010) 21:2 EJIL 387.
Villiger, ME, 'The Rules on Interpretation: Misgivings, Misunderstandings, Miscarriage? The 'Crucible' Intended by the International Law Commission' in E Cannizzaro (ed.), *The Law of Treaties Beyond the Vienna Convention* (Oxford University Press 2011) 105.
Commentary on the 1969 Vienna Convention on the Law of Treaties (Martinus Nijhoff 2009).
Customary International Law and Treaties (Kluwer Law International 1997).
Customary International Law and Treaties (Martinus Nijhoff 1985).
Virally, M, 'The Sources of International Law' in M Sørensen (ed.), *Manual of Public International Law* (MacMillan 1968) 116.
Vité, S, 'The Interrelation of the Law of Occupation and Economic, Social and Cultural Rights: The Examples of Food, Health and Property' (2008) 90:871 Int'l Rev of the Committee of the Red Cross 629.
Vöneky, S, 'Analogy in International Law' in R. Wolfrum (ed.), Max Planck Encyclopedia of Public International Law (2008-), online edition, www.mpepil.com, accessed 4 July 2014.

Voigt, C, 'The Role of General Principles of International Law and their Relationship to Treaty Law' (2008) 2:121 (38) Retfærd Årgang 3.

von Bogdandy, A and Venzke, I, 'Beyond Dispute: International Judicial Institutions as Lawmakers' (2011) 12 German LJ 979.

von Feuerbach, PJA Ritter, 'The General Principles of International Criminal Law: The Foundations of Criminal Law and the Nullum Crimen Principle' in *Lehrbuch des gemeinen in Deutschland gültigen peinlichen Rechts*, 11th edn (Heyer 1832) 12–19, translation by IL Fraser in(2007) 5 J Int'l Crim Justice 1005.

von Hebel, H, 'The Decision to Include Elements of Crimes in the Rome Statute' in RS Lee and Others (eds.), *The International Criminal Court: Elements of Crimes and Rules of Procedure and Evidence* (Transnational 2001) 3.

von Hebel, H, and Robinson, D, 'Crimes within the Jurisdiction of the Court' in RS Lee and Others (eds.), *The International Criminal Court: The Making of the Rome Statute* (Kluwer Law International 1999) 79.

von Liszt, F, 'The Rationale for the Nullum Crimen Principle' (2007) 5 J Int'l Crim Justice 1009.

Waldock, H, 'Sixth Report on the Law of Treaties' (1966) II Ybk of the ILC 51.
'Fourth Report on the Law of Treaties' (1965) II Ybk of the ILC 49.
'Third Report on the Law of Treaties' (1964) II Ybk of the ILC 5.

Wald, PM, Interview for The Third Branch (2002), www.uscourts.gov/ttb/mar02ttb/interview.html, accessed 21 April 2010.

Waldron, J, 'The Concept and the Rule of Law', Paper read at the NYU Colloquium in Legal, Political and Social Theory (14 September 2006) (on file with author).

Weigend, T, '"In General a Principle of Justice" – The Debate on the 'Crime against Peace' in the Wake of the Nuremberg Judgment' (2012) 10 J Int'l Crim Justice 41.
'Intent, Mistake of Law and Co-perpetration in the Lubanga Decision on Confirmation of Charges' (2008) 6 J Int'l Crim Justice 471.

Weil, P, 'Towards Relative Normativity in International Law?' (1983) 77 AJIL 413.

Werle, G, *Principles of International Criminal Law* (TMC Asser Press 2005).
and Jessberger, F, 'Unless Otherwise Provided: Article 30 of the ICC Statute and the Mental Element of Crimes under International Criminal Law' (2005) 3 J Int'l Crim Justice 35.

Wessel, J, 'Judicial Policy-Making at the International Criminal Court: An Institutional Guide to Analyzing International Adjudication' (2006) 44 Columbia J Transnat'l L 377.

White, N, and Cryer, R, 'The ICC and the Security Council: An Uncomfortable Relationship' in J Doria, H-P Gasser and MC Bassiouni (eds.), *The Legal Regime of the International Criminal Court: Essays in Honour of Professor Igor Blishchenko* (Martinus Nijhoff 2009) 455.

Wise, EM, 'General Rules of Criminal Law' (1997) 25 Denv J Int'l L & Pol'y 313.

Wolfke, K, 'Can Codification of International Law be Harmful?' in J Makarczyk (ed.), *Essays in International Law in Honour of Judge Manfred Lachs* (Martinus Nijhoff 1984) 313.

Wouters, J and Odermatt, J, 'Quis Custodiet Consilium Securitatis? Reflections on the Lawmaking Powers of the Security Council', Working Paper No. 109, Leuven Centre for Global Governance Studies (June 2013), http://papers.ssrn.com/sol3/papers.cfm?abstract˙id=2286208, accessed 3 July 2014.

Young, R, '"Internationally Recognized Human Rights" before the International Criminal Court' (January 2011) 60 Int'l Crim LQ 189.

Zacklin, R, 'Some Major Problems in the Drafting of the ICTY Statute' (2004) 2 J Int'l Crim Justice 361.

Zahar, A, and Sluiter, G, *International Criminal Law* (Oxford University Press 2008).

Zimmermann, A, 'Article 5' in O Triffterer (ed.), *Commentary on the Rome Statute of the International Criminal Court*, 2nd edn (CH Beck/Hart/Nomos 2008) 129.

'Article 8' in O Triffterer (ed.), *Commentary on the Rome Statute of the International Criminal Court*, 2nd edn (CH Beck/Hart/Nomos 2008) 275.

'Article 124' in O Triffterer (ed.), *Commentary on the Rome Statute of the International Criminal Court*, 2nd edn (CH Beck/Hart/Nomos 2008) 1767.

'Israel and the International Criminal Court – an Outsider's Perspective' (2006) 36 Israel Ybk of Human Rights 231.

INDEX

Lightning Source UK Ltd.
Milton Keynes UK
UKOW05f1956210916

283480UK00013B/707/P